Guide to
Tactical Perimeter Defense: Becoming a Security Network Specialist

by Randy Weaver and Dawn Weaver

COURSE TECHNOLOGY
CENGAGE Learning™

Australia • Brazil • Japan • Korea • Mexico • Singapore • Spain • United Kingdom • United States

COURSE TECHNOLOGY
CENGAGE Learning

**Guide to Tactical Perimeter Defense:
Becoming a Security Network Specialist**
is published by Cengage Course Technology

Vice President, Technology & Trade,
Academic Business Unit: Dave Garza

Director of Learning Solutions: Sandy Clark

Executive Editor: Steven Helba

Managing Editor: Larry Main

Product Manager: Robin M. Romer

Editorial Assistant: Dawn Daugherty

Developmental Editor: Lisa M. Lord

Technical Editor: Sydney Shewchuk

Quality Assurance: Green Pen Quality
Assurance

Print Buyer: Justin Palmeiro

Content Product Managers: Heather Furrow,
Pamela Elizian

Art Director: Kun-Tee Chang

Compositor: GEX Publishing Services

Cover Design: Abby Scholz

Marketing Manager: Gayathri Baskaran

Proofreader: Chris Clark

Indexer: Kevin Broccoli

Photo Credit: Alloy Photography/Veer

For product information and technology assistance, contact us at
Cengage Learning Customer & Sales Support, 1-800-354-9706

For permission to use material from this text or product, submit all
requests online at **www.cengage.com/permissions**
Further permissions questions can be emailed to
permissionrequest@cengage.com

ISBN-13: 978-1-4283-5630-6

ISBN-10: 1-4283-5630-4

Course Technology
20 Channel Center Street
Boston, MA 02210
USA

Cengage Learning is a leading provider of customized learning solutions
with office locations around the globe, including Singapore, the United
Kingdom, Australia, Mexico, Brazil, and Japan. Locate your local office at:
international.cengage.com/region

Cengage Learning products are represented in Canada by Nelson
Education, Ltd.

To learn more about Course Technology, visit
www.cengage.com/coursetechnology

To learn more about Cengage Learning, visit **www.cengage.com.**

Purchase any of our products at your local college store or at our preferred
online store **www.cengagebrain.com**

Printed in the United States of America
3 4 5 6 7 8 9 14 13 12 11

Contents

TABLE OF
Contents

Introduction

Perimeter defense is the collective result of using layers of hardware and software to control the flow of traffic into and out of the network perimeter. It includes firewalls, intrusion detection and prevention, secure remote access, auditing, and more. An effective perimeter defense strategy allows necessary communication to flow between the internal network and external resources, such as the Internet, yet prevents harmful or unauthorized traffic from gaining access. This book examines the technologies involved in securing the network perimeter.

This book was written with two goals. The first goal is to give you a solid foundation in advanced network security fundamentals. Essential security practices, such as TCP/IP addressing, routing, packet filtering, and installing proxy servers, firewalls, and virtual private networks (VPNs) are explained. The second goal is to prepare you to take the Tactical Perimeter Defense exam for the Security Certified Network Specialist (SCNS) certification.

Intended Audience

Guide to Tactical Perimeter Defense: Becoming a Security Network Specialist is intended for students and professionals who need hands-on introductory experience with installing firewalls and intrusion detection systems (IDSs). This book assumes you are familiar with the Internet and fundamental networking concepts, such as TCP/IP, gateways, routers, and Ethernet networks. It also assumes you have prerequisite knowledge and experience that's equivalent to CompTIA's Security+ certification.

How to Use This Book

This book should be studied in sequence. The first chapter offers a solid refresher on network security and establishes the basis for the running case project (discussed later in "The Running Case Project"). Each chapter builds on the previous one and expands on knowledge from prerequisite courses.

The Running Case Project

This book's running case project is designed to give you practical experience in applying skills and concepts and attempts to mirror a real-life setting as closely as possible. Throughout the book, you work on a full-scale network security project for a fictitious company, Green Globe R&D, Inc., an environmental research and "green" design company. Green Globe works with architects, construction companies, and others in designing environmentally sound structures and conducts independent environmental impact studies for government agencies, corporations, and educational institutions. Some field work is outsourced, with one or more project managers and several engineering staff overseeing short-term projects in more than 100 countries. Long-term studies often use doctoral students from American universities in addition to a small group of Green Globe staff. The company's employees are highly diversified.

Green Globe has recently closed a deal to provide design oversight and research services to a large international construction corporation. It has also been negotiating with the EPA to provide impact studies on a wide range of projects. As a result, the company needs to expand its base of operations to support expected growth of more than 300% over the next 18 months and 150% per year for the next five years.

Because of the sensitive nature of the company's work and the competition it faces, it requires high security. Additionally, it has received threats from unknown sources. Federal law enforcement agencies are investigating these threats, but the company is concerned about being a target for cyberterrorists, especially when working in socially and politically volatile regions.

Green Globe has one location capable of supporting expansion in terms of space and needs secure mobile services for staff in the field around the globe as well as at its main offices. It has no plans to move or open satellite offices at this time but is considering adding on to its current building, a large warehouse in an airpark. It has allocated a generous budget to purchase equipment.

Your firm has been hired to design a secure network for Green Globe. Your supervisor has dispatched you to its location to evaluate its needs, assess the location, and complete a preliminary design. The facility layout is shown in a diagram your instructor will provide.

Your design should meet these major requirements:

- One fully networked location, 100% company owned, in Phoenix, AZ. This location will be the permanent base of operations.
- Capable of supporting up to 200 full-time users in these departments: Account Management; Project Management; Research and Development; Engineering; Sales and Marketing; Legal; Administration (includes office staff and management); Reports and Publications; Client Services; and Facilities and Technology Support.
- High security required. Extremely sensitive data must remain secure.
- Temporary access to specific resources must be available for external entities, which includes some limited mobile access.
- The company must adhere to applicable state and federal laws on information security and privacy.

Chapter Descriptions

Here is a summary of the topics covered in each chapter of this book:

Chapter 1, "Network Defense Fundamentals," is intended as a review of previously learned concepts. This chapter reviews common security threats and vulnerabilities that security devices need to address and offers an overview of basic tools for blocking those threats, including packet filters, antivirus software, log files and analysis software, and IDSs. The defense in depth strategy, using network security in layers, is discussed as well as examining the goals of a network security program, which balances the need for connectivity and access with the need to maintain privacy and integrity.

Chapter 2, "Advanced TCP/IP," reviews TCP/IP version 4, the version widely used on the Internet and most networks. You revisit the fundamentals of TCP/IP, including subnetting, supernetting, and the TCP life cycle. IPv4 packet structure is examined in detail, and then you learn the basics of the new version, TCP/IP version 6, including IPv6 addressing, core protocols, configuration, and useful utilities.

Chapter 3, "Router Fundamentals," introduces the routing process. You learn about routing tables, static and dynamic routing, routing metrics, and routing loops and examine routing protocols, including Routing Information Protocol, Open Shortest Path First, and Interior Gateway Routing Protocol.

Chapter 4, "Fundamentals of Cisco Router Security," builds on Chapter 3 to explain the fundamentals of Cisco router security, including how access control lists are used for advanced packet filtering at the network perimeter. You also learn how Cisco passwords control access to the router and the importance of removing unneeded protocols and services from routers.

Chapter 5, "Designing Firewalls," explains the functions of a firewall and describes how perimeter networks are designed. This chapter provides an overview of basic types of firewalls and their main functions, explains how proxy servers work to shield hosts on an internal network, and covers selecting and configuring a bastion host. You also learn about common security functions that firewalls perform, including NAT, authentication, and encryption.

Chapter 6, "Configuring Firewalls," discusses how to design a firewall topology and position firewalls at optimum locations. Packet filtering on firewalls controls traffic flow in and out of the network, and firewalls are capable of authenticating users, clients, and sessions. You also learn about several measures for securing connectivity, such as passwords, smart cards, digital signatures, and public and private keys.

Chapter 7, "Managing Firewalls to Improve Security," discusses how to maintain and edit a rule base, manage log files, and improve firewall performance. In addition, this chapter guides you through installing Microsoft ISA Server 2006 and offers guidelines on using Linux's packet-filtering tool, Iptables.

Chapter 8, "Implementing IPSec and Virtual Private Networks," explains the basic VPN components and describes the three core activities a VPN performs: encapsulation, encryption, and authentication. You also learn about tunneling protocols, IP Security (IPSec), and Internet Key Exchange (IKE).

Chapter 9, "Designing Virtual Private Networks," explains how business needs figure into designing and deploying VPNs, how to configure VPNs, how to use different topologies to secure a network, and how VPNs and firewalls work together. You also learn how to modify firewall packet-filtering rules to accommodate a VPN and how to set up a VPN in Windows Server 2003.

Chapter 10, "Designing Intrusion Detection Systems," introduces fundamental IDS concepts, including components that make up an IDS and the basic step-by-step process of intrusion detection. Options for setting up an IDS are also covered, such as network-based, host-based, and hybrid IDS configurations.

Chapter 11, "Configuring and Using Intrusion Detection Systems," explains how to develop and refine IDS filtering rules. You learn options for assembling a security incident response team, ways to deal with false alarms and actual attacks, and guidelines for preparing evidence for prosecution. You also install WinSnort, an open-source IDS package that includes a MySQL database to store log information and GUI utilities for analysis and management.

Chapter 12, "Wireless Network Fundamentals," explains how electromagnetic radiation is harnessed and modified to enable wireless communication. You learn about wireless standards and regulations, including the IEEE and Federal Communications Commission, a major player in wireless communication. Finally, you learn the components and configuration of wireless networks.

Chapter 13, "Securing Wireless Networks," examines security concerns for wireless networks and countermeasures for protecting wireless networks. You learn about inherent vulnerabilities of wireless technology and review methods for addressing physical security, planning access point deployment, ensuring strong encryption and authentication, and auditing wireless networks.

Appendix A, "SC0-451 Objectives," maps the objectives in the Security Certified Professional (SCP) SC0-451 Tactical Perimeter Defense exam to this book's corresponding chapter and section. If you need to brush up on a specific topic to prepare for the exam, you can use this appendix as a handy reference.

Appendix B, "Additional Resources," lists several security-related organizations, groups, and other information sources you can turn to for up-to-the-minute news about virus attacks and security problems. This appendix also provides several tables listing common commands used with Cisco routers.

Features

To help you fully understand networking security concepts, this book includes many features designed to enhance your learning experience:

- **Chapter Objectives.** Each chapter begins with a list of the concepts to be mastered in that chapter. This list gives you a quick reference to the chapter's contents and serves as a useful study aid.

- **Figures and Tables.** Numerous diagrams of networking configurations help you visualize common perimeter defense setups. In addition, tables provide details and comparisons in an organized, easy-to-grasp manner. Some tables include specific examples of packet-filtering rules you can use to build a firewall rule base. Because most labs use Microsoft operating systems, Microsoft products are used for most of the screenshots and Hands-On Projects in this book.

- **In-Chapter Activities.** Each chapter has projects integrated into the main text. The purpose of these activities is to provide immediate reinforcement of a newly learned skill or concept and give you an opportunity to apply knowledge and skills as a way to maintain interest and motivation.

- **Chapter Summaries.** Each chapter's material is followed by a summary of the concepts introduced in that chapter. These summaries are a helpful way to review the ideas covered in each chapter.

- **Key Terms.** Following the Chapter Summary, a list of all terms introduced in the chapter with boldfaced text is gathered together in the Key Terms list, with full definitions for each term. This list encourages a more thorough understanding of the chapter's key concepts and is a useful reference.

- **Review Questions.** The end-of-chapter assessment begins with a set of review questions that reinforces the main concepts in each chapter. These questions help you evaluate and apply the material you have learned.

- **Hands-On Projects.** Although understanding the theory behind networking technology is important, practice in real-world applications of this theory is essential. Each chapter includes projects aimed at giving you experience in planning and development tasks or hands-on configuration tasks.

- **Case Projects.** Each chapter closes with the corresponding segment of this book's running case project (described previously in "The Running Case Project"), which gives you a chance to draw on your common sense as well as skills and knowledge you have learned.

Lab Setup

The lab setup for this book is straightforward, requiring Internet access for projects and research and access to a computer capable of supporting Windows XP Professional with Service Pack 2 and Windows Server 2003 in a dual-boot configuration.

Text and Graphic Conventions

Where appropriate, additional information and exercises have been added to this book to help you better understand the topic at hand. Icons throughout the text alert you to additional materials. The following icons are used in this book:

The Note icon draws your attention to additional helpful material related to the subject being covered.

Tips based on the author's experience offer extra information about how to attack a problem or what to do in real-world situations.

The Caution icon warns you about potential mistakes or problems and explains how to avoid them.

Each in-chapter activity is preceded by the Activity icon and a description.

Each hands-on project in this book is preceded by the Hands-On icon and a description of the exercise that follows.

These icons mark Case Projects, which are scenario-based assignments. In these projects, you're asked to apply independently what you have learned.

INSTRUCTOR'S RESOURCES

The following supplemental materials are available when this book is used in a classroom setting. All supplements available with this book are provided to instructors on a single CD. You can also retrieve these supplemental materials from the Course Technology Web site, *www.course.com*, by going to the page for this book, under "Download Instructor Files & Teaching Tools."

Electronic Instructor's Manual. The Instructor's Manual that accompanies this book includes additional instructional material to assist in class preparation, including suggestions for classroom activities, discussion topics, and additional case projects.

Solutions. Solutions to all end-of-chapter material are included, with answers to Review Questions and, when applicable, Activities, Hands-On Projects, and Case Projects.

ExamView. This book is accompanied by ExamView, a powerful testing software package that instructors can use to create and administer printed, computer (LAN-based), and Internet exams. ExamView includes hundreds of questions that correspond to the topics covered in this book, enabling students to generate detailed study guides that include page references for further review. The computer-based and Internet testing components allow students to take exams at their computers and have them graded automatically to save instructors time.

PowerPoint presentations. This book comes with Microsoft PowerPoint slides for each chapter. These slides are meant to be used as a teaching aid for classroom presentation, to be made available to students on the network for chapter review, or to be printed for classroom distribution. Instructors can also add their own slides for other topics introduced to the class.

Figure files. All figures in the book are reproduced on the Instructor's Resources CD. Similar to the PowerPoint presentations, they are included as a teaching aid for classroom presentation, to make available to students for review, or to be printed for classroom distribution.

COPING WITH CHANGE ON THE WEB

Sooner or later, all the specific Web-based resources mentioned in this book will become out of date or be replaced by newer information. In some cases, the URLs listed might lead you to their replacements; in other cases, the URLs will lead nowhere, leaving you with the dreaded "not found" error message.

When that happens, don't give up! There's always a way to find what you want on the Web, if you're willing to invest some time and energy. Most Web sites offer a search engine, and if you can get to the main site, you can use this tool to help you find what you need. You can also use general search tools, such as *www.google.com* or *www.livesearch.com*, to find related information. In addition, although standards organizations offer the most specific information on their standards, many third-party sources of information, training, and assistance are available. The bottom line is that if you can't find something where the book says it's located, start looking around, which is an excellent way to improve your research skills.

Visit Our Web Site

Additional materials designed especially for you might be available for your course. Go to *www.course.com* periodically and search for this book title for more details.

ACKNOWLEDGMENTS

We would like to thank Course Technology for the opportunity to write this book on a topic of such value and importance. Thanks also go to the editorial and production staff, including Robin Romer, Product Manager, and Pam Elizian, Content Product Manager. Thanks also to Lisa Lord, Development Editor, for her guidance, her words of encouragement, and her periodic reminders that kept us on track. Sydney Shewchuk, the Technical Editor, went above and beyond the call of duty to provide suggestions based on his experience and knowledge. We would also like to thank Green Pen Quality Assurance for ensuring technical accuracy and the following reviewers, who guided us with helpful feedback on each chapter:

Michael Anderson, ECPI College of Technology, Newport News
Julia Bell, Walters State Community College
Dr. Philip Craiger, University of Central Florida
Keith Elijah, Digital Network Analysis and Joint Network Attack School, Department of Defense
Mark Krawcyzk, Greenville Technical College
David Pope, Ozarks Technical Community College

Special thanks go to our family for their patience and support through this demanding and time-intensive process.

1

NETWORK DEFENSE FUNDAMENTALS

After reading this chapter and completing the exercises, you will be able to:

♦ Describe the threats to network security

♦ Explain the goals of network security

♦ Describe a layered approach to network defense

♦ Explain how network security defenses affect your organization

This chapter reviews the fundamental network security concepts you need to know. First, you learn about different kinds of intruders and threats to network security, such as malicious code and natural disasters. Attackers have many motivations for hacking into networks, and your job is to figure out what they're doing (before they do it, if possible) and prevent them from carrying out their plans. The Internet is widely used in most network environments, so you also review some concerns about Internet access.

Next, you learn about the goals of network security and the challenges of ensuring privacy, confidentiality, integrity, and availability for network resources. After reviewing the basics, you delve into network defense technologies. You discover how layering technologies can ensure better protection than any single technology used alone. The method of layering defensive technologies is called defense in depth (DiD) and includes physical, logical, and virtual security concepts. Auditing is the mainstay of troubleshooting and monitoring a network, so you also review log file basics. Finally, you see how security efforts affect an organization and learn that information security isn't the sole domain of IT.

OVERVIEW OF THREATS TO NETWORK SECURITY

A variety of attackers might attempt network intrusions, causing loss of data, loss of privacy, and other consequences. This threat concerns a growing number of corporate managers. More businesses are actively addressing this problem, but many others haven't taken steps to secure their systems from attack.

This section gives you a general overview of who might want to attack your systems and other threats you might encounter. The first step in defeating the enemy is to know the enemy. Next, you learn about major security concerns on the Internet and see how network security and defensive technologies are used to combat threats.

Types of Attackers

When planning network security measures, knowing the types of attackers (discussed in the following sections) who are likely to attempt breaking in to your network is important. This knowledge can help you anticipate and set up detection systems, firewalls, and other defenses to block them. Before getting into the types of attackers, an overview of motivations for attempting to break into systems can be helpful:

- *Status*—Some attackers attempt to take over computer systems just for the thrill of it. They like to keep count of how many systems they have access to as a sort of notch on their belts.

- *Revenge*—Disgruntled current or former employees might want to retaliate against an organization for policies or actions they consider wrong. They can sometimes gain entry through an undocumented account (a backdoor) on the system.

- *Financial gain*—Other attackers have financial profit as their goal. Obviously, attackers who break into a network can gain access to financial accounts. They can steal individual or corporate credit card numbers and make unauthorized purchases. Just as often, attackers defraud people out of money with scams carried out via e-mail or other means.

- *Industrial espionage*—Proprietary information is often valuable enough that it can be sold to competing companies or other parties who want to upgrade their technological capabilities in some way.

- *Principle*—Attacks might be carried out in support of certain beliefs, as a protest for perceived injustices, or for a variety of other reasons. Cyberterrorists, for example, are acting based on principles (whether good or bad).

Crackers

A **cracker** is anyone who attempts to gain access to unauthorized resources on a network, usually by finding a way to circumvent passwords, firewalls, or other protective measures. They seek to break into computers for different reasons:

- "Old school" hackers consider themselves seekers of knowledge; they operate on the theory that knowledge is power, regardless of how they come by that knowledge. They are not out to destroy or harm; they want to discover how things work and access any sources of knowledge they can find. They believe the Internet was intended to be an open environment and anything online can and should be available to anyone. In fact, most attackers' main goal is to improve technology.

- Other less "ethical" crackers pursue destructive aims, such as the proliferation of viruses and e-mail bombs, much like vandals and graffiti artists.

- Sometimes bored people who are highly adept with computers try to gain control of as many systems as possible for the thrill of it. They enjoy disrupting systems and keeping them from working, and they tend to boast about their exploits online.

Disgruntled Employees

Who would try to access customer information, financial files, job records, or other sensitive information from *inside* an organization? Disgruntled employees. These employees are usually unhappy over perceived injustices and want to exact revenge by stealing information. Often they give confidential information to new employers. When employees are terminated, security measures should be taken immediately to ensure that they can no longer access the company network.

Sometimes an organization's most serious vulnerabilities are those inside the firewall, not outside it. In addition, often the culprit isn't a disgruntled former employee, but a perfectly satisfied current employee. For example, in May 2006, the personal data of millions of American veterans was stolen from a Veterans' Administration (VA) employee's home. He had taken a laptop and an external hard drive home to work on, which he had been doing routinely for three years, and his home was robbed. The laptop was recovered a few weeks later, and according to federal investigators, it seemed unlikely that identity theft resulted from the stolen data. However, the VA recalled all laptop computers for a security audit, during which any unauthorized data was removed. Some veterans' groups have filed lawsuits because of this security breach, but so far, no reports of identity theft have surfaced. You can well imagine what could be done with that information, so those veterans whose data was stolen will have to monitor their credit closely.

TIP The 2005 CSI/FBI Computer Crime and Security Survey tracks computer crime and security incidents at major companies, providing quantified data for assessing business losses caused by computer crimes and security breaches. It provides data about the sources of intrusions, preparedness, and other relevant information and is available at *www.gocsi.com*. Click the CSI/FBI Survey link on the right, and follow the instructions to download the survey. You need to register, but registration is free.

Criminals and Industrial Spies

No matter how ethical attackers consider themselves to be, crackers are out to steal anything they can get their hands on or cause as much damage as possible. Industrial spies might be interested in selling information to the top bidder or using it to influence potential victims. Many companies would be interested in getting the plans for a new product from their competitors. Criminals might simply want to cause harm, for profit or for fun.

Script Kiddies and Packet Monkeys

The term **script kiddie** is often used to describe young, immature computer programmers who spread viruses and other malicious scripts and exploit weaknesses in computer systems. They lack the experience to create viruses or Trojan programs on their own, but they can usually find these programs online and spread them for their own aims. The assumption among supposedly more sophisticated crackers is that script kiddies seek only to break in to as many computers as possible to gain attention and notoriety.

Another type of mischievous attacker is a **packet monkey**, who's primarily interested in blocking Web site activities through a distributed denial-of-service (DDoS) attack. In a DDoS attack, the attacker hijacks many computers and uses them to flood the target with so many false requests that the server can't process them all, and normal traffic is blocked. Packet monkeys might also want to deface Web sites by leaving messages that their friends can read.

Terrorists

Until September 11, 2001, most people didn't consider a terrorist attack on an information infrastructure a likely threat. Since that awful day, however, the threat posed by terrorists has been taken more seriously. A terrorist group might want to attack computer systems for several reasons: making a political statement or accomplishing a political goal, such as the release of a jailed comrade; causing damage to critical systems; or disrupting the target's financial stability. Attacking the World Trade Center and Pentagon certainly accomplished the latter goal, given the nature and location of these structures. Terrorists might also want to cause fear.

To understand the seriousness of a terrorist attack on computers, think about how many critical systems are controlled by computers. Consider the chaos caused by a successful attack on a computer system controlling power grids or a nuclear power plant's reactors. The psychological effect can be just as detrimental as the damage to the infrastructure.

Malicious Code

In 2001, the Code Red worm infected millions of computers, costing around $2.4 billion in cleanup, lost productivity, and so on. (For more information, see the story "Code Blue Worm Strikes in China, May Migrate" at *www.newsfactor.com/perl/story/13405.html.*) This self-propagating malicious code (**malware**) exploited systems using Internet Information Services (IIS, Windows Web server software) that were susceptible to a buffer overflow vulnerability in the Indexing Service. When the worm appeared, Microsoft had already released a patch. The vulnerability was well known, and instructions were available explaining how to exploit it, yet many administrators hadn't taken steps to protect their systems by installing the patch.

More recently, the MSBlast worm of August 2003 spread to more than 120,000 systems in less than 24 hours, crashing systems all over the world. Although its spread wasn't as fast or impressive as Code Red, it continues to infect systems today. MSBlast (also known as Lovsan, W32.Blaster, and other names) exploited a vulnerability for which Microsoft had released a patch almost a month earlier. The goal of MSBlast was to launch a DDoS attack against the Windows Update Web site. Experts say that only poor programming of the worm slowed its progression. Just a few months before MSBlast, the Slammer worm inflicted similar damage on computer systems but spread faster, shutting down databases and bank ATMs all over the world.

Information security has come a long way since these famous worms, but a new vulnerability is always right around the corner, and security professionals must stay one step ahead of attackers. The following sections review types of malware you might encounter.

Types of Malware

Although most users think of any type of virus, worm, or Trojan program as a virus, they are completely different types of attacks. A **virus** is computer code that copies itself from one place to another surreptitiously and performs actions that range from benign to harmful. Viruses are spread by several methods: running executable code, sharing disks or memory sticks, opening e-mail attachments, or viewing Web pages that use malicious ActiveX objects.

A **worm** creates files that copy themselves repeatedly and consume disk space. Worms don't require user intervention to be launched; they are self-propagating. Some worms can install **backdoors**—a way of gaining unauthorized access to a computer or other resource, such as an unused port or terminal service that allows attackers to access and gain control over a computer. Others can destroy data on a hard disk.

A **Trojan program** is also a harmful computer program, but it appears to be something useful—a deception much like its namesake, the Trojan horse of Greek legend. The difference between a virus and a Trojan program is in how the malicious code is used. Viruses replicate themselves and can potentially cause damage when they run on a user's computer. Trojan programs can also create a backdoor. In addition, the hidden or obscure nature of a backdoor makes an attacker's activities difficult to detect.

Viruses, worms, and Trojan programs are major security threats. They can damage files, enable attackers to control computers, and cause applications to stop functioning correctly. In creating a network defense perimeter, you must guard against them. Firewalls and intrusion detection systems don't block malicious code on their own; you need to install antivirus software or proxy servers that can be configured to filter them out and delete them before they cause harm.

A macro is a type of script that automates repetitive tasks in Microsoft Word or similar applications. When you run a macro, a series of actions are carried out automatically. Macros are a useful way to make performing some tasks more efficient. Unfortunately, **macro viruses** perform the same functions, but they tend to be harmful.

In the past, **spyware**, which includes adware, tracking cookies, dialers, and spam, was considered more of a nuisance than something harmful. However, it has fast become a more serious threat. Some spyware isn't overtly harmful, but the impact it has on networks can range from consuming resources to wasting time. The effects are difficult to quantify because productivity depends on so many factors. Other types are harmful and represent even more of a threat than viruses. They might carry additional malware, they can generate additional traffic and use processors and other system resources, or they might steal personal information. According to some estimates, as many as 90% of computers connected to the Internet are infected with some type of spyware. In Activity 1-1, you download and run a popular spyware scanner to determine whether your computer is infected with spyware.

ACTIVITY

Activity 1-1: Scanning for Spyware

Time Required: 30 minutes

Objective: Download and run Spy Sweeper to scan your computer for spyware.

Description: In this activity, you download Webroot Software's Spy Sweeper, a well-known free spyware scanner. (The free scanner only identifies spyware; you must purchase the full version to remove it with a spyware cleaner.)

1. Start your Web browser, and go to **www.webroot.com/consumer/downloads/**.

2. At the top of the page, click the **Download Free Scan** button.

3. Save the program to your desktop, and then follow the instructions to install and run it. You need to provide a valid e-mail address and restart your computer before you can run the program. Figure 1-1 shows the user interface.

Figure 1-1   The Spy Sweeper user interface

4. Click the **Start Full Sweep** button. Did Spy Sweeper find any spyware on your system? How many spyware programs did you have that you weren't aware of? Are they harmful? Did you find any mistakes, such as legitimate programs flagged as spyware?

_____

_____

_____

5. Exit Spy Sweeper, and leave your computer running for the next activity.

One of the biggest problems with spyware is its overwhelming presence. It's everywhere, and even systems you scanned and cleaned this morning can be reinfected by afternoon. Sometimes users don't understand the differences between spyware, viruses, and worms, so they aren't cautious about their Web surfing or communication habits. Even system administrators have spyware on their personal computers. For that reason, any antivirus program should include antispyware capabilities, or you should install separate antispyware programs. Today's computer systems require comprehensive antivirus protection that's kept updated and run daily.

Other Threats to Network Security

It isn't possible to prepare for every possible risk to your systems. At best, you can maintain a secure environment for today's threats and have a comprehensive plan for integrating safeguards against tomorrow's threats into your defenses. The next threat might be infection by a new virus or the exploit of a recently discovered vulnerability, or it might be an earthquake that destroys your facility.

There are many threats you can't mitigate entirely, such as a natural disaster. Even if you have prepared for natural disasters by maintaining an alternative site complete with all necessary equipment, you could still suffer loss of network equipment at your primary site. Because the risks can't be eliminated, many insurers now offer cyber risk insurance to cover damages or loss related to a disaster or an attack. The costs and details vary, but for critical systems, insurance can be a business-saving investment.

NOTE

For more information on cyber risk insurance, see *Guide to Strategic Infrastructure Security: Becoming a Security Network Professional* (Course Technology, 2008, ISBN 1418836613).

Social Engineering: The People Factor

Another common way in which attackers gain access to an organization's resources is one that can't be defended against with hardware or software. The vulnerability, in this case, is gullible employees who are fooled by attackers into giving out passwords or other access codes. Attacks that involve employees who don't observe accepted security practices (or who willfully abuse them) can best be addressed with a strong and enforced security policy and regular, thorough security awareness training.

Common Attacks and Defenses

Table 1-1 describes some common attacks you need to guard against and the defensive strategies you can use to defeat them. These concepts are discussed in more depth throughout the remainder of this book.

Table 1-1   Attacks and defenses

Attack	Description	Defense
Denial-of-service (DoS) attack	Traffic into and out of a network is blocked when servers are flooded with malformed packets (bits of digital information) that have false IP addresses or other data inserted into them or contain other fake communications.	Keep your server OS up to date, and log instances of frequent connection attempts against one service.
SYN flood	A network is overloaded with packets that have the SYN flag set.	Keep your firewall and OS up to date so that these attacks are blocked by means of software patches and updates, and review your log files of access attempts to see whether intrusion attempts have been made.
Malware	Network computers are infected by viruses, Trojans, worms, spyware, or other forms of malicious code.	Install antivirus software and keep malware definitions up to date.
Social engineering	An employee is misled into giving out passwords or other sensitive information.	Educate employees about your security policy, which is a set of goals and procedures for making an organization's network secure.
Malicious port scanning	An attacker looks for open ports to infiltrate a network.	Install and configure a firewall, which is hardware or software designed to filter out unwanted network traffic and protect authorized traffic.
Internet Control Message Protocol (ICMP) message abuse	A network is flooded with a stream of ICMP Echo Request packets to a target computer.	Set up packet filtering.
Finding vulnerable hosts on the internal network to attack	An attacker who gains access to one computer on a network can get IP addresses, hostnames, and passwords, which are then used to find other hosts to attack.	Use proxy servers.
Man-in-the-middle attack	An attacker operates between two computers in a network and impersonates one computer to intercept communications.	Use virtual private network encryption.

Table 1-1   Attacks and defenses (continued)

Attack	Description	Defense
New files being placed on the system	A virus or other malware causes new files to proliferate on infected computers, using up system resources.	Install system-auditing software, such as Tripwire.
Remote Procedure Calls (RPC) attacks	The OS crashes because it's unable to handle arbitrary data sent to an RPC port.	Set up an intrusion detection system, and keep systems updated with the latest patches and hot fixes.

Internet Security Concerns

As you probably know from your study of basic networking concepts and TCP/IP, a port number combined with a computer's IP address constitutes a network connection called a **socket**. Software commonly used by attackers attempts to identify sockets that respond to connection requests. The sockets that respond can be targeted to see whether they have been left open or have security vulnerabilities that can be exploited. HTTP Web services, which use port 80, are among the most commonly exploited services.

The following sections review some aspects of using the Internet that you need to be aware of from a security standpoint. These sections cover e-mail vulnerabilities such as viruses, scripts that enter the network through e-mail or downloaded files, and broadband connections that enable computers to connect to the Internet with IP addresses that never change and can easily be attacked.

E-mail and Communications

For a home user who regularly surfs the Web, uses e-mail, and engages in instant messaging, a firewall's primary job is to keep viruses from infecting files and prevent Trojan programs from entering the system through hidden backdoors. Personal firewall programs, such as Norton Internet Security, come with an antivirus program that alerts users when an e-mail attachment or a file containing a known virus is found.

Scripting

A widespread network intrusion that's increasing in frequency and severity is the use of scripts—executable code attached to e-mail messages or downloaded files that infiltrates a system. It can be difficult for a firewall or intrusion detection system (IDS) to block these files, so specialty firewalls and other programs should be added to keep scripts from infecting a network.

A specialty e-mail firewall can monitor and control certain types of content that pass into and out of a network. These firewalls can be configured to filter out pornographic content, junk e-mail, and malicious code. MailMarshal STMP (*www.marshal.com/mailmarshal_*

1

smtp/), for instance, unpacks and scans the content of each e-mail before it reaches the recipient and includes antivirus and anti-phishing features.

E-mail is a vital tool for business communications. Unfortunately, e-mail is also one of the primary avenues for malware attacks. In addition, current laws on privacy, protection against offensive content, and liability for damages resulting from e-mail require companies to show they have taken all reasonable steps to protect their e-mail systems.

ACTIVITY

Activity 1-2: Examining E-mail Content Filters and Security Suites

Time Required: 30 minutes

Objective: Evaluate e-mail security software.

Description: In this activity, you search the Internet for e-mail content filters and security suites to discover what options are available. Although e-mail is indispensable in business, many risks are associated with it. Fortunately, products are available to help mitigate this risk, but keep in mind that sometimes the most complete product isn't the best for your organization's needs. To make the best choice, you need to know how and where to find products and documentation.

1. Start your Web browser, and go to **www.marshal.com/pages/products.asp**.

2. Read about the features of MailMarshal. Using a word processing program or paper and pencil, create a comparison chart, and use it to enter your findings as you investigate program features.

3. Go to your favorite search engine, and search on **e-mail content security**.

4. Visit three product pages and record the vendor, product features, and product cost on the comparison chart.

5. When you have finished recording product information, turn your comparison chart in to your instructor.

6. Leave your computer running for the next activity.

E-mail filtering programs introduce privacy issues that need to be balanced against an organization's need for protection—a trade-off that applies to almost all aspects of network security, not just e-mail. Another problem you might encounter with the plethora of security software available is redundant programs functions that are incompatible. For example, if you have Windows Firewall (included in Windows XP with SP2) and another personal firewall program running, you could have problems with your connection and with some programs or communications being blocked.

Always-on Connectivity

The proliferation of affordable high-speed connections, such as cable modems and DSL lines, brings up additional security concerns for network administrators. Computers with always-on connections are easier to locate and attack because their IP addresses remain the same as long as they're connected to the Internet—which might be days at a time if computers are left on overnight. Some users pay extra for static IP addresses that never change and enable them to run Web servers or other services. Static IP addresses, however, make it easier for attackers to locate a computer and scan it for open ports.

Another problem happens when remote users (employees who are on the road, contractors who work at home, or business partners) want to connect to your organization's internal network. These connections used to be made through temporary dial-up connections that used protocols such as Point-to-Point Protocol (PPP). Now remote users typically connect through an always-on connection, which means they might be connected to your network for hours at a time.

Always-on connections extend the boundaries of your corporate network, and you should secure them as you would any part of your network perimeter. At the very least, your network security policy should specify that remote users have firewall and antivirus software installed. If attackers can break in to a remote user's computer while that user is connected to your network, your network becomes vulnerable as well.

ACTIVITY

Activity 1-3: Identifying Open Ports

Time Required: 15 minutes

Objective: Use the Netstat command to look for open ports on your computer.

Description: A computer you're securing, particularly one that's hosting firewall or IDS software, should have a minimal set of resources and open ports on it. How do you determine which ports are open on your computer? You can do so with the Netstat utility, which is built in to both UNIX and Windows systems. The following steps apply to a Windows XP computer, but you can also run the Netstat -a command on a UNIX system to get the same information.

1. Click **Start**, point to **All Programs**, point to **Accessories**, and click **Command Prompt** to open a command prompt window.

2. At the command prompt, type **netstat -a** (leave a blank space between "netstat" and the hyphen) and press **Enter**.

3. Netstat presents information in columns. The first column, Proto, indicates the protocol being used. The last column, State, tells you whether a connection has been established or the computer is listening for connections. How many TCP ports were reported in the State column as listening? How many UDP ports? Write your findings here:

_____

_____

4. Type **exit** and press **Enter** to close the command prompt window.

5. Leave your computer running for the next activity.

GOALS OF NETWORK SECURITY

So far, you have reviewed the threats networks face. In the following sections, you learn what's needed to begin building secure systems. You need to enable business partners, mobile workers, and contractors to connect to the main network securely, and you need a way to authenticate authorized users reliably. You must also have a clear picture of the major goals of a network security effort, including privacy and data integrity.

Providing Secure Connectivity

In the early days of the Internet, network security emphasized blocking attackers and other unauthorized users from accessing the corporate network. Now secure connectivity with trusted users and networks is the priority. When people go online to conduct business, they often engage in the following activities that could make them vulnerable:

- Placing orders for merchandise online and revealing personal and financial information during payment

- Paying bills by transferring funds online

- Accessing account information

- Looking up personnel records

- Creating authentication information, such as usernames and passwords

The growth of the Internet and e-commerce isn't likely to slow down, so methods to secure these transactions must be set up and maintained. Several methods can be combined in a layered security scheme, as you see later in "Using Network Defense Technologies in Layers."

Securing Remote Access

One of the biggest security challenges for organizations that communicate via the Internet is the need to secure remote access for contractors and employees who are traveling. A virtual private network (VPN), with its combination of encryption and authentication, is an ideal and cost-effective solution (see Figure 1-2). (VPNs are covered in Chapters 8 and 9.)

Ensuring Privacy

Corporations, hospitals, and other organizations with databases full of personal and financial information need to maintain privacy to protect their customers and to maintain their integrity and credibility. In addition, laws protect private information and mandate severe penalties for failure to protect private information adequately. Examples of these laws include Sarbanes-Oxley, Health Insurance Portability and Accountability Act (HIPAA), and Gramm-Leach-Bliley Act. You probably won't need to know much about these laws for the SCO-451 certification exam, but if you work in an industry affected by laws governing privacy protection, you should familiarize yourself with them.

One of the most important and effective ways to maintain the privacy of information in an organization's network is to educate employees about security dangers and explain security policies. Employees are the ones most likely to detect security breaches *and* to cause security breaches accidentally. They can also monitor their co-workers' activities and stay aware of suspicious activity that could indicate a security problem.

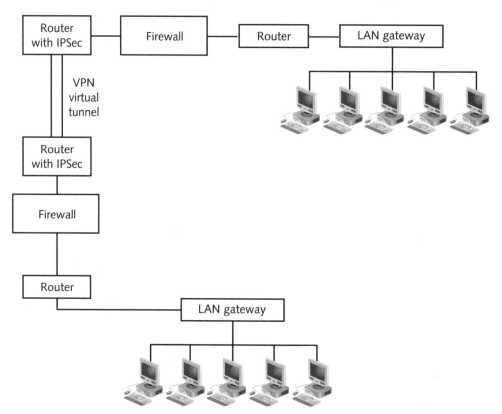

Figure 1-2   Providing secure connectivity with VPNs

Providing Nonrepudiation

Nonrepudiation is an important aspect of establishing trusted communication between organizations that conduct business across a network rather than face-to-face. Encryption protects the integrity, confidentiality, and authenticity of digital information. Encryption can

1

also provide **nonrepudiation**, which is the capability to prevent a participant in an electronic transaction from denying that it performed an action. Nonrepudiation simply means ensuring that the sender can't deny sending a message and the receiver can't deny receiving it.

Confidentiality, Integrity, and Availability: The CIA Triad

Security professionals are familiar with the term "CIA triad" (not to be confused with the organization in Langley, Virginia) to refer to the goals of ensuring confidentiality, integrity, and availability—the tenets of information security. **Confidentiality** refers to preventing intentional or unintentional disclosure of communications between a sender and recipient. **Integrity** ensures the accuracy and consistency of information during all processing (storage, transmission, and so forth). **Availability** is making sure those who are authorized to access resources can do so in a reliable and timely manner. The CIA triad is often represented as a triangle (see Figure 1-3).

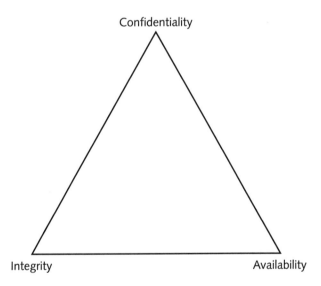

Figure 1-3   The CIA triad

USING NETWORK DEFENSE TECHNOLOGIES IN LAYERS

No single security component or method can be expected to ensure complete protection for a network—or even one host computer. Instead, you need to assemble a group of methods that work in a coordinated fashion to protect against a variety of threats.

The components and approaches described throughout the rest of this book should be arranged to provide layers of network defense. This layering approach to network security is often called **defense in depth (DiD)**. The National Security Agency (NSA) designed DiD as a best practices strategy for achieving information assurance. In general, the layers are as follows (each layer is discussed in the following sections):

- Physical security
- Authentication and password security
- Operating system security
- Antivirus protection
- Packet filtering
- Firewalls
- Demilitarized zones (DMZs)
- Intrusion detection systems (IDSs)
- Virtual private networks (VPNs)
- Auditing and log files
- Routers and access control

For more information on DiD, visit *http://nsa2.www.conxion.com/support/guides/sd-1.pdf.*

Physical Security

The term **physical security** refers to measures taken to physically protect a computer or other network device from theft and environmental disasters. Along with installing computer locks that attach the device to a piece of furniture in your office, critical servers should be in a room protected by a lock and/or burglar alarm. It's been said many times but is worth repeating: "If the bad guys can touch it, they own it." It takes only seconds for a computer to be compromised. Within minutes, an attacker can defeat most common locks and steal anything from a password file to a server.

Use an engraving tool to mark serial numbers, phone numbers, or other identifiers on portable devices, such as laptops, that can be lost or stolen easily. Specialized locks are available for PCs and laptops; many have alarms that go off if someone tries to take the device. You can also store portable computers in locked cabinets or other secure areas.

In addition, uninterruptible power supply (UPS) devices help maintain a steady level of electrical power, thus avoiding possible damage from voltage spikes—sudden and dramatic increases in power that can damage hardware. Additional physical security measures include fire suppression systems, video cameras, security guards, and generators.

Keep in mind that a standard water sprinkler fire suppression system destroys computer equipment. Usually a gaseous agent, such as argon or FM-200, is used. Fire suppression systems are based on four methods used to put a fire out. First, fires need oxygen, so agents that remove or consume oxygen cause the fire to go out. Second, removing the fuel the fire burns causes the fire to die. Third, removing the heat from a fire prevents combustion; some gaseous fire suppression agents absorb the heat from a fire faster than it can be generated. Fourth, fires involve a chemical reaction. Some fires can't be extinguished with the other three methods, but disrupting the chemical reaction causes the fire to go out or prevents it from igniting. Many fire suppression systems operate on this fourth method because a server room fire can't be extinguished by water to remove the heat, nor can the fuel be removed.

Authentication and Password Security

After you have physically secured your computers, you can protect them from the inside, too. One simple but effective strategy is **password security**—having your employees select strong passwords, keep them secure, and change them regularly. Using multiple passwords, including screensaver passwords and passwords for protecting critical applications, is also a good idea to guard against unauthorized employees gaining control of unattended computers.

Authentication uses one of three methods: something the user knows, something the user possesses, and something the user is. In network computing, authentication is performed in one of several ways. Basic authentication makes use of *something the user knows*, such as a username/password. In challenge/response authentication, the authenticating device generates a random code or number (the challenge) and sends it to the user who wants to be authenticated. The user resubmits the number or code and adds a secret PIN or password (the response) or uses *something the user possesses*, such as a smart card swiped through a card reader.

In large organizations, a centralized server typically handles authentication. The use of *something the user is*—biometrics (retinal scans, voiceprints, fingerprints, and so on)—is becoming more common because of increasing concerns over terrorist attacks and other criminal activities.

TIP

You can provide extra protection for a laptop by setting the Basic Input/Output System (BIOS) password—a password that keeps intruders from starting a computer. However, this protection can be circumvented easily if the computer is started from boot media.

Operating System Security

Another way to secure computers and their data from the inside is by installing OS patches that have been issued to address security flaws. It's your responsibility to keep up with patches, hot fixes, and service packs and install them when they become available. In addition, stopping any unneeded services and disabling guest accounts help make an OS more secure.

Antivirus Protection

Virus scanning refers to examining files or e-mail messages for filenames, file extensions such as .exe (for executable code) or .zip (for zipped files), or other indications that viruses are present. Many viruses have suspicious file extensions, but some seem innocuous. Antivirus software uses several methods to look for malware, including comparisons to the software's current signature files, which contain a pattern of known viruses. Signature files are the main reason for keeping your antivirus software updated; antivirus software vendors create updates frequently and make them available for customers to download. When antivirus software recognizes the presence of viruses, it deletes them from the file system or places them in a storage area called a "quarantine" where they can't replicate themselves or do harm to other files.

Firewalls and IDSs aren't equipped to scan for malware and eliminate it. However, many enterprise-level firewalls come with integrated antivirus protection. Antivirus software is a necessity for every computer in a network; if your firewall doesn't include antivirus software, install it on the computer that hosts the firewall and on all network computers. The most critical component of malware management, however, is up-to-date software.

The term "antivirus" implies protection against all forms of malicious code.

NOTE

Packet Filtering

Packet filters block or allow the transmission of packets of information based on port, IP address, protocol, or other criteria. Like firewalls and IDSs, they come in many varieties. Some are hardware devices, such as routers placed at a network gateway. Others are software that can be installed on a gateway or computer. Here are a few examples:

- *Routers*—These devices are probably the most common packet filters. Routers process packets according to an access control list (ACL) the administrator defines. Router security and ACLs are covered in Chapters 3 and 4.

- *Operating systems*—Some OSs, such as Windows and Linux, have built-in utilities for packet filtering on the TCP/IP stack of the server software. Linux has a kernel-level packet filter called Iptables; Windows has a feature called TCP/IP Filtering. Iptables is covered in Chapter 7.

- *Software firewalls*—Most enterprise-level programs, such as Check Point, perform stateful packet filtering. Personal firewalls, such as ZoneAlarm and

Sygate Personal Firewall, have a less sophisticated version called stateless packet filtering.

Whatever type is used, a packet-filtering device evaluates information in the packet header and compares it to established rules. If the information corresponds to one of the "allow" rules, the packet is allowed to pass; if the information matches one of the "deny" rules, the packet is dropped. The key point of most packet filters is that they process rules in the order they appear in the rule base. Once a packet is matched to a rule, the appropriate action is taken and the packet is not processed further, so be careful of the ordering of rules. Rule bases are explained more in Chapters 6 and 7.

Firewalls

The foundation for installing a firewall is your organization's security policy. With a solid security policy as your guide, you can design security configurations to support your organization's goals. Specifically, you can create a packet-filtering rule base for your firewall that reflects the organization's approach to network security. (You learn all about firewalls in Chapters 5 to 7.) The following section describes two ways in which a firewall can control the amount of protection for a network: permissive versus restrictive policies.

Permissive Versus Restrictive Policies

Based on the security policy, a firewall typically uses one of these general approaches to security (see Figure 1-4):

- *Permissive*—Calls for a firewall and associated security components to allow all traffic through the network gateway by default, and then block services on a case-by-case basis.

- *Restrictive*—Calls for a firewall and associated network security components to deny all traffic by default. The first rule denies all traffic on any service and using any port. To allow a specific type of traffic, a new rule must be placed ahead of the "deny all" rule.

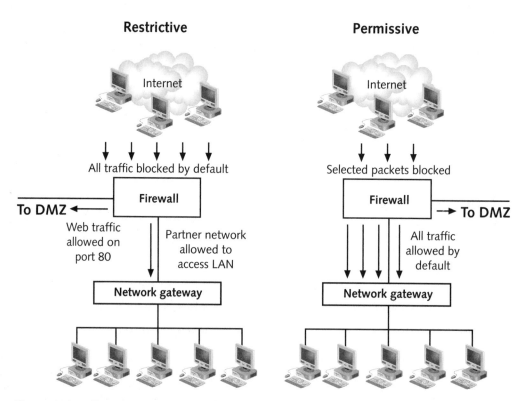

Figure 1-4   Permissive versus restrictive policies

A firewall should enforce the policy established by the network administrator. Enforcement is handled mainly by setting up packet-filtering rules contained in a rule base.

Demilitarized Zones

A subnet called a **demilitarized zone (DMZ)**, which is a network that sits outside the internal network but is connected to the firewall, makes services publicly available yet protects the internal network. A DMZ might also contain a Domain Name System (DNS) server, which resolves domain names to IP addresses. The subnet attached to the firewall and contained in the DMZ is sometimes called a "service network" or "perimeter network."

Intrusion Detection Systems

Firewalls and proxy servers ideally block intruders or malicious code from entering a network. However, an IDS used with these tools offers an additional layer of protection for a network. An IDS works by recognizing the signs of a possible attack and sending a notification to an administrator that an attack is underway. The signs of possible attacks are called **signatures**—combinations of IP address, port number, and frequency of access attempts. You learn about IDS design and configuration in Chapters 10 and 11.

Virtual Private Networks

When companies need to share files or exchange confidential information, often they turn to expensive leased lines from telecommunications companies. Although these lines create a point-to-point connection between company networks and, therefore, ensure a high level of security, the monthly costs are excessively high for budget-conscious companies. Many organizations are turning to VPNs to provide a low-cost and secure connection that uses the public Internet.

Network Auditing and Log Files

Auditing is the process of monitoring computers accessing a network and resources being accessed, and then recording the information in a log file. IT managers often overlook detailed, periodic review of log files generated by firewalls and IDSs. By reviewing and maintaining log files, you can detect suspicious patterns of activity, such as unsuccessful connection attempts that occur at the same time each day. You can identify—or at least gather enough information to begin to identify—those who have attacked your network. You can set up rules to block attacks and keep your network defense systems up to date by examining attack attempts that have penetrated firewalls and other protective devices. Effective management of log files is an essential activity in perimeter security.

Analyzing Log Files

Compiling, reviewing, and analyzing log files are among the most tedious and time-consuming tasks in network security. Network administrators read and analyze log files to see who is accessing their networks from the Internet. All connection attempts that were rejected should be recorded to identify possible intruders and detect vulnerable points in the system.

When you first install IDS or firewall hardware or software on your network, you'll probably be asked to prepare reports stating how the network is being used and what kinds of filtering activities the device is performing. Sorting logs by time of day and per hour produces more organized material that's easier to review and incorporate into reports than the log files the device typically produces.

Be sure to check logs to learn the peak traffic times on your network and identify the services that consume the most bandwidth. If your firewall or IDS can display log file entries graphically, showing these graphs to management is a good idea because they illustrate trends with more impact than lists of raw data.

In addition to the logs generated by firewalls, IDSs, VPNs, routers, and other security devices, the simple event logs in Windows XP can be useful in troubleshooting and detecting some types of attacks. Event Viewer isn't very helpful in reviewing these logs, however. Fortunately, some third-party log analyzers are available that work with Event Viewer and transform cryptic data into a readable, easy-to-understand GUI interface.

Configuring Log Files

The log files compiled by firewalls or IDSs give you different options. You can view active data (data compiled as traffic moves through a gateway in real time) or data that the device has recorded recently. You can also view information in these ways:

- *System events*—These events usually track operations of a firewall or IDS, making a log entry whenever it starts or shuts down.

- *Security events*—These events are records of any alerts a firewall or IDS has issued.

- *Traffic*—This is a record of the traffic that passes through a firewall.

- *Packets*—Some programs enable you to view information about packets that pass through them.

With more elaborate programs, you can customize what you see in log files and search for specific items or events.

Using GUI Log Viewers

You can always view log files with a text editor, but if you have ever used this method, you know how tedious it can be. A graphical tool organizes logged information into easy-to-read columns and enables you to sort them by date, IP address, protocol, or other criteria. When you're reviewing log files in raw format, the lines tend to run together, and it's easy to miss something.

Several log management tools are available that compile logs and present them in an easy-to-read format to make log review and network monitoring easier. Some firewall log analyzers even automate log file reviews and can compile data from several devices into one report. For example, ManageEngine Firewall Analyzer is available for firewalls, VPNs, and Squid proxy servers (used in many Linux and UNIX systems). This tool doesn't include IDS traffic, but it does have a centralized repository and reporting tool for other devices. It's compatible with many firewalls, including Check Point, Cisco PIX and VPN, and FreeBSD, and offers instant virus, security, and attack analysis in real time with configurable alert settings.

Even personal (or desktop) firewalls generate log files for review. One well-known personal firewall product is ZoneAlarm by Check Point, which generates an easy-to-read log viewer for program access and firewall activity (see Figure 1-5).

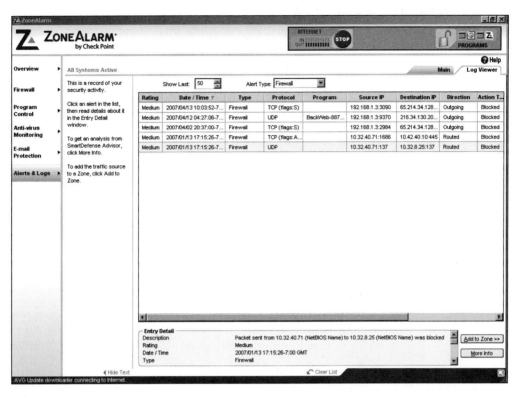

Figure 1-5   ZoneAlarm's log viewer

Routing and Access Control Methods

Routing and access control are important because routers at the network perimeter are critical in the movement of network traffic, whether the traffic is legitimate or harmful. Because of routers' positions on the perimeter, they can be equipped with firewall software to perform packet filtering and other functions.

To set up a defense, you need to know what kinds of attacks to expect and which services and computers might create openings that could be exploited. Security professionals must ensure that no unauthorized access occurs and find vulnerable points that would allow attackers to access the network. An attacker might attempt to access points of entry such as the following:

- *Vulnerable services*—Attackers might be able to exploit known vulnerabilities in a server program.

- *E-mail gateways*—Attackers might be able to attach a virus payload to an e-mail. If a recipient clicks the attachment to open it, the program runs and the virus installs itself on the user's system.

- *Porous borders*—Computers on the network might be listening (waiting for connections) on a port that's not being used. If attackers discover a port that the computer has left open and isn't being used, this open port can give them access to the computer's contents.

Users must have access to the resources needed to do their jobs, but unauthorized people must not be able to gain access to exploit resources. Access control is a vital component of network security and encompasses everything from complex permission configurations on domain controllers to a locked door. You should be familiar with three main methods of access control:

- *Mandatory Access Control (MAC)*—This method defines access capabilities rigorously in advance. System administrators establish what information users can and cannot share.

- *Discretionary Access Control (DAC)*—With this method, network users are given more flexibility in accessing information. Users are allowed to share information with other users; however, the risk of unauthorized access is higher than with the MAC method.

- *Role Based Access Control (RBAC)*—This method establishes organizational roles to limit information access by job function or job responsibility. An employee could have one or more roles that allow access to specific information.

THE IMPACT OF DEFENSE

Although the cost of securing systems and their data might seem high, in terms of **return on investment (ROI)**, the cost of a security breach can be much higher. As mentioned, several laws exist to protect privacy, and those laws can carry severe monetary penalties. When added to the direct and indirect costs of a security breach, a sound security scheme can seem inexpensive by comparison.

A key factor in securing systems successfully is the support you get from upper management. Before security efforts start, executives and managers have to be sold on the idea. Gaining management support serves several important purposes:

- First, the project is going to cost money, and you need to have funding for the project approved beforehand.

- Second, the project requires IT staff time, and managers, supervisors, and employees from all departments must participate to create clear priorities and carry out the security plan.

- Next, setting up and configuring security systems might require downtime for the network, which translates into lost productivity and inconvenience to everyone.

■ Last, and most important for the long-term success of security efforts, executives and management need to support the project from start to finish. If they don't, development, testing, implementation, and maintenance are nearly impossible to carry out because the necessary resources and enforcement won't be available. If management doesn't support security efforts, no one else will.

In addition, remember that planning and implementing security systems aren't enough. Probably the most challenging part of information security is keeping up to date on new threats and other developments in the industry. Security systems must be maintained continuously and updated to provide protection against new threats.

This chapter has given you an overview of network security fundamentals. If you find you aren't familiar with a concept discussed in this chapter, you might want to refer to *Guide to Networking Essentials, Fifth Edition*, by Greg Tomsho, Ed Tittel, and David Johnson (Course Technology, 2007, ISBN 1418837180). Most network professionals keep a library of reference materials to use as quick refreshers or to double-check facts. The computing and security fields are constantly changing, and many employers consider the ability to adapt and learn new concepts a prized "soft skill."

CHAPTER SUMMARY

❏ Network intruders might simply be motivated by a desire to see what kind of data is available on a network and to gain control of computers. Revenge by disgruntled current or former employees might be the primary motivation, however. Some attackers break into accounts and networks for financial gain. Others want to steal proprietary information for their own use or for resale to other parties.

❏ Because the Internet plays an important role in moving business-related traffic from one corporate network to another, an understanding of network security concerns pertaining to online communication is essential. E-mail is one of the most important services to secure because of the possibility of malware in e-mail attachments. In addition, always-on connections present security risks that need to be addressed with firewall and VPN solutions.

❏ Goals for a network security program come from an analysis of risks and an assessment of resources you want to protect. An important goal of any network security effort is maintaining the privacy of customer and employee information. Other goals include preserving data integrity, authenticating approved users of network resources, and enabling remote users to connect to the internal network securely.

❏ An effective network security strategy involves many layers of defense working together to prevent security threats.

❏ Auditing is the process of recording computers accessing a network and resources being accessed and then recording the information in a log file. Review firewall, packet-filtering, and IDS logs regularly to detect vulnerable points that should be closed.

❐ Routers at the network perimeter are critical to the movement of traffic into and out of the network. Access control ensures that users can access resources they need, but unauthorized people can't access network resources to exploit them.

❐ Defense affects the entire organization. Before beginning a security project, management must agree on and support the project. IT staff need input from managers, supervisors, and employees from all departments to create an effective policy and carry out security measures.

KEY TERMS

availability — Making sure those who are authorized to access resources can do so in a reliable and timely manner.

authentication — The process of determining authorized users' identities through matching a username and password, a fingerprint or retinal scan, a smart card and PIN, and so on.

backdoors — A way of gaining unauthorized access to a computer or other resource, usually through an opening in a program that's supposed to be known only to the program's author.

confidentiality — The goal of preventing intentional or unintentional disclosure of communication between a sender and recipient.

cracker — A person who attempts to gain access to unauthorized resources on a network, usually by finding a way to circumvent passwords, firewalls, or other protective measures.

defense in depth (DiD) — A layering approach to security that protects a network at many different levels by using a variety of strategies and methods.

demilitarized zone (DMZ) — A subnetwork of publicly accessible Web, e-mail, and other servers that's outside the LAN but still protected by the firewall.

integrity — The goal of ensuring the accuracy and consistency of information during all processing (storage, transmission, and so forth).

macro viruses — A type of malware that performs the same functions as a macro but tends to be harmful.

malware — Software, such as viruses, worms, and Trojans, designed to cause harm, allow theft, or otherwise compromise a computer system.

nonrepudiation — A method for ensuring that the sender can't deny sending a message and the receiver can't deny receiving it.

packet filters — Devices or software that block or allow transmission of packets of information based on port, IP address, protocol, or other criteria.

packet monkey — An attacker who's primarily interested in blocking Web site activities through a distributed denial-of-service attack.

password security — Measures to protect passwords, including selecting good passwords, keeping them secure, and changing them as needed. Using multiple passwords, including screensaver passwords and passwords for protecting critical applications, also helps guard against unauthorized access.

physical security — Measures taken to physically protect a computer or other network device from theft or environmental disasters.

return on investment (ROI) — The total value gained after a solution has been deployed. A positive ROI means the solution has solved more problems than it creates.

script kiddies — Attackers (often young people) who spread viruses and other malicious scripts and use techniques to exploit weaknesses in computer systems.

signatures — Combinations of flags, IP addresses, and other attack indicators that are detected by a firewall or IDS.

socket — A network connection that uses a TCP/IP port number combined with a computer's IP address.

spyware — A type of malware that includes adware, tracking cookies, dialers, and spam.

Trojan programs — A type of program that appears harmless but introduces viruses or causes damage to a computer or system.

virus — Computer code that copies itself from one place to another surreptitiously and performs actions that range from benign to harmful.

worm — A type of malware that creates files that copy themselves repeatedly and consume disk space. Worms don't require user intervention to be launched; they are self-propagating.

REVIEW QUESTIONS

1. Most network threats originate from what location?

   a. inside the company

   b. script kiddies

   c. backdoors

   d. industrial spies

2. Which of the following is a reason for network attacks? (Choose all that apply.)

   a. social engineering

   b. revenge

   c. financial gain

   d. all of the above

3. Preventing a participant in an electronic transaction from denying that it performed an action is called which of the following?

   a. plausible deniability

   b. integrity

    c. nonrepudiation

    d. undeniability

4. Firewall enforcement of policies is handled primarily by setting up packet-filtering rules contained in which of the following?

    a. routing table

    b. rule base

    c. access control list

    d. packet filter

5. Servers with outside access to the public should never be located where?

    a. on their own subnet

    b. on a DMZ

    c. on an internal LAN

    d. on a network perimeter

6. Packets filters can block or allow transmission of packets based on which of the following criteria? (Choose all that apply.)

    a. port number

    b. open ports

    c. time of access attempts

    d. IP address

7. An attacker who causes harm to systems in support of some principle is categorized as which of the following?

    a. cracker

    b. hacker

    c. industrial spy

    d. cyberterrorist

8. A IP address combined with a TCP/IP port number is called which of the following?

    a. network address

    b. socket

    c. script

    d. port ID

9. A major challenge of network security is the balance of privacy with security needs. True or False?

10. Name four goals of network security.

11. A UPS unit is a component of ——————— security.

    a. virtual

    b. auditing

    c. physical

    d. logical

12. Which of the following is one of the most critical aspects of security?

    a. password security

    b. updated software

    c. antivirus protection

    d. packet filtering

13. A packet-filtering device evaluates data in the payload and compares it with a defined set of rules. True or False?

14. Why is support from management important to network security efforts?

    a. technical input

    b. project management

    c. funding

    d. training

15. In a restrictive firewall policy, what is the starting point for developing a rule base?

    a. allow all traffic

    b. block all traffic except specified types

    c. allow all traffic except specified types

    d. block all traffic

16. In IDSs, the signs of a possible attack are called ———————.

    a. signatures

    b. signals

    c. definitions

    d. alerts

17. Reviewing log files manually is critical to identify possible attacks. True or False?

18. Which of the following types of events can be viewed in log files? (Choose all that apply.)

    a. application events

   b. system events

   c. traffic

   d. information events

19. Which of the following is a type of access control method? (Choose all that apply.)

   a. Mandatory Access Control

   b. Flexible Access Control

   c. Role Based Access Control

   d. Discretionary Access Control

HANDS-ON PROJECTS

**HANDS-ON
PROJECTS**

Hands-On Project 1-1: Learning More About Spyware

Time Required: 10 minutes

Objective: Visit the Anti-Spyware Coalition to learn more about efforts to contain spyware.

Description: In this project, you visit the Anti-Spyware Coalition to learn more about the problem of spyware and other harmful programs. The coalition provides common definitions and guidelines for handling spyware and offers a lot of useful information. You also visit the Center for Democracy and Technology to learn about its efforts to maintain privacy, freedom of expression, and access on the Internet. You need a workstation with Internet access, a pencil, and a piece of paper. A class discussion on findings is highly recommended.

1. Start your Web browser, and go to **www.antispywarecoalition.org/ documents/DefinitionsJune292006.htm**.

2. Read the introduction and the definitions of types of spyware.

3. On a separate piece of paper, write a brief description of the Anti-Spyware Coalition (ASC).

4. Next, go to **www.cdt.org/**, the Center for Democracy and Technology.

5. Click the **About Us** tab and read the statement at the top of the page.

6. Click the **Mission and Principles** link on the right.

7. Do you agree with the CDT's principles? Why or why not? Write a brief explanation.

8. When you're finished, turn your paper in to your instructor, and leave your computer running for the next project.

Hands-On Project 1-2: Downloading and Installing LanSpy

Time Required: 15 minutes

Objective: Download and install LanSpy, a port-scanning utility.

Description: LanSpy is a port-scanning utility that gives you all kinds of information about remote computers, such as DNS servers, MAC addresses, services, processes, users, sessions, shares, and more.

1. Start your Web browser and go to **http://lantricks.com/download/**.

2. Click the **LanSpy Setup.exe (from LanTricks.com)** link to download the software. Save the file to your desktop.

3. In Windows Explorer, double-click the installation program file for LanSpy, and follow the prompts to install it. Accept all default installation settings.

4. Start LanSpy by double-clicking the desktop shortcut. Figure 1-6 shows the LanSpy user interface.

5. Leave LanSpy running for the next project.

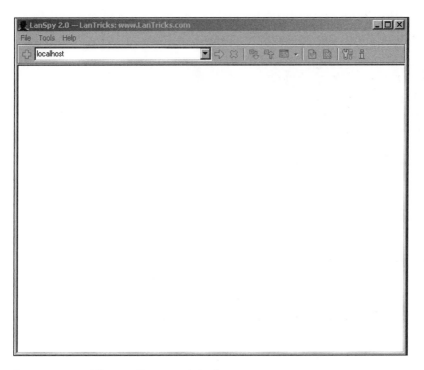

Figure 1-6   The LanSpy user interface

Hands-On Project 1-3: Using LanSpy

Time Required: 45 minutes

Objective: Use LanSpy to examine a remote computer.

Description: In this project, you use LanSpy to scan a classmate's computer. You examine the information LanSpy collects and assess how an attacker could use this information to launch an attack. You need the IP address of a classmate's computer before starting this project.

1. If necessary, start LanSpy.

2. You need to make sure you have valid logon credentials, or LanSpy might not be able to scan. You need the correct domain, logon name, and password.

Of course, an attacker wouldn't have this logon information, but you're experimenting to see what information a port scanner can gather from an unsecured remote computer.

NOTE

3. Click **File**, **Options** from the LanSpy menu, and then click **Autentification** (yes, it's misspelled) in the pane on the left (see Figure 1-7).

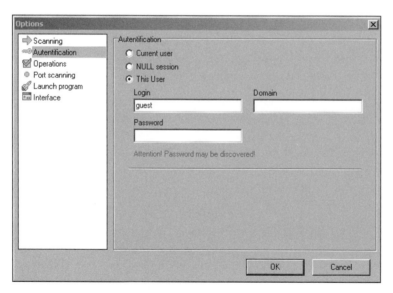

Figure 1-7   LanSpy authentication options

4. Enter information in the Login, Domain, and Password text boxes, and then click **OK**.

5. Enter your classmate's IP address at the top of the LanSpy window. Click the green arrow to begin the scan, which might take up to 30 minutes to complete.

6. When LanSpy has finished scanning, examine the results. They should look similar to Figure 1-8. What information did LanSpy discover that an attacker could exploit?

_____

_____

_____

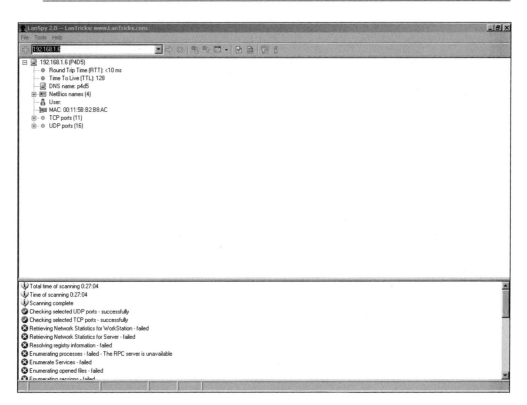

Figure 1-8   LanSpy authenticated scan results

7. Click **Tools**, **Another LanSpy** from the menu to open a second instance of the program. Don't close the results window for the previous scan.

8. Click **File**, **Options** from the menu to open the Options dialog box, click **Authentification** in the left pane, click the **NULL session** option button, and then click **OK**.

9. Enter the IP address again (if necessary) and rescan. The results of your null session scan should be similar to the results in Figure 1-9. Were the results the same?

_____

_____

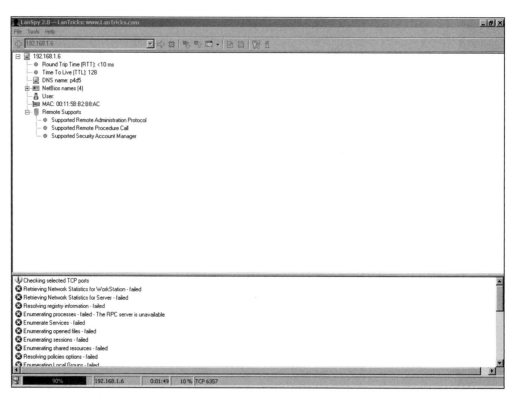

Figure 1-9   LanSpy null session scan results

10. Compare the results of the two scans. What information was found in the authenticated scan and the null session scan? What are the security implications?

_____

_____

_____

_____

11. Exit LanSpy, and close any open windows.

CASE PROJECTS

CASE PROJECTS

Case Project 1-1: Preliminary Research for Green Globe

Review the description of this book's running case project in the front matter. This information should guide you in completing each chapter's case project.

NOTE
Your instructor might decide to assign project teams to work on this case because a project as complex as this one would rarely be handled by one person. If you're assigned to a project team, you might want to review some IT project management resources for guidelines on how to split up the work, establish milestones, and keep on track to complete the assignment on time.

Your firm has been hired to design a secure network for Green Globe. Your supervisor has dispatched you to the Phoenix location to evaluate needs, assess the location, and complete a preliminary design. The facility layout is shown in the diagram your instructor will provide. These are the major requirements your design must meet, although you might think of others not listed here:

- One fully networked location, 100% company owned, in Phoenix. This location is the permanent base of operations.

- Capable of supporting up to 200 full-time users in these departments: Account Management; Project Management; Research and Development; Engineering; Sales and Marketing; Legal; Administration (includes office staff and management); Reports and Publications; Client Services; and Facilities and Technology Support.

- High security is required because extremely sensitive data must remain confidential.

- Temporary access to certain resources must be available for external entities, which include some limited mobile access.

- The company must adhere to applicable state and federal laws on information security and privacy.

- The network must support local and global mobility. Approximately half the employees based at the main office require mobility, and all field staff require some level of mobile services.

- The company is concerned about staff retention and wants to offer flexible working arrangements as an additional benefit, if possible.

In this project, you (and your team, if assigned) review and collect project management materials to prepare for this project. The most well-known project management resource is the Project Management Institute at *www.pmi.org*. Other IT-specific resources can be found with an Internet search. Download any templates, worksheets, or software to help with this project, as long as you violate no copyright laws or your school's guidelines.

2

ADVANCED TCP/IP

After reading this chapter and completing the exercises, you will be able to:

♦ Explain the fundamentals of TCP/IP networking

♦ Describe IPv4 packet structure and explain packet fragmentation

♦ Describe Internet Protocol version 6 (IPv6)

This chapter introduces you to the fundamentals of TCP/IP networking. To secure a network, understanding the TCP/IP protocol suite is vital. You review IP addressing briefly, revisit the TCP life cycle, and review how TCP communications sessions work. Then you move on to learn about Internet Protocol version 6 (IPv6), the next generation of IP.

Even if you're familiar with TCP/IP and IPv4, IPv6 involves some new protocols and functions you need to know. In this chapter, you examine the core protocols of IPv6 and learn about IPv6 addressing and utilities.

TCP/IP FUNDAMENTALS REVIEW

Transmission Control Protocol/Internet Protocol (TCP/IP) is actually a suite of many protocols for transmitting information from point to point on a network. You're probably already familiar with TCP/IP, but it never hurts to brush up. With the dynamic nature of information technology, it's easy to forget even simple details, so this section gives you a quick refresher on TCP/IP basics, such as the Open Systems Interconnection (OSI) model, IP addressing, and subnetting.

The OSI Model and TCP/IP Protocols

You're probably familiar with the OSI model of network communications, which divides communications into seven separate layers. TCP/IP has its own stack of protocols that correspond roughly to these layers. The two models are shown in Figure 2-1.

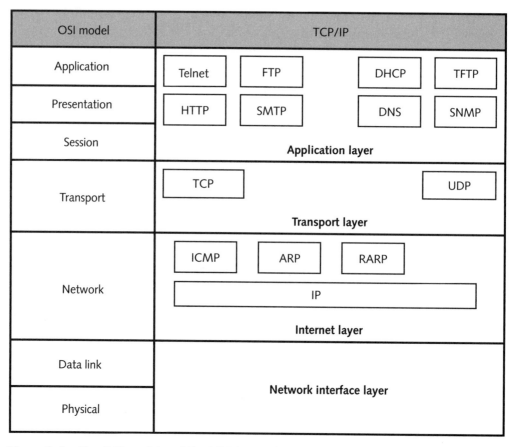

Figure 2-1   The OSI model and the TCP/IP stack

You should be familiar with most of these protocols and their functions. If you need a more detailed refresher on the TCP/IP stack, the OSI model, and the major protocols operating at different layers, do an Internet search on "TCP/IP and the OSI Model." Dozens of helpful sites are available for every level of knowledge, such as *www.tcpipguide.com/free/index.htm.*

TCP/IP Addressing

IP addresses currently in use on the Internet conform to **Internet Protocol version 4 (IPv4)**, which calls for addresses with 32 bits of data. Each 32-bit address is divided into four groups called octets; each octet contains 8 bits of data. In binary, an IP address looks like this: 10000000.00100110.00101100.11100010. Because this notation is a bit unmanageable, IP addresses are usually converted to the more familiar dotted decimal notation, such as 192.168.10.1. As you know, an IP address consists of two main parts:

- The **network address**, the part of an IP address shared among computers in a network
- The **host address**, which is unique to a computer in its subnet

These two parts are combined with a third dotted decimal value, the **subnet mask**, which tells another computer which part of the IP address is the network address and which part is the host address. You learn more about subnet masks in "Subnetting" later in this chapter.

One way attackers can gain access to your network is by determining the IP addresses of computers. After they have an address, they can attempt to take over the computer and use it to launch attacks on other computers in the network or access resources on the network. Therefore, one of the fundamental requirements of network security is to understand IP addresses and other network addresses so that you can conceal or change them to deter attackers.

IP addresses are valuable commodities. If attackers can find a computer's IP address, they can run a port scan to look for open ports that can be exploited. If you can hide IP addresses, you can prevent certain attacks. To hide the addresses of computers on your network, you can use Network Address Translation (NAT) to translate your private network's nonroutable internal addresses into the address of the NAT server's external interface connected to the Internet, thereby hiding the internal addresses.

Security is not the only reason for using NAT. The Internet has grown at a rate not expected by those who created the IPv4 32-bit addressing scheme. Today, IP addresses are in short supply, so Internet Protocol version 6 (IPv6) is under development. By sharing one or more of the NAT server's IP addresses with internal hosts, NAT has allowed more time to work out the details of IPv6. You can also use a proxy server to effectively conceal IP addresses of internal machines (see Figure 2-2).

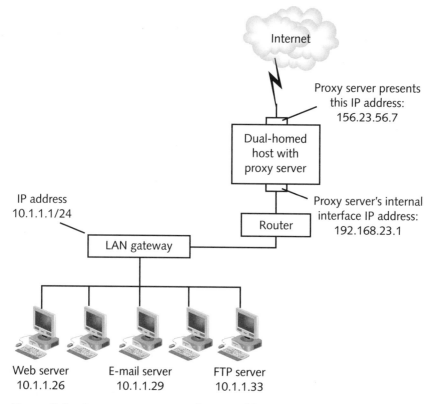

Figure 2-2   Proxy servers concealing IP addresses on the internal network

Address Classes

In IPv4, addresses are separated into address categories called "classes." An IP address class is determined by the number of its networks compared to the number of its hosts. For example, a Class A address uses 8 bits for the network portion of the address and 24 bits for the host portion. The classes have been divided as shown in Table 2-1. Remember that private network addresses can never be used on the public Internet.

Table 2-1   IP address classes

Class	First octet decimal range	Default subnet mask	Reserved private address range	Purpose
Class A	1–126 Note: 127.x.x.x is reserved for TCP/IP local interface testing.	255.0.0.0	10.0.0.0 to 10.255.255.255	Large corporations and governments
Class B	128–191	255.255.0.0	172.16.0.0 to 172.31.255.255	Medium networks
Class C	192–223	255.255.255.0	192.168.0.0 to 192.168.255.255	Small networks
Class D	224–239	N/A	N/A	Multicasting
Class E	240–254	N/A	N/A	Experimentation

TIP   You can find a number of IP address calculators on the Web; an excellent one is at *www.subnetmask.info/*. For more on IP addresses and subnets, refer to *Guide to TCP/IP, Third Edition*, by Ed Tittel and Laura Chappell (Course Technology, 2006, ISBN 1418837555).

Subnetting

As mentioned, an IP address identifies both the network and the host. Because address classes already have octets set (Class A has the first octet set, Class B the first two, and so on), the remainder of the address is available for masking. For example, a default Class B address has 16 bits available for the host portion of the address. This means the network has a total of more than 16,000 host addresses! However, most networks use some of the host bits to identify the network, essentially creating several smaller subnetworks instead of one large network. Using more host bits to identify the network gives addressing flexibility, in that the entire range of addresses can be divided into smaller, more manageable subnetworks. This is where subnetting comes in. A subnet mask identifies what portion of the IP address contains the network ID and what portion contains the host ID.

Subnet masking is used to logically segment internal networks, as described previously. It can also be used for the following purposes:

- Mirror the organization's physical layout.

- Mirror the organization's administrative structure.

- Plan for future growth.

- Reduce and control network traffic.

When administrators create subnetworks that mirror the organization's structure or physical layout, managing security, access needs, and auditing is easier. This concept is similar to creating sites and domains. Trying to manage many different user groups gets complicated. If all users with similar security and access needs are grouped into a single subnet, the entire group can be managed instead of managing each user separately. Subnets are used to make network management easier and to optimize security, performance, and access.

When administrators create subnets, they borrow bits from the host portion of the IP address to make a set of subnetworks. The number of borrowed bits determines how many subnets and hosts are available. An administrator can use up to 14 bits for subnetting a Class B network. (Two bits must be available for hosts.) When you subnet, you lose some addresses that would have been available for hosts, but a network of 16,000 hosts would be unwieldy to manage, and performance would suffer with so much traffic on a single network segment. Table 2-2 shows how subnetting is used on Class B networks.

Table 2-2   Class B subnetting

Subnet	Number of subnetworks	Usable hosts per subnet
255.255.192.0	2	16382
255.255.224.0	6	8190
255.255.240.0	14	4094
255.255.248.0	30	2046
255.255.252.0	62	1022
255.255.254.0	126	510
255.255.255.0	254	254
255.255.255.128	510	126
255.255.255.192	1022	62
255.255.255.224	2046	30
255.255.255.240	4094	14
255.255.255.248	8190	6
255.255.255.252	16382	2

Although you should already have a good working knowledge of subnetting, a brief refresher is useful. You might find it helpful to remember how binary stacks up to decimal in IP addressing. Table 2-3 shows the decimal equivalents of binary place values.

Table 2-3   Binary-to-decimal values

Binary digit	1	1	1	0	0	0	0	0
Decimal equivalent	128	64	32	16	8	4	2	1

Now that you remember what decimal value each binary digit in an IP octet represents, you can review subnetting. First, you select the mask that meets your needs, and then you assign the mask to your network. To do this, you must find the usable IP address ranges for the host address and broadcast address. Converting the last masking octet to binary does this most easily. Find the binary place value of the last masking digit, and that's the block size. (Block size refers to the maximum number of usable hosts in a subnet.) Subnetting a Class C address goes something like this:

Class C address: 199.1.10.0 (major network number)

Default mask: 255.255.255.0

Selected mask: 255.255.255.224

Mask converted to binary: 11111111.11111111.11111111.11100000

Notice that the last masked digit occupies the binary place value of 32 (which is the block size). Starting with the major network number, increment by 32 until you reach the mask's number (224). It looks like this:

- 0 (00000000) Unusable; cannot be all zeros

- 32 (00100000)

- 64 (01000000)

- 96 (01100000)

- 128 (10000000)

- 160 (10100000)

- 192 (11000000)

- 224 (11100000) Unusable; same as the subnet mask

Table 2-4 shows the host address ranges, broadcast addresses, and subnets for this example.

Table 2-4   Subnetting example

Subnet identifier	Valid host range	Broadcast address for subnet
199.1.10.32	199.1.10.33–199.1.10.62	199.1.10.63
199.1.10.64	199.1.10.65–199.1.10.94	199.1.10.95
199.1.10.96	199.1.10.97–199.1.10.126	199.1.10.127
199.1.10.128	199.1.10.129–199.1.10.158	199.1.10.159
199.1.10.160	199.1.10.161–199.1.10.190	199.1.10.191
199.1.10.192	199.1.10.193–199.1.10.222	199.1.10.223

NOTE   This example shows only the usable host addresses. Remember that the broadcast address for a subnet can't be used as a host address, and an address that's the same as the subnet identifier (the first address in a subnet range, such as 199.1.10.32) is not a valid address.

Here is the formula for calculating subnets:

$2^y - 2$ = number of usable subnets (y is the number of borrowed bits)

$2^x - 2$ = number of usable hosts per subnet (x is the number of unborrowed bits)

Variable Length Subnet Masking

Networks that don't have a large number of available IP addresses can use **variable length subnet masking (VLSM)**, which involves applying masks of varying sizes to the same network. VLSM can help an organization with a limited number of IP addresses and subnets of varying lengths use address space more efficiently. VLSM is a means of allocating IP addressing according to the network's needs. This allocation method creates subnets within subnets and multiple divisions of an IP network. VLSM is often used to secure stub networks or serial lines, making those subnets only as large as needed.

ACTIVITY

Activity 2-1: Determining Your Computer's IP Address

Time Required: 10 minutes

Objective: Determine the IP address of your computer.

Description: Every computer connected to the Internet is assigned an IP address. Often the address is generated dynamically, so it changes from session to session; for dial-up users, for example, an ISP assigns an address dynamically at the time of connection. With some DSL, ISDN, and T-1 or other connections, however, a static IP address is used. In this activity, you use the Ipconfig command to determine your computer's IP address. Ipconfig can be used on Windows NT 4.0 and later.

1. Click **Start**, **Run**, type **cmd**, and click **OK** to open a command prompt window.

2. At the command prompt, type **ipconfig /all** and press **Enter**. The screen displays your IP address as well as other information. In some cases, you might have several addresses. The IP address assigned to your Ethernet adapter is the external address.

3. Write down your IP address, subnet mask, and default gateway address on the following lines. In addition, write down the address assigned to your Ethernet adapter, if applicable.

_____

_____

_____

_____

4. Type **exit** and press **Enter** to close the command prompt window.

For a complete listing of Ipconfig commands, type ipconfig /? at the command prompt.

2

Classless Interdomain Routing

Classless Interdomain Routing (CIDR) is an address notation scheme that specifies the number of masked bits in an IP address/subnet mask combination. Instead of using standard notation for subnet masks, with CIDR you can simply list the number of masked binary bits. The subnet mask 255.255.255.224, for example, has a total of 27 masked bits (eight in each of the first three octets and three in the last octet). In CIDR notation, it's 192.168.6.0/27. (Remember that the last address before the next subnet identifier is always the broadcast address for the range.) CIDR overcomes the limitations of the default subnet masks of 8, 16, and 24 bits for Classes A, B, and C so that unused addresses don't go to waste.

If you use subnet masks to segment network traffic into a series of smaller subnetworks, plan in advance how you will allocate nodes to each segment and assign subnet masks to those segments. Your planning might include network growth projections for the next two to five years so that you won't have to set up different subnet designations with each future network change.

Supernetting, also known as summarization, is used to summarize multiple routing table entries into one entry. In addition, classless routing is used to exchange subnet mask information between routers in routing updates. Classless routing allows VLSM and supernetting to work.

Unicasting, Multicasting, and Broadcasting

Each IP address class (Class A through Class E) is used with a different type of network. The address classes reflect the network's size and whether the packet is unicast or multicast. In a **unicast** transmission, one packet is sent from a server to each client that requests a file or application, such as a streaming video presentation. If five clients request the video presentation, the server transmits the video presentation separately to each of the five clients. In the same example, a **multicast** transmission means the server can treat all five clients as a group and send one transmission that reaches all five clients. Multicasts can be used to reduce network traffic when transmitting bandwidth-intensive applications or files to multiple hosts. Instead of sending one to each host separately, the files or applications can be sent to all recipients at once.

A third type of network communication is called a **broadcast**, which sends a communication to all points on a specific network. (Routers are often configured so that they don't forward broadcasts to other networks.) There are two types of broadcasts:

Flooded

- Broadcasts for any subnet

- Routers don't forward because they are considered local

- Uses the address 255.255.255.255

Directed

- For a specific subnet

- Routers forward directed broadcasts

- Uses the broadcast address for the intended subnet

EXAMINING INTERNET PROTOCOL VERSION 4

TCP/IP is packet-based; it gives computers a fairly simple framework for transmitting information in small packages called packets or datagrams. Unfortunately, TCP/IP packets give attackers another way to gain entry into a network. Attackers can intercept packets and falsify the information in them or manipulate the packets in a way that makes it impossible for receiving servers to respond, which then disables those servers and opens the network to attack.

IP Datagrams

TCP/IP is transmitted along networks as discrete chunks called packets or **datagrams**. Each complete message is usually separated into multiple datagrams. Each datagram contains information about the source and destination IP addresses, a variety of control settings, and the actual data client and host exchange.

Each IP datagram is divided into different sections. The primary subdivisions are the header and the data, described in the following sections. Some packets have another segmented section at the end called a **footer** (or "trailer") containing data that indicates it's the end of the packet. An error-checking algorithm called a Cyclic Redundancy Check (CRC) might also be added in the footer.

IP Header Structure

The data in an IP packet is the part that end users see, but the **header** is the part that computers use to communicate, and it plays an important role in network security and intrusion detection. An IP header (similar to a TCP header, described in "TCP Headers" later in this chapter) contains a number of fields. Figure 2-3 shows a common way of depicting information in an IP header, which is divided into sections of 32-bit layers.

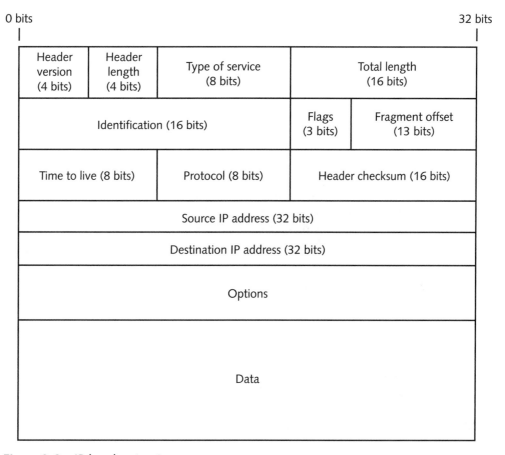

Figure 2-3   IP header structure

It's helpful to divide IP header sections into fields because their value in configuring packet filters differs. Each section has varying importance to attackers, too, so it's vital to know what each one does to protect against different types of attacks. These are the fields in the IP header structure:

- *Header version*—This field identifies the IP version used to generate the packet.

- *Header length*—This field describes the length of the header in 32-bit words and is a 4-bit value. The default value is 20. A "word" is the size of information a computer can move as it's working with it; more specifically, it's the width of the processor's registers. As you should recall from your hardware classes, registers are the storage areas where the processor does calculations. Most computers since the 386 have a 32-bit word size; some newer processors, such as the Intel Itanium and the AMD Opteron, have a 64-bit word size.

- *Type of service*—This field expresses the quality of service in the packet's transmission through the network. Four options are available: minimize delay, maximize throughput, maximize reliability, and minimize cost. Most IP network setups don't enable an application to set this value.

- *Total length*—This 16-bit field specifies the packet's total length to a maximum of 65,535 bytes.

- *Identification*—This 16-bit value helps divide the data stream into packets of information. The receiving computer (possibly a firewall) uses each packet's identification number to reassemble the packets that make up the data stream in the correct order.

- *Flags*—This 3-bit value indicates whether the packet is a fragment—one packet within a sequence of packets that make up an entire communication—and whether it's the last fragment or more are to follow.

- *Fragment offset*—If the data received is a fragment, this value indicates where it belongs in the sequence of fragments so that a packet can be reassembled.

- *Time to live (TTL)*—This 8-bit value identifies the maximum time the packet can remain in the system before it's dropped. Each router or device the packet passes through reduces the TTL by a value of one.

- *Protocol*—This field identifies the type of transport packet being carried (for example, 1 = ICMP, 2 = IGMP, 6 = TCP, and 17 = UDP).

- *Header checksum*—This field is the sum of the 16-bit values in the packet header, calculated by the CRC algorithm and expressed as a single value.

- *Source IP address*—This field is the address of the computer or device that sent the IP packet.

- *Destination IP address*—This field is the address of the computer or device receiving the IP packet.

- *Options*—This field can include items such as a security field and several source routing fields that the packet sender uses to supply routing information. Gateways can then use this routing information to send the packet to its destination.

Programs that capture packets as they pass through a network interface give you another way to view packet header information. Most network operating systems (NOSs) have some type of built-in or add-on program to monitor network activity, such as Windows Network Monitor. Many security administrators, however, prefer third-party applications for their versatility and extra features. Wireshark (formerly Ethereal; *www.wireshark.org*), for example, is an open-source network analysis utility that tracks packets and supplies detailed information on them. You use Wireshark in Activity 2-2.

ICMP Messages

Internet Control Message Protocol (ICMP) is designed to assist TCP/IP networks with troubleshooting communication problems. When used correctly, ICMP produces messages that tell a host whether another host can be reached through a ping signal.

A firewall or packet filter must be able to determine, based on a packet's message type, whether an ICMP packet should be allowed to pass. Table 2-5 lists some common ICMP types.

Table 2-5   ICMP types

ICMP type	Name	ICMP type	Name
0	Echo Reply	17	Address Mask Request
3	Destination Unreachable	18	Address Mask Reply
4	Source Quench	30	Traceroute
5	Redirect	31	Datagram Conversion Error
6	Alternate Host Address	32	Mobile Host Redirect
8	Echo	33	IPv6 Where-Are-You
9	Router Advertisement	34	IPv6 Here-I-Am
10	Router Solicitation	35	Mobile Registration Request
11	Time Exceeded	36	Mobile Registration Reply
12	Parameter Problem	37	Domain Name Request
13	Timestamp	38	Domain Name Reply
14	Timestamp Reply	39	SKIP
15	Information Request	40	Photuris
16	Information Reply	41	Used by experimental mobility protocols
19–29, 42–255	Reserved	1–2, 7	Unassigned

TIP

Many ICMP types have codes associated with them. Some common ones include codes for type 3 (Destination Unreachable) ICMP messages. For example, a type 3 ICMP message with a code of 13 indicates the message was administratively prohibited, usually meaning that an access list or firewall rejected the message. You can find a complete list of ICMP types and their codes at *www.iana.org/assignments/icmp-parameters*.

TCP Headers

TCP/IP packets don't contain just IP header information. They also contain TCP headers (shown in Figure 2-4) that provide hosts with a different set of flags—and give attackers a different set of components they can misuse in an attempt to attack networks.

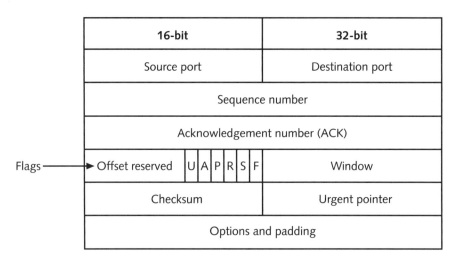

16-bit	32-bit
Source port	Destination port
Sequence number	
Acknowledgement number (ACK)	
Offset reserved · U A P R S F	Window
Checksum	Urgent pointer
Options and padding	

Flags ──────▶ Offset reserved

Figure 2-4   A TCP header

From a security standpoint, the Flags section of a TCP header (labeled as "Offset reserved" in Figure 2-4) is important because it's the one you can filter for when you create packet–filtering rules. For example, the TCP header portion of a TCP packet that has an acknowledgement (ACK) flag set to 1 rather than 0 indicates that the destination computer has received the packets that were sent previously. RFC 793 includes specifications for these six control flags in a TCP header:

- URG (urgent)

- ACK (acknowledgment)

- PSH (push function, which forces TCP to forward and deliver data)

- RST (reset the connection)

- SYN (synchronize sequence numbers)

- FIN (no more data from sender)

NOTE

Technology standards are explained in Requests for Comments (RFCs), which you can look up *www.rfc-editor.org*. Often an RFC is updated to add new information, so you should make a habit of checking to see what the current standards are and what has been added. For example, RFC 3168 defines the addition of Explicit Congestion Notification (ECN) to TCP and IP and adds two flags to the TCP header: ECN-Echo and CWR. Bits 8 and 9 of the reserved field in the TCP header are used for these two new flags. You can learn more about this update at *www.faqs.org/rfcs/rfc3168.html*.

UDP Headers

User Datagram Protocol (UDP) provides a datagram transport service for IP, but this protocol is considered unreliable because it's connectionless. In other words, a UDP packet doesn't depend on an actual connection being established from host to client. UDP is much faster than TCP and is appropriate when delivery doesn't need to be guaranteed. TCP establishes a connection and checks on delivery with acknowledgements, but UDP simply ships the packets and relies on other protocols to ensure delivery, perform error checking, and so on. It's especially useful for real-time applications, multimedia, or anything that requires speed over reliability.

UDP is used for broadcasting messages or for protocols that don't require the same level of service as TCP. For example, Simple Network Management Protocol (SNMP) and Trivial File Transfer Protocol (TFTP) are normally used on LANs, where packet loss is less of a problem. On the other hand, attackers can scan for open UDP services to exploit by sending empty UDP datagrams to a suspected open port. If the port is closed, the system sends back an ICMP Destination Unreachable message (type 3). UDP packets have their own headers, as shown in Figure 2-5, in addition to the data part of packets.

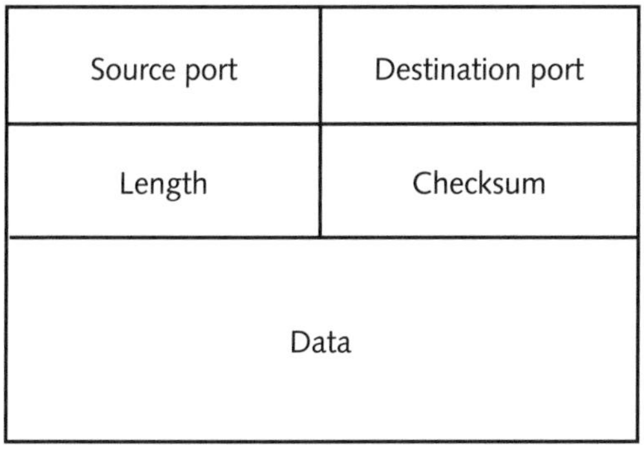

Source port	Destination port
Length	Checksum
Data	

Figure 2-5   A UDP packet header and data

 UDP is described in detail in RFC 768.

TIP

ACTIVITY

Activity 2-2: Using Wireshark

Time Required: 45 minutes

Objective: Download, install, and explore software for monitoring and analyzing network traffic.

Description: To get a better idea of what TCP/IP packet headers look like, using a network traffic analyzer to capture packets as they enter or leave your network can be helpful. In this activity, you download and use Wireshark to observe packets. You also need to install a packet capture utility called WinPcap for running Wireshark.

To do this activity, you must stop any firewall programs you're running.

NOTE

1. Start your Web browser and go to **www.wireshark.org/download.html**.

2. Under Windows 2000/XP/2003/Vista installer, click the link to start downloading Wireshark. (If the download sites have changed, as they often do, download the latest stable version of Wireshark.)

3. Save the installation setup file to your desktop. When the download is finished, double-click the Wireshark setup file on your desktop to start the installation.

Note that version 0.99.5 was used for this activity. If you download a different version, your screens and steps might vary slightly.

NOTE

4. You're prompted to install WinPcap during the installation because Wireshark needs it to capture packets. Follow the instructions to install it, and don't restart your computer after installing WinPcap.

5. Follow the prompts to install Wireshark and WinPcap. Accept all default installation settings. After the installations are finished, start Wireshark. Figure 2-6 shows the user interface.

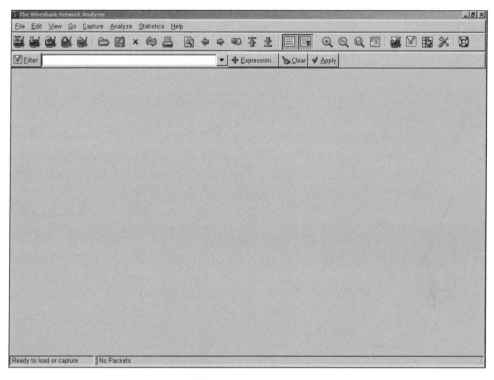

Figure 2-6   The Wireshark interface

6. To list available capture interfaces, click the far-left button on the toolbar.

Hovering the mouse over an icon displays a description.

TIP

7. Click the **Start** button for your Ethernet interface to begin capturing packets. Your list of interfaces should look similar to the one in Figure 2-7.

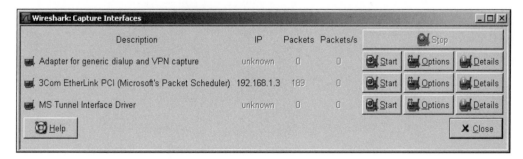

Figure 2-7   The Wireshark: Capture Interfaces dialog box

8. Allow Wireshark to capture packets for a few minutes or long enough to capture a variety of packet types. Packet types are color-coded for easier identification. Figure 2-8 shows a list of packets that Wireshark captured.

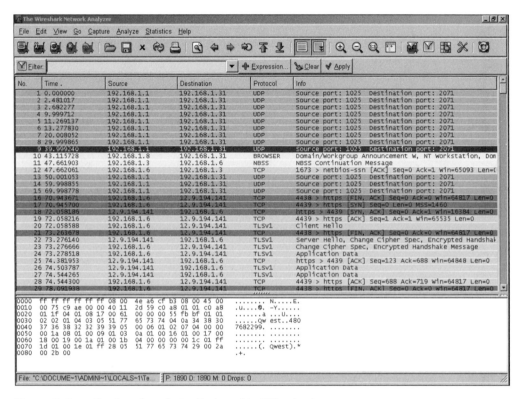

Figure 2-8   Captured packets displayed in Wireshark

9. Examine the types of packets and what they look like. Note that the time each packet was captured is represented as number of seconds since the first packet.

10. Click **Edit**, **Preferences** from the menu to open the Preferences dialog box. In the pane on the left, click to expand the **User Interface** category, if necessary, and then click **Columns** (see Figure 2-9).

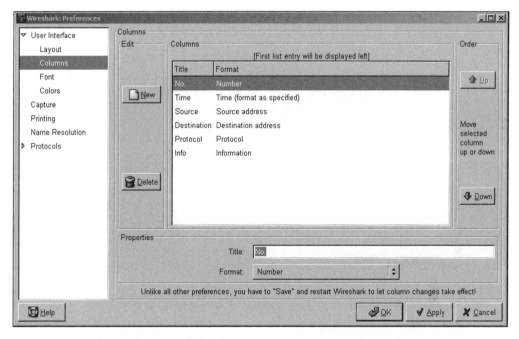

Figure 2-9   The Preferences dialog box

11. On the right, click **Time** in the list box to set preferences for the Time column in your capture window. Click the **Format** list arrow at the bottom, and click **Absolute time**. Click **OK**.

12. Save the capture to your desktop by clicking **File**, **Save As** from the menu. In the Save in list box, click **Desktop**, type **capture1** for the filename, and then click **Save**.

13. Exit Wireshark. Changes to the Column preferences are applied after restarting the program.

14. Restart Wireshark. Open capture1 by clicking **File**, **Open Recent** from the menu, and clicking it in the list. (It should be the first capture listed.) Notice that the time of capture is now shown in international standard time notation.

By default, the Wireshark layout is three horizontal panes, and you might need to adjust them to see data. Use the adjustment handles to resize panes, if necessary, so that you can see the packet list, details, and bytes.

TIP

15. Examine the middle and bottom panes showing packet details and packet bytes. Selecting any part of packet details highlights corresponding packet bytes and vice versa. Figure 2-10 shows information for a captured packet.

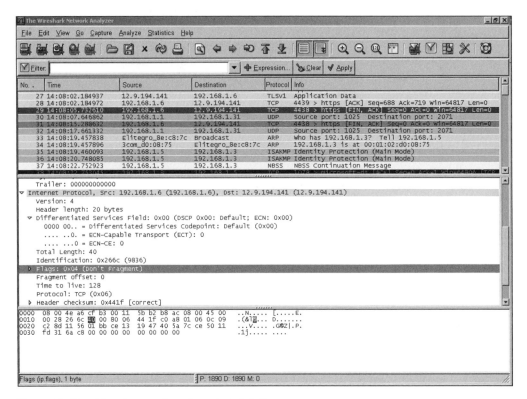

Figure 2-10   Viewing captured packet details

16. Examine the information, and when you're finished, exit Wireshark. Leave your system running for the next activity.

Packet Fragmentation

Fragmentation of IP packets was originally developed as a means of allowing large packets to pass through routers that had frame size limitations. Routers were then able to divide packets into multiple fragments and send them along the network, where receiving routers reassembled them in the correct order and passed them along to their destination.

Fragmentation creates a number of security problems, however. Because the TCP or UDP port number is supplied only at the beginning of a packet, it appears only in fragment number 0. Fragments numbered 1 or higher pass through the filter without being scrutinized because they don't contain any port information. An attacker simply has to modify the IP header to make all fragment numbers start at 1 or higher. All fragments then go through the filter and can access internal resources.

To improve security, you should configure the firewall or packet filter to drop all fragmented packets; in addition, fragmentation is seldom used now with improvements in routers. You could also have the firewall reassemble fragmented packets and allow only complete packets to pass through.

TIP

You can use your Wireshark capture from Activity 2-2 to examine packet fragmentation flags (and other packet fields discussed in this section). In the packet details pane, expand the Internet Protocol details and look at the flags. For example, in Figure 2-10, the packet details show a Flags value of 0x04, which means the Don't Fragment flag is set. A value of 0x00 means the Don't Fragment flag is not set. Examining packet captures is the best way to learn the fields of different packet types.

The TCP Life Cycle

Before a client initiates a TCP session, it must determine the port number that identifies the session and the starting sequence number. The port number is the source port for packets from the client to the server and the destination port for packets from the server to the client. The sequence number is determined based on an internal 32-bit clock that ensures randomness and makes sure sequence numbers don't overlap if lost packets arrive late. After determining these two items, the client initiates a session with the TCP three-way handshake.

TCP Three-Way Handshake

The TCP three-way handshake (see Figure 2-11) establishes a reliable connection between two points. Three methods are used to control the flow of data:

- Buffering
- TCP sliding windows
- Congestion avoidance

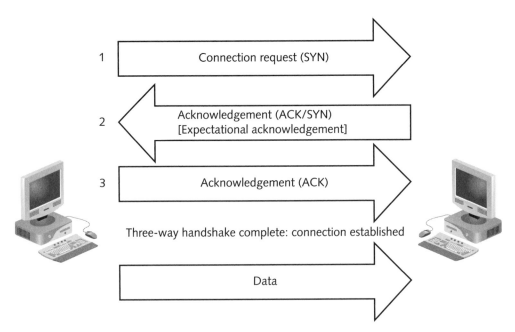

The first frame has the same sequence number and ACK
as the third packet of the three-way handshake

Figure 2-11   TCP three-way handshake

After a connection is established, TCP sliding windows control the flow and efficiency of communications. The size of the sliding window determines the number of ACKs sent for a data transfer and constrains the amount of data that's sent before the receiving host sends an ACK to the sending host. The sender controls the size of the sliding window.

After data has been exchanged, either party can end the session by sending a packet with the FIN flag set to indicate to the other side that the session can be terminated. The station receiving this initial FIN flag sends a response packet with the ACK flag and its own FIN flag set to acknowledge receipt of the FIN packet and show that it's also ready to end communications. If the receiving side still has data to send, however, it sends only an ACK back and continues sending data until it's done.

After all data has been sent, the side that first received the FIN sends its own FIN to show that termination can commence. During this lapse between the sender FIN and the responder FIN, the sender and responder are in the FIN WAIT 2 (sender of the first FIN flag) and CLOSE WAIT (recipient of the first FIN flag) status. Some applications, such as Web browsers, often use this type of half-closed connection so that a connection can be brought back into use without having to initiate the session again.

Domain Name System

Domain Name System (DNS) is a general-purpose service used mainly on the Internet. DNS servers translate host names to IP addresses used to identify the host computer. To connect to Web sites, users need a DNS server that can translate the **fully qualified domain names (FQDNs)** they enter, such as *www.course.com*, to the corresponding IP addresses so that the right computers can connect to one another.

In terms of network security, DNS is important because it gives network administrators another tool for blocking unwanted communication. With firewalls, Web browsers, and proxy servers, administrators can enter DNS names to block Web sites containing content that's considered offensive or unsuitable. In addition, networks that use DNS servers need to enable traffic through the DNS servers when packet filtering is set up.

DNS can be exploited in many ways. Attackers often attempt buffer overflow, zone transfer, or cache poisoning attacks. In a DNS buffer overflow attack, an overly long DNS name is sent to the server. When the server is unable to process or interpret the DNS name, it can't process other requests. A DNS cache poisoning attack exploits the fact that every DNS packet contains a "Question" section and an "Answer" section. An older, more vulnerable server has stored answers sent in response to requests to connect to DNS addresses. Attackers can break into the cache to discover the DNS addresses of computers on the network. Most (but not all) DNS servers, however, have been patched to eliminate this vulnerability.

DNS zone files contain a list of every DNS-configured host on a network as well as their IP addresses. Microsoft DNS-enabled networks also list all services running on DNS-configured hosts. When an attacker attempts to penetrate a network, the DNS zone file can provide a list of exploitable targets on that network. When configuring DNS servers connected to the Internet, disable zone transfers to all hosts except those internal to the network. Internal hosts must be able to transfer zone information to update their records.

Encryption

Packet filters, firewalls, and proxy servers provide protection for packets that pass through a gateway at the perimeter of a network or subnet. However, corruption can also occur between the sending gateway and the destination network's gateway. To protect a packet's contents from being intercepted, firewalls and other security devices often encrypt the contents of packets leaving the network and decrypt incoming packets. Encryption is the process of concealing information to render it unreadable to all but the intended recipients. Encryption turns ordinary (plain text) information into encoded cipher text.

Encryption on the Internet often makes use of digital certificates—electronic documents containing encrypted numerals and characters called a digital signature, which authenticates the identity of the person sending the certificate. Certificates make use of keys, which are long blocks of encoded text generated by algorithms. The sending host uses a key to encrypt data before transmission, and the receiving host uses the key to decrypt data. The encryption key can be any length, but most encryption methods use key lengths from 40 to 256 bits. Longer keys are more secure but at the cost of performance.

An organization that wants to encrypt data often needs to set up Public Key Infrastructure (PKI), which is needed to use digital certificates and public and private key distribution. The PKI framework is the foundation of some highly trusted security schemes, such as Pretty Good Privacy (PGP) and Secure Sockets Layer (SSL).

NOTE

Digital signatures and PKI are crucial to security on the Internet. For more information on these topics, do an Internet search or consult related RFCs. (Try *www.rfc-editor.org/rfcxx00.html* for current Internet standards.)

ACTIVITY

Activity 2-3: Examining a Digital Certificate

Time Required: 20 minutes

Objective: Examine a default digital certificate on a Windows XP computer.

Description: A digital certificate can be difficult to conceptualize. However, your Windows XP computer already has a number of digital certificates issued by organizations called certification authorities (CAs). You can view them to get a better idea of the information they contain. In this activity, you add the Certificates snap-in to the Microsoft Management Console (MMC), and then view the components of a certificate.

1. Click **Start**, **Run**, type **mmc**, and then click **OK**. The Microsoft Management Console window (labeled Console1) opens.

2. Click **File**, **Add/Remove Snap-in** from the menu.

3. In the Add/Remove Snap-in dialog box, click **Add**. In the Add Standalone Snap-in dialog box, click **Certificates**, and then click **Add**.

4. In the Certificates snap-in dialog box, verify that **My user account** is selected, and then click **Finish**.

5. In the Add Standalone Snap-in dialog box, click **Close**. Click **OK** to close Add/Remove Snap-in and return to Console1.

6. Click to expand **Certificates – Current User** and **Trusted Root Certification Authorities**.

7. Under Trusted Root Certification Authorities, click **Certificates**, and scroll down the list of certificates in the pane on the right. Double-click the first certificate labeled **VeriSign Trust Network**.

8. In the Certificate dialog box (which lists the certificate's components), click **Details**.

9. Click **Public key** to see the public key associated with the digital signature. Click **Enhanced key usage (property)** to see the ways in which the digital certificate can be used. Click **OK** to close the Certificate dialog box.

10. Click **File**, **Exit** from the menu to close the MMC. When prompted to save the settings, click **No**. Leave your system running for the next activity.

EXAMINING INTERNET PROTOCOL VERSION 6

IPv4 has some serious drawbacks. Although it was an engineering masterpiece in 1981, the Internet has grown at a rate the creators of the IPv4 32-bit addressing scheme didn't expect. IP addresses are now in short supply, so **Internet Protocol version 6 (IPv6)**, which has a larger address space of 128 bits, is under development to allow an almost endless supply of IP addresses.

IPv4 also presents problems with the routing system. Routers on the Internet backbone have routing tables with tens of thousands of entries. They get the job done, but because most computers aren't connected directly to the Internet backbone, a packet must traverse several extra hops along the route to its destination. In IPv6, backbone routing tables need only entries of other routers connected directly to them. The information in an IPv6 header contains the rest of the information needed to get a packet to its destination, so the process is streamlined.

Security is another concern with IPv4. Although it does support IPSec, IPv4 has no native encryption methods. Plenty of encryption methods are available, but the lack of standardization can create compatibility problems, and encryption can increase overhead on the network. IPv6, on the other hand, has integrated support for IPSec.

Another major advantage of IPv6 is its autoconfiguration capabilities. Instead of relying solely on Dynamic Host Configuration Protocol (DHCP) or manual configuration, IPv6 can determine its own settings based on two different models. **Stateful autoconfiguration** is basically an improved version of DHCP, referred to as "stateful" because the DHCP client and server must keep their information updated to prevent addressing conflicts. **Stateless autoconfiguration** allows the computer attempting to connect to determine its own IP address based on its Media Access Control (MAC) address. This method is much simpler because there's no need for a server to issue address configurations. In addition, although DHCP has made administration easier, it still requires configuration and management, and errors can still happen. In the next few sections, you learn about the core IPv6 protocols and see how the next generation of IP works.

NOTE

IPv6, specified in RFC 2460, has several improvements over IPv4. Reading RFCs can help you better understand IPv6 and its related protocols. Specific RFCs are included in Tips when possible throughout this chapter.

IPv6 Core Protocols

You have probably read brief descriptions of IPv6, but most networking books and articles haven't explored it in detail until recently. You might be a whiz at IPv4, but IPv6 has some major differences in its core architecture and functions and uses some different core protocols. For example, IPv4 uses Address Resolution Protocol (ARP), ICMPv4 Router Discovery, and ICMPv4 Redirect messages to manage node-to-node communications, but IPv6 uses the Neighbor Discovery protocol. The next few sections explain the core architecture and protocols of IPv6.

Internet Protocol Version 6

IPv6 is a connectionless, unreliable datagram protocol used mainly for addressing and routing packets between hosts. Being connectionless, IPv6 doesn't establish a session before data is exchanged, and delivery isn't guaranteed. IPv6 makes a best-effort attempt to deliver a packet but relies on higher-layer protocols, such as TCP, for acknowledgement and recovery of lost packets.

An IPv6 datagram consists of the IPv6 header and the IPv6 payload. The IPv6 header is made up of the IPv6 base header and IPv6 optional extension headers. For functional purposes, the optional extension headers and upper-layer protocols are considered part of the IPv6 payload. Figure 2-12 shows a comparison of IPv4 and IPv6 headers.

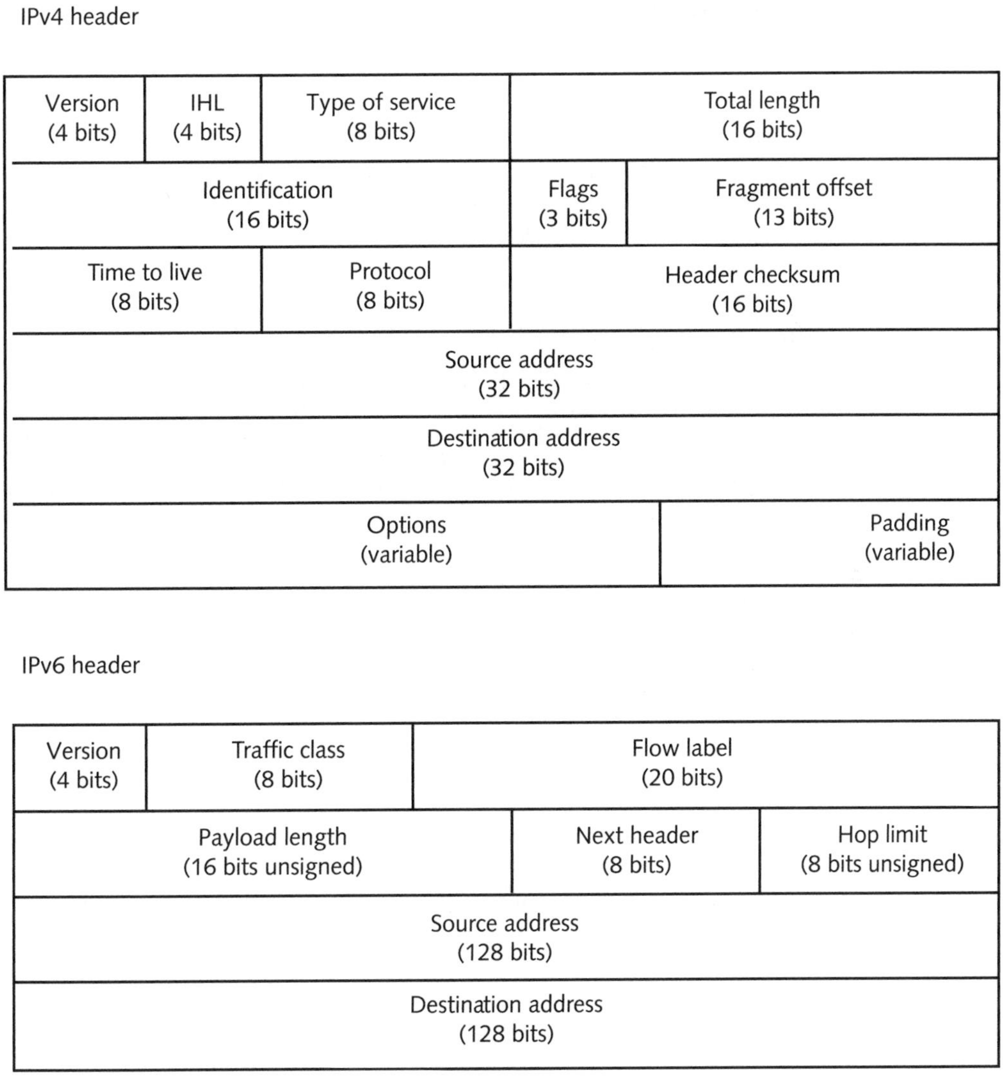

IPv4 header

Version (4 bits)	IHL (4 bits)	Type of service (8 bits)	Total length (16 bits)	
Identification (16 bits)			Flags (3 bits)	Fragment offset (13 bits)
Time to live (8 bits)		Protocol (8 bits)	Header checksum (16 bits)	
Source address (32 bits)				
Destination address (32 bits)				
Options (variable)			Padding (variable)	

IPv6 header

Version (4 bits)	Traffic class (8 bits)	Flow label (20 bits)	
Payload length (16 bits unsigned)		Next header (8 bits)	Hop limit (8 bits unsigned)
Source address (128 bits)			
Destination address (128 bits)			

Figure 2-12   IPv4 and IPv6 packet headers

As you can see in Figure 2-12, an IPv6 header is more streamlined than an IPv4 header. The fields in the IPv6 header are as follows:

- *Version*—This field specifies the IP version number (6 for IPv6). Note that the Internet header length (IHL) field has been removed in IPv6.

- *Traffic class*—Also known as the priority field, this field distinguishes between traffic that can be flow-controlled and traffic that can't. A value of 1 to 7 indicates lower priority transmissions that can be slowed down when encountering congestion, and values 8 to 15 represent real-time traffic that must have a constant sending rate.

- *Flow label*—This experimental field allows different connections between different sources and destinations to specify handling for connections. For example, a connection could be specified as "no delay allowed on this connection."

- *Payload length*—This field indicates the length of the IPv6 payload in octets and replaces the IPv4 total length field.

- *Next header*—This field identifies the type of header immediately following the IPv6 header and is important because it allows simplification of the header structure. The next header field selects which, if any, extension header follows the IPv6 header. If no extension headers are present, the next header field indicates the name of the transport protocol handler for that packet. (This field makes the IPv4 protocol field redundant.)

- *Hop limit*—This field indicates the maximum number of hops the packet is allowed before it's dropped. This number is decreased by 1 each time it's forwarded by a node. When the value in this field reaches 0, the packet is dropped. This field replaces the IPv4 time to live field.

- *Source address*—This field contains the 128-bit address of the packet source.

- *Destination address*—This field contains the 128-bit address of the packet's intended recipient. It might not be the final destination if a routing extension header (discussed in the following list) is present.

Extension headers include the following:

- *Routing*—Similar to IPv4's loose source and record routing (lsrr) option, this header is used to list one or more intermediary nodes on the way to a packet's destination. A next header value of 43 indicates that a routing header is present. A routing header isn't examined until it reaches the destination node.

- *Fragment*—This header is used to send a packet larger than the maximum transmission unit (MTU) value allows. The source node divides large packets into fragments and generates an identification value. (Fragmentation in IPv6 is performed only by source nodes, not by routers along the delivery path.) A next header value of 44 indicates a fragment header's presence, but only the destination node processes this header, using it to reassemble fragmented packets on receipt.

- *Authentication*—This header provides authentication and integrity for IPv6 packets. The payload is sent unencrypted, but the extension header is algorithm independent and supports many authentication techniques. This header provides no confidentiality for packet contents but verifies the packet's source.

2

- *Encapsulating*—This field provides integrity and confidentiality to IPv6 datagrams by using Encapsulating Security Payload (ESP) extension headers. This header is also algorithm independent.

- *Destination options*—This header carries optional information that only the destination node needs to examine. A next header value of 60 indicates this header's presence.

- *Hop by hop*—This header carries information that every node along the delivery path must examine and process. If this extension header is present, it must immediately follow the IPv6 header and is indicated by a next header value of 0 in the IPv6 header.

Remember that IPv4 and IPv6 headers aren't interoperable. A host or router must be configured to support both so that it can recognize and process both formats.

Internet Control Message Protocol for IPv6

ICMPv6, an integral component of IPv6 communications, is used by IPv6 nodes for reporting errors and for diagnostic purposes. As in ICMPv4, ICMPv6 uses the Ping and Tracert commands as well as other diagnostics you already know.

ICMPv6 messages are grouped into two classes: error messages and informational messages. Error messages are identified by message type codes 0 to 127, and informational messages are identified by message type codes 128 to 255. Table 2-6 shows common message type codes for ICMPv6.

Table 2-6   Common ICMPv6 message type codes

Message type	Code	Class
Destination Unreachable	1	Error
Packet Too Big	2	Error
Time Exceeded	3	Error
Parameter Problems	4	Error
Echo Request	128	Informational
Echo Reply	129	Informational

TIP

ICMPv6 is specified in RFC 2463.

An ICMPv6 message is preceded by an IPv6 header and sometimes by extension headers. An ICMPv6 header is identified by a next header value of 58 in the IPv6 header and follows the IPv6 header. An ICMPv6 header has the format shown in Figure 2-13.

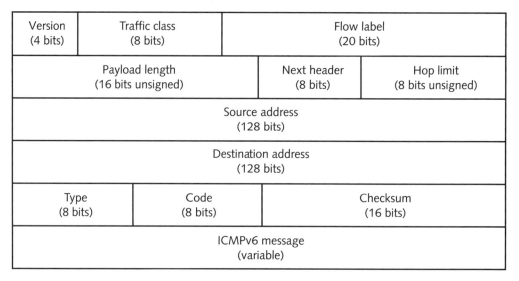

Version (4 bits)	Traffic class (8 bits)	Flow label (20 bits)		
Payload length (16 bits unsigned)			Next header (8 bits)	Hop limit (8 bits unsigned)
Source address (128 bits)				
Destination address (128 bits)				
Type (8 bits)		Code (8 bits)	Checksum (16 bits)	
ICMPv6 message (variable)				

Figure 2-13   An ICMPv6 header

The type field in Figure 2-13 indicates the type of message and contains the value for a type of ICMPv6 message; for example, a value of 128 indicates an Echo Request message. The code field specifies additional parameters for the message. For example, if a Destination Unreachable (type 1) message is received, it might contain 1 in the code field, indicating that the destination address was unreachable because the firewall configuration or other security protocol denied the packet access, thus prohibiting communication with the destination. Next, the checksum field is used to detect data corruption in the ICMPv6 message and parts of the IPv6 header.

ICMPv6 also provides the framework for additional IPv6 features, as shown in Table 2-7. These features are discussed in more detail in the following sections.

Table 2-7   ICMPv6 features

Feature	Description
Multicast Listener Discovery (MLD)	MLD replaces IGMPv3, which is used in IPv4. MLD is a series of three ICMPv6 messages used to manage subnet multicast membership.
Neighbor Discovery (ND)	ND replaces ARP, ICMPv4 Router Discovery, and ICMPv4 Redirect and has other functions, including prefix detection, duplicate address detection, and automatic address configuration. ND is a series of five ICMPv6 messages used to manage node-to-node communications on a link.

Multicast Listener Discovery

Multicasts are used for a variety of network functions and connectionless delivery of information to multiple subscribers at the same time. Unlike conventional data streaming with one stream per recipient, multicasting has a single stream on any link with at least one recipient. Instead of consuming bandwidth to distribute multiple copies, routers assume the task of tracking subscribers (group members) and creating copies only on an as-needed basis.

IP multicast traffic is sent to a single address but is processed by all members of a multicast group. Hosts listening on a specific multicast address are part of that multicast group. Group membership is dynamic, with hosts joining and leaving the group at any time. A host doesn't need to be a member of a group to send messages to the group. There are no limits to group size, and members can be on different subnets as long as the connecting routers support multicast message forwarding between those subnets. Multicast group members can be members of multiple groups simultaneously.

Multicast addresses can be permanent or transient. A permanent multicast address has an administratively assigned IP address. However, the address is permanent, not the group members. In IPv6, **Multicast Listener Discovery (MLD)** enables IPv6 routers to discover multicast listeners on a directly connected link and decide which multicast addresses are of interest to those nodes. MLD uses a series of ICMPv6 messages to track membership, as shown in Table 2-8.

Table 2-8   MLD message types

MLD message type	Description
Multicast Listener Query	Multicast routers send queries to poll a network segment for group members. Queries can be general, can request membership for all groups, or can be for a specific group.
Multicast Listener Report	This message is sent by a host when it joins a multicast group or in response to a Multicast Listener Query.
Multicast Listener Done	This message is sent by a host when it leaves a host group and is the last member of that group on the network segment.

TIP

MLD for IPv6 is specified in RFC 2710, with updates added in RFCs 3590 and 3810. Be sure to check for other updates because Internet drafts change often.

Neighbor Discovery

In IPv4, ARP is used to resolve addresses, and ICMP Router Discovery and ICMP Redirect are used to locate neighboring routers and redirect hosts to better routes to reach destination addresses. IPv6 uses a new protocol, **Neighbor Discovery (ND)**, to handle these tasks and provide additional functions. ND uses ICMPv6 messages to manage node-to-node communications. Table 2-9 summarizes the functions of ND.

Table 2-9   IPv6 ND functions

Process	Description
Router discovery	Discovers neighboring routers
Prefix discovery	Discovers local network prefixes
Parameter discovery	Discovers additional parameters, such as MTU and default hops for outbound packets
Address autoconfiguration	Automatic address configuration
Address resolution	Resolves neighboring node's address to its link-layer address
Next-hop determination	Determines the next-hop node address
Neighbor unreachability detection	Determines whether neighboring hosts or routers are no longer available
Duplicate address detection	Determines that an address considered for use is not already in use by a neighboring node
Redirect function	Process by which a router informs a host of a better first-hop IPv6 address to reach a destination

TIP   ND for IPv6 is specified in RFC 2461.

ND defines five different types of ICMP messages:

- Router Solicitation messages are sent by hosts when an interface is enabled. A Router Solicitation message requests that routers send a Router Advertisement message immediately rather than at the next scheduled time.

- Router Advertisement messages inform hosts about router presence and additional parameters about the link or services, such as address configuration or suggested hop limits. A Router Advertisement message is sent at defined intervals or in response to a Router Solicitation message.

- Neighbor Solicitation messages are sent by a node to determine the link-layer address of a neighbor or to verify that a neighbor is still reachable. Neighbor Solicitation messages are also used for duplicate address detection.

- Neighbor Advertisements are sent in response to a Neighbor Solicitation message or to update neighbors of a link-layer address change.

- Redirect messages are sent by routers to tell hosts about better first-hop addresses to reach a destination.

ICMP is an efficient method of managing many underlying networking functions, such as those formerly assumed by Internet Group Management Protocol (IGMP) and ARP. ND and MLD take care of these housekeeping jobs, such as managing group membership and managing node-to-node communications. Each message takes the form of an ICMP message and is identified in the packet header by the corresponding ICMPv6 message type code, as shown in Table 2-10. (In addition to these ICMPv6 message types, remember the common message types in Table 2-6.)

Table 2-10   ICMPv6 with MLD and ND message types

Message type	Code	Class
Group Membership Query (MLD)	130	MLD
Group Membership Report (MLD)	131	MLD
Group Membership Reduction/Done	132	MLD
Router Solicitation	133	ND
Router Advertisement	134	ND
Neighbor Solicitation	135	ND
Neighbor Advertisement	136	ND
Redirect	137	ND

NOTE   This section gives you an overview of IPv6 because the details would require an entire book. The purpose of this book is to prepare you for the SCNP Tactical Perimeter Defense exam (SCO-471), so this coverage is enough to help you answer questions on the exam and give you a solid introduction to this protocol. If you're interested in learning more about the next generation of IP, start with the RFCs listed in this section, and then search the Internet for more information.

IPv6 Addressing

An IPv6 address is 128 bits long, which would mean a very long number if you used the same decimal numbering scheme as in IPv4. To make IPv6 addresses manageable, the hexadecimal numbering format known as base 16 (or just "hex") is used. An IPv6 address consists of eight hex groups separated by colons. Each hex group contains a 16-bit value, and each digit represents a 4-bit value. The following examples show what an IPv6 address looks like:

```
4EDC:0000:7654:3210:F3DC:BA98:7654:AB1F
1080:0:0:0:8:800:200C:417A
```

Including leading zeros in a group isn't necessary, and hex letters aren't case sensitive. You can also replace consecutive zeros with a double colon, as shown in this modification:

```
1080::8:800:200C:417A
```

This "compression" of leading zeros comes in handy when typing long strings, but remember that the double colon can be used only once in an address. In a mixed environment of IPv6 and IPv4, you can use the colon hexadecimal notation of IPv6 addresses and the 32-bit dotted decimal notation of IPv4 addresses, as shown in the following examples:

```
0:0:0:0:0:0:22.1.68.45
0:0:0:0:0:FFFF:131.123.2.8
```

Using the double colon, these addresses can be condensed to the following:

```
::22.1.68.45
::FFFF:131.123.2.8
```

You might have wondered what the address is for the loopback. It looks like this: 0:0:0:0:0:0:0:1. This form can be compressed to ::1. You learn more about loopback addresses later in this chapter in "IPv6 Utilities."

Activity 2-4: Viewing Your IPv6 IP Address with Ipconfig

Time Required: 5 minutes

Objective: View your IPv6 IP address with Ipconfig.

Description: In this activity, you use Ipconfig to view your IPv6 address. Although IPv6 has additional utilities to view interface information, Ipconfig works, too.

 Windows XP SP2 has built-in support for IPv6, but you still must install the protocol as instructed in this activity. Users of earlier Windows versions must download the IPv6 support kit for their OSs from Microsoft because earlier versions do not have built-in support for IPv6.

1. Open a command prompt window.

2. Type **ipv6 install** and press **Enter**. You should see status and completion messages about the installation.

3. After IPv6 has been installed, type **ipconfig** and press **Enter**. Notice that two IP addresses are shown: your IPv4 address and subnet mask and your IPv6 address. Write down your IPv6 address:

_____

4. Type **exit** and press **Enter** to close the command prompt window. Leave your system running for the next activity.

Unicast, Multicast, and Anycast Addressing

IPv6 uses three types of addresses: unicast, multicast, and anycast. Notice that it doesn't use broadcast addresses.

Unicast is used for one-to-one communication, such as between a single host and a single receiver. One example is communication between two routers. A unicast address is configured for each interface connected to the network. There are actually several forms, or **scopes**, of unicast addresses in IPv6. These scopes identify the application suitable for the address and include global unicast, site-local unicast, and link-local unicast. There are a few other special-purpose types as well as the option to define new types in the future.

Multicast is used for one-to-many communication, in which a single host can send packets to a group of recipients. Multicast addresses also use scopes: global, organization-local, site-local, link-local, and node-local. Organization-local could be used in an organization with several sites in its network design, for example.

Anycast addresses are not assigned a specific range; instead, they are created automatically when a unicast address is assigned to more than one interface. This means anycast addresses are assigned from unicast address ranges and have the same scopes as unicast addresses. The idea behind anycast is to offer flexibility in providing services. For example, a service might be provided by a group of servers. Using anycast, the service can be provided by any one of the servers—usually the one that's closest. Anycast addresses are now used only by routers, but their use will expand as the technology becomes widespread.

TIP

IPv6 addressing details are specified in several RFCs. IPv6 stateless address autoconfiguration is specified in RFC 2462; reserved IPv6 subnet anycast addresses are explained in RFC 2526. The format for literal IPv6 addresses in URIs is covered in RFC 3986, and default address selection is explained in RFC 3484. The global unicast address format is in RFC 3587, and MLD source address selection is in RFC 3590. In addition to the RFCs, a number of Internet drafts deal with aspects of IPv6. They change fairly often, and Internet drafts eventually become standards. There are also competing drafts for some proposed standards, but usually only one is chosen as the standard. Check with the IETF at *www.ietf.org/rfc.html* for new additions or changes.

IPv6 Configuration

Microsoft OSs since Windows XP SP 1 have IPv6 support built in. These platforms support stateless autoconfiguration and don't usually need manual configuration of IPv6 addresses, although you might have to install the protocol (see Activity 2-4). By default, a link-local address is assigned to every Ethernet interface during startup. IPv6 addresses, such as site-local addresses or global addresses, are assigned automatically based on the receipt of IPv6 Router Advertisement messages. You must have a correctly configured IPv6-capable router on your network segment to receive additional addresses through IPv6 Router Advertisement messages.

NOTE

Some manual configuration is required for more advanced features and setups of IPv6. You can find procedures for your equipment with an Internet search or by contacting the vendor for instructions.

IPv6 Utilities

IPv6 includes several integrated utilities for configuration, troubleshooting, and other administrative tasks. Some are familiar because they are used in IPv4 and haven't changed much. IPv6 can be configured largely from the command line. In many ways, it has been designed for easier administration, lower overhead, increased security, and more efficient communications. In the following sections, you examine some major Windows IPv6 utilities. Some utilities, such as Ping and Tracert, are largely the same as in IPv4.

Net.exe

Net.exe is used to start and stop IPv6. It has several other applications, but only the two covered in this section are relevant to IPv6. The following command starts IPv6 and loads any new Tcpip6.sys driver files in *systemroot*\System32\Drivers into memory:

```
net start tcpip6
```

The following command stops IPv6 and unloads it from memory. This command fails if any IPv6 sockets are open.

```
net stop tcpip6
```

Ipv6.exe

The Ipv6.exe tool is for all Microsoft IPv6 configurations and is used to view the state of interfaces, neighbor caches, the binding cache, the destination cache (called the route cache in Microsoft), and the route table. It's also used to manually configure interfaces, addresses, and route tables. This is the general syntax for the Ipv6.exe command:

```
ipv6 if if#
```

This command displays information about interfaces. (For example, *if#* indicates the interface number.) If an interface number is specified, only information about that interface is shown. The output of this command displays the link-layer address, the list of IPv6 addresses assigned to that interface, and the current and supported MTUs. A number of subcommands, listed in Table 2-11, can be used for a wide range of tasks.

NOTE

The brackets shown in Table 2-11 aren't actually part of commands. They indicate options used with command-line utilities, much like DOS commands use switches.

Table 2-11   Subcommands for Ipv6.exe

Command	Description
ipv6 ifc *if#* [forwards] [advertises] [-forwards] [-advertises] [mtu #*bytes*] [site *site-identifier*]	Controls interface attributes. Interfaces can be forwarding or advertising, and you can set the MTU or change the site identifier.
ipv6 ifd *if#*	Deletes an interface.
ipv6 ncf *if# address*	Displays the contents of the neighbor cache. You can specify which interface and IP address to display.
ipv6 rc *if# address*	Displays the contents of the route cache. You can specify which interface and IP address to display.
ipv6 rcf *if# address*	Flushes the specified route cache entries.
ipv6 bc	Displays the contents of the binding cache.
ipv6 adu *if#/address* [lifetime VL[/PL]] [anycast] [unicast]	Adds or removes a unicast or an anycast address assignment on an interface. Unless anycast is specified, unicast is the default. Lifetime can be abbreviated as life, and if the life isn't specified, the default is infinity.
ipv6 spt	Displays the current contents of the site prefix table.
ipv6 spu prefix *if#* [lifetime L]	Adds, removes, or updates a prefix in the site prefix table.
ipv6 rt	Displays the current contents of the route table.
ipv6 rtu prefix *if#* [/*nexthop*] [lifetime L] [*preference* P] [publish] [age] [sp1 *site-prefix-length*]	Adds or removes a route in the routing table. The route (rtu) prefix is not optional. If the lifetime is set to zero, the route is deleted.

Ipsec6.exe

Ipsec6.exe is used to configure IPSec policies and security associations for IPv6. Like Ipv6.exe, it has several subcommands, shown in Table 2-12.

Table 2-12   Ipsec6.exe subcommands

Command	Description
ipsec6 sp *interface*	Displays active security policies. If no interface is specified, displays all interfaces.
ipsec6 sa	Displays active security associations.
ipsec6 c *filename with no extension*	Creates files used to configure security policies and security associations. Filename.spd is created for security policies and filename.sad for security associations. These files can be customized with a text editor. Do not enter a file extension; .spd and .sad are the defaults.
ipsec6 a *filename with no extension*	Adds a security policy or security association files to the list of active policies and associations.
ipsec6 i [policy] *filename with no extension*	Adds the security policy or security association files to the list of active policies and associations referenced by policy number.
ipsec6 d [type = sp sa] [index]	Deletes the specified security policy or security association file from the list of active policies and associations as referenced by their index number (displayed by ipsec6 sa or ipsec6 sp commands).

Other utilities you can use to configure IPv6 are listed in Table 2-13.

2

Table 2-13   Other IPv6 utilities

Command	Syntax (if applicable)	Description
ttcp.exe	ttcp -r -p*port* For additional switches and options, type ttcp at the command prompt.	Ttcp.exe (Test tcp) is a benchmarking tool used to send informational messages between nodes or to test a port for connectivity and performance. This command supports both IPv4 and IPv6. Ttcp.exe can listen or send on only one port at a time.
6to4cfg.exe	6to4cfg [-r] [-s] [-u] [-R *relay*] [-b] [-S *address*] *filename* Switches: -r: Becomes a 6to4 gateway router for the local network -s: Enables site-local addressing -u: Reverses the 6to4 configuration -R *relay*: Specifies the name or IP address of a 6to4 relay router -b: Tells 6to4cfg.exe to pick the best relay address instead of the first -S *address*: Specifies the local IPv4 address for the 6to4 prefix	This tool is used to configure IPv6 connectivity over an IPv4 network.
checkv4.exe	checkv4 [*filename*] Replace *filename* with the name of the file you want to check.	This tool is used to scan source code files to identify code that must be changed to support IPv6. It displays a line number and recommendation about how the code should be changed.

NOTE   Of course, IPv6 supports many different tools, and an Internet search for IPv6 tools yields many sites offering handy utilities. Some helpful ones are *www.ipv6tools.com*, *www.ipv6.org*, and *www.microsoft.com/technet/network/ ipv6/default.mspx*.

CHAPTER SUMMARY

❑ Transmission Control Protocol/Internet Protocol (TCP/IP) is a suite of many protocols for transmitting information from point to point on a network.

❑ IP addresses currently in use on the Internet conform to IPv4, with addresses of 32 bits (4 bytes) of data. An IP address consists of two main parts: a network address and a host address. The two values are combined with a subnet mask, a value that identifies the network and host portions of the address.

❑ Classless Interdomain Routing (CIDR) is an address notation scheme that specifies the number of masked bits in an IP address/subnet mask combination.

- TCP/IP is transmitted along networks as discrete chunks called packets or datagrams. Each IP datagram is divided into header and data sections. The data in an IP packet is the part users see, but the header is the part computers use to communicate.

- Fragmentation of IP packets was originally developed so that large packets could pass through routers that had frame size limitations.

- Attackers can misuse ICMP messages to intercept traffic and direct it to a server they control or to flood a server with so many requests that it can no longer handle other traffic.

- Domain Name Service (DNS) is a general-purpose service that translates fully qualified domain names, such as *www.course.com*, into IP addresses.

- Encryption protects data as it passes from one network to another, and authentication limits access to authorized users.

- Before a client initiates a TCP session, it must determine the port number that identifies the session and the starting sequence number.

- The TCP three-way handshake establishes a reliable connection between two points.

- IPv4 presents problems with the current routing system, requiring routers on the Internet backbone to store tens of thousands of entries. Security is another concern with IPv4. Although it does support IPSec, IPv4 has no native encryption methods.

- IPv6 was designed to address some problems with IPv4. IPv6 has a much larger address space of 128 bits, native support for IPSec, and the addressing architecture requires routers to store routing table entries only for nodes connected directly to them. The IPv6 packet contains all other information required for delivery.

- IPv6 is a connectionless, unreliable datagram protocol used mainly for addressing and routing packets between hosts. An IPv6 datagram consists of the IPv6 header and IPv6 payload. The IPv6 header has been streamlined considerably more than IPv4 headers. IPv4 and IPv6 headers are not interoperable.

- ICMP is used for reporting errors and for diagnostic purposes. As in ICMPv4, ICMPv6 uses the Ping and Tracert commands as well as other familiar diagnostics. ICMPv6 uses error messages and informational messages. ICMPv6 also enables two new protocols in IPv6: Multicast Listener Discovery (MLD) and Neighbor Discovery (ND).

- MLD enables IPv6 routers to discover multicast listeners on a directly connected link and to decide which multicast addresses are of interest to those nodes.

- IPv6 uses ND to perform the tasks that ARP, ICMP Router Discovery, and ICMP Redirect handled in IPv4. ND uses ICMPv6 messages to manage node-to-node communications.

2

❑ To make IPv6 addresses manageable, the hexadecimal numbering format is used. An IPv6 address consists of eight hex groups separated by colons. Each hex group contains a 16-bit value, and each digit represents a 4-bit value.

❑ IPv6 uses three types of addresses: unicast, multicast, and anycast. IPv6 does not use broadcast addresses.

❑ IPv6 supports stateless address autoconfiguration. By default, a link-local address is assigned to every Ethernet interface during startup. Site-local addresses or global addresses are assigned automatically based on receipt of IPv6 Router Advertisement messages.

❑ IPv6 includes several integrated utilities for configuration, troubleshooting, and other administrative tasks. Net.exe is used to start and stop the IPv6 protocol. Ipv6.exe is used for all Microsoft IPv6 configurations and to manually configure interfaces, addresses, and the route table. Ipsec6.exe is used to configure IPSec policies and security associations.

KEY TERMS

anycast — An address created automatically when a unicast address is assigned to more than one interface. Anycast addresses are assigned from unicast address ranges and have the same scopes as unicast addresses.

broadcast — A communication sent to all points on a specific network.

Classless Interdomain Routing (CIDR) — An IP address notation method that uses a slash (/) followed by the number of masked bits for an address—for example, 192.168.6.5/27 instead of 192.168.6.5 255.255.255.224.

datagrams — Discrete chunks of information; each datagram contains source and destination addresses, control settings, and data. Also called "packets."

footer — A section sometimes added to a TCP/IP packet that tells a computer it's the end of the packet.

fully qualified domain names (FQDNs) — Complete DNS names of computers that include the computer name, domain name, and domain name extension, such as *www.course.com*.

header — The part of a packet containing source and destination information and general information about the packet.

host address — The part of an IP address that's unique to a computer in its subnet.

Internet Control Message Protocol (ICMP) — A protocol that reports network communication errors to support IP communications. The Ping command is a common troubleshooting utility based on ICMP.

Internet Protocol version 4 (IPv4) — The IP addressing system currently in widespread use on the Internet, in which addresses are created with 32 bits (4 bytes) of data.

Internet Protocol version 6 (IPv6) — A new version of IP that's gaining support among software and hardware manufacturers and that will eventually replace IPv4; this version calls for 128-bit IP addresses.

multicast — A transmission used for one-to-many communication, in which a single host can send packets to a group of recipients.

Multicast Listener Discovery (MLD) — A core IPv6 protocol that enables IPv6 routers to discover multicast listeners on a directly connected link and to decide which multicast addresses are of interest to those nodes.

Neighbor Discovery (ND) — A core IPv6 protocol used to resolve addresses, locate neighboring routers, and redirect hosts to better routes to reach destination addresses. ND uses ICMPv6 messages to manage node-to-node communications.

network address — The part of an IP address that a computer has in common with other computers in its subnet.

scopes — Unicast addresses used in IPv6 to identify the application suitable for the address; scopes include global unicast, site-local unicast, and link-local unicast.

stateful autoconfiguration — In IPv6, this feature is basically an improved version of DHCP. It's referred to as "stateful" because the DHCP client and server must keep their information updated to prevent addressing conflicts.

stateless autoconfiguration — A feature of IPv6 that allows the computer attempting to connect to determine its own IP address based on the addressing of neighboring nodes.

subnet mask — A value that tells another computer which part of a computer's IP address is its network address and which part is the host address.

Transmission Control Protocol/Internet Protocol (TCP/IP) — A suite of protocols for transmitting information from point to point on a network.

unicast — A transmission in which one packet is sent from a server to each client that requests a file or application.

User Datagram Protocol (UDP) — A core transport protocol of the TCP/IP suite. UDP is connectionless, meaning it doesn't ensure delivery or provide ordering, as TCP does. UDP is much faster and is useful for transmissions that require speed over reliability. UDP relies on upper-level protocols for error-checking and sequencing services.

variable length subnet masking (VLSM) — A means of allocating IP addressing according to the network's needs that involves applying masks of varying sizes to the same network. This method creates subnets within subnets and multiple divisions of an IP network.

REVIEW QUESTIONS

1. What advantages does IPv6 have over IPv4? (Choose all that apply.)

    a. IPv6 uses DHCP for its configuration settings.

    b. IPv6 uses a 128-bit address space.

    c. IPv4 cannot support IPSec.

    d. IPv6 incorporates IPSec.

2. A Class C address has a first octet decimal range of _____ to _____.

    a. 172, 191

    b. 191, 224

    c. 192, 239

    d. 192, 223

3. Which of the following is a method of hiding internal host IP addresses? (Choose all that apply.)

    a. Network Address Translation (NAT)

    b. configuring the computer to insert a fake source IP address into outgoing messages

    c. proxy servers

    d. setting up software firewalls on all internal hosts

4. The reserved Class A address 127.0.0.1 is used for which of the following?

    a. broadcasting to all hosts on a subnet

    b. testing the TCP/IP local interface

    c. experimentation

    d. a firewall's internal interface address

5. What are the primary subdivisions of an IP datagram? (Choose all that apply.)

    a. data

    b. flags

    c. body

    d. header

6. Why is UDP considered unreliable?

    a. The header does not contain a checksum.

    b. The data is transmitted in clear text.

    c. It is connectionless.

    d. Routers typically drop a large number of UDP packets.

7. In CIDR notation, the IP address and subnet mask 191.9.205.22 255.255.192.0 are written as _____.

   a. 191.9.205.22\19

   b. 191.9.205.22/18

   c. 191.9.205.22\18

   d. 191.9.205.22/24

8. How do routers handle packets that are too large to pass through because of frame size limitations?

   a. Routers drop packets that are too large.

   b. Routers bounce packets back to the sender to be resized.

   c. Routers adjust their MTUs to accommodate the oversized packet.

   d. Routers break packets into smaller pieces called fragments.

9. Fragmentation of IP packets causes several security problems. How should you configure the firewall or packet filter to prevent harm from fragmented packets? (Choose all that apply.)

   a. Reassemble packets and allow only completed packets to pass.

   b. Forward fragments to the destination address for reassembly.

   c. Drop all fragmented packets.

   d. Request authentication from the source.

10. Which of the following is an IPv6 protocol? (Choose all that apply.)

    a. Multicast Listening Detection

    b. IGMPv6

    c. Multicast Listener Discovery

    d. Neighbor Detection

11. A DNS server translates _____ to _____.

    a. encrypted IP addresses, clear text

    b. IP addresses, MAC addresses

    c. FQDNs, IP addresses

    d. static addresses, DHCP

12. Why is fragmentation considered a security risk?

    a. Fragments numbered 0 contain port information.

    b. Fragments numbered 1 or higher are passed through filters.

    c. Fragmented packets can't be assembled.

    d. Fragmentation is frequently used.

13. Which of the following is used for one-to-many communication, in which a single host can send packets to a group of recipients?

    a. multicast

    b. unicast

    c. anycast

    d. netcast

14. Which of the following is used to display interface information in IPv6?

    a. Ipv6cfg.exe

    b. Ipsec6.exe

    c. Ipv6-ifcfg.exe

    d. Ipv6.exe

15. Before a client initiates a TCP session, it must determine which two items?

    a. sequence number

    b. sliding window size

    c. transmission rate

    d. port number to use for the session

16. When one party in a TCP session is ready to end the session, it sends a packet with the _____ flag set.

    a. SYN

    b. ACK

    c. RST

    d. FIN

17. An ICMPv6 header is indicated by a next header value of _____.

    a. 60

    b. 54

    c. 58

    d. 22

18. Sent by a node to determine a neighbor's link-layer address, the Neighbor Solicitation message has an ICMPv6 type code of _____.

    a. 4

    b. 137

    c. 134

    d. 135

19. Compressing the IPv6 address 1080:0:0:0:8:800:200C:417A results in which of the following?

    a. 1080::8:8:::2::C:417A

    b. 1080::8:800:200C:417A

    c. 1080::8:8::::20:C:417A

    d. :1080::8:800:200C:417A

20. The loopback address in IPv6 is 0:0:0:0:0:0:0:1, which can be compressed to _____.

    a. ::0:1

    b. :0::1

    c. ::1

    d. 0::1

21. Which of the following commands is used to delete an IPv6 interface (replacing *if#* with the interface number)?

    a. ipv6 ifd *if#*

    b. ipv6 del *if#*

    c. ipv6 flush *if#*

    d. ipv6 -d *if#*

Hands-On Projects

HANDS-ON PROJECTS

Hands-On Project 2-1: Assessing Your Network Interface

Time Required: 10 minutes

Objective: Examine active connections to computers with the Netstat utility.

Description: Netstat can provide a wealth of information. In this project, you use it to learn more about active connections to your computer.

1. Click **Start**, point to **All Programs**, point to **Accessories**, and then click **Command Prompt** to open a command prompt window.

2. Type **netstat** and press **Enter** to view the current active connections.

3. Type **netstat -a** and press **Enter** to view the currently established connections and the ports on which your computer is listening for new connections.

4. Type **netstat -pTCP** and press **Enter** to view information about TCP connections.

5. Type **netstat -pUDP** and press **Enter** to view information about UDP connections.

6. Type **netstat -n** and press **Enter** to view the IP address of any remote computers connected to your computer. This information can be useful in tracking an attacker connected to your network.

7. To get a summary of Netstat's switches, type **netstat /?** and press **Enter**.

8. Type **exit** and press **Enter** to close the command prompt window. Leave your system running for the next project.

Hands-On Project 2-2: Determining Network Connectivity with Linux

Time Required: 15 minutes

Objective: Use a Linux terminal window to observe the output from the Ifconfig command.

Description: In this project, you view network connectivity in Fedora or Red Hat Enterprise Linux, which is already configured with the X-Window Gnome interface. You need to log in with the root account or an account that has superuser (root) permissions. (*Note:* The steps are similar for other Linux versions and some UNIX versions.)

1. Right-click the Gnome desktop and click **Open Terminal**.

2. At the command line, type **ifconfig** and press **Enter**.

3. Notice the entries at the left. An entry for "eth0" means your system is configured to access an Ethernet network, such as through a network interface card. An entry for "ppp" means your system is configured for access to the Internet, such as through a dial-up modem. A "lo" entry is a local loopback connection used for diagnostic testing of the network connection.

4. Type **exit** and press **Enter** to close the terminal window. Leave your system running for the next project.

For detailed information on the Linux ifconfig command, type man ifconfig and press Enter. Press the spacebar to scroll through the pages, and press q to quit.

TIP

Hands-On Project 2-3: Calculating Subnets

Time Required: 15 minutes

Objective: Use a subnet calculator to automate the process of calculating subnets for an IP network.

Description: In this project, you use a subnet calculator to examine how subnetting works and discover how different methods of segmenting an address block can produce different results. As you work on this project, think about ways similar tools could help you with subnetting.

1. Start your Web browser and go to **www.subnetmask.info/**.

2. In the TCPIP Network Address text box, type **192.168.10.0**.

3. Type **8** for the required number of subnetworks, and then click **Calculate**. What subnet mask should you use? How many hosts per network do you have?

_____

4. Click the **Class C** option button, and click **512** in the Required number of subnetworks drop-down list. Click **Calculate**. What network class do you have? What is your subnet mask? Are there 512 subnets? Why or why not? How can you obtain 512 subnets from this address?

_____

_____

5. Return to the top, type **223.141.15.24** in the TCPIP Network Address text box, and click **64** in the Required number of hosts per network drop-down list. Click **Calculate**. How many networks does this configuration provide? How many hosts per network? What is its CIDR notation?

_____

6. Close your Web browser, and leave your system running for the next project.

HANDS-ON PROJECTS

Hands-On Project 2-4: Working with Wireshark

Time Required: 20 minutes

Objective: Use Wireshark to correlate user actions with network traffic.

Description: In this project, you perform another packet capture with Wireshark. During the capture, you use simple TCP/IP tools to generate traffic. Then you examine the captured traffic and identify the packets sent as a result of your actions.

1. Start Wireshark. Click the far-left button on the toolbar to open the Capture Interfaces dialog box, click to select your Ethernet interface, and then click the **Start** button to begin the capture.

2. Open a command prompt window. Type **ping 127.0.0.1** and press **Enter**.

3. Type **ping ::1** and press **Enter**.

4. Ping a classmate's computer by computer name or IP address. (*Hint:* Ipconfig can be used to determine an IP address.)

5. Type **tracert *ipaddress*** and press **Enter**.

6. Type **telnet *ipaddress*** to attempt to access another student's computer remotely, replacing *ipaddress* with the actual IP address, and press **Enter**. Don't worry if the connection can't be established; it shouldn't be. Your screen should be similar to Figure 2-14.

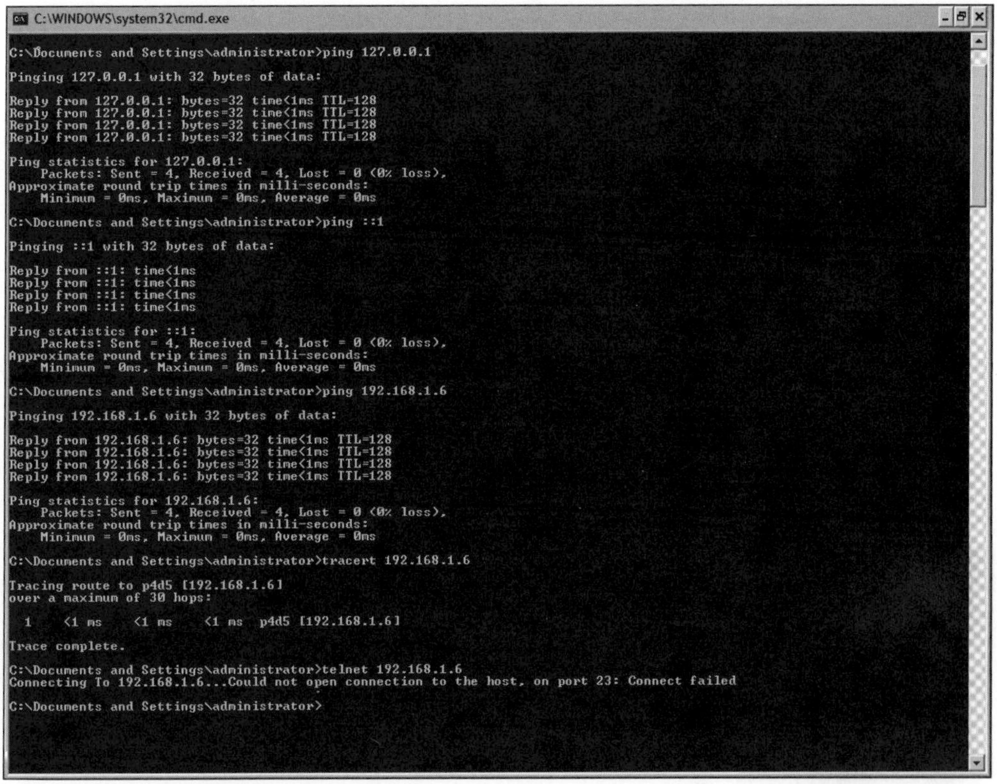

2

```
C:\WINDOWS\system32\cmd.exe                                                    _ 8 x

C:\Documents and Settings\administrator>ping 127.0.0.1

Pinging 127.0.0.1 with 32 bytes of data:

Reply from 127.0.0.1: bytes=32 time<1ms TTL=128
Reply from 127.0.0.1: bytes=32 time<1ms TTL=128
Reply from 127.0.0.1: bytes=32 time<1ms TTL=128
Reply from 127.0.0.1: bytes=32 time<1ms TTL=128

Ping statistics for 127.0.0.1:
    Packets: Sent = 4, Received = 4, Lost = 0 (0% loss),
Approximate round trip times in milli-seconds:
    Minimum = 0ms, Maximum = 0ms, Average = 0ms

C:\Documents and Settings\administrator>ping ::1

Pinging ::1 with 32 bytes of data:

Reply from ::1: time<1ms
Reply from ::1: time<1ms
Reply from ::1: time<1ms
Reply from ::1: time<1ms

Ping statistics for ::1:
    Packets: Sent = 4, Received = 4, Lost = 0 (0% loss),
Approximate round trip times in milli-seconds:
    Minimum = 0ms, Maximum = 0ms, Average = 0ms

C:\Documents and Settings\administrator>ping 192.168.1.6

Pinging 192.168.1.6 with 32 bytes of data:

Reply from 192.168.1.6: bytes=32 time<1ms TTL=128
Reply from 192.168.1.6: bytes=32 time<1ms TTL=128
Reply from 192.168.1.6: bytes=32 time<1ms TTL=128
Reply from 192.168.1.6: bytes=32 time<1ms TTL=128

Ping statistics for 192.168.1.6:
    Packets: Sent = 4, Received = 4, Lost = 0 (0% loss),
Approximate round trip times in milli-seconds:
    Minimum = 0ms, Maximum = 0ms, Average = 0ms

C:\Documents and Settings\administrator>tracert 192.168.1.6

Tracing route to p4d5 [192.168.1.6]
over a maximum of 30 hops:

  1    <1 ms    <1 ms    <1 ms  p4d5 [192.168.1.6]

Trace complete.

C:\Documents and Settings\administrator>telnet 192.168.1.6
Connecting To 192.168.1.6...Could not open connection to the host, on port 23: Connect failed

C:\Documents and Settings\administrator>
```

Figure 2-14   Wireshark testing

7. Minimize the command prompt window and return to Wireshark. Stop the capture in progress.

8. You should have captured the packets you sent in the previous steps. Try to identify the Ping packets. How many packets were captured for each Ping operation?

_____

9. Were the packets different for the IPv4 and IPv6 loopbacks? Why or why not? Can you identify the Telnet connection attempt?

_____

_____

10. Exit Wireshark. When prompted to save your Wireshark capture, click **Continue without Saving**. Close any other open windows.

CASE PROJECTS

CASE PROJECTS

Case Project 2-1: Evaluating IP Addressing and Subnetting Hierarchy for Green Globe

For this project, you determine an IP addressing scheme for Green Globe, including naming conventions and subnets needed for security and connectivity. You might need to revise the organizational hierarchy as you progress through the book, but you're determining a starting point for this project. You might have to come up with your own data if it isn't available, such as the number of employees in a business group or department.

Examine the facility diagram, and identify groups needing remote access. Decide how many subnets are required to serve the central office. External access is provided through a Class C IP address block statically assigned to the company. Design an internal addressing scheme that isolates high-security areas, manages bandwidth efficiently, and uses a restrictive security model for access. Your scheme can be presented as a written list identifying the IP address block, subnets, and groups served, or it can be a graphic.

Green Globe requires a service provider for communication access, so develop a simple comparison chart of at least three providers for international service as well as local access. Be sure to note support options, service-level agreements, and disaster recovery options these providers offer, and you should include any additional services that meet Green Globe's needs. (*Hint*: Visit each provider's Web site to search for information.) When your service provider chart and addressing scheme are finished, turn them in to your instructor.

3

ROUTER FUNDAMENTALS

**After reading this chapter and completing
the exercises, you will be able to:**

♦ Describe the basics of the routing process

♦ Explain how routers use routing protocols and describe common
routing protocols

This chapter introduces you to the fundamentals of Cisco routers. Traffic between nodes on different networks must pass through routers to reach their destinations. Routers are also a vital part of the Internet's infrastructure, enabling different networks, protocols, hardware, and applications to communicate via common communications channels.

You begin by reviewing the routing process and learning how address resolution takes place. Then you learn how routers make forwarding decisions for traffic based on information in routing tables. Finally, you learn how routing protocols work and examine common protocols routers use.

UNDERSTANDING THE ROUTING PROCESS

Routing is the process of transporting packets of information across a network from the source to the destination. At its most basic, routing involves two main functions: determining the best path for a packet to travel and moving the packet along its path. Path determination can involve using routing protocols with metrics (variables such as hop count, bandwidth, or link state), following a programmed route the administrator has assigned, or taking the default path, also determined by the administrator.

The routing process can be complex, but it generally follows these steps:

1. An application on a source computer creates a packet to send to a specific destination. The source computer determines whether the destination address is on the same or a different subnet. If the packet is destined for a different network, the source computer knows the packet must be sent to a gateway router.

2. The source computer checks for its configured default gateway router and sends the packet to it.

3. The gateway router receives the packet, strips off the Layer 2 header, and examines the destination address. The packet contains information telling the router which interface the packet entered from.

4. Based on the destination address and information the router has in its routing table, the router determines on which interface the packet should be routed out.

5. The router builds a header appropriate for the selected outbound interface. For example, if the outbound interface is a token ring interface, the router builds a token ring header so that the interface can understand the information and process the packet. The header contains Layer 2 source and destination addresses and protocol information.

6. The packet is sent out through the selected interface to the next hop.

This explanation of routing has been simplified. Typically, each packet requires the router to perform additional processing tasks, such as checking access control lists or tunneling different protocols (sending an IPX packet through an IP network, for example). Generally, protocols don't "talk" to each other without an intermediary device translating.

Exploring the Address Resolution Protocol Process

For data to be routed on an IP network, the packet must contain a source and destination IP address and a source and destination MAC address. **Address Resolution Protocol (ARP)** maps IP addresses to MAC addresses. Unique MAC addresses reference the endpoints (sending and receiving computers) in information exchanges. Many network devices maintain **ARP tables** listing the MAC and IP addresses of other devices on the network. Normally, devices obtain and update their ARP tables automatically.

When a computer prepares to transmit a packet to a destination on the local network, it checks its ARP table for an IP-to-MAC address mapping for the destination node. If the computer finds a mapping, the source computer uses the information to encapsulate the data it's ready to transmit. The source computer can then send the packet directly to the destination computer.

If the sending computer doesn't find an entry for destination IP address in its ARP table, the source host issues an ARP broadcast requesting the MAC address for the corresponding IP address. Every station on the local subnet receives the ARP broadcast, but only the destination host answers with the requested information. The rest of the devices on the segment discard the packet.

ARP packets have 28 octets (28 sets of eight binary digits) that identify hardware types, protocol types, and message lengths. The ARP request packet is broadcast to all MAC addresses (FF-FF-FF-FF-FF-FF), and all devices on the local segment check to determine whether their IP addresses match the destination's IP address.

The device that discovers its own IP address in the IP header returns an ARP reply. The source computer extracts the MAC address from the ARP reply and updates its ARP table. Then the source computer creates and addresses its data packet and sends it.

TIP   Remember from Chapter 2 that in IPv6, Neighbor Discovery (ND) replaces ARP.

Reverse Address Resolution Protocol

Reverse Address Resolution Protocol (RARP) is similar to ARP, except RARP maps MAC addresses to IP addresses. RARP is generally used for diskless workstations (dumb terminals). When a dumb terminal starts, it has its MAC address available because that information is hard-coded in the network interface card (NIC). Because the terminal has no hard disk, however, it has no way to store IP address information. At startup, the terminal broadcasts a RARP packet requesting IP addressing information.

Figure 3-1 shows the differences between an ARP and a RARP packet. Notice that the RARP header enters the destination address as the broadcast address, 255.255.255.255, but doesn't know its own source IP address, so it's entered as 0.0.0.0, indicating any node and any subnet.

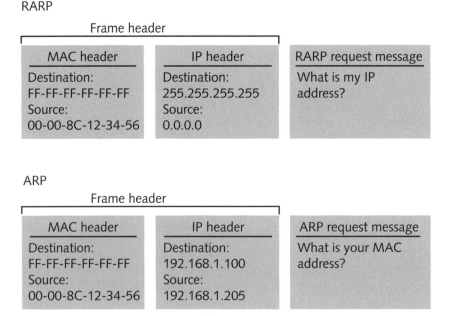

Figure 3-1   RARP versus ARP packets

Proxy Address Resolution Protocol

Proxy ARP is easy to understand if you know how proxy services work: One node acts on behalf of another (or several others) to provide a service or information. As mentioned, in the ARP process, a station broadcasts a request for the MAC address to be used for a specific IP address. Often, however, the node the requester is seeking isn't on the same network, and the request has to travel through a router to reach its destination.

Proxy ARP is used because routers, by default, don't forward broadcast traffic, and ARP requests are broadcasts. So the ARP request reaches the router, and the router doesn't forward it. If the router won't forward the request, the requester can't receive the information needed to address and send the packet. So how does internetwork ARP happen?

Routers act as proxies and provide their own MAC addresses. The router receives the ARP request packet, reads the information, and finds out that the destination host is on a different subnet. Instead of forwarding the ARP request, the router enters its own MAC address in an ARP reply and sends it to the original requester. That node receives the reply, updates its ARP table to reflect that the destination's IP address maps to the router's MAC address, and addresses and sends its data with the destination IP and the router's MAC address.

When the router receives the packets, it examines the addressing, determines the path needed to reach the destination, and rebuilds the packet header information. The router then sends the packet back out through the appropriate interface, and neither endpoint of the exchange realizes there was an intermediary proxy. Routers commonly act as ARP proxies, and the hosts sending ARP broadcasts have the router's MAC address in their ARP tables. Figure 3-2 shows how proxy ARP works.

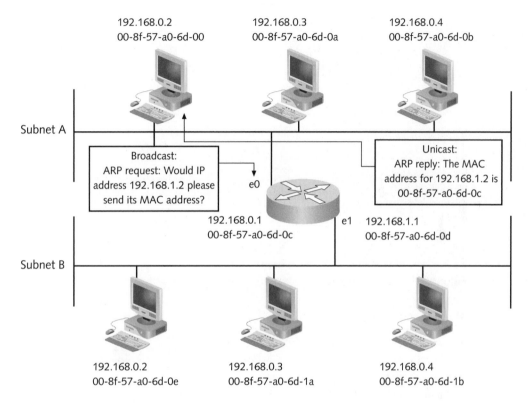

Figure 3-2 Proxy ARP

Accessing a Router

To understand router commands and configurations, you need to know how to work at the Cisco Internetwork Operating System (IOS) command-line interface (CLI). Before you can do that, however, you have to know how to gain access to the router. A few different methods are commonly used.

On the back of most Cisco routers are several ports; network modules such as frame relay, TI, and Fibre Channel interfaces; the power switch; and other devices specific to the router model. The auxiliary (AUX) and console (CON) ports are particularly important when you're accessing the CLI for configuration, troubleshooting, and maintenance. When you have physical access to the router, the easiest method is using the CON port with a rollover cable attached to a laptop or other workstation. You can use a number of terminal emulation programs; HyperTerminal, which comes with Windows, is easy to use. Attach the Ethernet jack of the rollover cable to the router's CON port, and attach the other end (usually a serial connection but could be an RJ-45 Ethernet jack) to a serial or Ethernet port on your laptop or workstation. Start your terminal emulation program, and set the connection attributes. Figure 3-3 shows the defaults for a serial connection using COM1. After the connection is set up, power on the router and wait for it to start.

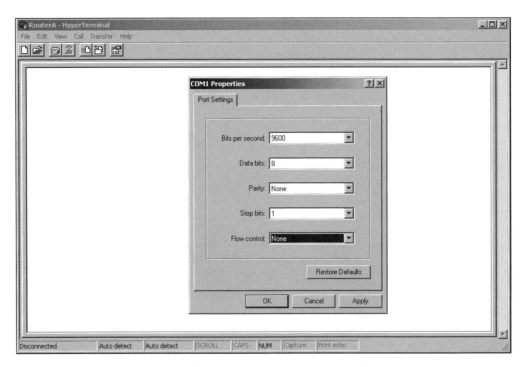

Figure 3-3   HyperTerminal default settings for a router console connection

You can also access a router with Telnet, although remote access requires some planning and caution. First, you must have passwords assigned to the Telnet lines. A router has five virtual terminal (VTY) lines for inbound Telnet access, numbered VTY 0 through VTY 4. The AUX port is sometimes used for access, but like the CON port, it requires physical access to the router. Routers also have asynchronous (TTY) lines for inbound or outbound modem and terminal connections. For all these lines, you can assign passwords and specify whether a password is required at logon. You can set up passwords for different users and lines, or use an authentication server for username and password access. In the activities in this chapter, you use a router CLI simulation program to see how to work with the Cisco IOS CLI, also called EXEC access.

A full discussion of router connections, lines, authentication servers, and CLI access is beyond the scope of this book. If you want more information, you can find technical documentation and product-specific instructions on Cisco's Web site at *www.cisco.com/univercd/home/home.htm*.

You can find Cisco routers and networking equipment on Internet auction sites, such as eBay, for a reasonable price. Equipment from auction sites is useful for getting practice at home working with these devices.

3

ACTIVITY 3-1: DOWNLOADING AND INSTALLING A ROUTER SIMULATION PROGRAM

Time Required: 10 minutes

Objective: Download and install a router simulation program.

Description: In this activity, you download and install a free router simulation program. Most router configuration is done from a command-line interface, and the program you install in this activity gives you practice in working with the Cisco IOS CLI.

A router command-line interface isn't that complicated, and most programs support the basic commands you're learning. Stick to trusted sources for downloading software to avoid potential malware.

1. Start your Web browser and go to a search engine. Type the keywords **free router sim** and press **Enter**. Select a simulator that enables you to practice the commands the Cisco Certified Network Associate (CCNA) exam covers. (Although this book isn't targeted for the CCNA exam, aiming for this level of capability makes it easier to perform the activities in this book.)

The program used as an example in this activity is Lab 1.0 of ToggIT Router Simulator downloaded from *www.freedownloadscenter.com*. Because the availability of freeware programs can change, the activities in Chapters 3 and 4 don't specify a router simulation program. You can do the activities no matter what program you're using.

2. Download and install the program, and then start it. You should see a window similar to Figure 3-4.

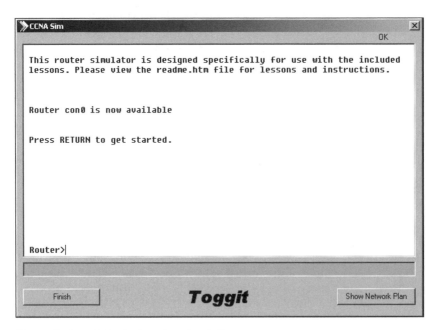

Figure 3-4   A typical router simulation program

3. Leave the router simulation program running for the next activity.

Routing Tables

Routing tables are lists of routes containing address, metric count, and link–state information about neighboring routers. These tables have three types of entries. **Static routes** are entered in a routing table by an administrator. **Dynamic routes** require routing protocols and routing algorithms that the router uses to calculate the best path, communicate routing table information to other routers, and update the routing table with information from other routers. **Default routes** are manually configured routes that direct all packets not specifically configured in the routing table. A packet that can't be routed to its destination via other learned or static routes is routed to the specified interface or next hop automatically.

NOTE   Remember that metrics are measurements, such as hop count, that routers use to determine the best route to take. Some metrics are automatic and depend on the routing protocol; others can be manually adjusted to fine-tune traffic flow.

Cisco routers use three main processes in building and maintaining routing tables:

- Routing processes that actually run a routing protocol, such as Interior Gateway Routing Protocol or Open Shortest Path First

- The forwarding process, which requests information from the routing table for making a forwarding decision

- Routing tables from other routers, which are sent as replies to requests for information about routing and forwarding processes or are automatically sent as default updates depending on the routing protocol in use

NOTE

You learn more about routing protocols and default updates in "Understanding Routing Protocols" later in this chapter.

A typical routing table is shown in Figure 3-5. Notice that the routes indicated by an R were discovered via Routing Information Protocol (RIP); routes noted with a C are directly connected.

```
Router1#sh ip route
Codes: C - connected, S - static, I - IGRP, R - RIP, M - mobile, B - BGP
   D - EIGRP, EX - EIGRP external, O - OSPF, IA - OSPF inter area
   N1 - OSPF NSSA external type 1, N2 - OSPF NSSA external type 2
   E1 - OSPF external type 1, E2 - OSPF external type 2, E - EGP
   i - IS-IS, L1 - IS-IS level-1, L2 - IS-IS level-2, ia - IS-IS inter area
   * - candidate default, U - per-user static route, o - ODR
   P - periodic downloaded static route

Gateway of last resort is not set

      172.16.0.0/24 is subnetted, 8 subnets
R        172.16.8.0 [120/3] via 172.16.1.1, 00:00:09, Ethernet0/0
C        172.16.4.0 is directly connected, Ethernet1/0
R        172.16.5.0 [120/1] via 172.16.1.1, 00:00:09, Ethernet0/0
R        172.16.6.0 [120/1] via 172.16.1.1, 00:00:09, Ethernet0/0
R        172.16.7.0 [120/2] via 172.16.1.1, 00:00:09, Ethernet0/0
C        172.16.1.0 is directly connected, Ethernet0/0
R        172.16.2.0 [120/2] via 172.16.1.1, 00:00:09, Ethernet0/0
R        172.16.3.0 [120/1] via 172.16.1.1, 00:00:09, Ethernet0/0
```

Figure 3-5   A typical routing table

Static Routing

Sometimes routing protocols are unnecessary, or you need to specify a route for traffic flow control or security reasons. For example, on a small network, routing protocols' update requests and replies can create unnecessary traffic and consume resources. In addition, a network might have only one point of access; this type of network is called a **stub network** (see Figure 3-6). A router with only one route out is called a **stub router**. A stub router is usually at the end of the network line, connected to only one other router. Stub networks are generally at the network's edge and are more or less dead-end segments.

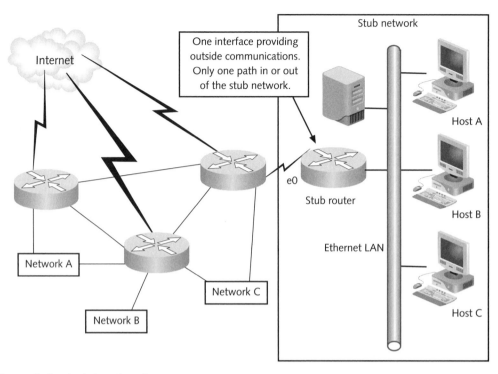

Figure 3-6 A stub network

Often you need to specify certain routes or adjust traffic flow to maximize efficiency, improve security or performance, and conserve bandwidth. In these cases (and for other reasons), an administrator can enter the route manually in the routing table. Using static routes gives an administrator full control over the flow of traffic. A static route, by default, has a lower metric than one determined via a dynamic routing protocol. Static routes are preferred because they have been programmed by an administrator. These routes are configured manually on Cisco routers with the ip route command, which uses the following syntax:

```
ip route [destination network] [destination network mask]
[IP address next hop interface] [administrative distance]
```

To make a static route permanent, you must add the word "permanent" to the end of the ip route command. Otherwise, the route is deleted from the routing table when the interface is shut down. (An administrative distance, discussed more in "Routing Metrics" later in this chapter, is simply a value telling the router which route is preferred if there are two or more possible routes.)

The main disadvantages of static routing are the time required to configure routes and the effort of maintaining the routing table when the network's topology changes. Also, static routes must be entered manually in each router, which can become time consuming as a network grows and changes. Administrators must also be familiar with the network's topology and have a thorough understanding of the routing process.

The advantages of static routing are the fine-tuned control administrators have over traffic flow and little to no resource overhead. Because a static route is preferred over a dynamic route, the router doesn't need to expend resources deciding which route to use. In addition, routers don't generate network traffic for route discovery because the static route is configured manually, thus reducing overall traffic load on the network.

ACTIVITY 3-2: WORKING AT THE COMMAND-LINE INTERFACE

Time Required: 10 minutes

Objective: Learn basic router command-line modes and navigate between them.

Description: In this activity, you learn how to log on to a router and move between different EXEC modes. You learn about basic commands for viewing configuration information and how to navigate between configuration modes to configure, maintain, and troubleshoot Cisco routers.

1. Return to your router simulation program from Activity 3-1, and press **Enter** to get started. You should see the > prompt, called the user mode prompt. From this prompt, you can view certain settings and enter privileged mode, where you can make changes to the router's configuration.

2. Type **enable** and press **Enter**. (The router simulation might ask for a password. You haven't programmed one yet, so just press **Enter** again.) You should then see a # prompt to indicate you're in privileged mode, where you can change the router's name, program banners, set passwords, and enter other configuration modes.

3. Type **configure terminal** and press **Enter**. The prompt changes to Router(config)#, which is global configuration mode. Type **hostname RouterA** and press **Enter**. The router has now been named, so the prompt changes to RouterA(config)#.

The Cisco IOS provides context-sensitive help, so if you're working with a real Cisco router, you can type ? to get a list of available commands. You can also type partial commands with a ? for subcommands and options. Most simulators don't offer this feature, however.

4. Type **interface ethernet 0** and press **Enter**. The prompt changes to RouterA(config-if)#, which is interface configuration mode for the Ethernet 0 interface. Type **exit** and press **Enter** to return to global configuration mode.

5. Type **interface serial 0** and press **Enter**. You're now in interface configuration mode for the serial 0 interface. Press **Ctrl+Z** (CTRL^ in Cisco syntax) to return to privileged mode.

6. Next, type **show running-config** and press **Enter**. Examine the output, which shows information about the IOS version, hostname, services, line, and interfaces. Return to global configuration mode (the RouterA(config)# prompt), type **line vty 0 4**, and press **Enter**. The prompt changes to RouterA(config-line)#.

7. Press **Ctrl+Z** to return to privileged mode, and then type **exit** and press **Enter** to return to user mode. If time permits, continue practice in navigating the CLI.

8. Leave your router simulation program running for the next activity.

Default Routes

Default routes ensure that packets not addressed to configured destinations can still reach their destination. A default route is also known as a quad zero route because it's configured as follows:

```
ip route 0.0.0.0 0.0.0.0 [next hop router ip address]
[administrative distance]
```

The zeros represent any destination network with any subnet mask.

ACTIVITY 3-3: ASSIGNING IP ADDRESSES TO INTERFACES

Time Required: 10 minutes

Objective: Configure IP addresses for Ethernet and serial router interfaces.

Description: In this activity, you configure the Ethernet 0 and serial 0 router interfaces with IP addresses. You then use the show commands to see how the interfaces change as you work with them.

The simulator used as an example in this chapter doesn't allow random IP addresses, so specific addresses must be used. Refer to your program's tutorials, instructions, or labs for addresses to replace variables such as *network* or *network mask* (subnet mask). If you need more help, ask your instructor.

If you have trouble remembering how to navigate the CLI modes referred to in this activity, return to Activity 3-2 for more practice.

1. If necessary, start your router simulation program, and enter privileged mode (RouterA# prompt). Type **show interface ethernet 0** and press **Enter**. Notice that the Ethernet 0 interface is up, but the line protocol is down.

In the show interface output, the Ethernet interface refers to the router's physical Ethernet interface. The line protocol refers to the line carrying the signal. If the line is usable, this field states that the line protocol is up, meaning the line is usable and keep-alives are successful. "Up" and "down" are straightforward: Up means it's working, and down means it isn't or the administrator has taken it down, in which case the output is "administratively down."

NOTE

3

2. Enter global configuration mode by typing **configure terminal** and pressing **Enter**. Type **interface ethernet 0** and press **Enter** to switch to Ethernet 0 interface configuration mode, prompt RouterA(config-if)#. Type **ip address** *ip address network mask* and press **Enter**. Type **no shutdown** and press **Enter** to enable the interface.

Cisco routers allow truncating many commands. For example, a real router would accept "en" instead of "enable" or "config t" in place of "configure terminal." Some simulation programs also accept shortened commands, but because many do not, complete commands are used in these activities.

NOTE

3. Exit to privileged mode, type **show interface ethernet 0**, and press **Enter**. The output now shows that Ethernet 0 is up and the line protocol is up. The IP address you just programmed is displayed along with statistics for the interface (see Figure 3-7).

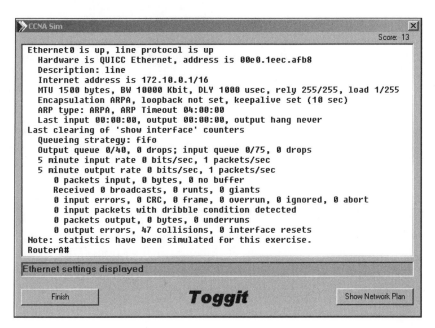

```
CCNA Sim                                                    X
                                                    Score: 13
Ethernet0 is up, line protocol is up
  Hardware is QUICC Ethernet, address is 00e0.1eec.afb8
  Description: line
  Internet address is 172.10.0.1/16
  MTU 1500 bytes, BW 10000 Kbit, DLY 1000 usec, rely 255/255, load 1/255
  Encapsulation ARPA, loopback not set, keepalive set (10 sec)
  ARP type: ARPA, ARP Timeout 04:00:00
  Last input 00:00:00, output 00:00:00, output hang never
Last clearing of 'show interface' counters
  Queueing strategy: fifo
  Output queue 0/40, 0 drops; input queue 0/75, 0 drops
  5 minute input rate 0 bits/sec, 1 packets/sec
  5 minute output rate 0 bits/sec, 1 packets/sec
     0 packets input, 0 bytes, 0 no buffer
     Received 0 broadcasts, 0 runts, 0 giants
     0 input errors, 0 CRC, 0 frame, 0 overrun, 0 ignored, 0 abort
     0 input packets with dribble condition detected
     0 packets output, 0 bytes, 0 underruns
     0 output errors, 47 collisions, 0 interface resets
Note: statistics have been simulated for this exercise.
RouterA#

Ethernet settings displayed

    Finish              Toggit            Show Network Plan
```

Figure 3-7   Sample output from the show interface ethernet 0 command

4. Return to interface configuration mode for Ethernet 0, type **shutdown**, and press **Enter**. Exit back to privileged mode and check the show interface output for Ethernet 0 again. Now Ethernet 0 is up, but the line protocol is down.

5. Enter interface configuration mode for the serial 0 interface. Type **ip address** *ip address subnet mask* and press **Enter** to assign the IP address to the interface. Serial interfaces are a little different from Ethernet interfaces. For a serial interface, you must also set the clock rate. Type **clock rate 56000** and press **Enter**. Enable the interface by typing **no shutdown** and pressing **Enter**, and then press **Ctrl+Z** to exit back to privileged mode.

6. Type **show running-config** and press **Enter**. Note that Ethernet 0 and serial 0 now show IP addresses.

7. Leave your router simulation program running for the next activity.

Dynamic Routing

All routing protocols use algorithms that enable routers to communicate with each other and essentially map the network in the form of routing tables. This function is what dynamic routing is all about. Routers are capable of maintaining route information by using routing protocols; routing tables are updated at regular intervals or when a route changes, depending on the protocol.

To understand the difference between static routing and dynamic routing, think of the difference between static IP addressing and Dynamic Host Configuration Protocol (DHCP). On a small network, static addressing works fine, but as the network grows, managing IP addressing is difficult, and the risk of communication failures increases. DHCP maintains and assigns IP addresses automatically. Static routing has its place in small networks, but managing it on a large network would be almost impossible. By using dynamic routing with routing protocols, routers can handle matters more easily.

Routing protocols are different from routed protocols, such as TCP/IP. A **routed protocol** is used to provide addressing for a packet being transported; a **routing protocol** allows routers to maintain information about network links in the routing tables they use. The two main types of routing protocols are discussed in the following sections.

Distance-Vector Routing Protocols

A **distance-vector routing protocol** uses mathematical calculations to compare routes based on some measurement of distance, such as hops. This protocol requires routers to send full or partial routing table updates periodically to neighboring routers.

Link-State Routing Protocols

Link-state routing protocols require each router to maintain at least a partial network map. Routers monitor link status, and when topology or link state changes, updates are sent to neighboring routers to inform them of the change. Link-state routing protocols use a notification called a link-state advertisement to broadcast changes. Because link-state routing protocols don't use the default periodic updates every 30 or 90 seconds, less network traffic is generated, although link-state protocols do require slightly more router memory.

Routing Metrics

As mentioned, routing protocols use metrics to determine the best path for packet routing. **Metrics** are cost values that help routers assess the desirability of a link and include hop count, load, bandwidth, delay, and reliability of links.

The idea of link "cost" isn't a matter of money; it's a method of assigning reliability ratings to a route. For example, if you have a T1 link and a redundant dial-up WAN link, a router running a distance-vector routing protocol could assign an equal value to each link. The router views both links as equally desirable, even though the T1 link is clearly preferable to the dial-up link.

Because older routing protocols, such as RIP, use only hop count to calculate the best path, the accuracy of the assessment is prone to errors. Other routing protocols use multiple metrics, such as reliability and bandwidth, for path determination.

Some metrics are fixed values, and others are variable. Load and reliability are measured over time intervals, generally 5 seconds. Routers observe attached links and report errors. A link that reports problems, such as interface errors on lost packets, is considered less reliable than a link reporting no errors. In this case, the reliability value of the link reporting no errors is a lower number, indicating a more reliable path. A link reporting consistently lower loads is considered less congested and, therefore, more reliable. Both load and reliability use the numbering scheme 1 to 255, with 1 being the best rating and 255 the worst. Table 3-1 summarizes the metrics common routing protocols use.

Table 3-1 Routing protocol metrics

Metric	Description	Values	Administrator can modify
Hop count	Indicates the number of hops between source and destination.	Variable depending on path	No
Reliability	Routers observe links and report on errors. Links with fewer errors reported are considered more reliable.	Measured from 1 to 255, with 1 being the most reliable and 255 the least	Can be configured as a fixed value
Load	Indicates traffic load over a specific link.	Measured from 1 to 255, with 1 being the lowest load and 255 the highest, representing 100% utilization	Can be configured as a fixed value
Bandwidth	Indicates the capacity of a link, measured from source to destination. The path with the overall highest bandwidth is considered the best path.	Variable depending on path; measured in bits per second	No
Delay	Represents the amount of time for a router to process, queue, and transmit a packet. A delay is measured from source to destination, and the route with the lowest cumulative delay is the preferred route.	Variable depending on path; measured in tens of microseconds, represented by the symbol μ	No

Administrative Distances

The **administrative distance** is a value used to establish a route's reliability (cost). Table 3-2 shows the default administrative distances of some common routing protocols. An administrative distance of 0 is the preferred route; a route with an administrative distance of 255 should never be used. The larger the number, the less reliable the route is considered.

Think of administrative distance as the sum of metrics. Dynamic routing protocols use algorithms to determine the best path. Metrics are the measurements entered into an algorithm to determine the result: administrative distance or cost value. One major difference between an administrative distance and a metric is that most metrics are automatic, but administrators can adjust administrative distances manually to optimize performance or control traffic for other reasons, such as a slow link, heavy congestion for a segment, or security concerns.

As you can see in Table 3-2, a static route has a default administrative distance of 1, making it the preferred route unless the administrator changes the administrative distance of another route managed via routing protocols. Normally, however, there's no good reason to do so. In the early days of networking, bandwidth was a commodity to be managed carefully. Today, high-speed, high-capacity transmission lines are common, and bandwidth isn't such an issue. Even so, some situations require managing traffic loads, so it's worth knowing that the administrative distances of routing protocols can be changed to have more control over traffic.

Table 3-2   Administrative distances

Route learned via	Administrative distance
Directly connected network	0
Static route	1
Enhanced Interior Gateway Routing Protocol (EIGRP)	90
Interior Gateway Routing Protocol (IGRP)	100
Open Shortest Path First (OSPF)	110
Routing Information Protocol (RIP)	120
Unknown	255

Administrators can change the way routers make path decisions by setting cost values on links. Usually, this process means entering a lower number reflecting a better path or setting values that prevent a route from being used unless all other routes are down. An administrator might choose this method for several reasons, such as controlling traffic over a backup link or reducing the load on a heavily used link. For some networks, links used for replication between sites might require careful traffic management or security controls, so tweaking the way routers handle traffic is necessary to optimize traffic flow.

ACTIVITY

ACTIVITY 3-4: CONFIGURING STATIC ROUTES

Time Required: 10 minutes

Objective: Configure a static route.

Description: Using the router simulation program, you enter a static route in the routing table and then view the routing table.

   1. If necessary, start your router simulation program. Type **show ip route** at the privileged mode prompt and press **Enter**. If you completed Activities 3-2 and 3-3, you should see a "C" before the IP address for an interface, indicating a directly connected route and the route's IP address and interface.

2. Enter global configuration mode. Type **ip route** *network network mask route*, replacing the variables *network*, *network mask*, and *route* with the addresses for your network, and press **Enter**. Enter one other network destination via the route, such as ip route 192.168.50.0 255.255.255.0 210.16.54.1; in this command, 192.168.50.0 255.255.255.0 is the destination to be reached and 210.16.54.1 is the route (interface address) to reach that destination.

3. Exit to privileged mode. Type **copy running-config startup-config** (often truncated to "copy run start") to copy your running configuration to the startup configuration and press **Enter**. Type **show ip route** again and press **Enter**. Two additional routes should be displayed now. The "S" indicates that the routes are static.

4. Leave your router simulation program running for the next activity.

NOTE

For more information on commands you might not understand in these activities, *visit www.cisco.com* and do a search for specific commands. Many Web sites offer tutorials and router command summaries, which you can find with an Internet search.

Route Summarization

Summarization allows service providers to assign addresses in a classless fashion, making more efficient use of available Internet addresses. As discussed in Chapter 2, IPv6 will eventually provide more IP addresses, but IPv4 isn't going to be phased out overnight. Until then, better ways to use IPv4 addresses are needed.

For example, to provide an organization with 2000 IP addresses, eight traditional Class C networks must be used. Table 3-3 compares a classful IP addressing example with classless routing, using network prefixes and supernetting for the same number of usable hosts. Clearly, this method would make a big difference in a routing table update. Instead of all routes of traditional addresses being sent, the supernetted network has only one address to advertise for all these networks.

Table 3-3 Traditional IP addressing to assign 2000 addresses

Traditional Class C address range	Subnet mask (network prefix)	Number of hosts	Supernetted address range (summarization)	Subnet mask (network prefix)
194.28.0.x	255.255.255.0 (/24)	254	194.28.0.x–194.28.7.x	255.255.248.0 (/21)
194.28.1.x	255.255.255.0 (/24)	254		
194.28.2.x	255.255.255.0 (/24)	254		
194.28.3.x	255.255.255.0 (/24)	254		
194.28.4.x	255.255.255.0 (/24)	254		
194.28.5.x	255.255.255.0 (/24)	254		
194.28.6.x	255.255.255.0 (/24)	254		
194.28.7.x	255.255.255.0 (/24)	254		
Total number of usable host addresses		2036	2046	

In the example in Table 3-3, 194.28.0.x/24, the router knows by the network prefix of /24 that the first 24 bits (three octets) of the address identify the network, and the remaining 8 bits are for host addressing within that network. With the supernetted example, 194.28.0.x/21, the first 21 bits identify the network, leaving the remaining 11 bits for host addressing. (Remember that the first and last address of an IP address range are reserved for the network address and broadcast address, respectively.) Even better, with supernetting, only the first 21 bits must match for all the traffic addressed to the block 194.28.0.x through 194.28.7.x to be routed to that network. So instead of having to maintain a list of all eight networks in the routing table, as the router would have to do in classful routing, the routing table can have just one entry that covers all eight.

Summarization is used for large networks or when bandwidth management is important. Large routing tables are a concern because they decrease router performance and generate network traffic in the form of routing table updates. (Remember that routers broadcast the routing table to other routers periodically.)

Deciding how to summarize a group of subnets is fairly straightforward. You count the number of bits that are common to all the networks you want to advertise, and then identify the number of common bits by using a network prefix. A network prefix is the

Classless Interdomain Routing (CIDR) notation rather than the traditional classful subnet mask. For example, /24 is the default CIDR notation for a Class C network prefix, and the corresponding default subnet mask is 255.255.255.0, meaning only the last octet is left for host addressing, and the first three octets identify the network. The only problem with using prefixes in routing is that RIP version 1 doesn't support sending network prefixes in the routing information. Because RIPv1's features are limited and difficult to secure, RIP version 2 is recommended, which does support sending network prefixes.

Variable length subnet masking (VLSM, discussed in Chapter 2) is another method of using classless routing to maximize the IP addresses allocated to your network. VLSM uses subnet masks of different lengths on the same network to assign network addresses based on need instead of using a generic masking scheme. For example, you have a Class C network divided into subnets, with each one supporting 62 hosts. In reality, only 15 to 20 hosts are attached to each subnet, so the additional addresses are wasted. With VLSM, you can divide the network into subnets of varying sizes to support your users but make better use of your available addresses, instead of using networkwide classful routing.

UNDERSTANDING ROUTING PROTOCOLS

As described previously, routers use routing protocols to make path determination choices and to share those choices with other routers. Routing protocols come in two major categories: **Interior Gateway Protocols (IGPs)** and **Exterior Gateway Protocols (EGPs)**. IGPs usually operate within the network boundary and are under a network administrator's control. EGPs are used between different networks (autonomous systems, discussed in the next paragraph) and are outside the local administrator's control.

Routing protocols work within frameworks called autonomous systems. An **autonomous system (AS)** is a network or group of networks controlled and managed by an administrator on behalf of an organization, such as a corporation or university. Autonomous systems are assigned a designation called an **Autonomous System Number (ASN)** in the form of an integer or in dotted decimal IP address format. Routers in the same AS communicate routing table information to one another with an IGP. Communicating routing information to other ASs requires a border router running an EGP.

NOTE

Internet Assigned Numbers Authority (IANA) assigns ASNs and allocates them to five regional registries. You can find more information on ASNs and regional registries at *www.iana.org/assignments/as-numbers*.

Interior Gateway Protocols

Routers used in an organization for intranet routing run IGPs, which exchange routing table information with other routers within a single AS. Some commonly used IGPs are discussed briefly in the following sections.

Routing Information Protocol

Routing Information Protocol (RIP) has been around for many years and is still used in many systems. RIP is defined in RFC 1058 and Internet Standard (STD) 56. In 1993, the IETF released an update to the RIP standard in RFC 1388, and then issued RFC 1723 to specify RIP version 2. RIPv2 added functionality to its predecessor; support for subnet masks was particularly important, given the growth of the Internet and the likelihood of running out of IP addresses. RFC 1723 didn't make RIP obsolete, however, and RIP is still widely used because it's easy to configure and maintain.

RIP is a distance-vector routing protocol with the following characteristics:

- A maximum hop count of 15 helps prevent routing loops from continuing indefinitely but makes RIP unsuitable for large networks.

- Hop count is the only metric used in path determination.

- Routing updates sent every 30 seconds create extra traffic.

- Timing mechanisms (holddown, update timer, timeout timer, flush timer) and split horizons prevent errors in routing information from being propagated. These features are explained in "Routing Loops" later in this chapter.

- RIP can't support variable length subnet masking.

- RIP has a slow convergence time. (Convergence is the time required for all routers to receive updates to routing tables.)

- RIP supports equal-cost load balancing (on pure Cisco networks only).

- RIPv2 supports subnet masks; RIP does not. RIPv2 also supports simple authentication to provide basic security for routing table updates.

To install RIP on Cisco routers, you must enable RIP and then configure RIP routing for each major network you want to advertise. (Basically, the addresses assigned to your physical interfaces are your routes.) To enable RIP, simply enter the following commands (indicated with bold type to differentiate from the prompt):

```
RouterA>enable

Password:

RouterA#config t

RouterA(config)#router rip
```

```
RouterA(config-router)#network network#

RouterA(config-router)#^Z
```

> **TIP**
>
> The RouterA(config-router)# prompt is called router configuration mode. In the preceding example, router is the primary command, and rip specifies what you're configuring (the RIP routing protocol).

You can use the show ip route command to display the routing table and use the show ip protocol and debug ip rip commands to monitor RIP. Show ip protocol can be entered at the user mode or privileged mode prompt. It displays all RIP timers, the administrative distance, network routing, version control, and routing information sources.

> **NOTE**
>
> Keep in mind that most free router simulation programs aren't fully functional duplications of the Cisco IOS. They are partial representations that can imitate common commands. For this reason, you might not be able to test all the commands discussed in this chapter in your router simulation program, and the prompts or output shown might not be exactly the same as what you see in your simulator. The command sequence examples in this chapter are what you would see if you were entering the commands into a real router.

ACTIVITY 3-5: ENABLING RIP

Time Required: 10 minutes

Objective: Enable and disable dynamic routing with RIP.

Description: Using the router simulation program, you enable and disable dynamic routing with RIP.

1. If necessary, start your router simulation program, and enter global configuration mode.

2. Type **router rip** and press **Enter** to enable RIP. Type **network** *ip address* and press **Enter**. Type **network** *ip address* again and press **Enter**. (Use two different IP addresses in these commands: the IP addresses you used in previous activities for your serial and Ethernet interfaces. Remember, you're telling RIP which routes you want to advertise.)

3. Exit to privileged mode. Type **copy running-config startup-config** and press **Enter** to copy your running configuration to the startup configuration.

4. Type **show ip route** and press **Enter**. You should see both directly connected and static routes. Return to global configuration mode and remove RIP by typing **no router rip** and pressing **Enter**.

5. Leave your router simulation program running for the next activity.

The debug ip rip command, which displays real-time RIP updates being sent and received, must be used from the privileged mode prompt. It uses a tremendous amount of processing power and network resources, so it should be used only for troubleshooting RIP and turned off with the "no" form of the command when you're done.

Open Shortest Path First

Open Shortest Path First (OSPF) was developed to address some limitations of RIP and because a common, interoperable IGP for the Internet was needed. OSPF is a link-state routing protocol that authenticates routing updates, includes route summarization, and supports VLSM.

OSPF uses areas (the router equivalent of domains) to control the boundaries of link-state updates. Routers that have all interfaces in a single area are referred to as **internal routers** and can communicate only with routers in the same area. Routers that have interfaces in multiple areas are called **area border routers (ABRs)**. A router that acts as a gateway or an intermediary between OSPF and other routing protocols (or other instances of the OSPF routing process) is called an **autonomous system boundary router (ASBR)**. Any router can be an ABR or ASBR. Routers are configured with area IDs assigned to the area an interface is in. An **area ID** can take the form of a randomly chosen integer between 0 and 4,294,967,295 or can be in dotted decimal format like an IP address, such as 0.0.0.0.

Routers that are in the same area and use simple password authentication must share the same key (password). To enable password authentication, use the following commands, replacing *key* with the password and *areaID* with the area ID for that interface:

```
ip ospf authentication-key key

area areaID authentication
```

OSPF has the following characteristics:

- No hop count limitation.

- More complex to configure than RIP.

- IP multicasts are used to send link-state updates, reducing the processing load on routers not listening for OSPF updates.

- Updates are triggered by changes instead of being sent periodically, which uses less bandwidth.

- Better convergence time and allows load balancing.

- Supports VLSM.

- Supports route summarization and aggregation, which are needed to manage large, complex networks.

- Supports basic password authentication for routing protocol exchanges.

- External routes injected into the AS routing table can be tagged, making it easier to keep track of them.

- Requires more CPU and memory overhead than RIP.

- Designed for use on a single AS. Each OSPF router in an AS maintains an identical database describing the AS topology. Each router constructs a shortest path tree from this database to build a routing table.

NOTE   OSPF's technical details are beyond the scope of this book. To learn more about OSPF, search at Cisco's Web site or refer to RFCs 1246 and 2328.

Interior Gateway Routing Protocol

Interior Gateway Routing Protocol (IGRP), like RIP, is a distance-vector routing protocol, but IGRP uses a composite metric that's calculated by factoring weighted mathematical values for internetwork delay, bandwidth, reliability, and load. IGRP routing can be influenced by using user-definable constants, including variance, which allows administrators to set acceptable ranges of deviation from the best path value for multipath routing.

NOTE   The latest Cisco IOS version no longer supports IGRP.

IGRP offers a lot of control over metrics, so administrators can fine-tune traffic flow and routing patterns. IGRP also uses methods to control routing loops, including holddowns, split horizon, and poison reverse (explained later in "Routing Loops"). IGRP has the following characteristics:

- Larger hop count; the default is 100, but it can support up to 255 if hop count is configured as a metric.

- Routing table updates (entire table) are sent every 90 seconds.

- Uses bandwidth and delay as default metrics.

- Can be configured to use load and reliability metrics.

- Can use several different cost paths for redundancy and load balancing.

- Uses split horizon and poison reverse to control routing loops and inconsistencies in the routing table.

- Can't support VLSM.

- Metrics can be configured to control path selection: hops, load, bandwidth, reliability, delay, and maximum transmission unit (MTU; size of the packet).

Configuring IGRP requires the following commands:

```
RouterA>enable

RouterA#config t

RouterA(config)#router igrp AS#

RouterA(config-router)#network network#

RouterA(config-router)#^Z
```

All routers configured to share routing table information via IGRP must use the same AS# parameter. As with RIP, after IGRP is configured, you can use the show ip route command to monitor all available IGRP routes. The show ip protocol command displays IGRP timers, and the debug ip igrp command is used for troubleshooting. As with any debug command, it uses a considerable amount of processing power, so it should be used only when necessary and turned off by using the "no" form of the command.

Enhanced Interior Gateway Routing Protocol

Enhanced Interior Gateway Routing Protocol (EIGRP) is a hybrid protocol, blending distance-vector and link-state capabilities into a single protocol. EIGRP is compatible with IGRP and contains an automated redistribution mechanism that allows IGRP routes to be imported into EIGRP and vice versa. EIGRP also contains several protocols for determining whether a route is looping or loop free and discovering alternate paths without waiting for updates from other routers. EIGRP treats IGRP routes as external, so administrators can customize them. EIGRP's major characteristics are summarized in the following list:

- It's a Cisco proprietary protocol.

- It supports VLSM.

- It uses bandwidth, delay, load, and reliability as metrics. Bandwidth and delay are used by default, and MTU is required in some EIGRP-related commands.

- Routing updates are multicast and triggered by topology changes.

NOTE

This section is a brief overview of EIGRP. If you're interested in learning more, Cisco's Web site offers several white papers and technical documentation at *www.cisco.com/univercd/cc/td/doc/cisintwk/ito_doc/en_igrp.htm#xtocid9*.

Routing Protocol Timers

Routing protocols use timers to control tasks, such as sending routing table updates or removing a route from the table. An administrator can usually reset these timers. For example, the update timer in RIP can be reset from the default of 30 seconds if your network is small and link or topology changes are infrequent. There's no reason to send updates every 30 seconds and consume bandwidth if an update time of 90 seconds, for example, is enough to keep the routing table accurate.

Exterior Gateway Protocols

Routers use EGPs to communicate with routers in other ASs. Routers exchange route information in much the same way that routers using IGPs do, by polling neighbors at intervals. The neighbors respond by sending their routing tables. Two common EGPs are Border Gateway Protocol (BGP) and Exterior Gateway Protocol (EGP). EGP offers simple exchanges, but BGP has additional capabilities, including partial updates, cost metric configuration, and support for CIDR. BGP also uses TCP to exchange only the part of the routing table that has changed.

 Although the internal workings of EGPs are as fascinating as IGPs, the focus of this chapter is on the internal network routing process. For your purposes, you need to know only the basics of EGPs.

NOTE

Routing Loops

Routing loops can occur when there's a link failure or a change to network topology. When a change occurs, an update is sent to neighboring routers and passed from node to node until all routers have received the update. The problem is that in large networks, updates might take several minutes to reach the farthest routers. This problem is referred to as a slow convergence time.

Having a slow convergence time causes inconsistencies in routing tables throughout the network. Distant routers still believe the path is good and propagate that information to other routers. Neighboring routers receive updates from these distant routers containing erroneous information and update their routing tables. This means packets are sent to routers that assume a certain path can be used to reach a destination, and the packet is sent from router to router, looping through the network.

This type of problem is referred to as "routing by rumor." The packet keeps looping forever, which is called "counting to infinity." The network can quickly become overwhelmed by undeliverable packets bouncing between routers, and network performance is severely degraded or grinds to a halt. Routing protocols use several methods of controlling routing loops, discussed in the following sections.

Maximum Hop Count

Routing protocols have a maximum hop count. Each time a packet passes through a router, it's considered one "hop." The packet's hop count (indicated in the packet header, explained in Chapter 2) is increased by one as each router forwards the packet to the next hop. Routing protocols have a default maximum hop count—when this number is reached, the network is deemed unreachable, and the packet is considered undeliverable and is destroyed. So instead of propagating forever through a network, an undeliverable packet is forwarded only until it reaches the maximum hop count configured for the network or the default hop count for the routing protocol.

Split Horizon

Split horizon is used in distance-vector routing protocols to help prevent incorrect routing information updates from propagating through the network. Split horizon is simply a rule that prevents information from being sent back out the same interface it was received from. For example, if Router A learns all its routes from Router B, it doesn't make sense to have Router A advertise those same routes back to Router B. Without split horizon or other methods of controlling erroneous information from circulating, a routing loop can occur.

There are two categories of split horizon: simple split horizon and split horizon with poison reverse. Simple split horizon works by keeping update advertisements for routing tables from being sent back through the same interface from which routes were learned. Split horizon with poison reverse advertises the route but adds an "unreachable" metric, so the route isn't used. The idea behind split horizon with poison reverse is that bad news is better than no news. The unreachable route is marked as unreachable in all routing tables as the network converges, so there are no routers advertising the route as good.

You might hear poison reverse referred to as "route poisoning," too. Route poisoning operates under the same idea, sending an unreachable metric for a route to prevent it from being used. The two techniques are similar, with the notable difference being the direction the poisoned updates are sent: forward, reverse, or both. Poison reverse is the poisoning of all possible reverse paths. But what happens when the route comes back up? That's where holddowns and timers come in, discussed in the next section.

Holddowns and Timers

Holddowns prevent routers from accepting and entering updates about paths that might be down. When a router receives an update that indicates a route is down, a holddown timer is started. Any updates about that path are ignored until the holddown timer expires, which prevents an interface from changing state (often called "flapping") and allows time for the network to stabilize. The default holddown timer varies depending on the routing protocol. Protocols also have **update timers** that control how often updates are sent and **flush timers** that control when a route is flushed from the routing table. Default times are shown in Table 3-4.

Table 3-4   Default holddown times

Routing protocol	Default update time	Default holddown time	Default flush time
Static route	NA	NA	NA
EIGRP	Hello time varies but is generally 5 seconds; does not have a periodic update timer	Three times the Hello time	Three times the Hello time; neighbors are removed if no Hello packet is received by the time the holddown expires
IGRP	90 seconds	280 seconds; default is three times the update timer plus 10	630 seconds; seven times the update period is the default
RIP	30 seconds	180 seconds	240 seconds

In EIGRP, the Hello packet is a multicast used for neighbor discovery and recovery. Hello packets are small and don't require acknowledgements. By using these packets instead of periodic updates, EIGRP reduces the load on resources. Updates to route information are sent only when necessary, and only pertinent changes are sent. If a neighboring router doesn't receive a Hello packet from a neighbor within the time allowed (the default flush time), it assumes that neighbor is no longer reachable, and the route is flushed from the routing table. This method makes EIGRP efficient in maintaining its routing tables without clogging the network with periodic updates. It also makes EIGRP one of the fastest converging routing protocols. The major drawback of EIGRP is that it's a proprietary Cisco protocol.

CHAPTER SUMMARY

- ☐ Routing is the process of transporting packets of information across a network from the source to the destination. Routing involves two primary functions: determining paths and forwarding traffic.

- ☐ Path determination involves using measurements, such as the number of nodes (or hops), that help a router decide the best path for a packet to take to reach its destination.

- ☐ For data to be routed on an IP network, the packet must contain a source and destination IP address and a source and destination MAC address. Address Resolution Protocol (ARP) maps IP addresses to MAC addresses.

- ☐ Many network devices maintain ARP tables, listing the MAC and IP addresses of other devices on the network. Normally, devices obtain and update their own ARP tables automatically.

3

- When a computer prepares a packet for transmission, it checks its ARP table for an IP-to-MAC address mapping for the destination node. If the sending computer doesn't find an entry in its ARP table, it sends an ARP broadcast requesting the MAC address for the destination. Every station on the local subnet receives the ARP broadcast, but only the destination host answers with the requested information.

- Reverse ARP (RARP) is similar to ARP, except RARP maps MAC addresses to IP addresses. RARP is generally used for diskless workstations (dumb terminals).

- In proxy ARP, routers receive ARP requests destined for a node outside the sending station's local subnet. Routers do not forward broadcasts, so the router provides its own MAC address in the ARP reply and acts as an intermediary between subnets.

- There are different types of routing table entries. Static routes are manually entered into the routing table by the administrator. Dynamic routes require routing protocols and routing algorithms that the router uses to maintain its routing table. Default routes are manually configured routes that apply to traffic not meeting other criteria.

- A distance-vector routing protocol uses mathematical calculations to compare routes based on some measurement of distance, such as hops. Link-state routing protocols require each router to maintain at least a partial network map and send full or partial updates when something changes.

- Metrics are cost values that help routers decide the reliability of a link and include hop count, load, bandwidth, and delay. Routing protocols use a variety of metrics for path determination.

- The administrative distance is a value used to determine the reliability (cost) of a route. Administrators can adjust a route's administrative distance if needed.

- Routing protocols are used by routers to make path determination choices and share those choices with other routers. Routing protocols come in two major categories: Interior Gateway Protocols (IGPs) and Exterior Gateway Protocols (EGPs).

- IGP routing protocols include Interior Gateway Routing Protocol (IGRP), Open Shortest Path First (OSPF), and Routing Information Protocol (RIP). IGPs are used in an autonomous system (AS), and EGPs are used to route information between different ASs.

- Routing loops can occur when there's a failure or change to network topology. When a change occurs, an update is sent to neighboring routers and passed from node to node until all routers have received the update. The problem is that in large networks, updates might take several minutes to reach the farthest routers. The time required for all routers to receive updates to routing tables is called convergence.

- Routing protocols use maximum hop count, split horizon, poison reverse, route poisoning, holddowns, and other timers to help prevent routing loops.

KEY TERMS

Address Resolution Protocol (ARP) — A protocol included in the TCP/IP protocol stack that maps IP addresses to MAC addresses.

administrative distance — A value calculated by a routing protocol algorithm or assigned by the administrator, used to determine the reliability (cost) of a route. Routing protocols use metrics to calculate an administrative distance.

area border routers (ABRs) — In OSPF, routers that have interfaces in multiple areas. *See also* Open Shortest Path First (OSPF).

area ID — A designation to differentiate between different OSPF areas. An area ID can take the form of a randomly chosen integer between 0 and 4,294,967,295 or can be in dotted decimal format like an IP address, such as 0.0.0.0. *See also* Open Shortest Path First (OSPF).

ARP table — A listing maintained by network nodes for routing purposes. Routers also maintain ARP tables, enabling a router to respond to an ARP broadcast with the needed information without having to forward a broadcast. *See also* proxy ARP.

autonomous system boundary routers (ASBRs) — Routers that act as gateways or intermediaries between OSPF and other routing protocols or between other instances of the OSPF routing process. *See also* Open Shortest Path First (OSPF).

Autonomous System Number (ASN) — An integer or IP address representing an autonomous system. ASNs are assigned by IANA and allocated to regional registries. *See also* autonomous systems (ASs).

autonomous systems (ASs) — A network or group of networks controlled and managed by an administrator on behalf of an entity, such as a corporation or university.

default routes — A statically configured route that directs all packets not configured in the routing table to a particular route. A packet to a destination that a router has no other table entry for is sent to a default route automatically for processing.

distance-vector routing protocol — A routing protocol that uses mathematical calculations to compare routes based on some measurement of distance, such as hops.

dynamic routes — Entries in a routing table that use routing protocols and routing algorithms to calculate the best path.

Exterior Gateway Protocols (EGPs) — Protocols used to enable routers to communicate routing information between different autonomous systems.

flush timers — Timers that control when a route is flushed from a routing table.

holddowns — Timers used to help prevent routers from accepting and entering updates about paths that might be down.

Interior Gateway Protocols (IGPs) — Protocols used to enable routers in an autonomous system to communicate routing information to each other.

Interior Gateway Routing Protocol (IGRP) — A distance-vector routing protocol that uses a composite metric calculated by factoring weighted mathematical values for internetwork delay, bandwidth, reliability, and load.

internal routers — In OSPF, routers that have all interfaces in a single area and can communicate only with routers in the same area. *See also* Open Shortest Path First (OSPF).

link-state routing protocol — A routing protocol that requires each router to maintain at least a partial network map. Routers monitor link status, and when topology or link state changes, updates are sent to neighboring routers informing them of the change.

metrics — Cost values that help routers decide the reliability of a link and include hop count, load, bandwidth, and delay.

Open Shortest Path First (OSPF) — A link-state IGP routing protocol developed to address some problems in RIP. OSPF uses areas to control link-state update boundaries.

proxy ARP — A service provided by routers when the target of an ARP request is on a different subnet, and the intermediary router returns an ARP reply with its own MAC address designated as the MAC-to-IP mapping for that IP address destination. The router doesn't forward broadcasts, so it acts as a go-between.

Reverse Address Resolution Protocol (RARP) — An address resolution protocol used primarily by diskless workstations that know their MAC addresses when they boot but have no hard disk to store IP addressing information. The workstation boots and sends a RARP request packet to find out its own IP address.

routed protocols — Protocols, such as IP, used to provide addressing about a packet being transported. Routed protocols contain Layer 3 addressing information about packets being transmitted. (Don't confuse them with routing protocols, which facilitate communication between routers updating their routing tables.)

routing — The process of transporting chunks of information (usually called packets) across a network from the source to the destination.

Routing Information Protocol (RIP) — A distance-vector IGP routing protocol that uses only hop count as a metric.

routing protocols — Protocols that allow routers to maintain information about network links in the routing tables they use.

routing tables — Lists of routes containing information about neighboring routers, such as the address, metric count, and link state.

static routes — Routes that an administrator enters manually in a routing table.

stub networks — Networks with only one outbound route.

stub router — A router at the edge of a network with only one way out.

summarization — A method used to keep routing tables smaller by addressing a block of contiguous networks as a single subnet. Also called supernetting because the network/node boundary in the subnet mask moves to the left rather than to the right, as with subnetting. (Supernetting, subnetting, and summarization are implementations of CIDR, discussed in Chapter 2.)

update timers — Timers that control how often routing updates are sent.

REVIEW QUESTIONS

1. A RARP broadcast requests the _____ of the _____ .

   a. MAC address, gateway

   b. IP address, gateway

   c. MAC address, source

   d. IP address, source

2. An ARP packet has the destination MAC address set to which of the following?

   a. 00-00-00-00-00-00

   b. 0.0.0.0

   c. 255.255.255.255

   d. FF-FF-FF-FF-FF-FF

3. A route that an administrator manually enters in a routing table to automatically forward packets not meeting other criteria to a particular interface is called which of the following?

   a. default route

   b. default table entry

   c. administrative route

   d. static route

4. In a routing table, a route designated by an "R" is which of the following?

   a. a static route assigned by the administrator

   b. a route discovered by RIP

   c. a route directly connected to the interface

   d. a route discovered by OSPF

5. A static route is deleted from the routing table when an interface is shut down, unless you enter the keyword "permanent" where?

   a. beginning of the show ip route command

   b. end of the ip route command

   c. beginning of the administrative distance

   d. end of the show ip table command

6. Which of the following is a value that helps routers determine the reliability of a link?

   a. delay

   b. bandwidth

   c. hops

   d. all of the above

7. A static route has a default administrative distance of _____.

    a. 0

    b. 1

    c. 90

    d. 255

8. IGRP has the following default timers: update = _____ seconds, holddown =_____ seconds, and flush =_____ seconds.

    a. 30, 180, 240

    b. 90, 280, 630

    c. 60, 190, 630

    d. IGRP doesn't use timers in this way.

9. Routing loops occur when there is a link failure or a change in the network's topology and updated routing information hasn't reached all routers before packets or updates containing erroneous route information are sent. True or False?

10. Split horizon is a technique used to control routing loops and works by doing which of the following?

    a. preventing routers from accepting or entering updates about paths that might be down

    b. preventing routing table information from being sent back out on the same interface it was received from

    c. triggering the router to flush the bad route from its routing table

    d. causing a packet to be dropped after passing through a specified number of routers

11. Which of the following default metrics does IGRP use? (Choose all that apply.)

    a. delay

    b. bandwidth

    c. hop count

    d. reliability

12. Which routing protocols support VLSM? (Choose all that apply.)

    a. RIP

    b. OSPF

    c. IGRP

    d. EIGRP

13. Which of the following is a network or group of networks controlled and managed by an administrator on behalf of an entity such as a corporation or university?

    a. autonomous site (AS)

    b. area

    c. autonomous system (AS)

    d. router domain

14. OSPF area IDs can't take the form of an IP address. True or False?

15. One problem with _____ routing protocols is that routers must send out periodic updates to neighbors, increasing bandwidth, CPU, and memory use.

    a. link-state

    b. distance-vector

    c. IGP

    d. EGP

16. Which of the following statements describes link-state routing protocols? (Choose all that apply.)

    a. Routers must monitor link status.

    b. Each router must maintain at least a partial network map.

    c. Routers send updates to neighboring routers when topology or link status changes.

    d. all of the above

17. An administrator can modify the values of all metrics. True or False?

18. An administrative distance of _____ indicates a preferred route, and an administrative distance of _____ indicates a route that should never be used.

    a. 1, 16

    b. 0, 255

    c. 1, 256

    d. 0, 15

19. In OSPF, routers that have interfaces in multiple areas are called which of the following?

    a. area border routers (ABRs)

    b. autonomous border routers (ABRs)

    c. autonomous system boundary routers (ASBRs)

    d. area boundary routers (ABRs)

20. Routing protocols have _____ that control how often updates are sent and _____ that control when a route is removed from the routing table.

    a. holddown timers, flush timers

    b. update timers, flush timers

    c. update timers, holddowns

    d. update triggers, flush timers

HANDS-ON PROJECTS

HANDS-ON PROJECTS

Hands-On Project 3-1: Building a Networking Toolkit

Time Required: 30 minutes

Objective: Begin developing a toolkit containing all the networking software, hardware, and tools you need.

Description: In this project, you begin putting together an assortment of networking and security tools. Part of this kit consists of software, such as diagnostic and troubleshooting utilities, but you also need small hand tools, forensics tools, storage devices, and documentation templates. You begin by making a list of what you need to gather, and then start collecting your tools.

NOTE

This is a project you should continue working on throughout your career. As you encounter items that are useful, add them to your kit.

1. Make a list of the hardware tools you use in building or repairing computers. Your list should include items such as screwdrivers, pliers, hex keys, an assortment of fasteners, antistatic bags, wire strippers, crimpers, a punchdown tool, an antistatic wristband, and commonly used cabling.

2. Next, make a list of software you might use for network analysis, such as Wireshark, LanSpy, port scanners, security scanners, and command-line utilities. An assortment of boot disks and CDs is also useful. Thousands of freeware tools can be downloaded from the Internet, and they can be burned to CDs for convenience. Some good places to start include *www.majorgeeks.com*, *www.snapfiles.com*, and *www.freedownloadscenter.com*.

A complete security toolkit must include computer forensics tools. Because this book doesn't focus on forensics topics, discussing these tools is beyond the scope of the book. However, be aware that basic computer forensics knowledge is necessary in computer security. You can find some excellent information on computer forensics and forensics software at *www.accessdata.com* or *www.computerforensicsworld.com/*, and you can do an Internet search for more information.

3. Next, think about other items you might use frequently. Carrying spare parts, such as floppy disks or CD-ROM drives, can be helpful when you're troubleshooting hardware failures. A soldering iron is useful for fixing broken wiring when a replacement part isn't available. Voltmeters help with electrical issues, and cable testers and analyzers can be a lifesaver.

4. Finally, a complete and current list of contacts is essential. Keep names and contact information for vendors and support resources, local law enforcement and emergency services, telephone and utility providers, and anyone else you might need to contact. Create a sheet to store this information in your kit.

If you keep a contact list on your cell phone, make sure you have a backup hard copy. Cell phones and digital devices do fail.

5. Any tools you have can be placed into a small toolkit. Having all these items organized and available makes network maintenance, troubleshooting, and repair much easier.

6. Keep a list of items you still need to gather and mark them off as you collect them.

CASE PROJECTS

CASE PROJECTS

Case Project 3-1: Developing a Routing Plan for Green Globe

In previous chapters, you have planned your project and designed an addressing scheme for Green Globe. In this chapter, you examine your addressing and network segmentation scheme to identify where you need routers. You also formulate a preliminary outline of how those routers will be configured to manage traffic flow through Green Globe's network.

Using the documentation you created in Chapter 2, determine where you need routers to implement your subnets. You need internal routers (or intelligent switches) for communication between subnets and border routers for connecting to the service providers you researched in Chapter 2.

After identifying the physical and logical locations for routers, decide what types of interfaces each router needs. Routers are highly customizable, and modules can be added or removed to provide whatever connectivity is required. For example, if you have decided a dedicated T1 is the best option for external access, you need specialized modules (CSU/DSU) to enable that connection. For internal access, combinations of switches, patch panels, and routers are common.

Next, create a name for each router. Identify the interface on each router, noting the type of interface, IP address and subnet mask, physical location, and name of the segment. Make sure you use consistent naming conventions. For each segment, note the business group served. You might also want to note the security level required for inbound and outbound access.

You might want to diagram the routers, interfaces, and addresses and use arrows indicating the flow of traffic. A diagram helps you visualize how information moves through the network. Remember that you'll be revising and adding to this design as you progress. If you're working on a project team, make sure the work is divided fairly, and all team members work together to complete this design. When your routing scheme is finished, turn it in to your instructor.

3

4

FUNDAMENTALS OF CISCO ROUTER SECURITY

> **After reading this chapter and completing the exercises, you will be able to:**
> ♦ Describe the use of access control lists on Cisco routers
> ♦ Explain the options for logging with Cisco routers
> ♦ Describe how basic Cisco authorization and authentication are configured

This chapter introduces you to the fundamentals of Cisco router security. Cisco routers have many configurations for enhancing your security perimeter. Because Cisco has the majority of the router market, this chapter (and the TPD exam) focuses on routers from this vendor.

First, you see how access control lists are used on Cisco routers to control packet handling and make filtering decisions. You learn the basics of standard and extended ACLs and the guidelines access lists usually follow. Next, you examine Cisco router logging and learn about the different levels and options available for tuning logging. You also examine how log files can be stored in the router's buffer or a syslog server or even sent to the console.

Then you move on to Cisco authentication and authorization methods, passwords on routers, and banner messages and learn about a common remote access method that provides more security than Telnet or other less secure methods. Finally, you briefly examine issues of hardening routers. As with any operating system, network, or device, unnecessary services and protocols represent security vulnerabilities.

CREATING AND USING ACCESS CONTROL LISTS

Access control lists (ACLs) are permit or deny statements that filter traffic based on the source and destination address, port number, and protocol in the packet header. ACLs provide traffic-flow control and enhance network security. They can also be used to fine-tune performance and control client access to sensitive network segments. This section introduces ACLs you can create and use on a Cisco router and offers some guidelines on effective ACLs and traffic management.

Use and Rules

You can approach ACLs in two ways: specify what traffic to deny and permit all others, or specify what to permit and deny all others. The latter approach is more secure but requires a lot of planning and a more complex list. There are two factors to remember when configuring ACLs:

- ACLs end with an implicit "deny any" statement, which means any packet that doesn't match the requirements for passage is blocked. Although this approach is more secure, it might not serve the network's needs and could block desirable traffic. To remedy this problem in networks where you don't need to block all access, include a "permit any" statement at the end of an ACL.

- ACLs are processed in sequential order. Careful planning is necessary to ensure that allowed packets aren't blocked inadvertently and packets that should be blocked don't slip through.

Table 4-1 summarizes some problems you should be aware of when creating ACLs and their solutions.

Table 4-1   ACLs: Common problems and solutions

Problem	Solution
Lack of planning results in simple logic mistakes.	Plan carefully what needs to be filtered and what needs access.
Sequential processing results in errors in filtering. Statements can't be moved after they are entered; the list must be removed entirely and replaced with a corrected list.	Create the list in a text editor and paste it into the terminal window when needed. This method gives you time to fine-tune and check the list for errors.
Applying ACLs via Telnet can result in the administrator applying the list being blocked.	Use the reload command to restore access, as long as the running configuration wasn't copied to the startup configuration.

Unlike previous versions, Cisco's latest Internetwork Operating System (IOS) supports inserting or deleting statement lines in ACLs. For more information, read the article at *www.cisco.com/univercd/cc/td/doc/product/software/ ios122s/122snwft/release/122s14/fsaclseq.htm*.

Remember the following general rules for ACLs:

- Routers apply lists sequentially.

- Packets are processed only until a match is made, and then they are acted on.

- Lists always end with an implicit "deny any" statement.

- ACLs must be applied to an interface as inbound or outbound filters; they aren't active until they're applied to an interface.

- Only one list per protocol, per direction can be applied to an interface.

- ACLs take effect immediately, but if you want the list to be permanent, you must copy the running configuration to the startup configuration by using the copy running-config startup-config (copy run start) command.

Test ACLs thoroughly before applying them to any production router in your network to make sure they do what you intended and to correct any errors before you apply them. Of course, you should have a baseline for your network so that you know what "normal" traffic looks like. Remember: If you have a baseline before and after applying an ACL (ideally, in your test network first), you can determine where problems might occur.

Standard ACLs

Standard ACLs have minimal configuration options. They can filter on source IP address information only—such as a host, subnet, or network address. Of course, there's no need to create a complex ACL if a simple one will do the job. Increasing complexity leads to increased chances for errors. As a rule, keep it simple. Resort to extended ACLs only if there's a good reason for that level of control. Standard ACLs can be configured for IP, Internetwork Packet Exchange (IPX), AppleTalk, and other protocols. The most commonly used ACLs are for IP and IPX, so the next sections focus on these protocols. However, there are other options for ACLs.

After a standard ACL is configured, you must apply it to the interface and specify the direction of the filter. ACLs are applied to inbound or outbound packets, and only one ACL per direction can be applied to an interface at a time.

Standard IP ACLs

With standard IP ACLs, you can permit or deny traffic from a source host, a subnet, or an IP address. Destination addressing doesn't affect standard ACLs, which work well for simple packet filtering. Standard ACLs, like all varieties of ACLs, use an **inverse mask** (the "source wildcard mask" parameter in commands) that tells the router which bits in the address to be filtered are significant. A 0 bit in an inverse mask means check the corresponding bit value in the IP address, and a 1 bit means ignore the corresponding bit value in the IP address. An inverse mask of 0.0.0.0 means all bits are significant, so that specific IP address is filtered. To indicate filtering an entire subnet, mask only the host ID portion of the address. For example, the inverse mask to filter the entire 172.16.0.0 network is 0.0.255.255. The 0s are significant; the 255s are ignored.

NOTE
Remember that a 0 or 1 bit value in IP addresses refers to the address's binary format. For instance, the inverse mask 0.0.0.255 (decimal format) is the same as 00000000.00000000.00000000.11111111 (binary format).

Standard ACLs have the following characteristics:

- They can filter based on source address.

- They can filter by host, subnet, or network address using an inverse mask.

- They should be placed as close to the destination as possible.

- They have a default inverse mask of 0.0.0.0.

Standard ACLs use the following syntax:

```
access-list [list#] [permit|deny] [source address] [source
wildcard mask]
```

The following list explains the parameters in this syntax:

- *list#*—Standard IP ACLs are represented by a number from 1 to 99.

- *permit | deny*—Specifies a permit or deny statement.

- *source address*—Indicates the IP address of the source.

- *source wildcard mask*—Determines which bits of the source address must match.

Standard IPX ACLs

Standard IPX ACLs function the same way as standard IP ACLs, except they can filter on source and destination addresses. Standard IPX ACLs use the following syntax:

```
access-list [list#] [permit|deny] [source network|node
address] [destination network|node address]
```

The following list explains the parameters in this syntax:

- *list#*—Standard IPX ACLs represented by a number from 800 to 899.

- *permit | deny*—Specifies a permit or deny statement.

- *source network | node address*—Indicates the IPX address of the source network or node.

- *destination network | node address*—Indicates the IPX address of the destination network or node.

In IPX ACLs, the keyword "any" (or its numeric equivalent of –1) stands for all IPX networks and all IPX nodes. This keyword is used for the "permit any" statement at the end of the list: access-list 801 permit –1 –1. IPX ACLs must be applied to an interface.

Extended ACLs

Extended ACLs offer many more filtering options than a standard list. A standard list can filter based on source addressing, but an extended list can provide fine-tuned control over source and destination addresses, ports, and protocols that you want to filter. Of course, increased complexity means more chances of making a mistake, so be careful when creating and using extended ACLs. As with standard ACLs, extended ACLs are usually used in TCP/IP networks. However, you should pay attention to some details of IPX when using extended lists because real-life networks combine a multitude of hardware, software, applications, protocols, and transmission methods.

Extended IP ACLs

An extended IP ACL can filter based on source and destination address, port number, and protocol type. It uses the following syntax:

```
access-list [list#] [permit|deny] [protocol] [source IP
address] [source wildcard mask] [operator] [port]
[destination IP address] [destination wildcard mask]
[operator] [port] [log]
```

The following list explains the parameters in this syntax:

- *list#*—Extended IP ACLs are represented by a number from 100 to 199.

- *permit | deny*—Specifies a permit or deny statement; ACLs can have many lines specifying that a certain type of traffic is permitted or denied access.

- *protocol*—The IP protocol to be filtered; IP includes all protocols in the TCP/IP suite or a specific protocol, such as Transmission Control Protocol (TCP), User Datagram Protocol (UDP), or Internet Control Message Protocol (ICMP).

- *source IP address*—IP address of the source.

- *source wildcard mask*—Inverse mask of the source that determines which IP address bits must match.

- *destination IP address*—IP address of the destination.

- *destination wildcard mask*—Inverse mask of the destination that determines which IP address bits must match.

- *operator*—Less than (lt), greater than (gt), or equal to (eq); used if the ACL filters a port number, range of port numbers, or service.

- *port*—Port number of the protocol (or service, such as FTP or Telnet) to be filtered.

- *log*—Turns on logging of ACL activity.

Remember the following points about extended IP ACLs:

- Extended IP ACLs don't have a default inverse mask of 0.0.0.0. An inverse mask must be specified for the source. Keywords can also be used.

- Extended IP ACLs must be applied to an interface as close to the traffic source as possible.

- The "established" parameter can be used to allow incoming traffic responding to an internal request. For example, to allow the network 101.0.0.0 to receive DNS resolution or responses to other network service requests, enter the following line in the ACL:

```
access-list 100 permit tcp any 101.0.0.0 0.255.255.255
established
```

- Extended IP ACLs, like all ACLs, must be applied to an interface to be active. Also, remember that only one ACL per interface, per direction, can be active.

To monitor IP ACLs, use the show ip access-lists or show access-lists command.

Activity 4-1 Installing a Router Simulator

Time Required: 15 minutes

Objective: Download and install another router simulator for use in the remaining router configuration activities.

Description: In this activity, you download and install a router simulator for additional practice working at the command-line interface (CLI). Kenn Thompson's Router Simulator is a close approximation of the actual Cisco IOS, so you can see what a real router console looks like.

If this simulator is no longer available, you can search for and download a suitable alternative. TechRepublic is a helpful resource for finding free tools, white papers, Web casts, and more, so you should be able to find another simulator there.

1. Start your Web browser and go to **www.techrepublic.com**. To download this tool, you need to sign up for a free TechRepublic membership.

2. After completing your membership application, sign in and go to **http:// software.techrepublic.com.com/download.aspx?&docid=181788&pro mo=100511**.

3. Click the **Download** link and save the Sim.exe file to your desktop.

4. To start the simulator, double-click the **Sim.exe** file on your desktop. If you see a security warning, click **Run** to continue. The simulator interface is similar to what you would see when opening a HyperTerminal connection to a real router through a rollover cable attached to the router's console port.

5. Press **Enter**, and type **enable** at the > prompt. You're prompted for a password, but you haven't set one yet, so press **Enter** again.

One quirk of this simulator is that the first character you type at the prompt tends to be erased, causing your commands to fail. If you have trouble with commands not working, this is probably the reason, so make sure you're typing the command correctly. Typing the first character twice can help prevent this problem.

6. Next, you use the help feature to see how a Cisco router can guide you through using commands. At the privileged mode prompt, type **configure ?** and press **Enter**. You should see a list of options with descriptions for the configure command.

7. Type **configure terminal** and press **Enter**.

8. Type **?** to see a list of commands available in global configuration mode.

9. Press **Ctrl+Z** to exit global configuration mode. Type **show ?** and press **Enter** to see a list of available show commands (see Figure 4-1).

```
#show ?
  access-expression  List access expression
  access-lists       List access lists
  accounting         Accounting data for active sessions
  aliases            Display alias commands
  arp                ARP table
  async              Information on terminal lines used as router interfaces
  bridge             Bridge Forwarding/Filtering Database [verbose]
  buffers            Buffer pool statistics
  cdp                CDP information
  clock              Display the system clock
  cmns               Connection-Mode networking services (CMNS) information
  compress           Show compression statistics
  configuration      Contents of Non-Volatile memory
  controllers        Interface controller status
  debugging          State of each debugging option
  dhcp               Dynamic Host Configuration Protocol status
  dialer             Dialer parameters and statistics
  dnsix              Shows Dnsix/DMDP information
  dxi                atm-dxi information
  entry              Queued terminal entries
  flash              System Flash information
  flh-log            Flash Load Helper log buffer
  frame-relay        Frame-Relay information
  history            Display the session command history
  hosts              IP domain-name, lookup style, nameservers, and host table
  interfaces         Interface status and configuration
  ip                 IP information
  key                Key information
  line               TTY line information
  llc2               IBM LLC2 circuit information
  location           Display the system location
  logging            Show the contents of logging buffers
  memory             Memory statistics
  modemcap           Show Modem Capabilities database
  ntp                Network time protocol
  ppp                PPP parameters and statistics
  printers           Show LPD printer information
  privilege          Show current privilege level
  processes          Active process statistics
  protocols          Active network routing protocols
  queue              Show queue contents
  queueing           Show queueing configuration
  registry           Function registry information
  reload             Scheduled reload information
  rhosts             Remote-host+user equivalences
  rif                RIF cache entries
  rmon               rmon statistics
  route-map          route-map information
  running-config     Current operating configuration
  sessions           Information about Telnet connections
  smds               SMDS information
  smf                Software MAC filter
  snapshot           Snapshot parameters and statistics
  snmp               snmp statistics
  spanning-tree      Spanning tree topology
```

Figure 4-1 Results of the show ? command

10. Leave Router Simulator running for the next activity.

TIP

Cisco routers have a useful feature called context-sensitive help. When you type a ? at a router prompt, a full list of available commands is shown. You can then type the command name followed by a ? to see the parameters for that command, as you learned in Activity 4-1. This feature can walk you through router configuration commands, but most certification exams don't offer this feature in router simulations. So although it's a useful aid in real life, you still need to know commands for certification exams. In addition, many exams don't allow truncated commands. For example, if the command is show memory, you must give the full command as the answer, even though the shortened version (show mem or sh mem) works on a router.

Extended IPX ACLs

Like extended IP ACLs, extended IPX ACLs offer more filtering options than standard IPX ACLs. All IPX lists should be applied to the interface closest to the source address. Extended IPX ACLs can filter based on the following:

- IPX protocol type

- IPX socket number

- Source network or node address

- Destination network or node address

Extended IPX ACLs use the following syntax:

```
access-list [list#] [permit|deny] [protocol] [source
network/node address] [socket] [destination network/node
address] [socket]
```

The following list explains the parameters in this syntax:

- *list#*—Extended IPX ACLs are represented by a number from 900 to 999.

- *permit|deny*—Specifies a permit or deny statement.

- *protocol*—IPX protocol to filter; the keyword "any" (or its numeric equivalent of –1) specifies all IPX protocols.

- *source network|node address*—IPX address of the source node or network.

- *destination network|node address*—IPX address of the destination network or node.

- *socket*—Points to a service (such as port numbers in IP); the keyword "all" (or its numeric equivalent of 0) indicates all sockets.

IPX Service Advertisement Protocol Filters

IPX Service Advertisement Protocol (SAP) filters are used to filter SAP advertisements, which are IPX broadcasts that allow administrators to choose what services are advertised as available on the network and specify where they're located. Although routers don't forward broadcasts by default, they are required to pass SAP advertisements through an IPX network. Passing SAP advertisements creates excess traffic that can be controlled by using ACLs to filter the broadcasts, among other methods. The ACL method has the benefit of controlling access for security purposes as well as reducing traffic generated by SAP broadcasts. You can apply two types of SAP filters to an interface:

- *Input SAP filters*—Limits what SAP advertisements a router incorporates into its SAP table

- *Output SAP filters*—Limits what SAP entries are passed on to other routers

If routers filter SAP broadcasts, how do clients on an IPX network know about available services? The router acts as a proxy and builds and maintains a SAP table. Cisco routers can also be configured to send incremental SAP updates when there are changes. A full discussion of how routers work in IPX networks is beyond the scope of this book, and you should be familiar with the basics of IPX/SPX from prerequisite work.

SAP filters must be created and then applied to an interface, using the following syntax:

```
access-list [list#] [permit|deny] [source network|node]
[service-type|server-name]
```

The following list explains the parameters in this syntax:

- *list#*—SAP filters are represented by a number from 1000 to 1099.

- *permit | deny*—Specifies a permit or deny statement.

- *source network | node*—Indicates the IPX address of the source network or node. A network number of -1 indicates any network.

- *service-type | server-name*—Indicates the service to be filtered and the name of the server that should have this service type filtered. A service type of 0 indicates any service. The server name is optional, used if SAP advertisements from a particular server are to be permitted or denied.

Using Access Control Lists

ACLs can be tricky to create. The most important factor is placing entries in the correct order to prevent undesirable effects, such as blocking allowed traffic. As mentioned, if an ACL contains an error, the main way to correct it is to create a new list, remove the old one, and apply the new list to the interface. This doesn't necessarily mean you have to start from scratch. You can modify your existing ACL in Notepad or another text editor to make corrections or adjustments, and then reapply the modified ACL. Remember, only one list per protocol, per direction, is allowed per interface, so the no access-list command must be used to remove the old ACL before a new one can be applied.

Although the most recent Cisco IOS supports adding, reordering, or deleting lines in an ACL, you might encounter routers running an older version of the Cisco IOS. If you don't know what IOS version your router is running, use the show version command. For additional questions, go to Cisco's documentation Web site and search for information on your equipment.

The general advice on creating ACLs is to enter them in a text editor and then copy them to the router. Planning is key to a successful ACL. The best method is to use a network diagram and examine each interface to see what's connected, what traffic is necessary, and which traffic should be blocked. After you have this information, you can begin creating an ACL to carry out your traffic controls.

Editing an ACL is straightforward. Create a new ACL (or edit your existing one) in a text editor, making necessary adjustments to traffic controls. After checking the new ACL for accuracy, remove the old ACL from the router interface with the no access-list command, and then apply the new ACL. Remember that after an ACL has been applied to an interface, the order of statements can't be changed, so mistakes must be fixed before applying the list or by creating and applying a new list. Table 4-2 shows the number ranges for Cisco ACLs.

4

Table 4-2 Number ranges for Cisco ACLs

List type	Number range
Standard IP	1–99
Extended IP	100–199
IPX SAP	1000–1099
Extended 48-bit MAC address	1100–1199
IPX summary address	1200–1299
Protocol type-code	200–299
DECnet	300–399
Standard Xerox Network System (XNS)	400–499
Extended XNS	500–599
AppleTalk	600–699
48-bit MAC	700–799
Standard IPX	800–899
Extended IPX	900–999
Expanded IP ACLs (available in Cisco IOS 12.0.1 and later)	1300–1399
Expanded IPX ACLs (available in Cisco IOS 12.0.1 and later)	2000–2699

Cisco IOS 11.2 and later also supports named ACLs. All lists must have different names, regardless of protocol or interface. Giving an ACL a meaningful name makes it easier to keep track of lists. To name an ACL, use the following syntax:

`[protocol] access-list [list type] [name]`

The following list explains the parameters in this syntax:

- *protocol*—Protocol type for the list (IPX, IP, and so on)

- *list type*—Type of list, such as standard, extended, and so forth

- *name*—Name for the list

TIP

The Cisco Web site has helpful online documentation. You can find answers, how-to tips, product specifications, case studies, and more at *www.cisco.com/univercd/home/home.htm*.

EXAMINING CISCO ROUTER LOGGING

Logging is a vital component of security because it provides information for troubleshooting, monitoring traffic patterns, and discovering and tracking down possible security incidents. Cisco routers are capable of logging a variety of events. These are the main types of logging Cisco routers use:

- *AAA logging*—**Authentication, authorization, and accounting (AAA) logging** collects information about user dial-up connections, commands issued, logons, logoffs, HTTP accesses, and similar events. AAA logs are sent to an authentication server by using the Terminal Access Controller Access Control System Plus (TACACS+) and/or Remote Authentication Dial-In User Service (RADIUS) protocols.

- *SNMP trap logging*—**Simple Network Management Protocol (SNMP) trap logging** sends notifications of system status changes to SNMP management stations. This logging method is normally used with an existing SNMP infrastructure.

- *System logging*—Depending on the system configuration, **system logging** reports system logs to different locations, including the system console port, UNIX servers via the syslog protocol, or a local logging buffer in router RAM.

Log events can also be monitored via remote sessions by using virtual terminal (VTY) or TeleTypewriter or text telephone (TTY) lines. Remote access to the router command line can be done in several ways, but all inbound connections are made with TTY lines. The most important security-related events that system logging records are changes to system configuration, ACL matches, interface status changes, and optional firewall or intrusion detection system (IDS) events.

Logging Levels

Logging events are tagged with an urgency or severity level ranging from 0 to 7, with 0 being the highest urgency and 7 the lowest. Table 4-3 lists these severity levels.

Table 4-3   Cisco router logging severity levels

Level	Urgency
0	Emergency—means the system is unstable
1	Alert—requires immediate action
2	Critical—indicates a critical condition
3	Error—indicates an error condition
4	Warning—specifies a warning condition
5	Notification—means a normal but possibly significant condition
6	Informational—displays an informational message
7	Debugging—displays a debugging message

Logging destinations can be configured with a severity level so that events below that level aren't received. Obviously, if your router is logging all levels, your log files fill up quickly, increasing the risk of overwriting critical information. The destinations you can specify for logging vary, and logging messages can also be buffered and viewed by using the show logging command at the privileged mode prompt.

This method has disadvantages, however. First, you must be at the terminal or accessing it remotely to view logs. Second, and more important, buffered logging is limited by the amount of memory in the router. Large log files can't be stored in the router's memory buffer without possible serious performance problems and the risk of lost logs.

Logging Options

For larger log files, a **syslog server** can be used. Most servers (Windows or UNIX) can be configured to host router logs, and a router is directed to send logs to a specific location with the logging host command.

Figure 4-2 shows options for the logging command. As you can see, a number of options are available for logging destinations and severity levels. You can specify the name or IP address of the logging host and set logging levels for the console, terminal lines, or syslog server.

```
RouterA(config)#logging ?
  Hostname or A.B.C.D  IP address of the logging host
  buffered             Set buffered logging parameters
  console              Set console logging level
  facility             Facility parameter for syslog messages
  history              Configure syslog history table
  monitor              Set terminal line (monitor) logging level
  on                   Enable logging to all supported destinations
  source-interface     Specify interface for source address in logging
                       transactions
  trap                 Set syslog server logging level

RouterA(config)#logging
```

Figure 4-2 Options for the logging command

NOTE Syslog is a simple protocol that sends a small text message via UDP or TCP to the server hosting the logs. It was originally developed for UNIX and Linux systems, but variations for other systems are available. A detailed discussion is beyond the scope of this book, but you can learn more by reading RFCs 3164 and 3195.

Buffered Logging

You can also set parameters for **buffered logging**, which stores log output files in the router's memory (RAM). Although buffered logging does have limitations, it's useful for troubleshooting purposes. Figure 4-3 shows options for the logging buffered command.

```
RouterA(config)#logging buffered ?
   <0-7>                  Logging severity level
   <4096-2147483647>      Logging buffer size
   alerts                 Immediate action needed      (severity=1)
   critical               Critical conditions          (severity=2)
   debugging              Debugging messages           (severity=7)
   emergencies            System is unusable           (severity=0)
   errors                 Error conditions             (severity=3)
   informational          Informational messages       (severity=6)
   notifications          Normal but significant conditions (severity=5)
   warnings               Warning conditions           (severity=4)
   <cr>

RouterA(config)#logging buffered
```

Figure 4-3 Options for the logging buffered command

Most router commands have similar parameters, but with buffered logging, you can also specify the buffer size. This parameter is important because the buffer is usually in router RAM, and you're limited by how much RAM is available. Most routers don't have a lot of RAM; they don't need it to handle traffic. To find out how much RAM your router has for buffered logging, use the show memory command at the privileged mode prompt (see Figure 4-4). The show memory free command displays statistics on the amount of free memory. The output has been truncated in Figure 4-4, but it gives you enough information to determine the router's memory statistics and configure a suitable buffer size.

```
RouterA#show mem ?
   <0-4294967294>         Dump memory starting at <address>
   allocating-process     Show allocating process name
   dead                   Memory owned by dead processes
   failures               Memory failures
   fast                   Fast memory stats
   free                   Free memory stats
   io                     IO memory stats
   multibus               Multibus memory stats
   pci                    PCI memory stats
   processor              Processor memory stats
   summary                Summary of memory usage per alloc PC
   <cr>
```

Figure 4-4 Options for the show memory command

NOTE Remember: With a real router, you can use the shortened form of commands. Therefore, Figure 4-4 shows the command as "show mem" rather than the full "show memory."

Antispoofing Logging

Antispoofing is a way to prevent spoofing and ensure that no packets arrive at your security perimeter with a source address of your internal network or certain well-known or reserved addresses. Antispoofing is accomplished by using ACLs. Because ACLs are so vital to security and are the primary means of implementing basic security on a router, you learn more about them in this section.

Your ACL should instruct the router to deny any inbound packet with a source address matching your internal network, broadcast, and loopback addresses; illegal addresses, such as all 0s or all 1s; and multicast or experimental address classes. At the end of the ACL, specify that packets matching these conditions are logged, as shown in this example:

```
access-list 101 deny any 172.16.0.0 0.0.255.255 any log
```

The log keyword added to the end of an extended ACL tells the router to send information about matching packets to the router's log. If logging is already configured (for example, you have specified a syslog server for router logging), that's where log data is recorded, as shown in the following example:

```
access-list 101 deny icmp any any redirect

access-list 101 deny any 172.16.0.0 0.0.255.255 any log

access-list 101 deny ip 127.0.0.0 0.255.255.255 any

access-list 101 deny any 224.0.0.0 31.255.255.255 any

access-list 101 permit any any any log

logging buffered

interface ethernet 0

ip access-group 101 out
```

The log keyword at the end of a line tells the router to log information about packets matching this line. The logging buffered command tells the router to send log output to the router's memory buffer. You can also enter the IP address or hostname of the syslog server in this line. The next line specifies which interface the ACL applies to—in this case, Ethernet 0. The last command links the defined ACL (101) to the outbound interface, Ethernet 0.

NOTE   You might be wondering about the difference between access-list 101 and ip access-group 101. The access-list command defines list parameters, and 101 is the name of the defined ACL in the example. The ip access-group command assigns an ACL to an interface and specifies the direction, in or out. The two commands, access-list and ip access-group, have to use the same name (in this example, 101).

Remember the syntax for an extended IP ACL:

```
access-list [list#] [permit|deny] [protocol] [source IP
address] [source wildcard mask] [operator] [port]
[destination IP address] [destination wildcard mask]
[operator] [port] [log]
```

Older Cisco IOS versions support the "log" keyword in ACLs, which records information about the source IP address and port number of packets matching that entry. Newer versions support the "log-input" keyword, which adds information about the interface through which the packet was received and the MAC address of the sending host.

Also, remember that a wildcard mask is basically the opposite of a subnet mask; it tells the router to ignore the masked bits of an address. In the preceding example, the router ignores the last two octets of the source address. If the mask is all 0s, it can be omitted from the ACL. In other words, 172.16.1.4 0.0.0.0 is the same as 172.16.1.4 to the router. Finally, after an ACL has been defined, it must be applied to a router interface and specified as inbound or outbound.

TIP The Internet Assigned Numbers Authority (IANA) provides information on reserved or special-purpose address blocks that your router should drop at the network perimeter. See *www.rfc-editor.org* for information on assigned blocks and reserved or special addresses.

Remember a few laws of ACLs:

- There's an implied "deny all" statement at the end of every ACL. Traffic not matching any of the criteria is blocked by this statement. Adding an explicit "permit any" at the end solves this problem, although your security policy dictates how to handle this situation.

- Every statement you add to an ACL is added to the end.

- No statement can be deleted after it's created. In most Cisco IOS versions before 12.3, you must delete the entire ACL and create a new one with corrections.

- ACLs are processed in the order statements are entered. After a match is found, the router takes the specified action and stops processing ACL statements.

UNDERSTANDING CISCO AUTHENTICATION AND AUTHORIZATION

Authentication and authorization on a router are much the same as with a server. They identify users and allow or deny access based on their credentials. Authorization specifies what users are allowed to do after they have accessed the system. For example, Bob is allowed to *authenticate* to the router to check an interface's status, but he isn't *authorized* to change settings on the interface. For the TPD exam, remember there are two methods of authenticating to a Cisco router: AAA and non-AAA.

AAA, as mentioned previously, stands for authentication, authorization, and accounting. Cisco's AAA architecture uses one or more of the following security protocols to enhance security: TACACS+, RADIUS, and Kerberos. TACACS+ and RADIUS are the most commonly used. TACACS+ is a proprietary Cisco protocol that uses TCP for transport and encrypts all data. It also allows multiple levels of authorization and can use other authentication methods. RADIUS is an open standard that uses UDP and encrypts only passwords. It also combines authentication and authorization as a single service instead of separate services.

Accounting enables an administrator to keep track of connections, the amount of traffic, commands entered on the router, number of bytes, number of packets, and start and stop times.

To enable AAA authorization and authentication on a Cisco router, first enable AAA in global configuration mode with the aaa new-model command. Next, define a named list of authentication methods and apply that list to an interface. This list is checked in sequence until there's a response. If authentication is denied at any point, the authentication process stops. Next, issue the aaa authentication login command and, optionally, the aaa authorization and aaa accounting commands.

This information is just a brief overview of Cisco's AAA Security Services. For in-depth information on setting up access control on your router, see *www.cisco.com*.

Although AAA is the recommended method for access control, you can also use non-AAA, such as local username authentication or enable password authentication. Any method not using Cisco AAA Security Services is considered non-AAA. The following sections explain passwords that can be configured on Cisco routers.

Router Passwords

Passwords are the main defense against attacks on your router, but remember that if attackers can physically touch your router, they can access all its configuration settings. Cisco routers have five types of passwords you must be able to configure:

- Enable
- Enable secret
- AUX
- VTY
- Console

Because a router's main purpose is to connect networks, you might see Ethernet, token ring, Fibre Distributed Data Interface (FDDI), Integrated Services Digital Network (ISDN), or other interface modules. Many Cisco routers are modular in nature, so you can customize them by selecting the interface modules you want and specifying the encryption levels and RAM your router must have. As mentioned, setting AAA security is the preferred method of securing access to the router; however, you still need to have local access to privileged mode in case of router or network issues.

Before setting passwords, there are a few things to know. Password length must be between 1 and 25 characters. Leading spaces in the password are ignored, but any spaces in the password are considered part of the password. Also, the first character can't be a number. In addition, there are three levels of encryption on Cisco passwords: type 0, which is no encryption at all; type 7, which is encrypted but can be decrypted by router password-cracking tools; and type 5, which is a Message Digest 5 (MD5) hash. Although MD5 is a one-way hash and can't be decrypted, it's still susceptible to brute-force attacks.

Enable Passwords

The enable password's main purpose is to prevent casual or accidental access to privileged mode. Because it uses weak encryption, it provides no real security against more determined and knowledgeable attackers. You should set it as a first line of defense, however. Take a look at the following example:

```
RouterA(config)#enable password pa$$word
```

After setting this enable password, you type "pa$$word" at the prompt to access privileged mode. You don't see anything onscreen as you type, so if you make a mistake, press Enter and try again.

Enable Secret Passwords

The enable secret password uses type 5 encryption and overrides an enable password. You might be wondering why you would set an enable password if it's so easily cracked and overridden by the enable secret password. The purpose of having both is that the enable password deters casual or accidental access, and an enable secret password slows down more determined attackers. Also, make sure the enable secret password is different from the enable password; if the enable password is cracked, the enable secret password could be discovered, if it's the same as the enable password. Here's an example of setting an enable secret password:

```
RouterA(config)#enable secret Pa33m04d
```

NOTE

Remember that no password can defend against intrusion if an attacker can physically access your router; resetting a password on a router is simply too easy.

AUX Passwords

Normally, the auxiliary port on a router is connected to a modem to allow remote access for router configuration. Configuring an AUX password is much like configuring a console password (discussed later in "Console Passwords"):

```
RouterA(config)#line aux 0

RouterA(config-line)#password M0d3m

RouterA(config-line)#login
```

VTY Passwords

Most Cisco routers support up to five simultaneous VTY sessions, and by default, no passwords are assigned to these VTY sessions. Cisco's built-in security on VTY lines requires configuring passwords to access the router through a VTY session, usually with Telnet. The following example shows how to set all five lines at once, although you can set each line separately, if you want:

```
RouterA(config)#line vty 0 4

RouterA(config-line)#password Kodiak

RouterA(config-line)#login
```

Console Passwords

The console port is used to connect directly to a router with a laptop or other computer by using a program such as HyperTerminal. Normally used to set up a new router, the console port can also be used to reset a router's password. For this reason, physical security of the router is critical. The following example shows configuring a console password:

```
RouterA(config)#line console 0

RouterA(config-line)#password J3N1ff3R

RouterA(config-line)#login

RouterA(config-line)#end

RouterA#
```

Encrypting Passwords

By default, enable secret is the only password that's encrypted. The service password-encryption command in global configuration mode, shown in the following example, encrypts all passwords on the router by using reversible encryption:

```
RouterA(config)#service password-encryption
```

Activity 4-2: Setting Passwords on a Cisco Router

Time Required: 20 minutes

Objective: Practice configuring passwords on a Cisco router.

Description: Using Router Simulator, you configure the five types of passwords for a Cisco router. These passwords provide basic physical and remote access security for a router.

1. Start Router Simulator, if necessary, and enter privileged mode.

2. To configure the CON 0 (console) password, type the following commands, pressing **Enter** after each one:

```
configure terminal
line con 0
password password
login
```

3. Press **Ctrl+Z**. Next, configure the VTY passwords by typing these commands, pressing **Enter** after each one:

```
configure terminal
line vty 0 4
password password
login
```

4. Press **Ctrl+Z**. Next, configure the AUX password by typing the following commands, pressing **Enter** after each one:

```
configure terminal
line aux 0
password password
login
```

5. Press **Ctrl+Z**. Type **show run** and press **Enter** to display a list of all your passwords (see Figure 4-5). These passwords aren't encrypted, so they appear in the router configuration output as cleartext.

```
#show run
ROUTER 0
Building configuration ...

Current configuration:
version 10.2(8a)
interface Ethernet0
shutdown
interface Ethernet1
shutdown
interface Serial0
shutdown
interface Serial1
shutdown
----- More -----
ip classless
ip subnet-zero
line con 0
 password password
 login
line aux 0
 password password
 login
line vty 0 4
 password password
 login
end

#
#
```

Figure 4-5   Displaying router passwords

6. Exit Router Simulator, and leave your computer running for the next activity.

Banners

Banners are messages displayed to anyone logging on to a router to greet users and to provide information or warnings during logons, during executive (privileged level) processes, or to an incoming asynchronous line connection. The most common banners display legal disclaimers and warnings at logon, and all banners should include a legal warning that clearly states the company's policy on unauthorized access.

NOTE   Legal disclaimers are a complex issue, and legal counsel should be consulted, if your budget allows. You need to address different jurisdictions, as some vary in which notifications are required, particularly when transmissions are monitored.

A typical banner might look like this:

```
WARNING! Authorized access only. Unauthorized access
prohibited.
```

> This system is the property of [COMPANY NAME]. Disconnect
> IMMEDIATELY if you are not an authorized user!

A banner might be more explicit, such as this example modified from the Department of Energy Computer Incident Advisory Capability (CIAC):

> THIS IS A PRIVATE COMPUTER SYSTEM. It is for authorized
> use only.
>
> Users (authorized or unauthorized) have no explicit or
> implicit expectation of privacy.
>
> Any or all uses of this system and all files on this system
> may be intercepted, monitored, recorded, copied, audited,
> inspected, and disclosed to authorized site and law
> enforcement personnel as well as authorized officials of
> other agencies, both domestic and foreign. By using this
> system, the user consents to such interception, monitoring,
> recording, copying, auditing, inspection, and disclosure at
> the discretion of authorized site personnel.
>
> Unauthorized or improper use of this system may result in
> administrative disciplinary action and civil and criminal
> penalties. By continuing to use this system you indicate
> your awareness of and consent to these terms and
> conditions of use. LOG OFF IMMEDIATELY if you do not
> agree to the conditions stated in this warning.

A banner should never include wording that could give attackers information about your system or network, such as names, IP addresses, software versions, and so forth. Avoid displaying any information an attacker might seek in network reconnaissance.

To enter a banner on a router, in global configuration mode, type a delimiting character, such as #. The delimiting character signifies the beginning and end of message text. It can be any character you like but can't be used in the message body and must be the same character at the beginning and end. Then enter the text you want the router to display when the router is accessed, and type another # to signify the end of the banner's message of the day (motd).

Remote Access with Secure Shell

A major security problem with routers, especially remote routers, is that network sniffers can intercept packets. The problem is compounded with connections to routers because they usually control the gateway access to your network. Protocols such as Telnet and FTP send everything in cleartext, making them extremely vulnerable to packet sniffers. Standard remote shell programs, such as rlogin, rsh, and rcp, are just as susceptible to attack and should never be used to connect to a device outside your physically controlled network. To manage large network infrastructures, you can use **Secure Shell (SSH)**, a remote shell program, instead of Telnet or FTP.

SSH-2 is an update of SSH-1 and is more secure. Instead of being a single protocol like SSH-1, it's a suite of protocols. In addition, SSH-1 and SSH-2 encrypt at different parts of packets. Another difference is that SSH-1 uses server and host keys to authenticate systems; SSH-2 uses only host keys. SSH-1 isn't widely used now because SSH-2 has stronger security.

As an alternative to the proprietary SSH, the team at OpenBSD created OpenSSH and claim it's more secure because of the open nature of the code. OpenBSD includes several tools: secure copy (scp) as a replacement for rcp, secure ftp (sftp) as a replacement for standard FTP, and the SSH daemon (sshd). Several open-source variations are available for UNIX, Windows, and multiplatform networks.

NOTE   Setting up and configuring SSH servers and clients are beyond the scope of this book because of the complexities of installing on different OSs; however, you can find more information at *www.ssh.com* and *www.openssh.com*.

SSH-1 Server was introduced on some Cisco devices with IOS 12.0.5.S, and the SSH client was introduced with IOS 12.1.3.T. Although only SSH-1 is used in the Cisco IOS, support for SSH-2 was added to some implementations beginning with IOS 12.1.(19)E. The current Cisco IOS offers an SSH server and client so that you can connect to your router's SSH server from an SSH client or connect your router's SSH client to another SSH server. For routers without support for SSH, you need to upgrade your router software. At Cisco's Web site, search for your router model and IOS version, and download the upgrade. You can find full instructions for installing, too.

Enabling SSH on the Router

Before enabling SSH, you must configure the router with a hostname, domain name, and at least one interface with a static IP address. To determine whether your router supports SSH, issue the show flash command to verify your IOS version, and compare it to the current list at Cisco's Web site or do an online search. After these preliminaries, you can enable the SSH server on your router with the following command to generate an RSA key pair:

```
RouterA(config)#crypto key generate rsa
```

This command enables SSH automatically, and deleting the RSA key disables SSH automatically. Next, you choose a key size. Key sizes range from 360 to 2048, but be sure to use a key larger than the default of 512 to ensure strong encryption. (A key size of 1024 should work for most applications.) To create new host keys, issue the following command again, which overwrites the previous keys:

```
RouterA(config)#crypto key generate rsa
```

To delete all RSA keys and certificates and disable SSH, use this command:

```
RouterA(config)#crypto key zeroize rsa
```

After the key pair has been generated on the router, SSH is enabled. There are a few more steps to fine-tune your SSH server. First, configure your authentication timeout interval (the time in seconds the server waits for a client to respond with a password) with this command:

```
RouterA(config)#ip ssh time-out 60
```

The maximum (and default) is 120 seconds, but in this example, 60 seconds was configured. The next step is to configure the number of logon attempts before the router drops the connection with this command:

```
RouterA(config)#ip ssh authentication-retries 3
```

The maximum is five attempts, and the default is three.

NOTE See the Cisco documentation for a complete list of commands, or use the router's context-sensitive help feature.

Installing the SSH Client

Several clients can be used to connect securely to your Cisco router. A popular choice is PuTTy, which works on UNIX and Windows systems. PuTTy still supports SSH-1 but now has support for SSH-2. Another popular program is Terra Term Pro with the SSH extension TTSSH installed. Terra Term Pro doesn't include this extension by default, so be sure to check any Terra Term Pro clients before you use them.

Activity 4-3: Installing PuTTy

ACTIVITY

Time Required: 10 minutes

Objective: Install an SSH remote access client program.

Description: In this activity, you install PuTTy, a popular open-source SSH remote access program, and examine the user interface.

1. Start your Web browser and go to **www.putty.nl/download.html**.

2. Scroll down to the latest release version, and click **putty.exe**. Save the file to your hard drive or a location your instructor designates.

3. Navigate to the file you downloaded and double-click the **PuTTy** icon. If a security dialog box warns you of an unknown publisher, click **Run**.

4. In the PuTTy configuration dialog box, make sure Session is selected in the Category pane, and enter the name or IP address of the router you want to connect to. Make sure the port number is set to the default SSH port 22 and SSH is selected under the Connection type heading.

5. Next, click **Window** in the Category pane to configure the PuTTy interface. Under Control the scrollback, change the default 200 to **2000** so that more terminal text is saved if you use the copy-and-paste method of entering commands. This option uses more memory for that session, however.

6. Click each feature under the Window item in the Category pane, and modify it to suit your preferences.

7. Next, click to expand **Connection** (if necessary) and click **SSH**. If you're on a slow network, click the **Enable compression** check box. If SSH-2 is supported, you can select 2 as the SSH protocol version; otherwise, leave the default.

8. Click **Cancel** to exit the program, and leave your computer running for the next activity.

Verifying SSH

Verifying that the router's SSH server is enabled is critical to security. In router enable mode, issue the show ip ssh command. The following example shows the command and the output it returns:

```
RouterA#show ip ssh

SSH Enabled - version 1.5

Authentication timeout: 120 secs; Authentication retries: 3
```

If the SSH server is not enabled, you see this output:

```
%SSH has not been enabled
```

You can also verify connections to the SSH server with the show ssh command. If you encounter problems when checking your router, verify that you have specified a hostname and domain. Also, make sure you have generated an RSA key pair correctly with the crypto key generate rsa command. If you have difficulty connecting to the router, you might not have configured the router's VTY lines by setting a password on the VTY interface. Remember that without a password, the router rejects any attempts to connect to the VTY interfaces.

You should also set a session timeout on VTY interfaces to reduce the risk of administrators leaving their computers unattended while logged on. Use the exec-timeout command as shown to set a timeout value of 10 minutes:

```
RouterA(config-line)#exec-timeout 10 0
```

Removing Unneeded Protocols and Services

A router is not that different from a standard desktop system, in that it has a processor, RAM, and an OS, and you can harden it as you would any server or workstation by removing unnecessary protocols and services. As a general rule, your router should support only required traffic. In other words, disable any unnecessary service or protocol.

Determining What to Remove

The best place to start in determining what services and protocols to disable is your router security policy. This document should specify what traffic is allowed and whether traffic is incoming or outgoing. If a service or protocol is needed on one interface, check to see whether it can be disabled on other interfaces. Also, remember to check the router vendor's Web site for new patches and security notices. The CERT Coordination Center (*www.cert.org*) is a helpful source of information on new security issues.

Consider each service or protocol for its usefulness and security vulnerability. For example, IP source routing is seldom used but is a possible method of attack. Cisco's proprietary Cisco Discovery Protocol (CDP) is another potentially risky protocol that routers use to identify themselves to each other. To enable CDP for all interfaces, use the cdp run command in global configuration mode. When CDP is no longer needed, disable it by using the no cdp enable command. CDP can be enabled or disabled for specific interfaces by using the same commands in interface configuration mode. You can't enable or disable CDP on an interface, however, unless it's globally enabled on the router.

NOTE
You can learn more about services and protocols to remove by visiting Cisco's Web site or doing an Internet search for your router model. Because routers are often modular, available services and protocols vary widely.

CHAPTER SUMMARY

- ❑ Access control lists (ACLs) are permit or deny statements that filter traffic, provide traffic-flow control, and enhance network security. They can be approached in two ways: Specify what traffic to deny and permit all others, or specify what to permit and deny all others.

- ❑ Standard ACLs can filter on source IP address information only. Extended ACLs can filter based on source and destination addresses, ports, and protocols.

- ❑ Cisco routers perform three main types of logging. AAA logging collects information about dial-up connections, commands, logons, logoffs, and similar events. SNMP trap logging sends notifications of system status changes to SNMP management stations. System logging sends notifications of system changes to different location, such as a syslog server, the router's memory buffer, or the system console port.

- ❑ Logging events are tagged with a severity level ranging from 0 (highest urgency) to 7 (lowest urgency).

- ❑ Buffered logging tells the router to store log output in the router's memory buffer.

◻ Antispoofing logging is done by using ACLs to deny any inbound packet with a source address matching your internal network, broadcast, and loopback addresses; illegal addresses, such as all 0s or all 1s; and multicast or experimental address classes.

◻ In Cisco authorization and authentication, AAA stands for authentication, authorization, and accounting. Authentication is used to identify users, authorization specifies what users are allowed to do after accessing the system, and accounting maintains records of what users do while on the system.

◻ Five main password types are used on a Cisco router: enable, enable secret, VTY, AUX, and console.

◻ Banners are used to deliver messages to anyone logging on to a router. The message should include a legal warning about unauthorized system access and penalties.

◻ Secure Shell (SSH) was developed to help overcome the security limitations of other remote access shell programs, such as Telnet, rlogin, and rcp. Some Cisco routers can be configured to support SSH for remote management purposes.

◻ Removing unnecessary protocols and disabling unneeded services is a critical step in hardening routers. Unless a port, protocol, or service is needed, it should be removed or disabled to protect the router.

4

KEY TERMS

access control lists (ACLs) — A series of permit or deny statements applied to inbound or outbound router interfaces for each protocol the router processes. ACLs are used to permit allowed traffic and block denied traffic.

antispoofing — A method of preventing spoofed inbound packets that might contain source addresses matching the internal LAN addressing scheme. Antispoofing uses ACLs on the router that deny or drop packets matching criteria indicating that they might be spoofed.

authentication, authorization, and accounting (AAA) logging — A type of logging that collects information about user dial-up connections, commands, logons, logoffs, HTTP accesses, and similar events. AAA logs are sent to an authentication server.

banners — Messages a router can be programmed to display to anyone logging on to the router.

buffered logging — A type of system logging that stores log output files in the router's memory (RAM).

inverse mask — The inverse of the subnet mask, also called the wildcard mask. In a subnet mask, some octets indicate the network and the rest identify the host. An inverse mask tells the router to pay attention to certain bits and ignore others.

Secure Shell (SSH) — A more secure form of remote access developed to overcome some security limitations of other remote access and management methods.

Simple Network Management Protocol (SNMP) trap logging — A type of logging that sends notifications of system status changes to SNMP management stations.

syslog server — A type of server configured to host router log files, particularly when you have large log files. A syslog server can be a UNIX or Windows server or another designated machine.

system logging — A type of logging that sends notifications of system status changes to different locations, including the router's memory buffer, system console port, or syslog server.

Review Questions

1. An inverse mask of 0.0.0.255 tells a router to pay attention to which octets of the IP address?

   a. first

   b. last

   c. none

   d. first three

2. ACLs end with an implicit _____ statement, resulting in all traffic not meeting other requirements being blocked. To prevent this from happening, enter a _____ statement at the end of the ACL.

   a. deny any, permit any

   b. permit all, deny any

   c. drop all, permit all

   d. permit all, drop all

3. Standard IP ACLs can allow or deny traffic based on which of the following?

   a. destination IP addresses

   b. protocol

   c. source IP address

   d. port or socket number

4. To make an ACL permanent, which of the following commands do you use?

   a. copy running-config startup-config

   b. configure memory

   c. erase flash

   d. ACLs apply unless they are removed, so they are already permanent.

5. Which of the following shows the correct syntax for a standard IP ACL that filters the 172.16.0.0 network?

   a. access-list 44 permit 172.16.1.3 0.0.0.0

   b. access-list 101 deny 172.16.0.0 255.255.255.255

   c. access-list 99 permit 172.16.254.254 0.0.0.0

   d. access-list 99 deny 172.16.0.0 0.0.255.255

6. Which of the following is a type of logging Cisco routers use? (Choose all that apply.)

   a. authentication

   b. STMP

   c. system

   d. AAA

7. The most important security-related events system logging records include which of the following? (Choose all that apply.)

   a. HTTP accesses

   b. commands carried out

   c. changes to system configuration

   d. changes to interface status

8. Logging level 4 indicates which of the following?

   a. emergency

   b. error condition

   c. notification

   d. warning condition

9. What is a disadvantage of buffered logging?

   a. Logs overwrite the router configuration.

   b. The buffer size can't be adjusted.

   c. Routers don't have enough RAM to store large log files.

   d. An attacker can intercept transmitted log files.

10. Which password is encrypted by default on a Cisco router?

    a. VTY

    b. enable secret

    c. CON

    d. enable

11. Which command encrypts all passwords in a Cisco router's output?

12. Explain the three levels of encryption on Cisco passwords.

13. What built-in Cisco security measure prevents using a VTY line for remote access, usually Telnet?

    a. access control lists

    b. passwords

    c. The CON password must be set and encrypted on the router.

    d. The VTY password must be set.

14. AAA stands for which of the following?

    a. authorizing, accounting, and authentication

    b. authentication, authorization, and accounting

    c. authentication, authorization, and accountability

    d. authenticating, authorizing, and accounting

15. The first step to enable AAA authorization and authentication on a Cisco router is to issue the _____ command.

    a. aaa authorization

    b. aaa new model

    c. aaa methods

    d. aaa new-model

16. SSH is enabled on all Cisco routers by default. True or False?

17. What command is used to generate an RSA key pair?

    a. generate key-pair

    b. crypto

    c. generate rsa key

    d. crypto key generate rsa

18. What command is used to verify that SSH is running on your router?

    a. show flash

    b. show ip ssh

    c. show ssh

    d. show version

19. TACACS+ uses _____ and RADIUS uses _____ for their transport protocols.

20. Cisco's proprietary Cisco Discovery Protocol (CDP) is a potentially risky router protocol. What command do you use to disable CDP?

    a. disable cdp

    b. service cdp-stop

    c. no cdp run

    d. nocdp

21. The enable secret password uses which of the following encryption methods?

    a. RSA

    b. Triple DES

    c. MD5 hash

    d. none

22. What command do you use to set the router authentication timeout interval to one minute?

    a. ssh timeout 1

    b. ssh timeout 060

    c. ip ssh time-out 60

    d. ssh time-out 1:00

4

HANDS-ON PROJECTS

HANDS-ON PROJECTS

Hands-On Project 4-1: Writing ACLs

Time Required: 60 minutes

Objective: Learn to write effective ACLs to control traffic flow.

Description: In this project, you're given sets of criteria, and then you write standard or extended ACLs to control specific traffic. You need a pencil and paper for this project. Assume a Class B network masking of 255.255.0.0, unless otherwise specified.

1. Write an ACL to achieve the following:

    a. Allow Telnet connections to the 192.168.1.0 network from host 10.3.4.7.

    b. Allow established connections from network 172.16.0.0 to anywhere.

    c. Permit all other access.

2. Write an ACL to achieve the following:

    a. Prevent Telnet access from network 192.168.1.0 to network 172.16.0.0.

    b. Prevent reserved addresses from accessing any network.

    c. Deny spoofing from the default route and broadcast address.

    d. Permit all other access.

3. Write an ACL to achieve the following:

    a. Deny ICMP traffic.

    b. Permit access to FTPServer01.

    c. Permit SMTP to the e-mail server named XYZCorpMail01.

    d. Permit any host to access the Web server named XYZWeb01.

    e. Allow access to all unrestricted ports 1024 and higher.

    f. Deny all other access.

Hands-On Project 4-2: Recovering a Password

Time Required: 20 minutes

Objective: Locate the command sequences to recover a password on a router.

Description: Like any other password, sometimes router access passwords are forgotten. An enable password can be recovered, but according to Cisco, enable secret passwords can't. However, they can be reset if you have physical access to the router, so physical security for routers is important. In this project, you visit Cisco's Web site to find the procedure for recovering a password on a 2500 series Cisco router. (Router Simulator doesn't support this procedure.)

NOTE

If you have access to a router, you should practice performing this procedure. One word of caution: When copying the startup configuration into memory from NVRAM, don't type copy run start or write. It erases your startup configuration, and because you haven't reconfigured anything yet, you then effectively have a blank router.

1. Start your Web browser and go to **www.cisco.com**. In the Search text box, type **2500 router password recovery** and press **Enter**.

2. Click the **Password Recovery Procedure for the Cisco 2000, 2500, 3000, 4000, AccessPro, 7000 (RP), AGS, IGS, and STS-10x** link.

3. Read the information to answer the following questions:

   a. Can password recovery be performed through a Telnet connection?

   _____

   b. The configuration register is a value that tells the router what configuration to boot from: flash or the stored configuration file. What's the usual configuration register value?

   _____

   c. To boot from flash, bypassing the saved configuration (where passwords are stored), what value do you need to change the configuration register to?

   _____

   d. Can the enable secret password be recovered?

   _____

4. In a separate document, write the step-by-step procedure for resetting a password on a 2500 series router, and then turn the document in to your instructor.

Case Projects

Case Project 4-1: Creating Draft ACLs for Green Globe's Routers

The network design you're creating for Green Globe needs the router placement refined and some draft ACLs. Using your materials from previous chapters, review the locations where routers should be located. If you haven't determined where to place them, do so now. Make sure you place routers between internal and external hosts, such as between servers and the Internet. (Remember that you'll be placing firewalls and IDSs in subsequent chapters.) You might also have routers between segments, and some segments need to be secured. Design a high-security set of router ACLs for both internal and external routers to meet the project's requirements.

In a text editor, create a brief chart listing the ACLs you created and explaining the results of each line. Having a record of each router's configurations makes revisions, troubleshooting, and maintenance easier.

4

5

DESIGNING FIREWALLS

After reading this chapter and completing the exercises, you will be able to:

♦ Explain what firewalls can and cannot do
♦ Describe common approaches to packet filtering
♦ Compare hardware and software firewalls
♦ Explain how to supplement a firewall with a proxy server
♦ Describe factors in choosing a bastion host
♦ Set up Network Address Translation (NAT)

When you travel by air, you have to pass through several security checkpoints. Your bags are checked, you go through a security checkpoint, and when you board the plane, your tickets and identity are verified. The purpose of all this "filtering" is to keep people who shouldn't be on the plane from boarding.

In the same way, security devices are placed at a network perimeter to filter packets of digital information. This arrangement of security devices is collectively called a firewall or firewall perimeter. This chapter discusses the concept of firewalls—what they are and what they aren't. Then you learn about packet filtering and developing a rule base to carry out your security policy. You also learn about different types of firewall hardware and software, how to work with proxy servers to make network defense more effective, and how to choose a bastion host for your network. Finally, you learn about using Network Address Translation with firewalls.

OVERVIEW OF FIREWALLS

As you learned in Chapter 1, a **firewall** is hardware or software that can be configured to block unauthorized access to a network. "Firewall" is often viewed as a catchall term representing any device that can block attackers or viruses. Managers commonly ask their network administrators to "get a firewall and put it on the network so that we have better security." This request implies that a firewall is one device that can single-handedly keep attackers away from a network, which is an incorrect assumption. Firewalls can't protect against employees who send proprietary information out of the organization through a network connection or by copying data to a disk. A strong security policy and access controls on sensitive information must be used to protect against this type of incident. A firewall also can't protect connections that don't go through it, such as remote dial-up connections. These connections require a virtual private network (VPN) for protection. The following sections explain what firewalls are and are not so that you have a clearer idea of what they do.

What Firewalls Are

The term "firewall" doesn't necessarily refer to a single router, computer, VPN gateway, or software program. Any network firewall is actually a combination of software and hardware components. The term "firewall" can refer to all devices positioned on the network perimeter, so the term "firewall perimeter" might be more descriptive.

The earliest firewalls were packet filters; a single packet-filtering router was placed at the network perimeter to function as a firewall, although a rather weak one. Today's firewalls are more than just a hardware appliance, and many are strictly software. Some firewall programs are designed for general consumer use, such as Norton Personal Firewall, ZoneAlarm, or CA Personal Firewall. They have fairly simple interfaces that give non-technical users a few choices to make for configuration (see Figure 5-1).

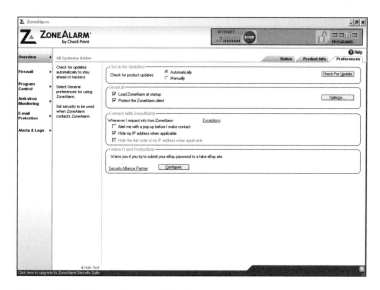

Figure 5-1 ZoneAlarm's interface

Much of the work in establishing rules and blocking traffic is done on a case-by-case basis: When a firewall encounters a type of traffic it doesn't recognize, it prompts you to decide whether the traffic should be blocked or allowed. This process can seem bothersome until the firewall "learns" what is and isn't acceptable traffic, but it's worth the effort.

In Figure 5-2, ZoneAlarm Personal Firewall is reporting that an ICMP Echo Request (ping) packet is attempting to access the trusted zone. The program offers the simple decision of allowing or denying the traffic. To prevent ZoneAlarm from asking about access rights for this program again, you can select the option Remember this setting. With this setting, ZoneAlarm remembers the rule and applies it automatically in the future.

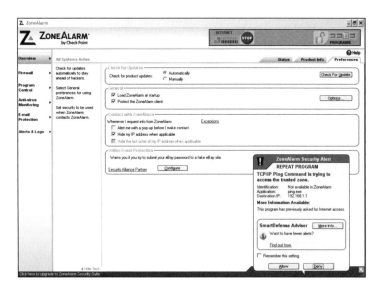

Figure 5-2 Personal firewalls establish rules on a case-by-case basis

Other firewall programs, such as Check Point NGX, are designed to protect and monitor large-scale networks. They come with a variety of GUI tools for configuring and monitoring network traffic. The range of options in these programs can be quite complex, and many offer integrated VPN, firewall, intrusion detection, and proxy services in one product.

Still other firewalls, such as the Cisco PIX line of **firewall appliances**, are self-contained hardware devices with firewall functions you can add to a network. For a list of links to firewall appliances, you can check *http://directory.google.com/Top/Computers/Security/Firewalls/Products*. For more information on the Cisco PIX line, visit *www.cisco.com* and search on "PIX."

Whether they are hardware or software, firewalls are effective only if they are configured correctly to block undesirable traffic, such as a SYN flood or an IP spoofing attack. The most sophisticated firewalls are useless if they have poorly configured rules that allow traffic from untrusted sources. In addition, because new threats and modes of attack are devised constantly, firewalls can be configured correctly and still fail to block some harmful traffic because they don't yet recognize the traffic as something to be blocked.

What Firewalls Are Not

Firewalls aren't a standalone solution, so they shouldn't be regarded as the only tool needed to protect a network. No firewall can protect a network from internal threats, such as disgruntled employees or users who try to find ways around security measures. A strong security policy and employee education are essential. Your organization's security policy should also include strict procedures for keeping patches updated and checking for any new vulnerabilities. Many cases have been reported of worms and viruses getting past expensive firewalls that weren't patched in a timely manner.

Ideally, a firewall should be combined with antivirus software and intrusion detection systems (IDSs) for a more comprehensive solution. Strong network security architecture encompasses many components, including IDSs, firewalls, antivirus software, access control, and auditing. The defense in depth (DiD) approach discussed in Chapter 1 is the most effective method of securing resources, so keep layered defense strategies in mind. Examples of products you might integrate with a firewall include the following:

- eSafe, a content security product by Aladdin Systems (*www.aladdin.com/esafe/default.aspx*) that scans traffic for malware and application-level threats and filters content to improve productivity

- ManageEngine's Firewall Analyzer (*http://manageengine.adventnet.com/index.html*), a Web-based monitoring and log analysis tool that collects logs from proxy servers, firewalls, and VPNs for monitoring performance, auditing traffic, and detecting intrusions

The expense of purchasing and installing several software programs can be considerable, easily running into many thousands of dollars. The most important consideration is the need for an integrated security system in which a firewall plays an important—but by no means solitary—role.

APPROACHES TO PACKET FILTERING

Chapter 4 introduced access control lists (ACLs) and packet filtering on routers. ACLs filter packets by using a rule base to determine whether to allow a packet to pass. In this chapter, you see how to develop a packet-filtering rule base for a firewall. First, you learn more about stateless and stateful packet filtering, and then see how a packet filter's activities depend on other security components it's intended to work with and its position in the perimeter's security configuration.

Stateless Packet Filtering

Packet filtering works by screening traffic that arrives on the network perimeter. **Stateless packet filters** determine whether to allow or block packets based on information in protocol headers. Most often, filtering is based on common IP protocol header features, such as the following:

- *IP address*—Each packet-filtering rule specifies a source IP address and a destination IP address.

- *Ports and sockets*—Ports give you more control over what's allowed and what's blocked when creating filtering rules. A socket is a software connection that enables an application to send and receive data via a network protocol.

- *ACK bits*—Packet filters can allow or block traffic based on the ACK (acknowledgement) bit in a TCP header.

Table 5-1 shows the simple set of rules for a firewall located at 192.168.120.1 on network 192.168.120.0.

Table 5-1   Stateless packet-filtering rules

Rule	Source IP	Source port	Destination IP	Destination port	Action
1	Any	Any	192.168.120.0	Above 1023	Allow
2	192.168.120.1	Any	Any	Any	Deny
3	Any	Any	192.168.120.1	Any	Deny
4	192.168.120.0	Any	Any	Any	Any
5	Any	Any	192.168.120.2	25	Allow
6	Any	Any	192.168.120.3	80	Allow
7	Any	Any	Any	Any	Deny

The following list describes the rules in Table 5-1 in more detail:

- *Rule 1*—Many external hosts contacted by a host on the internal network respond by connecting to TCP ports above 1023; this rule enables these connections.

- *Rule 2*—This rule prevents the firewall from connecting to any other hosts, external or internal. The firewall is supposed to monitor traffic, not make connections. An attacker who gets control of the firewall might try to use it to make a connection, and this rule blocks that attempt.

- *Rule 3*—This rule provides extra security for the firewall, in addition to Rule 2, by keeping external users from establishing a connection to the firewall.

- *Rule 4*—This rule enables internal hosts to make connections to computers outside the network.

- *Rule 5*—This rule enables external users to send e-mail into the network.

- *Rule 6*—This rule allows external users to access the network's Web server.

- *Rule 7*—This cleanup rule denies any other traffic that hasn't been allowed explicitly by previous rules.

However, intruders can still get around these defenses. For instance, the problem with Rule 1 (hosts responding to connections are allowed access to ports above 1023) is that it also allows faked (spoofed) connections to seem as though they're responding to connections to gain access.

Stateless packet filters do have the advantage of being inexpensive and often free. Some are included with routers or open-source OSs. On the other hand, stateless filters can be cumbersome to maintain in a complex network. They're vulnerable to IP spoofing attacks, and they have no form of authentication.

Stateful Packet Filtering

Stateless packet filters aren't enough for most organizations because they can't filter intrusions that occur when someone connects to a computer without the computer having initiated a connection. Without a connection in place, an attacker can spoof the computer into creating one, and denial of service (DoS) and other attacks can result. Another potential vulnerability is that a stateless filter handles every packet separately and doesn't record what packets have already passed through the filter. Previously forwarded packets belonging to a connection have no bearing on a stateless filter's decision to forward or drop a packet.

Stateful packet filters, however, keep a record of connections a host computer has made with other computers by maintaining a file called a **state table**. The packet filter allows incoming packets only from already connected external hosts with a record in the state table. For example, a firewall has Rule 1 from Table 5-1, allowing external connections on ports above 1023, in its rule base. One host on the internal network has certain connections underway, as shown in Table 5-2's excerpt from a state table.

Table 5-2   State table example

Source IP	Source port	Destination IP	Destination port	Connection state
192.168.120.101	1037	209.233.19.22	80	Established
192.168.120.104	1022	165.66.28.22	80	Established
192.168.120.107	1010	65.66.122.101	25	Established
192.168.120.102	1035	213.136.87.88	79	Established
223.56.78.11	1899	192.168.120.101	80	Established
206.121.55.8	3558	192.168.120.101	80	Established
224.209.122.1	1079	192.168.120.105	80	Established

NOTE   Ports 1023 and lower are reserved for specific protocols or other purposes. Therefore, when a Web page you request with your own port 80 is sent back, the Web server returns it by using a TCP port higher than 1023. That's why it's important for a firewall to allow these connections.

In the state table, internal hosts on the network with the address range 192.168.120.0 to 192.168.120.255 have established connections with hosts on the external network. Some are using HTTP port 80 to connect via the Web, and one has established a connection to an e-mail server on port 25. Near the bottom of the table, some external hosts have established connections to hosts on the internal network on port 80.

Suppose an attacker tries to connect to the network on port 10995 from IP address 201.202.100.1 by sending a packet with the ACK TCP header. The ACK header is normally sent at the end of a "handshake" between two networked computers and means that a connection is established. When a stateful firewall receives this packet, it checks the state table for an existing connection between any internal host and the computer at 201.202.100.1. If a connection isn't found in the state table, the packet is dropped.

One user-friendly packet filter is built into Windows XP. Windows Firewall is an improved version of XP's Internet Connection Firewall and offers more protection and control. You access it through Control Panel's Security Center, and then click the Windows Firewall link to open the dialog box shown in Figure 5-3. In the Exceptions tab, you can limit the amount of traffic with more precision and specify exceptions, such as ports or programs (see Figure 5-4).

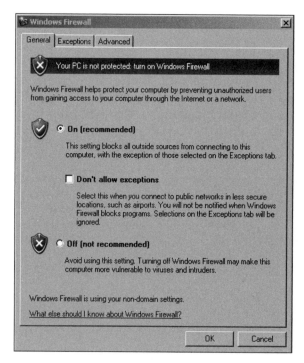

Figure 5-3 Packet filtering in Windows Firewall

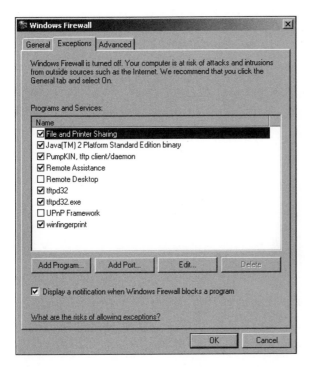

Figure 5-4 Specifying exceptions

In the Advanced tab, you can access settings for an interface, such as logging and Internet Control Message Protocol (ICMP) message handling. You can also control traffic for network services, such as Dynamic Host Configuration Protocol (DHCP), DNS, and FTP (see Figure 5-5). You can add, edit, or delete services and configure more specific control over ICMP responses. You can also reset Windows Firewall to its default settings, which can come in handy if a change you have made is causing problems, but you're unsure which change is the culprit.

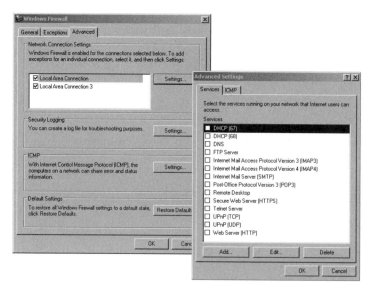

Figure 5-5 Configuring advanced settings in Windows Firewall

Stateful packet filtering doesn't necessarily address all problems with stateless filtering, such as authentication.

Packet Filtering Based on Position

The type of filtering that a firewall, router, or other device does depends on its position in the firewall perimeter and on the other hardware or software with which its activities need to be coordinated. For instance, a packet filter positioned between the Internet and a host that provides the only protection for that host must be configured carefully; all inbound and outbound traffic should be accounted for in the packet filter's rule base.

In contrast, a packet filter placed between a proxy server and the Internet needs to help in shielding internal users from external hosts. A company concerned about protecting its data warehouses and employees' privacy might install a proxy server on the network perimeter. A proxy server handles traffic on behalf of computers on the network it protects, rebuilding outbound and inbound requests to hide internal IP address information. A packet filter between a proxy server and the Internet must direct traffic to and from the proxy server. A main goal is to prevent direct connections between the internal network and the Internet (see Figure 5-6).

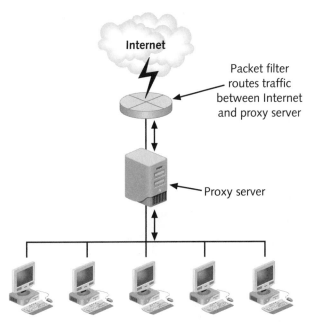

Figure 5-6 A packet filter connecting a proxy server with the Internet

Proxy servers can perform stateful packet filtering on their own. They operate at the OSI model's application layer, so they can make intelligent decisions about what traffic is allowed to pass. The tradeoff is the drop in performance that can result from the demand proxy servers place on the host computer, which is much higher than with a traditional firewall.

Another type of configuration combines packet filtering with a demilitarized zone (DMZ). One common setup is placing packet-filtering devices (routers or firewalls) at either end of the DMZ. The packet filter on the DMZ's external interface needs to allow Internet users to gain access to servers on the DMZ but block access to the internal network. The packet filter on the internal interface performs a similar function but for internal users; it enables them to access servers on the DMZ but not connect directly to the Internet. Instead, they connect to the Internet through a proxy server on the DMZ (see Figure 5-7).

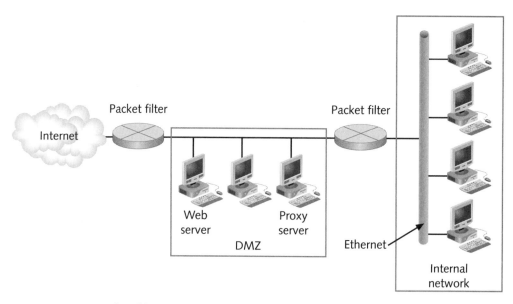

Figure 5-7 A packet filter routing traffic to and from a DMZ

The question of how many packet filters to use and where to place them depends on your needs. A simple home network might have adequate protection from a single well-configured stateful packet filter. A small network that needs to protect proprietary information can use a proxy server-packet filter combination to prevent IP or port information for internal hosts from being revealed to external users. If no IP addresses or ports can be discovered through port scans or other means, no attacks can be launched. For large companies that run public Web servers and have proprietary information to protect, placing packet filters on either side of a DMZ can provide effective multilayered protection for public servers and employees.

Activity 5-1: Installing a Freeware Firewall Program

Time Required: 30 minutes

Objective: Install a freeware firewall program.

Description: Freeware firewall programs aren't as full featured as commercial firewalls, but they're good for testing and learning how these programs work. In this activity, you need a Windows XP computer to download and use the freeware version of a popular personal firewall, ZoneAlarm by Check Point.

NOTE

You need to disable Windows Firewall or other firewall software before performing the activities in this chapter.

1. Start your Web browser and go to **www.zonealarm.com/store/content/company/products/znalm/freeDownload.jsp**.

2. Click the **I only want basic ZoneAlarm protection** link, and then click **Run** or **Save File** to begin downloading the program.

3. If a Security Warning dialog box opens, click **Run** or **OK**. Click the **XP/2000** option button, and then click **Next**.

4. Click the **Download and install** option button, and then click **Next**. When ZoneAlarm has finished downloading, follow the prompts to begin the installation.

5. After the installation is done, the ZoneAlarm Registration Survey opens. Complete the survey, and then click **Finish**.

6. When the ZoneAlarm setup dialog box opens and asks whether you want to start ZoneAlarm now, click **Yes**. Click **No Thanks** to continue installing the free version.

7. In the ZoneAlarm Configuration Wizard, click the **Scan my computer** option button, and then click **Next**. Click **Finish**, and then click **OK** to restart your computer.

8. Click **Finish** in the ZoneAlarm – Getting Started window to skip the video tutorial.

9. The first step is to configure the trusted zone. Until you enter the IP addresses you want to allow, ZoneAlarm blocks everything by default. Click **Firewall** at the left, and then click the **Zones** tab.

10. Click **Add**, point to **IP Range**, and then enter the subnet address range and a brief description for your classroom network. Click **OK**.

11. Click **Program Control** on the left, save your changes if prompted, and then click the **Programs** tab (see Figure 5-8). To add a new program to the list, click the **Add** button.

5

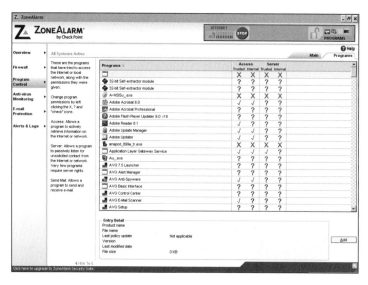

Figure 5-8 Configuring programs to add to the trusted zone

12. In the Add Program dialog box, click to open the **Internet Explorer** folder. Click the **iexplore.exe** file, and then click **Open**. Internet Explorer is added to the list of programs in the trusted zone.

13. Repeat Steps 11 and 12 for other programs allowed to access the Internet, such as your e-mail client, FTP programs, and so on. (For example, if you use Outlook Express for e-mail, the program name is Msimn.exe.).

14. When you're done, close the ZoneAlarm Control Center. To open the Control Center in the future, double-click the ZoneAlarm taskbar icon. Leave your system running for the next activity.

COMPARING SOFTWARE AND HARDWARE FIREWALLS

As a network administrator responsible for security, you need to evaluate firewall software and hardware packages and recommend the best choice for your company's needs. Firewalls come in many varieties, but they all handle these core functions: filtering, proxying, and logging. Some packages add "bells and whistles," such as caching and address translation. Many vendors now offer firewall packages that also include content filtering, antivirus, and intrusion detection. Security products can be affordable or extremely expensive, but don't let price rule your decision. Some freeware products have the same functions as a more expensive commercial package, and combinations of freeware and open-source security products can be effective. The following sections describe the software and hardware combinations you're likely to encounter in the workplace. This overview should help you choose a package when the time comes.

Software-Based Firewalls

Most people are familiar with software firewalls. They can be combined with hardware devices to create an extra-secure checkpoint. The downside of software-based firewalls is that they require a lot of work to configure the software and secure the OS by patching or removing vulnerable services. On the other hand, they're usually less expensive than hardware firewalls, so using them in several locations is affordable. Security professionals often debate whether software firewalls are more secure than hardware firewalls. Many believe the level of security depends more on skill in configuring the firewall and regularity of maintenance and updates than a specific program or device.

Free Firewall Programs

Free firewall programs aren't perfect. Their logging capabilities aren't as robust as in some commercial products, and configuration can be difficult. In addition, they might not include a way to monitor traffic passing through the firewall in real time or manage firewall settings for a network from a central location. Nonetheless, they have a place in small-business and home networks because of their convenience, simplicity, and unbeatable cost. Popular free firewall programs include the following:

- *Netfilter*—This program, which comes with the Linux 2.4 kernel, is a powerful solution for stateless and stateful packet filtering, Network Address Translation (NAT), and packet processing. Netfilter is good at logging detailed information about traffic in a well-organized, easy-to-review manner. For more information, visit *www.netfilter.org*.

- *ZoneAlarm*—The free version of this program (which you installed in Activity 5-1) is so effective that you might lose your Internet connectivity when you first set it up. Correct configuration that allows only the software and IP addresses you want is critical to maintaining Internet connectivity.

Many freeware firewall programs are stripped-down versions of more elaborate products from the same companies. You can try an evaluation version of ZoneAlarm Security Suite, for example, and then decide whether to purchase the commercial version.

Commercial Firewall Software: Personal Firewalls

Personal firewall products are located between the Ethernet adapter driver of the machine on which they're installed and the TCP/IP stack, where they inspect traffic between the driver and the stack. They include programs such as the following:

- *CA (Computer Associates) Personal Firewall*—This program includes security levels for grouping programs, protocols, and ports, automated configuration and help for novice users, and features for more experienced users to fine-tune control. You can also configure packet-filtering rules, real-time monitoring, and auditing. Visit *www.ca.com* for more information.

- *Norton Personal Firewall*—This easy-to-use program for home users comes as a standalone product or packaged with antivirus, antispam, and intrusion detection software. You can learn more at *www.norton-online.com/us/security/*.

- *ZoneAlarm Security Suite*—Along with firewall software, you get antivirus and spyware protection with the capability to block pop-up ads, cookies, and more. You can find ZoneAlarm and ZoneAlarm Security Suite at *www.zonealarm.com*.

- *BlackICE PC Protection*—This program combines intrusion detection with firewall functionality and offers protection against malware threats. You can find more information at *www.digitalriver.com/dr/v2/ec_dynamic.main? SP=1&PN=10&sid=26412*.

Despite the features in the preceding list, these personal firewall products are considered "lightweight" in terms of firewall protection. Some work with multiple protocols, but most guard only against IP threats. Some programs don't handle outbound connection blocking, and others do. Some are inconvenient to configure because they don't work on a "configure as you compute" basis. Instead, you set a general security level (such as Cautious, Nervous, or Paranoid), and the software adjusts its security settings accordingly.

Commercial Firewall Software: Enterprise Firewalls

Enterprise firewall programs come with a centralized management option and sometimes the capability to install multiple instances from a central location. Following are some examples:

- *Check Point NGX*—This suite of management and configuration tools offers real-time monitoring, remote administration, and log file analysis. For more information, search at *www.checkpoint.com*.

- *Proventia security products*—This program from IBM Internet Security Systems (*www.iss.net/products/index.html*) includes a variety of security tools and packages with an emphasis on centralized management for enterprise applications.

- *Novell's BorderManager*—This program uses directory-based access controls, content filtering, and secure VPN services in addition to firewall features. For more information, visit *www.novell.com/products/bordermanager*.

Firewalls that used to consist mostly of packet-filtering tools have added user authentication, NAT, encryption, and centralized management to stay ahead in an increasingly competitive market. Integrating other security and management features is becoming the rule rather than the exception.

Hardware Firewalls

One advantage of hardware firewalls is that they don't depend on a conventional OS, such as Windows or Linux, which can leave security vulnerabilities caused by bugs or other flaws. On the other hand, hardware firewalls *do* run on an OS—some Cisco hardware firewalls run on Cisco's Internetwork Operating System (IOS), for instance—and they can be subject to the same flaws as computer OSs. Hardware firewalls are usually more scalable than software firewalls, and they can handle more data with faster throughput. On the downside, hardware firewalls tend to be more expensive.

Hybrid Firewalls

A **hybrid firewall** combines aspects of hardware and software firewalls in one package. It can offer the high performance of a hardware appliance but also handle functions normally available only in software firewalls, such as protection against DoS attacks or integrated antivirus scanning. A hybrid solution is a good choice in a large organization when a firewall must protect hundreds or thousands of users and provide good throughput and virus protection.

Which firewall product is best for your needs? The choice depends on the number of users to protect, the amount of network traffic passing through the firewall, budget, and the organization's level of concern about security. Budget shouldn't always be the primary consideration. An inexpensive software firewall can become inadequate when a network grows, so buying the strongest one you can afford might be the wisest choice. Table 5-3 lists some advantages and disadvantages to consider when choosing a firewall.

Table 5-3   Firewall advantages and disadvantages

Type of firewall	Advantages	Disadvantages
Software—freeware	Unbeatable price; small file size; ease of installation	Only minimal features are offered; lack of technical support
Software—commercial personal firewalls	Simple to install; economical; auto-configuration features help novice users yet give advanced users more fine-tuned control	Not as full-featured as enterprise products and not as robust as hardware appliances; usually installed on single-computer systems, which reduces security
Software—commercial enterprise firewalls	Usually installed on a dedicated host for maximum security; centralized administration available for large networks; real-time monitoring and other administrative features	Can be difficult to install and configure; tend to be more expensive
Hardware appliances	More scalable than software firewalls, and offer faster throughput	Can be expensive and difficult to patch if bugs or security alerts require it
Hybrid firewalls	Combine the throughput and security of a hardware appliance with features of a software firewall	As expensive or more expensive than other firewalls

WORKING WITH PROXY SERVERS

Your organization's security policy might call for installing a **proxy server**—software that forwards packets to and from the network and caches Web pages to speed up network performance. In many organizations, a proxy server is the only type of firewall installed, except for a router. The following sections explain the goals of setting up a proxy server and how proxy servers work, how to choose a proxy server, and how proxy servers can filter content for a network.

NOTE Proxy servers provide effective protection because they work at the OSI model's application layer. They can interpret what application is used to make a request and forward the request on behalf of that application. In contrast, firewalls mainly interpret IP and TCP header information at the lower OSI levels.

Goals of Proxy Servers

Speeding up network communications was the original goal of proxy servers. The process, shown in Figure 5-9, works like this: As Web pages are requested from a company's Web server, the proxy server receives the Web pages and forwards them to the computer making the request. At the same time, it caches the page's text and image files—in other words, stores those files on disk for later retrieval if needed. With caching, the proxy server rather than the Web server can handle computers requesting the same Web page more than once. The proxy server checks its cache for the requested Web page and compares the page's contents against the contents currently published on the Web server. If no changes are found, files are retrieved from the proxy's cache rather than the Web server. Storing documents in disk cache reduces the load on the Web server and speeds up network traffic.

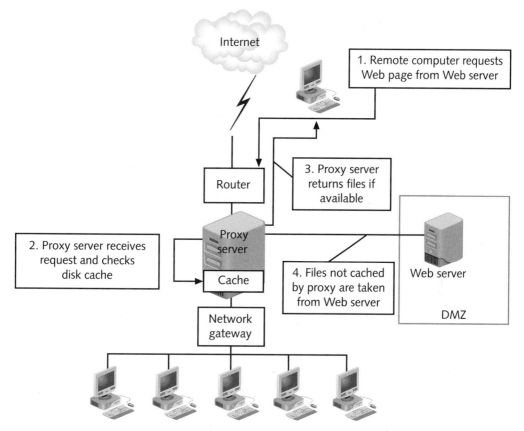

Figure 5-9 Proxy servers cache Web pages and other files

 Microsoft Internet Security and Acceleration (ISA) Server also caches documents to speed up network performance and is discussed in Chapter 7.
TIP

The main goal of proxy servers now is to provide security at the application layer and
shield hosts on the internal network. A secondary goal is controlling which Web sites
users are allowed to access. Proxy servers can use IP addresses or domain names to
block access to certain Web sites or top-level domains. For example, an administrator
could allow access to only the .gov top-level domain so that employees can view government forms online.

 Many proxy servers' default settings enable users to access the Internet by
using multiple services. However, these settings can open security holes. They
might enable Telnet access, for example, or allow Web access around the
CAUTION clock, which most users don't need. For better security, you should disable
services that most users don't need.

How Proxy Servers Work

Network-layer packet filters look only at the header of a TCP/IP packet. Their goal is to block unauthorized packets and allow only authorized packets to reach their destination. If packets are authorized, the packet filter enables host and client computers to communicate with one another directly.

In contrast, the goal of proxy servers is to prevent a direct connection between an external and internal computer. One way is by working at the application layer. When a proxy server receives a request from an internal computer, it opens the packet and examines the data. If the request is for a Web page and uses the standard GET method, the proxy server reconstructs the packet and forwards it to the requested Web server, acting as a proxy Web browser. By acting at the application layer, the proxy server can interpret which application was used to make a request and which application is needed to forward the request.

Reconstructing a packet means that when a proxy server receives a request, it replaces the original header with a new header containing its own IP address instead of the client's (see Figure 5-10). As you can see in this figure, the proxy server is in the DMZ. The following procedure occurs:

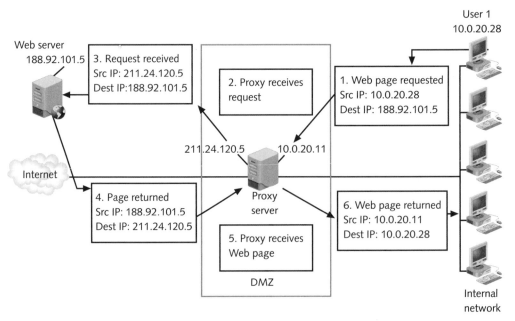

Figure 5-10 Proxy servers replace source IP addresses with their own addresses

1. User 1 requests the Web page at IP address 188.92.101.5.

2. The proxy server receives a request from User 1's Web browser in the internal network, examines the request, and strips off the packet header. The proxy

server replaces the header with its public source IP address before sending the packet on its way.

3. The Web server receiving the request interprets it as coming from the proxy server's IP address instead of from User 1's computer. In fact, the Web server (or an attacker who intercepts the request) has no way of knowing that User 1's computer exists.

4. The Web server then sends its response with the Web page to the proxy server.

5. The response goes through the proxy server for processing, and the IP header sent by the Web server is replaced.

6. The proxy server sends the requested Web page to User 1's computer, where the browser displays it.

The proxy server is configured to receive traffic before it goes to the Internet; client programs, such as Web browsers and e-mail programs, are configured to connect to the proxy rather than the Internet. Figure 5-11 shows a typical browser configuration.

Figure 5-11 Configuring client programs to connect to the proxy server rather than the Internet

In Figure 5-11, the proxy server's IP address of 192.168.0.1 has been entered in the Proxy address to use text box. Port 8080, normally used for proxy services, is also specified. This configuration results in the proxy server forwarding requests to external hosts over port 8080 with a source IP address of 192.168.0.1. Proxy servers require all network users to configure client programs accordingly. Depending on the number of users, configuration can be time consuming. If you don't have time to make all these configurations, you can prepare instructions that users follow to configure their own software so that you just have to deal with problems that come up.

Many older proxy server programs come with an auto-configuration script that sets the proxy server's address and port number for client programs automatically. Newer proxy servers, such as Microsoft ISA Server, no longer need a separate client program on users' computers. Table 5-4 summarizes some advantages and disadvantages of using proxy servers.

Table 5-4   Proxy server advantages and disadvantages

Advantages	Disadvantages
Examines contents of packets and filters on contents	Can be weak
Shields internal host IP address	Can slow down network access
Caches Web pages for faster access	Might require configuration of client programs to use the proxy server
Provides a single point of logging	Provides a single point of failure

ACTIVITY

Activity 5-2: Analyzing How Proxy Servers Handle Packets

Time Required: 20 minutes

Objective: Learn how proxy servers shield internal computers.

Description: Proxy servers shield internal computers by rebuilding packets and changing IP addresses. In this activity, you analyze the process step by step to see how proxy servers process IP addresses. Figure 5-12 shows network clients with Web browsers, a proxy server, and a Web server and how they interact. Use this diagram to guide you through this activity.

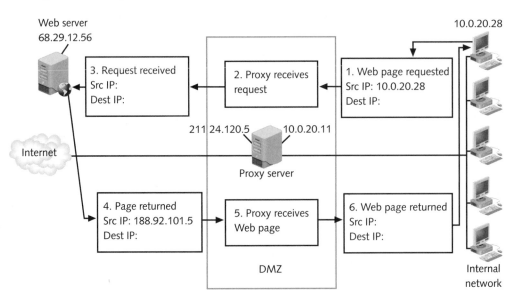

Figure 5-12   Interaction of elements in a packet transaction

List the source and destination IP addresses for each step in the process to show how IP addresses change as they go through the proxy server:

1. An internal host with the source IP address 10.0.20.28 makes a request to view a Web page from the server shown in the upper-left corner of Figure 5-12. Write the destination IP address for box 1 that appears in the packet the proxy server receives:

    _____

2. In box 3, what source and destination IP addresses appear in the packet the proxy server sends to the external Web server?

    _____

3. In box 4, what destination IP address does the proxy server receive in the response the external Web server sends?

    _____

4. In box 6, what are the source and destination IP addresses in the packet the proxy server sends to the internal host after processing the Web server's response?

    _____

Choosing a Proxy Server

Different proxy servers perform different functions to strengthen your firewall configuration. The type of proxy server you install depends on your network's needs. You can install a simple freeware proxy server if you're satisfied with your firewall's level of protection and simply want to add functions the firewall can't perform (such as filtering out pop-up ads and executable code).

If you want to strengthen existing firewall protection, however, a commercial proxy server can perform many functions that improve your network security, including a single point of logging and hiding internal IP addresses. If you need to save installation time and want only one program to manage, an enterprise firewall with proxy server, packet filtering, and other functions is a good choice. The basic types of proxy servers you can choose—freeware proxy servers, commercial proxy servers, or a firewall with proxy server functions—are described in the following sections.

Freeware Proxy Servers

Freeware proxy servers tend to offer a specific function rather than the full range of proxy server functions, so they're often described as "content filters." An Internet search for freeware proxy servers returns many links, but most of these products don't have the features business applications need. One freeware proxy server worth mentioning is Squid Proxy for Linux (*www.squid-cache.org*). It's an open-source product, so plenty of documentation and support are available.

Commercial Proxy Servers

The many benefits of commercial proxy servers are evident when you install a program such as Microsoft ISA Server. This program combines capabilities to cache Web pages and translate source and destination IP addresses with content filtering and traditional firewall functions, such as packet filtering and NAT. To compete with other security programs, most proxy servers aren't advertised as having these features. Instead, they're described as part of a comprehensive firewall package. A commercial proxy server is a good choice for a business network if you plan to upgrade the software when new versions are available. Any commercial program should offer technical support for installation and configuration problems.

Proxy Servers That Include Firewall Functions

Some proxy servers, such as ISA Server, can be set up to act as firewalls in addition to performing other functions. Having an all-in-one program simplifies installation, product updates, and day-to-day management. On the other hand, a single program is handling all your network security needs. If something goes wrong with the proxy server, the firewall also goes down. If feasible, using software and hardware devices in a coordinated network defense layer is preferable. For example, you could use ISA Server for the proxy server and Cisco PIX as the firewall.

Filtering Content

A useful feature of proxy servers is their capability to open TCP/IP packets, inspect the data portion, and take action based on the contents. This capability enables proxy servers to filter out content in a user's Web browser. In a business environment, proxy servers can be configured to block Web sites containing content employees shouldn't be allowed to view. They can also drop any executable programs, such as Java applets or ActiveX controls, embedded in Web pages that could damage or replicate files when they run on a user's computer.

NOTE   Most Web pages don't have embedded executable code. However, attackers have attempted to distribute malware by adding executable code to Web pages. An example is the W32/Nimda worm that, according to a CERT Coordination Center security alert (*www.cert.org/advisories/CA-2001-26.html*), can propagate itself when Web browsers open Web pages or when e-mail programs receive certain attachments.

CHOOSING A BASTION HOST

Security software doesn't operate on its own. It's installed on a computer that runs on an OS; this computer needs to be as secure as possible because of the important software on it and its position on the network perimeter. Often, this computer also functions as a server providing Web pages, e-mail, or other services to users inside and outside the network. This practice is discouraged because of vulnerabilities caused by the complexity of configuring this system; however, small companies might not have the resources to host these services separately. In this situation, a company should consider hiring a security specialist.

To protect security software as well as the network, the computer should be turned into a **bastion host**, a computer on the network perimeter that has been specially protected with OS patches, authentication, and encryption. A computer hosting a firewall that's riddled with OS vulnerabilities gives attackers a way to compromise the entire network. They might even be able to disable firewall software if they can gain administrative privileges or crack passwords on the server. The following sections describe how to choose and configure a bastion host that can safely host security software.

5

General Requirements

In general, a bastion host should be a computer running an OS that's already secure or has been in release long enough that patches for security vulnerabilities are available. When the OS is made as secure as possible by eliminating unnecessary software and services, closing potential openings, and protecting information with encryption and authentication, the computer is said to be **hardened**.

These are the general steps for creating a bastion host (covered in more detail in the following sections):

1. Select a machine with adequate memory and processor speed.
2. Choose and install the OS and any patches or updates.
3. Determine where the bastion host fits in the network configuration, and make sure it's in a safe and controlled physical environment.
4. Install the services you want to provide or modify existing services.
5. Remove services and accounts that aren't needed.
6. Back up the system and its data, including log files.
7. Conduct a security audit.
8. Connect the system to the network.

Selecting the Bastion Host Machine

You don't need to select the latest hardware and software combination to configure a bastion host. Instead, choose a combination of machine type and software that you're familiar with and can work with easily. You don't want to be repairing or rebuilding a machine under pressure and learning to operate it at the same time.

In an ideal situation, you can designate one host for each service you want to provide: one FTP server/bastion host, one Web server/bastion host, one SMTP server/bastion host, and so on. However, budget constraints might force you to combine services on one bastion host. In this case, a comprehensive risk analysis of the services and hardware you need to protect the most can be helpful. (For details on risk analysis, see *Guide to Strategic Infrastructure Security: Becoming a Security Network Professional*, Course Technology, 2008, ISBN 1418836613.) The following sections discuss essential components of a secure bastion host.

Operating System

The most important requirements for a bastion host are your level of comfort with the OS and its inherent security and reliability. Management probably isn't concerned about which OS you install; the priorities are ensuring that the machine protects the internal network and making sure you can get it running and maintain it easily.

Another top priority is the security level of the OS. Make sure you select a version that's stable and secure, and check the OS's Web site or well-known security sites (shown in the following list) for patches and updates for new vulnerabilities:

- Windows Server 2003 (*www.microsoft.com/windowsserver2003/default.mspx*)

- Red Hat Linux (*www.redhat.com*)

- Linux (*www.linux.org*)

- FreeBSD Project (*www.freebsd.org*)

- SANS Institute's list of the Top Twenty Most Critical Internet Security Vulnerabilities, which includes subsections on UNIX and Windows vulnerabilities (*www.sans.org/top20.htm*)

- U.S. Department of Energy's Computer Incident Advisory Capability (CIAC) site (*www.ciac.org/ciac*), which lists newly discovered security advisories

Memory and Processor Speed

Bastion hosts don't need to have the most recent or expensive memory-processor combinations. Memory is always important when operating a server, but because the bastion host might be providing only one service, you aren't likely to need several gigabytes of RAM. You might, however, need to match processing power to the server load, which could mean simply upgrading the processor or perhaps adding processors.

Location on the Network

Bastion hosts are usually located outside the internal network and often combined with packet-filtering devices, such as routers and firewall appliances, on either side (see Figure 5-13). This combination further protects the bastion host from attack because it can prevent tampered-with packets from ever reaching the bastion host. In addition, a packet-filtering server (proxy server) can filter out suspicious packets coming from *inside* the network as a result of Trojan programs or viruses.

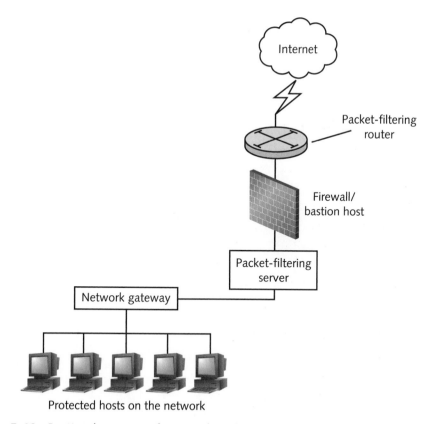

Figure 5-13 Bastion hosts are often combined with packet-filtering routers

More often, multiple bastion hosts are set up in the DMZ, with each machine providing a single service to the public (see Figure 5-14). This configuration is more secure because you can allow general access to the Web server yet limit mail server access to employees, for example.

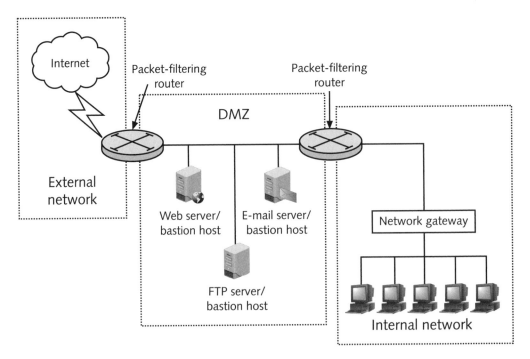

Figure 5-14   Bastion hosts in the DMZ

Hardening the Bastion Host

A bastion host can be any server hosting Web, e-mail, FTP, and other network services. However, the more services on the bastion host, the higher the chance of a security vulnerability in a service installed on the system. Therefore, one way to harden a bastion host is by removing all unnecessary software, services, and user accounts. The simpler your bastion host is, the easier it is to secure. In addition, services could have software bugs or configuration errors, which could lead to security problems. To give intruders fewer exploit opportunities, only the minimum number of services and open ports should be available.

Selecting Services to Provide

A bare-bones configuration reduces the risk of attacks and has the extra benefit of boosting efficiency. If you close unnecessary ports and disable user accounts and services you don't plan to use, attackers have fewer ways to access the system. Some critical services you should disable are those used to perform routing or IP forwarding—unless, of course, the bastion host is intended to function as a router. Disabling IP forwarding makes it more difficult for attackers to communicate with internal network computers.

When you're stopping or removing services, you shouldn't disable any **dependency services**—services the system needs to function correctly. For example, Telnet is usually disabled because other services don't normally require it. Remote Procedure Calls (RPC), however, shouldn't be disabled because almost everything depends on it to function correctly. In addition, stopping services one at a time to see what effect they have on the system is advisable. Get in the habit of documenting every change you make and how the system reacts so that you have a record in case you need to troubleshoot later. This documentation process, called **change management**, could be added as a requirement of your security policy.

TIP

Backing up the system before making major changes to services is a wise precaution.

5

ACTIVITY

Activity 5-3: Limiting Unnecessary Services

Time Required: 15 minutes

Objective: Stop unnecessary services to reduce security vulnerabilities.

Description: Often an OS has a number of services running by default that you don't need; for example, a Windows XP system with a typical setup might have as many as 80 services running at one time. The following steps show you how to inventory and stop running services on a Windows XP system.

1. Open Control Panel, and in Category view, click **Performance and Maintenance**.

2. Click **Administrative Tools**, and then double-click **Services**. If necessary, click the **Standard** tab at the bottom of the Services dialog box.

3. Scroll down the list of services and see whether there are any you don't need. (You might want to check Microsoft's Web site for Windows XP documentation to find out whether you can disable a service safely.) For instance, click **Routing and Remote Access**. If this service is listed as Started in the Status column, double-click it.

4. In the Routing and Remote Access Properties dialog box, click the **Stop** button to stop the service.

5. Click **Disabled** in the Startup type drop-down list to stop the service from restarting automatically in the future.

6. Click **OK** to close the Routing and Remote Access Properties dialog box and return to the Services dialog box.

7. Repeat Steps 3 through 6 for other services you want to stop.

8. When you're done, close all open windows to return to the Windows desktop. Leave your system running for the next activity.

Using Honeypots

A **honeypot** is a computer placed on the network perimeter to attract attackers so that they stay away from critical servers on the network (see Figure 5-15); it may or may not be a bastion host. This computer is equipped with software and perhaps data files that look like they're used by the company but aren't actually used. A honeypot might also be configured with security holes so that it seems vulnerable to known attacks. A honeypot can be located between the bastion host and internal network; if an attacker manages to get past the external packet filter to the DMZ and is scanning for open ports, the honeypot could act as a place for the attacker to get "stuck" (in other words, diverted from your real files by being misdirected to files of no value).

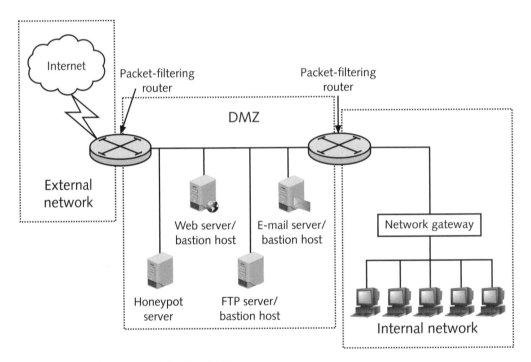

Figure 5-15   A honeypot in the DMZ

Network security experts are divided over honeypots. Some think they have value, some think they're outdated and not worth using, and some think they're unnecessary and even potentially dangerous if they contain information about your company and its bastion hosts. Laws on the use of honeypots are confusing at best, so consult your legal department before setting one up. Honeypots are worth mentioning not only because they're likely to be covered in certification exams, but also because they're still discussed as options in perimeter security.

Another goal of a honeypot is logging. Because intruders who can't tell the difference between the honeypot and a legitimate target can be expected to attack it, you can configure the honeypot to log every access attempt as a way to identify who's trying to attack your network. Because your employees aren't accessing resources in the honeypot, any access attempt is probably from an attacker. A honeypot can also give you an indication of how your real network computers might be attacked. By reviewing what OS flaws, open ports, or other vulnerabilities are exploited on the honeypot, you can take steps to address these vulnerabilities on other systems.

Disabling User Accounts

Default accounts are sometimes created during installation of OSs and other software, and some of these accounts have blank or default passwords. Accordingly, you should delete or disable all user accounts from the bastion host. They aren't needed because users shouldn't be able to connect to the bastion host from their computers. User accounts on the bastion host increase the chances of a security breach.

You should also rename the Administrator account as another way to thwart intruders. Many attackers can access computers through administrative accounts that use the default name "Administrator" and are never assigned a password. Renaming these accounts and using passwords of at least six or eight alphanumeric characters can prevent these attacks.

You should assume that the bastion host will be compromised in some way and take proactive steps to secure it. The bastion host is the system most likely to be attacked because of its availability to external users.

NOTE

Activity 5-4: Eliminating Unnecessary Accounts

ACTIVITY

Time Required: 10 minutes

Objective: Delete or disable unnecessary user accounts.

Description: The Guest account in Windows often gives attackers an opening to your network. In addition, you should have only one Administrator account to reduce the risk of attacks. The following steps show you how to eliminate or disable unnecessary accounts on a Windows XP computer.

1. Open Control Panel in Category view, and click **User Accounts**.

2. If you see the message "Guest account is on" at the bottom of the User Accounts window, click **Guest**. The User Accounts window for the Guest account opens. Click the **Turn off the guest account** link. The account is disabled, and you're returned to the previous User Accounts window.

3. If you see more than one account labeled Computer administrator, decide which administrator account you want to keep. Click the others in succession. In the next User Accounts window, click **Delete the account** or **Change the account type** to reduce access privileges.

4. Close Control Panel and return to the Windows desktop. Leave your system running for the next activity.

Handling Backups and Auditing

Setting up a bastion host requires being more systematic and thorough than you might be used to; backups, detailed recordkeeping, and auditing are essential steps in hardening a computer.

Bastion hosts can generate a lot of log files and other data, such as alert messages. You need to copy this information to other computers in your network regularly. When you do this recordkeeping, the information goes through network defense layers you have already set up. Because of its high security configuration, your bastion host will probably be in a vulnerable location on the DMZ and outside the internal network. Log files and system data, which need to be backed up regularly, should go through the firewall protecting the internal network to screen them for viruses and other vulnerabilities, such as manipulated packets. Attackers might insert falsified information into packets as a way to access computers on the internal network.

Auditing should be configured for all failed and successful attempts to log on to the bastion host and any attempts to access or change files. Administrators rarely have enough time to review log files, but you should make time every day to review logs for any devices in the DMZ as well as routers and packet-filtering servers. These logs can give you advance warning of intrusion attempts.

NOTE

To avoid using network resources, be sure that systems used as bastion hosts have CD-RW drives, removable disk drives, or tape drives so that you can make backups.

Using Network Address Translation

Network Address Translation (NAT) functions much like a mailroom worker routing letters addressed to "Santa Claus, North Pole" to people who reply to them; the senders don't know the locations and identities of the people who answer the letters. In NAT, computers outside the internal network don't see the IP addresses of host computers on the protected internal network. The NAT device (such as a firewall or router) acts as a go-between, receiving requests at its IP address and forwarding them to the correct IP addresses in the network. Using NAT means you don't have to assign public IP addresses to each computer in your network for it to send and receive information via the Internet. A NAT-enabled firewall or router is the only device that needs to have a public, routable IP address for use on the Internet. Internal hosts can be assigned private IP addresses set aside for use on networks.

NAT is one of the essential functions that many firewalls or routers perform. The reason for enabling NAT, from a security standpoint, isn't conserving IP addresses, however. By shielding IP addresses of internal hosts, a NAT-enabled device makes it more difficult for attackers to find computers to exploit. Many attacks begin with an intruder locating a computer with a static public IP address; the intruder can then scan the computer for open ports to exploit. If the intruder can't find the computer's IP address, attacks might never start. NAT can be carried out in two different ways—hide-mode mapping and static mapping—which are described in the following sections.

Hide-Mode Mapping

You might already be using a form of NAT called **hide-mode mapping**—the process of hiding private IP addresses behind one public IP address—in your home or classroom network. For example, you have a computer that functions as a network server, has a gateway to the Internet, and uses Dynamic Host Configuration Protocol (DHCP) to assign IP addresses dynamically to internal hosts. The server might have a public IP address, such as 213.141.56.8, but addresses on the internal network are private ones, such as 192.168.120.5, 192.168.120.6, 192.168.120.7, and so on. This address configuration enables computers on your network to share a single Internet connection at 213.141.56.8.

Hide-mode NAT enables multiple computers to communicate with the Internet yet keep their IP addresses hidden from other computers on the Internet (see Figure 5-16). Computers on the Internet see only the NAT device's IP address; packets from internal hosts seem to be coming from the NAT device. This mode has disadvantages, however. First, you can hide only so many clients behind a single IP address. For most networks, this limitation isn't a big problem; for a large network, however, performance can degrade as the number of connections increases. In addition, hide-mode NAT doesn't work with some types of VPNs because the two endpoints must have unique addressing. Finally, hide-mode NAT uses only a single public IP address, so you can't provide other services, such as a Web server, unless you have another IP address for them.

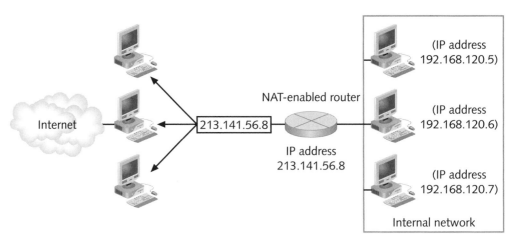

Figure 5-16 NAT in hide mode

NOTE A single NAT device essentially sets up a firewall for an internal network. In fact, any security scheme that shields computers from external attack is considered a firewall, regardless of whether the hardware or software device contains the label "firewall."

Static Mapping

Static mapping is a form of NAT in which internal IP addresses are mapped to external routable IP addresses on a one-to-one basis. Internal IP addresses are still hidden, but computers appear to have public routable IP addresses. Neither the public nor private IP addresses change dynamically; instead, they are static. Figure 5-17 shows a NAT device's static translation from private to public IP addresses.

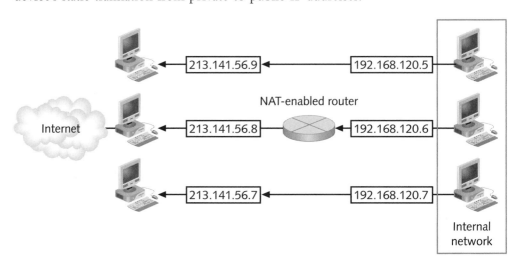

Figure 5-17 Static NAT translations

As you can see, each internal IP address has a corresponding public IP address that's visible to external hosts. External hosts think they're making a direct connection to an internal computer, but they're connecting to the NAT device, which forwards the request to an internal computer. Static NAT can be used when you have internal hosts that need more bandwidth instead of sharing available bandwidth with all other hosts.

NOTE
Because NAT devices function as a sort of go-between for internal and external computers, they can be confused with proxy servers. Proxy servers, too, shield internal hosts by forwarding requests from the Internet to computers, and vice versa. However, proxy servers rebuild packets before sending them on, and NAT simply forwards packets.

5

CHAPTER SUMMARY

- A firewall is hardware or software configured to block unauthorized access to a network. A firewall can be a combination of software and hardware components, and the term "firewall" can refer to all devices positioned on the network perimeter, whether they are hardware or software based.

- Firewalls aren't a standalone solution. Strong network security encompasses many components, including IDSs, firewalls, antivirus software, access control, and auditing.

- Software firewalls come in many varieties: freeware, shareware, and commercial enterprise. Hardware firewall appliances are more expensive, but they can handle more traffic. Hybrid firewalls combine the scalability of hardware devices with content filtering usually provided only by software firewalls.

- A proxy server forwards packets to and from the network and caches Web pages to speed up network performance. It also prevents direct connections between internal hosts and the Internet. Proxy servers work at the OSI model's application layer to interpret which application is making a request.

- A bastion host is a computer on the network perimeter that has been hardened with OS patches, authentication, and encryption. Bastion hosts can be combined with firewalls and packet-filtering devices for extra security and can provide Web, FTP, e-mail, and other network services. A honeypot is a vulnerable computer placed on the network perimeter to draw attackers' attention away from critical systems.

- Network Address Translation (NAT) conceals the IP addresses of internal hosts from external systems. NAT also enables networks to use private IP addressing for internal hosts, thus conserving public IP addresses. Hide-mode NAT conceals multiple IP addresses behind a single IP address; static NAT maps each internal IP address to a public IP address.

Key Terms

bastion host — A computer on the network perimeter that has been hardened with OS patches, authentication, and encryption.

change management — The process of documenting changes to hardware or software, which helps administrators roll back a configuration correctly if changes have an adverse affect.

dependency services — Services a computer system needs to function correctly. Key system processes usually depend on other processes to function.

firewall — Hardware or software configured to block unauthorized access to a network.

firewall appliances — Hardware devices with firewall functionality.

hardened — The process of making a computer more secure by eliminating unnecessary software and services, closing potential openings, and protecting information with encryption and authentication.

hide-mode mapping — NAT mode used to hide multiple private IP addresses behind one public IP address.

honeypot — A computer placed on the network perimeter to attract attackers and divert them from internal hosts.

hybrid firewall — A product that combines features of hardware and software firewalls in one package.

proxy server — Software that forwards packets to and from the network and caches Web pages to speed up network performance.

stateful packet filters — Similar to stateless packet filters, except they also determine whether to allow or block packets based on information about current connections.

stateless packet filters — Simple filters that determine whether to allow or block packets based on information in protocol headers.

state table — A file maintained by stateful packet filters that contains a record of all current connections.

static mapping — A NAT mode used to map internal IP addresses to external routable IP addresses on a one-to-one basis.

Review Questions

1. A firewall can do which of the following? (Choose all that apply.)

   a. Screen traffic for viruses.

   b. Prevent theft of proprietary information.

   c. Filter traffic based on rules.

   d. Provide a layer of protection for the network.

2. A firewall is an effective standalone security solution. True or False?

3. Name three functions most firewalls can't handle that need to be performed by other software products.

4. Stateless packet filters allow or block packets based on which of the following?

    a. status of the connection

    b. information in protocol headers

    c. state table

    d. packets that have been handled previously

5. Which of the following is an advantage of using a software firewall rather than a hardware firewall?

    a. throughput

    b. reliability

    c. cost

    d. availability

6. Which of the following is an advantage of using a hardware firewall rather than a software firewall? (Choose all that apply.)

    a. scalability

    b. cost

    c. ease of maintenance

    d. increased throughput

7. Almost every type of firewall depends on what configurable feature for its effectiveness?

    a. network connection

    b. state table

    c. rule base

    d. management console

8. Which of the following functions can a bastion host perform? (Choose all that apply.)

    a. FTP server

    b. e-mail server

    c. security management server

    d. domain controller

9. A packet filter between a proxy server and the Internet needs to route traffic to and from which of the following? (Choose all that apply.)

    a. Internet

    b. internal network

    c. DMZ

    d. proxy server

10. Which of the following can hide internal IP addresses from the Internet? (Choose all that apply.)

    a. packet filters

    b. NAT

    c. proxy servers

    d. state tables

11. Hardening a bastion host involves which of the following? (Choose all that apply.)

    a. disabling unnecessary services

    b. removing unnecessary accounts

    c. installing current patches

    d. selecting an OS

12. Which accounts should you delete on the bastion host?

    a. all system accounts

    b. all accounts

    c. all user accounts

    d. default administrator accounts

13. Goals of proxy servers include which of the following? (Choose all that apply.)

    a. enhancing network communication performance

    b. caching user account data and passwords

    c. hiding internal hosts

    d. facilitating communications between internal hosts and the Internet

14. What are the advantages of NAT? (Choose all that apply.)

    a. rebuilding packets from scratch

    b. storing files in a cache for improved performance

    c. shielding internal IP addresses from attackers

    d. using private IP addressing internally instead of public IP addresses

15. Why would you use static NAT mapping rather than hide-mode mapping? (Choose all that apply.)

   a. Static NAT mapping translates internal addresses to one IP address.

   b. Hide-mode mapping doesn't work with some VPNs.

   c. Static NAT mapping assigns IP addresses dynamically.

   d. With hide-mode mapping, performance on large networks could degrade as the number of connections increases.

16. What do proxy servers do that NAT doesn't do?

   a. perform encryption

   b. rebuild packets

   c. packet filtering

   d. work with static IP addresses

17. When you're stopping or removing services, you should be careful not to disable any _____ services.

   a. system

   b. remote access

   c. dependency

   d. encryption

5

HANDS-ON PROJECTS

HANDS-ON PROJECTS

Hands-On Project 5-1: Filtering UDP Traffic

Time Required: 10 minutes

Objective: Use advanced TCP/IP properties to configure UDP filtering.

Description: When you install and configure ZoneAlarm to send you alert messages, you'll probably notice many alerts from computers attempting to connect to yours on a UDP port. Because UDP is used less often than TCP and considered less secure than TCP, you might be inclined to block it altogether. However, computers on your network as well as your DNS server and your ISP's servers commonly use UDP. One way to block UDP communications selectively is to use Windows 2000/XP's built-in TCP/IP filtering function.

In this project, you configure which services are allowed to use specific UDP ports. To enter these ports, you need to know which services to run. You can review a list of ports at *www.iana.org/assignments/port-numbers*. For this project, you enable the common UDP ports for DNS (port 53) and NetBIOS (port 137).

1. Open Control Panel, and in Category view, click **Network and Internet Connections**.

2. Click **Network Connections**, right-click the icon representing your computer's connection to the Internet, and then click **Properties**.

3. In the General tab of the Properties dialog box, click **Internet Protocol (TCP/IP)**, and then click the **Properties** button.

4. Click the **Advanced** button, and then click the **Options** tab.

5. Click **TCP/IP filtering**, and then click the **Properties** button.

6. In the TCP/IP Filtering dialog box, click to enable the **EnableTCP/IP Filtering (All adapters)** check box. In the UDP Ports column, click the **Permit Only** option button.

7. Click **Add**. In the Add Filter dialog box, type **53**, and then click **OK**. The number 53 is listed under UDP Ports.

8. Click **Add** again. In the Add Filter dialog box, type **137**, and then click **OK**. The number 137 is added to the list of UDP ports.

9. Click **OK** to close all dialog boxes. Close any remaining open windows to return to the Windows desktop. If you're prompted to restart your computer, click **No**.

CASE PROJECTS

CASE
PROJECTS

Case Project 5-1: Firewall Planning for Green Globe

Green Globe's primary concern is ensuring strong security for the sensitive data on its computers. Your supervisor on this project wants you to begin planning to incorporate firewalls for protecting data and remote access. Before you begin, you need your most recent network design and materials from previous chapters for reference.

1. Using the documentation you have completed so far, evaluate types of firewalls. You can use a combination of hardware and software firewalls at the network and desktop level. Remember that Green Globe's security architecture must comply with government regulations.

2. Create a report explaining each type of firewall, where it should be located, and the functions it offers. (*Hint*: Potential locations include between the DMZ and Internet, on desktops, securing the Web server, and so on.)

3. Create a list of the hardware and software you need for your firewall design.

6

CONFIGURING FIREWALLS

After reading this chapter and completing the exercises, you will be able to:

♦ Design common firewall configurations

♦ Establish a set of rules and restrictions for a firewall

♦ Decide when to use user, session, or client authentication

You can incorporate firewalls into your security infrastructure in many different ways. You can use one or more firewalls to provide protection for publicly accessible Web or FTP servers, protect file servers from external attack while allowing internal hosts access, and more. In fact, you can design your security architecture to fit any requirements you have. In this chapter, you learn about common configurations for firewalls and how to select one best suited to your needs.

After determining the best firewall configuration for your network defense needs, you can set up firewall rules and restrictions to protect your network. This chapter explains considerations for creating a rule base and setting up a firewall policy.

Authentication, used to control access to your network, is an essential part of a network defense program. This chapter describes how to determine what to authenticate and explains the major types of authentication: user, client, and session authentication.

DESIGNING FIREWALL CONFIGURATIONS

You've learned about routing, router security, and firewalls. In this chapter, you see how these components are combined in the network perimeter to protect the internal network and provide and protect services in the DMZ. Businesses need a variety of services in their networks and on the Internet. They also need a network area where resource access is more flexible, allowing internal hosts and external systems to gain access. The problem is providing adequate access without jeopardizing confidential or mission-critical areas. To accomplish this goal, perimeter networks host Web servers, e-commerce servers, FTP servers, remote access services, databases, DNS servers, and more. Securing these systems requires firewalls, but firewalls can't do the job alone.

To design a secure perimeter network, you must understand how firewalls and other security measures are combined with bastion hosts, Network Address Translation (NAT), proxy servers, and authentication methods to provide the versatility needed for secure productivity. You've already learned about bastion hosts, NAT, and proxy servers in Chapter 5, and authentication methods are covered later in this chapter. In the following sections, you learn how to deploy firewalls in different ways on a network: as part of a screening router, a dual-homed host, a screened host, a screened subnet DMZ, multiple DMZs, multiple firewalls, or a reverse firewall setup.

NOTE

A secure perimeter network can also include Internet Protocol Security (IPSec), virtual private networks (VPNs), and intrusion detection systems (IDSs) and might also provide wireless access. These topics are covered in later chapters.

Screening Routers

A single router on the network perimeter configured to filter packets is the simplest kind of firewall. This **screening router** determines whether to allow or deny packets based on their source and destination IP addresses or other information in their headers (see Figure 6-1).

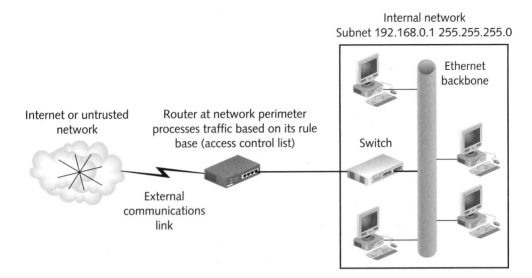

Figure 6-1 A screening router

However, this device alone doesn't stop many attacks, especially those using spoofed or manipulated IP address information. This type of router should be combined with a firewall or proxy server for added protection.

Dual-Homed Hosts

A common arrangement is installing firewall or other security software (such as a proxy server) on a **dual-homed host**, a computer configured with more than one network interface. The capability to forward packets is disabled on the computer, so only the firewall software can forward traffic from one interface to another (see Figure 6-2). Users connected to the Internet also use this type of setup. Rules are established so that the firewall moves traffic between the Internet and a home computer or network.

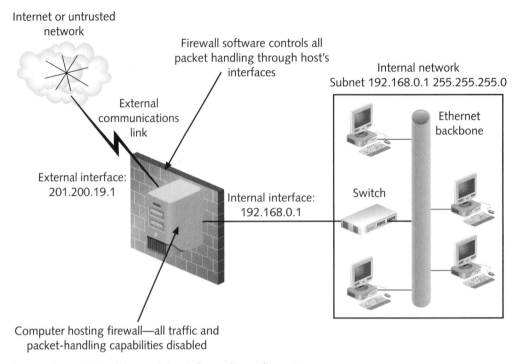

Figure 6-2 A dual-homed host firewall configuration

Originally, the term "dual-homed host" was used for a computer equipped with two separate network interface cards (NICs), with one NIC for each interface. Now this term is used to describe the setup in Figure 6-2, with a firewall placed between the network and the Internet. A dual-homed host is limited in the security it can provide because the firewall depends on the same computer used for day-to-day communication. Therefore, any problem with the host computer weakens the firewall. The big disadvantage is that the host serves as a single point of entry to the network, so attackers have to break through only one layer of protection to infiltrate the network. Therefore, a multilayered defense-in-depth (DiD) arrangement is even more important with a dual-homed host.

NOTE

The computer hosting firewall software might have more than two network interfaces. It might be connected to the demilitarized zone (DMZ), the Internet, and the internal network, for example. In that case, it's called a "multihomed host."

Screened Hosts

A **screened host** setup is similar to a dual-homed host, but the main difference is that a router is often added between the host and the Internet to carry out IP packet filtering.

It's essentially a combination of the dual-homed host and screening router configurations, blending the two for an added layer of functionality, security, and performance (see Figure 6-3). You might choose this setup for perimeter security on a corporate network, for instance. A common enhancement is having a screened host function as an application gateway or proxy server. The only network services allowed to pass through the proxy server are those for which proxy applications are already available.

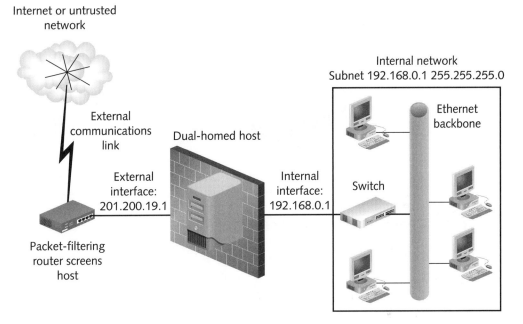

Figure 6-3 A screened host

Screened Subnet DMZs

As you learned in Chapter 1, a DMZ is a subnet of publicly accessible servers placed outside the internal network. Because this subnet contains important information, a packet filter or other security software should screen the DMZ. A common solution is making the servers a subnet of the firewall (see Figure 6-4).

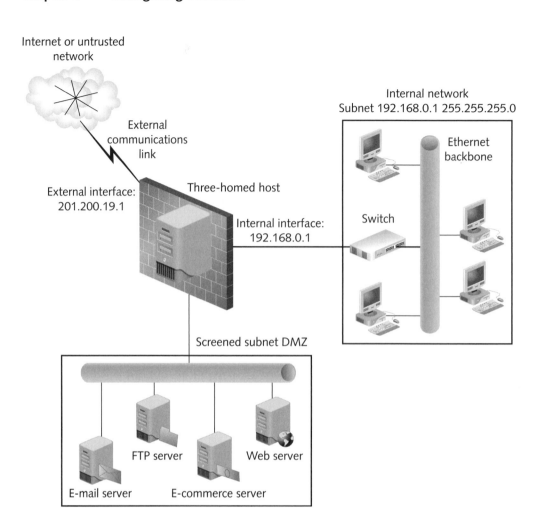

Figure 6-4 A screened subnet DMZ

Because the firewall protecting the DMZ is also connected to the Internet and can be connected to the internal network, it's often called a **three-pronged firewall**. You might choose this setup when you need to provide services to the public, such as an FTP server, a Web server, or an e-mail server, but want to make sure attackers can't access your Web site or FTP resources.

NOTE   The subnet attached to the firewall and contained in the DMZ is sometimes called a "service network" or "perimeter network" by those who dislike the military connotation of the term DMZ. The terms are used interchangeably in this book.

Multiple DMZ/Firewall Configurations

One DMZ isn't enough security for many large corporations that are connected to the Internet or do business online. To handle demand from the Internet and keep public servers' response time as fast as possible, you should set up multiple DMZs. Each DMZ is a **server farm**, a group of servers connected in a subnet that work together to receive requests with the help of **load-balancing software**. This software prioritizes and schedules requests and distributes them to servers based on each server's current load and processing power.

Installing clusters of servers in DMZs outside the internal network helps protect the internal network from becoming overloaded. Placing the company's Web server in the outer subnet mean it's better equipped to handle heavy traffic because there's less filtering of packets. If a Web server behind the firewall gets as many as 20,000 hits a minute, that amount of traffic could crash the server or seriously slow the firewall's performance as well as other traffic that needs to pass through. If the Web server is outside the protected network but in the DMZ, the firewall's performance isn't compromised. To protect the local network, inbound connectivity from the Web server to the internal network should be blocked, and access attempts should be logged carefully.

Each server farm/DMZ should be protected by its own firewall or packet-filtering router. One possible configuration is shown in Figure 6-5. The service networks don't necessarily need to be protected from one another; instead, they feed into a single router, which sends traffic to the internal network. The service subnets aren't connected directly to the Internet; a packet-filtering router screens each one.

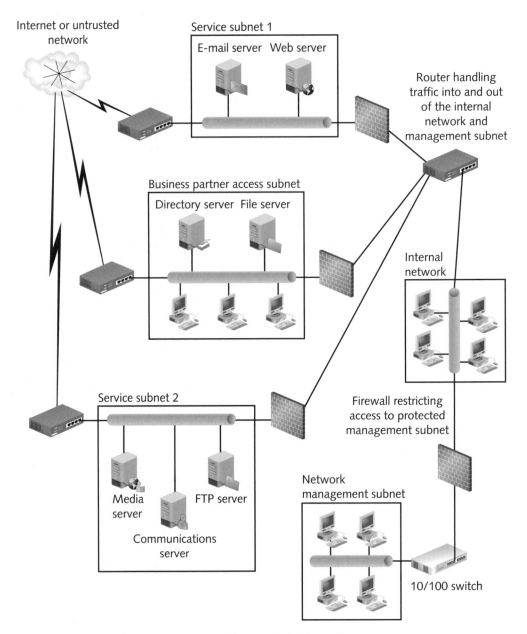

Figure 6-5 Multiple DMZs protected by multiple firewalls

A service network has also been established to allow sharing resources with a business partner. This network configuration should be handled with care, however, because some information could be sensitive; in this situation, placing a firewall between the packet-filtering router and business partner access subnet might be wise. A screened DMZ is also adequate, as long as the screening router is configured carefully, strict authentication methods are used, and access controls are placed on information at the file and folder level. Encrypting sensitive data can add another layer of protection.

Finally, an additional firewall is placed inside the internal network to protect network management systems. The advantage of locating management software out of band—outside the internal network on a protected subnet of its own—is that management servers get an extra level of protection against intruders. If intruders gain control of the firewall or network management software, they might be able to access hosts on the network.

TIP

A protected subnet in an already protected internal network could be used as an extra layer of protection for confidential information, such as customer or personnel data. The extra layer might protect servers from disgruntled employees in the organization as well as attackers from the Internet.

Multiple Firewall Configurations

As you learned in Chapter 1, DiD means multiple security devices configured to work together to provide protection. DiD makes use of many different layers of network security. To achieve this level of protection, many organizations find that they need more than one firewall, either throughout the network or on a subnet. The following sections describe using two or more firewalls to protect not only an internal network, but also one DMZ, two DMZs, and branch offices that need to connect to the main office's internal network. In addition, multiple firewalls can help you achieve load distribution that keeps heavy traffic flowing through the gateway smoothly.

Protecting a DMZ with Multiple Firewalls

When multiple firewalls are deployed around the network perimeter, they can work together to balance the network's traffic load. When multiple firewalls are used together, they must be configured identically and use the same firewall software. That way, traffic coming from the Internet can be balanced between them by using routers or switches on either side (see Figure 6-6).

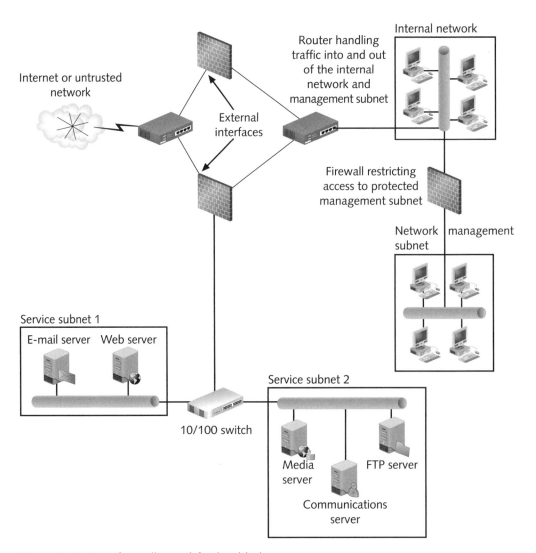

Figure 6-6 Two firewalls used for load balancing

The two firewalls in Figure 6-6 have an external interface on the Internet. You can also have one firewall with an interface on the Internet and the second with an interface on the internal network; the DMZ being protected is positioned between them. Using two firewalls helps in the following ways:

- One firewall can control traffic between the DMZ and the Internet, and the other can control traffic between the protected network and the DMZ.

- The second firewall can serve as a **failover firewall**, which is a backup that can be configured to switch on if the first one fails, thus ensuring uninterrupted service.

A major advantage of setting up a DMZ with multiple firewalls is that you can control where traffic goes in the three networks you're dealing with: the external network outside the DMZ, the external network within the DMZ, and the internal network behind the DMZ. You can identify certain protocols, such as outbound HTTP port 80, that should go to the external network within the DMZ and allow other protocols to pass through to the internal network.

Using multiple interior routers to connect your DMZ subnet to parts of your internal subnets can cause problems. For example, using Routing Information Protocol (RIP) on an internal system could determine that the most direct route to another internal system is through the DMZ. As a result, confidential internal traffic flows across your DMZ, where it can be intercepted if an attacker manages to break into a host computer. Having multiple interior routers also makes overall network configuration more difficult.

Activity 6-1: Designing a Failover Firewall

Time Required: 15 minutes

Objective: Analyze a set of requirements and design a configuration to meet those requirements.

Description: Your organization's security policy calls for your Web site to be online 95% to 100% of the time, even during a firewall failure caused by a denial-of-service (DoS) attack or other problem. You know that one way to ensure the availability of the Web server and other publicly accessible computers in your DMZ is to protect them with two firewalls. What are the requirements for this setup? How might you configure the two firewalls?

_____

_____

_____

_____

_____

_____

Protecting Branch Offices with Multiple Firewalls

A multinational corporation that needs to share information among branch offices in different locations can communicate securely by using a single security policy implemented by multiple firewalls. The main office has its own centralized firewall, which directs traffic for branch offices and their firewalls. The main office develops the security policy and deploys it through the centralized firewall with its rules on a dedicated computer called a **security workstation** (see Figure 6-7). Each branch office has its own firewall, but the main office develops and controls the security policy. The policy is then copied to other firewalls in the corporation.

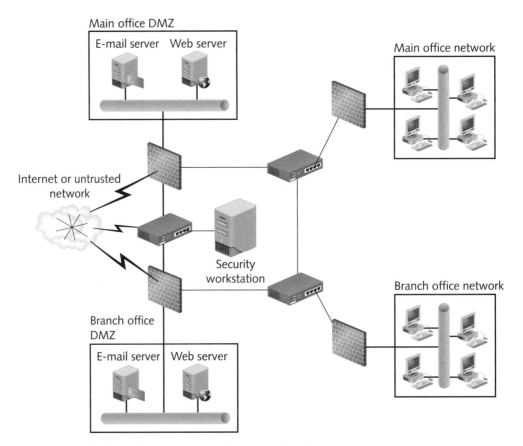

Figure 6-7 Multiple firewalls protecting branch offices

One notable aspect of Figure 6-7 is that the two firewalls have a path for communicating with one another and a router to direct traffic to each firewall. However, traffic from the Internet or the corporate network doesn't travel between the two firewalls; only traffic from the security workstation travels on the connection between DMZs, carrying configuration information to firewalls and receiving log file data from them.

Reverse Firewalls

Some forward-thinking companies install a **reverse firewall**, a device that monitors outgoing connections instead of trying to block incoming traffic. Sometimes the biggest threats to an internal network come from its own users. For example, a university makes certain applications available to researchers but restricts access to those applications to scientists who need them. Clever computer science students might try to break into the server storing these applications so that they can download and use them. A reverse firewall would help by monitoring outgoing connection attempts that originate from internal users and then filtering out unauthorized attempts. Reverse firewalls have other purposes. A company concerned about how its employees use the Web and other Internet services can set up a reverse firewall to log connections to Web sites. It can then block sites that are accessed repeatedly and considered unsuitable for employees to visit during work hours.

In a DoS or distributed denial of service (DDoS) attack, information floods out of a network from compromised computers (commonly called zombies), thus overloading the network. A reverse firewall, such as the hardware device Reverse Firewall sold by Cs3 (*www.cs3-inc.com/rfw.html*), inspects outgoing packets and tracks where they're originating from in the network. If the firewall detects many unexpected packets leaving the network, it sends a notification to the network administrator. This feature, however, could be part of any firewall and programmed into a hardware or software firewall so that you don't need to purchase a specialized reverse firewall.

6

NOTE

This chapter assumes you're building a firewall to protect your internal network from the Internet. However, you might also want to protect segments of the internal network from other segments—for instance, project development areas or segments where financial data or grades are stored. In these situations, internal firewalls can be positioned between two network segments or two organizations sharing a network. In this case, you need to set up packet-filtering rules that isolate the internal network from the Internet and from your bastion host. This way, if the bastion host is compromised, it won't lead to a compromise of the internal firewall. (Bastion hosts were covered in Chapter 5.)

TIP

Proxy servers also monitor traffic moving in the outbound direction—from the internal network to the Internet. However, proxy servers have the advantage of shielding information about internal computers by hiding internal IP addresses.

ACTIVITY

Activity 6-2: Monitoring Outbound Network Traffic

Time Required: 20 minutes

Objective: Analyze a problem scenario to determine a solution.

Description: Your company is concerned about the amount of employee time spent surfing entertainment and shopping Web sites during office hours. You're asked to come up with a way to monitor and track (and possibly block) connections from hosts on the internal network trying to make outbound connections to the Internet. How could you do this with a firewall?

_____

_____

_____

_____

_____

_____

Choosing a Firewall Configuration

Which firewall configuration is the best one for your needs? The advantage of many modern products is the amount of customization available and the capability to perform multiple functions, such as firewall and intrusion detection services. Remember that firewall setups aren't an either-or decision. You can combine a screened host with a multiple firewall setup, for instance; you can also have a reverse firewall in addition to a conventional firewall. Table 6-1 summarizes the advantages and disadvantages of each setup.

Table 6-1   Firewall configuration advantages and disadvantages

Configuration	Advantages	Disadvantages
Screening router	Simple, low cost; good for home applications if a stateful packet filter is used	Provides only minimal protection; viruses, Trojan programs, and some malformed packets might get through
Dual-homed host	Simple, economical; can provide effective protection if configured correctly	Provides a single point of entry (and fault); firewall depends entirely on the host computer
Screened host	Provides two layers of protection for home and small business networks	Provides a single point of entry (and fault); firewall depends on the host computer and router protecting it
Screened subnet DMZ	Protects public servers by isolating them from the internal network	Servers in the DMZ are highly vulnerable and need to be hardened
Multiple DMZ/firewalls	Provides layers of protection for a business network	Expensive
Single DMZ/two firewalls	Balances traffic load in high-traffic situations	Expensive
Branch offices/multiple firewalls	Provides protection for all offices in a corporate network as well as central administration	Firewalls must be purchased, installed, and configured at each office location
Reverse firewall	Monitors attack from inside the network; enables organizations to monitor user activity	Can slow down user access to external networks or other parts of the internal network

ESTABLISHING RULES AND RESTRICTIONS

After determining where packet-filtering devices should be positioned and their functions on the network, you need to establish the rule base that enables them to function. Most network security professionals agree that even the most full-featured firewall depends on a good **rule base**. This set of rules tells the firewall what action to take when a certain kind of traffic attempts to pass through. A simple firewall with well-constructed rules is more effective than a complex product with rules that don't block intrusion attempts.

A set of packet-filtering rules is often called an access control list (ACL) instead of a rule base.

What makes an effective firewall rule base? The following sections describe some points to consider:

- It should be based on the organization's security policy.
- It should include a firewall policy with rules for how applications can access the Internet.
- It should be as simple and short as possible.
- It should restrict access to ports and subnets on the internal network from the Internet.
- It should control Internet services.

This book refers to security policies as the basis of security, but they aren't included in the objectives for the Security Certified Program Exam SC0-451. Therefore, security policies aren't covered in detail in this book. Because they're so crucial to security, however, you should begin learning about them as soon as possible. Security policies and risk assessments are covered in *Guide to Strategic Infrastructure Security: Becoming a Security Network Professional* (Course Technology, 2008, ISBN 1418836613), which maps to the Security Certified Program Exam SC0-471.

Base the Rule Base on Your Security Policy

When you're configuring a firewall rule base, you have the opportunity to put your organization's security policy rules and procedures into practice. Certain elements of filtering packets are especially important to configuring rules and, therefore, implementing the organization's security policy:

- *Logging and auditing*—Most security policies require methods for detecting intrusions and other security problems, such as viruses.
- *Tracking*—The rule base should include a procedure for notifications so that you can follow response procedures in case of intrusions.
- *Filtering*—A primary objective of a rule base is to filter communications based on complex rules so that only traffic using approved protocols, ports, and source and destination IP addresses is allowed.
- *NAT*—The rule base should provide for concealing internal names and IP addresses from those outside the network.
- *Quality of Service (QoS)*—QoS rules can be set up to enable the firewall to maintain a baseline level of functionality, which can be specified in the organization's security policy.
- *Desktop security policy*—This policy enables you to specify the level of access remote users have when they log on to the network.

The following common guidelines should be reflected in the rule base to implement an organization's security policy:

- Employees can have access to the Internet with certain restrictions, such as content filtering or controls on downloads.

- The public can access the company's Web server and e-mail server.

- Only authenticated traffic can access the internal network.

- Employees aren't allowed to use instant-messaging software outside the internal network.

- Traffic from the company's ISP should be allowed.

- External traffic that attempts to connect to a port used by instant-messaging software should be blocked.

- Only the network administrator should be able to access the internal network directly from the Internet for management purposes.

Create a Firewall Policy for Application Traffic

A **firewall policy** is an addition to the security policy that describes how firewalls should handle application traffic, such as Web or e-mail applications. Risk assessment should provide a list of those applications and their threats and vulnerabilities, describe the impact if confidential data is compromised, and outline countermeasures for mitigating risks. Before developing a firewall policy, you must understand these factors because risk assessment results dictate whether firewalls block or allow your network's application traffic.

The firewall policy should explain how the firewall is set up, managed, and updated. Although each organization's needs are different, you follow the same general steps to create a firewall policy. First, you identify which network applications are needed and the vulnerabilities associated with each application. Next, you need to conduct a cost-benefit analysis to determine the most cost-effective and efficient method for securing application traffic. Remember that some traffic is more sensitive than others, and you must balance security and cost. Also, keep in mind that many networks have multiple firewalls at several locations, so you need to develop a traffic matrix such as the one in Table 6-2 for each location.

Table 6-2   Application traffic matrix

Application or service	Internal host type	Location	Host security policy	Firewall internal security policy	Firewall external security policy
FTP	Windows	Any	Client only; antivirus	Allow	Deny
FTP	UNIX	Any	Secure Shell (SSH); user ID/password; no anonymous traffic	Allow	Application proxy with user authentication
Telnet	Windows	Any	Client only	Allow	Application proxy with user authentication
Telnet	UNIX	Any	SSH	Allow	Application proxy with user authentication
NetBIOS over TCP/IP	Windows 95/98/NT	Any	Limit access to shares	Allow local domain only; deny all others	Deny

6

When the traffic matrix is finished, you can develop the firewall rule base. Firewalls enable you to control access to your computer or network by controlling access to particular applications. When computers listen for incoming connections on ports that certain applications use, such as instant-messaging programs, attackers can scan for these open ports. Firewall software gives you a way to block applications from accessing the Internet so that these ports aren't left open. If an application needs to be used, it can be flagged so that the user is prompted to specify whether access to the Internet is allowed. Typically, you have three options:

- *Allow*—The application can access the Internet at any time. (You'll probably want to establish this rule for Web browsers, e-mail applications, and other software used frequently.)

- *Block*—The application is blocked from accessing the Internet.

- *Ask or prompt*—The user is prompted when the application attempts to access the Internet.

Keep the Rule Base Simple

Keep the list of rules in your rule base as short as possible. The more complex the rule base is, the higher the chance of misconfiguring it. Some professionals suggest that a rule base contain no more than 30 rules and certainly no more than 50. Also, the shorter the rule base, the faster your firewall can process requests because it has fewer rules to review.

Typically, a firewall processes rules in a particular order. The rules are usually numbered 1, 2, 3, and so on, and a list of firewall rules is usually displayed in the form of a grid. The first cell in the grid is the rule number. Subsequent cells describe attributes the firewall should test for, such as an IP address or a protocol, and an action to be taken. Because rules are processed in order, the most important ones—the ones that should be processed first—are placed at the top of the list. (All firewalls have a way to reorder rules in the rule base.) It's a good idea to make the last rule in the rule base a **cleanup rule**, which is a rule that handles any other packets that haven't been covered in preceding rules. On a Cisco router, this cleanup rule is the explicit "deny all" statement at the end of an ACL.

When a packet hits a firewall, rules are tested one after another. As soon as a match is found, the action corresponding to the rule is followed. Usually, there are two possible actions: Allow (permit the packet to proceed through the firewall to its destination on the Internet or in the internal network) and Deny (drop the packet). Usually, no notification is sent to the sender for a Deny action because it might give attackers clues about the network's characteristics; the packet is simply dropped. A third option, Reject, typically isn't used because it notifies the sender and could give clues about the network.

Restrict Subnets, Ports, and Protocols

Packet filters can usually give you more control over what traffic can be blocked or allowed. The more flexibility you have, the better you can control specific types of traffic. The following sections give some examples of rules you can create to control traffic yet allow necessary connectivity.

Filtering by IP Addresses

One way to identify traffic is by IP address range. Some traffic comes from a network you trust, such as your own network or your ISP's servers, and shouldn't be blocked by the firewall. However, most firewalls start from the sensible premise that all traffic should be blocked by default, and you need to identify "trusted" networks whose communications should be allowed.

For instance, if your network subnet contains IP addresses in the range of 10.10.56.0 to 10.10.56.255, you would specify that the firewall regard them as "trusted," as shown in one of ZoneAlarm's configuration dialog boxes (see Figure 6-8). Remember that 10.10.56.0 is the subnet address and 10.10.56.255 is the broadcast address for this range, and they can't be used as valid IP addresses for hosts.

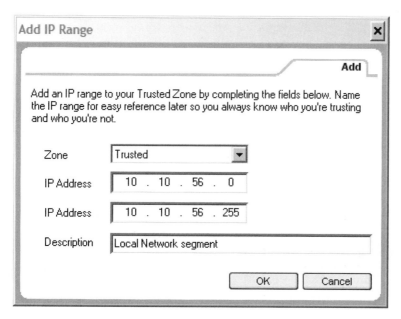

Figure 6-8   Identify trusted subnets or IP addresses

Filtering by Ports

TCP/IP and UDP transmit information by breaking it into segments of uniform length called packets (or datagrams). Packets can vary in length; however, what's important to remember is that a system using TCP or UDP sends packets of the same length in a transmission so that they can be sent and received more easily. A file might be divided into several packets, but all the packets are the same length.

Filtering by TCP or UDP port numbers is commonly called port filtering or protocol filtering. Using TCP or UDP port numbers can help you filter a wide variety of information, including SMTP and POP e-mail, NetBIOS sessions, Domain Name System (DNS) requests, and Network News Transfer Protocol (NNTP) newsgroup sessions. You can filter out everything but TCP port 80 for Web, TCP port 25 for e-mail, or TCP port 21 for FTP. Figure 6-9 shows the port-filtering process.

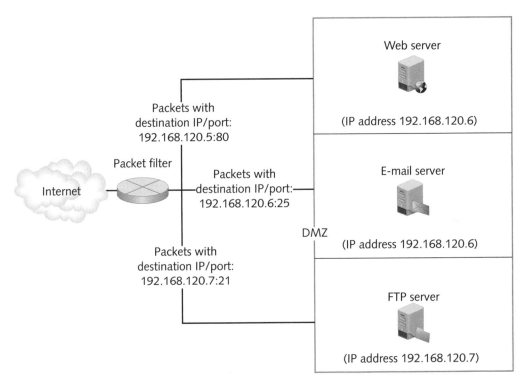

Figure 6-9 Port numbers direct packets to the client or server that needs them

Figure 6-9 indicates that ports are filtered by a router and directed to the correct combination of computer and software by their IP address and port number. The port numbers in this figure are technically correct; port 80 is reserved for HTTP Web pages, port 25 for SMTP e-mail, and so on. However, in practice, when two computers exchange information, they use two different port numbers: the port from which data is sent (the source port) and the port where the response data is received (the destination port). Network communication between two computers commonly uses different source and destination ports. (In fact, source and destination ports are rarely the same.) However, the fact that ports are different and the destination port is determined dynamically (determined on a per-connection basis and, therefore, impossible to predict) makes filtering by port number complicated.

NOTE   There isn't a magic solution to filtering services based on port number, especially when ports are above 1023 in the registered or dynamic port ranges IANA assigns. You have to know what services you're running on your network and what ports those services use; you block the ports you don't need and allow the ones you do. Refer to *www.iana.org/assignments/port-numbers* for current port number assignments.

For instance, on a Windows-based network, computers probably use the NetBIOS name service to find one another on NetBIOS ports 137, 138, and 139. NetBIOS traffic should originate inside your internal network and stay inside the firewall; any traffic from the Internet that attempts to use these ports should be dropped. You should also block inbound traffic that attempts to use ports assigned to other Windows networking services. Table 6-3 lists some examples of filtering common Windows services and ports. The EXT column refers to the external firewall.

Table 6-3   Filtering Windows services and ports

Rule	EXT	Protocol	Source IP	Source port	Destination IP	Destination port	Action	Service
1	X	TCP	Any	Any	Any	135	Deny	NetBIOS RPC
2	X	UDP	Any	Any	Any	135	Deny	NetBIOS RPC
3	X	TCP	Any	Any	Any	137	Deny	NetBIOS name service
4	X	UDP	Any	Any	Any	137	Deny	NetBIOS name service
5	X	TCP	Any	Any	Any	445	Deny	SMB/file sharing
6	X	UDP	Any	Any	Any	445	Deny	SMB/file sharing
7	X	TCP	Any	Any	Any	1720	Deny	NetMeeting
8	X	UDP	Any	Any	Any	1720	Deny	NetMeeting
9	X	TCP	Any	Any	Any	1755	Deny	Windows Media
10	X	UDP	Any	Any	Any	1755	Deny	Windows Media
11	X	TCP	Any	Any	Any	3389	Deny	Remote Desktop Protocol
12	X	UDP	Any	Any	Any	3389	Deny	Remote Desktop Protocol

NOTE   In Table 6-3, SMB stands for Server Message Block, and RPC means Remote Procedure Calls. RPC is a critical component of Windows communications, so be careful when filtering it. Be sure to check for dependencies, as with any service or protocol you're filtering.

UNIX also has its own set of services that should be blocked when they are inbound from the Internet. Table 6-4 lists some examples.

Table 6-4 Filtering UNIX services and ports

Rule	Protocol	Source IP	Source port	Destination IP	Destination port	Action	Service
1	TCP	Any	Any	Any	17	Deny	QOTD
2	UDP	Any	Any	Any	17	Deny	QOTD
3	TCP	Any	Any	Any	111	Deny	Portmapper
4	UDP	Any	Any	Any	111	Deny	Portmapper
5	TCP	Any	Any	Any	513	Deny	Remote Login
6	TCP	Any	Any	Any	514	Deny	Syslog
7	UDP	Any	Any	Any	514	Deny	Syslog
8	TCP	Any	Any	Any	635	Deny	mountd (NFS service)

CAUTION The problem with specifying a port number for filtering is that some applications, particularly instant-messaging programs, don't use a fixed port number when they reply to a client; they assign themselves dynamic port numbers, which are used only for the length of a particular communication. You have to filter these communications by IP address instead.

ACTIVITY

Activity 6-3: Adding Computers to a Trusted Zone

Time Required: 10 minutes

Objective: Specify trusted IP address ranges in ZoneAlarm.

Description: If you work on a network, you need to allow other computers to communicate with yours. By default, ZoneAlarm blocks all connections until you identify the computers that are allowed to access yours. The following steps add a computer to your trusted zone. (You installed ZoneAlarm in Activity 5-1.)

NOTE You need the IP addresses of other computers in your lab network, if you haven't already done so. Open a command prompt window, type ipconfig, and press Enter.

1. Open the ZoneAlarm window by double-clicking its taskbar icon.

2. Click **Firewall** in the list of program features.

3. Click the **Zones** tab to display a list of computers in your trusted zone. If only one machine is listed, you probably need to add others to your zone.

4. Click the **Add** button, and then click **IP Range** in the popup menu to open the Add IP Range dialog box.

5. In the first IP Address text box, enter the starting address for the first IP address in your lab network or other local network. Enter the ending address in the second IP Address text box. Enter a name for the network, and then click **OK**.

6. Click **Apply** to save the new configuration.

7. Minimize the ZoneAlarm window, and leave your system running for the next activity.

Filtering by Service

With some firewalls, you can filter by naming the service you want to use instead of specifying a port number. For example, instead of filtering port 23, you can simply specify the Telnet service. Remember that packets can also be filtered based on the ID field in the IP header. This method works much the same way for firewalls as it does for IDSs. Firewalls can also filter by the six TCP control flags you learned about in Chapter 2:

- URG (urgent)
- ACK (acknowledgement)
- PSH (push function)
- RST (reset the connection)
- SYN (synchronize sequence numbers)
- FIN (no more data from sender)

You have also learned about IP options, the set of optional flags in an IP header. Options add information to a packet, as in these examples:

- *Security*—This option enables hosts to send security parameters, handling restrictions, and other information.

- *Loose source and record routing*—This option enables the source computer to specify the routers used in forwarding the packet to its destination.

- *Strict source and record routing*—This option is the same as loose source and record routing, except the host computer must send the packet directly to the next address in the source route.

- *Internet timestamp*—This option provides a timestamp indicating when the packet was sent.

Packet-filtering rules should be tailored to meet a network's needs. However, every rule base should follow a few general practices:

- A firewall or packet filter that follows a "deny all" security policy should begin by allowing services selectively as needed and end by blocking all other traffic.

- The rule base should keep everyone except network administrators from connecting to the firewall. (Anyone who accesses the firewall can discover internal IP addresses and gain access to the internal network.)

6

- The rule base should block direct access from the Internet to any computers behind the firewall or packet filter. All inbound traffic, in other words, should be filtered first.
- The rule base should permit access to public servers in the DMZ and enable users to access the Internet.

A rule base, then, is a mixture of rules that selectively allow or deny access. Table 6-5 lists a typical set of rules that assume the firewall is at 192.168.120.1, the e-mail server is at 192.168.120.2, the Web server is at 192.168.120.3, and the DNS server is at 192.168.120.4. The internal network is represented by 192.168.120.0.

Table 6-5   A typical packet-filtering rule base

Rule	Source IP	Source port	Destination IP	Destina-tion port	Action	What it does
1	192.168.120.1	Any	Any	Any	Deny	Prevents the firewall from making any connections
2	Any	Any	192.168.120.1	Any	Deny	Prevents anyone from connecting to the firewall
3	192.168.120.0	Any	Any	Any	Allow	Allows internal users to access external computers
4	192.168.120.0	Any	192.168.120.4	53	Allow	Enables internal users to connect to the DNS server on port 53
5	Any	Any	192.168.120.2	25	Allow	Allows external and internal users to access the e-mail server via SMTP port 25
6	192.168.120.0	Any	192.168.120.2	110	Allow	Enables internal users to connect to the e-mail server using POP3 port 110
7	Any	Any	192.168.120.3	80	Allow	Enables both external and internal users to connect to the Web server on HTTP port 80
8	Any	Any	Any	Any	Deny	Blocks all traffic not covered by previous rules

NOTE   You can take one of two major approaches to security. The permissive approach leaves everything open and locks down only what must be secured on an as-needed basis. The restrictive approach locks everything down and opens only specific ports, protocols, and services that are needed.

Activity 6-4: Tracing a Blocked IP Address

Time Required: 15 minutes

Objective: Determine the source of packets logged by ZoneAlarm.

Description: ZoneAlarm blocks all external traffic unless you configure it to allow specific types of traffic. When you first start using the program, you're likely to get a flood of alert messages and corresponding log file entries for each connection attempt that's blocked. Some connections might be legitimate communications from your ISP. However, others might be from attackers. You can use the Tracert program, included with Windows XP (as well as Linux and other Windows versions), to determine whether the server from which the packet is originating is coming from your own ISP or school or from a server you don't recognize.

ZoneAlarm will probably ask whether to allow Tracert to access trusted and Internet zones. Allow the connection once only, so that Tracert isn't allowed access automatically in the future. Generally, if a program asks for access rights in ZoneAlarm and you didn't initiate any connections, deny access.

1. To use Tracert to determine a packet's origin, open a command prompt window, type **tracert *IPaddress*** (substituting the IP address you want to investigate), and press **Enter**.

2. Using the information you gathered in Step 1, determine which IP addresses aren't suspicious. To do this, contact your school's network administrator or the office managing Internet services, and ask what range of IP addresses are commonly used to give access to on-campus computers. If you use an ISP to connect to the Internet, contact the ISP and ask what IP address ranges it uses for customers.

3. Maximize the ZoneAlarm window (or, if necessary, double-click its taskbar icon).

4. To make sure alerts are on, click **Alerts & Logs** at the left of the ZoneAlarm window (see Figure 6-10), and click the **Log Viewer** tab, if necessary.

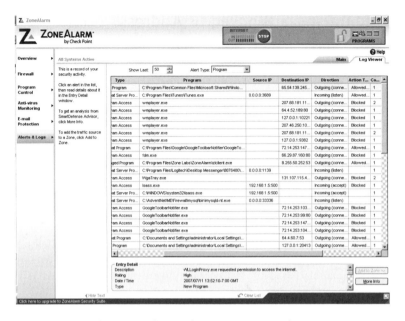

Figure 6-10 The ZoneAlarm Alerts & Logs window

5. Keep track of the kinds of alert messages you get. Do you receive any NetBIOS connection attempts from IP addresses that aren't on your network? What could be the source of a NetBIOS scan? Write down this information:

_____

_____

6. Do you get any attempts to connect on ports such as 1243 or 53001? Write down the port numbers in the Destination IP column after the IP addresses shown, and see whether any match the list of ports that well-known Trojan programs attempt to use. (Do an Internet search for "common Trojan ports" or similar keywords to find this information.)

_____

_____

7. Do you get any attempts to connect on port 137? This port is commonly used by Windows Internet Naming Service (WINS) registration. What could be the cause of this common connection attempt that's related to Windows networking services?

_____

8. When you're finished evaluating alert messages, click **Alerts & Logs** at the left, click the **Main** tab, and click the **Off** option button under Alert Events Shown to stop alert messages from being displayed.

9. Close all ZoneAlarm windows, and leave your system running for the next activity.

Control Internet Services

The goal in coming up with packet-filtering rules is to account for all possible ports a type of communication might use or for all variations of a protocol (for instance, passive and active FTP or standard and secure HTTP). Most businesses use the Internet heavily, and the challenge for security professionals is balancing the need for Internet connectivity with the need to secure network resources from the risks of Internet access. The following sections discuss how to control access to commonly used Web resources, such as surfing the Internet, sending and receiving e-mail, and using FTP as a secure means of centralized data storage.

Web Services Rules

A common priority of employees in a protected network is (not surprisingly) being able to surf the Web and exchange e-mails. Rules for accessing the Web need to cover standard HTTP traffic on TCP port 80 and Secure HTTP (S-HTTP) traffic on TCP port 443. These rules, shown in Table 6-6, assume that the local network has an IP address range of 207.177.178.0/24.

Table 6-6 Outbound Web access

Rule	Protocol	Transport protocol	Source IP	Source port	Destination IP	Destination port	Action
1	HTTP outbound	TCP	207.177.178.0/24	Any	Any	80	Allow
2	S-HTTP outbound	TCP	208.177.178.0/24	Any	Any	443	Allow

DNS Resolution

To connect to Web sites, users need to be able to resolve the fully qualified domain names (FQDNs) they enter, such as *course.com*, to their corresponding IP addresses by using DNS. Internal users connect to external hosts via a DNS server in the DMZ. DNS uses UDP port 53 for name resolution attempts and TCP port 53 for zone transfers. In addition, you need to set up rules that enable external clients to access computers in your network by using the same TCP and UDP ports, as shown in Table 6-7. (The rules in Table 6-7 assume that the DNS server is located at IP address 208.177.178.31.)

6

Table 6-7   DNS resolution rules

Rule	Protocol	Transport protocol	Source IP	Source port	Destination IP	Destina-tion port	Action
3	DNS outbound	TCP	208.177.178.31	Any	Any	53	Allow
4	DNS outbound	UDP	208.177.178.31	Any	Any	53	Allow
5	DNS inbound	TCP	Any	Any	208.177.178.31	53	Allow
6	DNS inbound	UDP	Any	Any	208.177.178.31	53	Allow

E-Mail Configuration

To set up configuration rules, assess whether your organization needs to accept incoming e-mail, whether internal users can access Web-based e-mail (such as Hotmail), and what e-mail clients your organization supports. This information helps ensure security without blocking e-mail access. Setting up firewall rules that permit filtering e-mails isn't simple, however. One reason is the variety of e-mail protocols that can be used:

- POP3 and IMAP4 for inbound mail transport
- SMTP for outbound mail transport
- Lightweight Directory Access Protocol (LDAP) for looking up e-mail addresses
- HTTP for Web-based e-mail service

To keep things simple, consider a configuration that uses only POP3 and SMTP for inbound and outbound e-mail, respectively. However, Secure Sockets Layer (SSL) encryption (a form of encryption between Web server and client) should be used for additional security. Table 6-8 outlines rules for e-mail access, which assume that the SMTP mail server is located at 208.177.178.29. Note that the S following a protocol, such as POP3/S, indicates SSL encryption.

Table 6-8   E-mail rules

Rule	Protocol	Transport protocol	Source IP	Source port	Destination IP	Destination port	Action
7	POP3 outbound	TCP	208.177.178.0/24	Any	Any	110	Allow
8	POP3/S outbound	TCP	208.177.178.0/24	Any	Any	995	Allow
9	POP inbound	TCP	Any	Any	208.177.178.0/24	110	Allow
10	POP3/S inbound	TCP	Any	Any	208.177.178.0/24	995	Allow
11	SMTP outbound	TCP	208.177.178.29	Any	Any	25	Allow
12	SMTP/S outbound	TCP	208.177.178.29	Any	Any	465	Allow
13	SMTP inbound	TCP	Any	Any	208.177.178.29	25	Allow
14	SMTP/S inbound	TCP	Any	Any	208.177.178.29	465	Allow

FTP Transactions

Two kinds of FTP transactions can take place on networks: active FTP or passive FTP. The rules you set up for FTP need to support two separate connections: TCP 21, the FTP control port, and TCP 20, the FTP data port. If some clients in your network support active FTP, you can't specify a port because the client can establish a connection with the FTP server at any port above 1023. Instead, you specify the IP address of your FTP server (in this example, 208.177.178.25), as shown in Table 6-9.

Table 6-9   FTP rules

Rule	Protocol	Transport protocol	Source IP	Source port	Destination IP	Destination port	Action
15	FTP control inbound	TCP	Any	Any	208.177.178.0/25	21	Allow
16	FTP data inbound	TCP	208.177.178.0/25	20	Any	Any	Allow
17	FTP PASV (passive)	TCP	Any	Any	208.177.178.0/25	Any	Allow
18	FTP control outbound	TCP	208.177.178.0/25	Any	Any	21	Allow
19	FTP data outbound	TCP	Any	20	208.177.178.25	Any	Allow

ICMP Message Type

Internet Control Message Protocol (ICMP) functions as a sort of housekeeping protocol for TCP/IP, helping networks cope with communication problems. The downside is that because ICMP packets have no authentication method to verify the packet recipient, attackers can attempt man-in-the-middle attacks, in which they impersonate the intended recipient. They can also send ICMP Redirect packets to direct traffic to a computer they control outside the protected network. A firewall/packet filter must be able to determine whether an ICMP packet, based on its message type, should be allowed to pass.

Table 6-10 lists some rules you can use to block common ICMP message types. The INT and EXT (internal and external) columns are left empty for Rules 1 and 7 so that those rules can apply to both inbound and outbound traffic. Rule 7 is a cleanup rule that drops all ICMP packets that haven't been filtered by previous rules.

Table 6-10   Filtering ICMP message types

Rule	INT	EXT	Protocol	ICMP type	Source IP	Source port	Destination IP	Destination port	Action
1			ICMP	Source Quench	Any	Any	Any	Any	Deny
2	X		ICMP	Echo Request	Any	Any	Any	Any	Deny
3		X	ICMP	Echo Reply	Any	Any	Any	Any	Deny
4	X		ICMP	Destination Unreachable	Any	Any	Any	Any	Deny
5		X	ICMP	Redirect	Any	Any	Any	Any	Deny
6		X	ICMP	Destination Unreachable	Any	Any	Any	Any	Deny
7			ICMP		Any	Any	Any	Any	Deny

Activity 6-5: Designing a Rule Base

Time Required: 30 minutes

Objective: Create a basic rule base for packet filtering.

Description: In this activity, you configure a set of basic rules for packet filtering for a network with the following characteristics: The internal network is represented by 192.168.120.0; the firewall is hosted at 192.168.120.1; the e-mail server is at 192.168.120.2; the Web server is at 192.168.120.3; and the DNS server is at 192.168.120.4.

You might find it helpful to use a table similar to Table 6-10 for writing your rules, although you can use the lines supplied in the following steps. Drawing the network configuration can also help you visualize the flow of traffic.

1. Create a rule that allows internal hosts to access the external network:

   _____

   _____

2. Create a rule that prevents any access to the firewall:

   _____

   _____

3. Create a rule that allows internal and external access to the e-mail server and Web server:

   _____

   _____

4. Create a rule that allows internal access to the DNS server:

   _____

   _____

5. For extra credit, what rule involving the firewall could you add?

   _____

   _____

6

AUTHENTICATING USERS

Authentication is the process of identifying users who are authorized to access the network. Many full-featured firewalls and IDSs handle this important task in a network defense program. In general, authentication depends on exchanging information that tells one entity that another entity is recognized as an authorized user. That information can be a password; a long encrypted block of code called a key; a checksum (a formula for verifying digital information); a physical object, such as a smart card; or biometric information from fingerprints, retina scans, or voiceprints. The following sections describe authentication schemes you can use when configuring a firewall.

Step 1: Deciding What to Authenticate

You're probably familiar with the type of authentication you use to get e-mail, access a file server, or dial up your ISP. Authentication by a firewall adds another level of security to these logons. When a connection is made to the firewall, you can have the firewall authorize it by requesting a username and password or by exchanging information "behind the scenes" so that users don't have to log on at every session. Of course, not all firewalls perform authentication, and the ones that do might handle only simple user authentication. In general, there are three different types of authentication—user, client, and session authentication—explained in the following sections.

User Authentication

User authentication is the process of identifying a person who has been authorized to access network resources. A user who submits the correct credentials can log on to the network from any location or any computer, which offers a measure of flexibility. You don't need to require users to log on every time they access the firewall; instead, you can configure the authentication to be automatic and based on the exchange of keys.

First, you define users and groups. To make management easier, you can assign a user to a group and set up access rules for that group instead of configuring each user's access rules separately. On a large network, specifying individual rights can become unmanageable and prone to errors. You can also specify source and destination addresses, which allows you to restrict resources the group is allowed to access.

In addition, you can specify time-based restrictions that control when a user is allowed to access the network, such as only on weekdays during daytime hours. Setting time-based restrictions adds another level of security if you don't have IT staff available around the clock to handle intrusion attempts. By blocking authorized access during overnight hours, you make it more difficult for attackers to launch exploits in the middle of the night.

If you prevent users from accessing the network on evenings or weekends, you might run into complaints from employees who need to work after hours. Make sure employees don't need to work during off hours before you set time-based restrictions.

Client Authentication

Client authentication is the process of granting access to network resources based on a source IP address, computer MAC address, or computer name rather than user information. As with user authentication, the identification process can be automatic or manual. If you require computers to authenticate themselves manually, users have to enter a username or password. Manual authentication requires extra effort for users to access the resources they want, but it increases security because you restrict access based on the source computer *and* username/password in one process.

If IP addresses on your network are assigned dynamically and change often, enterprise-level firewalls, such as Check Point NGX, account for this by using computer names (such as Email Server) rather than IP addresses for client authentication.

Even if an intruder steals a user's username and password, having that user log on with client authentication means the computer could be accessed only with the required IP address—or by spoofing the IP address, which the intruder would also have to obtain.

Session Authentication

Session authentication is the process of authorizing a user or computer on a per-connection basis by using authentication software installed on the client computer exchanging information with the firewall. Session authentication gives users more flexibility than user or client authentication; it enables any user and any computer (configured with the client software) to access network resources. The connection between the client computer and firewall is authorized instead of the person or a machine name or address.

In session authentication, the client computer and firewall authenticate in the background; however, the user making the connection does need to enter a password. You can configure session authentication so that a user is asked to enter a password every time a file or other resource is requested, once per session, or after a specified number of minutes of inactivity. The third option prevents unauthorized users from working at a machine connected to a protected resource that the original user has abandoned.

How do you decide which type of authentication is right for your needs? Table 6-11 compares the advantages and disadvantages of these three approaches.

Table 6-11   User, client, and session authentication

Method	Advantages	Disadvantages
User authentication	Gives the user flexibility in being able to access the network from any location	If username/password information is stolen, an unauthorized user can gain access
Client authentication	Provides better security than user authentication; can be configured to work with all applications and services	User must work at a computer configured for a client authentication
Session authentication	Gives the user the most flexibility; provides both password and session authentication	The Session Authentication Agent must be installed on each client computer

Step 2: Deciding How to Authenticate

Determining the type of authentication to use depends, in part, on that method's level of security, which is largely based on the type of information exchanged to verify the user or computer's identity. When you make a purchase at a retail store, often you're asked to show an ID card and sign a receipt to verify your identity. Over a network, computers or users present other types of digital information to declare who they are. The following sections examine types of information firewalls can exchange with clients for authentication purposes.

Password Security

Password-based authentication, in which a username and password are compared against a database of approved users, is probably the simplest and most straightforward authentication.

However, because passwords can be lost, cracked, or misappropriated by unauthorized users, some variations on the usual password system have been developed for increased security. Firewalls can use a number of password systems, including:

- *OS password*—The firewall refers to the user's password stored on the host computer's OS for authentication.

- *Firewall password*—Some firewalls include their own system of user passwords, such as the "enable" password on Cisco routers and PIX firewalls.

- *S/Key password*—S/Key uses a special application to generate a one-time encrypted password. The user is given the password and enters it once to authenticate. The password is not used again.

- *SecurID*—This form of two-factor authentication from RSA Security (*www.rsasecurity.com*) consists of a password (something the user knows) combined with something the user possesses (a small electronic device called a **token** that generates a random number every 60 seconds). Combining a random number with a password produces a one-time combination with secure authentication.

TIP

To learn more about security tokens, visit the RSA Security Web site (*www.rsasecurity.com*). RSA Security sells a variety of tokens for the SecurID system. According to RSA, SecurID has been used for 15 years with no reported breaches.

The OS password system is simple but won't work if the firewall is hosted on a stand-alone computer because users probably won't have an account on that computer. The S/Key one-time password system is far more secure and highly configurable. To use S/Key authentication, a seed is used to generate a one-time password. You can usually specify the number of one-time passwords generated by the seed and the secret password. You can also generate a list of passwords used in succession. These password lists are one type of one-time password. The other type is the challenge-response system, such as MS-CHAP in Windows. In this system, the client computer receives an identifier and then submits a challenge value. The authentication server or firewall returns a response value that the user submits to complete the process.

Smart Cards and Tokens

As mentioned, objects that a user possesses can be combined with passwords to create secure two-factor authentication. The most common objects are smart cards and tokens. You're probably familiar with smart cards in the form of credit cards and ATM cards; they're small plastic cards with a magnetic stripe that stores information about the card-holder. For smart cards to work, the user's computer needs a card reader installed.

Any object that enables users to authenticate themselves with a network can also be called a token. A smart card is a form of a token; other types are handheld or key fob electronic devices that generate random numbers changed periodically, such as RSA

Security's SecurID system. The user authenticates by entering the current number from the token as well as a PIN or password. Although smart cards and other tokens can be lost or stolen, requiring a PIN or password makes it difficult for a thief to use them.

Public and Private Keys

You use a password when you want to authenticate yourself on a network. Computers can also authenticate themselves to one another (or to programs that use encryption, such as enterprise-level firewalls) by exchanging codes. Because of computers' power in carrying out calculations and storing information, the codes they exchange can be long and complicated. The longer the code and the more complex the formula used to create it, the more secure the level of authentication.

The codes that computers exchange to be authenticated are called keys, which are blocks of encrypted code generated by mathematical formulas called algorithms. Keys are very long (1024, 2048, or 4096 bits or even longer) and, therefore, difficult (and sometimes nearly impossible) to crack. Keys can be issued to people as well as to computers. A popular and secure form of authentication on the Internet, **public key cryptography**, authenticates through the exchange of public and private keys.

How Public Key Cryptography Works

Data encrypted with your public key can be decrypted only with your private key. Figure 6-11 shows a simplified view of the way public key cryptography works.

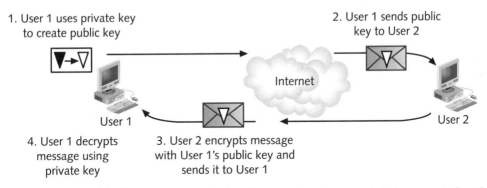

Figure 6-11 Public key cryptography involves exchanging a public key created with a private key

The encryption scheme shown in Figure 6-11 enables you to distribute a public key freely. Only you can read data encrypted with this key. In general, to send encrypted data to someone, you encrypt it with the recipient's public key, and the recipient decrypts it by means of the corresponding private key. Compared with symmetric key encryption (in which the same key is used rather than a pair of public and private keys), public key cryptography requires more computation, so it's not always suitable for large amounts of data.

The reverse of the encryption scheme shown in Figure 6-11 also works: Data encrypted with your private key can be decrypted only with your public key. This scheme isn't the best way to encrypt confidential data, however, because anyone with your public key could decrypt the data. Nevertheless, private key cryptography is useful because you can use your private key to sign data with your digital signature—an important requirement for e-commerce and other commercial applications of cryptography. Web browsers can then use your public key to confirm that the message was signed with your private key and hasn't been tampered with since being signed.

Digital Signatures

Encryption and decryption address the problem of eavesdropping but don't address two other security issues: tampering and impersonation. A **digital signature** is an attachment to an e-mail or other message that enables the recipient to verify the sender's identity. Some firewalls can generate digital signatures so that network users can identify themselves to one another. A digital signature provides tamper detection and identity verification with a mathematical function called a **message digest** (also called a one-way hash; a code of fixed length produced by processing input through a mathematical function). A message digest has the following characteristics:

- The value of the hash is unique for the hashed data. Any change in the data, even deleting or altering a single character, results in a different value.

- The content of the hashed data can't, for all practical purposes, be deduced from the hash, which is why it's called "one-way."

Instead of encrypting data, the signing software creates a one-way hash of it and then uses your private key to encrypt the hash. The encrypted hash along with other information, such as the hashing algorithm, creates a digital signature.

To validate data integrity, the receiving software uses the signer's public key to decrypt the hash and then uses the algorithm that calculated the original hash to generate a new one-way hash of the same data. (Information about the hashing algorithm is sent with the digital signature.) Finally, the receiving software compares the new hash against the original hash. If the two hashes match, the recipient can be certain that the public key used to decrypt the digital signature corresponds to the private key used to create the digital signature. If they don't match, the data might have been tampered with since it was signed, or the signature might have been created with a private key that doesn't correspond to the signer's public key.

You're probably familiar with Message Digest version 5 (MD5). Although MD5 was a great improvement over its predecessor, MD4, serious security vulnerabilities have been discovered, making its use for security purposes inadvisable. Secure Hash Algorithm version 1 (SHA-1) is used more commonly now. SHA-1 includes several different algorithms and is currently the standard of the U.S. government. However, a successful attack against it was discovered in February 2005, and more have been launched since then. Therefore, SHA-1 is now considered broken and is expected to be phased out by 2012 in favor of SHA-2, a more secure version. SHA-2 uses four hashing functions and longer digest lengths, and early examinations have revealed no weaknesses.

For more information on cryptography, refer to *Guide to Strategic Infrastructure Security: Becoming a Security Network Professional* (Course Technology, 2008, ISBN 1418836613).

6

Step 3: Putting It All Together

Passwords, tokens, keys, digital signatures, and certificates are often used on the Internet to secure communications and authenticate users, which has an impact on firewalls because they provide a gateway for communication between external computers on the Internet and internal network computers. If users on the internal network use encryption to authenticate themselves, that communication goes through the firewall. Firewalls, therefore, must be able to recognize and process a variety of authentication methods to enable users to make purchases from Web sites, send and receive encrypted e-mail, or log on to databases. The following sections explain some common authentication methods that firewalls use.

Secure Hypertext Transfer Protocol

Secure Hypertext Transfer Protocol (S-HTTP) uses a common security protocol, such as Secure Sockets Layer (SSL) or Transport Layer Security (TLS), to encrypt communication between a Web server and a Web browser. SSL, used more often than TLS, involves exchanging public and private keys and uses a digital certificate to verify the server's identity. SSL doesn't present a problem for firewalls. In an SSL packet, the data portion is encrypted, but the IP and TCP/UDP headers are not, so the firewall can filter and route the packet as needed. The firewall can't, however, scan or filter the data portion because it's encrypted. Although SSL does provide a way to encrypt confidential information when it's submitted to a Web site, it doesn't provide user authentication.

You can learn more about S-HTTP by reading its original proposal at *www.ietf .org/rfc/rfc2660.txt*.

Internet Protocol Security and Internet Key Exchange

IPSec works by encrypting communication at the network layer (Layer 3) of the OSI model. It can protect e-mail, Web traffic, and FTP file transfers automatically and is widely used because of its strong encryption algorithms and effective authentication methods. Firewalls that support IPSec give users a way to secure their network communications effectively.

NAT can interfere with some forms of IPSec and other encryption methods, however. If the firewall is used to configure rules for IPSec encryption, there should be no problem with NAT or filtering. However, if IPSec is implemented by software on the firewall (such as an OS or a VPN appliance) and IPSec communications are intended to pass through the firewall, the firewall doesn't read some IPSec-protected packets. Specifically, because Authentication Header (AH) encrypts packets' IP headers, firewalls performing NAT can't read the encrypted headers and, therefore, can't translate them into other IP addresses. In addition, because Encapsulating Security Payload (ESP) doesn't encrypt the IP header but does encrypt the TCP or UDP header port number, firewalls can't perform NAT on these packets because NAT changes port information as well as IP addresses.

NOTE   Refer to Chapter 8 for more details on AH, ESP, and IKE.

In addition to its encryption schemes, IPSec includes a variety of software components, including Internet Key Exchange (IKE), which provides for exchanging public and private keys to authenticate users. Another IPSec protocol, Internet Security Association Key Management Protocol (ISAKMP), enables two computers to reach agreed-on security settings and exchange security keys securely so that they can encrypt communications.

NOTE   IPSec incompatibilities with NAT have largely been addressed by NAT Traversal (NAT-T), which has been standardized by the IETF's IP Security Protocol Working Group and is defined in RFCs 3947 and 3948.

Dial-in Authentication

With laptops and handheld devices, employees can stay connected to the office while working at home or during business trips. Each time an employee accesses the corporate network remotely, however, a potential security breach is possible. An intruder or unauthorized user who gains access to the remote user's system could access files on the corporate network. To address this problem, firewalls can use special authentication systems designed for use with dial-up users. These are the two best-known systems:

- **Terminal Access Controller Access Control System (TACACS+)**, commonly called "Tac-plus," is a set of authentication protocols developed by Cisco Systems. TACACS+ uses TCP as its transport protocol and separates the authentication and authorization processes. TACACS+ also uses the MD5 algorithm to produce an encrypted digest of transmitted data.

- **Remote Authentication Dial-In User Service (RADIUS)** is generally considered less secure than TACACS+, even though it's supported more widely. RADIUS transmits authentication packets unencrypted across the network, which means they are vulnerable to attacks from packet sniffers. It combines authentication and authorization in a user profile.

These systems are becoming less critical because more remote employees and business partners have direct connections to the Internet and can establish connections through VPNs. However, they still play a role in many corporate networks' security schemes.

NOTE   TACACS+ is not backward compatible with Standard TACACS or Extended TACACS (XTACACS). For more information on TACACS, TACACS+, and XTACACS, search at *www.cisco.com*.

In TACACS+ or RADIUS, authentication is carried out by a server. A TACACS+ or RADIUS server is set up with the usual dial-up server used to receive connection requests from remote users, and the dial-up server can configure requests to the TACACS+ or RADIUS server for authentication. A TACACS+ or RADIUS authentication server needs its own IP address and uses special ports for communications, which means the network administrator must configure authentication for filtering, proxying, and NAT, as discussed in the following list:

- *Filtering characteristics*—TACACS+ uses TCP port 49; RADIUS uses UDP ports 1812 or 1645 for authentication and UDP ports 1813 or 1646 for accounting. (For more information on RADIUS client/server accounting, see RFC 2866.) You need to set up packet-filtering rules that enable clients to exchange authorization packets with the TACACS+ or RADIUS server.

- *Proxy characteristics*—A RADIUS server can function as a proxy server, but it doesn't work with generic proxy systems set up for Web access or other services. TACACS+, however, does work with generic proxy systems.

- *NAT characteristics*—RADIUS isn't compatible with NAT without additional configuration, but TACACS+ does work well with NAT systems. Static NAT works best because some TACACS+ systems use source IP addresses to create encryption keys.

NOTE

Wireless users connecting to the corporate network need to connect to a wireless access point. Ideally, VPNs should be used for wireless access because of the vulnerability of wireless transmissions; unauthorized users can intercept network traffic or Internet access via a wireless access point. The highly secure nature of VPN tunneling and encryption offers protection for wireless clients. RADIUS is also used in wireless networking, implemented as an 802.1x standard authentication protocol. You learn more about 802.1x, wireless communications, and securing wireless access in Chapters 12 and 13.

CHAPTER SUMMARY

- You can use several different firewall configurations to protect a network: screening routers, dual-homed hosts, multiple firewalls for load balancing or protecting branch networks, and reverse firewalls to monitor outbound communications.

- Firewalls are effective only if they are configured correctly to block undesirable traffic and allow necessary traffic.

- An effective firewall rule base should be based on the organization's security policy, provide rules for how applications can access the Internet, and be as simple and short as possible.

- A rule base should also restrict access to ports and subnets on the internal network from the Internet and control Internet services.

❑ Many firewalls perform user, client, or session authentication. They can authorize by accepting one-time or multiple-use passwords, using two-factor authentication systems such as SecurID, exchanging public and private keys, and issuing digital signatures.

❑ Many enterprise-level firewalls can operate with encryption schemes, such as Secure Sockets Layer (SSL) and Internet Protocol Security (IPSec). In addition, firewalls can work with a server configured so that employees can dial up the network remotely to access resources.

KEY TERMS

cleanup rule — A packet-filtering rule that comes last in a rule base; it covers any other packets that haven't been covered in preceding rules.

client authentication — The process of granting access to network resources based on a source IP address, computer MAC address, or computer name rather than user information.

digital signature — An attachment to an e-mail or other message that provides tamper detection and enables the recipient to verify the sender's identity.

dual-homed host — A computer that has been configured with more than one network interface.

failover firewall — A backup firewall that can be configured to switch on if the first one fails, thus ensuring uninterrupted service.

firewall policy — An addition to a security policy that describes how firewalls should handle application traffic, such as Web or e-mail applications.

load-balancing software — Software that prioritizes and schedules requests and distributes them to a group of servers based on each machine's current load and processing power.

message digest — A code of fixed length produced by processing input through a mathematical function, usually resulting in a shortened version of the original input. Also called a one-way hash.

public key cryptography — A form of network authentication that identifies participants through the exchange of public and private keys.

Remote Authentication Dial-In User Service (RADIUS) — An authentication method that identifies and verifies users who dial up a central server to gain access to networked resources.

reverse firewall — A device that monitors outgoing traffic instead of trying to block incoming traffic.

rule base — A set of rules for telling a firewall what action to take when a certain kind of traffic attempts to pass through.

screened host — Similar to a dual-homed host, except a router is often added between the host and the Internet to carry out IP packet filtering.

screening router — A router placed between the Internet and the protected network that determines whether to allow or deny packets based on their source and destination IP addresses or other information in their headers.

security workstation — A dedicated computer that deploys a security policy through a centralized firewall to other firewalls that protect branch offices or other networks in the organization.

server farm — A group of servers connected in their own subnet that work together to receive requests; the load is distributed among all the servers.

session authentication — The process of authorizing a user or computer on a per-connection basis by using authentication software installed on the client computer that exchanges information with the firewall.

Terminal Access Controller Access Control System (TACACS+) — A set of authentication protocols developed by Cisco Systems that uses the MD5 algorithm to produce an encrypted digest version of transmitted data. TACACS+ is usually used to authenticate dial-up remote users.

three-pronged firewall — A firewall that has three separate interfaces—for example, one to a DMZ, one to the Internet, and one to the internal network.

token — A small electronic device that generates a random number or password used in authentication.

user authentication — The process of identifying a person who has been authorized to access network resources.

6

REVIEW QUESTIONS

1. What's the main difference between a screened host and a dual-homed host?

   a. A dual-homed host has two NICs.

   b. IP forwarding is disabled.

   c. A packet filter shields the screened host.

   d. The host is screened by a firewall.

2. What's the main problem with a screening router?

   a. The router can be configured incorrectly.

   b. The router might not provide an adequate screen.

   c. The router can't be used with a firewall.

   d. The router alone can't stop many types of attacks.

3. What enables servers in a server farm to work together to handle requests?

   a. a router

   b. a switch

   c. a network hub

   d. load-balancing software

4. Why would a company consider the expense and extra work of purchasing and installing clusters of servers and creating multiple DMZs?

   a. The network can handle high traffic better.

   b. The company can put more information online.

   c. The company improves security.

   d. The company gains another layer of defense.

5. In which of the following situations would you consider creating a protected subnet within an already protected internal network? (Choose all that apply.)

   a. to protect Web servers

   b. to protect customer information

   c. to protect management servers

   d. to protect the company's reputation

6. A corporation with several branch offices has decided to maintain multiple firewalls, one to protect each branch office's network. What's the most efficient way to maintain these firewalls?

   a. Use a centralized security workstation.

   b. Send security policy information to each network administrator.

   c. Set up remote desktop management software.

   d. Broadcast configuration instructions periodically by e-mail.

7. Software or hardware configured to monitor traffic from the internal network to the Internet is called which of the following? (Choose all that apply.)

   a. stateful packet filter

   b. proxy server

   c. reverse firewall

   d. Network Address Translation (NAT)

8. Given that many kinds of traffic can pass through a network gateway, what's the problem with creating a long complex rule base designed to handle every possible situation? (Choose all that apply.)

   a. disk space

   b. slower performance

   c. danger of misconfiguration

   d. danger of missing attack attempts

9. Where should the most important rules in a rule base go?

   a. in the connection log file

   b. at the bottom of the rule base

   c. in the state table

   d. at the top of the rule base

10. Which of the following is a guideline for developing a firewall rule base?

    a. The rule base should restrict all Internet access.

    b. The rule base should restrict access to ports and subnets on the internal network from the Internet.

    c. The rule base should be as detailed as possible.

    d. The rule base should not interfere with application traffic.

11. A firewall policy does which of the following? (Choose all that apply.)

    a. describes how employees can use the firewall

    b. identifies and mitigates risks

    c. explains how the firewall is set up, managed, and updated

    d. specifies how the firewall should handle application traffic

12. A rule base should end with a(n) _____ rule.

    a. reject

    b. allow

    c. cleanup

    d. block

13. When you request a Web page, the Web server storing the page sends it back to you on which port?

    a. 80

    b. 443

    c. one higher than 1023

    d. one lower than 1023

14. Disabling _____ makes it more difficult for attackers to communicate with internal hosts.

    a. IP filtering

    b. IP forwarding

    c. IP routing

    d. IP lookup

15. In which situation should you choose user authentication rather than the more secure client authentication?

    a. Users move around a lot and need to log on from different locations.

    b. Client IP addresses are assigned dynamically.

    c. Client IP addresses are private.

    d. Users work at the same location and don't move around frequently.

6

16. What kinds of restrictions can you impose on user authentication? (Choose all that apply.)

    a. IP address

    b. network resources being requested

    c. time

    d. user's physical location

17. What would an attacker have to do to gain access to an account protected with client authentication? (Choose all that apply.)

    a. be physically located inside the company's building

    b. discover the correct username/password

    c. log on at the correct time

    d. discover the correct IP address

18. Which of the following characteristics describes TACACS+? (Choose all that apply.)

    a. works with NAT systems

    b. is backward compatible with Standard TACACS

    c. uses TCP port 49

    d. doesn't work with generic proxy systems

19. Which elements are used together to create two-factor authentication? (Choose all that apply.)

    a. something the user requests

    b. something the user lacks

    c. something the user possesses

    d. something the user knows

20. Name three methods that some firewalls use to incorporate encryption and protect users.

HANDS-ON PROJECTS

Hands-On Project 6-1: Creating a Firewall Configuration Diagram

HANDS-ON PROJECTS

Time Required: 30 minutes

Objective: Diagram firewall configuration designs.

Description: When you're asked to create and install a firewall configuration for a network, you need to be able to create a diagram showing how the system will be set up.

A diagram can be useful at the planning phase or when you're proposing a security setup for the network.

1. Draw a diagram of a screening router configuration. Use a simple circle or rectangle to represent the network being protected.

2. Draw a dual-homed host configuration. Be sure to label its external and internal interfaces.

3. Draw a screened host configuration. Again, be sure to label its external and internal interfaces.

Hands-On Project 6-2: Troubleshooting a Rule Base

6

Time Required: 15 minutes

Objective: Examine a rule base for any security concerns.

Description: As a security professional, you might be asked to edit packet-filtering rule bases or improve rules that leave security holes open. Analyze the rule base in Table 6-12, and then answer the following questions:

Table 6-12   Rule base

Rule	Source IP	Source port	Destination IP	Destination port	Action
1	Any	Any	192.168.120.0	>1023	Allow
2	192.168.120.1	Any	Any	Any	Deny
3	Any	Any	192.168.120.1	Any	Deny
4	192.168.120.0	Any	Any	Any	Any
5	Any	Any	192.168.120.2	25	Allow
6	Any	Any	192.168.120.3	80	Allow
7	Any	Any	Any	Any	Allow

1. Examine Rule 1 and explain what security risk it poses. Describe how this rule could be improved:

_____

_____

_____

_____

_____

_____

2. Describe a problem with the cleanup rule in the rule base:

_____

_____

CASE PROJECTS

Case Project 6-1: Designing a Perimeter Network for Green Globe

CASE PROJECTS

Green Globe's main concern is ensuring strong security for its sensitive data. You have been working on a preliminary design for this network, and your supervisor wants you to begin planning firewall configuration to protect data and remote access. In Chapter 5, you examined different firewalls. Refer back to that information to decide which products to use. Based on what you have learned in this chapter, determine where to place those firewalls and design a preliminary rule base for each one.

> **NOTE**
>
> You might be adding VPNs and intrusion detection to your design later in this book, so keep those expansions in mind when planning your firewall configuration.

1. Look at your most recent network diagram. Where do firewalls need to be added?

2. Examine your documentation on firewall products from Chapter 5 and your most recent network diagram. What products will you use at the network perimeter? On desktop computers? Do any machines require additional security? (*Hint*: Drawing the traffic flow can help you identify locations for security devices.)

3. After determining the products to use and identifying their locations, design a preliminary rule base for each firewall. (Remember to use consistent naming conventions for all devices to make identifying them easier.) Create a simple table such as the ones used in this chapter, or design your own method for organizing your rule bases.

Sometimes less is more. You might need only a few firewalls at key locations, so avoid the trap of throwing hardware at a design without a clear plan for its purpose. The more complex your design is, the more likely problems and configuration errors are.

Finally, remember that any technology infrastructure's purpose is to serve the organization's needs. Consider the organization's requirements, business environment, functions, and future when working on a network. Your clients will be much happier with your work and you will have far fewer problems to address.

7

MANAGING FIREWALLS TO IMPROVE SECURITY

After reading this chapter and completing the exercises, you will be able to:

♦ Explain how to edit a rule base

♦ Describe how to manage log files

♦ List measures for improving firewall performance and security

♦ Explain how to install and configure Microsoft ISA Server 2006

♦ Explain how to manage and configure Iptables for Linux

This chapter examines ways in which you can strengthen and manage firewall configurations. Firewalls can go a long way toward blocking traffic attempting to access your network from external networks, such as the Internet. However, focusing solely on inbound traffic could leave your network vulnerable. Malicious programs might install themselves on an internal host and then try to connect to an external location, for example. Your rule base must address outbound traffic as well.

First, you learn how to refine your rule base to filter potentially harmful traffic yet keep the rule base as efficient as possible. Then you learn more details about log files and analyzing log data and examine how to make your firewall perform better while maintaining the level of security you want.

After planning and fine-tuning, the next step is to put these principles into practice. The best way to learn firewall configuration and management is to practice with real firewall products. You have already installed ZoneAlarm and examined firewall fundamentals, but you probably don't have a Cisco PIX firewall available. Instead, you install and configure an enterprise-class software firewall, Microsoft ISA Server 2006. You also learn about the Linux packet-filtering tool, Iptables.

EDITING THE RULE BASE

Editing rules in a firewall's rule base is one of the best ways to improve security and performance. Making the rule base more effective also means the firewall can carry out your organization's security policies more effectively. Keep the following guidelines in mind to improve your firewall's rule base:

- Make sure the most important rules are near the top of the rule base.

- Make sure you don't make the firewall do more logging than it has to.

- Reduce the number of domain objects in the rule base.

- Keep rules that cover domain objects near the bottom of the rule base.

NOTE   Domain objects are named resources in an organization's domain—remember that a domain in this context is simply a security boundary.

The problem with using domain objects in the rule base is the possibility of a security breach. When the firewall encounters a rule including a computer or other domain object as the source or destination, it attempts to look up the object's domain name from its IP address. Through a DNS spoofing or DNS poisoning attack, an attacker who has gained control of the network's DNS server might be able to identify a computer on the internal network as a target. In addition, an intruder might attempt a zone transfer of the DNS database to acquire information about the internal network. A **DNS zone transfer** is a query that secondary DNS servers use to update their DNS records.

Reducing Rules

One of the simplest and most effective ways to reduce the number of rules in a firewall's rule base is to see whether it contains any unnecessary rules. There's no hard-and-fast rule for the number you should have; what's important is checking for duplicates or unnecessary entries.

Don't forget that the security policy plays a major role in determining what rules are necessary. For example, you have a network with IP addresses in the range 210.100.101.0 to 210.100.101.255. The firewall is at 210.100.101.1, and the Web server is at 210.100.101.2. Your organization's security policy calls for users on the internal network to be able to use HTTP to access Web sites and S-HTTP on the Internet, but not on the Web server in the organization's DMZ. You could write the rules as shown in Table 7-1.

Table 7-1   Inefficient firewall rules

Rule	Source IP	Destination IP	Protocol IP	Action	Track	Comments
1	Any	210.100.101.1	Any	Deny	Alert	Block access to firewall
2	210.100.101.0 to 210.100.101.255	210.100.101.2	S-HTTP	Deny	None	Block network access to Web server using S-HTTP
3	210.100.101.0 to 210.100.101.255	Any	HTTP, S-HTTP	Allow	None	Allow network access to all Web sites
4	Any	210.100.101.2	HTTP	Allow	None	Allow all computers to access the Web server using HTTP
5	Any	Any	Any	Deny	Log	Cleanup rule

This rule base has three rules to allow internal and external users to connect to the Web server with HTTP but not S-HTTP. A more efficient method is to consolidate two of the rules (2 and 3 in Table 7-1) into one rule (3 in Table 7-2).

Table 7-2   More efficient firewall rules

Rule	Source IP	Destination IP	Protocol	Action	Track	Comments
1	Any	210.100.101.1	Any	Deny	Alert	Block access to firewall
2	Any	210.100.101.2	HTTP	Allow	None	Allow full access to Web server using HTTP
3	210.100.101.0 to 210.100.101.255	All except 210.100.101.2	HTTP, S-HTTP	Allow	None	Enable network access to Web using HTTP and S-HTTP but not to DMZ Web server
4	Any	Any	Any	Deny	Log	Cleanup rule

NOTE   Tables 7-1 and 7-2 include a column called Track. Some firewall programs use this column to determine whether the firewall should record its actions when finding a match to a rule. Typical options in the Track column are Alert (which causes the firewall to send an alert message), Log (which tells the firewall to log the event), and None (which tells the firewall not to track the event). The Alert setting should be used only in emergencies because sending too many alerts can slow the firewall down and increase network traffic.

Reordering and Editing Rules

Another way to improve your rule base is to make sure the most frequently matched rules are near the top rather than the bottom. A firewall checks rules in top-to-bottom order until a match is found. If it has to proceed from rule 1 through rule 11 before finding the first match at rule 12, it spends unnecessary time processing rules 1 to 11. Moving rule 12 closer to the top makes it easier for the firewall to find the match quickly and allows traffic through with less delay.

To reorder rules, scan log files to find commonly used services (those with the most log file entries), and then move rules for those services closer to the top of the rule base. For example, one of the most common services is SMTP for outgoing e-mail. (This service is followed closely by POP3 for incoming e-mail and HTTP for the Web.) A rule that allows internal users to connect to the SMTP server in the DMZ, for example, should not be number 20; it should be in the top five. Similarly, rules for traffic to or from your network's DNS server should be near the top of the rule base, after the rule preventing access to your firewall.

The goal is to reduce the number of rules with Log as the action to the bare minimum to improve efficiency. You should log only events occurring as a result of attempts to access restricted resources (such as the firewall) or occurring on resources with activities you need to track (such as your external Web server's level of activity).

ACTIVITY

Activity 7-1: Improving a Rule Base

Time Required: 15 minutes

Objective: Review a sample rule base and make improvements.

Description: Reviewing and rewriting your firewall's rule base can speed up its performance and improve security. The sample rule base in Table 7-3 has some rules that could be edited and rearranged. The network has IP addresses from 210.100.101.0 to 210.100.101.255. The firewall is at 210.100.101.1, the Web server is at 210.100.101.2, the DNS server is at 210.100.101.3, the SMTP server is at 210.100.101.4, and the POP3 server is at 210.100.101.5. The firewall using this rule base works correctly, but some simple changes could improve its performance dramatically.

Table 7-3   Sample firewall rule base

Rule	Source IP	Destination IP	Protocol	Action	Track	Comments
1	Any	210.100.101.1	Any	Deny	Alert	Block access to firewall
2	210.100.101.0 to 210.100.101.255	210.100.101.2	S-HTTP	Deny	None	Block network access to Web server using S-HTTP
3	210.100.101.0 to 210.100.101.255	Any	HTTP, S-HTTP	Allow	None	Allow network access to all Web sites
4	Any	210.100.101.2	HTTP	Allow	Log	Allow all computers to access the Web server using HTTP
5	210.100.101.0 to 210.100.101.255	210.100.101.3	UDP	Allow	Log	Enable network to make queries to DNS server
6	210.100.101.3	Any except 210.100.101.0 to 210.100.101.255	TCP	Allow	Log	Enable DNS server to make lookups on the Web but not in the network
7	210.100.101.0 to 210.100.101.255	210.100.101.5	TCP	Allow	None	Allow network access to POP3 server
8	Any	210.100.101.4	TCP	Allow	None	Allow any computer to access the SMTP server
9	Any	Any	Any	Deny	Log	Cleanup rule

1. Which rules cover the same sort of communication?

   _____

   _____

2. Which rules are too far down the list and should be moved up?

   _____

3. Which rules give the firewall more work to do than is necessary? (*Hint*: Look in the Track column.)

   _____

   _____

   _____

4. On a separate piece of paper, create a rule base table like the following example. Using as few rows as possible, write a new rule base that addresses the questions in the preceding steps.

Rule	Source IP	Destination IP	Protocol	Action	Track	Comments

MANAGING LOG FILES

Log files generated by firewalls and other security devices provide critical information about network traffic and attempts to attack hosts on the internal network. You can control what the firewall records in log files and how these files are stored to improve the firewall's performance yet maintain network security. The following sections explain how to configure a firewall to generate log files more efficiently and how to use third-party software to get more information from your log files. You can also modify the log file format, prepare log file summaries, and generate reports that help you make changes to the firewall for more effective operation.

CAUTION Assembling a team of network administrators to manage tasks helps distribute the workload, but be aware that having too many administrators making changes can result in confusion and misconfiguration of the firewall. Make sure team members keep a record of every change they make, including the time the change was made and the reason for the adjustment. Keep the change management record accessible.

Deciding What to Log

Every firewall includes default settings for events it logs. Some firewalls log only packets subject to a rule with a Deny action. This setting makes sense because it enables administrators to keep track of unsuccessful attempts to access the network. However, you can choose to log all packets, including those that have been allowed, but this option slows operation of the firewall, proxy server, or IDS dramatically.

Many firewalls offer different kinds of log files, such as the following:

- *Security log*—Records any specific security events the firewall has detected, such as denial-of-service (DoS) attempts or port scans.

- *System log*—Records when the firewall was started and stopped so that you can keep track of who attempts to use or configure it.

- *Traffic log*—Captures each packet entering or leaving the firewall. You can use it for preparing reports that describe when traffic is heaviest, lightest, and so on.

Sometimes firewalls come with so many types of logging data that including them all would make log files enormous. On the other hand, some options that can give you useful information are overlooked simply because they make log file entries difficult to view without scrolling across a computer screen, or they won't fit on a standard sheet of paper. Some firewalls include a GUI interface that enables you to change the log file display by customizing which fields are included in the log. Table 7-4 lists some log file data you might find useful. The first seven types are "must haves"; the remaining types are useful but not essential.

Table 7-4   Types of log file data

Log file data	What it records
Date	The date when the event occurred
Time	The time when the event occurred, usually in Greenwich Mean Time (GMT)
Source IP	The IP address of the computer that made the request
Destination IP	The IP address of the computer being asked to provide a service to the requesting computer
Protocol	The name of the application protocol used to make the connection
Source port	The port number used to request a service
Destination port	The port number used to provide a service to the requesting computer
Authentication status	Whether the client making the request has been authenticated
Interface	The firewall interface on which the request was received (such as INT for internal interface or EXT for external interface)
Service	The name of the service (such as DNS, HTTP, or FTP) used to make the request or connection
Rule	The number of the rule used to process the request
Processing time	The time, in milliseconds, required to process the request
Bytes sent	The number of bytes sent from the internal host to the external computer as a result of the connection
Cache info	Indicates whether the requested object was cached

Configuring the Log File Format

Many firewalls and intrusion detection systems (IDSs) generate log files formatted in plaintext that you can view with a text editor, such as Notepad. Most text editors, however, require scrolling sideways to view lines, which makes viewing log files tedious. Additionally, plaintext log files can have a problem with field separators, such as commas or tabs, occurring within a field. For example, in the Date field, a tab might appear between the day and month, which can make a log entry difficult to read. Some sophisticated firewalls have the option to save log files in different formats, such as the following:

- *Native format*—You view log files within the firewall's interface.

- *Open Database Connectivity (ODBC) format*—You can view log files saved in this format with Microsoft SQL Server or another ODBC-compliant database program, which makes it easy to run reports on the data or extract certain fields for analysis.

- *W3C Extended format*—This customizable, ASCII text-based format, developed by the World Wide Web Consortium (W3C), is viewed with a text editor, not in a Web browser. You can choose which fields to include, and tools using this format can usually generate summaries. W3C also supports logging needs of proxy caches and captures more information. For more details on this format, visit *www.w3.org/TR/WD-logfile.html.*

You can edit and reconfigure log file formats as a first step toward improving firewall efficiency. Fine-tuning log file formats to log the information you actually need makes it easier to review files, helps with optimizing the rule base, and can improve performance and security by eliminating useless or duplicate entries. For example, you wouldn't want to log all connections to your Web server because that would produce a log file larger than the server could hold. Similarly, you wouldn't want to log internal DHCP broadcasts from hosts seeking IP configuration from the nearest available DHCP server.

Log files should also be reviewed regularly for any problems, signs of attacks, duplicate entries, or unnecessary logging (such as the DHCP broadcasts mentioned previously), and firewall rules should be edited to improve security. Here's the general process for reviewing log files and rules:

1. Start your log-viewing software and review the summary of recent log file events.

2. Display the raw data in the form of a report. You might create a report that sorts access attempts by source IP address so that you can see who's been attempting to connect to your network or by destination address to see where users are going on the Internet. (This information could be useful to track down the source of a downloaded Trojan program or a complaint of someone viewing objectionable content.)

3. Review the data and identify traffic patterns that point to problems with firewall rules. For instance, log files with duplicate entries are evidence that rules should be edited to eliminate repetition.

4. Adjust the rules accordingly.

5. Review subsequent log file data to make sure changes to rules reduced the number of unnecessary log file entries.

Log files can also indicate signatures of attack attempts, such as port scans. A signature might be a sequence of log file entries in which one computer makes connection attempts to consecutive ports on a single computer; this signature could indicate that the computer attempting connections is scanning for open ports. You should respond by blocking all connection attempts from the source computer and making sure no unnecessary ports are open on the targeted computer or others on the internal network.

Preparing Log File Summaries and Generating Reports

A log file summary shows the major events that generated log file entries over a particular period, such as a day, week, or month. These summaries aren't reports, but they list totals of how many events occurred and what type and can be used to prepare reports. Some firewall programs include log file analysis tools that prepare summaries of raw data over a certain period and have options for organizing the information into report forms.

Other programs require using an add-on log analyzer. ZoneAlarm, for example, is popular enough that MCS (*http://zonelog.co.uk*) created a log file analysis tool for it called ZoneLog Analyser. It enables you to import and work with ZoneAlarm log data, analyze log entries, and enter custom settings. You can get more information about a port by clicking to select it (see Figure 7-1). You can also download port assignments and descriptions. Updated port information is added automatically to the known ports list shown in Figure 7-1.

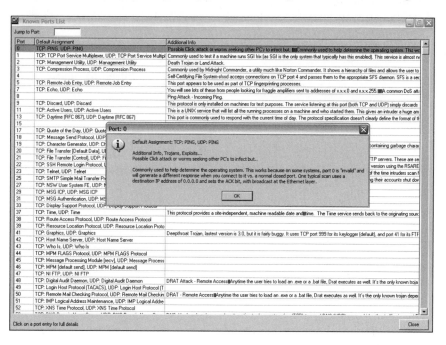

Figure 7-1   ZoneLog Analyser's known ports list

You can use the log import filters, shown in Figure 7-2, to omit certain IP addresses or ports or specify another database location for them.

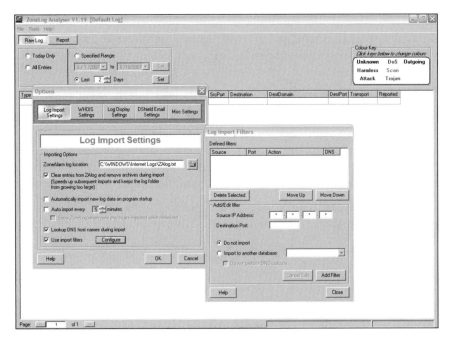

Figure 7-2   Using ZoneLog Analyser's log import filters

Notice in Figure 7-2 that the Options dialog box is also used to define Whois Internet lookup, log display, and DShield e-mail settings. There's also the Misc Settings tab (see Figure 7-3), where you can automate software and port database updates.

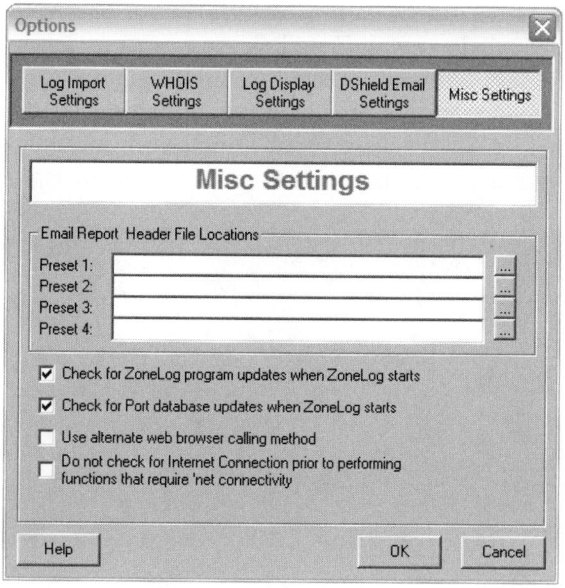

Figure 7-3 The Misc Settings tab

Viewing raw data can be tedious and prone to errors. As you can see in Figure 7-4, the raw data in ZoneLog Analyser is difficult to read and interpret. Some columns serve no purpose for a general log review and make the file harder to read.

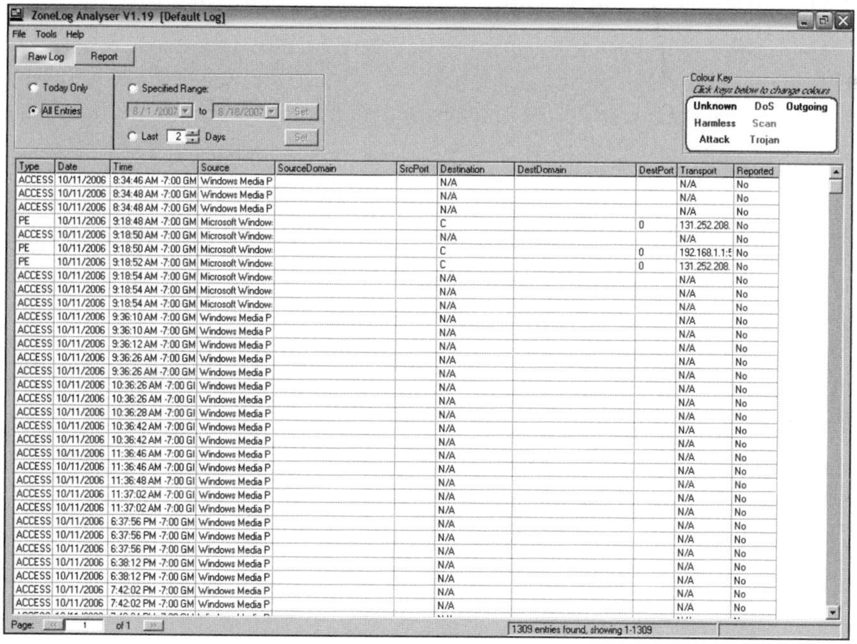

Figure 7-4 Raw data in ZoneLog Analyser

Generating a report that displays data in an easy-to-read format is preferable, and custom reporting features are particularly useful. ZoneLog Analyser can produce custom reports based on IP addresses, types of hits, or ports, for example. You can analyze attacks, IP addresses, and ports by using interactive automated tools and produce general or specific graphs and charts. Figure 7-5 shows an activity summary from January through March 2007, including outgoing attempts, in pie chart and graph formats.

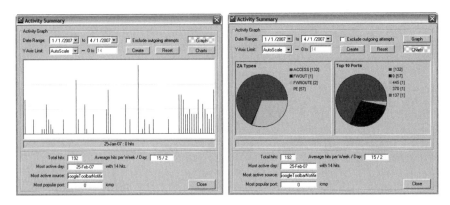

Figure 7-5   An activity summary in different formats

Reports can be analyzed to improve network security and performance and can be customized further. For example, in Figure 7-5, you can see days of heavier than normal activity. You can mouse over a bar on the graph to see the corresponding date below the graph. To generate a new report showing hits, double-click the bar.

You can use the pie chart to scrutinize the type of hits. In Figure 7-5, the majority of activity involves access, specifically when a program is blocked from accessing the network application's requests. ZoneAlarm's pop-up alerts asking for application access permission are designated PE in this chart.

A helpful feature of ZoneLog Analyser is the capability to resolve IP addresses by using a Whois lookup. Double-clicking a log file entry in Report or Raw Log mode opens a dialog box with details on that entry (see Figure 7-6).

You can resolve source and destination address details, enter notes for the entry, and click the WHOIS button to investigate the source by using Internet domain records. A Web browser opens with address lookup details, such as domain registrars for IP addresses, domain owners, and contact information (see Figure 7-7).

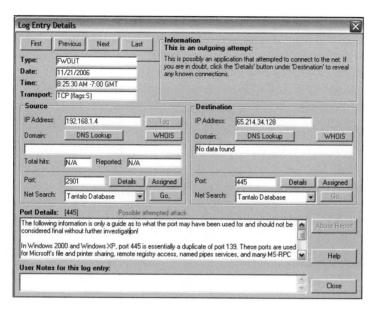

Figure 7-6   The Log Entry Details dialog box

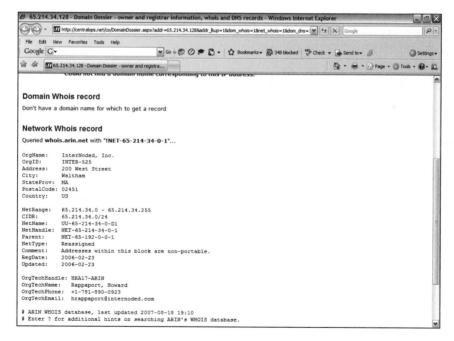

Figure 7-7   Address lookup details

ZoneLog Analyser is a helpful log file analysis tool capable of displaying considerable information about traffic ZoneAlarm has logged. More advanced firewall programs can produce a variety of reports and statistics, such as the number of visitors to your Web site, types of browsers visitors used, and pages that were accessed most often. These reports are similar to the reports a Web server generates, but firewall programs also report on security-related events, such as attack attempts. A Web server doesn't have a way to determine what constitutes a suspicious packet or an intrusion attempt; it simply serves Web pages and receives data submitted by clients.

IMPROVING FIREWALL PERFORMANCE AND SECURITY

After installing a firewall, you might notice that connecting to the Internet or receiving files from external hosts takes longer. The problem could be that the firewall's default settings are causing it to perform unnecessary operations. For example, a computer hosting a firewall can maintain a list of internal hosts the firewall can use for internal communications. Make sure the firewall uses its Hosts file instead of having to resolve IP addresses every time a request is received. For external communications, a DNS server is required to resolve names to IP addresses. If the network is large, an internal DNS server is more efficient. When configuring logs on the firewall, make sure the firewall isn't logging noncritical events, such as internal hosts using native Windows networking communications (WINS or NetBIOS). By changing default settings, you can reduce the disk space that log files take up.

Calculating Resource Requirements

It doesn't matter how advanced a firewall is if it doesn't have the hardware resources for optimum performance. It's worth the extra investment to make sure you have a host computer fast enough to keep up with traffic flow and security operations and with enough disk space to store the data being generated.

The host computer's processor speed has the most impact on firewall performance, and a multiple-processor configuration can maintain a better performance level when network traffic increases. Invest in equipment that can support multiple processors, use load-balancing when possible, and purchase the fastest processor chip your budget can handle.

Ensuring that the firewall has enough RAM is critical, too, because running out of memory results in dropped packets and traffic bottlenecks. System requirements are listed in the manual that comes with the software and on the manufacturer's Web site. For instance, ISA Server 2006 Standard Edition needs a minimum of 512 MB RAM, and more is recommended. (Typically, the minimum requirements don't result in optimum performance; for the firewall to operate at peak efficiency, use more than the minimum recommended amount of RAM.)

The host computer also requires storage space to **cache** Web pages and other files. A standard formula for determining cache space is 100 MB + (0.5 MB x number of users). If the firewall is intended to serve 500 users, for example, you need a minimum of 100 MB + (0.5 × 500), or 350 MB of cache space. With today's high-capacity hard drives, however, cache space isn't usually an issue.

NOTE Although firewall appliances have fewer problems meeting these hardware requirements, hardware upgrades might be necessary at some point. You might need to add RAM to meet a growing network's needs, add network interfaces, or use a third-party tool to increase functionality. Firewall appliances or preconfigured bundles also contain software that usually requires updating.

Testing the Firewall

After you have configured the firewall, testing it before and after it goes online helps ensure that users won't run into access problems. Ideally, you should test the firewall before you install it on the network so that you can shut down the software and make changes, if needed, without interrupting network traffic. One inexpensive option for testing is a lab with two client computers: one connected to the external interface (to simulate a computer on the Internet) and another on the internal interface (to simulate a computer on the internal network).

TIP If you don't have two computers, you can use one test machine and connect it to the internal interface, and then connect to the firewall's external interface through a dial-up connection.

For a large enterprise network, a full **test cell** (a dedicated test lab) that mirrors the architecture of the real network is best for testing new software, hardware, updates, and patches. It also provides a safe environment for testing security measures and designing auditing measures. A test cell is expensive to establish, requires staff to maintain it, and takes up extra space, but the benefit of ensuring network availability is worth the cost for enterprise networks. For example, some vendor patches cause problems with customized applications or have hardware incompatibilities. With a test cell, you can figure out how to make the patch work without affecting your production environment and make adjustments before carrying out changes on the actual network. You can also avoid the problems caused by a patch crashing a critical application on the network.

NOTE If you can't set up a test cell, have at least one test computer for patches, upgrades, hardware changes, and so on. A test computer should be the same type of hardware as in your production network.

Configuring Advanced Firewall Functions

After you have the firewall's basic functions set up, you can add advanced features if they are supported, such as the following:

- *Data caching*—Storing Web pages in cache was discussed in connection with proxy servers in Chapter 5, but firewalls can also cache Web pages.

- *Remote management*—You can install remote management software, if available, on remote computers to make monitoring and configuration easier, especially if you have several firewalls to manage or your firewalls aren't easy to access physically.

- *Application content filtering*—You can configure many firewalls to perform inspection at the application protocol level so that filtering is based on protocols such as HTTP, SMTP, POP3, and IMAP.

- *Voice protocol support*—Voice protocols, such as H.323v2 or Session Initiation Protocol (SIP), are used for Voice over IP (VoIP) services, in which the IP network also provides telephone service.

- *Authentication*—High-end firewalls include authentication methods as an additional security feature.

- *Time-based access scheduling*—You can configure policies (access control lists or rules) based on day of the week and time of day, for example.

In addition, you might also want to set up load sharing—configuring two or more firewalls to share the total traffic load. Each firewall in a load-sharing setup is active at the same time and uses a specialized protocol to communicate with the other firewalls.

ACTIVITY

Activity 7-2: Configuring Windows Firewall

Time Required: 15 minutes

Objective: Configure the Windows XP built-in firewall, Windows Firewall, and set up logging.

Description: Windows XP Professional has a built-in firewall called Windows Firewall, which is active by default when Service Pack 2 (SP2) is installed. If you aren't running SP2 or Windows Firewall is disabled, you need to install SP2 or enable Windows Firewall. In this activity, you configure Windows Firewall and learn how to adjust settings and enable logging. You can use any Windows XP Professional computer connected to the Internet.

1. Click **Start, Control Panel**. Make sure Control Panel is in Category View.

2. Click **Security Center**, and then click **Windows Firewall** to open the Windows Firewall dialog box. If necessary, click the **General** tab.

3. Windows Firewall has three settings: On (recommended), On with the Don't allow exceptions check box selected, and Off (not recommended). Click the **On (recommended)** option button, if it's not already selected.

4. Click the **Exceptions** tab to configure requests you want to allow. What programs are already added to the exceptions list by default?

_____

_____

_____

5. To add programs and services you want to allow, click their corresponding check boxes in the Programs and Services list.

6. To add programs or services that aren't listed, click the **Add Program** button. For ports, click the **Add Port** button. To change the default handling of a program or service, select it and click the **Edit** button.

7. Click the **Advanced** tab, and then click the **Settings** button in the Security Logging section (see Figure 7-8). Click the **Log dropped packets** and **Log successful connections** check boxes, if necessary. Write down the location of your log file on the following line (for example, C:\Windows\Pfirewall.log). Click **OK** to close the Log Settings dialog box and **OK** to close the Windows Firewall dialog box.

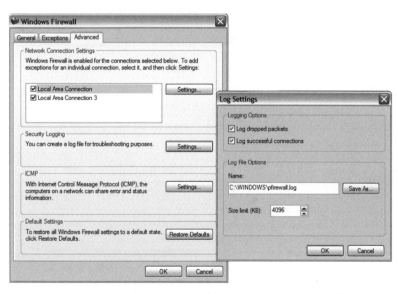

Figure 7-8   The Advanced tab and the Log Settings dialog box

8. Close any open windows, and leave your system running for the next project.

INSTALLING AND CONFIGURING MICROSOFT ISA SERVER 2006

Microsoft Internet Security and Acceleration (ISA) Server 2006 is more than just a firewall designed to protect business networks. It's an integrated security gateway that handles traditional firewall functions, filters at the application level, and caches Web pages to reduce network server load and improve the speed of accessing Web server pages. ISA Server 2006 offers many security, connectivity, and management functions in one product.

The first step in installation is selecting the version of ISA Server 2006. Table 7-5 summarizes the main differences between ISA Server 2006 Standard and Enterprise editions.

Table 7-5   ISA Server 2006 Standard and Enterprise editions

Feature	Standard Edition	Enterprise Edition
Caching	Single server store	Unlimited
Windows Network Load Balancing (NLB)	Not supported	Integrated
Multiple CPUs	Up to four	Unlimited, depending on OS
Multiple networks	Unlimited	Unlimited, adds enterprise networks
Policies	Local	Array and enterprise policies using Active Directory Application Mode (ADAM)

Table 7-5   ISA Server 2006 Standard and Enterprise editions (continued)

Feature	Standard Edition	Enterprise Edition
Monitoring and alerting	Microsoft Operations Manager (MOM) Management Pack, single server console	MOM Management Pack, multiserver console
Branch office management	Manual import and export of policies	Enterprise-level and array-level policies

After deciding which version best suits your needs, you need to configure a host machine for ISA Server 2006. Table 7-6 lists the minimum hardware requirements.

Table 7-6   Minimum hardware requirements for ISA Server 2006

Component	Minimum requirement
Processor	733 MHz Pentium III or higher
OS	Windows Server 2003 32-bit with SP1 or Windows Server 2003 RC 32-bit
Memory	512 MB (more is recommended)
Hard drive	NTFS partition with 150 MB of space (more is needed for Web caching)
Other components	CD-ROM or DVD-ROM, VGA or higher resolution monitor, NIC for the internal network (additional NIC for each extra connected network or for array communications), keyboard, and mouse

NOTE   ISA Server 2006 doesn't run on Windows XP Professional or earlier versions of Windows (Server or Professional). ISA Server runs on Windows Server 2003 and can be purchased as a preconfigured package (ISA Server, OS, and hardware) from a third-party vendor.

Licensing ISA Server 2006

You need a license to use ISA Server 2006 on a permanent basis. It's licensed on a per-processor basis, meaning you need to purchase one license for each processor on the host where ISA Server 2006 is installed. You can then use as many clients as you need to connect to the server.

Failing to purchase adequate licensing for software carries serious punishments, especially for trained IT professionals. In addition to legal penalties, you can be stripped of any certifications you have and will probably lose your job. Most vendor certifications require agreeing to a code of ethics that includes reporting software piracy. Part of your job is to ensure proper licensing for all software within your scope of responsibilities. An organization's security policy should state software licensing requirements explicitly, and these requirements must be enforced. Including software licensing issues and requirements in your security awareness training for users is a good idea, too.

Reviewing ISA Server 2006 Components

ISA Server 2006 Enterprise Edition has four major components that enable it to integrate into and work across the enterprise:

- *Configuration Storage server*—Configuration information for all arrays is stored on the **Configuration Storage server**. ISA Server 2006 array members access the Configuration Storage server to check for configuration changes and update their local storage with any changes. You can have multiple Configuration Storage servers and specify which one array members should contact. You can also specify an alternate Configuration Storage server in case the primary one fails.

7

- *ISA Server services*—This component is installed on array members, each of which is connected to the Configuration Storage server. **ISA Server services** perform firewall, VPN, and caching functions.

- *Array*—A group of ISA Server computers that are connected physically, share a common configuration, and run ISA Server services.

- *ISA Server Management*—You use this Microsoft Management Console (MMC) snap-in to manage the enterprise by connecting to a Configuration Storage server.

All these components can be installed on the same computer. The Configuration Storage server is vital to an ISA Server 2006 Enterprise deployment and must be available to install array members. It must also be available to all array members in the course of normal operations. If an array member can't communicate with the Configuration Storage server, it continues to provide services based on the last known configuration it received, but you can't monitor or change anything on it until the Configuration Storage server is restored. For large enterprises, Microsoft recommends installing the Configuration Storage server and array members on separate machines.

Installing ISA Server 2006

Before installing ISA Server 2006, you must attend to some planning tasks. As with any major deployment, consider where servers will be installed, how they will communicate with each other and the enterprise, and how they will be managed. Preparation makes installation progress more smoothly and produces better results.

You also need to collect some information before installing ISA Server 2006. First, you must have FQDN, DNS, and IP addressing details for the Configuration Storage server. Examining traffic flow in your network also helps you determine what ports and protocols are required so that you can design a solid rule base for your ISA server.

If the Configuration Storage server and array members will be in a single domain or a domain with trust relationships, encryption between servers is automatic. If not, create and export a server authentication certificate for the Configuration Storage server. The certificate enables encryption for communication between array members and the Configuration Storage server. It must be available to the computer hosting the Configuration Storage server during installation, and you need to install the root certificate (for the certification authority, or CA, issuing the server certificate) on array members.

The ISA Server 2006 installation should be completed in the following order:

1. Install the Configuration Storage server.

2. Create arrays and enterprise network rules and policies on the Configuration Storage server. This step is optional, depending on the topology you have designed.

3. Install ISA Server services on one or more computers. If you're installing an array, specify internal addressing information for the first new member of the array.

As part of the installation, Internet Connection Sharing, Internet Connection Firewall/Windows Firewall, and IP Network Address Translation (NAT) are disabled. Several services are stopped during installation and are restarted after the installation is finished, including Internet Information Services (IIS) Admin service, SNMP service, FTP Publishing, WWW Publishing, and Network News Transport Protocol (NNTP).

Installation of ISA Server 2006 is simplified by a wizard that guides you through the steps. Because ISA Server 2006 requires Windows Server 2003, you can't install it on a Windows XP system, but Microsoft has a way around this problem. On the Microsoft TechNet Web site, you can download a virtual version of ISA Server that's designed to simulate an actual deployment. The virtual hard drive (VHD) format requires about 10 GB of hard drive space and can run on Windows 2000, Windows Server 2003, Windows Vista, and Windows XP. The VHD format also requires installing virtualization software, such as Microsoft Virtual PC (free from Microsoft's Web site), to run the virtual machine.

7

Microsoft TechNet also has a online virtual lab environment you can use to evaluate software, and it includes many hands-on guided labs and manuals. With each lab module, you get 90 minutes of online access to the TechNet virtual lab. Lab topics range from learning the basics to testing deployment scenarios. The system requirements to use lab modules are lower than requirements for installing the actual software, so you have more options for evaluating software and learning about ISA Server 2006.

If you have a Windows Server 2003 computer, downloading and installing the evaluation software is helpful. If you don't have access to Windows Server 2003, the virtual labs are a good alternative. In fact, the virtual labs offer configuration options for main deployment scenarios, so you can practice more advanced techniques than you could without expensive equipment.

TIP
Microsoft offers a wide variety of software products for the virtual lab environment. If you have time, explore the available modules and complete any you find interesting or relevant. These lab modules are also a good way to evaluate software your company is considering. You can learn more about Microsoft TechNet Virtual Labs and VHD content at *http://technet.microsoft.com/en-us/default.aspx*.

Activity 7-3: Installing ISA Server 2006 Evaluation Software

ACTIVITY

Time Required: 30 minutes

Objective: Download and install ISA Server 2006 evaluation software.

Description: In this activity, you download and install ISA Server 2006 evaluation software. You need to restart your workstation and select Windows Server 2003 as the OS to boot. You also need an Internet connection for this activity.

1. Start your Web browser and go to **www.microsoft.com/technet/ downloads/isa/2006/trials/default.mspx**.

2. Under the Download ISA Server 2006 Trial Software heading, click the **ISA Server 2006 – Enterprise Edition** link. (You might need to register for access to the download. Registration is free and requires a valid e-mail address.)

3. Click the **Get Started Today** button. Sign in to Microsoft, if asked, and follow the instructions to download the software. Save the file to your hard drive.

NOTE   This download is large, so it takes some time. Your instructor might have downloaded the package and made it available on a network share.

4. Double-click the **ISA Server executable** file. Click the **Install ISA Server 2006** link, and then click **Next**.

5. Accept the license agreement, and enter the requested customer information. When you reach the Setup Scenarios window, click **Install Configuration Storage server**, and then click **Next**.

6. Review the components, and click **Next** to accept the default selection.

7. Click **Create a new ISA Server enterprise** in Enterprise Installation Options, and then click **Next**.

8. If you see the New Enterprise warning message, click **Next**. Enter a name and description for the enterprise, and then click **Next**.

9. In Enterprise Deployment Environment, click **I am deploying in a single domain or in domains with trust relationships**. Click **Next**, and then click **Install**.

10. After the server installation is finished, click **Invoke ISA Server Management when the wizard closes**, and then click **Finish**. When your server starts, you should see the ISA Server management console. As shown in Figure 7-9, this console has three main navigation areas.

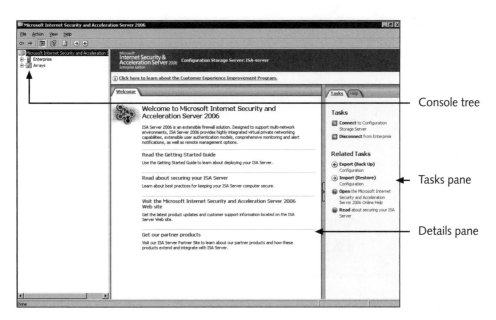

Figure 7-9   The ISA Server management console

    11. Close any open windows, and leave your system running for the next project.

Now that ISA Server 2006 is installed, you need to begin configuring it. ISA Server offers guidance on this process. As shown in Figure 7-10, the Enterprise management console lists the necessary configuration steps. (To see this console, you expand Enterprise in the console tree on the left.) ISA Server also has extensive help features and links to more information from the management console. As shown in Figure 7-10, there are four main configuration tasks. First, you assign administrative roles, which specify who is allowed to access ISA Server and what level of control they have. Next, you define your networks, and then you define enterprise policies. Finally, you configure array settings.

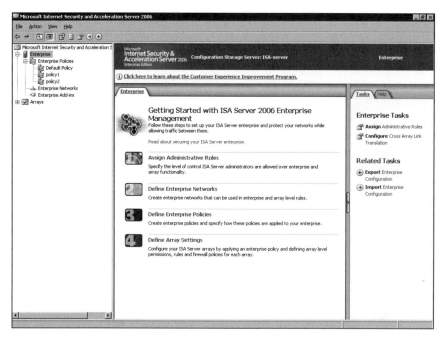

Figure 7-10 ISA The ISA Server Enterprise management console

ISA Server 2006 has a wizard for creating, editing, and deleting policies, but it does have default policies that can't be deleted or modified. As shown in Figure 7-11, the default enterprise policy rule is to deny all traffic from all networks going to all networks. Adding new policies that allow specific traffic gives your users the access they need.

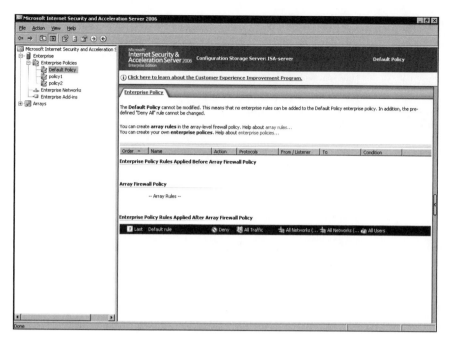

Figure 7-11   The default enterprise policy rule

After configuring enterprise administrative roles, networks, and rules, you can begin defining arrays, which involves configuring ISA Server array members to communicate with each other and the Configuration Storage server and specifying how the network is designed. Figure 7-12 shows several options for defining the network.

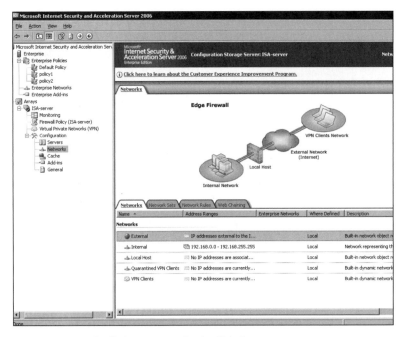

Figure 7-12   Defining networks in ISA Server arrays

When you begin entering access rules and working with ISA Server, all the objects you define are available to add as part of specific rules. If you have done your homework and planned your installation carefully, configuring ISA Server shouldn't be complicated. Activity 7-4 leads you through some major configuration tasks so that you can get comfortable working with the ISA Server management console.

Activity 7-4: Configuring ISA Server 2006

Time Required: 30 minutes

Objective: Configure ISA Server 2006 settings.

Description: In this activity, you perform general configuration tasks for ISA Server 2006: assigning administrative roles, defining networks, entering enterprise policy rules, and setting up basic firewall policies.

1. Open the ISA Server management console, and click to expand **Enterprise** in the console tree. The Getting Started with ISA Server 2006 Enterprise Management main window is displayed.

2. Click **Assign Administrative Roles** in the details pane. Click the **Assign Roles** tab, if necessary, and then click **Add**.

3. In the Administration Delegation dialog box, click **Browse**. Type **Administrator** in the text box, and then click **Check Names**. The entry should be in the *servername*\Administrator format. Click **OK**.

4. In the Role drop-down list, click **ISA Server Enterprise Administrator**, and then click **OK**. If you see a message stating the user/group has already been assigned the selected role, click **Cancel** and continue. Click **OK** in the Enterprise Properties dialog box to finish assigning administrative roles.

5. In the Getting Started window, click **Define Enterprise Networks** in the details pane. As shown in Figure 7-13, there are four default networks: External, Local Host, Quarantined VPN Clients, and VPN Clients.

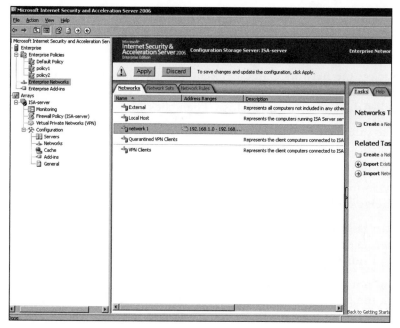

Figure 7-13   Configuring enterprise networks

6. Click the **Tasks** tab in the tasks pane, if necessary, and then click **Create a New Network** to start the New Network Wizard.

You can also right-click entries in the console tree to perform tasks.

7. Enter a name for your new network, and then click **Next**.

8. Click **Add Range**, enter the IP address range for the new network, and click **OK**. Click **Next**, and then click **Finish**.

9. In the details pane, click the **Network Sets** tab. In the tasks pane, click **Create a New Network Set** to start the New Network Set Wizard.

10. Enter a name for your new network set, and then click Next.

11. Click the **Include all selected networks** option button, and click the check box next to the network you just created. Click **Next**, and then click **Finish**.

12. In the details pane, click the **Network Rules** tab. In the tasks pane, click **Create a New Network Rule** to start the New Network Rule Wizard.

13. Enter a name for your new network rule, and then click **Next**.

14. To select the network traffic sources the rule applies to, click **Add**. In the Add Network Entities dialog box, click to select the network set you created in Steps 9 to 11, and then click **OK**. Click **Next**.

15. To select the network traffic destinations the rule applies to, click **Add**. In the Add Network Entities dialog box, click **All Networks (and Local Hosts)**. Click **Add**, and then click **Close**. Then click **Next**.

16. Make sure the **Network Address Translation (NAT)** option button is selected, and click **Next** and then **Finish**. You have defined your enterprise networks.

17. Return to the Getting Started window, and click **Define Enterprise Policies** in the details pane.

18. In the tasks pane, click **Create a New Enterprise Policy** to start the New Enterprise Policy Wizard. Enter a name for the policy, and click **Next** and then **Finish**.

19. Now you need to assign administrative roles to the policy. In the details pane, click the policy you just created, and then click **Edit Enterprise Policy Properties** in the tasks pane. Enter a description of the policy, if you want.

20. Click the **Assign Roles** tab in the details pane, and click **Add**. Click **Browse**, and type **administrator** in the text box. Click **Check Names**, and then click **OK**. In the drop-down list, click **ISA Server Enterprise Policy Editor**, click **OK**, and then click **OK** again.

21. In the console tree, click to select the policy you created. In the tasks pane, click **Create Enterprise Access Rule** to start the New Access Rule Wizard. Enter a name for the access rule, and then click **Next**.

22. Click **Allow** for the rule action, and then click **Next**.

23. Click **All outbound traffic** in the drop-down list, and click **Next**.

24. Click **Add**, click to expand **Network Sets**, and click the new network set you created. Click **Add**, and then click **Close**. Click **Next**.

25. Click **Add,** click to expand **Network Sets,** and click **All Networks (and Local Hosts).** Click **Add,** and then click **Close.** Click **Next.**

26. All Users is already selected as the user set, so click **Next,** and then click **Finish.** You can edit, reorder, and delete policies you create. Figure 7-14 shows your enterprise policy rules.

NOTE You've just created a policy that allows all outbound traffic from all users in your network set to access all networks. This rule isn't secure enough for a real network, so you shouldn't leave it in place, but it serves to give you practice in setting up rules. Allowing outbound access is fine, but in a real network, you would specify restrictions.

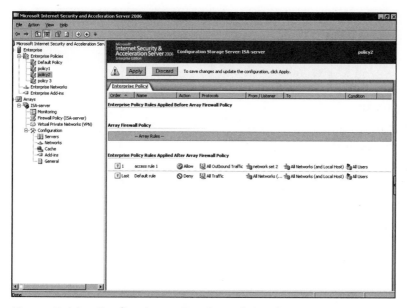

Figure 7-14   Configuring enterprise policy rules

27. You've assigned administrative roles, defined enterprise networks, and entered an enterprise policy. Leave the ISA Server management console open and your system running for the next activity.

For nearly every task in ISA Server 2006, a wizard and interactive tools are available to help you configure settings. The main chore in securing a network is planning the details for networks, users, access, and necessary security measures. In Activity 7-5, you configure some of ISA Server 2006's advanced security features.

Activity 7-5: Configuring Advanced Security Features in ISA Server 2006

Time Required: 30 minutes

Objective: Configure ISA Server 2006 security features.

Description: In this activity, you examine and configure filters and security features, create firewall policies, configure caching, and edit scheduling.

1. Open the ISA Server management console if necessary, and click **Enterprise Add-ins** in the console tree. The Application Filters tab, showing the application filters available in ISA Server 2006 Enterprise, is displayed (see Figure 7-15).

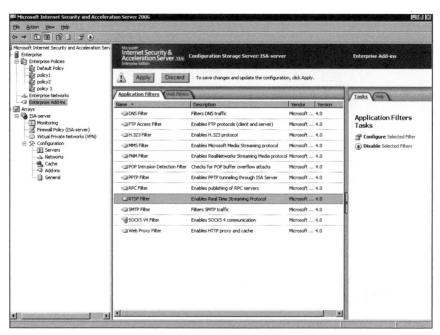

Figure 7-15 The Application Filters tab

2. Click **POP Intrusion Detection Filter** in the details pane. In the tasks pane, click **Configure Selected Filter**.

3. Click to enable the **Enable this filter on all arrays** check box, if necessary, and then click **OK**. Note that the filters enabled at the enterprise level can't be disabled at the array level. If you want a filter enabled for selected arrays only, enable it at the array level.

4. Disable the **POP Intrusion Detection Filter** at the enterprise level. You should see a red down arrow next to the filter name to indicate that it's been disabled.

5. In the console tree, click **Arrays**, click to expand your server, and click to expand **Configuration**. Click **Add-ins**. Right-click **POP Intrusion Detection Filter** and click **Properties**. Click to select the **Enable this Filter** check box. Click **OK**.

TIP

If you're working in a classroom setting, you can set up an ISA Server array by using the networked ISA Server systems in your class. Refer to the ISA Server help documentation for instructions.

6. Under Arrays in the console tree, click **General**. You access administrative tasks and global HTTP settings here as well as additional security features (see Figure 7-16).

7

Figure 7-16   General administration settings for arrays

7. Under Additional Security Policy in the details pane, click **Enable Intrusion Detection and DNS Attack Detection** to open the Intrusion Detection dialog box (see Figure 7-17).

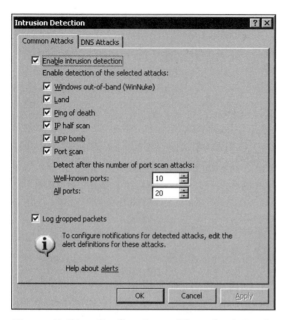

Figure 7-17   Configuring settings for intrusion detection

8. In the Common Attacks tab, click to select the **Port scan** check box to enable detection of a port scan attack. Accept the default threshold values of 10 and 20.

9. Click the **DNS Attacks** tab, review the available DNS attack detection methods, and then click **OK**.

10. Under Additional Security Policy in the details pane, click **Configure Flood Mitigation Settings**. In the Flood Mitigation dialog box, click the **Edit** button next to each attack to review the details, and then click **OK**.

11. Under Additional Security Policy in the details pane, click **Configure IP Protection**. Examine the settings in each tab of the IP Preferences dialog box, and then click **OK**.

12. Under Arrays in the console tree, click **Cache**, and then click **Define Cache Drives** in the tasks pane. Select the drive you want to use for caching (if necessary), and set the maximum cache size to use about half your free disk space (not half your total disk space). Click **OK**.

13. Under Arrays in the console tree, click **Firewall Policy**. In the tasks pane, click the **Toolbox** tab. Several categories of tools are available (see Figure 7-18).

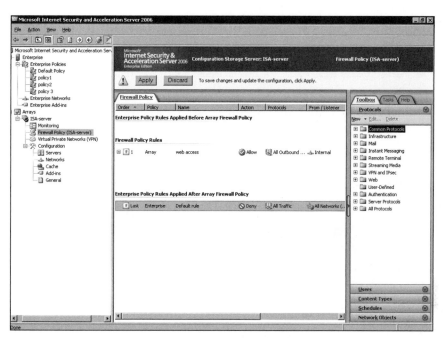

Figure 7-18   Available tools for the firewall policy

14. Click to expand the **Schedules** category at the bottom of the Toolbox tab. Click **Weekends**, and then click **Edit**. In the Weekends Properties dialog box, click the **Schedule** tab, and edit the template to allow work on Saturday from 8 a.m. through 2 p.m. Click **OK**.

15. Return to the Schedules category in the Toolbox tab, click **Work hours**, and then click **Edit**. Set a work week of Monday through Thursday from 7 a.m. to 6 p.m. and Friday from 7 a.m. to noon. Click **OK**.

16. In the tasks pane, click the **Tasks** tab. Under Firewall Policy Tasks, click **Create Access Rule** to start the Access Rule Wizard. Enter **firewall policy access rule 1** as the rule name, and click **Next**.

17. Click **Deny** as the action to take, and then click **Next**. In the drop-down list, click **Selected protocols** for the deny rule to apply to, if necessary, and then click **Add**. In the Protocols dialog box, click to select these protocols for the deny rule, making sure you click **Add** after selecting each one: **RIP, All instant messaging protocols except H.323 protocol and MSN Messenger, L2TP Server, PPTP Server**, and **Finger**. Click **Next**.

18. Apply the rule to traffic from external networks, and then click **Next**.

19. Set the rule to apply to traffic sent to your protected networks by clicking **Add**, clicking to expand **Network Sets**, and clicking **All Protected Networks**. Click **Add**, and then click **Close**. Click **Next**.

20. Click **Next**, accepting the default selection of All Users, and then click **Finish**. Explain what this rule accomplishes:

_____

_____

21. Now create a rule to allow all other traffic to pass through the firewall. Name it **firewall policy access rule 2**. Which rule should be first? Why?

_____

22. Your firewall policy rule base should look similar to Figure 7-19.

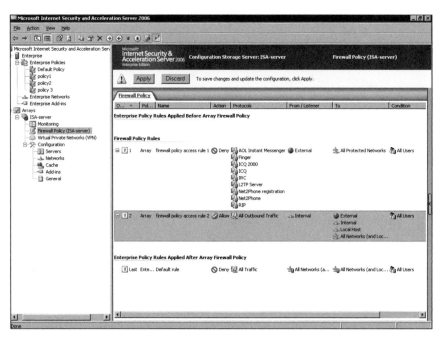

Figure 7-19   The firewall policy rule base

23. Click the **Apply** button above the details pane to apply and save your changes to the Configuration Storage server.

24. Leave your system running for the next activity. (You might find it helpful to refer to the ISA Server 2006 management console when reading the next section.)

You might have noticed that ISA Server 2006's VPN features aren't covered. VPNs are discussed in Chapters 8 and 9, and you configure ISA Server's VPN functions in those chapters.

NOTE

Monitoring Servers

When you have finished creating your enterprise and configuring rules, services, security, and connectivity, you still need to monitor your ISA Server 2006 deployment. Monitoring tools are integrated into the ISA Server management console and have many helpful features. Figure 7-20 shows the ISA Server Monitoring window, which you use to check connectivity, view alerts, monitor sessions, and check system performance.

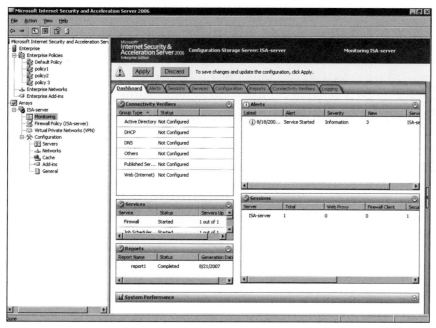

Figure 7-20   The ISA Server Monitoring window

The tabs offer many more options. For example, in the Reports tab, you can generate and customize reports, configure report jobs, and open saved reports. You use the Logging tab to configure and manage logging for your ISA server. Clicking Edit Filter in the tasks pane opens the Logging Properties dialog box (Firewall or Web Proxy), where you can specify the log format and log storage location and customize the fields included in logs. You use the Configuration tab to check array members' status to ensure that they're updated with current settings in the Configuration Storage server. The Connectivity Verifiers tab is where you monitor connectivity between servers.

You've learned the basics of navigating and configuring ISA Server 2006 Enterprise Edition, but to investigate its capabilities more thoroughly, visit Microsoft TechNet to complete the virtual labs for ISA Server 2006. With these labs, you can explore advanced features and practice configuring a virtual enterprise network. The labs include common deployment scenarios for ISA Server that prepare you for working with this software in a production environment. Part of being a good IT security administrator is continuous learning.

According to many employment forecasting experts, continuous learning will be the rule for jobs of the future. Those who want to succeed and move ahead will incorporate continuous learning into their work habits, so take advantage of all available learning opportunities.

 Many tools integrate with ISA Server 2006 to enhance its functionality and make management easier. You can find ISA Server 2006 tools on Microsoft's Web site or from numerous third-party vendors.

MANAGING AND CONFIGURING IPTABLES

Iptables, included in version 2.4.x and later of the Linux kernel, is used to configure packet-filtering rules for the Linux firewall Netfilter. It replaces Ipchains (which was developed for the Linux firewall Ipfwadm). Unlike Ipchains, Iptables enables Netfilter to perform stateful rather than stateless packet filtering. You can also filter packets based on a full set of TCP option flags instead of just the SYN flag, which was the only filtering flag available in Ipchains. Unlike ISA Server 2006, Iptables is a command-line tool. You can use it to set up logging, NAT, and forwarding packets from one port to another.

Like other packet-filtering programs, Iptables works with sets of rules. Unlike other programs, however, the rules are grouped in the form of **chains**. You can think of a chain as being similar to a rule base. The differences are that Linux makes use of multiple rule bases/chains, and a rule in one chain can activate a rule in another chain.

Built-in Chains

When Iptables receives a packet, the chains are reviewed. Iptables comes with three built-in chains:

- *Output*—This chain of rules is reviewed when packets are received from inside a network with a destination address on an external network.

- *Input*—This chain of rules is for packets from an external network destined for a location on the internal network.

- *Forward*—This chain is used when a packet needs to be routed to another location.

The packet moves through all rules in a chain until a match is found. If a match is found, one of four decisions is made on how to handle it:

- *Accept*—The packet is accepted.

- *Drop*—The packet is dropped without any error message, which provides effective security because it doesn't let external users know anything about the system processing the request.

- *Queue*—The packet is queued for processing by a specific application.

- *Return*—Iptables stops checking rules in the chain and returns to the original chain.

The chains of rules work together as shown in Figure 7-21, and the following process takes place:

1. Incoming packets that aren't forwarded go through the Input chain.

2. If a match is found, the action associated with the matched rule applies.

3. If no match is found, the packet moves to the Forward chain.

4. If no match is found, the packet moves to the Output chain.

5. If no match is found, the default action for the chain is carried out.

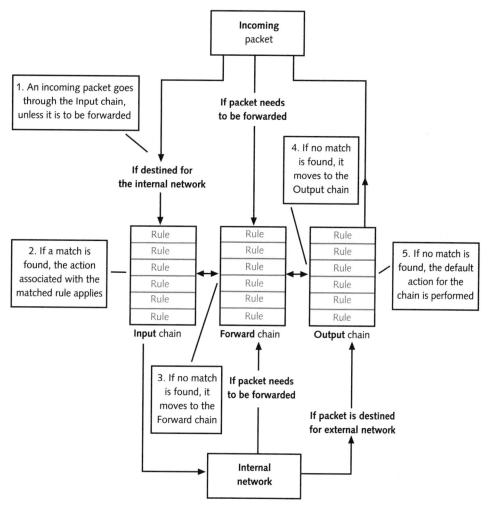

Figure 7-21   Built-in chains of packet-filtering rules in Iptables

An incoming packet goes through the Input chain, unless it's forwarded.

In the iptables command, you configure the default action for a chain with the -P option, which sets the default policy for a built-in chain. Then comes the chain name, OUTPUT, and the new policy, ACCEPT. The following command sets Accept as the default action for any packets going from the internal network to the Internet:

```
iptables -P OUTPUT ACCEPT
```

The following command blocks all incoming connection attempts by default:

```
iptables -P INPUT DROP
```

After setting the default action, you can configure more specific actions on a case-by-case basis. The two preceding commands are optional starting points for more restrictive rules that follow.

Another default command rejects all forwarded packets by default. For example, the following command blocks any packets the firewall forwards to a destination computer:

```
iptables -P FORWARD DROP
```

Blocking packets from being forwarded by default prevents external users from accessing internal computers in case a user activates a service on a port by accident, which could allow an attacker to exploit the opening.

To see other options for the iptables command, type iptables -h at the command prompt to access the Help file (see Figure 7-22). After you set the default rules, you can create specific rules by using the commands described in the following section.

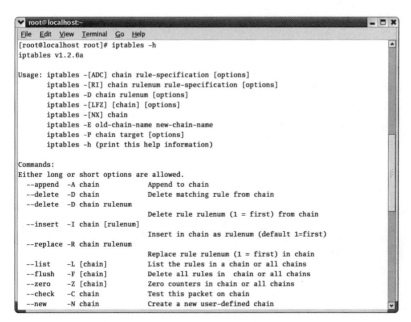

```
root@localhost:~                                                    _ □ x
File  Edit  View  Terminal  Go  Help
[root@localhost root]# iptables -h
iptables v1.2.6a

Usage: iptables -[ADC] chain rule-specification [options]
       iptables -[RI] chain rulenum rule-specification [options]
       iptables -D chain rulenum [options]
       iptables -[LFZ] [chain] [options]
       iptables -[NX] chain
       iptables -E old-chain-name new-chain-name
       iptables -P chain target [options]
       iptables -h (print this help information)

Commands:
Either long or short options are allowed.
  --append  -A chain             Append to chain
  --delete  -D chain             Delete matching rule from chain
  --delete  -D chain rulenum
                                 Delete rule rulenum (1 = first) from chain
  --insert  -I chain [rulenum]
                                 Insert in chain as rulenum (default 1=first)
  --replace -R chain rulenum
                                 Replace rule rulenum (1 = first) in chain
  --list    -L [chain]           List the rules in a chain or all chains
  --flush   -F [chain]           Delete all rules in  chain or all chains
  --zero    -Z [chain]           Zero counters in chain or all chains
  --check   -C chain             Test this packet on chain
  --new     -N chain             Create a new user-defined chain
```

Figure 7-22   Viewing Iptables options for chains

7

NOTE   One advantage of using Iptables rather than an add-on firewall is that because it's part of the Linux kernel, it runs through its packet-filtering rule base and makes decisions quickly.

User-Defined Chains

In addition to built-in chains, you can create user-defined chains by using commands for configuring rules. The following list explains some of these commands (with *chain* representing the name of the chain to which the rule belongs):

- -A *chain rule*—Adds a new rule to the chain

- -I *chain rulenumber rule*—Places a new rule in a specific location in the chain, as indicated by *rulenumber*

- -R *chain rulenumber rule*—Replaces a rule with a new one in the location specified by *rulenumber*

- -D *chain rulenumber*—Deletes the rule at the position specified by *rulenumber*

- -D *chain rule*—Deletes a rule

Commands for creating rules include the following:

- -s *source*—Identifies the source IP address
- -d *destination*—Identifies the destination IP address
- -p *protocol*—Identifies the protocol used in the rule (such as TCP or UDP)
- -i *interface*—Identifies the network interface the rule uses
- -j *target*—Identifies the action (or **target**) associated with the rule; the target can be an action (such as Allow or Drop), a network, or a subnet
- !—Negates whatever follows it, such as an IP address you want to exclude
- -l—Activates logging if a packet matches the rule

Some examples should make these commands clearer. Refer to the set of rules in Table 7-2 earlier in this chapter, and then see how the following commands create the same rules:

```
iptables -A OUTPUT -s any -d 210.100.101.1 -p any -j DROP
iptables -A OUTPUT -s any -d 210.100.101.2 -p HTTP -j ACCEPT
iptables -A OUTPUT -s 210.100.101.0-210.100.101.255 -d any !
   210.100.101.2 HTTP,HTTPS -j ACCEPT
iptables -A OUTPUT -s any -d any -p any -j DROP -l
```

In addition, you can identify a service rather than a protocol: www for the World Wide Web, smtp for outgoing e-mail, and pop3 for incoming e-mail. The following rule enables all users on the 10.0.20.0/24 network to access the Web server at 10.0.20.2 by using the World Wide Web service:

```
iptables -A OUTPUT -s 10.0.20.0/24 -d 10.0.20.2 www -j ACCEPT
```

Configuring Iptables is complex; this overview is intended only to give you a starting point. For more information, see the main pages for Iptables in the Linux Help files. An excellent resource for Netfilter and Iptables is *www.netfilter.org*.

NOTE

ISA Server 2006 and Iptables have many capabilities not mentioned in this chapter. Covering either one would take an entire book, so you should do extensive research and review product documentation before taking the certification exam.

Chapter Summary

- Improving a firewall configuration often involves optimizing the rule base to enhance efficiency and improve security. In addition, you can optimize logging to fine-tune control over what's logged and how log files are stored to improve firewall performance.

- Many firewalls and IDSs generate log files you can view with a text editor, but text-based log files can be difficult to read. With other firewalls, you can use different log file formats, such as ODBC or W3C Extended format. Another option for viewing log files is using a firewall's built-in interface.

❐ Fine-tuning log file formats to log only the information you need makes it easier to review files, helps optimize the firewall rule base, and can improve performance and security by eliminating useless or duplicate entries.

❐ Some firewall programs include log file analysis tools that prepare summaries of raw data over a certain period and include options for organizing the information into report forms. Other programs require using an add-on log analyzer.

❐ The host computer's processor speed has the most impact on firewall performance. Choose a machine with the fastest processor available and at least the minimum required RAM, if not more. A standard formula for determining requirements for cache memory is 100 MB + (0.5 MB x number of users).

❐ After configuring a firewall, testing before and after it goes online helps prevent user access problems. Ideally, you should test a firewall before installing it on the network so that you can shut down the software and make changes without interrupting network traffic.

❐ After installing a firewall, you need to configure basic functions and then add advanced features, such as data caching, remote management, application filtering, voice and multimedia application support, load balancing, and failover redundancy.

❐ Microsoft ISA Server 2006 incorporates firewall and caching functions with comprehensive security, connectivity, and management features.

❐ Iptables is a Linux command-line tool for creating packet-filtering rules. It includes three built-in chains of rules that monitor inbound and outbound packets as well as packets to forward to specific destinations.

KEY TERMS

cache — Store data on disk for later retrieval; also a hard disk area where files are stored.

chains — Sets of packet-filtering rules that Iptables uses. *See also* Iptables.

Configuration Storage server — In ISA Server 2006, the server that stores configuration information for all array members in the enterprise.

DNS zone transfer — A query used by secondary DNS servers to update their DNS records.

Iptables — A packet-filtering command-line tool used with the Linux firewall Netfilter.

ISA Server services — A component of ISA Server 2006 installed on array members that performs firewall, VPN, and caching services.

target — In Iptables, the command option that determines what action is taken on packets matching specific criteria.

test cell — A dedicated testing environment, ideally modeled after the production environment, used for testing new software or hardware to detect and correct problems before placing it into production.

REVIEW QUESTIONS

1. Which of the following guidelines should you keep in mind when editing your rule base? (Choose all that apply.)

   a. Place rules governing domain objects near the bottom of the rule base.

   b. Make your rule base as detailed as possible.

   c. Place the most frequently matched rules near the top of the rule base.

   d. Adjust default logging so that the firewall logs all traffic.

2. One of the simplest and most effective ways to improve a rule base is to do which of the following?

   a. Reduce the number of rules.

   b. Remove duplicate or unnecessary listings.

   c. Make sure the rule base contains the recommended number of rules.

   d. Reverse the order of rule processing.

3. You shouldn't log events resulting from attempts to access restricted resources. True or False?

4. The firewall host computer's _____ has the most impact on firewall performance.

   a. RAM cache

   b. network card speed

   c. available hard drive space

   d. processor speed

5. What critical information do firewall logs provide? (Choose all that apply.)

   a. information about potential attacks

   b. information about software errors

   c. application failure records

   d. information about network traffic

6. What is the advantage of saving firewall logs in Open Database Connectivity (ODBC) format?

   a. reading logs by using the firewall interface

   b. presenting logs in a graphical format

   c. opening logs in a Web browser

   d. opening logs with a database application

7. Having several administrators available to configure a firewall can _____. (Choose all that apply.)

   a. make developing content filters easier

   b. allow creating multiple packet-filtering rules

   c. distribute the load of firewall maintenance

   d. cause confusion

8. Why do so many firewalls, by default, log packets that are denied?

   a. to keep log file size to a minimum

   b. to track unsuccessful access attempts

   c. to have a record on file in case users complain

   d. to be able to correct rules to allow access to the same packets

9. If a firewall doesn't look up hostnames on the host computer, what happens? (Choose all that apply.)

   a. Performance slows.

   b. The firewall has to resolve domain names.

   c. The firewall drops all packets.

   d. The firewall could crash.

10. What happens when a firewall runs out of memory? (Choose all that apply.)

    a. It stops functioning and shuts down.

    b. It drops packets.

    c. It slows down traffic flow.

    d. It uses the page file.

11. Which of the following is a common formula for determining cache memory needs?

    a. 1 GB + (0.5 MB x [1.5 x number of users])

    b. 100 MB + (0.5 MB x number of users)

    c. 0.5 MB x number of users

    d. 350 MB + (0.5 MB x number of users)

12. ISA Server 2006 can be installed on which OS?

    a. Windows Vista

    b. Windows 2000 Server

    c. Windows XP Professional

    d. Windows Server 2003

13. Which of the following is an Iptables built-in chain? (Choose all that apply.)

    a. Inbound

    b. Output

    c. Reverse

    d. Forward

14. What do Iptables chains consist of?

    a. IP addresses

    b. packet-filtering rules

    c. log file listings

    d. encrypted packets

15. What benefits does a test cell provide?

    a. allows testing of live production equipment

    b. gives you the opportunity to discover problems before placing new equipment into production

    c. serves as a central location for deploying updates and patches

    d. gives administrators a quiet place to nap after a long day

16. Which of the following is the most critical component of an ISA Server 2006 Enterprise deployment?

    a. array

    b. Configuration Storage server

    c. ISA Server services

    d. MMC snap-in

17. The Configuration Storage server can't be installed on the same computer as ISA Server services. True or False?

18. In which order should ISA Server 2006 installation be performed?

    a. installing ISA Server services, installing the Configuration Storage server, creating arrays and enterprise policies

    b. creating arrays and enterprise policies, installing ISA Server services, installing Configuration Storage server

    c. installing the Configuration Storage server, creating arrays, installing ISA Server services, creating enterprise policies

    d. installing the Configuration Storage server, creating arrays and enterprise policies, installing ISA Server services

19. ISA Server 2006 can detect and prevent TCP flood attacks. True or False?

HANDS-ON PROJECTS

Hands-On Project 7-1: Configuring Iptables

Time Required: 20 minutes

Objective: Use a Linux system to configure Iptables rules.

Description: Iptables enables Netfilter to perform stateful packet filtering, NAT, logging, and other security functions for the Linux kernel. In this project, you activate Iptables and begin configuring it. You need a computer with Red Hat Linux 8.0 or later. Assume the following about the network you're configuring: The network is at 10.0.20.0/24, the firewall is at 10.0.20.1, the e-mail server is at 10.0.20.2, and the Web server is at 10.0.20.3.

1. Click the **Red Hat** icon or equivalent for your OS, point to **System Tools**, and click **Terminal**.

2. To configure Iptables to run whenever you start your computer, type **chkconfig --level 345 iptables on** and press **Enter**.

3. If necessary, turn off any other security programs you have running by entering the following (pressing **Enter** after each command):

    ```
    service ipchains off
    service ip6tables off
    ```

> If these services aren't running, the command returns an "Unrecognized service" error.

NOTE

4. Type **iptables –L** and press **Enter** to view default chains and their policies. What do you notice about the default actions?

   _____

   _____

5. Type the following commands to set default policies for built-in chains. After each line, press **Enter**:

    ```
    iptables -P OUTPUT ACCEPT
    iptables -P INPUT DROP
    iptables -P FORWARD DROP
    ```

6. Type **iptables –L** and press **Enter** to verify the policy changes. (*Hint:* You can press the up arrow key to cycle through previous commands.)

7. Create a rule for the security policy statement "Anyone on the internal network can access the Web server on the DMZ as well as external Web sites":

   _____

   _____

8. Create a rule that prevents hosts on the Internet from accessing internal hosts by using the World Wide Web service:

   _____

   _____

9. Create two rules that enable anyone on the internal network to connect to the company e-mail server but not to external e-mail servers via SMTP:

   _____

   _____

10. To save your changes, type **service iptables save** and press **Enter**.

HANDS-ON PROJECTS

Hands-On Project 7-2: Analyzing a Log File

Time Required: 15 minutes

Objective: Analyze a log file for duplicate entries.

Description: In this project, you analyze the log file entries in Table 7-7 so that you can eliminate duplicate entries to improve firewall efficiency and security. You also examine these entries for possible attacks and any missing information. The network has IP addresses from 210.100.101.0 to 210.100.101.255. The firewall is at 210.100.101.1, the Web server is at 210.100.101.2, the DNS server is at 210.100.101.3, the SMTP server is at 210.100.101.4, and the POP3 server is at 210.100.101.5.

Table 7-7   Sample log file entries

Entry	Date	Source	Destination	Destination port	Action	Type	Protocol
1	21Mar2007	67.23.89.9	210.100.101.23	137	Deny	Log	UDP
2	21Mar2007	67.23.89.9	210.100.101.23	137	Deny	Log	UDP
3	21Mar2007	189.101.10.88	210.100.101.151	114	Deny	Log	TCP
4	21Mar2007	189.101.10.88	210.100.101.151	115	Deny	Log	TCP
5	21Mar2007	210.100.101.3	155.201.8.83	37	Allow	Log	TCP
6	21Mar2007	67.23.89.9	210.100.101.23	137	Deny	Log	UDP
7	21Mar2007	210.100.101.35	210.100.101.3	137	Allow	Log	TCP
8	21Mar2007	189.101.10.88	210.100.101.151	116	Deny	Log	TCP
9	21Mar2007	189.101.10.88	210.100.101.151	117	Deny	Log	TCP
10	21Mar2007	210.100.101.126	210.100.101.2	80	Allow	Log	TCP
11	21Mar2007	225.23.202.5	210.100.101.2	80	Allow	Log	TCP
12	21Mar2007	189.101.10.88	210.100.101.151	118	Deny	Log	TCP

7

1. Are there any duplicate log file entries? What do they indicate, and how could you cut back on the duplication?

2. Are there any events that don't need to be logged?

3. Identify any attack attempts:

4. Is any type of information missing from the log files that should be there?

CASE PROJECT

CASE PROJECTS

Case Project 7-1: Developing a Firewall Architecture for the Green Globe Network

Using all previous work and what you have learned in this chapter, design an ISA Server 2006 Enterprise array for Green Globe. Update your network topology maps to show the locations of ISA Server systems and the Configuration Storage server. Be sure to include details about connectivity between array members and the Configuration Storage server, and construct a naming and addressing scheme for the ISA Server array.

Include information about services you plan to provide with ISA Server and how critical resources will be secured. For example, what authentication method will you use? If you've already settled on a RADIUS server, you would configure ISA Server to use it for authentication. In addition, include inbound and outbound filtering, Web content filtering and caching, communication services, and any security measures you plan to use.

Be sure to proofread carefully, and make sure formatting conforms to your instructor's or school's writing guidelines. Update any documentation, if needed, to reflect changes.

NOTE

8

IMPLEMENTING IPSec AND VIRTUAL PRIVATE NETWORKS

After reading this chapter and completing the exercises, you will be able to:

♦ Explain basic VPN concepts

♦ Describe encapsulation in VPNs

♦ Describe encryption in VPNs

♦ Describe authentication in VPNs

A virtual private network (VPN) combines two essential elements of a network defense strategy: security and connectivity. VPNs play important roles in businesses that rely on the Internet for critical communications and are attractive because of their low cost and efficiency.

In the past, companies conducting electronic transactions used leased lines—private connections rented from telecommunications companies, using technologies such as frame relay or T-carriers (T1, T3). Leased lines are expensive, however, so a VPN is a cost-effective way for networks to make a secure connection through the public Internet.

A VPN is said to be "virtual" because the connection between networks doesn't use a dedicated line. Rather, it uses the same public Internet connections that millions of people use. Users who make VPN connections gain privacy via a variety of technologies, such as encryption and authentication. In this chapter, you learn what VPNs are, why they are growing in popularity, and how they ensure private communication between networks. This chapter also explains the protocols that create a secure virtual tunnel between computers and describes encryption methods for maintaining the privacy and integrity of VPN communications.

UNDERSTANDING VPN CONCEPTS

A **virtual private network (VPN)** provides a way for two computers or computer networks to communicate securely by using the same public communication channels available on the Internet, where millions of computers and networks exchange data.

To understand what VPNs are, consider how regular mail works. Because you want your letter kept private, you place it in a sealed envelope (encapsulation). If you're concerned about the possibility of your message being intercepted and read by someone else, you could write it in code (encryption), but you would need a way to let the receiver decrypt it, which could be considered a "key exchange."

You need to tell the mail carrier where to deliver the envelope and exactly who's supposed to receive it, so you place a name and address on the outside (the destination address information). If your envelope can't be delivered, you put a return address on the envelope (the source address) so that the mail carrier can bring it back to you. As on the public Internet, your message can take several paths to its destination. This is the "virtual" part of a VPN.

Finally, the mail is processed through many different sorting centers, air and ground transportation systems, and post offices that form the United States Postal Service (USPS) "network," just as the Internet is a conglomeration of private LANs, public transmission lines, and other systems forming a giant mesh network.

Specified computers, users, or network gateways are identified as endpoints of the VPN connection, which is called a **tunnel**, and only those designated computers, users, or gateways can participate in the VPN (see Figure 8-1). A VPN is a network because it connects computers and extends an organization's network beyond its current boundaries. A VPN, then, is a virtual network connection that uses the Internet to establish a secure connection. VPNs enable computers to exchange private encrypted messages that others can't decipher.

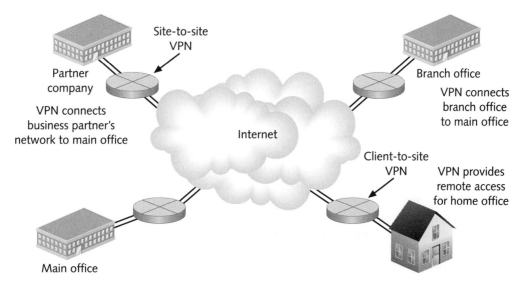

Figure 8-1 Establishing connections with a VPN

VPN endpoints represent extensions of participating networks. Those endpoints must be secured by a firewall, or they could give intruders a way to access the network. Unless your VPN client software incorporates its own firewall, you need to make sure any remote computers connecting to your organization's VPN are equipped with desktop firewalls.

VPN Components

VPNs can be assembled by using a variety of components. However, all VPNs contain some essential elements that enable data to be transmitted securely from one point to another:

- *VPN server or host*—A **VPN server** is configured to accept connections from clients who connect via dial-up or broadband.

- *VPN client or guest*—A **VPN client** can be a router that serves as the endpoint of a site-to-site VPN connection, which uses hardware to connect two networks. It can also be an OS configured to function as an endpoint in a VPN.

- *Tunnel*—The connection through which data is sent.

- *VPN protocols*—**VPN protocols** are sets of standardized communication settings that software and hardware use to encrypt data sent along the VPN. They include Internet Protocol Security (IPSec), Point-to-Point Tunneling Protocol (PPTP), and Layer 2 Tunneling Protocol (L2TP).

The number of components in a VPN depends on the number of networks in its configuration. For instance, if a VPN contains four networks, it has at least four separate servers and four tunnels; clients from each endpoint can participate in any of the VPN tunnels they have permission and credentials to access.

In general, you can set up two different types of VPNs. The first type links two or more networks and is called a **site-to-site VPN** (or a gateway-to-gateway VPN). The second type makes a network accessible to users who need remote access and is called a **client-to-site VPN** (or a remote access VPN).

TIP Some companies that maintain VPNs with partner organizations benefit by using the same ISP as their partners for an Internet connection. Positioning participants in the VPN on the same part of the Internet backbone can make the VPN run more smoothly and reliably.

Hardware VPNs

The components you choose to establish a VPN depend on whether you want to use existing hardware or software. Creating a VPN with new components increases costs but has the benefit of reducing the load on the other network security components (such as firewalls).

Hardware-based VPNs connect one gateway to another (gateway-to-gateway). Typically, the VPN hardware is a router at each network gateway that encrypts outbound packets and decrypts inbound packets. Another hardware option involves a **VPN appliance**, a hardware device designed to serve as the VPN endpoint and join LANs (see Figure 8-2).

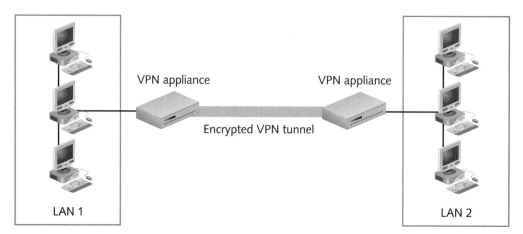

Figure 8-2 VPN appliances create secure connections between two or more LANs

In general, hardware products, such as routers, that are dedicated to VPN operation tend to handle more network traffic than software products. As a result, they are more scalable than software VPNs. They can also be more secure than software VPNs because they are designed from the ground up for a specific purpose and don't depend on an underlying OS that might have security flaws. Hardware VPNs should be the first choice for fast-growing networks that need to encrypt all traffic passing through the VPN device. They are also a good choice when VPN endpoints use the same type of routers and are controlled by the same organizations. Table 8-1 lists some examples of hardware VPN devices.

Table 8-1 Hardware VPN products

Manufacturer	Product name	Web site
Cisco Systems	VPN 3000 series concentrators, VPN 3002 Hardware Clients, 7600 series WebVPN Services Modules, 7600 series routers, PIX 500 appliances, and 6500 series Catalyst switches, among others	www.cisco.com
SonicWALL	SSL VPN Secure Remote Access appliance models 200, 2000, and 4000; PRO series; and the Unified Threat Management (UTM) platform combining security and access capabilities	www.sonicwall.com
Nokia	Nokia 5i, 10i, 50i, 105i, 500i, and Mobile VPN	www.nokia.com
Juniper Networks	Secure Access 700, 2000, 4000, 6000, and 6000 SP	www.juniper.net
WatchGuard	WatchGuard Firebox X series (integrated UTM)	www.watchguard.com

The security industry has moved toward integrated solutions, as discussed previously. The most common term you see with integrated security products is **Unified Threat Management (UTM)**. UTM describes integrating firewall, intrusion detection/ prevention, antivirus, e-mail, and communication security; VPNs and secure remote access; authentication; and other security-related functions into a single product suite. Many excellent products provide firewall, intrusion detection, VPNs, authentication, and more in a single platform. Integrated solutions have some major advantages, particularly cost, interoperability, and easier management. On the other hand, dedicating security devices to a particular function might be better because having a single device introduces a single point of failure and reduces layers of defense. In reality, even though a UTM product can perform multilayered defense functions, it's still a single product. An organization's security needs dictate whether a UTM product is appropriate.

Software VPNs

Most software-based VPNs are integrated with firewalls and are more cost-effective than hardware VPN devices. They also increase network security because they are integrated with functions that a firewall already performs, such as packet filtering and Network Address Translation (NAT). Software-based VPNs are appropriate when networks participating in the VPN use different routers and firewalls or when the endpoints are controlled by different organizations and network administrators.

The reason for using software VPNs to link networks is the flexibility they offer. They can, for instance, be configured to enable traffic based on domain name, protocol, or IP address. These restrictions prove useful when some, but not all, of the traffic passing through the VPN is meant to be encrypted and sent through the tunnel. Because software VPNs often rely on the OS they are installed on, configuring and using them are more complex, however. Table 8-2 lists some examples of VPN software solutions.

Table 8-2   Software VPN products

Manufacturer	Product name	Web site
Check Point	VPN-1 Power VSX, VPN-1 UTM, VPN-1 MASS, and Firewall-1 GX	*www.checkpoint.com*
NETGEAR	ProSafe VPN Client	*www.netgear.com*
3Com Corporation	OfficeConnect	*www.3com.com*
Open source	OpenVPN, VPN daemon, FreeS/WAN, SSL-Explorer, SSLBridge	Several sites; search for the product you want
Microsoft	Internet Security and Acceleration (ISA) Server 2006	*www.microsoft.com*

ACTIVITY

Activity 8-1: Direct-Connecting Two Lab Computers

Time Required: 15 minutes

Objective: Connect two lab computers with a null-modem/crossover cable.

Description: In this activity, you direct-connect two computers in your lab so that you can create a VPN between them in subsequent activities. You need two computers running Windows XP. One computer functions as the VPN host, and the other computer functions as the VPN guest.

1. Obtain a crossover, null-modem, or direct-connection cable.

2. The connectors at the end of the cable look the same, but they are not. Inspect them, explain the difference, and explain the purpose of this cable:

_____

_____

_____

TIP

You can download and install virtual null-modem software that emulates a null-modem cable connection. Some programs can also simulate a connection between two computers on a single machine, which is helpful for testing purposes. If you don't have access to two computers, or creating a physical cable connection isn't possible, simulation software is an excellent alternative.

3. Plug the cable into the corresponding port of each computer you want to connect.

4. On both computers, open Control Panel. In Category view, click **Network and Internet Connections**, and then click **Network Connections** at the bottom. Under Network Tasks at the left, click the **Create a new connection** link. If the Location Information dialog box opens, enter the area code for your location, and then click **OK**.

5. When the New Connection Wizard starts, click **Next**. Click the **Set up an advanced connection** option button, and then click **Next**.

6. Click the **Connect directly to another computer** option button, and then click **Next**.

7. To select the computer role, click **Host** on one computer and **Guest** on the other computer. To configure the VPN guest, enter the VPN host computer's name as the connection name, and then click **Next**.

8. In the Select a device (guest computer) or Device for this connection (host computer) drop-down list, click **Communications port (COM1)**. (COM2 might be available, too; either will work.) Click **Next**.

9. Select the users allowed to connect to the host. Usually the administrator is allowed to connect, but another user with administrative privileges might be allowed, too. You can also add a new user in this window by clicking **Add**.

10. Click **Next**, and then click **Finish**. Leave the Network Connections window open for the next activity.

VPN CORE ACTIVITY 1: ENCAPSULATION

VPNs can use public Internet connections and still provide a high level of security because they perform a core set of activities: encapsulation, encryption, and authentication. Together, these activities tunnel data from one network to another using the infrastructure of the Internet.

First, VPNs perform **encapsulation** of data: They enclose a packet within another packet that has different IP source and destination information for a high degree of protection. Encapsulation protects the integrity of data sent through the VPN by hiding the data packets' source and destination information. The VPN encapsulates the actual data packets in packets that use the VPN gateway's source and destination addresses, as shown in Figure 8-3. The gateway could be a router that uses IPSec, a VPN appliance, or a firewall that functions as a VPN and has a gateway set up.

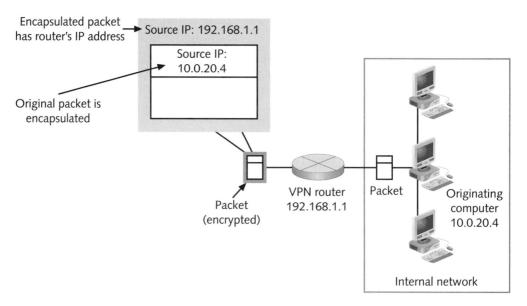

Figure 8-3 Encapsulating data to conceal source and destination information

When a VPN tunnel is in place, the source and destination IP addresses of the encapsulated data packets can be in the private reserved blocks that aren't routable over the Internet, such as the 10.0.0.0/8 addresses or the 192.168.0.0/16 reserved network blocks.

Understanding Tunneling Protocols

Because VPNs link networks and gateways that might have different OSs or hardware platforms, protocols need to be established so that communication can take place. When you configure a device to function as a VPN host, you need to choose the protocol you want to use. For instance, IPSec with Internet Key Exchange (IPSec/IKE) is fast becoming the protocol of choice among VPNs. A variety of common VPN protocols are discussed in the following sections.

Point-to-Point Tunneling Protocol

IPSec and Secure Shell provide VPN security in many circumstances, but they aren't appropriate for every application. Users who need to dial up a server on computers running older OSs might need to connect to VPN servers configured to support **Point-to-Point Tunneling Protocol (PPTP)**.

PPTP encapsulates TCP/IP packets and uses a proprietary technology called Microsoft Point-to-Point Encryption (MPPE) to encrypt data passing between the remote computer and the remote access server. PPTP should be used only in trusted networks where security is addressed by other means. Vulnerabilities in Microsoft Point-to-Point Encryption (MPPE) and Microsoft Challenge/Response Authentication Protocol (MS-CHAP) make PPTP a poor choice for high-performance networks with many hosts. Use PPTP only for a small-scale VPN that needs to support mobile users. The best option is to upgrade older clients to use more secure protocols when possible.

Activity 8-2: Setting Up a Remote Access Server

Time Required: 30 minutes

Objective: Configure a computer as a remote access/VPN server.

Description: In this activity, you configure Routing and Remote Access Services (RRAS) on one of the two computers you connected in Activity 8-1 so that it can accept incoming VPN connections. Then you can use it to set up a direct VPN connection or a dial-up connection using PPTP or L2TP.

1. If the Network Connections window isn't open, open it from Control Panel, and click the **Create a new connection** link.

2. When the New Connection Wizard starts, click **Next**.

3. Click the **Set up an advanced connection** option button, and then click **Next**.

4. Verify that the **Accept incoming connections** option button is selected, and then click **Next**.

5. If necessary, click **Communications cable between two computers**, and then click **Next**.

6. Verify that the **Allow virtual private connections** option button is selected, and then click **Next**.

7. In the User Permissions dialog box, click the box next to the user(s) who should be granted access to your computer. If necessary, click **Add** and create a username and password in the New User dialog box. When you're done, click **Next**.

8. In the Networking Software dialog box, verify that **Internet Protocol (TCP/IP)** and **File and Printer Sharing for Microsoft Networks** are selected. Click **Internet Protocol (TCP/IP)**, and then click the **Properties** button.

9. Verify that the **Allow callers to access my local area network** check box is selected, and then click **Specify TCP/IP addresses**.

10. In the From and To text boxes, specify a range of IP addresses for the VPN server to allocate. For this example, enter **192.168.1.1** in the From text box and **192.168.1.254** in the To text box. Click **OK**.

11. Click **Next**, and then click **Finish**. Close any open windows, and leave your system running for the next activity.

8

Layer 2 Tunneling Protocol

Layer 2 Tunneling Protocol (L2TP) is based on two older PPP tunneling protocols, Cisco's Layer 2 Forwarding (L2F) and PPTP, and uses UDP port 1701. Using L2TP, a host machine can connect to a modem and have its PPP data packets forwarded to another remote access server. L2TP encapsulates the PPP packets. When the data reaches the remote access server, its payload is unpacked and forwarded to the destination host on the internal network.

The endpoints of an L2TP tunnel are called the L2TP Access Concentrator (LAC) and the L2TP Network Server (LNS). Generally, the LAC is the initiator of the tunnel, and the LNS is the server waiting for tunnels (although either side can initiate tunnels). After an L2TP tunnel is established, it's bidirectional. L2TP exchanges two types of packets within the tunnel: control and data packets. Reliability features are provided for control packets but not for data packets. Reliability must be provided for data packets by higher-layer tunneled protocols.

Used alone, L2TP doesn't provide confidentiality or authentication, so it's usually combined with IPSec for improved security. This combination is referred to as L2TP/IPSec. Introduced with the release of Windows 2000, L2TP/IPSec is a more secure alternative to PPTP. IPSec enables L2TP to perform authentication and encapsulation as well as encryption. It encapsulates the entire L2TP packets, which has a couple of notable benefits. Because the L2TP packet is encapsulated in the IPSec packet, no information about the internal network can be gained from the encrypted packet. Also, the hidden L2TP packet is contained in the IPSec packet until reaching the endpoint, so UDP port 1701 doesn't need to be opened unless a firewall or packet filter is acting as an endpoint. (IPSec is explained in detail later in "Understanding IPSec/IKE.")

TIP

L2TP/IPSec is described in RFC 3193.

NOTE

A new version of L2TP, L2TP version 3 (L2TPv3), was published as a proposed standard in 2005. L2TPv3 has more advanced security features and better encapsulation and can carry data links other than PPP. You can learn more about L2TPv3 in RFC 3931.

ACTIVITY

Activity 8-3: Setting Up a Direct Client Connection

Time Required: 25 minutes

Objective: Configure a computer to act as a VPN client to the remote access server configured in Activity 8-2.

Description: After installing a null-modem cable between two computers, you can configure the second computer to function as the client. This activity assumes you have completed Activities 8-1 and 8-2.

1. Open the Network Connections window from Control Panel, and click the **Create a new connection** link.

2. When the Network Connection Wizard starts, click **Next**.

3. Click the **Set up an advanced connection** option button, and then click **Next**.

4. Click the **Connect directly to another computer** option button, and then click **Next**.

5. Click **Guest**, and then click **Next**.

6. In the Connection Name window, enter the name of the host computer, and then click **Next**.

7. In the Select a device drop-down list, select the direct cable connection you set up in Activity 8-1, and then click **Next**.

8. Click **Finish**. The Connect Direct dialog box opens.

9. Enter the username and password you created in Activity 8-2, and then click **Connect**. A message box states that the connection is being made. In a few seconds, a second message box should state that the connection has been established. Verify the connection by switching to the host computer and opening the Network Connections window. An icon representing the connection should be displayed. Click **OK** to close the Connection Complete dialog box.

10. Close any open windows, and leave your system running for the next activity.

Generic Routing Encapsulation

Generic Routing Encapsulation (GRE) is a tunneling protocol that can encapsulate a variety of Network-layer packets inside IP packets. GRE encapsulates the actual packet inside a GRE packet, which is then encapsulated in an arbitrary transport protocol for delivery. In IPv4 networks, the transport protocols are, of course, TCP and UDP. Other protocol stacks can also work with GRE, hence the "generic" in its name.

GRE is a stateless protocol, meaning endpoints don't monitor the status of other endpoints. This is useful because an endpoint might not be able to detect a service provider or network's internal tunneling architecture. Cisco designed GRE to create virtual point-to-point links to Cisco routers at remote locations, but it can be used for several applications. It can be combined with PPTP and IPSec and is commonly used with PPTP in Microsoft VPNs.

Here's how GRE works:

1. The packet to be transmitted is passed to the local endpoint of the VPN tunnel.

2. The packet is given a PPP header and encrypted.

3. GRE encapsulates the packet.

4. A transport protocol header is added.

5. The packet is transmitted through the tunnel.

6. At the endpoint, the transport protocol and GRE and PPP headers are stripped off.

7. The payload may or may not be decrypted, depending on the endpoint configuration and encryption used.

8. The payload is transmitted to its destination.

GRE uses IP protocol 47 and native IPv4 routing. Route filtering is not changed, but if packet filters are used, the filter must be configured to examine inside the GRE packet, or filtering should be done at tunnel endpoints. In this case, it might be wiser to terminate the tunnel at the firewall. IPv6 isn't currently included as a delivery or payload protocol with GRE.

CAUTION GRE can enable attacks against VPN client computers. The GRE protocol isn't attacked, but attackers can build a GRE packet and use it to initiate a connection to the client. Attacks on a protocol level require some effort to discover basic information about the target network. Used correctly, this type of attack can result in the attacker gaining a legitimate connection. For more information on attacks using GRE, visit *www.phenoelit-us.org/irpas/gre.html* or search for GRE protocol attacks.

Secure Shell

Like IPSec, Secure Shell (SSH) provides authentication and encryption of TCP/IP packets over a VPN or other connection. SSH works with UNIX-based systems to create a secure Transport-layer connection between participating computers. Versions for Windows are available, too. SSH also makes use of public-key cryptography (discussed later in "VPN Core Activity 2: Encryption").

When a client initiates an SSH connection, the two computers exchange keys and negotiate the algorithms for authentication and encryption to create a secure connection at the Transport layer. The username and password transmitted to the server are encrypted. All data sent subsequently is also encrypted. SSH is available free via the OpenSSH package of applications (*www.openssh.org*).

Socks

The **Socks** protocol is normally used as a way to provide proxy services for applications that don't usually support proxying. Socks version 5 adds encrypted authentication and support for UDP. With these new features, Socks v.5 can enable applications to set up a secure tunnel by using encryption and authentication.

NOTE

SSH and Socks v.5 aren't widely supported by VPNs, so they aren't covered extensively in this chapter. If you're interested in learning more about SSH, try *www.openssh.com* or *www.ssh.com*.

ACTIVITY

Activity 8-4: Establishing a VPN Connection

Time Required: 15 minutes

Objective: Establish a VPN connection with the VPN server and client configured in previous activities.

Description: After establishing a direct connection between two computers, you can establish a VPN connection on top of the direct connection that adds authentication and encryption. This activity assumes you have completed Activities 8-1, 8-2, and 8-3.

1. On the host computer, open a command prompt window.

2. Type **ipconfig** and press **Enter**. Details about your computer's IP addresses are displayed. Write down the IP address for the Ethernet adapter and the RRAS server you set up previously:

   _____

   _____

3. Switch to the client computer, and open a command prompt window. Type **ipconfig** and press **Enter**. Write down the PPP adapter IP address:

   _____

4. If necessary, open the Network Connections window from Control Panel. Write the name of the icon representing the direct connection you made to the other computer (probably the host computer's name):

   _____

5. Right-click any other network connections that might be active (such as Local Area Connection, if you use it to connect to the Internet) and click **Disable**.

6. Click the **Create a new connection** link. When the Network Connection Wizard starts, click **Next**.

7. Click the **Connect to the network at my workplace** option button, and then click **Next**.

8. In the Network Connections window, click the **Virtual Private Network connection** option button, and then click **Next**.

9. In the Connection Name window, enter **VPN Activity 8-4** as the connection name, and then click **Next**.

8

10. In the VPN Server Selection window, type the IP address of the host computer that you entered in Step 2, and then click **Finish**.

11. In the Connect VPN Activity 8-4 window, enter your username and password from Activity 8-2, and then click **Connect**.

12. When the progress window shows that you're connected, close any open windows, and leave your system running for the next activity.

If you can't connect, make sure all firewall software is disabled on both systems, and you've entered the correct server IP address, username, and password.

NOTE

Understanding IPSec/IKE

Internet Protocol Security (IPSec) is a set of standard procedures that the Internet Engineering Task Force (IETF) developed for enabling secure communication on the Internet. IPSec has become the standard set of protocols for VPN security for a number of reasons:

- IPSec works at Layer 3 and, therefore, provides a type of security not available with protocols that work at Layer 2.

- IPSec can encrypt an entire TCP/IP packet, instead of just the data portion, as with other protocols.

- IPSec was originally developed for use with IPv6, although it can also work with the current version, IPv4.

- IPSec provides authentication of source and destination computers before data is encrypted or transmitted.

Perhaps the biggest advantage of using IPSec is that it has gone through the process of standardization and is supported by a wide variety of VPN hardware and software devices. OSs such as Windows 2003 and XP enable you to set up an IPSec connection with another Windows computer that has IPSec enabled. In fact, you add IPSec security policy support as a snap-in to the Microsoft Management Console in Activity 8-5.

If you want more background on IPSec and related technologies, you can find links to the original RFC papers at *www.ietf.org/rfc/rfc2401.txt*.

TIP

When an IPSec connection is established between two computers, the computers authenticate one another and then establish the **Security Association (SA)** settings they use to communicate. An SA is a relationship between two or more entities that describes how they will use security services to communicate. Each IPSec connection can perform encryption, encapsulation, authentication, or a combination of the three. When determining which services to use, the entities in a connection must agree on the details, such as which algorithm to use for encryption. After that transaction is completed, the entities must share session keys. An SA is the method IPSec uses to track all the details of a communication session. SAs are unidirectional, meaning that an SA is set up in each direction of a communication, forming two one-way SAs between entities.

These transactions take place in the background. However, in an OS environment, you need to decide whether IPSec is required for all connections to the host machine or whether the host requests an IPSec connection for computers or other devices that support it. If IPSec is not supported on the client machine, it isn't used. You also have the option of requiring a secure connection to another computer over a VPN. If you want to connect to another computer while requiring IPSec, you need to adjust the packet-filtering rules; otherwise, your IPSec-enabled computer blocks all other connections by default.

Activity 8-5: Activating IPSec and Specifying a Policy

Time Required: 30 minutes

Objective: Configure the host (VPN server) to use IPSec.

Description: After you have two computers connected via a VPN, you can configure them to use IPSec to communicate. You can also set up a tunnel with L2TP or PPTP as the tunneling protocol. Follow these steps on the Windows XP host computer. This activity requires completing all previous activities.

1. Click **Start**, **Run**. In the Open text box, type **MMC**, and then click **OK**.

2. A Microsoft Management Console window opens, labeled Console1. Click **File**, **Add/Remove Snap-in** from the menu. In the Add/Remove Snap-in dialog box, click the **Add** button.

3. In the Add Standalone Snap-in dialog box, click **IP Security Policy Management** in the list of snap-ins (see Figure 8-4), and then click the **Add** button.

Figure 8-4 Adding the IPSec snap-in

4. When the Select Computer or Domain dialog box opens, verify that **Local computer** is selected, and then click **Finish**.

5. In the Add Standalone Snap-in dialog box, click **IP Security Monitor** in the list of snap-ins, and then click the **Add** button.

6. Click **Close** to close the Add Standalone Snap-in dialog box, and then click **OK** to close the Add/Remove Snap-in dialog box.

7. In the left pane of the MMC, click **IP Security Policies on Local Computer**.

8. In the right pane, right-click **Secure Server (Require Security)** and click **Assign**.

9. Right-click **Secure Server (Require Security)** again and click **Properties**.

10. In the Secure Server (Require Security) Properties dialog box, click **All ICMP Traffic**, and then click the **Edit** button.

11. Click **All IP Traffic**, and then click the **Edit** button to open the IP Filter List dialog box (see Figure 8-5). The Description text box explains that the rule blocks all IP traffic to and from the local computer that doesn't use IP security. You need to create a less restrictive rule—one that sets up a tunnel between the host computer and your VPN guest.

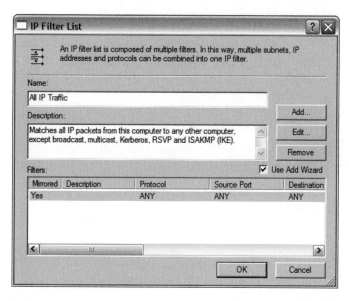

Figure 8-5   Viewing packet-filtering rules for an IPSec VPN connection

12. Click the **Edit** button. In the Filter Properties dialog box, click **A specific IP Address** in the Destination address drop-down list, and then enter the IP address of the client computer that's direct-connected to this host computer. Click **OK**.

13. Click **OK** to close the IP Filter List dialog box.

14. Click **All ICMP Traffic**, and then click the **Edit** button.

15. Repeat the procedure in Steps 12 and 13 to set up an ICMP traffic rule for the same IP address you entered in Step 12.

16. Click **Apply** and then click **OK** to close the Edit Rule Properties dialog box, and click **Close** to close the Secure Server (Require Security) Properties dialog box.

17. Click **File**, **Exit** from the menu to close the MMC window. When prompted to save your changes, click **Yes**, and then click **Save**. Close any other open windows, and leave your system running for the next activity.

IPSec Components

IPSec's many components provide encryption, encapsulation, key exchange, and authentication. These components include the following:

- *Internet Security Association Key Management Protocol*—**Internet Security Association Key Management Protocol (ISAKMP)** enables two computers to agree on security settings and establish an SA so that they can exchange keys by using Internet Key Exchange.

- *Internet Key Exchange (IKE)*—The **Internet Key Exchange (IKE)** protocol enables computers to exchange keys to make an SA. By default, IKE uses UDP port 500 on both the client and server. Different configurations might use different ports. IPSec Nat-T, for example, uses UDP port 4500 for IPSec traffic.

- *Oakley*—This protocol enables IPSec to use the Diffie-Hellman encryption algorithm to create keys. (You can learn more about Diffie-Hellman encryption at *www.ietf.org/rfc/rfc2631.txt*.)

- *IPSecurity Policy Management*—This service runs on Windows computers. It retrieves IPSec security policy settings from Active Directory and applies them to computers in the domain that use IPSec.

- *IPSec driver*—An **IPSec driver** is software that handles the tasks of encrypting, authenticating, decrypting, and checking packets.

Suppose you have configured a VPN connection between two computers and you want that connection to use IPSec. When one IPSec-compliant computer connects to the other, the following events occur:

1. The IPSec driver and ISAKMP retrieve the IPSec policy settings.

2. ISAKMP negotiates between hosts, based on their policy settings, and builds an SA between them.

3. The Oakley protocol generates a master key to secure IPSec communication.

4. Based on the security policy established for the session, the IPSec driver monitors, filters, and secures network traffic.

CAUTION   IPSec isn't foolproof. For instance, if the machine running IPSec-compliant software has already been compromised, no communication from it, including IPSec communication, can be trusted. IPSec isn't a substitute for firewall, antivirus, and intrusion detection software.

TIP   IPSec in tunnel mode isn't recommended for remote access VPNs. For this purpose, use L2TP/IPSec.

The two core IPSec components are the ones that protect TCP/IP packets exchanged in the VPN: Authentication Header and Encapsulating Security Payload, discussed in the following sections.

Authentication Header

Authentication Header (AH) is an IPSec component that authenticates TCP/IP packets to ensure data integrity. With AH, packets are signed with a digital signature that tells other IPSec-compliant devices the packet contains accurate IP header information because it originated from a computer using IPSec. Digitally signing a packet indicates that it hasn't been tampered with or that the IP information in the header hasn't been spoofed. It ensures integrity but not confidentiality.

To authenticate all or part of a packet's contents, AH adds a header calculated by IP header and data values in the packet, essentially creating a message digest of the packet. Security is achieved by calculating the values with a hashing algorithm and a key known only to entities in the transaction. (Keys are negotiated and exchanged when the SA is set up.) Because only authorized entities have the key, only they know how to run the algorithm to see whether the data has been tampered with. If the values match, the message's authenticity is considered intact.

An AH header doesn't change the contents of a message. It simply adds a field following the IP header. The field contains the computed value of the IP header (except any fields that change in transit, such as the time to live [TTL] field) and the data, as shown in Figure 8-6.

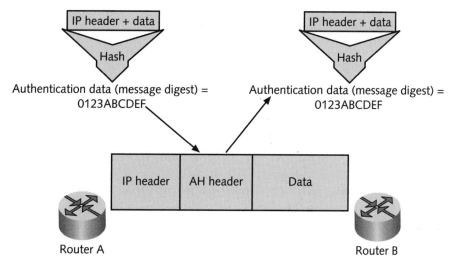

Figure 8-6 AH message exchange

AH works a little differently in the two IPSec modes: tunnel and transport (see Figure 8-7). In tunnel mode, AH authenticates the entire original header and builds a new IP header placed at the front of the packet. The only fields not authenticated by AH in tunnel mode are fields in the new IP header that can change in transit. In transport mode, AH authenticates the data and the original IP header, except fields that change in transit.

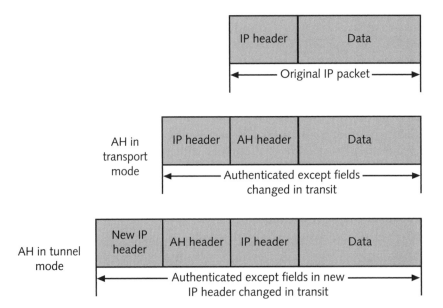

Figure 8-7 AH in tunnel and transport modes

Encapsulating Security Payload

As mentioned, AH ensures authentication and integrity for messages but not confidentiality. The confidentiality of data transmitted through a VPN tunnel using IPSec is ensured by means of **Encapsulating Security Payload (ESP)**. ESP encrypts different parts of a TCP/IP packet, depending on whether IPSec is used in transport or tunnel mode.

In tunnel mode, ESP encrypts both the header and data portion of a packet. This encryption protects data, but because the IP header is encrypted, the data can't pass through a firewall that performs NAT because the firewall doesn't know how to interpret the IP source and destination information in its encrypted form. In transport mode, only the data portion is encrypted. As a result, if the VPN is used with a firewall that performs NAT, IPSec should be configured to work in transport mode. Figure 8-8 shows the difference the IPSec mode makes to ESP.

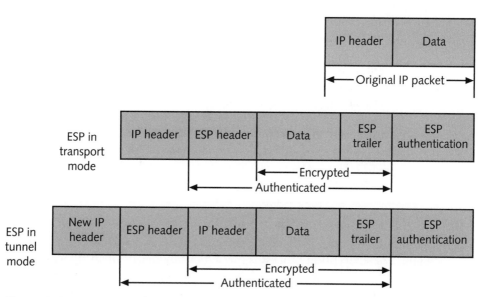

Figure 8-8 ESP in tunnel and transport modes

NOTE

Using AH and ESP together offers additional security, but you might not want to use ESP if another device or application is already providing encryption. ESP, like other forms of encryption, requires substantial processing resources and can slow the rate of data transfer through a VPN.

ACTIVITY

Activity 8-6: Configuring the Client VPN Tunnel with IPSec

Time Required: 15 minutes

Objective: Configure the VPN client computer to use IPSec.

Description: After you have set up the host computer in your VPN connection to require IPSec, you need to configure the client computer to use IPSec as well. This activity assumes you have completed Activities 8-1 through 8-5.

1. Open the Network Connections window from Control Panel.

2. Right-click the icon representing your VPN connection and click **Properties**.

3. In the Virtual Private Connection Properties dialog box, click the **Networking** tab.

4. In the Type of VPN drop-down list, click **Automatic**, if necessary, and then click **OK**.

5. Close all open windows except the Network Connections window. Right-click the icon representing your VPN connection and click **Connect**. Enter the username and password you created in Activity 8-2, and then click **Connect**. When you're finished, close all open windows.

NOTE

Multiprotocol Label Switching (MPLS) is an IETF initiative that provides efficient routing, forwarding, switching, and designation of traffic. It's independent of Layer 2 and 3 protocols and provides a way to map IP addressing information into a simple, fixed-length label. After a packet has been labeled, it's routed by label switching. MPLS shows promise for reducing latency and easing strained Internet backbone infrastructures and doesn't rely on encapsulation or encryption for security. Although MPLS is beyond the scope of this book, it's worth learning more about this technology. You can read more about MPLS (RFC 3031) at *www.faqs.org/rfcs/rfc3031.html*. For helpful tutorials, go to *www.iec.org/online/tutorials/* and search the list of tutorials.

VPN CORE ACTIVITY 2: ENCRYPTION

Encryption is the process of rendering information unreadable by all but the intended recipient. The encryption process is carried out by means of an algorithm that generates an encoded block of data called a **key**. The key is part of an electronic document called a **digital certificate**, which is obtained from a **certification authority (CA)**, a trusted organization that issues keys. The key is then used to encrypt data at the originating endpoint of the VPN and decrypt it at the destination endpoint (see Figure 8-9).

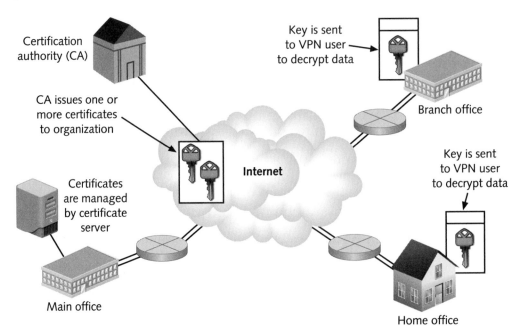

Figure 8-9 VPN endpoints encrypt and decrypt data by exchanging keys

To perform encryption at both endpoints of the VPN, the keys must be exchanged by participants who have an SA. The exchange can be performed by using a variety of encryption methods. In **symmetric cryptography**, the same key is exchanged by sender and recipient. In **asymmetric cryptography**, two different keys are used—a public key and a private key. When a person or an organization obtains a digital certificate from a CA, an encryption algorithm is used to generate a private key. This key is never exchanged but is maintained securely by the certificate holder. The private key is used to generate a public key, which can be exchanged freely among VPN participants.

Another type of key exchange method, Internet Key Exchange (IKE), uses **tunnel method encryption** to encrypt the header and data parts of a packet and encapsulate the packet within a new packet that has a different header. IKE is increasingly popular because it provides a high level of security, which outweighs the decrease in network performance caused by complex encryption.

Encryption Schemes

One advantage of a VPN is the capability to extend a wide area network (WAN) to multiple locations by using the Internet. However, the openness of the Internet creates security risks that need to be addressed by encryption. Encryption is one of the most important aspects of a firewall because it's how a VPN achieves its primary goal of preventing unauthorized users from reading the data payload.

Encryption schemes don't ensure a uniform level of security, however. Most older encryption algorithms, such as Data Encryption Standard, have been cracked. The reason is simple: As computers have grown faster and more powerful, more resources could be brought to bear on cracking algorithms. The approach is usually brute force, meaning all possible keys are tried. Generally, the longer the key, the more difficult the algorithm is to crack. So algorithms had to become more complex and use longer keys and more rounds of computations. Some encryption schemes provide strong encryption that uses long keys (for instance, 128-bit keys) or multiple keys. The following sections describe some encryption methods commonly used in VPNs.

Triple Data Encryption Standard

Many VPN products use **Triple Data Encryption Standard (3DES)** encryption. 3DES is a variation on **Data Encryption Standard (DES),** an older protocol standard IBM developed in the mid-1970s that was adopted as an encryption standard in 1977. DES is not a secure encryption method; it can be cracked, although it requires many computers working on it. For this reason, it's considered obsolete and is rarely used now. 3DES is far more secure because it uses three separate 64-bit keys to process data. The first key encrypts the data, the second key decrypts it, and the third key encrypts it again (see Figure 8-10).

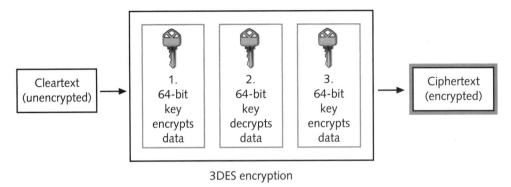

3DES encryption

Figure 8-10 Many VPNs use 3DES encryption

Although using three keys results in a strong level of encryption, the problem is the time and resources needed to encrypt the information. It takes three times as long as it does in DES, which uses only a single key. It's also more processing intensive, making its use a tradeoff. Although most modern computers are capable of using stronger encryption without intolerable performance degradation, encryption must be selected and managed carefully. Use stronger encryption to ensure confidentiality when needed and other forms of security, such as digital certificates, for authentication or integrity. In short, use only what's necessary; if you don't need to encrypt everything, don't.

Advanced Encryption Standard

The National Institute of Standards and Technology (NIST) developed a new encryption standard, Advanced Encryption Standard (AES), to replace 3DES as the U.S. government standard, effective May 26, 2002. AES is stronger than 3DES and works faster. It uses the Rijndael (usually pronounced Rhine-dahl) symmetric encryption algorithm that specifies how to use 128-bit, 192-bit, or 256-bit keys on 128-bit, 192-bit, or 256-bit blocks. The standard AES implementation has a fixed block size of 128 bits and uses keys of 128, 192, or 256 bits.

NOTE

In practice, the Rijndael algorithm can support a larger range of key and block sizes, and the AES standard supports key sizes of 128, 192, or 256 bits and has a fixed block size of 128 bits. The names Rijndael and AES are generally used interchangeably, but they aren't the same. Rijndael is the algorithm, and AES is the implementation.

AES is a block cipher, meaning mathematical computations are applied to blocks of data. Each iteration (application of the algorithm) is called a round. AES applies 10 rounds for 128-bit keys, 12 rounds for 192-bit keys, and 14 rounds for 256-bit keys, compared to the number of rounds the best-known attacks against block ciphers use, which are 7, 8, and 9, respectively.

Another concern centers on the mathematical structure of AES. Most ciphers don't have the neat algebraic description of AES, leading some cryptographers to speculate that a flaw in the mathematical structure could lead to successful attacks. As of this writing, some successful attacks have been launched against certain AES implementations, and others are theoretically possible. One successful type of attack is a **side channel attack**. A side channel attack doesn't attack the cipher directly; instead, it attacks the underlying systems that leak data. Some classes of side channels attacks include the following:

- *Timing attacks*—Attacks based on measuring how much time computations take to perform. For example, a timing attack might watch data move in and out of the CPU or memory. Watching how long it takes to transfer key information can yield clues about key length or eliminate certain key lengths.

- *Power monitoring attacks*—Attacks that use the varying power consumption by hardware during computation. Watching the power input to the CPU during computation offers information that can be used to determine the algorithm.

- *Acoustic cryptanalysis*—Similar to power monitoring attacks, acoustic cryptanalysis uses the sound produced by computations. The current used to power hardware produces heat, which is leaked into the atmosphere. The fluctuations of heating and cooling (thermodynamics) produce low-level acoustic noise that can be examined for clues about the underlying system.

- *Radiation monitoring (also known as van Eck or TEMPEST)*—Leaked radiation provides plaintext or other information that can be used to launch attacks. Electrical current fluctuations generate radio waves, which can occur in patterns. The patterns can be recorded and analyzed to gain information about associated hardware, and sometimes bits of actual data can be captured.

- *Thermal imaging attack*—If the surface of the CPU can be seen, infrared images can be taken that provide clues about the code being run.

Side channel attacks rely on emitted information, as in acoustic or radiation monitoring, and relational information, as in timing or power monitoring attacks. Countermeasures against side channels attacks include power conditioning and UPS systems to control power fluctuations and emissions, shielding to prevent radiation leakage, and strong physical security to prevent acoustic recorders or other monitoring devices from being installed.

TIP Another possible attack against AES is an XSL attack. An XSL attack is extremely complex and uses multivariate quadratic equations. Although this type of attack is possible, its complexity makes it unlikely to affect AES in practice in the foreseeable future. You can learn more about XSL attacks (and find more information on cryptography) at *www.cryptosystem.net/aes*.

Obviously, launching these attacks requires a high level of expertise, which eliminates many potential attackers. As successful attacks emerge, however, automated scripts and instructions invariably appear, making it possible for less knowledgeable attackers to use the techniques. Keep in mind, too, that any encryption algorithm can be broken. The most basic component of cryptography is mathematics. Every algorithm is based on a defined mathematical construct, so it's predictable to some degree. The major factors in cracking an algorithm are the amount of cryptographic knowledge required to design the attack and the amount of processing power needed to perform the attack.

In VPNs, AES is becoming more widely supported. As of 2006, AES was the most widely used encryption method, no doubt because of its status as the accepted government standard and its perceived strong security. Many vendors offer modules enabling AES as an encryption method for VPNs and remote access; these modules usually don't require much configuration.

NOTE For more information on AES, see *www.csrc.nist.gov/publications/ fips/fips197/fips-197.pdf* and *www.faqs.org/rfcs/rfc3268.html*. For more information on implementing cryptography consistent with U.S. government guidelines, read the NIST Special Publication 800-21, Guideline for Implementing Cryptography in the Federal Government (available at *http://csrc.nist.gov/publications/*).

Microsoft systems primarily use PPTP, L2TP/IPSec, and MPPE for VPN encryption. MPPE works with keys generated by MS-CHAP, MS-CHAPv2, and Extensible Authentication Protocol-Transport Level Security (EAP-TLS) authentication and supports 128-bit, 56-bit, and 40-bit encryption schemes. MPPE secures PPTP connections between VPN servers and clients. Microsoft systems also support TLS/SSL, discussed later in this chapter.

Secure Sockets Layer

Many VPNs use **Secure Sockets Layer (SSL)** to encrypt tunneled information via the Web. SSL was developed by Netscape Communications Corporation as a way of enabling Web servers and browsers to exchange encrypted information. SSL gets its name from the following:

- It uses public and private key encryption to create *secure* communications.

- It uses the *sockets* method of communication between servers and clients. (A socket is simply a combination of an IP address and a port number, such as 210.45.73.28/443.)

- It operates at the Network *layer* (Layer 3) of the OSI model. However, it can still provide a level of security that works between TCP and HTTP.

SSL is widely used on the Web; in fact, VPNs that use SSL can support only data that's exchanged by Web-enabled applications. For this reason, SSL is unlikely to replace IPSec as a security standard for VPNs, but it can be a useful adjunct to IPSec when Web browsers and Web servers need to connect securely.

An SSL session makes use of both symmetric and asymmetric keys. The asymmetric keys are used to start an SSL session, but symmetric keys are then generated dynamically for most of the transfer. It works like this:

1. The client connects to the Web server by using SSL.

2. The two machines authenticate each other and determine which ciphers and protocols to use. The client sends the server its preferences for encryption method, the SSL version number, and a randomly generated number to be used later.

3. The server responds with the SSL version number, its cipher preferences, and its digital certificate. The digital certificate tells the client who issued it, a data range, and the server's public key. The server can ask the client for its own digital certificate at this point.

4. The client verifies that the date and other information on the digital certificate are valid. If so, the client generates a "pre-master" code and sends it to the server, using the server's public key. The client's digital certificate is also sent, if the server requested one.

5. The server uses its private key to decode the pre-master code that the client sent. The server then generates a master secret key that both client and server use to generate session keys—symmetric keys used during the SSL session to verify the integrity of data that's exchanged.

6. The server and client exchange messages to the effect that future messages will be encrypted with the session key, and then they send each other a separate, encrypted message that their side of the handshake is complete.

7. The handshake is completed, and the SSL session begins. Either side can renegotiate the connection at any time, and the process repeats (which could happen because of a lost connection, timeout, or user intervention, such as logging out).

SSL is a secure way to transmit data on the Web, such as credit card numbers used for online purchases. However, SSL can cause problems for firewalls that can't interpret SSL data, in much the same way that firewalls can have trouble interpreting IPSec data that uses tunnel mode encryption.

Transport Layer Security

Transport Layer Security (TLS) was designed to provide additional security for Internet communication. Although it's similar to SSL in operation and design, TLS adds some notable improvements. First, it uses a hashed message authentication code (HMAC) that provides extra security by combining the hashing algorithm with a shared secret key. Both parties must have the same shared secret key to authenticate the data. Second, TLS splits the input data in half, processes each half with a different hashing algorithm, and then recombines them by using an exclusive OR (XOR) function. This method provides protection if one of the algorithms proves to be vulnerable.

TLS provides authentication and encryption mechanisms. It supports certificate-based authentication, as SSL does, and the handshake process is similar. For encryption, TLS can support a variety of ciphers, both symmetric and asymmetric, and several hashing algorithms, summarized in Table 8-3.

Table 8-3   TLS cryptography

Type of cipher	Cipher/algorithm
Public key (asymmetric)	Rivest-Shamir-Adelman (RSA), Diffie-Hellman, Digital Signature Algorithm (DSA)
Private key (symmetric)	Rivest Cipher (RC) 2, RC4, International Data Encryption Algorithm (IDEA), DES, 3DES, AES, and Camellia
Hashing algorithms	Message Digest (MD) 2, MD4, MD5, Secure Hash Algorithm (SHA), and SHA-1

TLS/SSL uses symmetric cryptography for bulk encryption and asymmetric cryptography for authentication and key exchange. TLS runs below Application-layer protocols, such as SMTP, FTP, HTTP, and LDAP, but above the UDP and TCP Transport-layer protocols. This makes TLS useful for securing a variety of protocols. For the most part, TLS takes place automatically, requiring no user action, and makes administering firewalls and NAT easier. The downside is that TLS requires more processing power and administration time for managing certificates.

Most new VPN hardware devices support TLS/SSL, and it's available in current OSs. OpenVPN uses TLS/SSL to tunnel the entire network protocol stack. Windows 2000, XP Professional, and Server 2003 support TLS/SSL, which is implemented as part of the Security Channel (Schannel) architecture.

TIP

You can learn more about TLS at *www.ietf.org/* or by searching on the keyword TLS. The first definition of TLS is in RFC 2246, and you can study the current approved version in RFC 4346. Many RFCs also deal with extensions of TLS.

VPN Core Activity 3: Authentication

The third core activity VPNs perform to ensure the security of tunneled communication is authentication. Authentication is essential because network hosts that receive VPN communications need to know that the originator of the communication is an approved user of the VPN.

The type of authentication used in a VPN depends on the tunneling protocol. A growing number of networks use IPSec to authenticate users; VPN participants establish an SA and exchange keys to authenticate one another. PPTP, which is used for dial-up access to a remote server, uses MS-CHAP, in which both computers exchange authentication packets. TLS/SSL uses certificate-based authentication. RADIUS is also commonly used for authentication services in VPN architecture.

VPNs use digital certificates to authenticate users and encryption to ensure that, even if communication is intercepted in transit, it can't be read. Figure 8-11 shows the VPN core activities of encapsulation, encryption, and authentication.

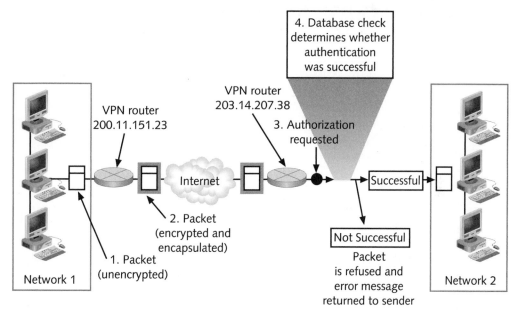

Figure 8-11 VPN core activities

In Figure 8-11, the following are the basic steps in the authentication process:

1. The source computer transmits the unencrypted packet on internal network 1.

2. After the VPN router at 200.11.151.23 encrypts and encapsulates the packet, the packet passes through the gateway into the Internet.

3. The VPN router at internal network 2 requests authentication.

4. A database check determines whether authentication is successful. If it is, the packet is allowed to reach its destination. If it's not, an error message is returned.

Kerberos

Kerberos is an authentication system developed at the Massachusetts Institute of Technology (MIT). The name refers to the three-headed dog in Greek mythology that was said to guard the gates of Hades. Kerberos authenticates the identity of network users by using a simple method called "authentication by assertion." The computer that connects to a server and requests services asserts that it's acting on behalf of an approved user of those services. Although this method sounds simple, the process by which computers communicate the assertion and response is not. Figure 8-12 shows how Kerberos works, and the following list outlines what happens at each step:

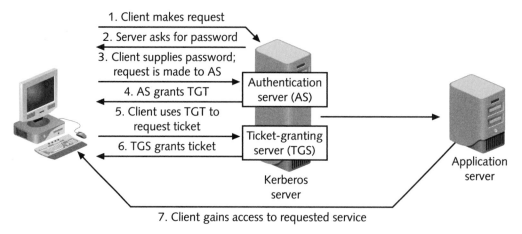

Figure 8-12 The Kerberos authentication process

1. A client requests a file or other service.

2. The server prompts the client for a username and password (user account credentials).

3. The client submits the credentials, and the request is sent to an authentication server (AS) that's part of the Kerberos system. The Kerberos AS is known as the **Key Distribution Center (KDC)**. A domain controller can also serve as the authentication server in Windows 2000 or XP.

4. The AS creates an encrypted code called a session key, based on the client's password plus a random number associated with the service being requested. This session key is called a **ticket–granting ticket (TGT)**.

5. The AS grants the TGT.

6. The client presents the TGT to the **ticket–granting server (TGS)**. The TGS is also part of the Kerberos system but may or may not be the same server as the AS.

7. The TGS grants the session ticket and forwards the session ticket to the server holding the requested file or service on behalf of the requesting client.

8. The client gains access to the requested service or file.

A major advantage of Kerberos is that passwords aren't stored on the system, so they can't be intercepted. A ticket is specific to a user and typically expires after a set period (usually eight hours). Kerberos does allow postdated tickets and renewable tickets, but users can't modify tickets directly; they must request these flags when requesting their tickets.

Kerberos has a lower "network overhead" than a Public Key Infrastructure (PKI) system, so you don't need to install a central server and manage a Kerberos system as you would a PKI system. This lower overhead is especially handy in a small network where only a few users need access to shared resources. Kerberos is also useful for single sign-on (SSO). Instead of having to sign on to each resource and keep track of all those credentials, the user simply signs on to the Kerberos authentication services and has access to all resources he or she has permission to use.

There is a major concern with Kerberos, however. The AS (KDC) is a single point of failure, so if it goes down (and no backup servers can take over this role), no one can be authenticated. Administrators using a single AS should take measures to ensure that authentication services can continue to function in the event of an AS failure. Other major security flaws in Kerberos have emerged, making it possible for attackers to run arbitrary code on KDCs, launch man-in-the-middle or DoS attacks, or cause the domain controller to shut down. Patches are available to address these vulnerabilities, however.

TIP

The current Kerberos version 5 is defined in RFC 1510.

8

CHAPTER SUMMARY

- ❏ VPNs are virtual in that they don't make use of dedicated leased lines; instead, they use public communication lines, such as the Internet.

- ❏ VPNs are private because they send data through a secure tunnel that leads from one endpoint to another.

- ❏ VPNs are networks that connect one network to one or more networks, one computer to another, or one computer to a network.

- ❏ VPN components include VPN servers, VPN clients, the tunnels through which data passes, and protocols that determine how to encrypt tunneled data. A site-to-site VPN uses these components to connect networks. A client-to-site VPN connects remote users to a network. VPN endpoints can be terminated by VPN hardware, VPN software, or a combination of both.

- ❏ VPN encapsulation encloses one packet in another to conceal the original packet's source and destination IP address and to protect the contents.

- ❏ VPNs use protocols to enable tunneled communication between endpoints. Point-to-Point Protocol Tunneling (PPTP), Layer 2 Tunneling Protocol (L2TP), and Generic Routing Encapsulation (GRE) are common tunneling protocols.

- ❏ Internet Protocol Security (IPSec) combined with Internet Key Exchange (IKE) is popular because of its wide support and high security provided by using Authentication Header (AH) authentication and Encapsulating Security Payload (ESP) encryption.

❑ Encryption is one of the technologies that make VPNs possible. Many VPNs use 3DES encryption, although Advanced Encryption Standard (AES) is becoming more common and is more secure.

❑ Some VPNs use Secure Sockets Layer (SSL) encryption when Web applications need to be connected securely. Digital certificates, symmetric and asymmetric cryptography, and IKE are also used to encrypt VPN transmissions. Transport Layer Security (TLS), designed to replace SSL, is becoming more common in VPNs.

❑ Authentication ensures that the computers participating in a VPN are authorized users. The authentication method depends on the tunneling protocol and can include IPSec, key exchanges, MS-CHAP, and digital certificates.

❑ Another strong authentication/encryption system, Kerberos, is used in Windows and other OSs to give employees access to network resources for short periods by issuing tickets.

KEY TERMS

Advanced Encryption Standard (AES) — An encryption standard that uses the Rijndael symmetric block cipher; it replaced 3DES as the U.S. government standard in 2002.

asymmetric cryptography — A type of encryption in which two different keys are used. A private key is kept by the certificate holder and never shared; a public key is shared among users to encrypt and decrypt communication. *See also* symmetric cryptography.

Authentication Header (AH) — An IPSec protocol that provides authentication of TCP/IP packets to ensure data integrity.

certification authority (CA) — A trusted organization that issues digital certificates that can be used to generate keys. *See also* digital certificate.

client-to-site VPN — A type of VPN connection that makes a network accessible to remote users requiring dial-up access; also called a remote access VPN.

Data Encryption Standard (DES) — An encryption scheme developed by IBM in the mid-1970s that was adopted as an encryption standard in 1977. It's now considered obsolete and is rarely used.

digital certificate — An electronic document issued by a certification authority that contains information about the certificate holder and can be used to exchange public and private keys. *See also* certification authority (CA).

Encapsulating Security Payload (ESP) — An IPSec protocol that encrypts the header and data parts of TCP/IP packets.

encapsulation — The process of enclosing a packet within another one that has different IP source and destination information to ensure a high degree of protection.

Generic Routing Encapsulation (GRE) — A nonproprietary tunneling protocol that can encapsulate a variety of Network-layer protocols.

Internet Key Exchange (IKE) — A form of key exchange used to encrypt and decrypt data as it passes through a VPN tunnel. IKE uses tunnel method encryption to encrypt and then encapsulate packets for extra security. *See also* tunnel method encryption.

Internet Protocol Security (IPSec) — A set of standard procedures that the Internet Engineering Task Force (IETF) developed for enabling secure communication on the Internet.

Internet Security Association Key Management Protocol (ISAKMP) — An IPSec-related protocol that enables two computers to agree on security settings and establish a Security Association so that they can exchange keys by using Internet Key Exchange. *See also* Internet Key Exchange (IKE) *and* Security Association (SA).

IPSec driver — Software that handles the actual tasks of encrypting, authenticating, decrypting, and checking packets in an IPSec connection.

Kerberos — An IETF standard for secure authentication of requests for resource access.

key — An encoded block of data generated by an algorithm and used to encrypt and decrypt data.

Key Distribution Center (KDC) — A Kerberos component that holds secret keys for users, applications, services, or resources; creates and distributes session keys by using symmetric cryptography.

Layer 2 Tunneling Protocol (L2TP) — A tunneling protocol derived from two older protocols, Cisco's L2F and Microsoft's PPTP. L2TP encapsulates PPP packets and is usually combined with IPSec for improved security.

Point-to-Point Tunneling Protocol (PPTP) — A tunneling protocol used for dial-up access to a remote server.

Secure Sockets Layer (SSL) — A protocol developed by Netscape Communications Corporation as a way of enabling Web servers and browsers to exchange encrypted information.

Security Association (SA) — A designation for users, computers, or gateways that can participate in a VPN and encrypt and decrypt data by using keys.

side channel attack — An attack method that exploits vulnerabilities of underlying hardware systems that leak data instead of exploiting vulnerabilities in a cryptographic algorithm.

site-to-site VPN — A VPN that uses hardware devices, such as routers, to connect two networks; also called a gateway-to-gateway VPN.

Socks — A communication protocol that provides proxy services for applications that don't normally support proxying and enables applications to set up a secure tunnel by using encryption and authentication.

symmetric cryptography — A type of encryption in which the sender and recipient exchange the same key. *See also* asymmetric cryptography.

8

ticket-granting server (TGS) — The part of the KDC that creates and distributes session keys clients use to access resources. *See also* Key Distribution Center (KDC).

ticket-granting ticket (TGT) — A digital token sent from the Authentication Server to the client. The client presents the TGT to the TGS to obtain a session key to access the resource. *See also* Key Distribution Center (KDC) *and* ticket-granting server (TGS).

Transport Layer Security (TLS) — A protocol designed to secure Internet traffic. Although it hasn't replaced SSL yet, it offers improvements and is used more widely now for a variety of applications.

Triple Data Encryption Standard (3DES) — A stronger variation of DES that uses three separate 64-bit keys to process data, making the encryption much harder to break. *See also* Data Encryption Standard (DES).

tunnel — The connection between two endpoints in a VPN.

tunnel method encryption — A method of key exchange that encrypts both the header and data parts of a packet and encapsulates the packet within a new packet that has a different header.

Unified Threat Management (UTM) — A term describing products that integrate a variety of security features, such as VPN and remote access services, firewall and intrusion detection functions, and management consoles, into a single application, device, or product.

virtual private network (VPN) — A cost-effective way for networks to create a secure private connection using public lines (usually the Internet). VPN endpoints establish connections (tunnels) to transmit and receive data, and then tear the connections down when they're no longer needed. Combinations of encryption, authentication, and encapsulation help ensure the confidentiality, privacy, and integrity of information.

VPN appliance — A hardware device designed to terminate VPNs and join networks.

VPN client — A router or an OS that initiates a connection to a VPN server.

VPN protocols — Standardized communication settings that software and hardware use to encrypt data sent through a VPN.

VPN server — A computer configured to accept VPN connections from clients.

REVIEW QUESTIONS

1. Which of the following VPN components is configured to accept connections?

   a. VPN server

   b. VPN client

   c. tunnel

   d. VPN protocol

2. VPNs differ from leased lines in that they use which of the following to make connections?

   a. hardware or software

   b. the public Internet

   c. operating systems

   d. all of the above

3. The VPN connection through which data passes from one endpoint to another is called which of the following?

   a. gateway

   b. extranet

   c. tunnel

   d. transport

4. Under what circumstances does a firewall need to be installed at the endpoint of a VPN connection, and why?

5. A VPN that uses hardware to connect two networks is called which of the following? (Choose all that apply.)

   a. gateway-to-gateway VPN

   b. hub-and-spoke arrangement

   c. tunnel

   d. site-to-site VPN

6. What term describes procedures for enabling a VPN to encrypt traffic?

   a. public key cryptography

   b. protocol

   c. encapsulation

   d. digital certificate

7. Which of the following protects the integrity of data sent through the VPN tunnel and hides packets' source and destination information?

   a. encryption

   b. a VPN appliance

   c. IPSec

   d. encapsulation

8

8. PPTP uses which of the following to encrypt data passing between the remote computer and remote access server?

   a. Layer 2 Tunneling Protocol (L2TP)

   b. Microsoft Point-to-Point Encryption (MPPE)

   c. MS-CHAP

   d. IPSec

9. What type of VPN is used to give remote users dial-up access to a central office?

   a. client-to-site

   b. site-to-site

   c. gateway-to-gateway

   d. mesh configuration

10. A group of authentication and encryption settings that two computers negotiate to set up a secure VPN connection is called which of the following?

   a. protocol

   b. Security Association (SA)

   c. handshake

   d. key exchange

11. Computers in a VPN authenticate one another by means of which encryption-related component?

   a. public key

   b. challenge/response

   c. digital certificate

   d. username/password

12. Which tunneling protocol can encapsulate many types of Network-layer packets in IP packets?

   a. L2TP

   b. PPP

   c. IPSec

   d. GRE

13. Which of the following provides authentication and encryption of TCP/IP packets over a VPN or other connection and is used primarily on UNIX systems?

   a. SSL

   b. SSH

   c. MPPE

   d. PPTP

14. IPSec allows which security activity to take place before data is encrypted or transmitted?

    a. encapsulation

    b. authentication

    c. establishing a Security Association (SA)

    d. applying security policy settings

15. To access an application protected by Kerberos, which of the following is required?

    a. certificate

    b. key

    c. username/password

    d. ticket

16. What is the block size in AES?

    a. 64 bits

    b. 128 bits

    c. 192 bits

    d. 256 bits

17. Internet Key Exchange (IKE) uses which of the following to encrypt a packet's header and data?

    a. asymmetric cryptography

    b. 3DES encryption

    c. TLS encryption

    d. tunnel method encryption

18. If a VPN is used with a firewall that performs NAT, IPSec should be configured to work in which mode?

    a. tunnel

    b. transport

    c. pass-through

    d. encapsulation

19. Transport Layer Security (TLS) has which of the following security improvements over SSL? (Choose all that apply.)

    a. TLS combines its hashing algorithm with a shared secret key.

    b. TLS provides authentication and encryption mechanisms.

    c. TLS supports certificate-based authentication.

    d. TLS splits data in half and processes each half with a separate key.

8

HANDS-ON PROJECTS

HANDS-ON PROJECTS

Hands-On Project 8-1: Combining a VPN with a Firewall

Time Required: 15 minutes

Objective: Troubleshoot a sample problem and propose solutions to correct the problem.

Description: You configured a VPN to use IPSec in its most secure mode—using ESP with tunnel mode. However, you encounter problems with the firewall, which is positioned between the VPN and the internal network. The firewall ends up dropping a substantial percentage of the packets that are terminated by the VPN device. Troubleshoot the situation by answering the following questions:

1. What could be causing the firewall to fail to process VPN traffic?

    _____

    _____

2. How could you solve the problem?

    _____

    _____

    _____

    _____

Hands-On Project 8-2: Adjusting a VPN for Scalability

Time Required: 15 minutes

Objective: Analyze a problem to determine possible solutions.

Description: Your security policy calls for your network defenses to provide maximum security and compatibility with other systems. Accordingly, you configure the VPN to use AH authentication and ESP encryption. You perform a network audit after a week and notice that performance has slowed dramatically. You have received user complaints about it and need to make adjustments. Use the following lines to summarize your options:

_____

_____

_____

_____

CASE PROJECT

Case Project 8-1: Planning Remote Access for Green Globe

In this book's previous case projects, you have designed a basic network and revised it as you've learned more in each chapter. In this chapter, you begin the important task of designing VPN remote access for Green Globe. Recall from the case project description that Green Globe has many employees who work from locations all over the world. Secure remote access is a critical component of Green Globe's network requirements, so for this chapter, revise your network plan to meet these requirements. Remember that Green Globe requires high security and has temporary workers who might need access to certain resources. All employees require some level of mobility, and government regulations apply to Green Globe's network security. For this project, you should prepare the following:

- A complete list of hardware and software needed

- Complete information about support options, costs, contact information, and warranties

- A plan for testing the new system

- An updated network diagram that shows the network's physical and logical layout and the remote access solution

- Any other information relevant to your design, such as dial-up numbers, encryption techniques, authentication and access controls, configuration of client machines, and so on

Submit your design proposal, cost breakdown, and updated diagrams to your instructor or for peer review. Remember that you will be submitting a complete project proposal at the end of this book, so don't wait until the last minute to begin working on your final proposal. Check with your instructor for details on your school's writing guidelines.

8

CHAPTER

9

DESIGNING VIRTUAL PRIVATE NETWORKS

After reading this chapter and completing the exercises, you will be able to:

♦ Explain considerations for planning VPN deployments

♦ Describe options for VPN configurations

♦ Explain ways to adjust packet-filtering rules for VPNs

♦ Describe ways to review VPN policies and procedures

♦ Explain how to set up a VPN in Windows Server 2003

Designed and deployed correctly, a virtual private network (VPN) is a secure, cost-effective way for remote users to access corporate resources, for remote sites to connect to one another or the central office, and for partners or vendors to share resources. Designed or deployed incorrectly, however, a VPN creates a security liability.

In this chapter, you build on the concepts you learned in Chapter 8 and learn the process of designing, testing, and deploying a VPN to meet an organization's needs. Like most technologies, VPNs exist to support business processes. You need to know about the business and its goals, needs, and plans before you can design an effective and secure VPN strategy. After you have a clear picture of what's needed and the resources you have to work with, you can decide where and how to place the VPN server and how to configure and control access. You also see how packet filtering and policies are used to further secure your VPN and learn the process of setting up a VPN in Windows Server 2003.

Planning VPN Deployment

Deciding whether a VPN is right for an environment requires careful examination. You need a thorough understanding of the organization—where it's going, where it has been, and what it needs. It isn't enough to simply know what remote access or connectivity needs are. You must understand the big picture of how technologies enhance a business environment.

You also need to know what advantages a VPN offers and any potential disadvantages the business might encounter. Assess the organization's goals, needs, personnel, operating environment, and more before you begin planning architecture. Client-side security must be enforced through some mechanism, whether it's hardware, software, policy, or access-based controls. The entire configuration should then be planned, equipment selected, physical and logical topology chosen, and a complete cost analysis conducted. These planning steps are crucial to predictable results; businesses don't like surprises that cost them money.

VPN Advantages and Disadvantages

VPNs have many advantages for businesses, but they have some disadvantages, too. They offer a high level of security—provided network administrators address inherent challenges. For instance, if a VPN device is configured incorrectly or remote users at a VPN endpoint disable their firewalls by mistake and let in an attacker, the protection the VPN normally provides can be circumvented. In addition, VPNs can be complex to configure, and the necessary hardware and software can represent a substantial investment. Table 9-1 summarizes some of the main advantages and disadvantages.

Table 9-1   Some advantages and disadvantages of VPNs

Advantages	Disadvantages
Far less expensive than leased lines	Can be complex to configure
Many elements working together provide strong security	Can result in slower data transfer rates than a leased line
Standards and protocols used in VPNs are well developed and widely used	Depends on the often unpredictable Internet; if your ISP or other parts of the Internet go down, your VPN goes down
Can result in less overall complexity in an organization's network	Requires administrators to install VPN client software on remote computers
Can make use of a company's existing broadband connection	VPN hardware and software from different vendors might prove incompatible because they use different protocols

By focusing on Internet-based technologies, VPNs simplify a network. You have only one Internet connection to manage instead of an Internet connection plus leased lines. In addition, running a VPN means you have even more ways to maximize network uptime. Downtime is expensive; in addition to the cost of repairs, it adds administrative time in troubleshooting and repairing problems and affects users' productivity. If your network is up and running smoothly, you don't need to spend time troubleshooting and making repairs.

Assessing Business Needs

As mentioned, planning a VPN deployment requires assessing an organization's goals. The need to keep business transactions private has prompted more organizations to adopt VPNs. The popularity of e-commerce is an incentive as well, and government and military agencies need to share information to provide effective homeland security.

A VPN is an excellent solution for an organization that needs to follow a budget while maintaining security. Budgetary considerations have always made VPNs an attractive business proposition. When you use a VPN, you're essentially spreading the cost of its operation over many users, which makes it cost effective.

In addition, many companies employ remote contractors who need to access the corporate network from their homes or offices. Employees who travel for business reasons need to check e-mail and transfer files with colleagues in the central office. Secure remote access is an essential requirement for many businesses and is an important reason for establishing a VPN. Another reason is the need to have a secure means of access for partners, suppliers, contractors, and others outside the company.

Considering the type of business, number of employees, existing infrastructure, and security required for data gives you the basis for planning VPN deployment. You should also review the company security policy for guidance on existing security goals and procedures. With this information, you can integrate a VPN with minimal disruptions and avoid unexpected and undesirable outcomes.

When considering the type of business, ask "What does it do? What product or service does it sell and who are its customers?" These questions might seem unrelated, but you need to know who you're providing access for and where VPN users are located.

Analyzing the existing infrastructure helps you determine how and where to place a VPN. If the network administrator has an accurate network map, this task is fairly easy. Often this documentation is unavailable, however, so you might need to examine the network and make your own map. It doesn't need to be complex. It just needs to accurately reflect the environment into which you're integrating VPN services.

After deciding on the placement of a VPN, you can begin researching hardware or software. Determine whether you should reconfigure existing hardware to support VPN connections or purchase a VPN appliance, server, firewall, or router to do the job. Your assessment of the organization's needs and existing infrastructure can guide you in this decision, and vendors are always happy to assist potential buyers. Use their knowledge to help you decide what's going to meet your needs, offer sufficient scalability, stay within budgetary constraints, and integrate with existing systems. You might want to

9

develop a list of requirements when meeting with vendors to ensure that nothing is overlooked. Remember to follow security policy guidelines, however, when giving out network information. Some information, such as trade secrets or business processes that give your company a competitive advantage, must remain confidential.

Cost is also a key factor and narrows down the choices of hardware and software. Beware of "bleeding edge" technology that could become outdated or unsupported just weeks after you purchase it. Also, realize that having unlimited funds doesn't mean your design will be foolproof. Regardless of budgetary factors, your design must integrate with existing technology and provide services without failure. In other words, you don't need to reinvent the wheel. For example, if you're installing VPN services on a network with older firewalls on the perimeter, you could configure those firewalls to provide VPN services instead of replacing them with newer ones. If the firewalls provide the necessary services with acceptable performance and security and offer adequate scalability, upgrading probably isn't necessary. Of course, if the CIO instructs you otherwise, buy the brand-new high-end solution and deploy it.

VPNs are as diverse as the needs they support. When you have a clear picture of the organization and its users, you can begin planning the configuration, testing, and deployment. A secure VPN design should address the following factors:

- Secure connectivity
- Encryption
- Availability
- Authentication
- Secure management
- Reliability
- Scalability
- Performance

Ensuring Client Security

Another critical aspect of deployment is enforcing security on the client side of the VPN tunnel. If remote users' computers are compromised, the internal network is at risk. Client-side issues to consider include whether to require clients to use a firewall and intrusion detection system (IDS) and whether policies should be enforced on client computers before allowing remote users to authenticate to the internal network.

Remember that a VPN extends the corporate network by using public communication channels. When it's set up and configured correctly, a VPN can supply inexpensive, secure access; set up incorrectly, a VPN is a tremendous security liability that can give intruders full access to your network. Failing to secure access to a remote network has legal implications, too. If your VPN connects to partner or vendor networks, and an intruder gains access to their network through your poorly configured VPN, your company could face litigation for damages resulting from the security breach. This situation isn't likely, but it isn't impossible. The point is that you must consider the security implications of any extension of your network.

There are several ways to increase VPN client security, from network configuration settings to third-party software solutions. For example, when a Windows client connects to a VPN server, select the Use default gateway on remote network option. This option prevents **split tunneling** by the client, which results in multiple paths. One path goes to the VPN server and is secured, but an unauthorized and unsecured path permits users to connect to the Internet or another network while still connected to the corporate VPN (see Figure 9-1). Split tunneling leaves the VPN server and internal network vulnerable to attack.

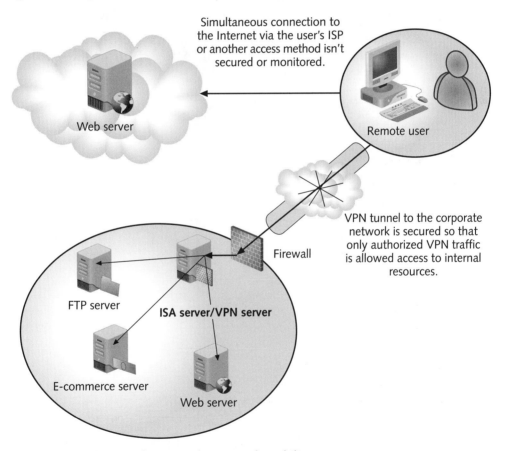

Figure 9-1 Split tunneling introduces a vulnerability

Small organizations without the resources to enforce total control over clients should at least require users to sign an acceptable use agreement. Remote users should be required to maintain an Internet firewall and current virus protection and secure the computer against unauthorized use and be prevented from enabling split tunneling while connected to the network.

Activity 9-1: Setting the Default Gateway on a Client Computer

Time Required: 15 minutes

Objective: Prevent split tunneling on a VPN client computer.

Description: Using the VPN connection you established in Chapter 8, you enable the default gateway option on the client computer's VPN connection.

1. Open Control Panel and double-click **Network Connections**.

2. Right-click the VPN connection you want to change and click **Properties**.

3. Click the **Networking** tab, click **Internet Protocol (TCP/IP)** in the This connection uses the following items list box, and then click **Properties**.

4. Click the **Advanced** button to open the Advanced TCP/TIP Settings dialog box, and in the General tab, click the **Use default gateway on remote network** check box (see Figure 9-2).

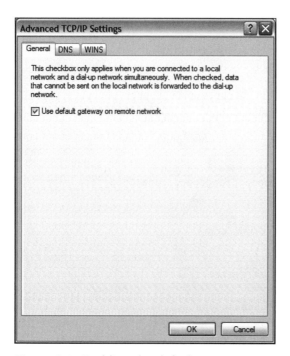

Figure 9-2 Enabling the default gateway option to prevent split tunneling

5. Click **OK** to close any open windows.

CONFIGURING VPNS

After you have a clear picture of the business, you can begin planning the VPN deployment. To set up a VPN, you need to define a **VPN domain**: a set of one or more computers that VPN hardware and software handle as a single entity. The computers in a VPN domain use the VPN to communicate with another domain. With a firewall, a domain might be a set of networked computers grouped under a name, such as Office_Network. If you set up Windows to function as a VPN host, you can designate a set of IP addresses for accessing that host (see Figure 9-3).

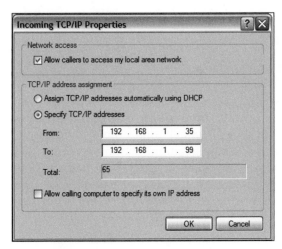

Figure 9-3 Specifying IP addresses for a VPN domain

Single and Multiple Entry Point Configurations

You also need to determine whether the network gateway is included in the VPN domain. This decision depends on whether your network has a site-to-site or client-to-site VPN configuration (as explained in Chapter 8). Small networks that use VPNs typically have only site-to-site connections and often have **single entry point configurations**: All traffic to and from the network passes through a single gateway, such as a router or firewall (or both). In a single entry point configuration, the gateway must be a member of the VPN domain. In the configuration shown in Figure 9-4, the VPN domain includes a group of computers in the internal network as well as the gateway.

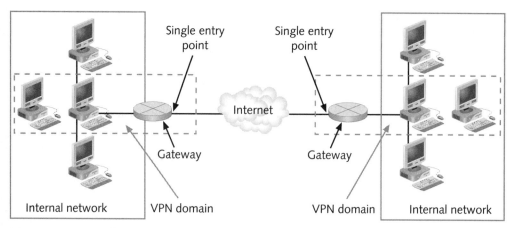

Figure 9-4 A single entry point configuration

In contrast, many large organizations have networks with several client-to-site connections. These connections require **multiple entry point configurations** in which multiple gateways are used, each with a VPN tunnel connecting a different location (see Figure 9-5). In a multiple entry point configuration, excluding the gateway from the VPN domain is important. If you don't exclude the gateway, all traffic to and from each gateway in the internal network is encrypted. This encryption reduces performance unnecessarily because you need to encrypt only the traffic from gateway to gateway.

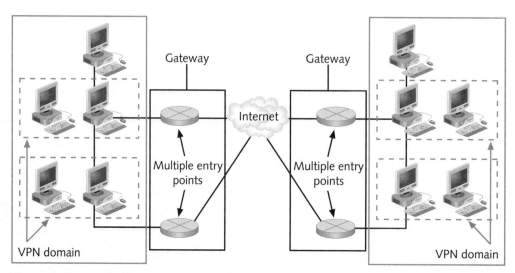

Figure 9-5 A multiple entry point configuration

Preventing VPN domains from overlapping is also important; having multiple routes in routing tables could cause some traffic to be routed incorrectly or not at all because of duplicate IP addresses. If a router has multiple paths for directing packets, it might not respond correctly. This problem can be fixed easily by configuring routing tables correctly.

Selecting a VPN Topology

A VPN's **topology**—the way components in a network are connected physically to one another—determines how gateways, networks, and clients are related to each other. As explained in the following sections, VPN topologies correspond to basic network physical and logical topologies. The three basic topologies are mesh, star, and hybrid VPNs.

Mesh Topology

In a **mesh configuration**, all participants in the VPN have Security Associations (SAs) with one another. (Refer to Chapter 8 for a review of SAs.) Two types of mesh arrangements are possible:

- *Full mesh*—Every subnetwork is connected to all other subnets in the VPN (see Figure 9-6). This topology is complex to manage and is best used with small VPNs.

- *Partial mesh*—Any subnet in the VPN may or may not be connected to the other subnets. This configuration offers more flexibility than a full mesh arrangement.

9

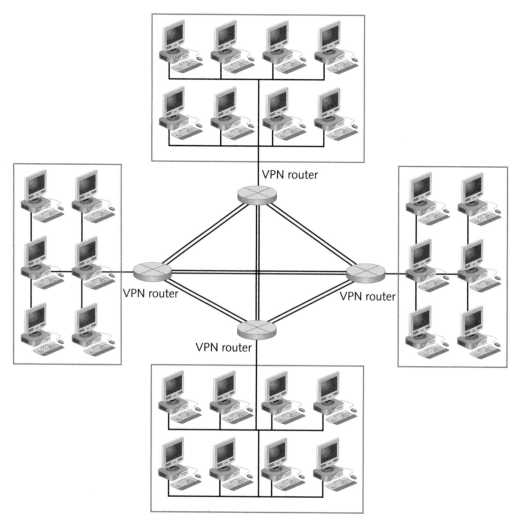

Figure 9-6 A full mesh VPN configuration

The advantage of a mesh configuration is that each participant can establish VPN communications with all other participants. However, if a new LAN is added to the VPN, all other VPN devices have to be updated to include information about new users. The problem with mesh VPNs is the difficulty in expanding the network and updating every VPN device whenever a host is added.

Star Topology

In a **star configuration** (also known as a hub-and-spoke configuration), the VPN gateway is the hub, and other networks participating in the VPN are called rim subnetworks (see Figure 9-7).

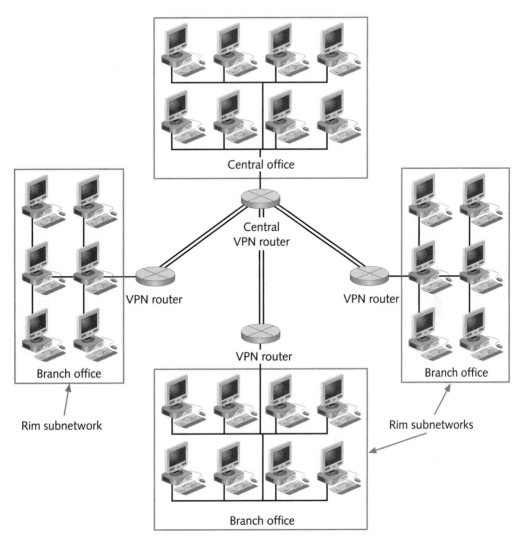

Figure 9-7 A star VPN configuration

In this configuration, separate SAs are made between each rim subnetwork's hub. The central VPN router is at the organization's central office because most star VPNs have communications go through the central office where the main IT staff is located. Any networks or computers that want to participate in the VPN need to connect only to the central server, not to any other systems in the VPN. This setup makes it easy to increase the VPN's size when more branch offices or computers are added. On the other hand, in star configurations, all communications flow in and out of a central router. This setup creates a single point of failure at the central router and can slow communication, especially if branch offices are far apart. One solution is to use two or more routers at the central office. They can be configured for load-balancing to improve performance and function as failover devices.

Hybrid Topology

As organizations with VPNs grow to include new computers and branch offices, they naturally evolve from a mesh or star configuration into a **hybrid configuration** that combines network topologies (see Figure 9-8). Because mesh configurations tend to operate more efficiently, the central core linking the network's most important branches should probably be a mesh configuration. However, branch offices can be added as spokes connecting to a VPN router at the central office. A hybrid setup combining these two configurations benefits from the star configuration's scalability and the mesh configuration's speed.

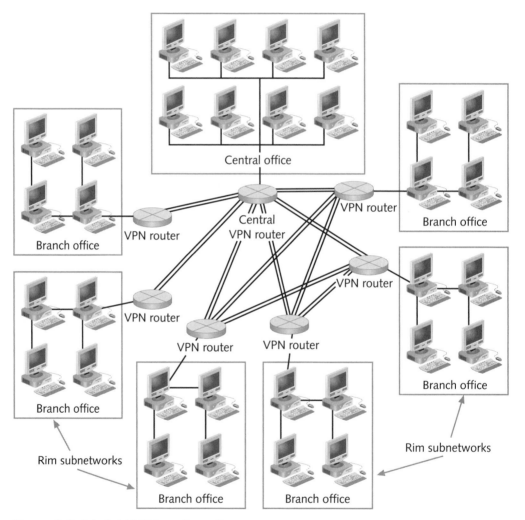

Figure 9-8 A hybrid VPN configuration

Activity 9-2: Designing a VPN Topology

Time Required: 30 minutes

Objective: Recommend a VPN solution for a company.

Description: Discuss the following scenario in class or research it on your own. You might want to use Microsoft Paint or another drawing program to illustrate the specifics of your design and help in your assessment. Evaluate the requirements, and present your recommendations in writing or orally, as directed by your instructor.

Scenario: You manage a network that connects via a VPN to a combination of branch offices and remote users. Four branch offices and one central office need to communicate securely to transfer files, especially confidential budget data. In addition, three remote users need to communicate with the network by using a VPN, but they don't need to talk to one another because they work in different areas of the company.

1. Describe a VPN configuration that would serve all parts of the extended corporate network.

   _____

   _____

2. What are your recommendations for securing remote users' connections? How would you enforce those recommendations?

   _____

   _____

9

Using VPNs with Firewalls

Having a VPN doesn't reduce the need for a correctly configured firewall. You should always use a firewall as part of your VPN security design. Using a VPN with a firewall, however, requires careful planning and configuration. Several different configurations are possible, and each option has advantages and disadvantages, as explained in this section. One option is to install VPN software on the firewall. Several commercial firewalls include VPN components as an added option. As you can see in Figure 9-9, this configuration has a single point of entry into the network:

- The firewall allows outbound access to the Internet.

- The firewall prevents inbound access from the Internet.

- The VPN service encrypts traffic to remote clients or networks.

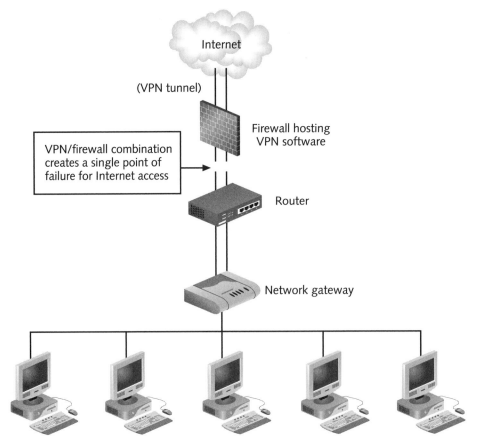

Figure 9-9 The VPN server on a firewall

The advantages of putting the VPN on a firewall include the following:

- You can control all network access security from one server.

- There are fewer computers to manage, meaning less chance of configuration mistakes.

- You can create and manage rules that apply to your VPN traffic with the same tools you already use to manage your firewall.

The disadvantages of installing the VPN on a firewall include the following:

- You have one server controlling all network access security. Any errors in configuring the VPN or firewall could leave your network open to attack.

- You must make sure to configure routes carefully so that traffic goes through the correct interfaces.

- Incorrect configuration of the firewall or VPN rules could allow traffic from the Internet to get past your security.

- Internet access and VPN traffic compete for resources on the server, so a more powerful computer might be necessary.

Another option, shown in Figure 9-10, is setting up the VPN parallel to your firewall inside the demilitarized zone (DMZ). Internal clients continue to point to the firewall as their default gateway and are unaware of the VPN connection. The firewall has a route to any networks accessible via the VPN server and instructs clients to send packets to the VPN server when appropriate.

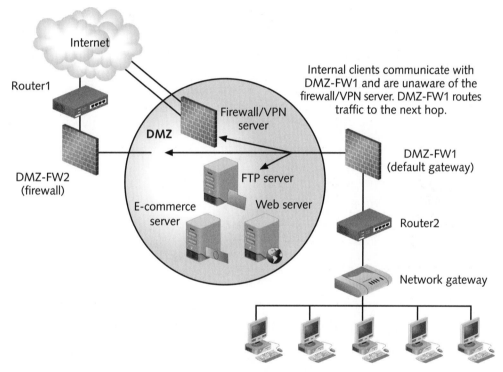

Figure 9-10 The VPN server parallel to a firewall

A DMZ can also be called a screened subnet or a perimeter network. If it's used for sharing files and access to company data with a business partner, a perimeter network is often referred to as an extranet.

These are the advantages of putting the VPN server parallel to the firewall:

- VPN traffic isn't going through the firewall, so there's no need to modify firewall settings to support VPN traffic.

- This configuration can be scaled more easily. New VPN servers can be added without having to reconfigure the firewall.

- If the VPN server becomes too congested, you can add another server and distribute the load.

The disadvantages of a VPN parallel to a firewall include the following:

- The VPN server is connected directly to the Internet, making it an ideal target for attackers.

- If the VPN server becomes compromised, the attacker will have direct access to your internal network.

- The cost of supporting a VPN increases with the addition of new servers and extra support staff.

Another location for the VPN server is behind the firewall connected to the internal network. As shown in Figure 9-11, the VPN server isn't accessible from the Internet. All packets must go through the firewall to reach the VPN server. As with the parallel configuration, you need to add a route to the firewall that redirects VPN traffic from internal clients to the VPN server. You also need to configure the firewall to pass encrypted VPN traffic directly to the VPN server.

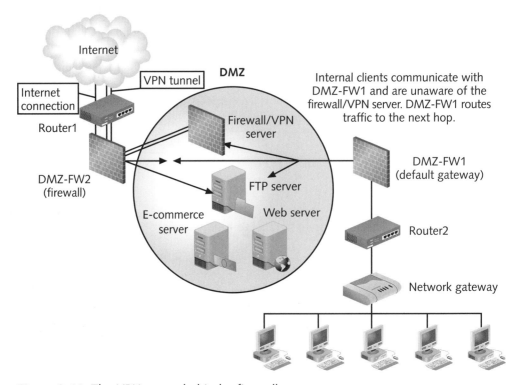

Figure 9-11 The VPN server behind a firewall

Putting the VPN server behind the firewall has some advantages:

- The VPN server is completely protected from the Internet by the firewall.

- The firewall is the only device controlling access to and from the Internet.

- Network restrictions for VPN traffic are configured only on the VPN server, making it easier to create rule sets.

The disadvantages of putting the VPN server behind the firewall include the following:

- All VPN traffic must travel through the firewall, which increases congestion and latency.

- The firewall must handle VPN traffic from the Internet to the VPN server. Getting the firewall to pass encrypted VPN traffic to the VPN server could require advanced configuration.

- The firewall might not know what to do with IP protocols other than ICMP, TCP, and UDP. Supporting VPNs that use IP protocols, such as ESP packets for IPSec or Generic Routing Encapsulation packets for PPTP, could be challenging.

NOTE

If you terminate the VPN connection in front of the firewall, VPN traffic will be on the unprotected external network for a brief period before passing through the firewall.

ACTIVITY

Activity 9-3: Setting up a VPN with a Firewall

Time Required: 30 minutes

Objective: Explore the placement of a VPN in relation to a firewall.

Description: In this activity, you explore where to place a VPN in relation to a firewall. In groups or individually, read the following scenarios and answer the questions. Your instructor might want you to present your recommendations to the class. Remember that effective communication and presentation skills are vital soft skills, which are as important as technical knowledge in earning you recognition and respect in your job.

Scenario 1: You configured a VPN to use IPSec in its most secure mode—using ESP with tunnel mode. However, you encounter problems with the firewall, which is positioned between the VPN and the internal network. The firewall ends up dropping a substantial percentage of the packets terminated by the VPN device.

    1. Troubleshoot the situation: What could be causing the firewall to fail to process VPN traffic? How could you solve the problem?

        _____

        _____

Scenario 2: You need to decide whether to put the VPN server in front of the firewall where it's exposed to the Internet or in the DMZ behind the firewall. Your organization's security policy calls for the firewall to implement NAT. In addition, the VPN needs to connect to only a single gateway. Members of the IT staff are in disagreement about where to place the firewall. One group argues that there's a security risk in putting the VPN in the DMZ because it creates two points of entry to the network (the firewall and the VPN device). Another group argues that placing the VPN in front of the firewall means the firewall needs to be configured carefully to let traffic through from the VPN without giving attackers a point of entry.

    2. You're asked to resolve the disagreement. What recommendation would you make?

_____

_____

ADJUSTING PACKET-FILTERING RULES FOR VPNS

A perimeter firewall is configured with rules that filter packets the VPN sends or receives. These rules control intranet traffic to and from VPN clients and should be based on your organization's security policies. Packet filtering is based on the header fields of inbound and outbound packets. However you configure your VPN and firewall combination, you need to set up packet-filtering rules that allow VPN traffic to pass through as needed. Packet filtering makes use of three IP packet header fields in particular:

- The source address is the 32-bit IP address of the host that sent the packet and generated the information in it.

- The destination address is the 32-bit IP address of the destination host expected to receive the packet and its information.

- The protocol identifier (protocol ID) is a number indicating to which upper-level protocol the data in the packet belongs.

You can conduct packet filtering based on any or all of these header fields. Using the source or destination address, for example, you can block all packets from an address or range of addresses, and you can route allowed packets to a range of addresses. The protocol ID field is used to refer to protocols such as the following:

- ICMP, protocol ID 1

- TCP, protocol ID 6

- UDP, protocol ID 17

- Generic Routing Encapsulation (GRE), protocol ID 47

- ESP, protocol ID 50

- AH, protocol ID 51

The Internet Assigned Numbers Authority (IANA) maintains a list of all protocol IDs at *www.iana.org/assignments/protocol-numbers*.

PPTP Filters

PPTP, the first widely supported VPN protocol, supports legacy authentication methods, doesn't require a PKI, and provides automated configuration. PPTP might be the
best option when VPN connections must pass through a NAT server or firewall. NAT
changes the internal computer's IP address to the address of the NAT device. For this
reason, NAT isn't compatible with many IPSec implementations. The problem comes
from the Internet Key Exchange (IKE) protocol that IPSec uses. IKE embeds the sending computer's IP address in its payload, and because the embedded address doesn't
match the source address of the IKE packet (which is the NAT device's address), the
receiving computer drops the packet.

The IPSec working group of the IEEE has created standards for NAT Traversal
(NAT-T) defined in RFCs 3947 and 3948. NAT-T is designed to solve some
problems of using IPSec with NAT.

9

PPTP comes into play when older clients need to connect to a network through a VPN
or when a tunnel must pass through a firewall that performs NAT but isn't compatible
with IPSec. For PPTP traffic to pass through the firewall, you need to set up packet-
filtering rules that permit this communication. PPTP uses two protocols: TCP and
GRE. A VPN server that has been configured to receive PPTP traffic listens for incoming connections arriving on TCP port 1723. It also needs to receive GRE packets (identified by protocol ID 47). Table 9-2 shows filtering rules you would use for your
gateway, if it had an IP address of 205.43.1.78 and a remote gateway with an IP address
of 77.127.39.2.

Table 9-2   PPTP packet-filtering rules

Rule	Source IP	Destination IP	Protocol	Source port	Destination port	Action
1	Any	205.43.1.78	TCP	Any	1723	Allow
2	Any	205.43.1.78	Protocol ID 47	Any	Any	Allow

In Table 9-2, two rules are established. Rule 1 allows incoming PPTP connections from
any computer to be received at the VPN server at 205.43.1.78 via port 1723. Rule 2
allows incoming traffic that uses protocol ID 47 (incoming traffic consisting of GRE
packets).

TIP   For increased security, in the Action column, you could specify an option such as "Drop all packets except those that meet this criteria," if your firewall enables you to make these distinctions. In your rule base, you must configure this option as any other rule, specifying source, destination, protocol, action to take (Deny, in this case), and so forth.

L2TP and IPSec Filters

If you use L2TP, you need to set up rules that permit IPSec traffic. You have to account for IKE using protocol ID 1701 and UDP on port 500. As listed previously, ESP uses protocol ID 50, and AH uses protocol ID 51. Table 9-3 shows the filter rules for a network gateway with an IP address of 205.43.1.78 and a remote gateway with an IP address of 77.127.39.2.

Table 9-3   L2TP packet-filtering rules

Rule	Source IP	Destination IP	Protocol	Transport protocol	Source port	Destination port	Action
1	Any	205.43.1.78	IKE	UDP	500	500	Allow
2	Any	205.43.1.78	ESP	Protocol ID 50	Any	Any	Allow
3	Any	205.43.1.78	AH	Protocol ID 51	Any	Any	Allow

In this example, Rule 1 covers inbound IKE traffic, which uses UDP port 500. Rule 2 allows traffic if you decide to use ESP, which requires a filter rule allowing protocol ID 50 packets. Rule 3 allows traffic if you use AH, which requires a rule for protocol ID 51. As with filters for PPTP, you achieve better security if, in the Action column, you specify a cleanup rule, such as "Drop all packets except those that meet this criteria."

REVIEWING VPN SECURITY POLICIES AND PROCEDURES

VPN endpoints are vulnerable to many of the same viruses, Trojan programs, and spyware as internal network computers, and an infected remote computer can spread viruses or malicious code to computers on the internal network. Because remote clients are outside an administrator's realm of control, the responsibility for remote client security falls mostly on end users. There are measures you can take to mitigate these risks, however, such as including VPN policies in your overall security policy, using VPN quarantine procedures, logging VPN connections, and auditing remote access activity logs. These measures are discussed in the following sections.

Using VPN Quarantine

A quarantine network is a segment of the network with limited access to resources, especially internal resources. Quarantine networks are logical topology structures and are used for untrusted clients, such as business partners, vendors, and consultants as well as remote access/VPN clients. Quarantined clients can be checked for policy compliance and then granted access to resources after compliance is verified, or a connection can be maintained in quarantine state for the duration of the session, depending on the nature of the connection (a remote access/VPN client or a limited access consultant, for example) and the client's access permissions.

VPN quarantine was created to address the problem of remote clients not meeting an organization's security standards. Although a VPN provides encryption and encapsulation to secure access, it can't check to make sure clients have the latest updates or check for malicious software. So a computer connecting to a network via a VPN can introduce malware and, if not updated, might contain software vulnerabilities that can be exploited. VPN quarantine provides a method to address these vulnerabilities by placing clients in a state of virtual solitary confinement while they're checked for policy compliance.

Clients are subjected to preconnection and post-connection checks by using custom scripts or a third-party add-on utility. The checks can examine service pack version, software update status, and whether an approved antivirus program and personal firewall are running and updated on the client. Other requirements can be specified in the scripts. While these checks are running to verify compliance with the remote access policy, computers attempting to connect are placed in a quarantine network. After computers have been examined and passed the checks, the quarantine is lifted, and clients are allowed access to network resources. VPN quarantine isn't a cure-all for security vulnerabilities but can help prevent computers with unsafe configurations from connecting to the internal network.

NOTE
Quarantine isn't used solely for remote access. It has been used to mitigate other threats as well. E-mail is a good example because it's a main source of malware infections. For this reason, corporations have taken a proactive approach, and many corporate e-mail systems use an approach similar to quarantine for screening suspicious e-mails or e-mails with attachments. If an e-mail contains viruses or doesn't comply with policies, it's dropped, and the recipient might receive an e-mail stating that a message was determined to be a threat and was dropped.

To use VPN quarantine, you must have quarantine-compatible remote access clients and server, resources for a quarantine network, an accounts database, and a quarantine remote access policy. VPN quarantine can use Windows authentication or a RADIUS server, but RADIUS is the preferred method.

Windows Server 2003 SP1 and Internet Security and Acceleration (ISA) Server 2006 support VPN quarantine scripts, and most other modern OSs can be configured to support quarantine procedures. Because VPN quarantine uses scripts and integrates with RADIUS servers, using it on varied platforms is possible and fairly simple. Refer to vendor instructions for exact procedures.

Some third-party applications that enable quarantine are available, too. VPN-Q 2006 from Winfrasoft, for example, is used for endpoint security on Windows clients. It integrates with ISA Server 2004/2006 and can be deployed on Windows Server 2003 without ISA Server installed. For more information on VPN-Q 2006, visit *www.winfrasoft.com/vpnq.htm*. Another third-party VPN quarantine application is Quarantine Security Suite (QSS), developed by Frederic Esnouf. QSS consists of three components: the QSS Security Client installed on the client workstation, the QSS Approval Server installed on the ISA Server 2004/2006 server, and the QSS Management Console for managing remote access security policies. For more information on QSS, visit *http://fesnouf.online.fr/qss_main.htm*.

Logging VPN Activity

In a Microsoft network, the Routing and Remote Access Services (RRAS) server can perform local machine event logging, recording events in the server's System, Security, and Application logs (viewed in Event Viewer). Typically, these logs are used to notify administrators of unusual events or for troubleshooting. Event logs provide limited information about remote access, but specific logs give you more useful data about remote clients.

The RRAS server hosting VPN services has additional logging capabilities beyond standard Event Viewer logs. It can also perform local authentication and accounting logging. Events are recorded in a separate log file in a Windows Internet Authentication Services (IAS) format or a database-compatible format. (Windows Server 2003 IAS is the Windows version of a RADIUS server and proxy.) These logs are used for tracking remote access authentication attempts and use. The applicable remote access policy's name is included with each connection attempt, making these logs useful for troubleshooting remote access policy problems. Windows Authentication and/or Windows Accounting might need to be enabled before you can configure what to log or where to store those logs. To do this, you use the Routing and Remote Access MMC snap-in to open the Local File Properties dialog box (see Figure 9-12). The Log File tab shown in this figure is where you configure logging settings, such as log file format and storage location.

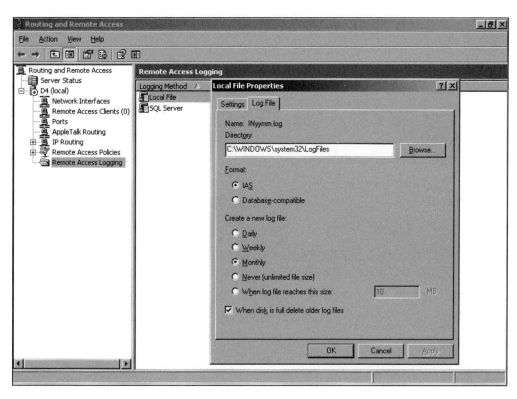

Figure 9-12 Configuring logging of accounting and authentication requests

Windows also provides support for RADIUS-based authentication and accounting logging. The RADIUS server stores logs in a separate file, which can be used for tracking remote access and use. RADIUS accounting and/or authentication must be enabled before you can configure logging.

NOTE Remember that the Windows RRAS server is a RADIUS client, and remote clients dialing up the RRAS server aren't connecting to the RADIUS server directly. The RRAS server relays authentication credentials to the RADIUS server for verification, acting as the go-between. After a remote client is authenticated, it accesses network resources through the RRAS server. The RADIUS server's primary function is authentication services.

To configure a Windows RRAS server to use a RADIUS server for accounting and authentication logging, you use the Routing and Remote Access MMC snap-in. Right-click the server name (D4 in this example) and click Properties. In the Security tab, select RADIUS Authentication in the Authentication provider drop-down list and RADIUS Accounting in the Accounting provider drop-down list (see Figure 9-13).

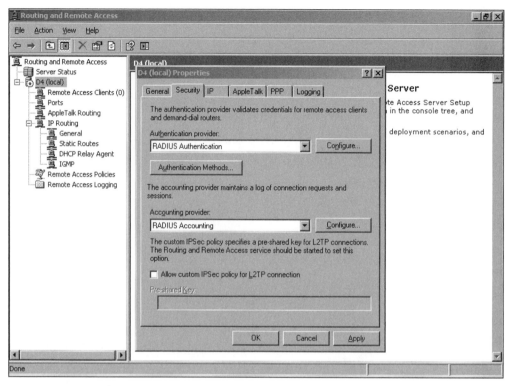

Figure 9-13 Configuring RADIUS accounting and authentication

Next, you specify where the RADIUS server is located and enter its shared secret, which acts as an account password. The shared secret must be used for the RRAS server to access RADIUS services. To do this, click the Configure button (next to Authentication provider) shown in Figure 9-13. Click Add to open the Add RADIUS Server dialog box, enter the required information (see Figure 9-14), and then click OK.

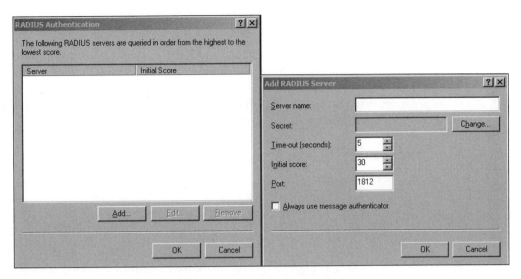

Figure 9-14 Configuring the RRAS server to use RADIUS

The same general rules for any security logging apply to remote access logging, too. You must make sure log files can't be tampered with, maintain a reasonable retention policy, and ensure consistent, regular review of log data. Storing a backup copy of log files on a separate computer is a good idea for sensitive data, and including log files in backups is a sensible precaution. Using a database with third-party log-file analysis tools can help you keep up with log file reviews, and using an integrated database that stores your remote access, firewall, and intrusion detection logs helps you compare logged events from all devices to get a clear picture of an event.

TIP

In Chapter 11, you install and configure a full WinSnort IDS with a MySQL database for log storage and tools for log analysis. This setup is good for storing remote access and firewall logs, so keep the log data generated by other security devices in mind as you progress through that chapter. Configuring the MySQL database to accept different logs is simple, and with most security devices, you can designate a database for log files.

Auditing Compliance with VPN Policies

An organization's VPN or remote access policy defines standards for connecting to the network from any host or remote system, and these policies must be integrated with an organization's overall security policies. Policies should be defined for different levels of restriction, such as what time of day access is allowed. You might also want to define tighter controls for business partners than you do for company employees working from home. Controls for administrators might be less restrictive; however, administrators should be required to have more secure passwords and change them more often.

You should audit these policies to confirm that they're being enforced and that all users are complying with them. Enforcing these policies can be difficult with remote users, however. Having strict policies on client-side OSs, configuration, and VPN client software makes this task easier. However, configuring each remote user's computer, often over the phone with the help of tech support, can be frustrating and time consuming. One solution is to standardize the VPN client for remote users. That way, tech support staff needs to learn how to support only one application, so there's less chance of errors.

In addition, test each client that will connect to the network to ensure smooth operation and help prevent security threats. After bugs are worked out and remote users can access the network, verify that everything is working according to the organization's policies and procedures. Remote users' connections should be monitored for performance and capability to connect. Is the connection maintained during file transfers? How long does a normal file transfer take? Is an idle connection terminated after a specified time? You should work with a knowledgeable remote user to help determine a baseline for future auditing, testing, and troubleshooting.

Guidelines for VPN Policies

Best practices to incorporate into your remote access/VPN policy include the following:

- Plan the most secure deployment possible, and keep careful records of all changes.

- Use strong authentication methods.

- Require password strength, length, and complexity and require passwords to be changed frequently. Also, make sure the password history setting is long enough to prevent reusing passwords.

- Have the remote access server use DHCP to assign addresses to remote clients or configure a static range of IP addresses on the VPN server so that it can assign addresses dynamically to remote clients.

- Log remote connections and use a centralized database or server for storing log files, if possible.

- Use VPN quarantine procedures, if available, to ensure policy compliance.

- Disable public peer-to-peer (P2P) file-sharing programs. If these programs are necessary for productivity, provide approved programs and ban all others.

- Preventing users from downloading and installing software is usually the safest route.

- Make sure user accounts don't have full administrative access to their systems.

- Ensure strong encryption for data, especially passwords.

- Disable split tunneling.

- Require remote clients to be configured automatically to limit or eliminate user intervention. Keep security decisions out of users' hands as much as possible.

- Disable or remove vulnerable protocols, such as Telnet, FTP, and rlogin.

- Use extra caution when configuring connectivity methods, especially wireless. Configure automatic disabling of wireless connectivity when users are connected directly or using another method of access.

- Prevent the use of removable storage devices, such as thumb drives or external hard drives, anywhere on the network.

- Install personal firewall and antivirus programs on remote devices and configure them for automatic updates.

- Make sure remote clients are self-defending, meaning remote users can't disable or bypass security measures. Measures should, as much as possible, take place automatically, without user intervention.

- Manage user audit information so that remote users receive policy updates and transmit their audit data before connecting.

- Conduct regular user training on security topics.

Strike the best balance between productivity and security in remote access/VPN policies. It's easy to err on the side of caution and lock a network down too tightly, which erases all the benefits of mobility. It's equally easy to err on the side of productivity and leave the network open to attack. Try to provide the best security possible, within the guidelines of your security policy, yet give remote users enough freedom to be productive. Remember that policies that are too stringent or too complex are likely to be bypassed or ignored.

CREATING A VPN IN WINDOWS SERVER 2003

Configuring VPNs is fairly straightforward in Windows Server 2003. Click Start, point to Administrative Tools, and then click Manage Your Server to open the Manage Your Server console, where you can start the Configure Your Server Wizard, shown in Figure 9-15.

In this wizard, you can specify which server roles you want to add. To enable and configure VPN or dial-up access, you add the Remote access/VPN server role to the server. The corresponding setup wizard then starts and finishes the role addition. For example, to add the Remote access/VPN server role, the Routing and Remote Access Server Setup Wizard starts (see Figure 9-16), which you use to specify the services you want the server to perform, such as VPN and NAT.

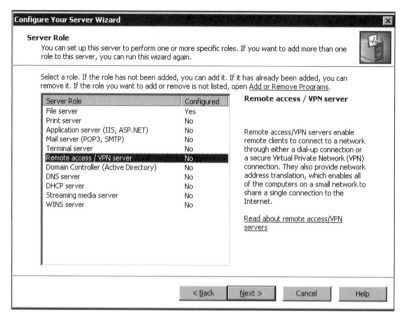

Figure 9-15 The Configure Your Server Wizard

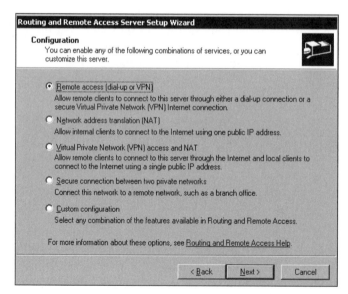

Figure 9-16 Selecting services for the remote access server to perform

You manage remote access server settings by using the Routing and Remote Access MMC snap-in. In this MMC snap-in, you can specify policies, configure authentication and encryption, and manage clients. The default policy applied to remote access in this example is ISA Server Default Policy because ISA Server is installed on this server and assumes control over remote access. To modify its settings, right-click the policy in the details pane and click Properties to open the Properties dialog box (see Figure 9-17).

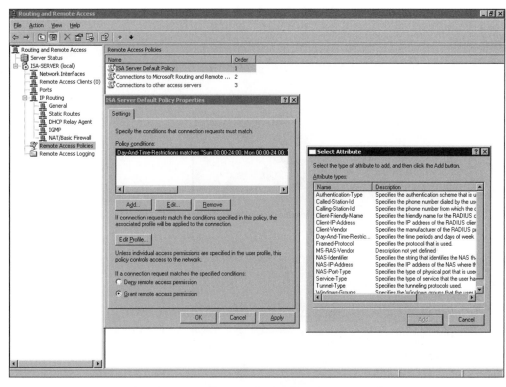

Figure 9-17 Settings for the ISA Server Default Policy

Activity 9-4: Exploring VPNs on Windows Server 2003 with ISA Server 2006

Time Required: 20 minutes

Objective: Examine using a Windows Server 2003/ISA Server 2006 computer for VPN access and security.

Description: In this activity, you examine how your Windows Server 2003 system running ISA Server 2006 provides VPN remote access services and VPN quarantine. This activity assumes you have installed and configured ISA Server 2006 as described in Chapter 7 and configured the server for VPN access as described in Chapter 8. You must start Windows Server 2003 to perform this activity.

1. Click **Start**, point to **All Programs**, point to **Microsoft ISA Server**, and click **ISA Server Management** to open the ISA Server management console.

2. In the console tree, click to expand **Arrays**, and then click **Virtual Private Networks (VPN)**. The Configure VPN Client Access details and tasks panes open.

3. Click **Configure Address Assignment Method** in the details pane. The Virtual Private Networks (VPN) Properties dialog box opens to the Address Assignment tab (see Figure 9-18). Notice that in other tabs, you can configure the RADIUS server and authentication and specify which networks can access your VPN server.

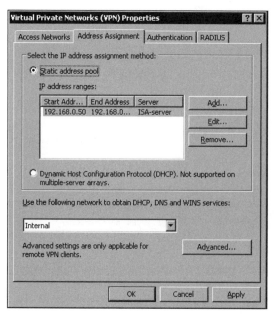

Figure 9-18 Configuring VPN properties

4. Make sure the **Static address pool** option button is selected, and then click the **Add** button to enter an IP address range. (You can also configure DHCP for VPN access in this tab.)

5. In the Select the server drop-down list, click **ISA Server**, enter a range of IP addresses, and then click **OK**.

To view details about IP address ranges you have assigned to the internal networks configured in ISA Server, click Enterprise in the console tree, expand Enterprise Policies, and click Enterprise Networks. You can't specify VPN address ranges that overlap your internal network addressing.

6. Under Arrays in the console tree, click to expand **Configuration**, and then click **Networks**. Click the **Network Rules** tab in the details pane. Notice that ISA now includes network rules related to VPN client access.

7. To configure rules, click the **VPN Clients to Internal Network** rule in the details pane (see Figure 9-19), and click **Edit Selected Network Rule** in the tasks pane. The Properties dialog box opens. Take a few moments to explore the settings, and then click **Cancel**.

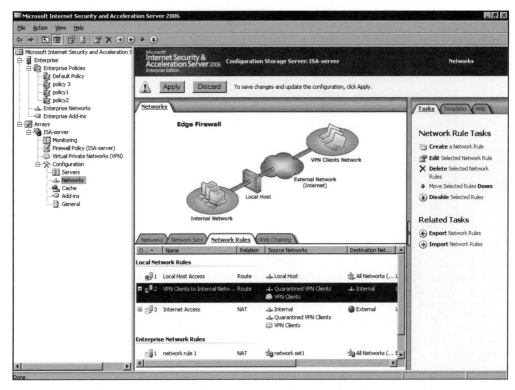

Figure 9-19 Selecting the VPN Clients to Internal Network rule

8. In the details pane, right-click **Quarantined VPN Clients** in the Source Networks column and click **Properties** to open the Quarantined VPN Clients Properties dialog box.

9. Click the **Quarantine** tab. As you can see in Figure 9-20, you can enable Quarantine Control in this dialog box and specify the ISA server or a RADIUS server as the source of quarantine procedures. You can also exempt certain users from quarantine procedures. VPN quarantine requires configuration on the server and clients. Review the settings in this dialog box, and then click **OK**.

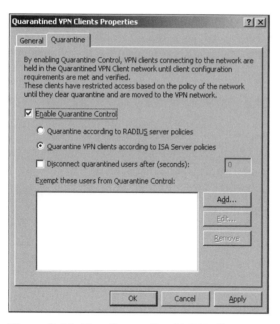

Figure 9-20 The Quarantined VPN Clients Properties dialog box

TIP

You can access VPN quarantine properties in several places in the ISA Server management console or the Routing and Remote Access MMC snap-in. Use the method most convenient to you, but remember that it's easy to lose track of changes you make, so try to be consistent and record your actions. For example, ISA Server doesn't apply changes unless you click the Apply button at the top of the details pane, but Windows Server 2003 does. Remember, too, that the golden rule of computing is to make only one change at a time. If something goes wrong, you know exactly what caused the problem.

10. Take a few moments to explore the changes to your ISA server with the addition of Routing and Remote Access Services. When you're finished, click **Cancel** to close the Properties dialog box.

By now, you understand that the most critical aspect of network security is careful, thorough planning. After you've planned configurations, it's a matter of entering information to carry out your design. There are many guides for effective planning, and most vendors offer detailed instructions and helpful tips. An additional benefit of thorough planning is the documentation you generate.

CHAPTER SUMMARY

- The type of business, its existing infrastructure, and its security policy help determine the VPN configuration and hardware or software you need.

- VPNs have several advantages: high security, low cost, and flexibility for remote access and extranets. They can simplify network management and maximize network uptime.

- VPNs also have disadvantages: serious security risks, performance slowdown caused by encryption, dependence on the sometimes unreliable Internet, complexity of remote client configuration, and compatibility issues between VPN products.

- Client-side issues in planning a VPN include whether to require a firewall and IDS software and whether policies should be enforced before authentication to the internal network.

- A VPN is often configured by establishing a VPN domain, which eases management and improves security. Whether the network gateway is included in the domain depends on your VPN configuration.

- VPNs can have single entry point configurations or multiple entry point configurations, and networks can be connected by using a mesh, star, or hybrid topology.

- VPNs need to be used with firewalls, and packet-filtering rules must be set up for them to work together. Packet filtering uses three IP packet header fields in particular: source address, destination address, and protocol ID.

- Packet-filtering rules cover ports and protocols such as PPTP, L2TP, and IPSec. Filter packets so that traffic between VPN endpoints passes through the VPN, and other traffic is filtered to reach specific destinations on the network.

- VPN quarantine places remote clients in a secured area while they're checked for compliance. Logging provides data for auditing, troubleshooting, and tracing network activity. Auditing confirms policy enforcement and user compliance.

- Best practices for remote access security include using strong encryption and authentication, logging remote access activity, ensuring policy compliance, and keeping security decisions out of users' hands.

- After you have installed and configured a VPN, you need to test clients for policy compliance, performance, and baseline measurements.

- Configuring a VPN in Windows Server 2003 isn't difficult if you have planned your design carefully. In Windows Server 2003, VPNs and remote access are managed through MMC snap-ins.

9

KEY TERMS

hybrid configuration — A VPN configuration that combines characteristics of the mesh and star configurations.

mesh configuration — A VPN configuration in which all participants in the VPN are connected to one another. This configuration is commonly arranged as a full mesh or partial mesh setup.

multiple entry point configuration — A type of VPN configuration in which multiple gateways are used, each with a VPN tunnel connecting a different location.

single entry point configuration — A VPN configuration in which all traffic to and from the network passes through a single gateway, such as a router or firewall.

split tunneling — The term used to describe multiple paths. One path goes to the VPN server and is secured, but an unauthorized and unsecured path permits the user to connect to the Internet or some other network while still connected to the corporate VPN.

star configuration — A VPN configuration in which a single gateway is the "hub" and other networks that participate in the VPN are considered "rim" networks.

topology — The way in which participants in a network are connected physically to one another.

VPN domain — A group of one or more computers that the VPN hardware and software handle as a single entity. This group uses the VPN to communicate with another domain.

VPN quarantine — A method created to address the problem of remote clients not meeting an organization's security standards. Quarantine places remote clients in a secured area while they are checked to ensure that software updates and current patches have been applied, antivirus software has been installed and updated, and other policies have been complied with.

REVIEW QUESTIONS

1. Which of the following factors should a secure VPN design address? (Choose all that apply.)

   a. authentication

   b. encryption

   c. ease of use

   d. perimeter security

2. A VPN domain is a group of computers that _____.

   a. share the same domain name

   b. are in the same subnet

   c. are handled as a single entity

   d. make up a VPN

3. In what type of VPN configuration must a router belong to the VPN domain?

   a. gateway-to-gateway VPN

   b. multiple entry point

   c. single entry point

   d. partial mesh

4. Which of the following is an advantage of using a mesh VPN topology?

   a. You need to configure only the central office's VPN server.

   b. All participants can communicate securely with each other.

   c. All participants can exchange encrypted communication.

   d. The VPN can be scaled along with the organization.

5. Which of the following is an advantage of using a star VPN topology?

   a. Fewer connections with ISPs need to be made.

   b. Fewer VPN hardware or software devices need to be used.

   c. Only the VPN server at the hub needs to be updated.

   d. All participants can communicate with each other.

6. Briefly describe split tunneling.

7. What client-side issues do you need to consider when planning a VPN deployment? (Choose all that apply.)

   a. whether to require the client to use a firewall

   b. the organization's current growth rate

   c. how policies should be enforced on the client computer

   d. cost of equipment employees need to buy

8. Determining whether the network gateway is included in the VPN domain depends on whether your network has a _____ VPN configuration.

   a. site-to-site

   b. client-to-gateway

   c. gateway-to-domain

   d. client-to-client

9. What problems could occur if VPN domains overlap? (Choose all that apply.)

   a. Packets could be dropped.

   b. Packets could be routed incorrectly.

   c. All domains could fail.

   d. The VPN server could become unstable and crash.

10. List three types of logging a Windows RRAS server can perform.

9

11. In a mesh topology, all participants in the VPN have ———————— with one another.

    a. tunnels

    b. SAs

    c. static routes

    d. trusts

12. What is a main disadvantage of mesh VPNs?

    a. They aren't reliable.

    b. There's a lack of confidentiality among peers.

    c. They are difficult to enlarge or change.

    d. The equipment must be the same at all sites.

13. What is a main disadvantage of star VPNs? (Choose all that apply.)

    a. Changes are hard to make.

    b. The central hub is a single point of failure.

    c. Performance can degrade, especially if sites are geographically dispersed.

    d. Communication is easy to intercept.

14. Putting a VPN on the firewall has which of the following disadvantages? (Choose all that apply.)

    a. There are more computers to manage.

    b. Only one server controls security, so any configuration errors leave the network open to attack.

    c. Internet access and VPN traffic compete for resources on the server.

    d. VPN traffic isn't encrypted.

15. A VPN server configured to receive PPTP traffic listens for incoming connections on port ———————— and needs to receive GRE traffic identified by protocol ID ————————.

    a. UDP 1443, 17

    b. TCP 1723, 47

    c. UDP 3349, 443

    d. UDP 1723, 47

16. Which protocols and ports must be allowed to pass when you're using L2TP and IPSec? (Choose all that apply.)

    a. protocol ID 50

    b. UDP 500

    c. TCP 50

    d. protocol ID 1701

17. Which of the following might be the best option when NAT traffic must pass through a firewall?

    a. IPSec

    b. PPP

    c. L2TP

    d. PPTP

18. There's no need to set up packet-filtering rules on the perimeter firewall for VPN traffic. True or False?

19. AH uses protocol ID _____.

    a. 50

    b. 171

    c. 500

    d. 51

9

HANDS-ON PROJECTS

HANDS-ON PROJECTS

Hands-On Project 9-1: Configuring L2TP Packet-Filtering Rules

Time Required: 10 minutes

Objective: Configure access for remote user VPN connections.

Description: In this project, you configure a set of packet-filtering rules that enable a remote user to connect to your VPN gateway at 101.26.111.8 from the user's gateway, which is assigned an IP address dynamically and uses L2TP. The packet-filtering rules should enable VPN traffic to pass through your firewall.

1. Write down the UDP source and destination ports that L2TP uses. (*Hint:* Refer to the "L2TP and IPSec Filters" section earlier in this chapter.)

   _____

2. Write two rules for inbound traffic. What are the two options you could specify as the action for these rules?

   _____

   _____

3. Write two rules for outbound traffic.

   _____

   _____

Hands-On Project 9-2: Recommending VPN Procurement

Time Required: 30 minutes

Objective: Research and recommend hardware to meet a specific VPN solution.

Description: In this project, you assess the following scenario and research different ways to meet the requirements. Your instructor might have you present your recommendations to the class or ask you for a written report.

Scenario: You manage all parts of an extranet that comprises several different subnets. Because you are the administrator for these subnets, you have control over what equipment each part of the network uses. You're expecting heavy traffic and have been asked to recommend VPN equipment.

1. What kind of VPN components make sense in this situation?

   _____

   _____

2. What kind of topology would be the easiest to configure and maintain?

   _____

   _____

CASE PROJECT

Case Project 9-1: Implementing a Remote Access Solution for Green Globe

Now that you have designed a secure remote access solution for the company, you must complete your documentation. In Chapter 8, you should have documented your remote access solution, including a complete list of equipment and software needed and a cost breakdown for the additions. You should also have revised your network diagram so that you know the logical and physical layout. For this chapter, check your design and make any revisions you think are needed.

The pivotal aspect of securing remote access for Green Globe is user awareness. Design a remote access training module for Green Globe's remote workers. The training module should be available in both hard-copy and electronic formats. Remember that it's intended for a nontechnical audience, so keep it simple and avoid technical jargon. It should explain remote access security, give instructions for connecting remotely, and cover safe handling of mobile devices, procedures in the event of device damage or theft, and any other user awareness topics relevant to your remote access design.

As always, you can use any available templates or resources, as long as you adhere to academic honesty guidelines and respect copyrights and related laws.

NOTE

10

INTRUSION DETECTION SYSTEM CONCEPTS

After reading this chapter and completing the exercises, you will be able to:

♦ Identify the components of an intrusion detection system

♦ Describe options for implementing intrusion detection systems

♦ Explain the steps of intrusion detection

A security policy is the basis for securing an organization's network. An intrusion detection system (IDS) adds another level of defense to firewalls, virtual private networks (VPNs), and other security devices. Like a burglar alarm, an IDS has sensors to detect when unauthorized users attempt to gain access and notifies you so that you can take countermeasures. Unlike a burglar alarm, however, some IDS devices can be configured to respond in a way that actually stops attacks.

Intrusion detection involves monitoring network traffic, detecting attempts to gain unauthorized access to a system or resource, and notifying the appropriate professionals to take countermeasures. This chapter discusses IDS components and then explains options for designing an IDS by distributing its components at critical locations and hosts. Finally, you examine how IDS components operate together to protect a network.

EXAMINING INTRUSION DETECTION SYSTEM COMPONENTS

A network **intrusion** is an attempt to gain unauthorized access to network resources. The term "intrusion" is a polite way of saying "attack," and often an attack is launched with the intention of compromising the integrity and confidentiality of network data or users' privacy. An **intrusion detection system (IDS)** consists of more than one application or hardware device and incorporates more than just detection. **Intrusion detection** involves three network defense functions—prevention, detection, and response. As shown in Figure 10-1, firewalls perform the prevention function, IDSs provide the detection function, and network administrators carry out the response function.

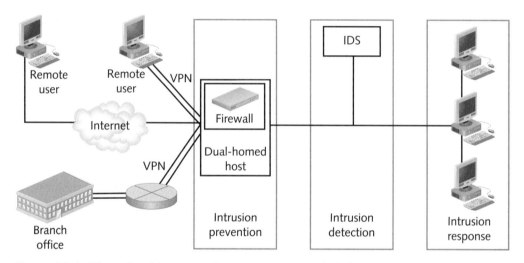

Figure 10-1 The role of intrusion detection in network defense

Modern products often blur these lines between functions, however. Firewalls might have built-in IDSs, and IDSs can often carry out responses automatically. All-in-one devices, sometimes called intrusion detection and prevention systems (IDPSs), are becoming more effective and less costly, so they are being used more widely. An all-in-one device has the advantage of increasing interoperability, addressing security concerns more thoroughly, and centralizing management. Some all-in-one products can be quite complex, however, and require extensive knowledge to configure and maintain.

The following sections describe typical components of an IDS:

- Network sensors or host-based agents that analyze and report activity; used with management servers that receive and manage information from sensors, analyze data, and identify some events

- Detection and prevention capabilities

- A command console for interfacing with the IDS

- A database server storing attack signatures or behaviors that an IDS uses to identify potentially suspicious traffic

The National Institute of Standards and Technology (NIST) publishes a variety of resources, including NIST Special Publications available at *http://csrc.nist.gov/publications/nistpubs*. This chapter is based on standards in NIST Special Publication 800-94, Guide to Intrusion Detection and Prevention Systems (IDPS).

Sensors and Agents

A sensor or agent functions as the electronic "eyes" of an IDS. In host-based IDS configurations, an IDS installed on a single host computer has its **agent** built in to the IDS software. In a network-based IDS, a **sensor** is hardware or software that monitors traffic passing into and out of the network in real time. (Host-based and network-based IDS configurations are discussed later in "Options for Intrusion Detection Systems.")

When a sensor detects an event it considers suspicious, an alarm is triggered. Attacks detected by an IDS sensor can take one of two forms:

- Single-session attacks, in which an intruder makes an isolated attempt to locate a computer on the internal network or gain access by other means

- Multiple-session attacks, such as port scans or network scans, that take place over a period of time and are made up of several events

An IDS that checks for intrusions on a network might have several sensors placed at strategic locations. Sensors should be placed at common entry points to the network (see Figure 10-2), such as the following:

- Internet gateways

- Connections between one network and another or between subnets separated by switches

- A remote access server that receives dial-up connections from remote users

- Virtual private network (VPN) devices that connect a LAN to a business partner's LAN

In some IDS configurations, sensor software collects data from a hardware device called a network tap, which gathers data from network traffic traveling over the physical media.

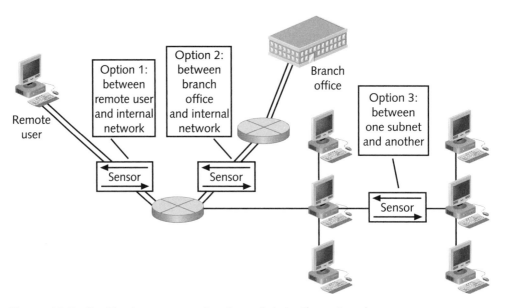

Figure 10-2   Positioning sensors at entry points to the network

If a firewall is used to protect the network, sensors could be positioned on either side of the firewall. However, if the sensor is placed outside the firewall at a point exposed to the Internet, it could become the subject of an attack. A more secure location is behind the firewall in the demilitarized zone (DMZ), as shown in Figure 10-3.

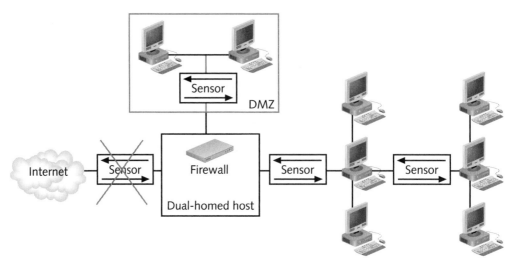

Figure 10-3   Positioning sensors behind the firewall in the DMZ

Management Servers

An **IDS management server** is the central repository for sensor and agent data. Sensors report log data to the management server, which analyzes and correlates the events received from several sensors. Some large networks have many management servers or even two tiers of servers, and small networks might not use any management servers.

Detection and Prevention Capabilities

Most IDSs support multiple detection capabilities for more flexibility in configuration and improved accuracy. When you're selecting an IDS, consider the customization options it offers. Detection capabilities that can be customized to improve accuracy include the following:

- *Thresholds*—A value that sets the limit between normal and abnormal behavior
- *Blacklists*—A list of entities, such as port numbers, URLs, or applications, that have been associated with malicious activity
- *Whitelists*—A list of entities known to be harmless
- *Alert settings*—Specifying default priorities or severity levels, determining which prevention capabilities should be used for certain events, and specifying what information should be logged and how alert messages are sent, for example

10

Administrators can also view detection-related code, such as traffic signatures. With some IDSs, administrators can review the application code of protocol analysis programs. Some alerts might be generated from a complex set of signatures, so being able to modify IDS signature code helps improve accuracy and is the only way to make the IDS recognize organization-specific characteristics. Writing custom IDS signature code is complex and requires programming expertise because software bugs can cause IDSs to malfunction or fail.

Any customization should be reviewed periodically to make sure it's still accurate and to account for changes in the environment; this advice applies to baseline measurements used for anomaly detection, too. Keep in mind that IDS updates and patches could affect custom settings.

Most modern IDSs have multiple detection methods. Intrusion detection is still the basis of their operation, but these integrated systems often use compliance monitoring, too. Enterprise-class IDSs, such as SecurVantage Enterprise by Securify (*www.securify.com*), monitor for vulnerabilities, access controls, logons, and host-level service behaviors and offer custom reporting and analysis tools. Most vendors also offer integrated management consoles for organizing data collected from several systems.

Prevention Capabilities

Many IDSs can be set up to take some preventive countermeasures, such as resetting all network connections when an intrusion is detected. Prevention capabilities vary by product. With some, administrators can specify what preventive measure should be taken for each alert type and decide to enable or disable prevention. Some IDSs have a simulation mode, in which all prevention capabilities are disabled, but the system generates reports of when they would be applied in response to different events. These reports are used to fine-tune prevention capabilities, which reduces the risk of blocking legitimate traffic.

IDS prevention capabilities shouldn't be considered a substitute for administrators taking countermeasures, however. Administrators can use their judgment to determine whether an alarm is being triggered by a false positive or a genuine attack. If the attack is genuine, administrators can gauge its severity and determine whether the response should be **escalated**—increased to a higher level.

Anomaly and Misuse Detection Systems

There are two general types of detection systems: anomaly detection and misuse detection. An **anomaly detection** system makes use of **profiles** for each authorized user or group that describe the services and resources normally accessed on the network. (Network baselines are associated with profiles, too.) You might use anomaly detection if you're especially concerned with misuse from inside the organization or you want to monitor all traffic into and out of e-mail, Web, and FTP servers.

Some IDSs can create baselines during a "training period"—during this time, the IDS monitors network traffic to observe what constitutes "normal" network behavior. Otherwise, you need to create profiles yourself. Because a large-scale network might consist of hundreds or thousands of users divided into many groups, profile configuration can be a lot of work.

The accuracy of profiles has a direct impact on effective detection of anomalies. If profiles are accurate, the IDS sends alarms only for genuine attacks. If profiles are incomplete or inaccurate, the IDS sends alarms that turn out to be **false positives**, alarms generated by legitimate network traffic rather than actual attacks. False positives waste valuable time and resources and, if they occur often, can result in IT employees not taking alarms seriously. You also need to configure an IDS accurately enough to avoid **false negatives**, genuine attacks that an IDS doesn't detect. False negatives have the most serious security implications. **True negatives** are legitimate communications that don't set off an alarm. The term **true positive** is sometimes used to describe a genuine attack.

 An anomaly-based system can also generate false positives caused by changes in user habits; after all, people don't use computer systems the same way all the time. When users vary a pattern (by attempting to access a database they've never used before, for instance), a false positive is likely.

In contrast to anomaly-based detection, which triggers alarms based on users' or groups' deviations from "normal" network behavior, **misuse detection** triggers alarms based on characteristic signatures of known external attacks. You might select misuse detection if you have the time and ability (and perhaps the software) to analyze the large amount of log file data this system generates.

NOTE   You might also see misuse detection referred to as signature-based detection or a knowledge-based IDS. The names for this detection technique vary, but the method is the same: using databases of signatures of known attacks to identify and possibly respond to intrusions.

Organizations that want a basic IDS and are mostly concerned with known attacks from intruders trying to access hosts from the Internet should choose a misuse-based IDS and update its signatures regularly. Network engineers research well-known attacks and record rules associated with each signature; a database of these signatures is then made available to IDSs so that they can begin protecting networks immediately after installation. An anomaly-based IDS, on the other hand, must be trained to recognize "normal" network traffic before it can protect a network. Table 10-1 summarizes the advantages and disadvantages of these detection systems.

10

Table 10-1   Advantages and disadvantages of detection systems

Detection method	Advantages	Disadvantages
Anomaly	Because an anomaly detection system is based on profiles an administrator creates, an attacker can't test the IDS beforehand and anticipate what will trigger an alarm.	Configuring the IDS to use profiles of network users and groups requires considerable time.
	As new users and groups are created, IDS profiles can be changed to keep up with these changes.	As new users and groups are created, profiles available to the IDS must be updated to remain effective.
	Because an anomaly detection system doesn't rely on published signatures, it can detect new attacks.	The definition of what constitutes normal traffic changes constantly, and the IDS must be reconfigured to keep up.
	The system can detect attacks from inside the network by employees or attackers who have stolen employee accounts.	After installation, the IDS must be trained for days or weeks to recognize normal traffic.
Misuse	This approach makes use of signatures of well-known attacks.	The database of signatures must be updated to maintain the IDS's effectiveness.

Table 10-1   Advantages and disadvantages of detection systems (continued)

Detection method	Advantages	Disadvantages
	This IDS can begin working immediately after installation.	New types of attacks might not be included in the database.
	This IDS is easy to understand and less difficult to configure than an anomaly-based system.	By making minor alterations to an attack, attackers can avoid matching a signature in the database.
	Each signature in the database is assigned a number and name so that the administrator can specify the attacks that should set off an alarm.	Because a misuse-based system makes use of a database, a lot of disk storage space might be needed.

A misuse-based system has another potential weakness you should keep in mind: the need to maintain **state information** (data about a connection) on a possible attack. When an IDS receives a packet, information about the connection between the host and remote computer is compared to entries in the state table. A state table maintains a record of connections between computers that includes the source IP address and port, destination IP address and port, and protocol. Furthermore, the IDS needs to maintain state information for the entire length of the attack, which is called the **event horizon**. Maintaining this information might require an IDS to review many packets of data; during long attacks, such as those that last from user logon to user logoff, the IDS might not be able to maintain the state information long enough, and the attack could circumvent the system.

NOTE   Monitoring an attack in progress can be helpful if you want to gather information for identifying, capturing, and prosecuting intruders or learn more about the vulnerability being exploited. The circumstances under which you allow an attack to progress should be spelled out clearly in the security policy. However, if the attack is causing severe harm, such as failure of network services or theft of proprietary data, stop the attack as quickly as possible.

Besides misuse and anomaly detection, an IDS can detect suspicious packets in other ways:

- *Traffic rate monitoring*—If a sudden and dramatic increase in traffic is detected, such as that caused by a denial-of-service (DoS) attack, the IDS can stop and reset all TCP traffic.

- *Protocol state tracking (stateful packet filtering)*—Some IDSs can go a step beyond matching packet signatures by performing firewall-like stateful packet filtering. The IDS maintains a record of the connection's state and allows packets to pass through to the internal network only if a connection has been established already.

- *IP packet reassembly*—Some IDSs can reassemble fragmented IP packets to prevent fragments from passing through to the internal network.

Alert Systems

A home burglar alarm system is configured to emit a sound if a certain event occurs, such as a window breaking or a door opening. An IDS operates in much the same way—it sends an alert when it encounters packets or traffic patterns that seem suspicious. In response to these events, the IDS uses a **trigger**—a set of circumstances that causes an alert message to be sent. Alert messages can take many forms, such as a pop-up window, an e-mail, a sound, or a message sent to a pager.

Alerts can result from two general types of triggers (discussed in more detail in the following sections):

- *Detection of an anomaly*—The IDS sends an alarm when it detects an event that deviates from behavior defined as "normal." Anomaly detection is sometimes called "profile-based detection" because it compares current network traffic to profiles of normal network use.

- *Detection of misuse*—An IDS configured to send an alarm in response to misuse makes use of signatures, which are sets of characteristics that match known attacks.

NOTE   Another detection method used sometimes is heuristics—using an algorithm to detect suspicious traffic. Although this method is useful for detecting certain attacks, it's resource-intensive and requires a lot of tuning and maintenance to conform to the environment. Generally, heuristics are used for specific reasons and situations, and for most large networks, the drawbacks often outweigh the advantages.

10

ACTIVITY

Activity 10-1: Analyzing Anomalies in User Behavior

Time Required: 30 minutes

Objective: Analyze a user's behavior to determine whether an event is normal or a possible intrusion.

Description: In anomaly-based detection, the administrator must determine whether an anomaly deviates from "normal" behavior severely enough to warrant investigation. For this activity, you use the information in Table 10-2 gathered from an anomaly-based IDS to answer the following questions.

Table 10-2   User profile analysis

User	Behavior	Date	Time
Bob	Network logon	M–F	8:00 a.m. to 9:00 a.m.
	Log on to e-mail account	M–F	8:30 a.m. to 5:00 p.m.
	Log on to file server	M–F	8:30 a.m. to 5:00 p.m.

1. Describe how you would respond to an alert notifying you that Bob logged on at 2 p.m. on a Friday and logged off at 7 p.m.

_____

_____

_____

2. Describe two possible causes (one legitimate, one suspicious) for this series of events: You get an alert stating that on Tuesday, Bob logged on at 2 a.m., logged off at 7 a.m., logged on again at 8:30 a.m., and logged off at 5 p.m.

_____

_____

_____

_____

3. Describe a suitable response to discovering that the situation in Step 2 was repeated every day during the previous week.

_____

_____

_____

Command Console

A **command console** is software that provides an interface to an IDS. It enables administrators to receive and analyze alert messages and manage log files. In large-scale networks with more than one IDS, a single console enables administrators to keep up with a large volume of events so that they can respond quickly. A program such as Enterasys Dragon IDS/IPS (under Advanced Security Applications at *www.enterasys.com/products/index.aspx*) provides a single interface for analyzing and managing security events. Dragon IDS/IPS also includes multiple detection and prevention capabilities.

An IDS can collect information from security devices throughout a management network, and they are connected to the command console where they can be evaluated. The command console shouldn't be slow to respond because its host computer is busy backing up files or performing firewall functions when a suspicious event is detected, so a command console is usually installed on a dedicated computer to maximize response speed.

NOTE

A management network can be on an organization's regular network, but ideally it should be separate. If this arrangement isn't feasible, a good alternative is a virtual management network, created by setting up a virtual LAN to segregate IDS devices. This configuration provides some protection for the IDS but not as much as a full management network would.

Database of Attack Signatures or Behaviors

IDSs don't have the capability to use judgment, so network administrators should exercise their own judgment when evaluating security alerts. However, IDSs can make use of a source of information for comparing the traffic they monitor. Misuse-detection IDSs reference a database of known attack signatures; if a sensor detects a packet or a sequence of packets matching a signature, it sends an alert. The SecurityFocus online database of known vulnerabilities (see Figure 10-4) is updated frequently, and you can search it online for a particular type of attack to find more information (*http://online.securityfocus.com/bid*).

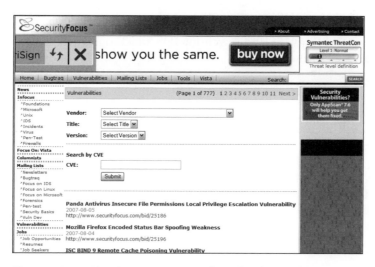

Figure 10-4   The SecurityFocus online database of known vulnerabilities

The key to attack signature databases is to keep them up to date; a new type of attack that hasn't been added to the database can defeat an IDS quickly. An IDS vendor that uses attack signatures should include a way to download new entries and add them to the database. The problem with systems that depend solely on signatures is that they are passive: They monitor traffic, compare it to the database, and send alerts whenever a packet matches a signature, which can result in many false positives. With most IDSs, however, administrators can address this problem by adding custom rules to the signature database. An anomaly-based IDS also makes use of a database of stored information against which network traffic is compared, so custom rules can also be used with these systems to reduce false alarms.

Activity 10-2: Examining an Attack Signature

Time Required: 30 minutes

Objective: Research well-known attack signatures to recognize the key components of common attacks.

Description: In intrusion detection, attack signature databases help identify traffic patterns that match known attacks. Understanding what an attack signature looks like is important so that you can analyze intrusions. Some IDS software automates analysis, but you need to be able to identify attacks your IDS misses and perhaps program custom signatures to improve your IDS's accuracy. You need a partner for this activity.

1. Start your Web browser, and search for IDS attack signatures. What are some common attacks and what characteristics does an IDS look for?

   _____

   _____

   _____

   _____

2. Start Wireshark (which you installed in Chapter 2) and open a command prompt window. Exchange IP addresses with your partner. (If needed, type **ipconfig** and press **Enter** to determine your IP address.) Write down both addresses:

   _____

   _____

3. Disable any firewalls that are running, and in Wireshark, start a packet capture on your Ethernet adapter.

4. Begin an attack on your partner's computer by typing **ping *IPaddress* -t** at the command prompt (replacing *IPaddress* with your partner's IP address) and pressing **Enter**. Your partner should launch an attack on your computer.

5. Allow Wireshark to capture packets from the attacks for two to three minutes, and then stop the capture. Close the command prompt window to stop the attack.

6. Examine the capture in Wireshark. What kind of attack is it? What characteristic identifies this attack?

   _____

   _____

   _____

   _____

7. Did the attack affect your computer's performance? Why or why not?

_____

_____

_____

_____

8. Optional, if you have enough time and resources: Open several command prompt windows and initiate a persistent ping against one target machine. The machine under attack should have Wireshark running to capture the attack.

9. Continue to escalate the attack by adding more command prompt windows running persistent pings. Were you able to cause any noticeable effect on the target machine's performance? What kind of attack is this?

_____

_____

10. Exit Wireshark, and close any open command prompt windows. Remember to restart your firewall, and leave your computer running for the next activity.

10

OPTIONS FOR INTRUSION DETECTION SYSTEMS

The preceding sections described different ways that IDSs detect suspicious events and send alarms. In this section, you examine another way to categorize IDSs: by their position on the network and how position affects their activities. In the following sections, you examine network-based IDSs, host-based IDSs, and hybrid IDSs.

Network-Based Intrusion Detection Systems

A **network-based IDS (NIDS)** is a set of components that contains the general components of any IDS, specialized for network use. It examines traffic on network segments by using sensors positioned at locations where they can monitor network traffic, management servers, a command console, and databases of signatures. It also has a mechanism for storing logs, backing up configurations, and sending alert messages to designated administrators.

Sensors on an NIDS can be hardware appliances or software. An appliance-based sensor usually has specialized NICs for packet capture and processing, designed to analyze traffic signatures. NIDS sensor appliances run an OS that's specially hardened and not usually accessed by administrators. Software-based sensors can be installed on hardened hosts or contain a specialized OS designed to run on hosts with specific configurations.

Positioning an NIDS on the Network

Common locations for NIDS sensors include behind the firewall and before the LAN, between the firewall and the DMZ, or on any network segment (see Figure 10-5).

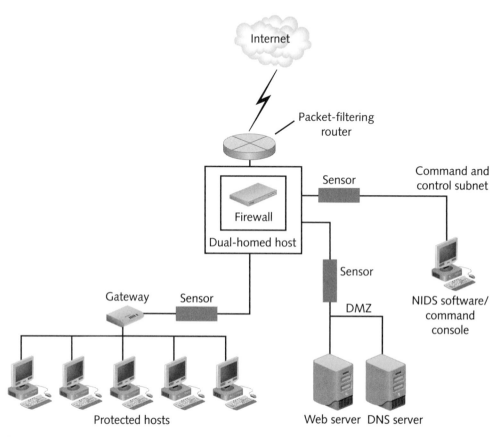

Figure 10-5 An NIDS monitoring traffic behind the firewall or in the DMZ

Positioning sensors at the network perimeter is ideal for enabling the IDS to sniff packets (receive and analyze them) as they pass into the network. Each IDS sensor is also equipped with its own NIC so that it can sniff packets in promiscuous mode, in which each packet is detected and analyzed in its entirety.

An NIDS can use inline sensors or passive sensors. An **inline sensor** is positioned so that network traffic must pass through it. This type of sensor is used to stop attacks from blocking network traffic and is usually placed where firewalls and other security devices are positioned, such as between network segments or at connections to external networks. The drawback of inline sensors is the potential to create a traffic bottleneck if the sensor becomes overloaded, but you have two possible workarounds for this problem. You can position the inline sensor on the more secure side of the network, such as behind the firewall, so that it has less traffic to process. You could also place the sensor on the less secure side to protect and lessen the load on the device dividing networks. Figure 10-6 shows an inline sensor positioned inside the firewall perimeter.

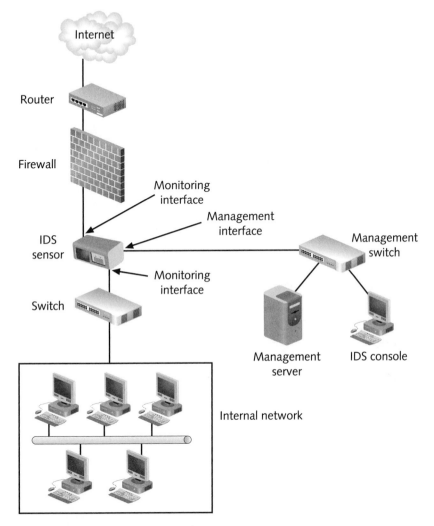

Figure 10-6 Positioning an inline sensor

Passive sensors monitor copies of actual traffic; no actual traffic passes through them. They are typically placed at key network locations, such as divisions between networks, or on key network segments, such as the DMZ (see Figure 10-7). Passive sensors monitor traffic by using these methods:

- *Spanning port*—A port on many switches that can see all network traffic passing through. A passive IDS sensor attached to this port can monitor traffic flow without the traffic actually passing through it.

- *Network tap*—A direct connection between a sensor and the physical network medium, such as a fiber-optic cable.

- *IDS load balancer*—A device that collects and directs traffic to monitoring systems. Administrators configure rules that tell the load balancer where to direct different types of traffic.

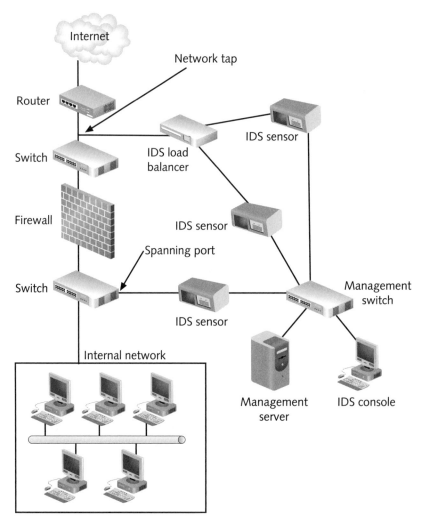

Figure 10-7 Positioning a passive sensor

NIDS Capabilities

NIDS capabilities vary, depending on the product. Some can collect information about hosts, OSs, applications, and network activities and characteristics. By identifying hosts, you could develop a list of all hosts on the network, organized by IP or MAC addresses. Tracking which ports are used on each host can indicate which OS is running, and knowing which OS versions are used can also help identify vulnerable hosts. An NIDS can also analyze packet headers to identify characteristics or unusual behavior of OSs. Identifying an application can be used to monitor which ports are being used and help identify misuse of the application. Collecting general information about network characteristics, such as hop count, can help identify changes to the network configuration, such as when a new device is added or removed.

A primary function of an NIDS is extensive logging of traffic. You can use traffic logs to identify and analyze potential attacks, locate vulnerabilities, assess network use and performance, and correlate with other device logs. NIDSs usually log the following types of information:

- Timestamp
- Event or alert type
- Protocols
- Connection or session ID
- Source and destination IP addresses and ports
- Size of transmissions, usually in bytes
- State-related information
- Application requests and responses
- Network, Transport, and Application layer protocols
- Preventive action taken, if any

10

Most NIDSs use a variety of detection capabilities, usually combinations of anomaly detection, misuse detection (signature based), and stateful protocol analysis. These capabilities work together to improve detection efficiency and accuracy. For example, stateful inspection might parse activity into requests and responses, which are then examined for anomalies and compared to signatures. This type of multilayered inspection is similar to the defense-in-depth strategy and increases accuracy more than using a single detection method does.

Prevention capabilities differ depending on the product and the sensor type: passive, inline, or a combination. Some preventive actions an NIDS can take include the following:

- *Passive only*—Ending the current TCP session (called session sniping, not commonly used now)

- *Inline only*—Inline firewalling, bandwidth throttling, and altering malicious content

- *Passive and inline*—Reconfiguring other network security devices, such as instructing a firewall to block certain types of activity, or running an administrator-defined script

With most NIDSs, administrators can configure specific actions for each type of alert. Some also offer simulation modes for fine-tuning alerts and prevention actions.

NIDS Management

After choosing an NIDS, an administrator should design the architecture and test and secure the NIDS components. Designing the architecture includes determining where sensors are located, how many are needed, and how they should be connected. Testing NIDS components includes accounting for network downtime while deploying sensors or network taps or activating spanning ports. Securing NIDS components involves making sure sensors aren't assigned IP addresses on monitoring interfaces so that other hosts can't initiate connections to them, hardening management networks, and configuring hosts for log files and backups.

As with any networking component, NIDS architecture, detection, and prevention configurations should be evaluated regularly. NIDS software and hardware systems must be updated and patched periodically, and custom configurations should be monitored and adjusted as needed to remain effective against network threats.

Host-Based Intrusion Detection Systems

In contrast to an NIDS on the network perimeter, a **host-based IDS (HIDS)** is deployed on hosts inside the network perimeter. On a small network, HIDS features might be hosted on the machine an HIDS is monitoring. The HIDS host could be a printer, Web server, computer, firewall, switch, router, or combination. HIDSs are generally deployed only on sensitive or mission-critical hosts because placing one on every host in the network would be cost prohibitive. (The costs of software and licensing are factors to consider.) HIDSs in a large network environment commonly use management servers, signature databases, and consoles for configuration and monitoring. Often, HIDSs use the same IDS infrastructure as NIDSs. Figure 10-8 shows a typical HIDS deployment.

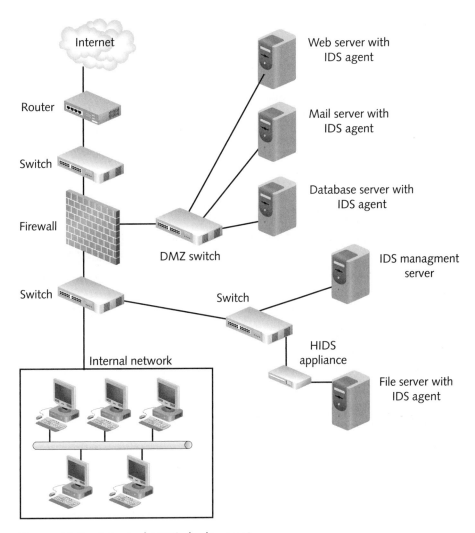

Figure 10-8 A typical HIDS deployment

NOTE

HIDSs can also consist of dedicated appliances running agent software that are positioned to monitor traffic on a particular host. Technically, this arrangement could be considered an inline NIDS, but this type of HIDS is highly specialized for monitoring a single host or type of traffic, so it's categorized as an HIDS. An HIDS appliance is often used to protect a Web or database server.

An HIDS monitors and evaluates packets generated by the host and gathers data from OS and application logs on the host. An HIDS also gathers system variables such as the following:

- System processes
- CPU use

- File accesses

- System logs

- System and application configuration changes

System events matching the signatures of known attacks reach the IDS on the host, which sends an alert message to users or the administrator. An HIDS doesn't sniff packets as they enter the network. Instead, it monitors log file entries and user activity and is highly effective at tracking internal users' misuse of resources.

Configuring an HIDS

An HIDS can have two configurations: centralized or distributed. In a centralized configuration, the HIDS sends all data that's gathered to a central location (the command console or management server) for analysis. In a distributed configuration, data analysis is distributed among hosts; each host analyzes data and sends only alert messages (not the data) to the command console.

In a centralized configuration (see Figure 10-9), the host's performance is unaffected by the IDS. However, because data is sent to the command console where it's analyzed, any alert messages that are generated don't occur in real time.

The process in Figure 10-9 is as follows:

1. An event is generated on the host.

2. Data gathered by the IDS agent (a software program running on the host) is transmitted to the command console, where analysis is performed.

3. A log file entry is created.

4. If necessary, an alert is generated.

5. The IDS responds.

6. Finally, data is stored in a database for long-term analysis.

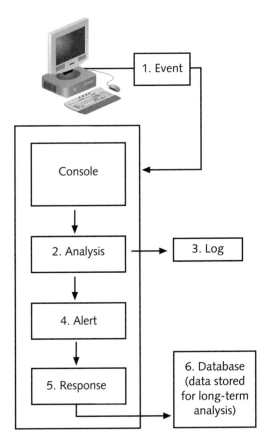

Figure 10-9 A centralized HIDS

In a distributed configuration, event data processing is distributed between the host and command console. The host generates the data and analyzes it in real time. As a result, analysis can be performed without a delay, but the tradeoff is reduced performance on the host. The host processes all data, whether alerts are required or not. Data is then transmitted to the command console in the form of alert messages, as shown in Figure 10-10.

10

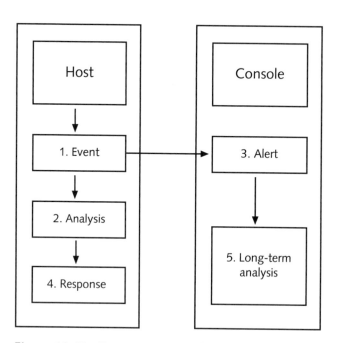

Figure 10-10 Processing event data from an HIDS

Choosing the Host

The RAM, hard disk space, and processor speed required on the host depend on the type of HIDS. In a centralized configuration, processing is performed on the command console, so the host's performance requirement is minimal. However, in a distributed configuration, the host gathers intrusion data and analyzes it in real time, so it should be equipped with the maximum memory and processor speed. Check the vendor's IDS requirements for recommendations.

Comparing NIDSs and HIDSs

An HIDS can tell you whether an attack attempt on the host was successful. An NIDS, on the other hand, provides alerts on suspicious network activity but doesn't tell you whether an attack attempt reached the targeted host and whether an intrusion actually occurred. HIDSs can detect attacks that would get past an NIDS. For example, fragmentation, out of sequence, or other masking techniques might bypass firewalls and NIDSs as legitimate traffic.

On the other hand, an HIDS provides only the data pertaining to the host on which it's installed, not the network as a whole. An HIDS can't detect an intrusion attempt that targets the entire network, such as a port scan on a range of computers. If you use an HIDS, you need to install it on several hosts on the network, which takes time and can be more expensive than an NIDS.

In addition, HIDSs can compare records stored in audit logs to detect inconsistencies in how applications and systems programs are used. However, they are susceptible to some DoS attacks and could create increased performance overhead on host systems.

Hybrid IDSs

A **hybrid IDS** combines the capabilities of HIDSs and NIDSs for more flexibility and security. The challenge in using a hybrid IDS is getting the components to work together, although many IDS products have built-in hybrid capabilities. Variations of hybrid IDSs—combined IDS sensor locations and combined IDS detection methods—are described in the following sections.

Combining IDS Sensor Locations

One type of IDS hybrid combines host-based and network-based systems. The combination enables sensors to be positioned on network segments and as agents on hosts. As a result, the network can report on attacks aimed at network segments or the network as a whole. In addition, computers storing confidential information, such as databases of job records, can be protected with an HIDS. An IDS on a host (especially one with a distributed configuration) can analyze data in real time and send an alert immediately that notifies the administrator of a possible unauthorized access attempt.

10

Combining IDS Detection Methods

Another IDS hybrid combines anomaly and misuse detection. The combination helps overcome the limitations of each detection method in the following ways:

- Having a database of known attack signatures enables the system to start running immediately and effectively wards off most well-known external attack methods.

- Having an anomaly-based system keeps the system flexible and capable of detecting internal misuse that deviates from normal use patterns.

A hybrid IDS that combines anomaly with misuse detection can respond to the latest, previously unreported attacks and to attacks from both external and internal sources. A drawback is that administrators have more configuration and coordination work to do. Data from multiple sources must be collected in a central location, where it can be reviewed and analyzed.

Advantages and Disadvantages of Hybrid IDSs

Hybrid IDSs have the advantage of being able to combine aspects of NIDS and HIDS configurations. You can monitor the network as a whole with network-based sensors and monitor attacks that reach computers with host-based sensors. The drawback of a hybrid IDS is the need to get disparate systems to work in a coordinated fashion. In addition, data gathered from multiple systems can be difficult to analyze easily.

Activity 10-3: Redistributing Network Sensors

Time Required: 15 minutes

Objective: Optimize sensor placement and discuss the pros and cons of the change.

Description: You have installed an NIDS in a traditional design: A sensor is placed on each network segment, and alarms are transmitted to the command console where you can review and evaluate them. A comparison of firewall logs with IDS alarms indicates that the sensors can't capture every packet passing through the network. Based on this situation, answer the following questions:

1. Describe how you could troubleshoot this configuration by rearranging the sensors:

   _____

   _____

   _____

2. What are the pros and cons of making this change?

   _____

   _____

Evaluating IDS Products

Some IDS products include antivirus or firewall capabilities, and IDS products can be integrated and combined for comprehensive protection. The options for custom defenses that include an IDS are numerous, so you should focus on evaluating the system that best fits your needs.

As with any network security component, the most expensive or full-featured product isn't always the best option. Considerations such as availability of staff to install and support technologies, the organization's security stance, and the operating environment are important. The best approach is to know what you need before you invest resources. Here are the basic factors in evaluating IDS products:

- Determine whether an IDS product is necessary. Sometimes the existing network components can perform IDS functions well enough to meet security requirements.

- Conduct a risk assessment to decide what network resources require protection and at what level.

- Define general requirements and goals the IDS should meet. Assess security policies and other related organizational policies that affect security and IDS goals.

- Evaluate the technical specifications of IT systems so that you have an estimate of how many products are needed and where they should be positioned.

- Determine your external security requirements, such as applicable laws, security audit requirements, results of investigations of security incidents, or organizational cryptography specifications.

- Evaluate your needs for security capabilities, information gathering, and logging.

- Review the detection and prevention capabilities of IDS products you're considering.

- Identify performance and management requirements for the IDS.

- Define the interoperability and scalability potential for each product you're considering.

- Determine a reasonable cost estimate that includes acquisition, testing, installation, daily use, maintenance, and updates to keep the IDS operating at peak efficiency.

- Identify resource limitations, such as budget, staff, or hardware.

- Identify any training, documentation, and support required for IDS products.

10

EXAMINING INTRUSION DETECTION STEP BY STEP

IDSs operate in different ways, depending on whether they are configured to react to anomalies or misuse. Despite differences in operation, the process can be divided into general steps, shown in Figure 10-11, that apply to most IDSs. These steps are described in the following sections.

TIP

The SANS Institute maintains a useful FAQ on intrusion detection at *www.sans.org/resources/idfaq*.

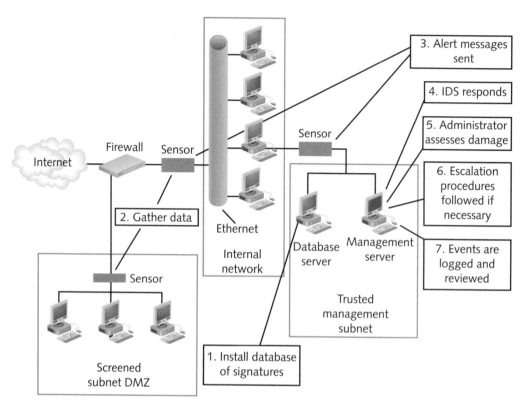

Figure 10-11 Steps in intrusion detection

Step 1: Installing the IDS Database

The first step in intrusion detection occurs before any packets are detected on the network. Along with the IDS software and hardware, you need to install the database of signatures or user profiles, which gives the IDS a set of criteria against which it can compare packets passing through the sensor.

In an anomaly-based system, installing the database can take as much as a week after installing IDS devices so that the IDS can observe network traffic and compile baseline data on normal network use. Some data can take a week to record because it occurs over a period of days—for example, a series of daily logons to the network. In a misuse-based IDS, you can install the database of attack signatures included with the software, or you can add your own custom rule base to account for new attacks or special situations that generate false positives.

Step 2: Gathering Data

After the IDS and database are installed, network sensors and agents can gather data by reading packets. Agents installed on hosts observe traffic entering and leaving those hosts, and sensors placed on network segments read packets passing through those segments.

Sensors need to be positioned where they can capture all packets entering and leaving a host or network segment. Sensors placed on network segments can't always capture every packet if the traffic level becomes too heavy, however. Repositioning agents on each network host improves accuracy, even though the expense of purchasing new agents and the effort of installing them can be considerable. What's important is being able to capture all packets so that none can circumvent the IDS.

Step 3: Sending Alert Messages

The IDS detection software compares packets it observes with signatures stored in its database. An alert message is transmitted when a packet matches an attack signature or deviates from normal network use. The alert message goes to the IDS command console, where the network administrator can evaluate it.

Step 4: The IDS Responds

10

When the command console receives an alert message, it notifies the administrator in a way that the administrator has configured beforehand. The console might display a pop-up window or send an e-mail, for instance. An IDS can also be configured to take action when a suspicious packet is received and an alert message is sent. The following list describes some typical preventive or response actions an IDS can take:

- *Alarm*—An alert message is sent to the command console or another designated location.

- *Drop*—The packet is dropped without an error message being sent to the originating computer.

- *Reset*—The IDS is instructed to stop and restart network traffic, thus halting severe attacks.

- *Code analysis*—The IDS can prevent malicious code from running or stop certain applications from opening shells used to launch some attacks.

- *File system monitoring*—The IDS can prevent files from being modified, accessed, replaced, or deleted.

- *Network traffic filtering*—The IDS can act as a host-based firewall to stop violations of unauthorized access or acceptable use policies, based on IP address or protocol or port information.

- *Network traffic analysis*—The IDS can stop incoming traffic from reaching a host or leaving it. This action is useful for stopping Network, Transport, or Application layer attacks as well as unauthorized applications and protocols.

NOTE   An IDS stops TCP traffic by sending a TCP packet with the RST (reset) flag set, which terminates the connection with the computer attempting to attack the system. Resetting TCP traffic doesn't affect UDP or other types of traffic, however. This action, called session sniping, isn't used often in modern IDSs.

Step 5: The Administrator Assesses Damage

An automated response sent by an IDS is like a call to action. It's the administrator's responsibility to monitor alerts and determine whether countermeasures need to be taken. When an IDS is first installed, it might send many alerts that are false positives, depending on the accuracy of information in the database. Administrators usually have to fine-tune databases to account for situations that seem to be intrusions but are actually legitimate traffic.

In an anomaly-based system, for example, an adjustment might be needed for an employee who logs on over the weekend instead of during the standard weekdays. In a misuse-based system, an adjustment can be made to allow traffic that the IDS might determine to be suspicious, such as a vulnerability scan performed by a device at a particular IP address; you could add a rule that changes the IDS action in response to traffic from that IP address. Figure 10-12 shows the dividing line between acceptable and unacceptable network use.

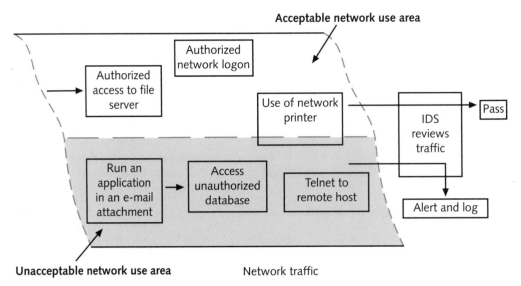

Figure 10-12 Differentiating acceptable and unacceptable network use

The line dividing acceptable from unacceptable network use isn't always clear, however. In Figure 10-12, for example, the box indicating network printer use overlaps into the unacceptable area because acceptable use of this resource depends on the purpose. Printing office-related documents constitutes acceptable use, but printing personal photos, for example, probably falls on the unacceptable side of the line.

The goal of adjusting the IDS database is not to avoid false positives because they're almost inevitable. False positives do consume an administrator's time and energy, but they don't compromise network security. The goal is avoiding false negatives—incidents that should cause an alarm but do not. False negatives occur without anyone's knowledge and are a potentially serious breach of security. Although false positives are often seen as nuisances, they are far less serious than false negatives.

Step 6: Following Escalation Procedures

Escalation procedures are a set of actions spelled out in the security policy and followed if the IDS detects a true positive (a legitimate attack). These procedures vary, depending on the severity of the incident. A Level One incident might be managed quickly with only a single security professional, a Level Two incident represents a more serious threat and must be escalated to involve a security professional with more authority, and a Level Three incident represents the highest degree of threat.

10

NOTE

Escalation procedures, part of an overall organizational security policy, are covered in more detail in *Guide to Strategic Infrastructure Security: Becoming a Security Network Professional* (Course Technology, 2008, ISBN 1418836613).

Step 7: Logging and Reviewing Events

After an IDS has sent an alert to the command console and responded as necessary, the event that caused the alert is entered in the IDS log. The event can also be sent to a database file, where it can be reviewed along with other previous alerts. Reviewing a number of alerts sent over a period of time enables administrators to determine whether patterns of misuse have been occurring. This review also gives administrators the opportunity to spot a gradual attack, such as a series of logons occurring only once every few days or a series of ping sweeps (attempts to solicit a response from IP addresses inside a network) taking place once a week over a few months.

An IDS should also provide **accountability**—the capability to track an attempted attack or intrusion back to the responsible party. Some systems have a built-in tracing feature that attempts to locate the IP address associated with an event. Identifying the person who used the source computer can be difficult, but a trace can at least provide a starting point for identifying an attacker.

Chapter Summary

❑ Intrusion detection systems (IDSs) add another line of defense behind firewalls and antivirus software. Many IDSs can go a step beyond transmitting alarms and actually respond to an event, making intrusion prevention systems (IPSs) or intrusion detection and prevention systems (IDPSs) more common.

❑ IDS components include sensors or agents, management servers that gather and analyze data from sensors and agents, command consoles that provide an interface for administrators, and databases of attack signatures (for misuse detection) or user profiles (for anomaly detection).

❑ A network-based IDS (NIDS) uses sensors positioned at key points on the network. A host-based IDS (HIDS) deploys agents on selected hosts in the network. A hybrid IDS combines aspects of network-based and host-based IDS configurations. Many IDS products can also combine detection and prevention capabilities.

❑ Selecting an IDS requires evaluating the organization's needs, the product features, and security goals.

❑ The steps of intrusion detection typically follow this process: installing the IDS and database of attack signatures or user profiles, gathering data, sending an alert, responding to the alert, assessing damage, following escalation procedures, and logging and reviewing events. Specified actions, such as sending alerts or responding to the incident, are taken when a packet matches an attack signature or deviates from normal network use.

Key Terms

accountability — The capability to track an attempted attack or intrusion back to its source.

agent — An IDS component (hardware, software, or combination) that monitors traffic on a specific host.

anomaly detection — A type of detection system based on profiles that sends an alarm when it detects an event deviating from behavior defined as "normal."

command console — Software that provides a graphical interface to an IDS.

escalated — The process of increasing the response to an intrusion to a higher level.

event horizon — The entire length of an attack, from the first packet the IDS receives to the last packet needed to complete the attack.

false negatives — Attacks that occur but aren't detected by the IDS.

false positives — Alarms generated by legitimate network traffic rather than actual attacks.

host-based IDS (HIDS) — An IDS deployed on hosts inside the network perimeter.

hybrid IDS — An IDS that combines the capabilities of HIDSs and NIDSs for more flexibility and security.

IDS management server — An IDS component that serves as the central repository for sensor and agent data.

inline sensor — An NIDS sensor positioned so that all traffic on the network segment is examined as it passes through. *See also* network-based IDS (NIDS).

intrusion — An attempt to gain unauthorized access to network resources and to compromise the integrity and confidentiality of network data or users' privacy.

intrusion detection — The process of monitoring network traffic to detect unauthorized access attempts and sending notifications so that countermeasures can be taken.

intrusion detection system (IDS) — A network security measure that can consist of applications and hardware devices deployed on the network, hosts, or both to prevent, detect, and respond to traffic interpreted as an intrusion.

misuse detection — A type of detection system that sends an alarm in response to characteristic signatures of known external attacks.

network-based IDS (NIDS) — A set of IDS components specialized for network use. It examines traffic on network segments by using sensors positioned where they can monitor network traffic, management servers, a command console, and databases of signatures.

passive sensor — An NIDS sensor that examines copies of traffic on the network; no actual traffic passes through the sensor. *See also* network-based IDS (NIDS).

profiles — Sets of characteristics that describe network services and resources a user or group normally accesses.

sensor — An IDS component (hardware, software, or combination) that monitors traffic on a network segment.

state information — Data about a network connection, which is typically kept in a state table.

trigger — A set of circumstances that causes an IDS to send an alert.

true negatives — Legitimate communications that don't cause an IDS to set off an alarm.

true positive — A genuine attack detected successfully by an IDS, in contrast to a true negative or false positive.

10

REVIEW QUESTIONS

1. How can data gained from intrusion detection be used to improve network security? (Choose all that apply.)

   a. prevent future attacks

   b. route traffic more efficiently

   c. shield IP addresses on the network

   d. help determine how to respond to security incidents

2. Name the three network defense functions in intrusion detection.

3. Network sensors should be positioned where on the network?

    a. external or internal interfaces

    b. entry points to the network

    c. before the firewall

    d. between the DMZ and the network

4. An IDS management server performs which of the following functions?

    a. monitoring inbound and outbound traffic

    b. modifying state information

    c. storing and analyzing sensor data

    d. providing an IDS interface

5. Which of the following is an IDS detection capability you can customize? (Choose all that apply.)

    a. blacklists

    b. signatures

    c. state tables

    d. thresholds

6. Misuse detection is based on which feature of network traffic?

    a. user profiles

    b. normal traffic

    c. signatures

    d. user accounts

7. An anomaly-based IDS can be circumvented in which of the following ways?

    a. new attacks

    b. changes in user habits

    c. changes in published signatures

    d. minor changes in attack methods that don't match known signatures

8. A misuse-detection IDS can be circumvented in which of the following ways?

    a. changes in attack methods

    b. a stolen user account

    c. making traffic appear normal

    d. attacks made during the IDS training period

9. Which intrusion detection method can begin protecting a network immediately after installation?

10. Which intrusion detection method is almost impossible for intruders to test before attempting an attack?

11. Which IDS activity could detect a DoS attack?

    a. protocol state tracking

    b. misuse detection

    c. traffic monitoring

    d. IP packet reassembly

12. What is a potential weakness of misuse detection?

    a. changing user habits

    b. training period after installation

    c. the need to maintain state information

    d. alert settings

13. Which of the following events has the most serious security implications?

    a. true positive

    b. true negative

    c. false positive

    d. false negative

14. What type of IDS should you use if you're mainly concerned with preventing known attacks?

    a. misuse-based IDS

    b. network-based IDS

    c. host-based IDS

    d. anomaly-based IDS

15. An HIDS can detect an intrusion attempt that targets the entire network, such as a port scan on a range of computers. True or False?

16. What preventive or response actions can an IDS take to respond to a possible attack? (Choose all that apply.)

    a. prevent malicious code from running

    b. drop the suspicious packet

    c. allow, reset, alarm

    d. reset all network connections

17. Which of the following is almost inevitable and should be expected after installing an IDS? (Choose all that apply.)

    a. false negatives

    b. huge log files

    c. signatures that become outdated

    d. false positives

10

18. What advantage does IDS simulation mode offer?

19. How can an inline sensor be positioned to reduce the load on a perimeter security device, such as a firewall or router?

    a. place the sensor inside the security perimeter

    b. replace the firewall or router with the sensor

    c. position the sensor outside the security perimeter

    d. add another firewall or router

HANDS-ON PROJECTS

HANDS-ON PROJECTS

Hands-On Project 10-1: Using Port Attack Information

Time Required: 15 minutes

Objective: Assess potential security risks to your computer by using the DShield list of Top 10 Target Ports.

Description: DShield gathers log files from users around the world and prepares reports they can analyze to determine whether intrusion attempts have been made on their networks. You can view reports on the DShield site and apply them to your own firewall or IDS.

1. Start your Web browser and go to **www.dshield.org/reports.php**.

2. Click the **Top 10** link to view the DShield – Top 10 Reports page. (You can register with DShield to get additional information.)

3. To determine whether your computer has connections open on a frequently targeted port to computers outside your network, open a command prompt window and use the **netstat -a** command to view a list of open network connections.

4. Note how many connections are open on frequently targeted ports, such as TCP/UDP ports 137 and 139. Are there any suspicious connections, such as ones from unknown sources? How could you trace the source of these connections?

   _____

   _____

   _____

5. When you're finished, close any open windows, and leave your system running for the next project.

Hands-On Project 10-2: Analyzing a Suspicious Signature

Time Required: 20 minutes

Objective: Analyze an attack signature to determine details about the intrusion, identify the type of attack taking place, and suggest methods to prevent these attacks.

Description: An IDS that depends on a database of known attack signatures is vulnerable to attacks that aren't already in its database. Systems that enable the administrator to create custom rules depend on the administrator to analyze attack signatures.

1. Review the data in Figure 10-13. In particular, note the destination IP addresses and ports.

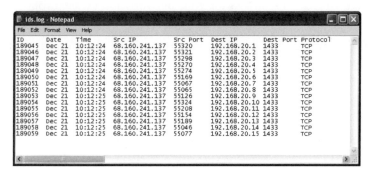

Figure 10-13 Destination IP addresses and ports

2. Identify the possible intruder. How could you trace the intruder and determine whether this person has been responsible for any other attacks? (*Hint:* Review preceding activities and projects in this chapter.) Record your answer here:

_____

_____

_____

_____

3. Where is the source IP computer located? Is the computer known to have been involved in any other attacks?

_____

_____

4. Describe what kind of event is happening in Figure 10-13:

_____

_____

_____

_____

10

5. Suggest how you could prevent similar intrusion attempts from succeeding in the future:

_____

_____

_____

_____

Hands-On Project 10-3: Designing an IDS

Time Required: 45 minutes

Objective: Prepare a report on an IDS for your network and create a topology map to aid in your IDS design.

Description: In this project, you prepare a report explaining what an IDS is and how to create one for your network. You need word processing and drawing programs or pencil and paper to answer the following questions and create diagrams.

1. To describe your lab network, use the following lines to list the number of computers and the OSs running on them. (If you don't have access to a lab network, assume you're working in a lab with 10 computers, 8 running Windows XP and 2 running Fedora Core Linux.)

_____

_____

_____

_____

2. Draw a topology map of your network using a drawing program or pencil and paper.

3. List the components needed to create an IDS:

_____

_____

_____

_____

4. Position an NIDS in a distributed configuration on your topology map.

5. Map out the IDS process in steps that include the following:

- Packet detected
- Detection method processes packet
- Alert transmitted
- Notification sent
- Alert logged
- Analysis and countermeasures

CASE PROJECTS

Case Project 10-1: Setting up a Two-Tiered IDS Response

You administer a network configured with two separate subnets: 10.8.1.1/16 and 10.9.1.1/16. You add a new subnet, 10.10.1.1/16, to the network. Each subnet has a separate Ethernet interface on the IDS device (designated by e0, e1, and e2). The IDS also has an external interface on the Internet (designated by s0) at IP address 210.10.1.1. Because your network has expanded, you need to configure the IDS. You don't want it to interfere with traffic originating from the e0, e1, and e2 interfaces by resetting the TCP connections if a packet matches the database and an alarm is sent. On the other hand, you *do* want the IDS to send an alarm and reset TCP connections if a suspicious packet reaches the external interface s0. How could you accommodate both types of responses?

Case Project 10-2: Using an IDS to Trace Internal Misuse

An IDS can be used to detect and track unauthorized access attempts that come from inside the organization's network as well as outside. For example, your SMTP server's log files indicate that the server has been sending hundreds of e-mails every Monday morning at 8:00 a.m. for the past three weeks. You suspect that the SMTP server is being used to distribute mass e-mails by an employee who manages an e-mail newsletter. How could you verify this problem by using the IDS?

10

Case Project 10-3: Selecting an IDS for Green Globe

You have designed Green Globe's network using a distributed and layered security approach. In this project, you evaluate IDS products and design an IDS solution for Green Globe's network resources. There are several decisions you must make during this process. First, you must decide what the goals are for the IDS. Next, you must determine where sensors should be deployed. Do you need a centralized or distributed design? Then you must decide what administrative tools you need and begin investigating products that provide services you need. Follow these general steps to create your design:

TIP

You might want to do some research and find sample IDS designs to help you in this project. Cisco's *SAFE: IDS Deployment, Tuning and Logging in Depth [SAFE Blueprint]* is a great place to start (*www.cisco.com/warp/public/cc/so/neso/vpn/vpne/safwp_wp.pdf*).

NOTE

Remember that some steps might not apply, and you might have to add others not listed here, depending on your design.

1. Determine the goals for your IDS. Does it need to examine all network traffic or only traffic on specific segments? Should each host be monitored or only servers and workstations hosting confidential data or applications? After defining your goals, you can decide where sensors should be positioned.

2. Review your current network diagram to locate all entry points to your network. Don't forget to include remote access, dial-up, VPN, and even any deliberate administrative "backdoors." Mark these entry points on your network diagram.

3. Locate any internal hosts that are critical, such as research and development servers, database servers storing customer or employee information, domain controllers, global catalog servers, and so forth. Mark them on your diagram.

4. Determine which segments, switches, or routers provide access to the internal hosts noted in Step 3 and any others that serve critical or confidential areas. Mark these hosts on your diagram.

5. Use your updated network diagram to determine optimum sensor placement. The goal is to use as few sensors as possible (to reduce costs and minimize administrative effort) yet provide coverage of all critical areas. Mark sensor locations on your diagram. Be sure to check them to make sure you haven't missed anything.

Consider having a classmate review your design at this point. A fresh pair of eyes often spots overlooked problems and can offer unbiased insight. Never underestimate the value of peer review.

NOTE

6. Remember to look for alert and response capabilities, and don't forget signature files and updating.

7. Now you have the information to decide on administrative tools you need. Look at your diagram again. Is there a secure server where you can install the IDS command console? Do you need to purchase extra hardware for IDS administration and logging?

8. Next, make a list of your needs. How many sensors do you need? How many hosts require software? What type of administrative software will you use? How will log files be managed?

9. Using the Internet or other resources, find an IDS product that meets your needs. Be sure to consider the vendor's stability and reputation, available support options, cost, and scalability. For the Green Globe network, remember that governmental regulations apply, so be sure the product you choose meets or exceeds those guidelines.

10. Document your configuration. Update your network diagram to reflect the final design, sensor locations, hosts where the product is installed, server configurations, log file storage, alerts and analysis, and so on. Establish how and where signature files are obtained and how software will be updated.

11. Update your documentation to reflect any changes to the network configuration and relevant policies, such as incident response. List contact information for the vendor and support staff and note escalation procedures, if necessary.

12. Place your updated diagrams and details on new software and hardware in an appendix. Submit a management summary of the design, a copy of your current network design showing your IDS deployment, and supporting documentation of the product and configurations to your instructor. Specifically, your submission should include:

   ■ A summary of the IDS stating what it is, where it's deployed, and how it's intended to work. Include a brief statement of how this IDS supports Green Globe's standards and requirements. This management summary should be written for a nontechnical audience and give an overview of the IDS.

   ■ A network diagram showing locations of software and hardware deployments.

   ■ Product details, including alert and response capabilities, scalability potential, vendor and support options, log file storage and analysis methods, and specific network configurations.

   ■ Signature file availability and updating and any other update issues for the software or hardware IDS.

   ■ *Optional*: You might also want to include ideas for testing the IDS and devising change techniques and management for signatures and handling false positives, false negatives, and so on.

10

11

CONFIGURING AND USING
INTRUSION DETECTION SYSTEMS

**After reading this chapter and completing the
exercises, you will be able to:**

♦ Install and configure an intrusion detection system

♦ Explain considerations for setting up a security incident
response team

♦ Describe the six-step incident response process

♦ Explain options for dealing with false positives and legitimate
security alerts

In previous chapters, you learned how intrusion detection systems work, what components they use, and how to interpret signatures of legitimate traffic and attack attempts. In this chapter, you learn how to install and configure an intrusion detection system (IDS). You begin by installing and configuring an IDS featuring Snort, a MySQL database for log storage, and the Basic Analysis and Security Engine (BASE) console for real-time alert viewing. After installing and configuring an IDS, you need to know how to respond to alert messages it generates. Therefore, you also learn how to develop a security incident response team, respond to an incident, and deal with false positives and legitimate alarms (true positives).

INSTALLING AND CONFIGURING AN INTRUSION DETECTION SYSTEM

The key to a successful IDS is planning, so take the time to plan carefully. By the time you've finished planning, most of the work involved in an IDS is already done. Implementation is far easier and more accurate and certainly provides a more effective IDS.

After selecting a product and designing an architecture, IDS installation isn't difficult, but it does require time and attention to detail. Modern self-install executables make installation a point-and-click task for many software packages, but IDS products haven't gotten quite that far yet. You still spend a lot of time working at the command line for configuration and maintenance.

In the past, a major problem with installing Snort on Windows was compatibility. Fortunately, excellent resources are available to make the process easier. For example, *www.winsnort.com* has instructions for installing and configuring a WinSnort IDS as well as fully tested, compatible files. In the following section, you install and configure Snort, the industry-standard IDS product, along with several support programs designed to make Snort administration easier and increase IDS functionality.

Working with Snort

Snort is an open-source IDS created by Martin Roesch and Brian Caswell that combines anomaly, signature, and protocol detection and can run on several platforms, including Windows, Linux, and Mac OS. It doesn't consume a lot of system resources and is ideal for monitoring traffic on a small network or a host. Snort is intended for installation on a computer positioned at the network perimeter. It can also function on a dedicated computer in a home or small business network. Combined with a database and various utilities, Snort becomes a powerful tool.

It comes with a collection of rule files customized for different types of network traffic; these rules are activated in the Snort.conf configuration file (see Figure 11-1). Separate rules exist for port scans, backdoor attacks, Web attacks, and many other kinds of intrusions. The rule files are text based, so you use a text editor to view them and edit them to conform to your network. The files can be customized easily for a variety of other events.

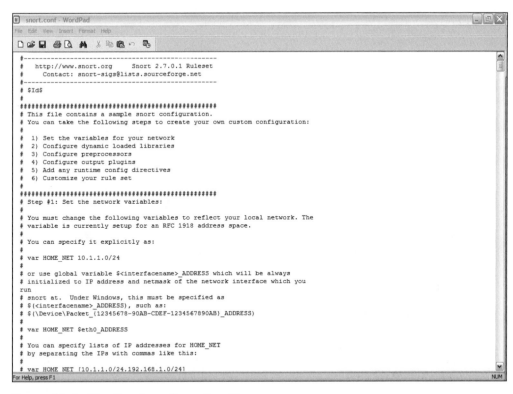

```
#-------------------------------------------------------
#   http://www.snort.org      Snort 2.7.0.1 Ruleset
#      Contact: snort-sigs@lists.sourceforge.net
#-------------------------------------------------------
# $Id$
#
#######################################################
# This file contains a sample snort configuration.
# You can take the following steps to create your own custom configuration:
#
#  1) Set the variables for your network
#  2) Configure dynamic loaded libraries
#  3) Configure preprocessors
#  4) Configure output plugins
#  5) Add any runtime config directives
#  6) Customize your rule set
#
#######################################################
# Step #1: Set the network variables:
#
# You must change the following variables to reflect your local network. The
# variable is currently setup for an RFC 1918 address space.
#
# You can specify it explicitly as:
#
# var HOME_NET 10.1.1.0/24
#
# or use global variable $<interfacename>_ADDRESS which will be always
# initialized to IP address and netmask of the network interface which you
run
# snort at.  Under Windows, this must be specified as
# $(<interfacename>_ADDRESS), such as:
# $(\Device\Packet_{12345678-90AB-CDEF-1234567890AB}_ADDRESS)
#
# var HOME_NET $eth0_ADDRESS
#
# You can specify lists of IP addresses for HOME_NET
# by separating the IPs with commas like this:
#
# var HOME_NET [10.1.1.0/24,192.168.1.0/24]
```

Figure 11-1   The Snort configuration file

In addition, other configuration files have variables that enable you to protect SMTP, HTTP, and SQL servers on your network, which can cause false alarms because of the amount of traffic passing through them. Sourcefire, in cooperation with Snort.org, provides updated rules for Snort that are tested and can be integrated manually or by using an add-on tool, such as Oinkmaster. (You install Oinkmaster later in this chapter.)

Choosing a Computer to Run Snort

Windows is resource intensive. Adding Snort and support tools to a Windows machine results in an effective IDS configuration but requires a lot of memory and processor speed. These are the minimum requirements to install and run Snort:

- A computer running Windows NT, Windows 9x, Windows 2000 Server or Professional, Windows XP Home or Professional, or Windows Server 2003

- A packet capture driver for Windows (WinPcap is currently the only viable option)

- One or more NICs

- A network connection

Of course, minimum requirements don't allow much functionality. Without additional programs, Snort is a command-line utility and difficult to use. Installing Snort with a database, a GUI interface, and reporting tools makes it easier to use and produces more useful data. This is the recommended configuration for installing a full WinSnort IDS:

- At least two partitions, one for the OS and another for the WinSnort IDS installation (although an additional partition can be useful for installing the database separately)

- A hardened computer running Windows 2000/XP Professional or Windows Server 2000/2003 (for high-traffic environments and for better multiple-CPU support)

- At least 60 MB of hard drive space to install Snort and support programs (doesn't include space for the data Snort gathers)

- One or more fast processors

- As much RAM as the machine can support, at least 1 GB

If you plan to run Snort, the database, and the GUI console from the same computer, you need a very fast machine. When Snort runs out of resources, it drops packets, which makes it useless. Make sure you have enough log storage space, too. Depending on your network traffic and how you intend to use Snort, your log files can become quite large. The average size for a log alert in text format is about 5 KB, so the determining factors are how many are generated and how long log entries are stored. Of course, log files shouldn't be retained forever, and custom rules can affect how much log information is produced.

For the best performance on a single host computer running the Snort IDS, install the OS and applications on one partition and Snort on another. This setup makes backups easier and helps prevent partitions from corrupting each other. In a high-traffic network, consider installing Snort, the database, the Web server, and IDS sensors on different computers.

After you have the hardware set up and the OS installed, you need to harden and secure the computer, which includes the following tasks:

- Place the computer is a secure area.

- Disable, remove, or otherwise secure the floppy and CD/DVD drives so that security can't be bypassed by starting from boot media. For example, you can install hardware locks on the front of the computer to prevent access to the CD/DVD and floppy drives.

- Configure the computer to start only from the hard drive, and password-protect the BIOS.

- Remove or disable all unnecessary services, and remove all protocols except TCP/IP.

- Change the administrator account name, disable or rename the guest account, and remove all other accounts.

- Choose strong passwords, and change passwords often.

- Log all user access activity on the computer.

- Use secure protocols, such as Secure Shell (SSH), Secure Sockets Layer (SSL), and Internet Protocol Security (IPSec), for any remote access to and from IDS sensors. If strictly local administration is possible, disable remote access.

- Keep the computer updated with current patches, service packs, and updates.

NOTE Hardening and maintaining a Windows system for any purpose is an ongoing process. New exploits emerge constantly, and many recent malware exploits have taken advantage of computers that hadn't installed available patches for vulnerabilities. Make sure all computers have patches applied regularly.

Even without a database installed, you could still configure Snort for text-based logging and alerts, but this configuration doesn't produce the neatly organized, easy-to-interpret information that a database can. There are some good reasons to configure a database for Snort. First, text-based log files are difficult to manage. Second, you can't classify alerts or produce reports effectively from a text-based log. Third, add-on tools for Snort management, such as the BASE console, require a database. Snort can log to Microsoft Access, SQL, Oracle, and other relational databases, but it logs to MySQL natively. Configuring Snort to work with other databases takes more configuration and add-ons to translate data into the correct format. In addition, Snort can't log to Access in real time. If possible, installing MySQL for Snort is a better option.

11

Activity 11-1 guides you to the information and files you need to install Snort. Be aware that the installation is detailed and takes considerable time, so don't plan to rush through it.

Activity 11-1: Installing a WinSnort IDS

ACTIVITY

Time Required: 60 to 90 minutes

Objective: Download and install Snort and related programs to create a full WinSnort IDS.

Description: Snort is an open-source IDS program that's available for both Linux and Windows systems. In this activity, you download and set up the program on Windows XP Professional, along with MySQL, BASE, and other utilities for using and managing Snort. The time needed for installation varies, depending on how fast you type and how many errors you make.

You might also need to troubleshoot your installation and find workarounds for problems. This task reflects the real IT world: Things seldom go according to plan, and you often have to figure out how to make a program work. This activity includes installation notes about common problems you might encounter when installing WinSnort, but remember to check WinSnort's forums and FAQs for updated or additional information. You can also post questions or problems to the forum. In the open-source community, your input is crucial to continuing improvements.

Make sure you follow instructions exactly. If even one character is typed incorrectly, the installation won't work. Make sure any firewall software on your computer is turned off for these activities. Snort can't connect to its MySQL database if a firewall is running.

1. Start your Web browser and go to **www.winsnort.com/index.php**. Click **Installation Guides**, and then click **WinIDS Install Guides Using MySQL**.

2. Next, click **Installing a complete IDS using the IIS 5/6 Webserver**.

3. When you reach the "WinIDS – All in One Software Pak" section, download the software or obtain it from the location your instructor specifies.

4. Read the instructions and follow them carefully to install all required software.

5. Installation notes:

   a. Your command prompt might have C:\Documents and Settings*username* as the default startup directory. Most commands in the Snort installation require being at the root of the C or D drive. To return to the root of a drive, type **cd ** and press **Enter**.

   b. At the time of this writing, the WinSnort instructions contained an error. In the "Test IIS and PHP" section, the files hadn't been uncompressed, so these tests failed. If your installation also fails these tests, double-check to make sure all configurations up to this point are correct. If your configurations are accurate and the problem persists, skip this section and proceed with the remainder of the installation as instructed.

   c. In the MySQL installation, if there's no "Skip sign-up" option, click **Next** to proceed.

   d. In the "Configure IIS for the WinIDS BASE Security Console" section, the instructions say "Enable Default Content Page," but they should be "Enable Default Document."

6. When you see the BASE console, similar to Figure 11-2, you have installed and configured a full WinSnort IDS successfully.

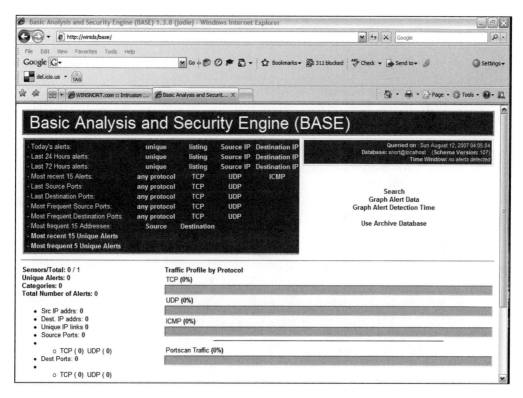

Figure 11-2   The Basic Analysis and Security Engine console

7. Create a restore point, and then leave the BASE console open for the next activity.

A major aspect of intrusion detection is maintaining updated signatures and rules. You might also need to add custom signatures. Activity 11-2 walks you through updating Snort signatures in Oinkmaster.

ACTIVITY

Activity 11-2: Installing Oinkmaster

Time Required: 30 minutes

Objective: Install and configure Oinkmaster, a GUI tool for managing Snort IDS signatures.

Description: In this activity, you install and configure Oinkmaster for the WinSnort IDS you installed in Activity 11-1. Oinkmaster makes managing Snort IDS signatures easier.

You need a valid e-mail address for this activity.

1. Start your Web browser, if necessary, and go to **www.winsnort.com/index.php**.

2. Click **Installation Guides**. On the Guides and Information page, click **WinIDS Companion Documents**, and then click **Installing Oinkmaster into an existing WinIDS**.

3. Read the document and install Oinkmaster as instructed. (Oinkmaster was downloaded with the Windows All-in-One Software Pak in Activity 11-1.)

4. Before you can access the official VRT Snort rules, you must go to **www.snort.org/** to register. Under Account (located below the navigation pane on the left), click **NOT REGISTERED?**.

5. After you have your "oinkcode," return to the installation guide and proceed with the activity.

6. After your rules have been updated successfully and Snort has stopped and restarted, Oinkmaster is installed. The Oinkmaster interface should look similar to Figure 11-3.

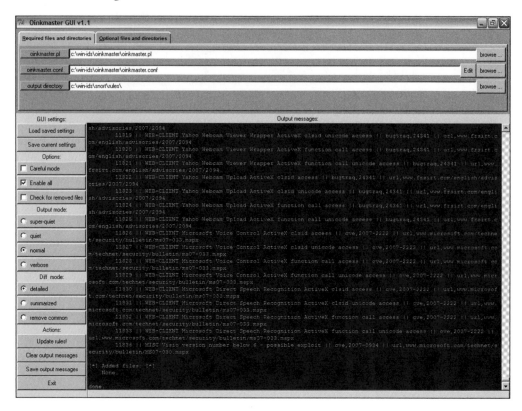

Figure 11-3 The Oinkmaster interface

7. Leave your system running for the next activity.

Now you have everything installed to run Snort, log events to your MySQL database, examine alerts with the BASE console, and manage rules. Next, you need to set up e-mail alerts to help monitor for potential intrusions. The BASE console is helpful for monitoring MySQL databases in real time, but it isn't as useful for more advanced functions. Therefore, in Activity 11-3, you install and configure EventwatchNT, a GUI plug-in for Snort that enables e-mail alerts.

ACTIVITY

Activity 11-3: Installing and Configuring EventwatchNT

Time Required: 20 minutes

Objective: Install and configure EventwatchNT to work with your WinSnort IDS.

Description: In this activity, you download and install EventwatchNT, an e-mail alert plug-in that works with your existing Windows IDS. Snort sets priorities, or importance levels, for alerts that range from 1 to 3, with 1 being the highest and 3 the lowest.

1. Start WordPad, and open the **Snort.conf** file. Usually, it's in the D:\ Win-ids\Snort\Etc path, but make sure you enter the correct path on your system, or Snort will fail. Change the # output alert_syslog: LOG_AUTH LOG_ALERT line to remove the # symbol (which indicates a comment), as shown in this example:

   ```
   output alert_syslog: LOG_AUTH LOG_ALERT
   ```

2. Save the Snort.conf file and exit WordPad.

3. You downloaded EventwatchNT with the Windows All-in-One Support Pak in Activity 11-2. Unzip the EventwatchNT folder into D:\Win-ids\ Eventwatchnt (creating the Eventwatchnt folder, if needed).

4. In the D:\Win-ids\Eventwatchnt folder, double-click **eventwatchnt.exe**. The EventwatchNT Configuration dialog box opens (see Figure 11-4).

11

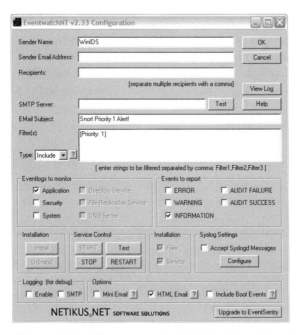

Figure 11-4   The EventwatchNT Configuration dialog box

5. Enter the following information:

   a. Sender Name: **WinIDS**

   b. Sender Email Address: ***eventwatchnt@yourdomain.com*** (substituting your domain name)

   c. Recipients: Enter e-mail addresses for the people who should receive an alert. Separate multiple addresses with a comma.

   d. SMTP Server: Enter the name or IP address of your SMTP server. If you don't know it, open your e-mail client and look for it in your e-mail account settings.

   e. Email Subject: **Snort Priority 1 Alert!**

   f. Filter(s): **[Priority: 1]** (*Caution:* You must type this information exactly, including the brackets.)

6. In the Type drop-down list box, click **Include**, and then click the **Test** button next to the SMTP Server text box. If you see a message that the e-mail was sent, and the e-mail arrives in your inbox, your SMTP configurations are correct.

7. In the Events to report section, click the **INFORMATION** check box, and in the Options section at the bottom, click the **HTML Email** check box.

8. In the Installation section, click the **Install** button.

9. In the Service Control section, click the **START** button, and then click **OK** at the top of the dialog box.

10. Open Event Viewer by clicking **Start**, pointing to **Administrative Tools**, and clicking **Event Viewer**.

11. In the pane on the left, right-click **Application** and click **Properties**. In the General tab of the Application Properties dialog box, click the **Overwrite events as needed** option button. Click **OK**, and then close Event Viewer.

Now you have installed and configured an advanced IDS. You've learned how to update rules and set up e-mail alerts, but these tasks are only the beginning of intrusion detection. You must still monitor and update the system and respond to alerts when they happen. You also need to know how to write your own rules to address problems specific to your network environment, which is discussed in the following sections.

Developing IDS Rules

An IDS's effectiveness depends on how complete and up to date signatures or user profiles in its database are. If an IDS command console receives alarms from well-known intrusion signatures or suspicious events, you should respond by:

- Adjusting packet-filtering rules
- Creating rules on the IDS

An IDS, like a firewall or packet-filtering router, has rules you edit in response to network scans and attacks. It can do more than simply react to undetected attacks, however. An IDS can be used proactively to block attacks and move from intrusion detection to intrusion prevention. The following sections examine configuring an IDS to filter out potentially harmful traffic by specifying rule actions, rule data, and rule options.

Rule Actions

By configuring an IDS to take actions other than triggering an alarm when it encounters a suspicious packet, you gain another layer of network defense. You have more control over how attacks are recorded and handled, and you can reduce false positives after you have worked out all the bugs. Finally, you also help the IDS handle new intrusion attempts that attackers develop.

Most IDS products include documentation about rule writing, and Snort is no exception. Because some actions, options, or data can differ between platforms, referring to the product documentation for help in rule writing is best. Customizing rules can also increase false positives during the learning process, so be aware that your customizations might not help the situation. If you can develop a test lab that mimics your production environment, however, you can develop and test rules before applying them. Often, thorough testing enables you to work out bugs in a new product or configuration without any negative effect on your live network.

Snort gives you an idea of the kinds of actions that can be carried out when it encounters a packet matching one of its rules. Actions are set in the Snort.conf file, which you can edit with a text editor. (You can also create a custom rules file and have Snort refer to it.) Generally, these are the available actions for rules:

- *Alert*—Sends an alert message that you define ahead of time when setting up the IDS. For your WinSnort IDS, you installed and configured EventwatchNT to send alerts via e-mail.

- *Log*—Records the packet in the log files.

- *Pass*—Allows the packet to pass through to the internal network.

- *Activate*—Creates an alert message along with a dynamic rule that covers subsequent logging.

- *Dynamic*—Enables Snort to continue logging subsequent packets when a certain packet is detected. For instance, if a port scan packet is detected, you could call a dynamic rule that tells Snort to log the next 100 packets.

Other IDSs also give you the option to terminate the originating computer's TCP connection if an attack is detected. With Snort's BASE interface, you can examine each alert and use a variety of tools to trace its source.

Rule Data

After you specify the action you want Snort to perform, you specify the rest of the data that applies to the rule, which includes the following:

- *Protocol*—Snort supports IP, TCP, UDP, and ICMP.

- *Source and destination IP addresses*—You can use the word "any" to specify any IP address or the netmask format for indicating a subnet mask. A Class A IP address uses the 255.0.0.0 netmask, a Class B address uses the 255.255.0.0 netmask, and a Class C address uses the 255.255.255.0 netmask.

- *Port number*—You can specify a port or use the word "any."

- *Direction*—The direction from the source computer and port to the destination computer and port is specified with the -> characters. For rules that affect traffic heading in both directions, use <>.

For instance, a rule that logs traffic from any computer to a computer at 192.168.10.1 on port 23 looks like the following:

```
Log tcp any any -> 192.168.10.1 23
```

A rule that logs traffic in both directions between two subnets looks like this:

```
Log tcp 10.1.20.0/24 any <> 200.156.15.0/24 any
```

More specific attributes, such as ACK flags, are covered by the rule options, which follow the rule actions and data.

Rule Options

Snort rules become more precise when you add rule options. Options are enclosed in parentheses, placed after the rule data, and separated from the data by a blank space. Options in parentheses are separated by a semicolon and a blank space, as shown in the following example with two options. The msg option prints the specified text message with the alert message and the data recorded in log files. The flags option triggers a specified action when the indicated flags are detected in a packet—in this example, the SYN and FIN flags (SF).

```
alerttcp any any -> 192.168.10.0/24 any (msg: "SYN-FIN
scan packet"; flags: SF;)
```

The most useful Snort options include the following:

- *msg*—Tells the logging and alerting engine what message to print with a packet dump or an alert.
- *ttl*—Tells Snort to match the time to live (TTL) value in a packet's IP header.
- *id*—Tells Snort to match a packet's fragment ID number.
- *flags*—Tells Snort to match specified TCP flags set in a packet.
- *ack*—Tells Snort to match the ACK flag in a packet.
- *content*—Tells Snort to match a defined string in the packet's data payload.
- *logto*—Tells Snort to log files to a specified filename instead of the default log files.

TIP　　You can find a complete list of options for Snort rules at *www.snort.org/docs/ writing_rules/*.

TCP flags are usually designated in Snort rules by a single character, as shown in the following list:

- F (FIN)
- S (SYN)
- R (RST)
- P (PSH)
- A (ACK)
- U (URG)

11

- 2—Reserved bit 2

- 1—Reserved bit 1

- 0—No TCP flags set

- + ALL—Matches all specified flags plus any others

- * ANY—Matches any of the specified flags

- !—Matches all flags except the flag you specify

Proactive Rules

After you understand the available options, you can set up proactive rules that cover many suspicious traffic signatures. An IDS rule base is different from a packet-filtering rule base because it assumes that firewalls or routers are already filtering packets. Therefore, any traffic that gets through the packet filter and matches an IDS signature should be logged. That way, you can analyze what traffic is getting through the filter so that you can adjust the rules.

For example, examine the following rules. The first two rules tell Snort to log any TCP and UDP traffic that reaches the IDS. The third rule sends an alert if any ICMP Echo Request packets or other ICMP packets reach the IDS.

```
logtcp any any -> any any (msg: "TCP traffic log";)
logudp any any -> any any (msg: "UDP traffic log";)

alerticmp any any -> any any (msg: "ICMP traffic
alert";)
```

After you set up these general rules, you can create rules for specific traffic signatures, as shown in the following examples. The following rule sends an alert if a packet with the SYN, FIN, and ACK flags is detected:

```
alerttcp any any -> 192.168.1.0/24 any (flags: SFA; msg:
"SYN-FIN-ACK packet detected";)
```

On the other hand, the following rule sends an alert if a packet with no flags set is detected:

```
alerttcp any any -> 192.168.1.0/24 any (flags: 0; msg:
"null packet detected";)
```

The following two rules send an alert if the IDS detects any packets with the two most frequently watched for IP options: **loose source and record routing (lsrr)** and **strict source and record routing (ssrr)**. The lsrr option specifies a set of hops the packet must traverse, but not necessarily every hop along its path. The ssrr option specifies every hop the packet traverses from source to destination. (Only one IP option can be specified per rule.)

```
alerttcp any any -> 192.168.1.0/24 any (ipopts: ssrr;
msg: "strict source routing packet";)
alerttcp any any -> 192.168.1.0/24 any (ipopts: lsrr;
msg: "loose source routing packet";)
```

The following rule sends an alert if the word "Password" is detected in a packet's data payload:

```
alerttcp any any -> any any (content: "Password"; msg:
"password transmitted?";)
```

The following rule is intended to address a path obfuscation attack:

```
alerttcp any any -> any 80 (content: "/. /. /. /"; msg:
"possible Web URL path obfuscation";)
```

After you have configured a rule base, the IDS can begin monitoring your network for suspicious activity.

Analyzing Log Files

You must monitor traffic logs for signs of intrusion or attack, although reviewing logs has some disadvantages. Even minimal logging can generate thousands of entries daily, and examining these entries manually is time consuming and tedious. Reviewing log files manually is also prone to errors, and log entries show you only what happened in the past, so they aren't useful for real-time monitoring. Finally, log files have a size limit, so when they reach that limit, they overwrite older entries, possibly deleting important information.

Fortunately, tools that monitor IDS logs on a real-time basis are available, including the BASE console you installed with Snort. Most can send an alert if suspicious activity is detected, and some can even mount a defense under certain conditions indicating an attack. Many tools perform other tasks, too. There are several factors to consider when choosing a log-monitoring tool:

- *Compatibility*—Is the tool compatible with your existing systems? Refer to the hardware and software inventory you completed in Chapter 1 to answer this question. Check the platform the tool runs on, programming languages required for the tool, and hardware the tool supports, such as IDSs, firewalls, servers, routers, and so on.

- *Scalability*—Can the tool support the company's projected growth for the next 5 or 10 years? Can it be upgraded or updated to keep up with new threats, attack signatures, and so forth?

- *Cost*—How much does the tool cost to set up? To maintain?

- *Vendor*—Is the vendor reputable and stable? What kind of long-term support can you expect?

- *Portability*—Can the tool be used with (ported to) different platforms or products?

- *Tracking*—Does the tool offer reverse DNS lookup, Whois, and other features for tracing attacks and connections?

- *Report format*—How does the tool organize and display reports? GUI or command-line interface?

- *Response and alerts*—Can the tool send alerts? Can you customize alerts (specify alert-triggering conditions and people to send the alert to) and configure a response if certain conditions are met?

- *Security flaws*—Does the tool have any known security vulnerabilities? Keep in mind that any software can have bugs.

- *Management and configuration*—How is the tool managed? Centrally? Remotely? Does configuration require editing one or many files? Does it use a GUI or command-line interface? Does the tool require knowing a programming language, script, or platform unfamiliar to support personnel?

The next step in protecting your organization is developing response procedures, as discussed in the following section. Because you can't be there around the clock to monitor for alerts and respond to incidents, you need to organize a security incident response team to take action if an incident occurs.

DEVELOPING A SECURITY INCIDENT RESPONSE TEAM

You can respond to a security incident in a number of ways, such as taking countermeasures designed to block intrusions, making corrections to packet-filtering rules to block intrusions an IDS has detected, and modifying security policies to cover new vulnerabilities. Developing a security incident response team (SIRT) gives your organization the flexibility to carry out these response options. The following sections examine the functions of a SIRT, discuss considerations for selecting team members, and explore options for staffing this team.

Functions of a SIRT

A SIRT, also known as a computer incident response team (CIRT), is a group of people assigned to respond to security breaches. The team's primary functions consist of six steps:

1. *Preparation*—Begin with a risk analysis and security policy, and create the SIRT.

2. *Notification*—Send news of security incidents to SIRT members; determine communication methods.

3. *Response*—React to internal and external security breaches and policy violations; determine who to notify; determine whether the attack is legitimate or a false alarm; and assess the level of damage.

4. *Countermeasures*—Contain the damage and remove any harmful or unauthorized files that have been introduced. These countermeasures are strategies that address threats to network security. Also, take corrective measures to prevent attacks from recurring.

5. *Recovery*—Restore damaged files and compromised resources.

6. *Follow-up*—Record what happened; conduct a forensics examination, if necessary; decide whether to prosecute offenders; and adjust security policies as needed. (Forensics is discussed briefly in "Gathering Data for Prosecution" later in this chapter, but computer forensics techniques are beyond the scope of this book and the certification exam.)

The six steps of **incident response**, discussed in more detail in "How to Respond: The Incident Response Process" later in this chapter, are part of a larger workflow that encompasses everything from risk analysis to the reevaluation of security policies and procedures after an event occurs. The incident response process isn't a separate series of events but an ongoing process, as shown in Figure 11-5.

11

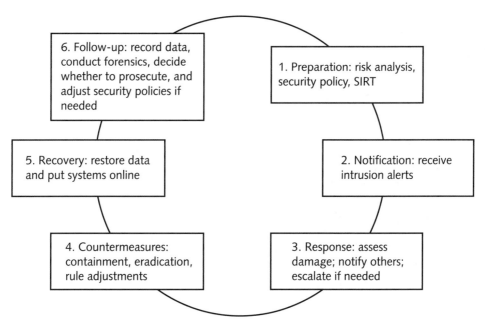

Figure 11-5   The intrusion response process

Selecting Team Members

Often, it makes sense to look within the organization for SIRT members. Employees who are already in-house are familiar with personnel and the organization's procedures and rules. Employees who are part of a SIRT need to be able to stop any ongoing work to respond to a security incident when it happens. They should also be given enough authority to make decisions if the organization's security policy calls for it, such as ordering employees to change passwords or disconnecting the network from the Internet.

SIRT members should represent a cross-section of the organization to ensure that all parts of the organization are involved in responding to incidents. Each member can then report to his or department about any security concerns that might require changes in how jobs are performed. Having all parts of the company represented in the SIRT reduces the chance of conflict that can result if files are lost or resources are damaged. Typically, SIRT members are drawn from the following departments:

- *Management*—At least one member of the SIRT should be upper-level management with the authority to make decisions affecting the entire company, such as shutting down the Web server or taking the network offline.

- *Legal*—An attorney in the Legal Department should be part of the SIRT to give advice if the company needs to take legal action against an intruder.

- *Information Technology (IT)*—At least one member of the IT staff should be on the SIRT. IT staff members know where the affected data is located and what parts of the network should be off limits to unauthorized users.

- *Physical Security*—A representative from security guard personnel should be on the SIRT for guidance if an incident involves physical damage to computer resources.

- *Information Security Services (ISS)*—ISS staff are trained to handle computer- and network-related security incidents.

- *Human Resources (HR)*—Many security incidents originate from within the company. If so, HR should be notified so that appropriate disciplinary measures can be taken.

- *Public Relations (PR)*—For well-known companies with a public profile, security incidents can affect business. A PR person on the SIRT can convey accurate information to the media and the public.

- *Finance/Accounting*—Placing a dollar amount on a security incident might be required for insurance purposes, and having someone from the organization's financial staff on board can make the process go more smoothly.

Not all these people need to be available when an incident occurs. Because security breaches can occur any time of the day or night, you need to have at least one person who has been trained in incident response on duty at all times. This person can summon SIRT members with a higher level of authority if action needs to be taken. The team's organization and response procedures should be worked out at an initial meeting of all SIRT members. The SIRT should, however, include one person designated as the leader who calls other members to meetings and communicates SIRT activities to others in the organization. You might also want to call in people from outside the company who can contribute to the SIRT. You can gain expertise and perspective by including security consultants and law enforcement officers who can give advice if needed.

CAUTION

Serious consequences can result if you don't include enough people in the SIRT. If you neglect to include someone from the IT staff, for example, IT might simply replace data in a database with a backup copy after an attack instead of reporting the incident to the SIRT. Similarly, not having an HR representative on the SIRT could result in legal problems if employees are accused without evidence.

Staffing Options

A **virtual team** consists of employees with other jobs to perform during regular business hours who act as a team only during meetings or when an incident becomes serious. Using a virtual team can be an efficient use of personnel, but this type of team tends to need retraining. In contrast, a team devoted to incident response full-time can stay on top of technical issues as part of its normal activities.

How well your organization responds to security alerts depends largely on the number of employees involved and how many other duties they perform in the organization. A permanent, dedicated security officer or team of people who perform only security tasks result in the best level of response. If your budget allows, you can assemble a team devoted to incident response or other security matters, such as configuring firewalls and IDSs. However, this arrangement might be economically feasible only for large corporations. Small companies might need to assign people to handle incident response in addition to other responsibilities.

NOTE

Public resource teams that publish notices and articles about serious security incidents are available around the world. You can consult with one of these teams to benefit from its expertise and ability to coordinate resources. These teams also provide training for SIRT members. Consider contacting resources such as the CERT Coordination Center (*www.cert.org*) in the United States or DFN-CERT in Germany (*www.dfn.de/content/index.php?id=74989&L=2*).

Outsourcing Incident Response

Because of staff or budget constraints, you might need to outsource incident response activities. Outsourcing has its advantages and disadvantages. You might find that hiring an outside incident response team results in lower overall costs because the team has to deal only with actual incidents instead of managing firewalls, reviewing log files, and changing passwords and user accounts. On the downside, outsourcing security functions could decrease your organization's capability to carry out timely, effective incident response procedures. Your network might be attacked at the same time as your outside team's other customers, which makes it unlikely that you'll get priority assistance. To avoid this problem, make sure service standards are explicit in your contract with an incident response service, and be sure to get references from current and former customers before you hire one.

Staging Drills

After the SIRT has held an initial organizational meeting and completed training, you need to conduct a security drill, not unlike fire drills in schools. Because of the staff time involved, you might need to convince upper management that this drill is necessary. However, drills can pay off in the long run by making incident response more effective and coordinated.

You don't need someone to actually attack your network. Instead, pick a time for the drill, and then follow an attack scenario. Drills can be scheduled or unscheduled. When the "attack" takes place, contact team members to test the notification process and make sure all phone and pager numbers are correct. Then test the response process by assembling the team and giving them the scenario.

Drills are intended to identify any holes in security procedures and to make sure everyone on the SIRT knows his or her responsibilities. All procedures carried out during the drill should be documented, and after the drill, hold a meeting to discuss how the drill went and whether any procedures should be handled differently to respond more quickly or effectively. You might want to conduct subsequent drills periodically to reevaluate how well the response procedures work.

EXAMINING THE INCIDENT RESPONSE PROCESS

You should be able to describe your incident response process clearly in a short document of perhaps five or six pages that SIRT members can refer to if an event occurs and they need to know how to proceed. Although a security "incident" could be as simple as a lost password, this section focuses more on handling intrusions and attacks the IDS detects. The following sections examine the six-step incident response process outlined earlier: preparation, notification, response, countermeasures, recovery, and follow-up.

Step 1: Preparation

The two crucial preparation tasks are performing a risk analysis and developing a security policy. Risk analysis identifies and prioritizes assets to determine the impact of loss or damage and is also used to prepare a security policy, which describes how the organization should respond to intrusions. Many security policies contain a section on incident response; others note the location of current incident response protocols. Wherever this information is located, everyone involved in incident response should know where and how to get current response guidelines quickly. A security policy should include the following directives for incident response:

- A statement to the effect that incident response is mandatory for the organization

- The objectives of incident response

- The limits of incident response, including privacy violations and other prohibited actions, such as retaliation against attackers

- The relationship of the SIRT to the law enforcement community—in other words, when law enforcement officers should be brought in to the incident response process

Setting limits on incident response activities is important to help avoid lawsuits. People who contend they have been wrongly accused can file suit and force the company to respond in court and possibly pay damages.

Security policy development and risk analysis are covered in detail in *Guide to Strategic Infrastructure Security: Becoming a Security Network Professional* (Course Technology, 2008, ISBN 1418836613).

Another important preparation task is deciding how to monitor the network for suspicious traffic. In large organizations, SIRT members might be dedicated to this task; in small companies, the network administrator performs this task, or several people might take turns. In a proactive approach to network monitoring, you test the network to see how it responds to scans and other events and to determine where vulnerabilities might exist. In a passive approach, the IDS is set up to send alerts if activity is detected that warrants it, and traffic isn't monitored continuously. Although a proactive approach is best for preventing security incidents, many organizations don't have the resources for it. If a passive approach is the best your organization can do, you're less likely to catch an attack in progress, so reviewing logs is more critical.

Step 2: Notification

Notification is the process of sending news about security incidents to SIRT members. Notifications can come from the IDS, other SIRT members, or a network administrator who detects suspicious activity. In addition, employees should be instructed to notify the SIRT member on call when they detect a virus, find oddly named files on their systems, or notice other signs of a security breach.

Before calling in other members of the team, assess the potential damage, if any. As mentioned previously, not all team members need to be contacted for every incident. You might want to assign levels of impact to events that determine how many and which people are called in to respond. For example, you can designate beforehand who to summon for Level One (not serious, probably a false alarm), Level Two (could be serious), and Level Three (serious) incidents. Answering questions such as the following can help you evaluate which level is appropriate:

- How many network hosts are affected?

- How many networks or subnets are involved?

- What level of privileges did the intruder gain? (If root or administrator privileges were gained, the attack becomes serious immediately.)

- What assets are at risk?

- How many different types of attacks are involved?

You also need to figure out how people are going to be notified, including **out-of-band notification**, which occurs via a non-network communication device, such as a pager, telephone, or cell phone. You might want to avoid using e-mail to prevent intruders from knowing that you're responding, for example. In addition, if a natural disaster knocks out regular phone lines, you might have to rely on cell phones. Other notification methods include the following:

- *Set up a hotline*—Employees and SIRT members can call this number if someone isn't available immediately and an incident occurs.

- *Set up a list of people to contact by phone*—Determine whether the team leader should be contacted first, and then the leader can decide who else needs to be contacted based on the situation's severity. Keep contact information updated.

NOTE

If you encounter a serious security incident, consider informing the Current Activity section of the CERT Coordination Center (*www.us-cert.gov/current/ current_activity.html*) so that other security professionals are alerted to the possibility of similar network attacks.

Step 3: Response

After the appropriate SIRT members have been notified of an incident, response measures must be systematic and thorough. When an incident occurs, SIRT members should keep the following principles in mind:

- Don't panic.

- Follow established procedures.

First, take time to analyze all reported events. Don't simply react to the first event you encounter. Make sure auditing is enabled so that you can capture the necessary data, and document everything that happens.

Establish standard procedures in the form of a short, easy-to-read set of incident response instructions. The instructions might look similar to Figure 11-6. This type of diagram is called a flowchart. Although flowcharts can be complex, one used for incident response instructions should be kept simple to ensure that SIRT members can follow it easily.

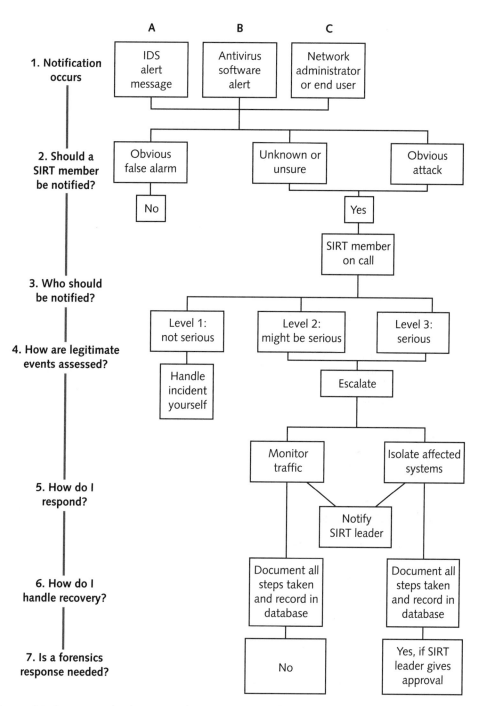

Figure 11-6 A sample diagram of incident response instructions

11

Determining How to Respond

Determining an incident's scope and severity tells you whether to escalate the incident (call in more security professionals and take immediate countermeasures). You can check risk analysis ratings to assess the value of assets that have been compromised; the higher the value, the more urgent and stronger your response should be. To determine how to respond based on asset value, answer questions such as the following:

- What are you trying to accomplish by your response? Determine whether you're interested primarily in protecting company data, recovering lost information, or maintaining a good reputation so that consumers have faith in your company and its products.

- How quickly can you respond consistently?

- Can you call in law enforcement or take legal action against offenders without exceeding your available budget?

After you have determined exactly what has happened and how severe the event is, decide whether the event should be escalated or you can handle it yourself. If the incident is obviously a false alarm and no damage has occurred, analyze what happened, make adjustments to prevent similar false alarms in the future, document what occurred, and move on.

If the incident is a legitimate attack, report it to other SIRT members. Provide the basic facts of the incident—what type of event occurred, the OS on the affected computer, when the event took place, and whether it's still ongoing. Describe the consequences of the attack—what systems have been accessed, what level of access privileges the attacker used, and any changes made to the targeted system. You might want to create a form for this report similar to the one in Table 11-1.

Table 11-1   Incident reporting form

Item	Description
Incident number	
Date	
Time	
Your name	
Description of event	
Origin	
Targets	
Data lost	
Current status	

You don't want to overreact to intrusions, however. It's more prudent to determine first whether any files have been damaged and consult with fellow SIRT members—especially those in upper management—who have the authority to make important decisions. On the other hand, if an intrusion is occurring and files have been compromised, you need to have clear procedures in place that tell you to shut down a server or Internet connections, if necessary. The time to work out these questions is at an initial meeting of the SIRT when rules and procedures should be discussed. All members should understand their roles and know what tasks they should carry out in case an incident happens.

Step 4: Countermeasures

After making an initial assessment and notifying the appropriate team members, you should take **countermeasures** to control any damage that has occurred. Two general types of countermeasures can be carried out: containment and eradication.

Containment is the process of preventing a malicious file, intruder, or compromised medium from spreading to other resources on the network. For example, you might shut down an affected system or disable user accounts or services. If the problem can be contained so that it affects only a single disk or computer, the attack can be curtailed or even thwarted.

Eradication usually follows containment and involves removing any files or programs that resulted from the incident, including malicious code, Registry keys, executable files, and malware, such as viruses and worms. The process of eradicating these files can be tedious and time consuming, but it should not be rushed. In many cases, the affected system simply has to be rebuilt or replaced by using the most recent clean backup. Remember that removing programs that attackers install or viruses produce doesn't prevent the problem from occurring again. Any backdoors that the attacker exploited to gain access to the system must be closed.

11

Step 5: Recovery

Recovery is the process of putting compromised media, programs, or computers back in service so that they can function on the network again. Don't simply plug machines or disk drives back in to the network and leave them to their users, however. Instead, monitor restored devices for at least 24 hours to make sure the network is operating properly.

SIRT members might even have users sign a statement agreeing that their computers have been serviced and returned and are in working order. This statement might seem like excessive detail, but it's part of documenting every step of incident response so that other team members and management can handle similar situations in the future. Monitoring systems closely for one or more days ensures that no undetected vulnerabilities remain. In addition, IT staff should adjust packet-filtering rules to block communications to or from any Web sites involved in the attack.

Step 6: Follow-Up

Follow-up is the process of documenting what took place after an incident was detected and a response occurred. By recording what happened in a file such as a database, information is stored where others can review it, which has many benefits. Keeping a record of events associated with a security incident has many benefits. Future SIRT members who encounter similar events can benefit from your notes. The company's legal representatives can also use the information in court, and public resource teams investigating security breaches can examine the data as well. Documentation is essential if you intend to prosecute offenders, and log files, hard drives, and alert messages are part of the trail of evidence. Any recommendations for changes in security policies or procedures as a result of security incidents should also be included in the follow-up database.

Follow-up can be a tedious part of incident response, however. When an incident is over, your first impulse is to move on to the next task, not record what happened in exhaustive detail. However, following steps you documented during previous events can make handling new incidents easier and less time consuming.

Even though you do all your work on computers, recording notes in electronic format might not be the best option. If the power goes out and your network is down, handheld devices or a pad and pen are your only options. After the incident, you can transfer your notes to a centralized database where all team members have access to it.

DEALING WITH FALSE POSITIVES AND LEGITIMATE SECURITY ALERTS

Now that you know the overall process of incident response, you can explore details of handling legitimate security alerts and dealing with a common problem of using IDSs: false positives.

Adjusting Rules to Reduce False Positives

False positives are the bane of many IDS administrators and probably the main complaint people have about using IDSs. The problem is that as you tune an IDS in an effort to eliminate false positives and false negatives (events that should have triggered an alert but didn't), its performance can become severely degraded and you can slow down the network. Suppose you create a new IDS rule for every false positive. Before long, your rule base will be so long that network traffic slows down while every rule is checked, one after another. It's much better to adjust existing rules when needed and create new rules only if necessary. When you get false positives, you should adjust your rules to reduce them in the future. You need to create rules that permit legitimate traffic to pass through without setting off an alarm.

One way to reduce the number of alerts is to exclude an address so that it doesn't generate an alarm or create a log record when its signature originates from the specified host or IP address. The addresses you exclude don't have to be external hosts. For instance, a management computer on your network might perform a ping sweep periodically. This event would trigger an alarm unless you exclude the management computer from the signature your IDS uses. You can extend this principle to encompass an entire subnet or network. You need to specify only a host subnet mask or a range of IP addresses, such as 10.0.0.0/8.

Disabling Signatures to Reduce False Positives

In some cases, you might want to disable entire signatures from triggering an alarm. If you're testing your network and doing a port scan, for instance, you want to disable any signatures that would match if the IDS detected a port scan. Even if an incident is a false positive, you should still record it in a tracking chart (see Table 11-2).

Table 11-2 Incident tracking form

Incident number	Type of incident	Location	Priority	Status	Last update	Team lead	Alternate team lead
28	Port scan through 255	192.168.20.1	Moderate	Inactive	5/25	JB	MK
29	Trojan program	192.168.20.39	High	Active	5/26	JB	GH

You might also want to exclude a signature on one IDS if another IDS contains the same signature. Reducing the number of duplicate signatures allows each device to operate more efficiently.

Dealing with Legitimate Security Alerts

When you get an alert from your IDS, how do you know the attack is legitimate? This section examines Step 3 of the intrusion response process—response—in more detail. First, you need to determine whether the attack is a false positive or a legitimate incident (true positive). Look for indications such as the following:

- System crashes are noticed or reported.
- Major changes in traffic patterns are noticed, without a valid cause, such as personnel or workload changes.
- New user accounts suddenly appear on the network.
- Sporadically used accounts suddenly have heavy activity.
- New files appear, often with strange filenames.
- A series of unsuccessful logon attempts occurs.

11

If the event turns out to be a legitimate security incident, you need to respond calmly and follow procedures spelled out in the security policy. To some extent, the way you respond to a legitimate attack depends on your organization's size and the nature of its activities. For a small company with fewer than a dozen employees, disconnecting the Web site from the Internet for a day or two might not have a big impact on sales. For a large company that depends on Internet revenue and receives thousands of Web site visits per day, the response should be more measured—more people need to be involved, you should take the Web site offline only if absolutely necessary, and you should get it running again as soon as possible.

Assessing the Impact

After you have determined that an incident isn't a false positive, find out whether any host computers on your network were compromised. If an intruder did get into your systems, determine the extent of the damage.

Next, define the scope and impact of the problem: Was one site affected or several different ones? How many computers were involved? There's no easy way to determine this information other than checking each computer, running virus scans, and examining logs for suspicious activity. If your firewall was compromised, any computer on the network could be accessed. The firewall must be reconstructed, which means the network will be down for a while. All host computers must then be checked for software consistency—making sure software on those computers hasn't been altered. This process, however, is only in response to the most serious incidents, ones that affect critical resources.

Developing an Action Plan

Many SIRTs like to develop an action plan—a series of steps to follow when a legitimate attack occurs. Writing down steps such as "disconnect the computer from the network" might seem obvious, but in the heat of the moment, having the list at hand can be a valuable aid. An action plan might have the following steps:

1. Assess the seriousness of the attack.

2. If a serious incident is involved, notify the team leader immediately. Determine whether a forensics investigation is required.

3. Document all actions, including who performed them and when.

4. Contain the threat by disconnecting the computer from the network.

5. Determine the extent of the damage. Were passwords compromised? Files accessed? New files added? Are Trojan programs present?

6. If you plan to prosecute, make a bit-stream image of the storage medium. A bit-stream image copies every bit on the disk, including free space, slack space (space between file clusters), and deleted files, essentially creating an exact

duplicate. A backup doesn't copy deleted files, slack space, and free space. Often evidence is hidden in these places deliberately, so making a bit-stream image is important. Be sure to keep the original medium for evidence, but never perform any analysis on it. The original should be stored securely.

7. Eradicate the problem.

8. Restore the system or medium and monitor it for integrity.

9. Record a summary of the incident. Send a memo to the CEO and Legal Department describing what happened.

After determining that an attack has occurred, you need to understand exactly how the attack was conducted so that you can configure countermeasures to prevent recurrences. For some network security analysts, the most effective tool for analyzing attacks is using **attack visualization**, which is the process of replaying the attack so that you can see what the attacker viewed.

Handling Internal Versus External Incidents

Intrusions and security breaches often originate from inside an organization. When you suspect that an employee is involved, your response needs to be more measured than if an attacker is compromising your network. You might want to avoid notifying the entire staff, for instance, so as not to alert the offender. Until you're sure who is involved, you might even want to keep affected computers online to keep intruders from knowing that you're on their trail. When you have identified the intruder, notify the Human Resources and Legal departments so that they can begin considering disciplinary action. Notify the entire staff only when they need to know that something serious happened and when they need to change passwords or take active steps toward preventing future incidents.

TIP Employees suspected of causing security breaches should be interviewed by trained, authorized personnel. Interviewers should explain that blame and punishment aren't the purpose of the incident investigation; instead, organizational security is. This explanation tends to put employees at ease so that they're more likely to provide information.

Taking Corrective Measures to Prevent Recurrence

After you have contained and eradicated the problem, you need to take steps to prevent it from occurring again. For instance, if a password was intercepted because an attacker planted a Trojan program on a network computer that sniffed passwords in transit, you need to track the following:

- Where the Trojan program came from
- Who transmitted the password

11

In response, you should download signatures of known Trojan programs that your IDS doesn't already include. You should also set up a rule that sends an alarm whenever a password is transmitted without being encrypted.

At times, you need to notify others on the Internet about your attack. Informing others in the industry that you have been hit by malicious code enables them to block incoming attacks and spread the workload of definition resolution. (In a nutshell, "definition resolution" is analyzing and defining malicious code to develop patches, antivirus signature updates, and removal tools to solve the problem.)

Working Under Pressure

In an ideal world, security incidents would occur one at a time and take place slowly enough that security professionals could respond before loss of data occurs. In the real world, incidents occur quickly, without warning, and simultaneously with other problems.

Incident response activities need to be carried out with discretion so that you don't alert the attacker. Regardless of who or where the attacker is, sometimes allowing the incident to continue for a while is best, if no serious damage is occurring. This method gives you time to monitor and record the attacker's activities and use this information for tracking, capturing, and possibly prosecuting him or her.

When you're working under pressure, the temptation is to proceed as quickly as possible and seal off any vulnerable computers or services so that nothing is lost. However, you need to remember the goal of your actions, whether it's to gather evidence for prosecution or simply discover the security flaw that allowed access so that it can be corrected. If prosecution is your goal, how you handle data collection can have a huge impact on how admissible the evidence is. If the information could have been tampered with between the time it was detected and the time of the court date, it could become invalid. Therefore, don't attempt to gather digital evidence unless you're competent in computer forensics techniques. Destroying potential evidence won't earn you a promotion. More likely, it will get you a one-way trip out of the building.

Filling out a response checklist, such as the examples in Table 11-3, is a good idea. Evidence intended for prosecution must be traceable, and this checklist keeps a record of incidents and responses, aside from log files. Also, you can determine what action caused a problem if, for example, a change to the rule base causes unexpected or undesirable results. It can't be said enough: Document everything! Even events that seem insignificant at the time can prove important later.

Table 11-3   Intrusion response checklist

Date/time	Occurrence	Response
10/20/07 07:58 a.m.	Alert from IDS that an Echo Request was received from IP address 62.126.0.34	Blocked request; changed rules to block Echo Requests from 62.126.0.34
10/20/07 10:14 a.m.	Alert from IDS that a series of Echo Requests was sent from internal computer 192.168.20.38 to the destination 200.46.101.1	Disconnected 192.168.20.38 from the network; ran anti-Trojan software; blocked communications with 200.46.101.1

Gathering and Handling Evidence for Prosecution

Although the following is by no means a complete list of computer forensics techniques, keep these guidelines for handling evidence in mind:

- *Make sure two people handle the data at all times*—Having one person look "over the shoulder" of the other is essential so that no one can argue that one person working alone could have fabricated or altered the data.

- *Write down everything*—Document every event that occurs and everything you do, no matter how trivial it might seem at the time.

- *Lock it up*—After data is collected, it should be locked away and protected so that there's no danger of tampering with it. As mentioned previously, duplicate storage media by making a bit-stream image and store the original in a safe location. Do your analysis on the duplicate and leave the original alone.

Early in the process of handling a legitimate security incident, SIRT members need to decide who will handle the evidence so that the chain of custody (the record of who handled an object that's used as evidence in court) is recorded. Before an incident occurs, determine whether you plan to prosecute offenders and include this decision in your security policy. If you intend to prosecute network intruders, you must respond with extra care and follow specific evidence-handling guidelines.

 CAUTION Don't attempt to perform computer forensics tasks (particularly if the evidence is important or related to a serious crime) if you don't know precisely what you're doing. Computer forensics is a highly specialized field, and becoming proficient at it takes extensive training and practice, not to mention specialized tools.

When you're investigating an incident within a legal framework, reliable and accurate electronic findings are critical. Computer forensics is a relatively new field, but the requirements for evidence handling and criteria for admissible evidence are well established. Consider the level of investigation required for the situation. If the issue is inappropriate use of the Internet and company resources, a full forensics investigation isn't warranted. If company computers might contain evidence of a criminal act, evidence gathering and handling must be considerably more detailed and careful. In this situation, you might recommend that your company hire a professional computer forensics examiner or call local law enforcement for guidance.

How you handle each case depends on the circumstances, but the general steps for handling and examining digital evidence are described in the following list:

1. *Secure the area*—Ask all unnecessary personnel to leave the area; make sure no one disturbs you while you work.

2. *Prepare the system*—Before you begin working on the system, photograph it so that you have a record of how it was arranged when you started your investigation. Be sure to photograph all cables and connections, front and back, so that the configuration can be duplicated if necessary.

3. *Examine the system*—You might want to examine the system while the attack is actually taking place, if possible, to identify services the attacker is exploiting and detect suspicious connections to other computers on the network.

4. *Shut down the system*—Disconnect the computer from the network. Note, however, that some malicious programs are configured to erase themselves when the computer is shut down. There are some steps you can take to prevent this, depending on the system, but computer forensics are beyond the scope of this book. If the situation warrants, calling in a forensics expert might be advisable. Otherwise, do some research to find methods of shutting down a computer safely without losing data.

5. *Secure the system*—After you disconnect the computer, if you plan to work on it in a lab, place it in an antistatic bag for transport. Insert blank disks in any drives so that the drives aren't damaged in transit.

6. *Prepare the system for acquisition*—Start the computer from a boot floppy disk or CD that has been configured so that it doesn't access the hard drive when the computer starts. Using boot media preserves the hard drive in its original state for examination.

7. *Examine the system*—Check the current system date and time to see whether it's accurate.

8. *Connect target media*—Connect a clean drive to the system and make a bitstream image of the affected drive.

9. *Secure evidence*—Turn off the computer, disconnect the target media, seal the machine, and connect the target media to a lab computer so that you can begin analyzing the data. Be sure to keep the original media in a secure location with an evidence log recording the chain of custody, and use the bitstream image for all investigation and analysis.

During these steps, take extensive notes on everything that's done to the scene and anything that might contain evidence. Your notes should keep track of when each step was performed and who performed it to maintain the chain of custody.

Advanced computer forensics techniques are well beyond the scope of this book. What's important to remember is that you must have considerable training and experience to become proficient enough to collect, analyze, and preserve digital evidence. If you don't have this training, the smartest move is to call in someone who does. In reality, you probably wouldn't conduct computer forensics beyond securing the scene, which simply involves keeping the location from being disturbed until a qualified computer forensics examiner arrives to investigate. The Federal Rules of Evidence apply to digital data, and failure to maintain the strictest controls can result in data being lost or deemed inadmissible as evidence.

TIP

You can learn more about the Federal Rules of Evidence and guidelines for computer investigations by reading the federal guide "Searching and Seizing Computers and Obtaining Electronic Evidence in Criminal Investigations" at *www.cybercrime.gov/s&smanual2002.htm*. In addition, Course Technology offers an excellent book on computer forensics, *Guide to Computer Forensics and Investigations*, Third Edition (2008, ISBN 1418063312).

CHAPTER SUMMARY

11

- ☐ The open-source IDS Snort, available for several platforms, combines anomaly, signature, and protocol detection. You can install it with a database, a GUI interface, and reporting tools to make it easier to use and produce more useful data.

- ☐ Any IDS must be monitored and kept up-to-date with current signatures. Review logs regularly, using tools that aid in monitoring and organizing data to maximize an IDS's effectiveness.

- ☐ IDSs can have packet-filtering rules, as routers and firewalls do, that detect suspicious packets. Rule actions tell an IDS what to do (such as log the packet or send an alert) when it encounters a packet matching one of its rules. Rule data specifies additional information that applies to a rule, such as protocol or port number. Rule options can assist in interpreting log files and determining how to react to attack attempts.

- ☐ A security incident response team (SIRT) should have representatives from management, human resources, and legal counsel as well as all major departments. The team's primary functions are reflected in the six steps of incident response: preparation, notification, response, countermeasures, recovery, and follow-up.

- ☐ The incident response process should be based on risk analysis and the company's security policy and defined clearly in a brief document to which all SIRT members can refer.

- When notification of a security event occurs, the SIRT member on call should assess the incident. After the initial response and assessment, countermeasures should be taken. The two general types of countermeasures are containment and eradication.

- In recovery, the compromised media, programs, or computers are put back into service so that they can function on the network again. Finally, in follow-up, the incident should be described fully and stored in a database or other file where future SIRT members can access it if similar incidents happen.

- False positives are almost inevitable with any IDS. You can reduce their recurrence by adjusting rules and disabling signatures.

- Legitimate security alerts require a calm, systematic, and thorough response. Assess the impact, develop an action plan, and take corrective measures to prevent recurrence.

- When gathering evidence for prosecuting attackers, you need to document all steps and maintain a record of the chain of custody. Review computer forensics techniques to make sure digital evidence will be admissible in court, but realize that hiring professional computer forensics examiners is often the best course of action.

KEY TERMS

attack visualization — The process of replaying an attack so that you can see what the attacker viewed.

chain of custody — The written record of who handled an object; used as evidence in court.

containment — The process of preventing a malicious file or compromised media from spreading to other network resources.

countermeasures— Strategies that address threats to network security.

eradication— The process of removing any files or programs that result from an incident, including malicious code or malware, Registry keys, and unnecessary executable files.

follow-up— The process of documenting what happened when an incident was detected and a response occurred.

incident response— The actions taken after a security incident to determine what happened and what countermeasures should be taken to ensure the network's continued security.

loose source and record routing (lsrr)— An IP option that specifies a set of hops the packet must traverse but not necessarily every hop in the path.

notification— The process by which SIRT members receive news about security incidents.

out-of-band notification— A method of sending news about a security incident on another communication device, such as a pager, rather than via the network.

recovery— The process of putting compromised media, programs, or computers back in service on the network.

strict source and record routing (ssrr)— An IP option that specifies every hop that the packet must traverse.

virtual team— A group of people who normally have other jobs and act as a team only during meetings or when an incident becomes serious.

REVIEW QUESTIONS

1. What is the advantage of configuring IDS rules if you already have packet-filtering rules in place? (Choose all that apply.)

   a. You can attach messages to the alerts.

   b. The IDS can contact incident response teams automatically by using out-of-band notification.

   c. The IDS can be configured to take actions.

   d. You can ensure that no attacks will be successful.

2. What are some actions available for rules?

   a. block

   b. deactivate

   c. pass

   d. alert

3. Which rule causes Snort to log traffic from any computer to a computer at 192.168.10.1, port 23?

   a. log udp all all -> 192.168.10.1 23

   b. logging tcp any -> 192.168.10.1 23

   c. log tcp any any -> 192.168.10.1 23

   d. log snmp any any -> 192.168.10.1/23

4. The Snort msg option tells the logging and alerting engine to do which of the following?

   a. Match the ACK flag in a packet.

   b. Log files to a specified filename instead of the default log files.

   c. Print a message along with a packet dump or an alert.

   d. Record all TCP flags to a message in the log files.

5. Why does it make sense to look in-house for SIRT members?

   a. You can assemble the team more quickly than by hiring outsiders.

   b. Current employees are familiar with the organization.

   c. Current employees already have the necessary incident response training.

   d. Current employees are more trustworthy than contractors brought in from outside.

11

6. Which Snort rule sends an alert if the word "Password" is detected in the packet's data payload?

   a. alert tcp any any -> any any (content: "Password" in data payload; msg: "password transmitted?";)

   b. alerttcp any any -> any any (content: "Password"; msg: "password transmitted?";)

   c. alerttcp any any -> any any (content Password; msg: password transmitted;)

   d. alert tcp all-> all (content "Password"; msg "password transmitted?";)

7. Determining the level of damage caused by an incident falls into which of the following incident response steps?

   a. response

   b. detection

   c. follow-up

   d. recovery

8. The ssrr IP option specifies a set of hops that a packet takes between source and destination, but not every hop in the path. True or False?

9. Which of the following applies to drills that test incident response procedures?

   a. They should be unscheduled.

   b. They should be scheduled.

   c. They should involve an actual attack.

   d. They should follow a scenario.

10. A group that helps organizations with incident response, training, and security information is called which of the following?

    a. public resource team

    b. incident response group

    c. incident coordination center

    d. distributed intrusion detection system

11. Why would you consider outsourcing your incident response needs?

    a. better security

    b. lower cost

    c. faster response

    d. less strain on in-house staff

12. Which of the following is a way of reducing false positives? (Choose all that apply.)

    a. adjusting rules

    b. decreasing network gateways

    c. excluding signatures or IP addresses

    d. restricting access control lists

13. When transporting a system or media for analysis in a lab, you should do which of the following? (Choose all that apply.)

    a. Place the evidence in plastic bags.

    b. Place the evidence in antistatic bags.

    c. Insert boot media in all drives.

    d. Photograph the area before anything is disturbed.

14. Which of the following is a record of who handled evidence that can be used in court?

    a. incident tracking form

    b. follow-up

    c. chain of custody

    d. audit

15. Who is likely to review the detailed information you record during follow-up after an incident? (Choose all that apply.)

    a. supervisors who are planning to leave the organization

    b. public resource teams aiding in the investigation of a security breach

    c. IT staff trying to determine whether new hardware or software is needed to enhance network performance

    d. future SIRT members who weren't involved in the original incident

16. What is a system requirement for installing Snort with a database and console?

    a. a network operating system, such as Windows Server 2003

    b. at least two hard drive partitions

    c. dual processors

    d. multiple NICs

17. When you encounter a false positive, you should create a new rule to eliminate it. True or False?

18. Why would you want to disable a signature on an IDS? (Choose all that apply.)

    a. You're upgrading your network.

    b. The signature is generating too many alerts.

    c. The signature is duplicated on another network segment.

    d. none of the above

19. What's the first thing you should do when handling evidence for prosecution?

    a. Call all senior staff members.

    b. Log the current user off the system and log on as administrator.

    c. Turn off the system and unplug it.

    d. Secure the area.

11

20. Which of the following events can help you differentiate a false positive from a legitimate security alert? (Choose all that apply.)

    a. New files appear with strange filenames.

    b. Power fluctuations are noticed.

    c. Strange people are seen in the building.

    d. System crashes are reported.

HANDS-ON PROJECTS

Hands-On Project 11-1: Keeping Users Informed

Time Required: 30 minutes

Objective: Analyze incident scenarios and determine notification procedures.

Description: Keeping employees informed about security incidents when they occur and in their aftermath is important. However, not all employees should be asked to respond to every security incident, or they will become unduly alarmed or stop taking notifications seriously. In this project, you analyze some common situations and answer questions about how to handle them.

1. Someone gains access to your Web server, which hosts the company Web site and is used to sell goods and services. You realize you have to disconnect the Web server from the Internet while you respond. Name four user groups in your organization who should be notified in this situation:

    _____

    _____

2. A password was used, apparently by someone in the company, to gain access to a file server containing company financial data. Which user groups should get full information about the incident? What information should you convey to rank-and-file employees while you attempt to determine who's responsible for the unauthorized server access?

    _____

    _____

    _____

    _____

Hands-On Project 11-2: Responding to an Intrusion Alert

Time Required: 30 minutes

Objective: Evaluate an alert scenario and explain the correct response.

Description: You get an alert from the IDS telling you that a Trojan attack has been detected on port 31337 of the computer at 192.168.3.33. You run an antivirus program on the affected computer and find that the Trojan program is indeed present. While you're sitting at the computer, Outlook Express opens without prompting and begins sending e-mails. Answer the following questions to indicate how you would respond.

1. Describe what your mental approach to these events should be:

2. Explain what you should do to isolate the affected computer:

3. After the computer is isolated, describe what should be investigated next:

4. List people who should be notified:

5. Describe what you could learn by a subsequent review of logs:

11

CASE PROJECTS

CASE
PROJECTS

Case Project 11-1: Designing an Incident Response Strategy

Now that Green Globe has a well-designed and documented network configuration, it's time to develop an IDS and incident response strategy for this chapter's running case project. First, you need to decide whether a WinSnort IDS, such as the one you used in this chapter, is suitable for Green Globe. Examine the functionality, security, and regulatory compliance requirements for Green Globe. Does a full WinSnort IDS meet the company's needs? Would another design be more suitable?

Next, you need to assemble a SIRT responsible for determining whether incidents are legitimate or false positives, deciding how to escalate responses, and assessing whether prosecution is viable or necessary. The team should be drawn mainly from current Green Globe employees. Include IT staff and representatives from upper management, finance, and human resources. Also, designate a person to handle public relations. Include contact information for the company's legal counsel, and identify a local law enforcement officer to contact if necessary. Follow these steps to help plan Green Globe's SIRT:

1. List who should be included in the SIRT, and explain briefly why you selected each member. It doesn't need to be a specific list of names, but a general guide for selection (including information such as skills needed, responsibilities the member is suited for, and so forth). For example, you might list the Human Resources director because she's familiar with all employees and can handle staff notification, if needed. This list is intended for upper management, which will coordinate organizing the team with your guidance.

2. Plan the general agenda for the team's first meeting. The team must select a team leader, discuss how responsibilities should be divided, and design a plan for developing, testing, and maintaining incident response procedures. Prepare a short list of items the team should address.

3. Guide the SIRT leader to develop an initial response checklist that includes responsible parties, contact information, and notification and escalation procedures. This checklist should be posted for employees but not available for the general public (to protect team members' privacy). Develop a sample document the SIRT leader could use to organize this information.

You can find more information on incident response at the CERT Coordination Center, SANS Institute, and FEMA Web sites. Do an Internet search to find these Web sites and to locate additional examples to follow.

Be sure to update your network diagrams and documentation, and record IDS configurations, such as names and locations of databases, contact information for e-mail alerts, and other details needed for the installation. In addition, draft guidelines for hardware to set up the IDS you have selected, including any software or licensing costs. You might want to include flowcharts, sample documents, or other supporting material for your design. For example, if you've selected a command-line tool, include a chart listing commonly used commands.

After you have developed your list for upper management, the SIRT meeting agenda, and the sample incident response checklist and revised your network documentation to include your IDS proposal, proofread all documents carefully and submit them to your instructor.

Begin thinking about finalizing your final draft soon. Be sure to review all previous chapters' case projects and incorporate any feedback you have received. Don't wait until the last minute to do this because it's easy to overlook errors or omissions. Make sure you have included a references page listing all resources you've used for your project.

12

WIRELESS NETWORK FUNDAMENTALS

> **After reading this chapter and completing the exercises, you will be able to:**
> ♦ Explain wireless communication concepts
> ♦ Describe factors in wireless network design

Wireless networking is used in government and private industry for an array of services, and this chapter introduces you to the fundamentals of wireless communication and wireless design considerations.

First, you learn the fundamentals of how wireless communication works and how radio communication laws affect it. Wireless standards change rapidly, so you learn the basic standards and then examine more recent developments. The Federal Communications Commission is the regulatory body governing wireless use, so this chapter reviews laws you must adhere to. Finally, you examine how wireless networks are designed.

WIRELESS COMMUNICATION CONCEPTS

Wireless networking is any exchange of data between computers and other devices that doesn't use cables. Wireless networking is used in many situations, including mobile computing, setting up or adding to a network when running physical cabling is difficult or expensive, and temporary business locations. When a business occupies temporary facilities, setting up a wired network doesn't make sense; a wireless network is easier, faster, and less expensive. When the business moves, all the equipment can be moved and reused easily in a new location.

Wireless networking follows the same general principles of any computer network—sharing information and resources—but has some major differences. First and most important, wireless networking uses certain types of electromagnetic radiation, specifically **radio frequency (RF) waves** or **infrared (IR) radiation**, to communicate instead of sending electrical signals over physical cabling. In wireless networks, RF waves are used most commonly; infrared is used mainly for communication with peripheral devices, such as printers, and short-range communication between laptop IR ports.

Understanding electromagnetic radiation, explained in the following section, is important so that you know what's involved in designing and administering a secure wireless network.

Electromagnetic Radiation

Cosmic objects emit different types of energy, known as **electromagnetic (EM) radiation**. "Electromagnetic" means made of electrical and magnetic fields, and radiation is energy that travels and spreads out as it moves. So EM radiation is electromagnetic energy traveling as a self-propagating wave and spreading out as it moves.

A **wave** is simply a means of transporting energy from one place to another without physical movement of material. In wave motion, energy is transported by a disturbance that occurs in a distinct repeating pattern. The maximum departure of the wave from the undisturbed state is called the **amplitude**. Figure 12-1 shows basic wave properties and amplitude.

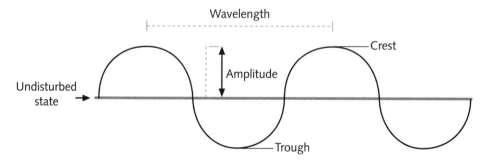

Figure 12-1   Wave properties

EM radiation types are (from highest energy to lowest) gamma rays, x-rays, ultraviolet light, infrared light, visible light, microwaves, and radio waves. (There are more precise classifications for these forms of radiation, but they are unnecessary for this material.) All these radiation types are collectively called the **EM spectrum**, which is expressed in terms of energy (temperature), wavelength, or frequency. **Frequency** is the number of times an event occurs in a specified period. For example, frequency in EM radiation is measured in hertz (Hz)—how many waves occur per second. The higher the number of hertz (also measured in KHz, MHz, GHz, and so on), the higher the frequency and the more energetic the radiation.

Frequency has an inverse relationship with **wavelength**, which is the distance between repeating units (usually the midpoint or crest) of the wave. So frequency is the number of waves per second, and wavelength is the distance between waves. Hotter objects produce higher-frequency, shorter-wavelength radiation than cooler objects.

The atmosphere blocks most of the EM spectrum from striking the earth's surface and allows only visible light, some radio waves, and a small amount of ultraviolet light through. Higher-frequency EM radiation (above 300 GHz), such as microwaves, x-rays, and gamma rays, is lethal.

Wireless Networking Standards

In the early years of wired networking, interoperability was a problem because the wide variety of proprietary protocols and devices didn't work together. In response to customer demands, technology and standards were developed to make widespread interoperability a reality. The wireless market is still in the process of achieving interoperability, but progress has been made with the advent of third-generation (3G) cellular technologies.

Cellular standards are important to wireless networks because wireless LANs (WLANs), mobile Internet, cell phones, and other widely deployed wireless services use RF waves, and the standards for radio communications apply regardless of the application. The basic signaling technologies in radio and wireless communication are similar, and adhering to cellular standards increases interoperability.

IT security professionals often forget that **IEEE 802.11 Wireless Ethernet standards** aren't the sole guideline for the wireless industry. They do govern WLANs, but the IEEE is only one organization collaborating with others worldwide on global communication standards. For example, in 2000, the International Telecommunications Union (ITU), after more than a decade of collaboration with other global standards organizations, unanimously approved the International Mobile Telecommunications 2000 standard (IMT-2000). A key feature of IMT-2000 is a framework for global interoperability for telecommunications systems. IMT-2000 is discussed more in "RF Signaling" later in this chapter.

TIP

Some international standards are compatible, and others still aren't. If a company requires international compatibility for wireless services, make sure service is available where it's needed, and no unforeseen compatibility problems are discovered after funds and resources have been expended on wireless.

NOTE

Another widely used technology is Bluetooth, which operates at 2.4 GHz. Part of its popularity stems from a low production cost, which is appealing to device manufacturers. Because of its short range and low bandwidth, it's used primarily for networking PDAs, headsets, printers, and cell phones. One challenge in WLANs is making Bluetooth devices interoperate with WLANs on the same frequency.

Radio Frequency and the FCC

Because wireless uses RF primarily, it can interfere with radio and TV broadcasts, military and aviation communications, maritime communications, emergency services communications, satellite navigational systems, radar, and cellular telephone services, among other critical applications. For this reason, most radio and some infrared and microwave frequencies are regulated strictly by the **Federal Communications Commission (FCC)** in the United States (and similar agencies internationally).

The FCC regulates what frequencies wireless communications can use, how much power antennas can emit, and other matters concerning the use of radio waves, infrared, and microwaves used for communication. If your transmission strengths, frequencies, and directions violate FCC rules, your organization has to pay heavy fines. If your transmission interferes with police or fire services bands, you could also be held liable for injuries or deaths caused by that interference. When planning wireless deployment, be sure to check with your local FCC office for any regulations or requirements you must meet. Many frequencies are licensed to commercial, industrial, government, and military entities and can't be used by anyone other than the licensee. Even though wireless hardware vendors can sell only devices that meet FCC regulations, sometimes your location has special circumstances. The person using the devices is the person who's fined if wireless devices cause a problem or don't comply with applicable laws. Also, some states have additional laws on wireless devices.

ACTIVITY

Activity 12-1: Researching First-Responder Interference Cases

Time Required: 20 minutes

Objective: Using the Internet, research wireless interference cases that involved emergency services or liability for the wireless operator.

Description: In this activity, you search the Internet for records, reports, or articles about emergency services experiencing interference from wireless devices. Select a case and write a brief presentation to give to your class.

1. Start your Web browser and go to **www.usatoday.com/tech/news/ 2001-03-12-cell-phones-cops.htm**.

2. Read the article. What kinds of problems are cellular and wireless interference causing for emergency bands?

3. Search for more news on this topic.

4. For class discussion: What are the primary problems that caused this event? What plans exist to solve the problem?

In general, home or small business wireless networks don't involve major regulatory headaches and can usually be set up with off-the-shelf products. Integrating wireless into an enterprise network might require using antennas for site-to-site communication, however, and these antennas must meet FCC regulations (discussed in "Wireless Network Components" later in this chapter). You might also have to meet licensing or other requirements. Always check regulations to prevent your company from losing communication services or paying fines. The FCC can order wireless communication causing harmful interference to other licensed entities to shut down immediately.

The good news is that there are some unregulated frequencies and some methods of modifying transmissions that eliminate potential interference with regulated bands. Some of these methods are discussed in the following sections.

Infrared Transmissions

Wired networks send information as electrical signals, but **infrared transmissions** use infrared light pulses and require an emitter and a detector. The emitter is usually a laser diode or LED. The detector is sometimes combined with the emitter and detects IR transmissions and generates the corresponding electrical current for wired communication, much like a standard network interface card (NIC) translates data into electrical current (voltage). The intensity of the light pulse in IR indicates the on or off status of each bit of data, just as the presence or absence of voltage indicates the bit status for a wired transmission.

IR communications can be directed or diffused. A **directed IR transmission** requires the emitter and the detector to be pointed directly at one another; a **diffused IR transmission** relies on reflected light that can bounce off walls or other objects. The emitter and detector don't have to be pointed at one another for a diffused IR transmission.

IR wireless has some advantages. It doesn't interfere with other signals and isn't susceptible to interference from them. Signals can't pass through walls (but can pass through glass), so IR transmissions are usually confined to a room. The disadvantages of IR are its limited range, low speeds of only up to 4 Mbps, and the requirement for direct line-of-sight or in-the-room conditions. For these reasons, IR is generally used for short-range applications, such as a TV remote, wireless headsets, or short-range data transfers between laptops or handheld computers. Some specialized WLANs use IR, as in hospitals where RF would interfere with other signals or high-security environments, but in most office settings, IR isn't robust enough for WLANs.

12

Activity 12-2: Exploring IR Transmissions

Time Required: 10 minutes

Objective: Experiment with an IR device to test the transmission properties of IR.

Description: In this activity, you test the directed and diffused properties of IR transmissions. A TV remote is the preferred equipment for this activity, but another IR remote signaling device will work.

1. Get your TV remote control. Most use IR, although some use RF (UHF) to pass through walls, such as multiroom satellite TV systems.

2. Look at the front of the remote, where you should see one or more small bulbs. They are IR emitters.

3. Look at the front of your TV to find the detector.

4. Point the remote emitters directly at the detector. Turn the TV on and off.

5. Turn around and point the remote at a wall. Turn the TV on and off. Experiment with positioning to test the reflected signal. Are there any positions where the remote doesn't work?

6. Go into another room with the door closed, and try to use the remote. Does it work? What property of IR transmissions does this test demonstrate?

   _____

7. Now open the door and try to bounce the signal off a wall to turn on the TV. If you have a mirror, try bouncing the signal off it.

8. If you have a laser pointer, try using it to control your TV. Does it work? Why or why not?

   _____

   _____

   _____

9. For class discussion: How does a TV remote using IR tell the TV how to change channels and mute, increase, or decrease volume?

Radio Frequency Transmissions

RF wireless transmissions overcome some limitations of infrared, making it the most commonly used transmission medium for WLANs. RF can pass through walls and other nonmetallic objects and travel great distances, but it's a bit more complex than IR, involving transmission ranges, signal modulation, and interference (discussed in the following sections). Table 12-1 summarizes the most commonly used RF bands.

Table 12-1 Common RF bands

Band and abbreviation	Frequency	Common uses
Extremely low frequency (ELF; maritime use) Super low frequency (SLF; maritime use) Ultra low frequency (ULF) Very low frequency (VLF)	3–30 Hz 30–300 Hz 300–3000 Hz 3–30 KHz	Naval and maritime
Low frequency (LF)	30–300 KHz	Cordless telephones
Medium frequency (MF)	300 KHz–3 MHz	AM radio
High frequency (HF)	3–30 MHz	CB and shortwave radio
Very high frequency (VHF)	30–144 MHz 144–174 MHz 174–328.6 MHz	FM radio, TV channels 2–6 Taxi radios TV channels 7–13
Ultra high frequency (UHF)	328.6–806 MHz 806–960 MHz 960 MHz–2.3 GHz 2.3–2.9 GHz	Public safety Cell phones Air traffic control radar WLANs
Super high frequency (SHF)	2.9–30 GHZ	WLANs
Extremely high frequency (EHF)	30–300 GHz	Radio astronomy
Atmosphere blocks frequencies	Above 300 GHz	N/A

NOTE

WLANs using RF operate in the UHF and SHF bands, using primarily the 2.4 GHz and 5 GHz frequencies.

12

Transmission Ranges

A wireless network's transmission range varies depending on the standard in use and the environment. Generally, lowering bandwidth increases coverage area, and throughput decreases with distance. Higher frequencies usually mean less range.

NOTE

Throughput is the amount of information being transmitted, which is lower than the signaling rate because of overhead. For example, a typical 802.11g 54 Mbps network might have an actual throughput of only 30 Mbps.

The range your network needs depends on the site. One pitfall is the urge to increase coverage by placing too many access points (APs). Although overall performance and coverage would seem to be better, having stray wireless signals outside your security perimeter is risky. Unlike a wired network with a clearly defined area of operation, wireless is transmitted through the air, so enforcing physical security for wireless means careful placement of APs. There's also the risk of **co-channel interference**, in which signals from APs interfere with each other. In a multiple-AP environment, you must be careful to arrange APs so that overlapping signals don't share the same channel (frequency).

Walls, metal, and other solid objects impede wireless transmissions, although as a low-frequency radio signal, wireless can pass through walls and other objects to a certain extent. Too many objects or metallic constructions have a detrimental effect on the wireless signal, however. You can overcome this effect by strategic placement of APs, adjustment of antennas, or just removing the obstacles. For example, if a wireless work-station is having trouble with its connection, a minor adjustment of an antenna might correct the problem. If this adjustment doesn't work, you need to examine objects between the wireless NIC (WNIC) antenna and the AP and look for other potential sources of interference.

Interference

Radio frequencies can be highly susceptible to interference from electrical storms, solar activity, laser printers, and other forms of EM radiation as well as other RF transmissions. An old microwave oven, for example, can cause major problems for wireless network because the oven emits RF interference. This interference source might be missed easily if the oven isn't in use when you perform an RF sweep to determine sources of interference in your site. (RF sweeps are part of a wireless site survey, discussed in Chapter 13.) A nearby cordless phone can also cause problems. The factor to remember is transmission power. Devices using the same or close frequencies compete and interfere with each other, but the device with the higher transmission power continues to operate. The FCC regulates the transmission power of antennas and RF devices.

ACTIVITY

Activity 12-3: Identifying Potential Interference Sources

Time Required: 10 minutes

Objective: Examine your classroom for potential interference sources.

Description: In this activity, you examine your classroom to identify any possible sources of interference that might impede the performance of a wireless network. Remember that a wireless transmission can travel in all directions, so look up and down, too. You need a pencil and paper for this activity.

1. Select a starting point in the room where your imaginary AP would be located. Regard all workstations in the room as wireless stations. Make sure to select a different location than your classmates.

2. Examine all areas and don't forget to consider what's behind the walls and above and below your AP.

3. Write down all items that could cause communication problems for a wireless network.

4. When you're finished, turn your paper in to your instructor or use it for class discussion.

There are a couple of major interference problems in wireless communications. In **multipath**, a signal has more than one path from the transmitter to the receiver. If the signal is reflected or refracted by the atmosphere, ground, or other obstacles, the reflected path can interfere with the direct path. This problem is called **fading**. Co-channel interference, discussed in the previous section, is another source of interference.

One of the biggest problems in using RF is that concurrent use of the same bands as other entities results in one or both experiencing interference, usually severe enough to disrupt communications. As you have learned, several RF bands are licensed and can't be used by anyone but the licensee on record with the FCC. Unlicensed bands, however, can be used for different purposes by anyone. They are shown in Table 12-2.

Table 12-2   Unlicensed radio frequency bands

Unlicensed band	Frequency	Total bandwidth	Common uses
Industrial, Scientific, and Medical (ISM)	902–928 MHz 2.4–2.4835 GHz 5.725–5.85 GHz	234.5 MHz	Cordless phones, WLANs, wireless Public Branch Exchanges (PBXs)
Unlicensed Personal Communications Systems	1910–1930 MHz 2390–2400 MHz	30 MHz	Wireless PBXs
Unlicensed National Information Infrastructure (U-NII)	5.15–5.25 GHz 5.25–5.35 GHz 5.725–5.825 GHz	300 MHz	WLANs, wireless PBXs, campus applications, long outdoor links
Millimeter Wave	59–64 GHz	5 GHz	Home networking applications

12

Radio Frequency Signal Behavior

RF signal behavior is characterized by whether a factor contributes to an increase (gain) or decrease (loss) in power. **Gain** is the positive difference in amplitude between two signals and is achieved by magnifying the signal. Although gain and amplitude are sometimes used synonymously, gain is actually a measure of amplification. Gain can occur intentionally, when you use a device that provides more power, or unintentionally, when the signal bounces off an object and recombines with the original signal, thus increasing its strength.

Loss, sometimes referred to as attenuation, is the negative difference in amplitude of signals. Sometimes loss is intentional, when you use a device to reduce signal power to comply with regulations on maximum signal strength, for example. Most of the time, however, loss is unintentional. Loss can be the result of many factors, but the following are the most common:

- In **absorption**, certain types of material can absorb RF signals, including wood, concrete, and asphalt.

- In **reflection**, an RF signal can bounce off some materials, which is the opposite of absorption. Objects that cause reflection are usually large in relation to the signal's wavelength and smooth, such as walls or buildings. The earth's surface can also reflect signals, and metals are generally reflective.

- In **scattering**, small objects and rough textures can disperse the signal. Trees, foliage, rocks, and sand are common objects causing scattering. Certain weather conditions can cause scattering, such as blowing dust or rain.

- In **refraction**, differences in density between air masses over distances can cause refraction. When moving through these differences in density, the signal actually bends instead of traveling in a straight line.

- **Diffraction** is similar to refraction, except that the signal bends around an object in its path, instead of bending as it moves through it.

- **Voltage standing wave ratio (VSWR)** is caused by differences in equipment rather than external influences, as in previous examples. If one part of the equipment has a different impedance than others, the signal can be reflected back within the device, and the reflected power can cause the device to burn out (see Figure 12-2).

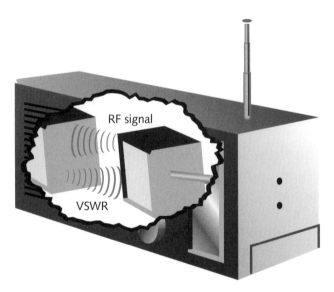

Figure 12-2 Voltage standing wave ratio

Measuring RF Signals

RF measurement requires some knowledge of mathematics. Because the TPD certification exam doesn't focus on wireless design, you don't need an in-depth lesson in RF math. You just need to know how RF power is measured and the 10s and 3s rules of RF math.

RF power is measured in two ways. The first is on a linear scale using milliwatts (mW). One mW is equal to one thousandth of one watt of power. In linear scale systems, everything is relative to a starting point of zero. When calculating gain or loss, however, this linear scale isn't helpful because the important part is the relation to the whole. For example, a loss of 50 mW could be major or minor in relation to the transmission's total power. If the total power is 100 mW, a loss of 50 mW is major. If the total power is 30,000,000 mW, a loss of 50 mW is minor.

When the transmission power is the point of reference, you get a better measurement of the impact of loss or gain. A 50 mW loss when the power is 100 mW means a 50% loss. If the total power is 30,000,000 mW, a loss of 50 mW is insignificant. This doesn't mean a relative scale is more precise than a linear scale, only that a relative scale provides a better picture of the loss or gain in relation to the whole.

The industry-standard measurements of power are mW and dBm. dBm is the reference point that relates the decibel scale to the linear milliwatt scale and specifies that 1 mW = 0 dBm. RF power gains and losses on a relative scale are measured in decibels (dB) instead of mW. dBs are a logarithmic method of expressing power and voltage ratios and are used because they're easier to add and subtract than ratios or percentages when calculating power levels. Decibels aren't exact, however; small differences are generally rounded off for the purpose of easy calculations.

For example, +10 dBm means 10 times the power, so −3 (3 dB minus 1 mW) actually means roughly half the power because −3 dB is equal to a ratio of about 2. About double the power is represented by +3 (3 dB plus 1 mW). If +10 dB means 10 times the power, +3 dB is like saying you have to multiply the power by $10^{3/10}$, which comes out to 1.9953, rounded up to 2.

12

The other relative scale power measurement of importance to WLAN administrators is **Equivalent Isotropically Radiated Power (EIRP)**. EIRP is the power radiated by a wireless system's antenna and includes the intended transmission power as well as the unintended gain. Although RF gain and loss are measured in decibels, EIRP uses a slightly different measurement known as isotropic decibels (dBi) that applies only to an antenna's gain. The reference point of EIRP is a theoretical antenna operating at 100% efficiency.

There are other measurements of RF power, but most measurements for WLANs are in dBm or mW. WLAN measurements are defined in the United States by FCC Part 15.247 and limit the distance a WLAN can transmit. EIRP measures the gain of the antenna; Transmitter Power Output (TPO) measures the power being delivered to the transmitting antenna and is also regulated by the FCC. The maximum TPO the FCC has established for WLANs is 1000 mW or 30 dBm. The maximum EIRP for 802.11b and 802.11g WLANs varies with speed and is shown in Table 12-3.

Table 12-3   802.11b and 802.11g maximum EIRP

Transmission speed	802.11b	802.11g
24 Mbps or less	40 mW (16 dBm)	50 mW (17 dBm)
36 Mbps	25.1 mW (14 dBm)	40 mW (16 dBm)
48 Mbps	20 mW (13 dBm)	31.6 mW (15 dBm)
54 Mbps	20 mW (13 dBm)	20 mW (13 dBm)

RF Signaling

RF transmits a **carrier signal**, which can change based on the signal's voltage and direction. A change in voltage doesn't change the transmission frequency; rather, it determines how long the transmission takes to reach the maximum voltage, fall to the minimum, and return to a neutral charge. In an unmodified RF transmission, however, the signal contains nothing to distinguish between the carrier wave and any other aspects of the signal, such as data. For this reason, changes to the carrier wave are needed to transmit data, video, audio, and so forth on the RF signal.

RF data is transmitted as analog or digital signals. An **analog RF signal** is a continuous wave that oscillates between positive and negative voltage, such as an audio or a video broadcast. **Digital RF signals** also oscillate between positive and negative voltage, but they are divided into discrete segments with many starts and stops in the data stream. If you understand how the binary code system works, you know that "digital" signal is synonymous with "binary" signal.

A carrier signal alone can't carry information, so how can data be transmitted? The answer is **modulation**, which means changing characteristics of the signal. Computers transmit, interpret, and store information in digital format, so an analog RF signal must be converted into digital format. Converting analog to digital and vice versa requires a modulator. Several modulation methods for analog and digital signals are used in wireless networking. Three characteristics of the carrier wave signal can be changed to enable it to carry information:

- Height (amplitude)

- Frequency

- Relative starting point of the signal

Analog Modulation

Analog modulation methods (shown in Figure 12-3) are as follows:

- In **amplitude modulation (AM)**, the height of the carrier wave is changed so that a higher wave represents a 1 bit and a lower wave represents a 0 bit. (Remember that 1 or 0 is the binary representation of on or off.)

- In **frequency modulation (FM)**, the number of waves representing one cycle is changed so that the number representing a 1 bit is higher than the number representing a 0 bit.

- In **phase modulation (PM)**, the cycle's starting point is changed when the bit being transmitted changes from 1 to 0. Instead of the wave oscillating from maximum to minimum regularly, when the bit changes, the wave oscillates from minimum to neutral and then back to minimum before returning to neutral and back to maximum.

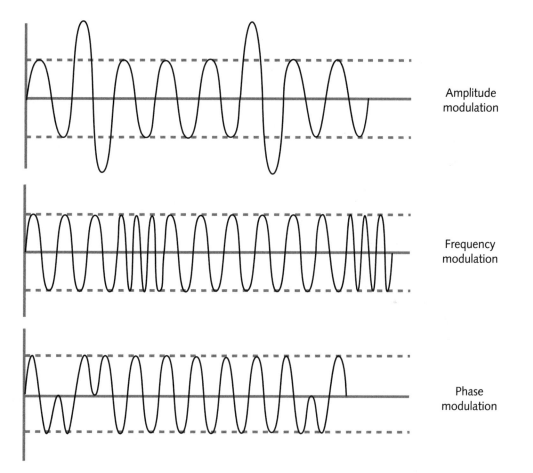

Amplitude modulation

Frequency modulation

12

Phase modulation

Figure 12-3 Modulation techniques

NOTE Although analog RF can be used to transmit data, most WLANs use digital signals. Until recently, IEEE standards required providing analog services. Because these services are no longer required, analog modulation isn't critical for WLANs. Support for analog services is expected to be phased out in favor of more robust digital techniques.

Digital Modulation

Digital modulation techniques still use changes in signal frequency, amplitude, and starting point (phase) but are superior to analog methods for four reasons:

- Better use of bandwidth

- Fewer interference problems

- Error correction more compatible with other digital systems

- Less power required to transmit

A digital signal is the same as a binary signal. Three binary signaling techniques can be used with digital modulation:

- *Return-to-zero (RTZ)*—Voltage increases to represent a 1 bit, with zero voltage representing a 0 bit. The voltage for a 1 bit drops back to zero before the end of the bit period. A bit period (T) is the amount of time required to transmit a logical 1 or a logical 0.

- *Non-return-to-zero (NRZ)*—Voltage increases to represent a 1 bit, with zero voltage representing a 0 bit. The voltage for a 1 bit doesn't drop back to zero before the end of the bit period; it remains high for the duration of the bit period.

- *Polar non-return-to-zero (polar NRZ)*—Voltage increases to represent a 1 bit and drops to negative voltage to represent a 0 bit.

RF signals are by nature **narrowband** transmissions, meaning they transmit on one frequency or a very small frequency range. Narrowband transmissions are particularly vulnerable to interference from any signals operating in or near the frequency being used. Radio and TV stations operate with little disruption on a narrowband frequency because no one else is allowed to use their FCC-licensed frequencies. These are the most common digital signal modulation methods:

- *Amplitude shift keying*—**Amplitude shift keying (ASK)** is a binary modulation technique in which the height of the carrier can be changed to represent a 1 or 0 bit. In ASK, a 1 bit has a carrier signal, and a 0 bit has no signal (basically, voltage versus no voltage).

- *Frequency shift keying*—**Frequency shift keying (FSK)** is a binary modulation technique in which the carrier signal's frequency is changed to represent a 1 or 0 bit.

- *Phase shift keying*—**Phase shift keying (PSK)** is a binary modulation technique similar to phase modulation, in which the signal's relative starting point is changed to represent a 1 or 0 bit and changes whenever the bit changes from one to the other. Because PSK is a binary method, the signal starts and stops.

- *Frequency division multiplexing*—**Frequency division multiplexing (FDM)** is an RF signaling method in which multiple base signals are modulated on different carrier waves and combined to form a composite signal.

These methods work much like analog modulation techniques, except digital signals start and stop, and ASK uses NRZ coding instead of both the 1 and 0 bits having carrier signals. A narrowband signal is shown in Figure 12-4.

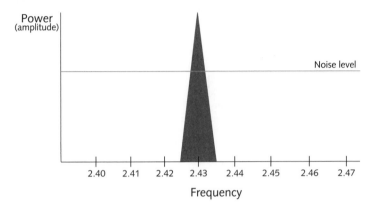

Figure 12-4   Narrowband transmission

Spread Spectrum

An alternative to narrowband transmissions is **spread spectrum**, which spreads a narrow signal over a broader portion of the radio band. Aside from reducing interference vulnerability, it has some major advantages over narrowband. First, the transmitted signal's bandwidth is much higher than that of the original message. Second, bandwidth is determined by the spreading function and is known only to the transmitter and receiver, which is especially important for security reasons. A spread-spectrum transmission is shown in Figure 12-5.

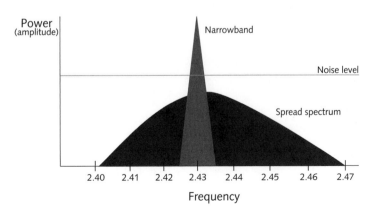

Figure 12-5   A spread-spectrum transmission

12

The more technical definition of spread spectrum is an RF communication system in which the base signal is spread over a larger bandwidth by injecting a higher frequency signal. The spreading function attaches a key, also called a spreading code or sequence, to the communication channel. The method of inserting the key defines the spread spectrum technique. These are the major methods of spread spectrum used in wireless networks:

- In **direct sequence spread spectrum (DSSS)**, shown in Figure 12-6, the key is applied at the data level. The spreading code (key) is the chip sequence used to represent message bits.

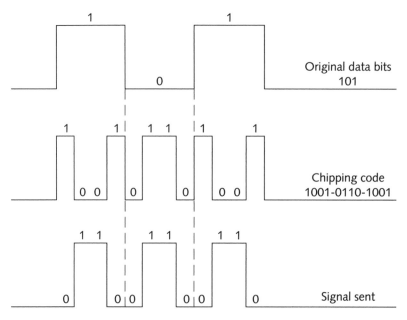

Figure 12-6   A DSSS transmission

- In **frequency hopping spread spectrum (FHSS)**, shown in Figure 12-7, the key is applied at the carrier frequency level. The spreading code (key) is the list of frequencies used for the carrier signal.

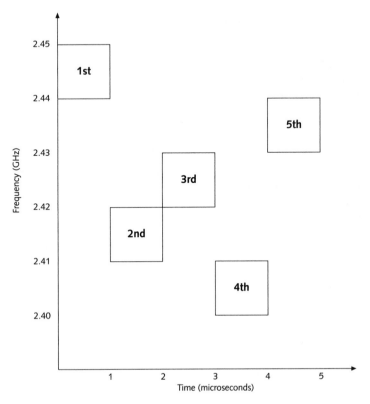

Figure 12-7   An FHSS transmission

- In **orthogonal frequency division multiplexing (OFDM)**, which is technically a modulation technique, a high-speed signal is divided into smaller pieces that are sent simultaneously across many lower-speed channels.

In DSSS, an expanded redundant chipping code is used to transmit each bit. **Chipping code** is the term for the bit pattern. (A single radio bit is often called a chip.) Because the chipping code is applied directly to data entering the carrier modulator, the modulator sees a higher bit rate corresponding to the code sequence's chip rate. Every chip carries data bit information. Provided interference noise doesn't affect every chip, information can be recovered, making DSSS less vulnerable to data loss from interference. The downside of DSSS is that spreading sequences tend to be very long, so high bandwidth is needed. The signal strength is low enough, however, that the signal isn't likely to be intercepted because it can barely be detected at all. To potential eavesdroppers, it appears as a slight increase in noise.

In FHSS, the carrier hops frequencies over a wide band according to a sequence defined by the key. The speed of the hops depends on the data rate of the original information. FHSS transmits a short burst on one frequency, hops, transmits another short burst, and so on until the transmission is completed. The key in FHSS is called the **hopping code**, and it determines the sequence and speed of frequency hops. The major advantages of FHSS are immunity to jamming and interference and low probability of interception, making it fairly secure.

Redundancy of the transmitted message is achieved by the potential to retransmit on different carrier frequencies (in FHSS) and through the message bit on each chip of the spreading code (in DSSS).

With DSSS or FHSS, multiple wireless or RF systems can coexist if different keys (spreading sequences) are used. With the demand for higher wireless data rates to support bandwidth-heavy applications, ways of maximizing transmission frequency (spread spectrum) and allocating the transmission to multiple users (multiplexing) are developing.

Access Methods

The following are the major wireless/cellular telephony methods for optimizing use of RF bands and providing apparent simultaneous service to multiple connections:

- In **Code Division Multiple Access (CDMA)**, transmissions are separated by codes. The full available spectrum is divided by using pseudorandom codes. CDMA is a form of spread spectrum signaling because the signal has a higher bandwidth than the data being transmitted. CDMA is also a wideband method. Wideband CDMA in three modes—IMT-DS, IMT-MC, and IMT-TC—will be the dominant radio interface methods for 3G networks.

- In **Frequency Division Multiple Access (FDMA)**, multiple transmissions are separated by frequencies. Communication signals are allocated carrier frequencies within the RF bandwidth to share the band spectrum. FDMA is a narrowband method and has been used for first-generation (1G) analog systems.

- In **Time Division Multiple Access (TDMA)**, multiple transmissions on a frequency are separated by time. Communication signals share the same channel but are assigned time slots (much like a single CPU processes multiple threads). TDMA is a narrowband method and the dominant technique in second-generation (2G) systems.

Figure 12-8 shows the differences in these three methods.

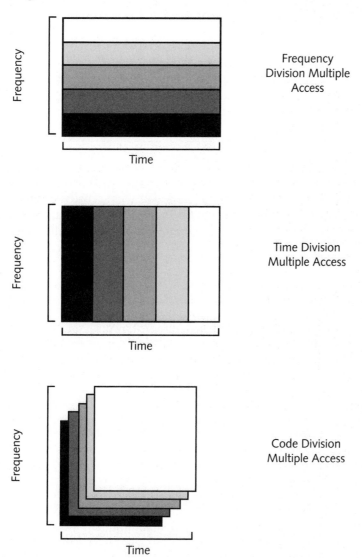

Figure **12-8**   Multiple access methods

Of these three methods, the one used most often in WLANs is CDMA. The original standard defined by QUALCOMM (a company specializing in wireless communication; see *www.qualcomm.com*) was IS-95. IS refers to Interim Standard of the Telecommunication Industry Association (TIA). IS-95 is sometimes called 2G cellular. Several revisions to 2G have emerged; the most common is the 3G standard, IS-2000, which supersedes IS-95.

IS-2000 addressed some requirements specified by the current global standard for 3G wireless communication, IMT-2000. The IMT-2000 standard specifies five radio interfaces, with a sixth, IP-OFDMA, submitted by the IEEE based on its 802.16e standard.

 You can visit the ITU's Web site at *www.itu.int/home/imt.html* for more information on 3G cellular and the IMT-2000 standard and radio interfaces.

WIRELESS NETWORK DESIGN

For any LAN, you must determine what the network needs to do, who will be using it, and what future changes are possible. You must also consider security requirements and operating environment (competition, potential for attacks, critical operations, and so on). When you're designing a WLAN, however, you also need to be familiar with wireless components, topologies, transmission and frequency ranges, and methods of identifying and eliminating interference sources.

Wireless Network Components

Wireless communication devices include cell phones, wireless access points, TV remote controls, radios, satellites, medical diagnostic equipment, and more. In WLANs, however, you spend most of your time dealing with networking components that enable wireless communication to take place or enable integrating wireless with wired networks.

Wireless NICs

Wireless NICs (WNICs) are the unwired counterpart of standard NICs found in networked computers and devices. Instead of placing messages on the wire, however, a WNIC formats messages for transmission without wires. When a WNIC prepares to transmit, it does the following:

1. Changes the computer's internal data from parallel to serial transmission.

2. Divides the data into packets and attaches the sending and receiving computer's address information.

3. Determines where to send the packet (access point, wireless router, and so forth).

4. Transmits the packet.

A variety of WNICs are available for desktop computers, laptops, handheld devices, and more. As with standard NICs, WNICs are often added to devices as an on-board feature. Figure 12-9 shows some common add-on types.

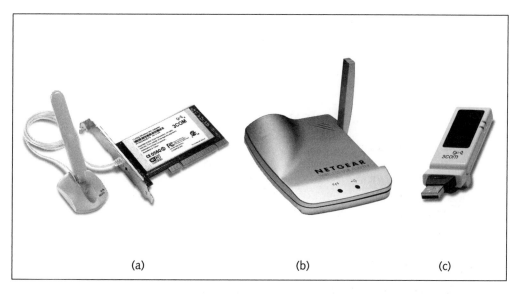

(a)   (b)   (c)

Figure 12-9   Desktop computer WNICs: (a) PCI internal NIC, (b) standalone USB device, and (c) USB key fob

Access Points

12

An **access point (AP)** consists of the antenna and radio transceiver used to transmit to and receive from wireless nodes, an RJ-45 jack for a connection to a wired network, and bridging software to translate communications between wired and wireless devices (see Figure 12-10). APs perform two major functions: acting as the base station for the wireless network segment and serving as the bridge between wired and wireless segments.

TIP

A standard desktop computer can be used as a wireless AP with a standard NIC, a wireless NIC, and special software.

Figure 12-10   A wireless access point

The range of an AP varies depending on the type of AP, the wireless standard, and environmental factors, such as walls, doors, and interference sources. The number of wireless clients an AP can support varies depending on where clients are located and what they are doing. Because the radio signal is being shared, clients performing high-bandwidth activities reduce the total number of clients the AP can support.

Generally, APs mounted on desks are subject to interference from solid objects. The preferred placement is on the ceiling or high on a wall, but electrical power is a problem because outlets aren't usually on or near the ceiling. The solution is **Power over Ethernet (PoE)**, in which power for the AP unit is supplied by the unused wire pairs in standard twisted-pair Ethernet cabling, eliminating the need for electrical wiring.

   PoE is now the IEEE 802.3af standard.

NOTE

Antennas

RF waves are transmitted and received by an **antenna**; this device has one end in the air and the other end fixed to the ground directly or via a grounded device. Antennas are generally made of copper wire or another conductive medium, and radio waves striking the wire during transmission or reception cause electrical pressure (voltage) on the wire. The voltage forces the wire to oscillate at the same frequency as the radio waves striking it or being emitted. So RF waves are broadcast by applying an electrical current to the antenna, causing the antenna's wire to oscillate at the same frequency as the radio signal (see Figure 12-11).

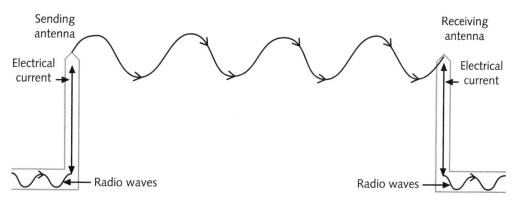

Figure 12-11   Antenna sending and receiving radio signals

EIRP is the measurement of the total power radiated by a wireless system's antenna, but the FCC uses the term **intentional radiator** to describe a device that's not the antenna and is designed to generate radio signals. The FCC regulates the power an intentional radiator can generate.

Antennas have these fundamental characteristics:

- As the frequency gets higher, the wavelength gets smaller, requiring a smaller antenna. Generally, antenna length should be about one fourth the wavelength.

- As antenna gain increases, the coverage area narrows.

Other characteristics of RF antenna transmissions include polarization, wave propagation, multipath distortion, the Fresnel zone, and free space path loss. **Polarization** refers to the plane in which radio waves propagate or the orientation of radio waves as they leave the antenna (usually vertical or horizontal but can be any direction or even circular). Remember that antennas are basically wires with electrical currents applied. The current forces the wire to oscillate, thus generating waves. In basic wave motion, waves follow the plane of their electrical fields, and the electrical field is parallel to the radiating element. An antenna perpendicular to the ground is said to be vertical, and an antenna parallel to the ground is said to be horizontal. Therefore, a vertical antenna radiates a signal horizontally across the ground. Antennas that are polarized differently from each other can't communicate effectively because most of the signal doesn't strike the receiving antenna. For example, a horizontal antenna and a vertical antenna couldn't communicate because the signals radiate toward the tip of the antenna rather than down its length.

Wave propagation is the pattern of wave dispersal as waves travel from sending to receiving antennas. Waves can bounce off the Earth's ionosphere (sky wave propagation) or follow a direct path to the receiving antenna (RF line of sight). Multipath distortion isn't usually a problem with sky wave propagation, but in line of sight (LOS) transmission, objects can interfere with the signal, causing refraction or diffraction. The refracted

12

or diffracted signal still reaches the receiver but might reach it at a different time than the signal propagated directly between antennas. Multipath distorted signals actually reduce the power of a straight-line transmission. One solution to multipath distortion is antenna diversity, which uses multiple antennas, inputs, and receivers.

The **Fresnel zone** (pronounced fra-nel) is a series of ellipsoidal shapes in the wave calculated to determine the signal strength and identify potential obstacles and potential for multipath distortion between sending and receiving antennas (see Figure 12-12). As a general rule, zone 1 of the Fresnel zone should be 60% free of obstacles.

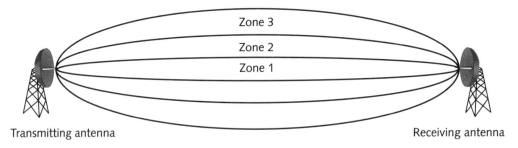

Figure 12-12   The Fresnel zone

As an RF signal travels from the sending antenna, it disperses (spreads out). The more it spreads out, the weaker the signal becomes. This phenomenon is known as **free space path loss**. No action of the antenna can counteract free space path loss. The antenna is only a piece of equipment that radiates or absorbs a signal. Antenna gain can occur in response to a change in the antenna's shape by focusing RF radiation into a tighter beam of energy, measured by beam width in horizontal and vertical degrees. For example, focusing a 360-degree beam into a directed 30-degree beam causes the signal to travel much farther without requiring additional power.

There are three basic types of antennas: omnidirectional (also known as dipole), semidirectional, and highly directional. Table 12-4 lists their characteristics.

Table 12-4   Basic antenna types

Type of antenna	Radiation direction	WLAN installation
Omnidirectional	All directions equally	Most common for a WLAN AP in one building
Semidirectional	Focuses energy in one direction	Used for short- or medium-range remote wireless bridges, such as a point-to-point link between neighboring buildings
Highly directional	Tightly focuses signal beam in one direction	Long-distance, point-to-point links, as in a wireless link between buildings separated by up to 25 miles; not commonly used for WLANs

ACTIVITY

Activity 12-4: Researching Antenna Types

Time Required: 30 minutes

Objective: Research types of radio antennas.

Description: In this activity, you use the Internet to research types of radio antennas, identify what they look like, and see what applications they're used for.

1. Start your Web browser and go to a search engine.

2. Find at least two examples each of omnidirectional, semidirectional, and highly directional antennas.

3. Draw (or print) a picture of each example, and note the maximum transmission distance.

4. For each example, write down (on a separate piece of paper) a situation in which it might be used and a situation that might create a need to change the antenna. (*Hint:* What would happen if a high-rise were built in the path between sender and receiver?)

Remote Wireless Bridges

A remote wireless bridge connects wired and/or wireless network segments, much as an AP or regular bridge does, with two major exceptions. First, a remote wireless bridge transmits at higher power than an AP, which increases its range. Second, instead of the omnidirectional transmission used by APs, a remote wireless bridge uses a directional antenna to focus transmissions in one direction. Remote wireless bridges can be used to connect wireless segments in a point-to-point configuration, as shown in Figure 12-13. Remote wireless bridges can also be used in a point-to-multipoint configuration, connecting network segments as shown in Figure 12-14.

12

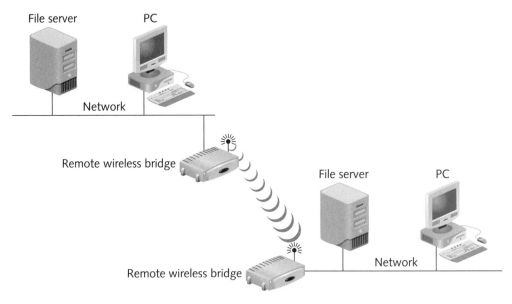

Figure 12-13 Point-to-point bridging

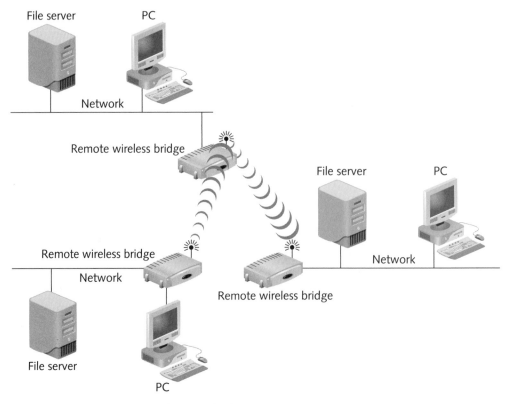

Figure 12-14 Point-to-multipoint bridging

A remote wireless bridge operates in four modes:

- *Access point mode*—The bridge functions as a standard AP and doesn't communicate with other remote wireless bridges.

- *Root mode*—The bridge, called the root bridge, can communicate only with other bridges that aren't in root mode. It can't communicate with other root bridges or wireless clients.

- *Nonroot mode*—The bridge can communicate only with root bridges. Some manufacturers make remote wireless bridges that can also be configured as APs, enabling them to communicate with wireless clients and the root bridge simultaneously.

- *Repeater mode*—The bridge extends the range, as a hub or repeater does in a wired network. Repeater bridges can be used to extend the distance between network segments and can be positioned between other bridges.

Wireless Gateways

A wireless gateway combines management and security into a single appliance and can perform the following functions:

- Authentication

- Encryption

- Intrusion detection

- Malicious program protection

- Bandwidth management

- Centralized network management

WLAN Configurations

IEEE Wireless LAN standards define three basic WLAN configurations: Basic Service Set, Extended Service Set, and Independent Basic Service Set. In a **Basic Service Set (BSS)**, a group of wireless devices is served by a single AP. A BSS is sometimes called infrastructure mode. A BSS must be assigned a unique identifier known as the **service set identifier (SSID)**, which is the network (domain) name for the BSS. The geographical coverage for the BSS is called the **Basic Service Area (BSA)**, and the actual coverage varies, depending on environmental factors, types of equipment, and number of users. Some devices are advertised as having a range up to 375 feet from the AP, but in reality, their range is usually much shorter. Figure 12-15 shows a BSS configuration.

12

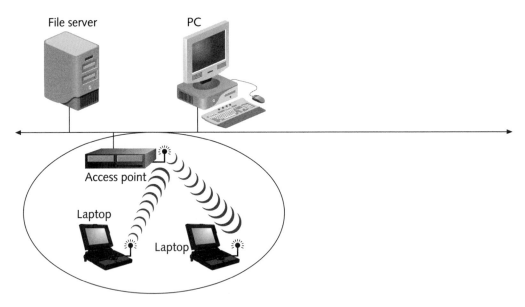

Figure 12-15   A BSS configuration

For an **Extended Service Set (ESS)**, BSS networks are connected through a common distribution system, and APs are strategically placed so that users can move through a wider BSA. Although APs are often configured with different channels to prevent co-channel interference, the range of channels (the WLAN's frequency range) is part of the ESS, and, like a BSS, the entire network has a unique SSID.

In an ESS (see Figure 12-16), APs are set up to provide some overlap. The coverage areas are called cells, and the WLAN is set up like a cell phone system. Movement between AP coverage areas (cells) is called **roaming**. When mobile users move into a new coverage area, their devices select the AP with the strongest signal strength. After the AP accepts the roaming device, that device tunes to the AP's channel but continues to survey radio frequencies at regular intervals to see whether another AP can provide better service (a stronger signal).

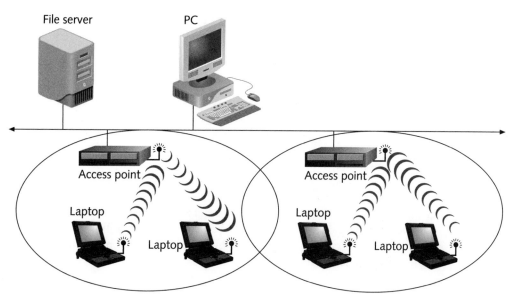

Figure 12-16   An ESS configuration

Finally, an **Independent Basic Service Set (IBSS)** is a wireless network that doesn't use an AP. Instead, wireless devices communicate directly with one another, as computers in a peer-to-peer network do. In wireless, IBSS is also known as ad-hoc mode.

Now that you understand the basics of how radio waves work and how they are used to form wireless networks, you can move on to the specifics of wireless security in the next chapter.

12

CHAPTER SUMMARY

- Wireless transmissions use electromagnetic (EM) radiation, specifically radio frequency (RF) waves or infrared (IR) radiation, to communicate instead of sending electrical signals over physical cabling. For wireless networks, RF is used most commonly. Infrared is mainly used for communication with peripheral devices,

- EM radiation travels in waves. A wave's maximum departure from the undisturbed state is the amplitude. Frequency is the number of times an event occurs in a specified period, and wavelength is the distance between repeating units (usually the midpoint) of the wave.

- Wireless communication has several standards. The one used most often for WLANs in the United States is IEEE 802.11 Wireless Ethernet standards. The most common WLAN standards for devices in the United States are 802.11b, 802.11a, and 802.11g.

- ❏ RF is subject to strict regulations by the FCC because of the potential for interference with radio, TV, maritime, emergency services, and other critical communications.

- ❏ The RF spectrum is divided into bands based on frequency. Most WLANs use frequencies in the 2.4 GHz and 5 GHz bands.

- ❏ The speed and transmission range of a wireless network varies depending on the standard, equipment, environmental factors, number of users, location of clients, and purpose.

- ❏ RF is highly susceptible to interference from solar activity, electrical storms, manmade radiation, and other RF emissions. Cross-channel interference, multipath distortion, and fading are common types of interference.

- ❏ RF signal behavior is characterized by whether a factor contributes to a gain or loss of power. RF power is measured on a linear scale using milliwatts (mW) or on a relative scale using decibels (dB). dBm is the reference point that relates the decibel scale to the milliwatt scale.

- ❏ RF transmits a carrier signal, which can be changed via modulation to allow RF radiation to carry information. A carrier signal's amplitude, frequency, or relative starting point can be changed.

- ❏ RF data can be analog or digital. Analog modulation methods are amplitude modulation, frequency modulation, and phase modulation. Digital modulation methods include amplitude shift keying, frequency shift keying, phase shift keying, and frequency division multiplexing.

- ❏ Spread spectrum spreads a narrowband signal over a broader portion of the RF band. The major methods are direct sequence spread spectrum, frequency hopping spread spectrum, and orthogonal frequency division multiplexing.

- ❏ The major wireless/cellular telephony methods for optimizing use of RF bands and providing simultaneous service to multiple connections are Code Division Multiple Access (CDMA), Frequency Division Multiple Access (FDMA), and Time Division Multiple Access (TDMA).

- ❏ Wireless network components include wireless NICs, access points, antennas, remote wireless bridges, and wireless gateways.

- ❏ Antennas transmit and receive radio waves and can be omnidirectional, semidirectional, and highly directional.

- ❏ A remote wireless bridge operates in four modes: access point, root, nonroot, and repeater. Wireless gateways act as centralized management and security appliances and can perform authentication, encryption, intrusion detection, malicious program protection, bandwidth management, and centralized network management.

- ❏ IEEE 802.11 standards define three WLAN configurations: Basic Service Set (BSS), Extended Service Set (ESS), and Independent Basic Service Set (IBSS).

KEY TERMS

absorption — A type of loss in which certain materials absorb the RF signal.

access point (AP) — A wireless device that acts as the base station for a wireless network segment and serves as the bridge between wired and wireless segments.

amplitude — Maximum departure of a wave from its undisturbed state; the height of the carrier wave.

amplitude modulation (AM) — An analog modulation method in which the height of the carrier wave is changed.

amplitude shift keying (ASK) — A binary modulation technique similar to AM that changes the height of the carrier wave. With ASK, instead of both the 1 and 0 bits having carrier signals, the 1 bit has positive voltage, and the 0 bit has zero voltage.

analog RF signal — A continuous RF wave that oscillates between positive and negative voltage.

antenna — A device used to transmit or receive radio waves. An antenna usually has one end in the air and the other end fixed to the ground directly or via a grounded device. Antennas are generally made of copper wire or other conductive material.

Basic Service Area (BSA) — The geographical area of coverage for a WLAN.

Basic Service Set (BSS) — An IEEE-defined WLAN configuration in which a group of wireless devices is served by a single AP.

carrier signal — The signal on which a radio transmission is sent.

chipping code — The bit pattern used in direct sequence spread spectrum. *See also* direct sequence spread spectrum (DSSS).

co-channel interference — Interference from two or more wireless access points transmitting with the same frequency.

Code Division Multiple Access (CDMA) — A form of spread spectrum signaling in which sender and receiver share a common code to differentiate their communications from other transmissions.

diffraction — Similar to refraction, except the signal bends around objects in its path, usually objects with a rough surface. *See also* refraction.

diffused IR transmission — An infrared transmission that relies on reflected light rather than a line-of-sight connection between the IR emitter and detector.

digital RF signals — RF signals that oscillate between positive and negative voltage but are broken into discrete segments with many starts and stops in the data stream, instead of a constant stream, as in analog transmissions.

directed IR transmission — A form of IR transmission that requires the emitter and the detector to be pointed directly at one another.

direct sequence spread spectrum (DSSS) — A wireless modulation technique that uses an expanded redundant code to transmit each data bit. The spreading code (key) is the chip sequence used to represent message bits, and the key is applied at the data level.

12

electromagnetic (EM) radiation — Electromagnetic energy traveling as a self-propagating wave and spreading out as it moves.

EM spectrum — All forms of EM radiation collectively. EM radiation forms are (from highest energy to lowest) gamma rays, x-rays, ultraviolet light, infrared light, visible light, microwaves, and radio waves.

Equivalent Isotropically Radiated Power (EIRP) — The power radiated out by a wireless system's antenna, including not only the intended transmission power, but also unintended gain.

Extended Service Set (ESS) — An IEEE-defined WLAN configuration in which multiple BSS networks are connected through a common distribution system.

fading — A form of interference/power loss where the signal is reflected or refracted by the atmosphere, ground, or other obstacles, and the reflected path interferes with the direct path.

Federal Communications Commission (FCC) — The primary regulatory agency in the United States for wireless communication.

free space path loss — The loss of signal strength resulting from the dispersion of the signal over distance.

frequency — The number of times an event occurs in a specified time period; the rate at which an electrical current alternates, creating different radio transmissions.

Frequency Division Multiple Access (FDMA) — An access method in which multiple transmissions are separated by frequencies for each communication.

frequency division multiplexing (FDM) — An RF signaling method that enables multiple users to share a communication channel. Base signals are modulated on different carrier waves and combined to form a composite signal.

frequency hopping spread spectrum (FHSS) — A modulation technique in which the range of frequencies used for transmission changes during the transmission. The time spent on a particular frequency is called the dwell time.

frequency modulation (FM) — An analog modulation technique that changes the number of waves used to represent one cycle, so the number of waves representing a 1 bit is higher than the number of waves representing a 0 bit.

frequency shift keying (FSK) — A binary modulation technique that changes the frequency of the carrier signal.

Fresnel zone — An area in which the RF signal strength can be calculated to determine the signal strength, identify potential obstacles, and determine the potential for multipath distortion between sending and receiving antennas.

gain — The positive difference in amplitude between signals.

hopping code — The sequence of changing frequencies in FHSS that determines the sequence and speed of frequency hops.

IEEE 802.11 Wireless Ethernet standards — A series of standards specifying transmission speeds, ranges, and other aspects of wireless networks.

Independent Basic Service Set (IBSS) — A wireless network that doesn't use an AP; also known as ad-hoc mode.

infrared (IR) radiation — A type of radiation with a shorter wavelength than radio waves but a longer wavelength than visible light.

infrared transmissions — IR uses infrared light pulses. Infrared transmissions require an emitter and a detector. The emitter is usually a laser diode or LED. The detector is sometimes combined with the emitter and does just what its name implies: It detects IR transmissions and generates the corresponding electrical current for wired communication.

intentional radiator — A device that's not the antenna and is designed to generate radio signals.

loss — The negative difference in amplitude between signals.

modulation — The process of varying the wave form to transmit a signal, such as modulating between on and off to create 1s and 0s.

multipath — A signal has more than one path from the transmitter to the receiver.

narrowband — An RF transmission on one frequency or a very small frequency range.

orthogonal frequency division multiplexing (OFDM) — A modulation technique that breaks a high-speed signal into smaller pieces and sends it in parallel across many lower-speed channels.

phase modulation (PM) — An analog modulation technique that changes the cycle's relative starting point when the bit being transmitted changes from 1 to 0.

phase shift keying (PSK) — A binary modulation technique that starts and stops the signal to represent a binary digit.

polarization — The plane on which radio waves propagate; the orientation of the radio waves as they leave the antenna, usually vertical or horizontal.

Power over Ethernet (PoE) — A technology that sends power for the AP unit over unused wire pairs in standard twisted-pair Ethernet cabling.

radio frequency (RF) waves — A type of EM radiation used most commonly for wireless networks.

reflection — A type of loss in which the RF wave bounces off certain materials.

refraction — Signals traveling through different air masses can be bent rather than traveling in a straight line. The signal changes in response to atmospheric conditions.

roaming — A wireless device moving between access points, or cells, without losing transmit/receive capabilities. Cells are interconnected so that as the wireless device moves between cells, the device/cell negotiates a new connection, depending on signal strength.

scattering — A type of loss in which small objects, such as raindrops, dust, or foliage, scatter the signal.

service set identifier (SSID) — A unique identifier up to 32 characters that serves as the wireless network name.

spread spectrum — An alternative to narrowband transmissions that spreads a narrow signal over a broader portion of the radio band.

12

Time Division Multiple Access (TDMA) — An access method that uses different time slots to allow devices to share a frequency channel.

voltage standing wave ratio (VSWR) — A type of loss caused by differences in the equipment itself. For example, if one part of the equipment has a different impedance than others, the signal can be reflected back within the device, and the reflected power can cause the device to burn out.

wave — A means of transporting energy from one place to another without physical movement of material.

wave propagation — The pattern of wave dispersal as waves travel from sending to receiving antennas.

wavelength — The distance between two successive amplitude peaks.

wireless networking — Any exchange of data between computers and other devices that uses RF transmission methods instead of traditional wired cables.

REVIEW QUESTIONS

1. In which of the following situations would a wireless network be an effective alternative?
   a. a business that occupies temporary space
   b. a network with employees who travel
   c. an older building with no existing wiring
   d. all of the above

2. Wireless communication emits which types of EM radiation? (Choose all that apply.)
   a. gamma rays
   b. infrared radiation
   c. ultraviolet light
   d. radio frequency waves

3. The maximum departure of a wave from its undisturbed state is called which of the following?
   a. frequency
   b. wavelength
   c. amplitude
   d. hertz

4. All types of electromagnetic radiation are collectively called which of the following?

   a. EM spectrum

   b. EM field

   c. light spectrum

   d. visible light spectrum

5. Frequency is which of the following?

   a. distance between repeating units of a wave

   b. number of times an event occurs in a specified period

   c. method of transporting energy without physical movement of material

   d. radiation spreading out as it moves

6. The distance between midpoints of a wave is called which of the following?

   a. frequency

   b. wavelength

   c. amplitude

   d. hertz

7. What frequency range does Bluetooth use?

   a. 5 GHz

   b. 2 to 11 GHz

   c. 5.15 to 5.35 GHz

   d. 2.4 GHz

8. What type of infrared transmission relies on reflected light?

9. Infrared wireless is extremely fast, can travel long distances, and is not susceptible to interference. True or False?

10. Which of the following is a common type of signal loss? (Choose all that apply.)

    a. deletion

    b. diffraction

    c. deflection

    d. scattering

11. Refraction occurs when the RF signal is scattered by small objects, such as raindrops or foliage. True or False?

12. RF power is measured on a relative scale by which of the following?

    a. milliwatts

    b. decibels

    c. watts

    d. 10s and 3s rules of RF math

12

13. The reference point that relates relative and linear RF power measurement scales is dBm, which specifies that _____ mW is equal to _____ dBm.

   a. 1, 1

   b. 0, 0

   c. 0, 1

   d. 1, 0

14. Why is digital modulation superior to analog modulation?

15. Which of the following is the power radiated by a wireless system's antenna, including the intended power and any gain?

   a. Equivalent Isomeric Radiant Power (EIRP)

   b. Equivalent Isotropically Radiated Power (EIRP)

   c. Voltage Standing Wave Ratio (VSWR)

   d. Transmitter Power Output (TPO)

16. Which of the following multiple access methods separates transmissions by pseudorandom codes?

   a. OFDMA

   b. TDMA

   c. FDMA

   d. CDMA

17. How does a semidirectional antenna transmit its signal?

   a. in all directions equally

   b. in opposite directions

   c. in one general direction

   d. in a tight beam in one exact direction

18. Briefly describe the four modes in which a remote wireless bridge can operate.

HANDS-ON PROJECTS

HANDS-ON PROJECTS

Hands-On Project 12-1: Researching the FCC

Time Required: 30 minutes

Objective: Explore the FCC Web site to learn more about wireless communication.

Description: In this project, you explore the FCC Web site to learn some basics about frequencies commonly used for wireless. You also use the FCC license search tool to see what types of wireless communication entities operate in your area. You need a workstation with Internet access for this activity.

1. Start your Web browser and go to **http://wireless.fcc.gov/services/ index.htm?job=wtb_services_home**.

2. In the list of wireless services, click the **Advanced Wireless Services (AWS) Spectrum** link. Examine the page and explore the links.

3. What services are included in this spectrum?

   _____

   _____

4. On the AWS Spectrum home page, click **Industry Data**.

5. Click **ULS License and Application Search** and then click **License Search**. Conduct some searches on local radio, TV, or cellular service providers. Try entering just your state and county and then searching for all frequencies. How many licensees did you find?

   _____

6. What types of licensees operate in your area? How could interference cause problems for them? (Use an additional sheet of paper, if needed.)

   _____

   _____

   _____

   _____

   _____

HANDS-ON PROJECTS

12

Hands-On Project 12-2: Installing NetStumbler

Time Required: 15 minutes

Objective: Download and install a freeware program for detecting wireless networks.

Description: In this project, you install NetStumbler, a freeware wireless networking utility for Windows. You use this program in Chapter 13 if you have wireless equipment available. If you don't have a WNIC and wireless AP, this project at least familiarizes you with the interface and some features of the program.

1. Start your Web browser and go to **www.netstumbler.com**.

2. On the NetStumbler page, click **Downloads**.

3. Click **NetStumbler x.x.x Installer** (substituting the latest version for x.x.x, which is 0.4.0 at the time of this writing).

4. When the File Download box opens, click **Save**.

5. Select your desktop as the file target location. After the file has been downloaded, click **Run** in the Download complete dialog box. If the Security Warning dialog box opens, click **Run** again.

6. Follow the prompts to install the program with default configurations. After the installation is finished, the NetStumbler Help dialog box opens automatically. Click **Usage and Configuration Examples** and read the information. How could you use this program to design a wireless LAN?

_____

_____

_____

7. Close the Help dialog box, and start NetStumbler by clicking **Start**, pointing to **All Programs**, and clicking **Network Stumbler**.

8. Examine the interface, shown in Figure 12-17, and note the categories of information that are gathered:

_____

_____

_____

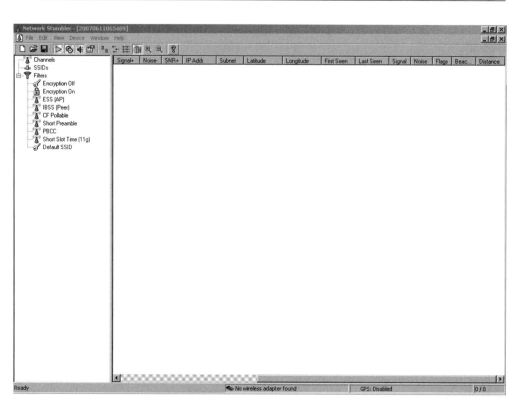

Figure 12-17   The NetStumbler interface

9. Exit NetStumbler, and close any open windows.

Hands-On Project 12-3: Researching Access Points

Time Required: 30 minutes

Objective: Research the Internet to identify several wireless access points.

Description: In this project, you research wireless access points from different vendors. You determine which APs are suitable for home use and which are for businesses. You also examine at least one enterprise-class access point.

1. Start Microsoft Word (or another word-processing program), and create a table with four columns and five rows. Label the columns Access Point, Features, Cost, and Recommended Use.

2. Start your Web browser and search for wireless access points.

3. Visit vendor Web sites to gather information on at least five APs, including one enterprise-class AP. Enter the information in the table you have created.

4. When you're done, turn your table in to your instructor.

CASE PROJECTS

Case Project 12-1: Planning Mobile Access

Green Globe's network design is almost complete. One final design consideration is the integration of mobile devices, including PDAs, cell phones, laptops, and specialized scientific instruments that interface with a custom application. Security for wireless communication must be tight but allow access for temporary employees. You must also plan for employees at the home office to be mobile.

Using the work you have completed in previous chapters, begin to develop a plan that addresses how to meet Green Globe's mobility needs. At a minimum, answer the following questions:

- How many access points will likely be needed in the facility? What other equipment is needed?

- What network equipment might be needed to provide access for mobile employees?

- Are there any sources of interference within range? How can it be addressed?

Keep in mind that Chapter 13 covers wireless security, so you might be modifying your plan based on information in that chapter. You won't submit your project for this chapter, unless instructed to do so. It's your preliminary assessment based on what you've learned in this chapter.

As the course draws to a close, continue working on your final submission, paying attention to spelling, grammar, and professional appearance. Make sure your citations are accurate and complete and your documents are formatted according to your school's writing guidelines.

12

13

SECURING WIRELESS NETWORKS

> **After reading this chapter and completing the exercises, you will be able to:**
> ♦ Explain basic concepts in wireless security
> ♦ Describe security solutions for wireless networking

This chapter introduces you to the fundamentals of wireless security. You learn about the threats wireless networks face and solutions for defending against them. Passive attacks, active attacks, rogue devices, and key management concerns are explained so you can identify major weaknesses in wireless network design and determine possible solutions.

In most organizations, the most critical resource, and the biggest threat to security, is the people using the systems. Therefore, comprehensive security policies and security awareness training programs are crucial to ensure the secure use of mobile devices. Countermeasures to security threats also include physically securing devices, using strong authentication and key management, and using strong encryption to protect data stored on portable devices or transmitted wirelessly.

UNDERSTANDING WIRELESS NETWORK SECURITY FUNDAMENTALS

Although wireless networking offers many advantages, the predominant challenge has always been security. From the beginning of wireless networks, IT professionals have struggled with comprehensive, efficient, and effective security solutions. The original IEEE 802.11 standard didn't incorporate security adequately, so vendors, developers, and the IEEE have spent several years coming up with solutions to flaws in the early 802.11 standards. Wireless networks continue to suffer from the stigma of not being secure, however, so many businesses still refuse to use them. They consider wireless networks dangerous, with no effective alternatives for securing them. That's not the case, as you learn in this chapter.

The newest implementation of the IEEE 802.11 standard, 802.11i, does provide effective security mechanisms, but most current deployments use 802.11b or 802.11g. Upgrading to 802.11i-compliant hardware and configurations can be complicated and costly for many companies. You learn more about 802.11i later in this chapter.

Security Concerns

Wireless networks face different threats than wired networks do. Wireless networks don't have physical cabling that can be secured, so packets literally travel the airwaves and are vulnerable between transmitter and receiver. If no encryption is used, everything, including passwords and confidential data, is sent in cleartext.

This section explains the evolution of wireless security concerns. Wireless communication relies heavily on the Media Access Control (MAC) sublayer of the Data Link layer in the OSI model. MAC frames and MAC addresses play an important role in wireless communication, but they also create vulnerabilities.

Then you learn about passive and active scanning of wireless networks. Scanning for wireless signals is a valid activity, allowing wireless stations to find and connect to available networks, but these methods are also used to find networks to attack.

The basic authentication methods in IEEE 802.11 networks also caused security problems, and you learn about the inherent vulnerabilities of IEEE 802.11's authentication mechanisms. Then you examine wireless networks attacks and major security vulnerabilities, such as the challenge of managing keys and the dangers of using default settings.

Next, you examine common methods for securing wireless networks. Wi-Fi Protected Access (WPA), WPA2, and 802.1x are some of the robust solutions for securing modern wireless networks and are discussed later in this chapter.

In wireless networks, a wireless device is called a "station," which is similar to the term "node" in wired networks.

IEEE 802.11 Media Access Control: Frames

The MAC sublayer of the OSI model performs many critical functions in a wireless network, which can be classified as the following:

- Discovering wireless access points, channels, and signal strengths

- Joining the wireless network, including authentication and association to the access point

- Transmitting data

- Maintaining the connection

Each access point (AP) has a 0- to 32-byte service set identifier (SSID), which is essentially its network name. SSIDs separate airwaves into segments so that wireless networks in the same physical area can operate independently of one another. SSIDs can also be mapped to virtual LANs, so some APs support multiple SSIDs.

When wireless stations communicate, they use MAC frames to locate wireless networks, establish and maintain the connection, and transmit data. All MAC frames contain a control field that identifies the 802.11 protocol version, frame types, and codes that specify wireless configurations. Frames also contain MAC source and destination addresses, a frame sequence number, and a frame check sequence (FCS) for error detection.

In the 802.11 standard, there are three types of MAC frames: management frames, control frames, and data frames. **Management frames** establish and maintain communications. They are always sent in cleartext, and many contain SSIDs. Even link encryption, such as Wired Equivalent Privacy (WEP), doesn't encrypt management frames. The security problem is that anyone intercepting a management frame can discover the SSID and then has part of the information needed to access that network. Figure 13-1 shows the structure of a management frame.

13

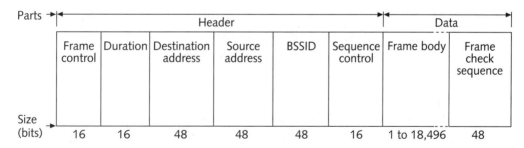

Parts

	Header						Data	
Frame control	Duration	Destination address	Source address	BSSID	Sequence control	Frame body	Frame check sequence
16	16	48	48	48	16	1 to 18,496	48

Size (bits)

Figure 13-1   An IEEE 802.11 management frame

The following list explains the fields in a management frame:

- *Frame control*—Information such as the IEEE standard version and whether encryption is used

- *Duration*—The amount of time in microseconds needed for transmission

- *Destination and source address*—Source and destination addresses of sending and receiving stations

- *BSSID*—Basic Service Set identifier (the network name), a variation of SSID

- *Sequence control*—The packet's sequence number and fragment number

- *Frame body*—The data payload

- *Frame check sequence*—Error detection

Table 13-1 describes common types of management frames.

Table 13-1   Management frame types

Frame type	Purpose
Association request	Allows an AP to allocate resources for a wireless station
Association response	Sent by the AP in response to an association request frame; indicates whether the request is accepted or rejected
Reassociation request	Sent to the new AP when a wireless station roams into a different AP coverage area (also called a "cell")
Reassociation response	Sent by the AP in response to a reassociation request frame; indicates whether the request is accepted or rejected
Probe request	Sent by a station when it needs to get information from another station
Probe response	Sent by a station in response to a probe request frame; indicates capabilities, supported data rates, and so on
Disassociation	Sent by a station to another station if the sender wants to terminate the connection
Authentication	Sent by the AP to determine whether to allow a wireless station to enter the network
Deauthentication	Sent by a station to another station if the sender wants to terminate the connection
Beacon	Sent by an AP to any listening stations to advertise services or information available on the wireless network; contain SSIDs, capabilities, supported rates, and other information about the AP and wireless network

Reassociation requests and responses might seem confusing because the station doesn't authenticate again. A station can be authenticated on multiple APs but associated with only one at a time. If a station leaves the network on which it's currently authenticated, it must authenticate to the new network. However, moving to a new coverage area doesn't necessarily mean the station has changed networks; it simply means it has left one AP's coverage area and moved into another.

Control frames help deliver data frames between stations and control access to the medium. Figure 13-2 shows a typical control frame. There are six types of control frames; the following list explains the four most common:

- *RTS*—A **request to send (RTS)** frame is the first step of the two-way handshake before sending a data frame. A station using the RTS/CTS mechanism sends an RTS frame when it wants to transmit data.

- *CTS*—In response to an RTS frame, a **clear to send (CTS)** frame gives a station clearance to send. It contains a time value that keeps all other stations from transmitting long enough to give the sending station time to transmit.

- *ACK*—After receiving a data frame, the receiving station performs error checking. If no error is found, it sends an **acknowledgement (ACK)** frame; if no ACK frame is received, the sending station retransmits the frame.

- *PS-Poll*—A **power-save poll (PS-Poll)** frame is used when a station has awakened from power-save mode and sees that an AP has frames buffered for it. The station sends this frame to let the AP know it can transmit the buffered frames.

Stations and APs have a configuration parameter called the RTS threshold that indicates whether the RTS/CTS process is used before transmitting. If a station is configured to use RTS/CTS frames, it transmits an RTS frame requesting access to the medium. After a CTS frame is received in response, the station knows it can transmit safely. All stations listening hear the exchange and hold transmissions long enough for data to be transmitted and an ACK frame indicating success to be received. This process is not foolproof, however. A station that isn't listening or isn't connected to hear the exchange could still transmit during the reserved time.

13

You can review IEEE 802.11 standards at *http://grouper.ieee.org/groups/ 802/11/*.

TIP

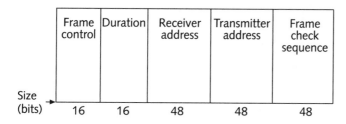

Frame control	Duration	Receiver address	Transmitter address	Frame check sequence
16	16	48	48	48

Size (bits)

Figure 13-2   An IEEE 802.11 control frame

The following list explains the fields in a control frame:

- *Frame control*—Information such as the protocol version, frame type, and whether encryption is used

- *Duration*—The amount of time in microseconds needed for transmission

- *Receiver address*—MAC address of the receiving station

- *Transmitter address*— MAC address of the transmitting station

- *Frame check sequence*—Error detection

Data frames carry the TCP/IP datagram, and the payload is encrypted (see Figure 13-3). Data from higher-layer applications, such as printer control data or Web pages, is carried in the data frame body. Data frame fields labeled Address 1, Address 2, Address 3, and Address 4 carry the BSSID, source MAC address, destination MAC address, and address of the transmitter or receiver, respectively.

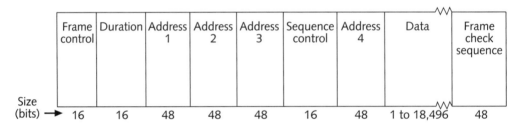

Figure 13-3 An IEEE 802.11 data frame

The following list explains the fields in a data frame:

- *Frame control*—Information such as the IEEE standard version and whether encryption is used

- *Duration*—The amount of time in microseconds needed for transmission

- *Destination and source address*—Source and destination addresses of sending and receiving stations

- *BSSID*—Basic Service Set identifier (the network name), a variation of SSID

- *Sequence control*—The packet's sequence number and fragment number

- *Frame body*—The data payload (information from higher OSI layers)

- *Frame check sequence*—Error detection

Unlike MAC addresses and fully qualified domain names (FQDNs), SSIDs aren't registered, so two wireless networks could use the same SSID. A station could also have a null SSID that allows it to match all SSIDs. If a beacon frame contains a null SSID, attackers just have to capture frames containing the correct SSID. Most current APs are capable of having beaconing turned off. This measure isn't that effective, however, as attackers can wait for management or control frames containing the information they want or spoof management frames and sniff the responses to find information. (Sniffing is capturing network traffic during transmission.)

In addition, several management frames contain the network's SSID, and management frames are always transmitted in cleartext, even when WEP is used. A passive scan can reveal SSIDs to attackers easily, and some APs send beacon frames as often as several times a second, so attackers don't have to wait long to intercept frames containing SSIDs.

Scanning and Attacks

When a wireless station wants to connect to a wireless network, it begins listening on each available channel for an AP's beacon frame broadcast. This listening process is called passive or active scanning.

In **passive scanning**, a wireless NIC (WNIC) listens to each channel for a few packets, and then moves to another channel. Because the station listens without transmitting, its presence isn't usually revealed. **Radio frequency (RF) monitor mode** allows passive scanning, although many WNICs have this capability disabled by default in their firmware. In RF monitor mode, the WNIC's equivalent of promiscuous mode in NICs, a WNIC can capture packets without authenticating or associating with an AP or ad hoc (peer to peer) wireless network. For this reason, passive scanning is difficult or impossible to detect.

A **passive attack** uses passive scanning to gather information about a wireless network for later use, such as SSIDs, MAC addresses, passwords, and usernames. Wireless networks are particularly vulnerable to passive attacks, such as sniffing and network reconnaissance. Because transmissions in wireless networks travel over airwaves, attackers simply need to be within range of an unsecured network to intercept packets and then analyze them to get more information for further attacks.

In **active scanning**, the station sends a probe request frame out on each available channel and waits for a probe response frame from available APs. Even after a wireless station is associated with a wireless network, it continues to scan for beacon frames. If a station is disconnected from the network, it can reconnect more quickly if it already has the information needed to connect to another AP or station. In general, stations select the strongest signal, unless they're configured to connect to a specific AP or other criteria are set. Occasionally, a station connects to the AP it receives a signal from first.

In **active attacks**, attackers use several techniques to probe wireless networks in an attempt to gather information. Unlike passive attacks, most active attacks can be detected by network security measures, although some bypass security measures and APs, sending traffic directly to the victim station. Table 13-2 lists some common active attacks; notice that some are types of denial-of-service (DoS) attacks.

13

TIP

Many free and easy-to-use tools that automate attacks are available. Some common ones are AirCrack, AirSnort, CoWPAtty WPA Cracker, and WepAttack. For more information, visit *www.wardrive.net/wardriving/tools*. However, be careful when you're testing wardriving software! You could connect to a wireless network inadvertently. If you cause harm, you could face charges, whether your actions were intentional or not.

Table 13-2   Common active attacks

Attack	Method
Jamming (DoS attack)	The attacker floods airwaves with noise to weaken the RF signal and cause the wireless network to stop functioning.
Association flood (DoS attack)	The attacker authenticates several fake stations to send a flood of spoofed association requests, which overflow an AP's association request table. An AP can have up to 2007 concurrent associations before the association request table overflows and refuses further associations.
Forged disassociation (DoS attack)	The attacker sends a forged disassociation frame containing the spoofed source MAC address of an AP. The target station attempts to reassociate, and the attacker continues to send disassociation frames to prevent reassociation or replies with a reassociation response.
Forged deauthentication	The attacker monitors transmissions to identify target stations. When a data or association response frame is captured, the attacker sends a spoofed deauthentication frame containing the AP's MAC address. To prevent reconnection, the attacker continues to send deauthentication frames for the duration of the attack.
MAC address spoofing	The attacker inserts spoofed values in a frame's sender MAC address field.
Session hijacking	The attacker causes valid users to lose their connections by sending a forged deauthentication or disassociation frame to their stations, for example. The attacker then assumes their identities and privileges by sending their stations' MAC addresses to the AP. The attacker disables users' systems by using a DoS or buffer overflow attack so that their stations can't reconnect.
Brute force	The attacker uses a program that attempts every possible key combination by changing one character at a time systematically; this attack is an attempt to decrypt a message to discover the default key.
Dictionary	In an attempt to determine passphrases, the attacker encodes dictionary words in the same way the passphrase was encoded. When the encoding matches, the attacker has found the passphrase.

Some of these attacks take advantage of Carrier Sense Multiple Access/Collision Avoidance (CSMA/CA) being used as a wireless access method. With CSMA/CA, stations listen before transmitting. If traffic is already in transmission, stations wait until airwaves are clear before transmitting. In wireless DoS attacks, simply flooding airwaves with transmissions prevents legitimate stations from transmitting.

Ethernet networks use the CSMA/CD access method, with stations listening for collisions and waiting a random amount of time before transmitting when they detect a collision.

NOTE

Activity 13-1: Analyzing a Wireless Frame

ACTIVITY

Time Required: 15 minutes

Objective: Analyze an 802.11 frame.

Description: In this activity, you examine a sample wireless frame header as it's usually displayed in standard packet-capturing tools, such as Wireshark. Note the ways an 802.11 packet can be identified. Write down your answers to questions on a paper you can turn in to your instructor.

1. Examine the following frame header details:

```
Type/Subtype: Data (32)
Frame Control: 0x4908 (Normal)
Version: 0
Type: Data frame (2)
Subtype: 0
Flags: 0x49
    DS status: Frame is entering DS (To DS:1 From DS:0)
(0x01)
    .... .0.. = More Fragments: This is the last
fragment
    .... 1... = Retry: Frame is being retransmitted
    ...0 .... = PWR MGT: STA will stay up
    ..0. .... = More Data: No data buffered
    .1.. .... = WEP flag: WEP is disabled
    0... .... = Order flag: Not strictly ordered
Duration: 015
BSS Id: ABC_12:34:56 (00:01:02:D0:55:44)
Source address: DEF_78:91:10 (08:01:4b:98:76:54)
Destination address: GHI_12:13:14 (00:4e:00:d5:c3:00)
Fragment number: 0
Sequence number: 1985
TKIP/CCMP parameters
    TKIP Ext. Initialization Vector: 0x000000000013
    Key: 0
```

2. List specific details that identify this packet as a wireless frame.

3. What aspects of this frame could be useful to attackers?

4. When you have finished, turn your paper in to your instructor. Leave your system running for the next activity.

13

MAC Address Filtering and Spoofing

Wireless networks don't depend on MAC addresses only for establishing, maintaining, and managing connections or transmitting data. Wireless stations also use MAC addresses rather than IP addresses for identification between stations and APs. IP addresses are Network layer identities and can't be used for addressing in a MAC frame.

MAC addresses are hard-coded into NIC firmware, but entering a different value into the frame is a simple matter with the right software tool. Most configuration tools included with hardware can be used to change a WNIC's MAC address, and you can find many free tools specifically designed for spoofing addresses.

One of the most basic security mechanisms in wireless networks is MAC address filtering. MAC addresses of legitimate stations are entered (manually in the configuration interface) into the AP's MAC address table, and only recognized stations can connect to the AP. Attackers get around this mechanism by sniffing the network to find legitimate MAC addresses, and then alter frames by using those values; this tactic is called MAC address spoofing. The injected frame appears to be from a legitimate source, so attackers can connect to the AP and network.

Wireless Authentication

When a wireless station wants to connect to a network, it authenticates to an AP or another station first in a process called **IEEE 802.11 authentication**. A key difference between wireless and wired networks is that the wireless station, not the user, is authenticated before being connected to the network. To access resources, users are then prompted to authenticate after the connection has been made. However, the AP doesn't typically perform user authentication; that process is handled by a Remote Authentication Dial-In User Service (RADIUS) or Terminal Access Controller Access Control System (TACACS+) server, directory services, or another means of network authentication.

Early 802.11 standards provide two basic authentication methods: open system authentication and shared key authentication. In **open system authentication**, as long as a station has an SSID that matches the network it's attempting to join, it's authenticated without further checking (see Figure 13-4). In ad-hoc mode (a peer-to-peer network), one station sends an authentication frame to another and receives a frame indicating recognition. In infrastructure mode (another term for a BSS configuration, with APs connecting stations), a station transmits its request to the AP and is authenticated as long as it has the correct SSID. Open system authentication provides little security because SSIDs are transmitted in management frames in cleartext. Attackers can easily use passive scanning to find this information from other authenticated stations or from the AP if it's broadcasting beacon frames.

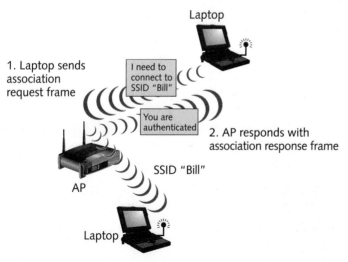

Laptop

1. Laptop sends association request frame

I need to connect to SSID "Bill"

You are authenticated

2. AP responds with association response frame

SSID "Bill"

AP

Laptop

Figure 13-4   Open system authentication

Shared key authentication uses a standard challenge-response process with shared key encryption. A wireless station sends an authentication frame to an AP, which returns an authentication response frame containing the challenge text. The station encrypts the text with its shared key and returns it to the AP. Using its own copy of the shared key, the AP decrypts the text and compares it to the original challenge text. If they match, the AP sends another authentication frame with the results, and the station is authenticated. If they don't match, the station's connection attempt is rejected.

A single shared key is distributed to all stations on a wireless network before they can communicate (see Figure 13-5). The IEEE standards don't specify any mechanisms for key management, so vendors, administrators, developers, and others must devise their own key management schemes. Managing shared keys effectively is a challenging aspect of securing wireless transmissions, as discussed later in "Key Management Concerns in 802.11 Networks." Shared key authentication is also considered weak because it uses WEP for encryption. Attackers can use passive scanning to capture packets and crack the shared key; after they have the key, they can be authenticated to the network easily and then launch attacks.

13

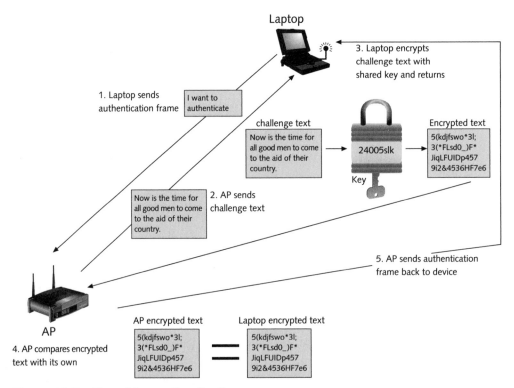

Figure 13-5   Shared key authentication

WEP Vulnerabilities

The 802.11 standard includes WEP and outlines several cryptographic objectives but doesn't specify how to achieve these objectives. The objectives include the following:

- *Efficiency*—The encryption algorithm must be efficient enough to be used in hardware or software.

- *Exportable*—U.S. Department of Commerce security guidelines must be met so that WEP-enabled devices can be exported outside the United States.

- *Optional*—WEP must be an optional feature.

- *Self-synchronizing*—Each packet must be encrypted separately so that a single lost packet doesn't result in all packets being unreadable.

NOTE   U.S. computer security guidelines change often and apply to industries, devices, and international exportation rules differently. If you're interested in a specific rule on a device, visit the Department of Commerce's Web site at *www.commerce.gov*, and search for the device there.

Shared key encryption in WEP uses the Rivest Cipher version 4 (RC4) encryption algorithm, which allows keys up to 128 bits. 802.11 uses a 40-bit or 104-bit key with a 24-bit **initialization vector (IV)** added to the beginning of the key. The IV initializes the key stream generated by the RC4 algorithm and is transmitted in cleartext.

To understand WEP's weaknesses, you need to understand IV vulnerabilities. The IV is part of the RC4 encryption key, and because it's transmitted in cleartext, it gives attackers 24 bits of the key. The IV is a short stream by cryptographic standards, and reusing the same key results in keys repeating after a short time. All users use the same key, so capturing enough packets to crack the key and decrypt transmissions isn't hard.

Often, the IV starts at 0 and increments by 1 each time a key is generated, so not only does it repeat, it does so in a predictable pattern. Because the IV is a 24-bit value, only 16 million combinations are possible. Therefore, in a busy network, the IV can reinitialize and start over at 0 in only about 6 hours. After enough packets have been captured, attackers can crack the key with a brute-force or dictionary attack.

Because the challenge text in shared key authentication is sent in cleartext, attackers can capture it along with the IV and then capture the challenge response. With this information, they can crack the key. Even though the RC4 specifications make it clear that keys should never be reused, inevitably they are in WEP.

WEP provides adequate protection against casual users with no ill intent but not against attackers determined to gain access. Dynamic WEP, a newer version, offers slightly better protection because it rotates keys frequently, which solves the IV problem. It also uses different keys for broadcast and unicast traffic and changes them frequently. It requires minimal effort to set up but isn't used much because it provides only a partial solution. Another option is WEP2, which was developed to address some vulnerabilities in WEP. It uses a 128-bit key and Kerberos authentication. Although these enhancements helped, WEP2 ended up being no more secure than WEP and isn't used widely.

13

NOTE   WEP is often disabled to increase throughput. Even though it doesn't provide much security, you should still make sure it's enabled as a first line of defense to prevent casual users from connecting.

Default WEP Keys

Even though the 802.11 standard states that APs and wireless stations can hold up to four keys simultaneously (see Figure 13-6), only one is chosen as a station's **default key** for encrypting messages for transmission. The default key doesn't have to be the same on every station, but the same key must be used for both encryption and decryption. Each station must contain the key used for encryption to decrypt a message. For example, if a sending station uses Key3 for encryption, the receiving station must use its copy of Key3 to decrypt the message.

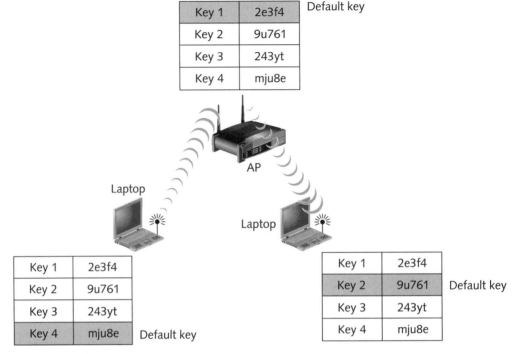

Figure 13-6 Default WEP keys

Key Management Concerns in 802.11 Networks

Key management is a challenge in wireless security. The 802.11 standard leaves the details of key management up to vendors and users, so many companies still rely on WEP or WEP2, thinking that its encryption and security mechanisms are adequate.

WEP was integrated into devices to prevent casual eavesdropping and unauthorized access. It works well to prevent eavesdropping but has shortcomings in preventing unauthorized access. Further, WEP keys must be installed on all stations in a network before they can communicate. This procedure takes a lot of time, resulting in keys being changed infrequently or not at all. WEP and WEP2 shouldn't be used alone for security, but if they are, make sure keys are changed often.

Even if stronger encryption methods are used, an effective key management method is still crucial. In wired networks, many organizations use some form of Public Key Infrastructure (PKI). If a comprehensive PKI system is already in place, it should also be used for wireless segments to make sure keys are managed effectively.

NOTE

The technical details of WEP in 802.11 networks are beyond the scope of this book, but relying solely on WEP as a security measure is strongly discouraged for most wireless applications. If you're interested in more details on how it works, search the Internet for the many available articles on the IEEE 802.11 implementation of WEP. You can find information on methods and tools to secure (or crack) WEP, too. One helpful resource for wireless security information is *www.wardrive.net*.

Association with a Wireless Network

To access services and resources, a station must be associated with an AP (in infrastructure mode) or another station (in ad-hoc mode). **Association** is a two-step process. First, a station listens for beacon frames to locate a network to join, and then goes through the authentication process; a station can't be associated without being authenticated first. Second, the station sends an association request frame. If the AP accepts, it reserves memory space for the station and sends back an association response frame containing the association ID and connection information, such as supported data rates. A station can be authenticated on several APs simultaneously but can be associated with only one network at a time.

Wardriving and Rogue Devices

In **wardriving**, a potential attacker (or two working in tandem) drives around with a laptop and WNIC in RF monitor mode to detect unsecured wireless signals. With inexpensive hardware and free software, accessing an unsecured wireless network, whether it's part of an enterprise or a home network, is too easy. The myth is that wardrivers are simply hijacking the connection, but they are stealing information, violating data privacy, and using their access to cause malicious damage.

Rogue devices are wireless devices that employees connect and use without authorization or verification of configurations. Many administrators still consider an employee connecting a rogue device a minor problem, but any unauthorized device represents a security vulnerability that can be exploited. In addition, rogue devices are usually poorly configured, so attackers can often locate them quickly and easily.

For example, Betty, an accounts payable manager, wants a mobile connection because she goes to the file room often to review or file paperwork or reconcile accounts. If she were able to take her laptop with her, she wouldn't have to haul files between her office and the file room. She asked the IT Department about setting up this connection but was told no. Betty knows the salespeople use laptops to connect wirelessly, so she concludes that the IT Department just doesn't want to bother with setting up her laptop.

Betty researches wireless connections and finds out that all she needs is a wireless router and WNIC. Her laptop has an onboard WNIC, so she buys an inexpensive wireless router. She follows the simple instructions to attach the router and then uses the Windows XP wizard to configure the WNIC and connect to the corporate network.

13

She thinks the IT Department was too lazy to help her because the wireless connection wasn't hard or time consuming to set up, but she's satisfied that she was technically savvy enough to do it herself.

Meanwhile, a wardriver is cruising around the neighborhood. Looking at his laptop, he sees that his antenna has detected a WLAN broadcasting advertisements as "linksys." He knows immediately that it's a wireless router configured with default settings, and the open-source software he's using tells him it's broadcasting unencrypted packets, so he connects to it and starts capturing packets. He examines the packets and finds what he's looking for: a valid username and password. With this information, he can probably gain full access to the network, including sensitive information. With a little more effort, he can disable software, infect the network with a virus, delete or corrupt data, or worse.

This situation happens every day, but companies usually don't realize that well-intentioned employees are too often the source of wireless security breaches. Worse, IT might not have configured wireless network security and auditing correctly, so rogue devices often go unnoticed until a breach is discovered (if it ever is). According to some surveys over the past few years, 40% to 60% of wireless networks use default configurations, have no intrusion detection, emit signals far beyond the necessary range, and don't even use weak WEP encryption. With the proliferation of wireless devices, these lax security measures cause headaches for security professionals and make intrusions easy for attackers.

Although it might seem that Betty is solely responsible for any harm to the network that might occur, the IT Department shares responsibility. Too often, IT personnel are unresponsive or abrupt with users. Had an IT Department employee politely explained to Betty why her request couldn't be accommodated, she might not have taken steps to set up her own wireless connection. Unfortunately, she wasn't as knowledgeable as she thought she was, so her laptop's connection wasn't secured correctly. A comprehensive security awareness training program with information about wardriving and rogue devices would have also helped prevent Betty's actions. IT professionals should remember to treat users with respect to help ensure that network security is maintained. If you maintain a good working relationship with users, they're usually willing to follow security procedures. If you refuse to help them, they can and will circumvent procedures you've set up.

Wireless Man-in-the-Middle Attacks

In a man-in-the-middle (MITM) attack, attackers intercept the transmissions of two communicating nodes without the users' knowledge. The transmissions can be modified and then forwarded to the intended destination, blocked from being delivered, or simply read and passed on. Most wired networks have taken countermeasures to reduce the risk of MITM attacks, but wireless networks give attackers new opportunities to use this attack method. A wireless MITM attack follows the same general procedure as on a wired network, but attackers often set up a fake AP to intercept transmissions and make stations think they're connecting to an authentic AP. Figure 13-7 shows a typical wireless MITM attack.

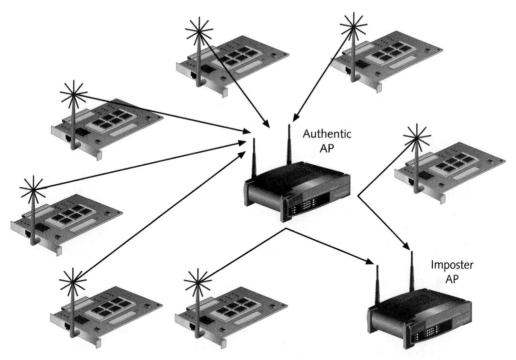

Figure 13-7   A wireless man-in-the-middle attack

Wireless Device Portability

The primary purpose of wireless devices, such as laptops and PDAs, is mobility, but this capability makes them vulnerable in many ways. First, they are designed to be portable, which makes them vulnerable to theft, use by unauthorized users, improper or unsafe storage and handling, established connection protocols being bypassed, and more.

For example, a company-owned computer stays on a user's desk unless authorized personnel move it. If someone else moves or tampers with it, measures are in place to spot these events quickly, locate the device, and deal with the problem. In addition, to steal a company computer, an attacker must gain entry to the facility. Other security measures include protecting established channels through which connections to the corporate network and Internet take place, scheduling and installing software updates automatically, and ensuring that devices remain within the corporate security perimeter, under IT's control.

Not so with mobile devices. Employees take these devices with them and use them to connect from home, their cars, and hotel rooms, and they might allow others to use the devices. Theft is a problem, too. For example, a U.S. Department of Veteran's Affairs employee had a laptop stolen from his car. It contained the personal information of more than 50 million veterans. All those veterans had to be notified, even though the laptop

13

was recovered and didn't seem to have been tampered with. However, these people still have to worry and watch for signs of identity theft because of the possible breach of a single mobile device.

Also, mobile devices might not be backed up or have updates installed if they aren't connected to the corporate network when those procedures take place. Mobile devices can be compromised in countless ways when they aren't protected by security personnel. For this reason, make sure highly sensitive data isn't stored on mobile devices, and ensure that strong encryption and authentication are used.

EXAMINING WIRELESS SECURITY SOLUTIONS

As in the early years of wired networking, the original focus in wireless standards wasn't on security but on connectivity. So wireless security is a few years behind wired network security, but the IEEE, Wi-Fi Alliance (*www.wi-fi.com*), and other standards and security organizations are working to address the inherent security problems in wireless networks.

TIP

You can find additional resources, including the Wi-Fi Alliance and IEEE 802.11 Working Group, in Appendix B. Collecting online resources that you check frequently to update your knowledge is particularly wise in wireless networking because technology changes so rapidly, and new vulnerabilities and exploits emerge daily.

After learning about 802.11 security issues, you might think the best option is to simply avoid using wireless networks. For some businesses, the risks of wireless are too high to justify using it, and many organizations simply don't want the headaches of securing wireless networks. However, wireless networking offers too many advantages to abandon it just because security is challenging. In the following sections, you learn some common solutions for addressing the security flaws in wireless networks. With a little extra work, wireless can be a secure, effective enhancement to networking technology.

Countermeasures for Wireless Threats

Wireless networks require special security measures, and the following sections explain common configurations to mitigate wireless vulnerabilities and protect against wireless networking threats.

Incorporating a Wireless Security Policy

A main component of security is a wireless security policy. The key differences between wireless and wired networks are in the Physical and Data Link layers, so your wireless security policy should focus on issues in those two OSI layers. A wireless security policy should address the following:

- Scope and goals of the policy
- Responsibilities for wireless matters and contact information for responsible parties
- Physical security of APs to prevent tampering, unauthorized access, interference sources, and so on
- Approved hardware and software
- Procedures for requesting, testing, installing, and configuring hardware and software
- Assignment of responsibilities for installing, maintaining, and managing wireless devices
- Guidelines and penalties for scanning or accessing the wireless network without authorization
- Explicit statements of the nature of wireless communications, including measures to protect the rest of the network from potential harm from wireless communication
- Details on wireless security awareness training
- Internet access via wireless connections
- Assignment of responsibilities for protecting data, privacy, and devices
- Penalties for attempting to bypass security measures willfully

The policy should also address other details related to the wireless environment, such as requirements for encryption methods, authentication, and storage of confidential data.

Ensuring Physical Security

Just as no computer can be made completely secure, there's no way to ensure absolute physical protection for mobile devices. The best tool for ensuring physical security of mobile devices is security awareness training for users. They should be made aware of the potential for theft and the consequences of stolen devices and be trained not to leave their mobile devices where they can be stolen or used by unauthorized people or to leave them logged on to the network.

Include training about protecting mobile devices from damage, too, such as making sure mobile devices are stored in an appropriate environment. Remind users that some protective measures are simply common sense; for example, they shouldn't leave laptops in cars during the summer or winter or outside during rainstorms.

13

Activity 13-2: Examining Physical Security for Wireless Devices

Time Required: 30 minutes

Objective: Research physical security for wireless devices.

Description: In this activity, you search the Internet to find examples of devices for physically securing wireless components. Select one and write a summary of it.

1. Start your Web browser, and do an Internet search for wireless physical security devices.

2. Visit several sites, and examine at least three different devices.

3. Select one device and write a brief summary of it, about two to three paragraphs. Include cost, purpose, how it works, and where to get it. Be sure to cite your sources.

4. Proofread your paper, and submit it to your instructor.

Planning AP Placement

You can avoid many pitfalls of wireless security by careful planning. Because RF signals propagate in different directions at different rates and distances and are affected by interference sources, determining exactly where the signal is going is difficult. A **site survey** is a procedure for assessing the environment and determining where APs are needed to provide adequate coverage. Site surveys can also help determine whether to use directional or omnidirectional antennas and how much power is necessary for the required signal performance.

Most important from a security standpoint, a site survey tells you where your signal is going that it shouldn't. Careful placement to provide adequate coverage yet prevent indiscriminant radiation of the signal can mitigate the risk of many vulnerabilities because attackers can't detect and infiltrate your network if they can't detect a signal.

A site survey follows these general steps:

1. Get a facilities diagram showing walls, walkways, wiring, elevators, other WLANs (if applicable), and planned locations of wireless stations.

2. Examine the facility for potential sources of interference with the RF signal, such as metal racks, microwave ovens, and so forth. Be sure to check the diagram for accuracy and note any discrepancies.

3. Determine the coverage areas needed, identify roaming areas, and specify where there will be no coverage. You can limit potential problems by limiting roaming areas.

4. Determine preliminary AP locations. There should be some overlap in coverage, but make sure the channels are far enough apart to avoid interference.

5. Identify suitable mounting locations for APs, antennas, patch cabling, and power lines, and consider different antenna needs based on location. For example, you don't want an omnidirectional antenna for an AP mounted on or near an outside wall. A high-gain directional antenna oriented to transmit and receive within the facility is more suitable.

6. Test AP placement before running the wiring and mounting APs permanently. Several RF site survey tools are available that can identify the AP, its signal strength and quality, and its data rate. Remember to test coverage on lower and upper floors of a multifloor facility.

7. Walk the entire outside of the facility to discover any signals leaving the building. If you find any, identify exactly where they go. Check upper or lower floors in the building for signals, too. Completely preventing signals from radiating outside might not be possible, but you need to assess the potential risk. For example, you might have an RF signal radiating 10 feet outside the office but in an area that's not easily accessible to attackers or is secured by external fencing or security patrols.

8. Document the results of the site survey, and on the facilities diagram, note each AP's location, signal coverage, and antenna type. This information also helps you identify rogue devices and aids in troubleshooting.

Changing Default Hardware and Software Settings

Default settings for hardware and software wireless configurations create serious vulnerabilities, so you should change a number of settings before installing a new device. For example, most APs include a simple HTTP interface for configuration, but after you configure the AP, you should disable this interface to prevent attackers from being able to access and tamper with the AP. If you don't want to disable HTTP access, you can password-protect access to the interface if the AP supports it. Disabling the HTTP interface is the preferred method, however.

Default settings that should be changed before connecting to the network include the following:

■ The default SSID should be changed so that it doesn't give attackers any information about the type or location of equipment. Default SSIDs commonly include a device's manufacturer, as in the "linksys" SSID for Betty's wireless router, used earlier in the rogue device example. Attackers discovering a default SSID can assume that other values, such as the administrator password, are defaults and use this information to attack the network.

■ The default administrator password should be changed so that it's as strong as the AP will support.

■ The default beaconing interval should be changed, primarily to reduce traffic and improve throughput for data.

- Manufacturers' default keys are well known, too. When configuring a device, specify another key. Remember to write it down, however, because all devices must have the same key to communicate.

- Retaining default channels can increase the likelihood of co-channel interference, which might reduce performance or disable the network entirely. Also, attackers frequently scan for vulnerable wireless networks by using known default channels. If default channels aren't changed, attackers might discover the device vendor and other default values they can use in attacks.

- By default, most security measures aren't enabled on wireless equipment. Before placing a device on the network, configure it with appropriate security settings, such as enabling WEP, configuring MAC ACLs, and configuring authentication and encryption.

As you can see from this list, changing default values is important to make it harder for attackers to find a network and gain access to it.

ACTIVITY

Activity 13-3: Finding Default Values for Wireless Devices

Time Required: 15 minutes

Objective: Research default values for popular wireless devices.

Description: In this activity, you search the Internet to find default values for popular wireless devices.

1. Start your Web browser, and go to a search engine to find Web sites for the manufacturers listed in the following steps.

2. What is the default IP address for a Netgear wireless router? The default password? The default username?

\
\

3. What is the default IP address for a Linksys Wireless-G Broadband router? The default SSID? The default username? The default password?

\
\

4. What is the default password for a Cisco Aironet AP? The default username? The default IP address?

\
\

5. Be prepared to discuss your findings in class. Leave your system running for the next activity.

Strong Encryption and Authentication

Strong authentication and encryption weren't addressed in the original IEEE 802.11 standard, but newer methods, discussed in the following sections, have been developed to improve security.

802.1x and Extensible Authentication Protocol

The **IEEE 802.1x** standard was developed to provide a means of port-based access control on Ethernet LANs and has been revised to work for wireless networks. It uses **Extensible Authentication Protocol (EAP)** and encrypted tunnels for data exchange. EAP is a group of extensible management protocols that stations use to request port access, and it includes a method of secure key exchange.

In 802.1x authentication, there are three players: supplicant, authenticator, and authentication server (see Figure 13-8). The supplicant is the station requesting access through the authenticator, which is usually an AP in wireless networks. The authenticator passes the request to the authentication server, which stores authorized users' credentials. An important strength of 802.1x is that the supplicant never communicates directly with the authentication server, thus reducing the chance of compromising sensitive data stored on the server.

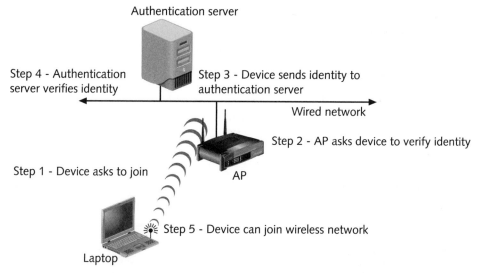

Figure 13-8 802.1x authentication

Often a RADIUS server is used for the authentication server. When the authentication server receives a request, it checks to see whether the authenticator is authorized to send requests. If so, it checks its database for the user's name. If it finds the user's name, it checks the password to see whether to grant access. Depending on the authentication method, the authentication server might respond with a challenge message that the user must respond to correctly. The authentication server notifies the authenticator of its decision, and the authenticator passes that decision back to the supplicant. The authenticator relays all messages between the authentication server and supplicant.

 NOTE Although not defined by standards, wireless user credentials can also be stored in an external database, such as SQL, LDAP, or Active Directory databases.

The 802.1x standard is based on EAP, which includes the following in its collection of extensible protocols:

- *EAP-Transport Layer Security (EAP-TLS)*—Requires using certificates to validate supplicants.

- *EAP-Tunneled TLS (EAP-TTLS)*—Supports advanced authentication, such as tokens.

- *Protected EAP (PEAP)*—Uses certificates from supplicants but doesn't require certificates from the authentication server. After authentication, the authenticator builds an encrypted tunnel to authenticate the supplicant.

- *Lightweight EAP (LEAP)*—This Cisco-proprietary standard authenticates based on the Windows username and password. No certificates are required.

- *Flexible Authentication via Secure Tunneling (FAST)*—Sets up a tunnel without checking digital certificates and supports tokens.

802.11i and Advanced Encryption Standard

Ratified in 2004, the **IEEE 802.11i** standard addresses encryption and authentication. It uses 802.1x authentication and **Advanced Encryption Standard (AES)**, a symmetric block cipher, for encryption. AES is strong enough to meet the U.S. Federal Information Processing Standard (FIPS) and has replaced the Data Encryption Standard (DES) encryption algorithm.

Unlike a stream cipher that substitutes character for character, a block cipher breaks data into blocks of 8 to 16 bits, and then encrypts each block separately. For additional security, blocks can also be arranged randomly rather than sequentially. Several iterations (rounds) of complex multiplication operations are performed on each block to substitute and rearrange bytes, and then encrypt the new arrangements of bytes again. The number of rounds depends on the key length. With a key length of 80 bits, breaking the AES key with a brute-force attack would take 800 years and $1 million worth of computers. At 256 bits, breaking the AES key would take 10^{56} years. That's 10 followed by 56 zeros, which is a *very* long time, but attackers will probably discover a way to break the AES key sooner than that.

For details on block and stream ciphers and AES, see *Guide to Strategic Infrastructure Security: Becoming a Security Network Professional* (Course Technology, 2008, ISBN 1418836613).

Wi-Fi Protected Access

Wi-Fi Protected Access (WPA) was developed as a subset of the 802.11i standard and replaces WEP encryption with **Temporal Key Integrity Protocol (TKIP)**. TKIP is based on the same RC4 mechanisms used in WEP but includes a method for generating new keys for each packet, which addresses WEP's problem of static keys that repeat. TKIP also incorporates automatic AP-client synchronization of unicast encryption keys on a frame-by-frame basis, so keys don't have to be changed manually, as in WEP.

In TKIP, different keys are used for authentication and encryption. Keys used between a pair of stations are called **pairwise keys**. After a station's credentials are accepted, the authentication server produces a master key for that session, and TKIP distributes this key to the station and AP. This **pairwise master key (PMK)** generates data encryption keys, data integrity keys, and session group keys for multicasts. The PMK isn't used for any other purpose, which makes it less vulnerable to attack.

At the start of a session, the PMK is used to compute keys for encryption, data integrity, and authentication. The **pairwise transient key (PTK)** is the first key created from the PMK. It's actually four keys shared between the AP and wireless client. PTKs are used to generate more keys according to the cryptographic algorithm in use, whether it's TKIP or AES. Keys are transient, meaning they change in real time during a session, and a new key is generated dynamically for each packet.

To learn more about how TKIP, WPA, and the 802.11i standard work, search the Internet for articles. You can also download the IEEE 802.11i standard at *http://standards.ieee.org*.

WPA also uses **Message Integrity Check (MIC)**, which is a mathematical function similar to Cyclic Redundancy Check (CRC) that checks whether a message has been tampered with (see Figure 13-9). The MIC implementation in TKIP is referred to as Michael and uses a longer IV of 48 bits. If the MIC value for a received message doesn't match the value sent with the message, the packet is assumed to have been tampered with and is dropped. Unlike CRC, however, MIC includes an optional measure that deauthenticates a station and prevents new associations for one minute if MIC errors are detected. MIC also includes a frame counter, which prevents replay attacks.

13

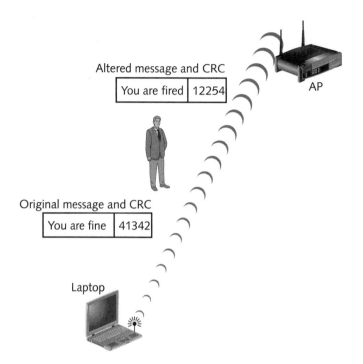

Figure 13-9 The MIC process

WPA authentication can be accomplished with 802.1x or a preshared key. If a preshared key is used, it must be entered on the AP and station first and is used as a seed for generating encryption keys. A major disadvantage of using a passphrase and preshared keys is that to prevent the passphrase from being cracked, it must be very long (more than 20 characters) and very complex (no dictionary words and consisting of letters, numbers, and symbols).

WPA has these notable improvements over WEP:

- Minimum key length is increased for stronger data encryption.
- IV sequencing is enforced so that IVs aren't reused.
- IV length is doubled, from 24 bits to 48 bits.
- Packet-tampering detection is built into MIC.
- Key rotation is automatic.

Wi-Fi Protected Access version 2 (WPA2) is based on the final ratified 802.11i standard and uses AES for encryption and 802.1x or preshared keys for authentication. One notable difference between 802.11i and WPA2 is that WPA2 allows both TKIP and AES clients to communicate, whereas 802.11i recognizes only AES.

WPA and WPA2 can be used in Personal Security and Enterprise Security modes of operation, which provide guidance on how to use WPA and WPA2 for different purposes. Personal Security mode is designed for single users or small office/home office (SOHO) settings, and Enterprise Security mode is designed for medium to large businesses.

Table 13-3 summarizes the major wireless security solutions.

Table 13-3   Wireless security solutions

Type	Encryption	Authentication	Key length	Security level
WEP	WEP	Shared key	40–104 bits with a 24-bit IV	Low
WEP2	WEP2	Kerberos	128 bits	Low
Dynamic WEP	Dynamic keys	Various	128 bits	Low
WPA Personal Security	TKIP	PSK	128 bits	Medium
WPA2 (802.11i) Personal Security	AES	PSK	128 bits	Medium to high
WPA Enterprise Security	TKIP	802.1x	128 bits	Medium to high
WPA2 Enterprise Security	AES	802.1x	128 bits	High

WPA2 Enterprise Security provides the highest security available and should be used for a wireless network when an authentication server is available, as an authentication server is required for 802.1x authentication to work. If an authentication server isn't available, WPA2 Personal Security should be used.

13

Wireless Auditing

An integral part of security management, auditing wireless networks can be more important than auditing wired networks because ensuring that only authorized users can access data is critical in wireless networks, which are more vulnerable to interception. Audits are based on security policies, so auditors review the security policy first, and then test the system to ensure compliance. Next, they assume the role of an attacker to check for vulnerabilities. On the Internet, you can easily find all the tools and information needed to attack any network, and many of these resources are free.

Security auditors are often called "penetration testers" or "ethical hackers."

Hiring third-party experts to conduct security audits can be a good idea for the following reasons:

- First, they will be looking at your network with fresh eyes and no preconceived ideas. When you have worked with your system for a long time, you might miss even obvious problems.

- Second, they are likely to have different skills and an extra arsenal of tools and techniques.

- Third, they usually do more wireless security audits than administrators, so they have the focus and experience of a specialist.

If you hire a third-party expert, make sure to check credentials and ask for references because unfortunately, some unscrupulous people pretend to be qualified, trustworthy experts. Also, make sure responsibilities, fees, and permissions are spelled out in a contract (which genuine auditors almost always require).

NOTE   Attackers are usually considered to be bad people, an attitude that's reflected in the media. Of course, they *are* breaking the law and causing damage. However, their ingenuity in exposing security flaws has forced the technology community to come up with solutions, and these advances have resulted in better, faster, and more secure technologies.

Risk and Security Assessments

An early step in developing a security policy is a comprehensive risk assessment. You must know what your assets are and how critical they are to your organization before you can protect them effectively. Similarly, you need to prioritize your assets and know what threats your organization faces to ensure that assets are protected. Risk assessments help with these critical tasks.

Most basic security audits don't include a comprehensive risk assessment; they're intended to evaluate policy compliance, determine the effectiveness of existing security, and identify unknown vulnerabilities. A security assessment differs from a risk assessment, in that it identifies existing security measures. To upgrade security and possibly performance and function, you need to evaluate the starting point accurately. This security assessment is then used during a security audit to evaluate the effectiveness of your security measures.

NOTE   For more information on security policy development and risk assessments, see *Guide to Strategic Infrastructure Security: Becoming a Security Network Professional* (Course Technology, 2008, ISBN 1418836613).

Auditing Tools

After an auditor completes a security assessment, the next task is to use a variety of tools and techniques to attempt to break into the network. This task, formally known as **penetration testing**, is intended to identify security vulnerabilities that attackers could exploit. Attackers use sniffers in the network reconnaissance phase to capture packets so that they can gather information about targets. Auditors use sniffers to see what kind of information attackers can gain by using them. Table 13-4 describes several popular wireless sniffers and the types of information they can gather. Hundreds of sniffing programs are available for PCs and handheld devices and any OS available, and many add-ons can be combined with these programs.

Table 13-4   Wireless sniffers

Name	OS	Description
AirCrack	Mac OS X, Windows, Linux	A sniffer and WEP/WPA key cracker that can be used to launch attacks. Consists of airodump (packet capture), airdecap (decrypts WEP/WPA capture files), aircrack (WEP and WPA/PSK cracker), and aireplay (packet injection).
Kismet	POSIX, Linux, BSD, Mac OS X, Win32	This 802.11 Layer 2 detector, sniffer, and IDS is passive and undetectable in operation and capable of detecting hidden networks, rogue devices, attacks, and unauthorized users.
NetStumbler	Windows	An 802.11a, 802.11b, and 802.11g WLAN detecter and analyzer. WebStumbler is an add-on that converts files to HTML.
Wireshark (previously Ethereal)	Windows, UNIX, Linux, and other OSs and UNIX variations	A network protocol analyzer capable of live monitoring or capture. Live data can be read from FDDI, PPP, token ring, Ethernet, and 802.11 networks.
AirSnort	Windows, Linux	This tool recovers encryption keys by using passive monitoring. It requires 5 to 10 million packets.
FakeAP	Linux, BSD UNIX	This tool generates thousands of counterfeit 802.11b APs and is useful as a honeypot tool.
WPA Cracker	Linux	A dictionary/brute-force attack tool against WPA.

13

AP Logging Functions

A network that can't be monitored can't be secured, so being able to maintain and review a record of activity is essential for security. Lower-end APs might not have the capability to generate more than simple connection statistics and a basic event log, but many enterprise-class models can maintain more sophisticated event logs and connection statistics and interface with a Simple Network Management Protocol (SNMP) tool. Figure 13-10 shows an AP event log.

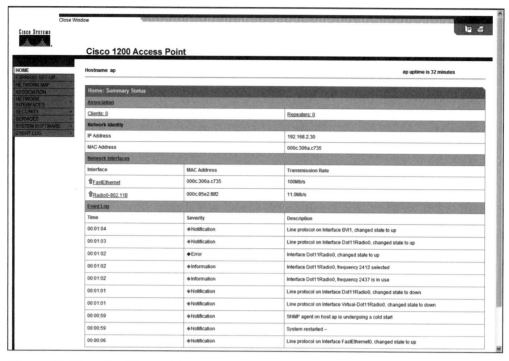

Figure 13-10   An AP event log

SNMP requires installing an SNMP agent on the device to be monitored (in this case, the AP), and logged information is stored in the SNMP agent's management information base (MIB), also housed on the monitored device. The MIBs gather data and report it to an SNMP management station that produces overall network statistics. SNMP configuration is shown in Figure 13-11. Using these network statistics, you can set an SNMP alarm that sends an alert message, called an SNMP trap, to the management station when specified limits are exceeded. The management station then queries all stations for details of the event that triggered the alert.

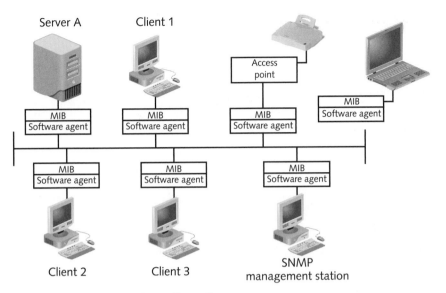

Figure 13-11   SNMP configuration

NOTE

Another method of managing AP logs and monitoring activity is Remote Monitoring (RMON), an SNMP-based tool used to monitor LANs connected via a WAN. The RMON standard, specified in RFC 1757, enables network monitors, network probes, and console stations to exchange and organize network information. For more information, visit *www.cisco.com/univercd/ cc/td/doc/cisintwk/ito_doc/rmon.htm*.

Wireless Security Best Practices

There are a number of methods for protecting wireless devices. This section summarizes some best practices, but it's not an all-inclusive list. First, and most important, make sure personnel using wireless devices have received thorough training on corporate security policies. Second, restrict data that can be transferred to a portable device. Highly sensitive data should never be stored on a portable device unless absolutely necessary. Third, try to break into your wireless network (see the Caution). You can use the same tactics and tools attackers do as well as others based on your knowledge of the network's configuration that attackers might not know. If your budget allows, a third-party wireless security audit is a sound investment.

CAUTION

You must have written permission from an authorized person before performing penetration testing on any network. You should also have legal counsel review a contract that specifies what will be done, possible effects, timelines, and expectations of both parties.

13

The following list summarizes other best practices to follow:

- Use strong authentication, such as 802.1x.

- Use strong encryption, preferably end to end.

- Perform a site survey and place APs strategically.

- Make sure a comprehensive wireless security policy is kept up to date, and users are trained to follow it.

- Ensure that default settings, such as SSIDs, are changed.

- Avoid using protocols that send traffic in cleartext.

- If appropriate, use VPNs for wireless transmissions.

- Use wireless IDSs and IPSs.

- Make sure all stations are running up-to-date antivirus protection.

- Make sure firewalls are used on wireless devices.

- Audit the wireless network periodically.

- Make sure you monitor your wireless network traffic by using the best means available.

CHAPTER SUMMARY

- A major challenge for wireless networking is security. The IEEE, vendors, and developers have worked to come up with solutions to wireless security threats.

- Wireless networks use the airwaves as a transmission medium, so packets are more vulnerable to interception.

- The Media Access Control (MAC) sublayer of the OSI model performs many critical functions in a wireless network. Each access point (AP) has an SSID (network name) and communicates by using management, control, and data MAC frames.

- Passive scanning involves a wireless station listening for beacon frames. A passive attack uses passive scanning to gather information for later use. Active scanning involves a station sending out probe request frames on each available channel and waiting for a response.

- Before a station can be associated with an AP and join a wireless network, it must be authenticated. The IEEE 802.11 standard includes open system and shared key authentication.

- SSIDs, as well as other information about the wireless network, are vulnerable in standard 802.11 transmissions because management frames send network information in cleartext.

❑ WEP was implemented in the original 802.11 standard and uses the Rivest Cipher version 4 (RC4) encryption algorithm. A default key is used for encryption, and the IV in a WEP key is vulnerable to being cracked.

❑ Even though wireless networking has inherent security problems, a number of effective security solutions and standards are available, including IEEE 802.1x, WPA/WPA2, and IEEE 802.11i.

❑ Auditing a wireless network is crucial to maintaining and improving security. Security assessments, third-party audits and penetration testing, and logging are part of a comprehensive auditing plan.

❑ Lower-end APs might generate only simple logs, but many enterprise-class models can maintain an event log and connection statistics and interface with a Simple Network Management Protocol (SNMP) tool.

❑ Some wireless security best practices include training users, developing a wireless security policy, restricting what data can be stored on portable devices, and ensuring that default settings are changed.

Key Terms

acknowledgement (ACK) — A type of control frame that a receiving station sends when a packet has been received successfully with no errors.

active attacks — Attacks that use active scanning (sending out probe request frames on each available channel) in an attempt to gather information for subsequent attacks.

active scanning — The process of a wireless station sending out a probe request frame on each available channel and waiting for a probe response frame from available APs.

Advanced Encryption Standard (AES) — A symmetric block cipher used for encryption in IEEE 802.11i.

association — A two-step process of being accepted into a wireless network. First, a station listens for beacon frames to locate a network to join, and then it goes through the authentication process. Second, the station sends an association request frame; if it's accepted, it receives an association ID and connection information. A station can be associated with only one network at a time and must be authenticated before being associated.

clear to send (CTS) — A type of control frame sent in response to a request to send (RTS) frame; it gives the sender clearance to begin transmitting packets.

control frames — A type of MAC frame used to help deliver data frames between stations and control access to the medium.

data frames — A type of MAC frame that contains the TCP/IP packet sent over a wireless network or between wireless devices. It carries data from higher-layer applications, such as printer control data or Web pages.

13

default key — A wireless station or AP's key for encrypting messages for transmission. The default key doesn't have to be the same on every station, but the same key must be used for both encryption and decryption.

Extensible Authentication Protocol (EAP) — A group of extensible management protocols used in IEEE 802.1x. EAP includes a method of secure key exchange, and wireless stations use it to request port access.

IEEE 802.11 authentication — The process by which an AP accepts or rejects a wireless device's connection attempt.

IEEE 802.11i — A wireless security standard intended to replace the IEEE 802.11 WEP-based standard. It uses 802.1x authentication and AES for encryption. *See also* Advanced Encryption Standard (AES).

IEEE 802.1x — A standard developed to provide a means of port-based access control on Ethernet LANs; it has been revised for wireless networks to incorporate authentication and key management.

initialization vector (IV) — In WEP's shared key encryption, a 24-bit value added to the beginning of a key to initialize the key stream generated by the RC4 algorithm.

management frames — A type of MAC frame used to establish and maintain communications between wireless devices or between a wireless device and an access point.

Message Integrity Check (MIC) — A mathematical function used in WPA that replaces the Cyclic Redundancy Check (CRC); it's designed to detect tampering in packets. *See also* Wi-Fi Protected Access (WPA).

open system authentication — This 802.11 authentication method relies on a station having an SSID that matches the network it's attempting to join as the only criteria for acceptance. Its security drawback is that SSIDs are transmitted in cleartext in management frames.

pairwise keys — Any keys used between a pair of devices in TKIP. *See also* Temporal Key Integrity Protocol (TKIP).

pairwise master key (PMK) — The TKIP key used to generate data encryption keys, data integrity keys, and session group keys, among others. This key is used only once at the start of a session.

pairwise transient key (PTK) — The first TKIP key generated by the pairwise master key (PMK) and used for further key generation, according to the cryptographic algorithm in use.

passive attack — An attack that uses passive scanning to gather information for later use in other attacks; also called network reconnaissance.

passive scanning — The process of a wireless station listening on each available channel for an AP's beacon frame, and then moving on to the next channel without sending anything.

penetration testing — The process of using a variety of tools and techniques to attempt to break into a network. Penetration testing, also called ethical hacking, is used legitimately as part of security audits to identify security vulnerabilities that attackers could exploit.

power-save poll (PS-Poll) — A type of control frame that a station sends on awakening from power save mode; it indicates to the access point that it's ready to receive any frames the AP has buffered for it.

radio frequency (RF) monitor mode — A wireless NIC mode (equivalent to promiscuous mode in wired NICs) that allows a WNIC to capture packets without authenticating or associating with an AP or ad hoc (peer to peer) wireless network.

request to send (RTS) — A type of control frame that a station sends when it wants to transmit. The RTS frame sender requests that the medium be reserved long enough for the transmission to be completed and an acknowledgement control frame to be received from the destination.

rogue devices — Wireless devices installed on a network without authorization or verification of configurations.

shared key authentication — An 802.11 authentication method that uses a standard challenge-response process with shared key encryption. It relies on a wireless station having the correct key to encrypt the AP's challenge text as the criteria for acceptance. Its security drawback is that it uses WEP, which is easily cracked, for encrypting the shared key.

site survey — An in-depth examination of a proposed wireless network site designed to determine AP placement and identify stray signals, noise, and obstacles.

Temporal Key Integrity Protocol (TKIP) — An encryption method devised as a replacement for WEP in WPA. TKIP is based on the same RC4 mechanisms used in WEP but includes a method for generating new keys for each packet. It also incorporates automatic AP-client synchronization of unicast encryption keys, so keys don't have to be changed manually, as in WEP.

wardriving — Driving around with a laptop and WNIC in RF monitor mode to detect unsecured wireless signals.

Wi-Fi Protected Access (WPA) — A subset of the 802.11i standard that addresses encryption and authentication; it uses IEEE 802.1x or preshared keys for authentication and TKIP for encryption. *See also* IEEE 802.1x *and* Temporal Key Integrity Protocol (TKIP).

Wi-Fi Protected Access version 2 (WPA2) — The encryption and authentication architecture based on the final ratified IEEE 802.11i standard. WPA2 uses preshared keys or IEEE 802.1x for authentication and AES for encryption. *See also* Advanced Encryption Standard (AES) *and* IEEE 802.1x.

13

REVIEW QUESTIONS

1. What function does an SSID serve on a wireless network?

   a. identifies an access point's location

   b. monitors a station's connection properties

   c. identifies the network name

   d. encrypts network traffic

2. Which of the following OSI layers is the most important in a wireless network? (Choose all that apply.)

   a. Physical

   b. Network

   c. Session

   d. Data Link

3. Which of the following frames carries TCP/IP packets in a wireless network?

   a. management

   b. data

   c. control

   d. MAC

4. When a station needs information from another station, it sends which of the following frames?

   a. association request

   b. beacon

   c. probe request

   d. probe response

5. What is the purpose of a beacon frame?

   a. An AP sends it to determine whether to allow a device to enter the network.

   b. It advertises services or information about the wireless network.

   c. It aids in establishing and maintaining communication.

   d. It assists in delivering frames that contain data.

6. Which of the following is the process of listening on each available channel for an AP's beacon?

   a. surfing

   b. monitoring

   c. scanning

   d. probing

7. The IEEE 802.11 standard provides which of the following authentication methods? (Choose all that apply.)

   a. asymmetric

   b. shared key

   c. open system

   d. closed system

8. A station can be authenticated without being associated. True or False?

9. Which TKIP key is used only once, at the start of a session?

   a. PTK

   b. pairwise key

   c. PMK

   d. PSK

10. Which authentication method does WPA2 Enterprise Security use?

   a. preshared key

   b. 802.1x

   c. EAP

   d. AES

11. Even though 802.11 wireless devices can hold up to four keys simultaneously, they have to use the same one to communicate with each other. True or False?

12. A site survey helps accomplish which of the following? (Choose all that apply.)

   a. determining placement of stations

   b. evaluating what type of antennas to use

   c. identifying where APs should be placed

   d. determining where data should be stored

13. Having an abundance of APs in a wireless network improves performance. True or False?

14. Some default settings that should be changed before connecting a device include which of the following? (Choose all that apply.)

   a. SSID

   b. channel

   c. keys

   d. MAC address

15. Which of the following provides the strongest wireless network security?

   a. WEP2 Enterprise Security

   b. WPA2 Enterprise Security

   c. WPA Enterprise Security

   d. WPA2 Personal Security

16. WPA2 uses which of the following for encryption?

   a. TKIP

   b. EAP

   c. AES

   d. EAS

13

17. EAP is used in 802.1x to provide which of the following? (Choose all that apply.)

    a. port access

    b. authentication services

    c. secure key exchange

    d. encryption keys

18. WPA2 supports which of the following authentication methods? (Choose all that apply.)

    a. preshared keys

    b. 802.1x

    c. 802.11i

    d. Kerberos

19. What part of an SNMP configuration resides on the device to be monitored? (Choose all that apply.)

    a. MIB

    b. SNMP trap

    c. SNMP agent

    d. SNMP alarm

20. To use WPA2 Enterprise Security, an authentication server must be available. True or False?

HANDS-ON PROJECTS

HANDS-ON PROJECTS

Hands-On Project 13-1: Observing Wireless Device Handling

Time Required: 2 to 3 hours

Objective: Observe your surroundings and note any security lapses in how wireless devices are handled.

Description: In this project, you observe how people handle their wireless devices, take notes on your observations, and report your findings to your classmates or instructor. You need a notepad and pencil for this project.

1. Choose a busy time to observe wireless users, such as rush hour in the morning or afternoon.

2. Select a location where you're likely to find wireless devices, such as your school's common areas or a cybercafe.

3. Watch people around you and observe how they handle their cell phones, laptops, and other wireless devices.

4. Did you notice any mishandling? Any security lapses? For example, did anyone place his or her cell phone where it could be stolen or tampered with? Leave a laptop unsecured? Place a device in a potentially damaging environment, such as next to a hot or cold beverage?

5. Write down your observations, and turn them in to your instructor or present them in class.

Hands-On Project 13-2: Creating Homemade Antennas

Time Required: 60 minutes

Objective: Research ways to make homemade wireless antennas from common household items and minimal hardware.

Description: In this project, you research the process of making a homemade wireless antenna, and then a write a report summarizing your findings.

1. Start your Web browser, go to a search engine, and search on the keyword **cantenna**.

2. Select at least three links containing information on making homemade wireless antennas.

3. Read the information, noting the components of each design and other pertinent information, such as antenna gain and loss, specifics on required parts, and variations you find interesting.

4. Next, search on the keywords **Marc Duggan's Lego Inventions**, and examine these designs.

5. What are some ways to automate a homemade antenna?

6. How do you boost a cantenna's gain?

7. Write a report summarizing your findings and answering the questions in these steps. Submit this report to your instructor, and be prepared to discuss your findings in class.

Hands-On Project 13-3: Developing a Wireless Security Policy

Time Required: 60 minutes

Objective: Research existing wireless security policies to use in developing your own.

Description: In this project, you research existing wireless security policies, examine components of these policies, and assess the reasons for including particular policy statements. When you have finished your research, write a comprehensive wireless security policy.

(*Hint*: A wireless security policy is part of your overall organizational security policy. Make it clear and concise, and use nontechnical terms so that users can understand it easily.)

1. Start your Web browser and search for wireless security policies.

2. Examine several examples of wireless security policies. A good starting point is the policy at the University of Westminster's Web site at *www.wmin.ac.uk/page-1237*.

3. When you have finished reading how others have approached creating wireless security policies, develop your own.

4. Submit your work to your instructor. Remember to check spelling and grammar, and submit a professional document.

HANDS-ON PROJECTS

Hands-On Project 13-4: Creating a Presentation on Wireless Attack Methods

Time Required: 2 to 3 hours

Objective: Research current wireless attacks and develop a presentation for use in security awareness training.

Description: In this project, you research current wireless attack techniques, and develop a presentation you can use in security awareness training.

1. Start your Web browser, and search for current wireless attack techniques.

2. Select a common attack technique, and develop a presentation to explain how it takes place, what network vulnerability the attack exploits, and what countermeasures can be used to defend against it. You can write a speech or memo, create visual aids (such as charts), or develop a PowerPoint presentation.

3. Make sure your presentation is geared to nontechnical users, but be sure you can answer any technical questions that might come up.

4. Submit your work to your instructor or present it in class, depending on your instructor's directions.

CASE PROJECTS

CASE PROJECTS

Case Project 13-1: Finalizing the Wireless Design Proposal

In Chapter 12, you began designing a wireless network segment for Green Globe. In this project, you revise and complete this design. Using the materials you have already completed, the facility diagram, and the Green Globe description from this book's front matter, evaluate your wireless network design for security. Be sure to describe the security architecture and include a list of hardware and software and approximate costs. Draw your final design on a separate sheet of paper or in a drawing program.

Case Project 13-2: Completing the Green Globe Project Proposal

At this point, you should have your network design proposal for Green Globe completed. Submit the following to your instructor:

- A written design proposal that includes all the documentation you have completed in each chapter.

- Include your research, drafts, and any worksheets at the end of your proposal as appendixes, unless instructed otherwise.

- Make sure sources are cited correctly and your paper conforms to your school or instructor's writing guidelines.

- Include a network diagram showing the physical and logical topology of your design; a list of all hardware, software, and other equipment needed with approximate costs; and any other relevant information and supporting documentation.

Congratulations! Your case project for this book is complete.

13

SC0-451 OBJECTIVES

Table A-1 maps the Tactical Perimeter Defense objectives in the Security Certified Professional's (SCP's) SC0-451 course to the corresponding chapter and section title where the objectives are covered in this book. Major sections are listed after the chapter number, and applicable subsections are shown in parentheses. Because the SCP exams undergo periodic updating and revising, you should check the SCP Web site for the latest developments at *www.securitycertified.net*.

Table A-1 Objectives-to-chapter mapping

Domain objective	Chapter and section(s)
Domain 1.0: Network Defense Fundamentals	
1.1: Examine Network Defense Fundamentals	Chapter 1: Overview of Threats to Network Security, Goals of Network Security
1.2: Identify Network Defense Technologies	Chapter 1: Using Network Defense Technologies in Layers
1.3: Examine Access Control Methods	Chapter 1: Using Network Defense Technologies in Layers (Routing and Access Control Methods)
1.4: Define the Principles of Network Auditing	Chapter 1: Using Network Defense Technologies in Layers (Network Auditing and Log Files)
1.5: Identify the Impact of Defense	Chapter 1: The Impact of Defense
Domain 2.0: Hardening Routers and Access Control Lists	
2.1: Implement Fundamental Cisco Router Security	Chapter 3: Understanding Routing Protocols Chapter 4: Creating and Using Access Control Lists, Examining Cisco Router Logging, Understanding Cisco Authentication and Authorization
2.2: Describe the Routing Process	Chapter 3: Understanding the Routing Process, Understanding Routing Protocols
2.3: Remove Unwanted Protocols and Services	Chapter 4: Removing Unneeded Protocols and Services
2.4: Create and Implement Access Control Lists	Chapter 4: Creating and Using Access Control Lists
2.5: Configure Cisco Router Logging	Chapter 4: Examining Cisco Router Logging

Table A-1   Objectives-to-chapter mapping (continued)

Domain objective	Chapter and section(s)
Domain 3.0: Implementing IPSec and Virtual Private Networks	
3.1: IPSec Fundamentals	Chapter 8: VPN Core Activity 1: Encapsulation (Understanding IPSec/IKE)
3.2: Implement IPSec on Windows Server 2003	Chapter 8: VPN Core Activity 1: Encapsulation (Understanding IPSec/IKE)
3.3: Identify Core VPN Concepts	Chapter 8: (All)
3.4: Examine VPN Design and Architecture	Chapter 8: Understanding VPN Concepts, VPN Core Activity 1: Encapsulation, VPN Core Activity 2: Encryption, VPN Core Activity 3: Authentication Chapter 9: Planning VPN Deployment, Configuring VPNs, Adjusting Packet-Filtering Rules for VPNs
3.5: Implement a VPN Using Windows Server 2003	Chapter 9: Creating a VPN in Windows Server 2003
Domain 4.0: Advanced TCP/IP	
4.1: Examine the Core Concepts of TCP/IP	Chapter 2: TCP/IP Fundamentals Review, Examining Internet Protocol Version 4, Examining Internet Protocol Version 6
4.2: Identify and Describe Packet Headers	Chapter 2: Examining Internet Protocol Version 4, Examining Internet Protocol Version 6
4.3: Examine the Session Setup and Teardown Process	Chapter 2: Examining Internet Protocol Version 4 (The TCP Life Cycle)
Domain 5.0: Securing Wireless Networks	
5.1: Describe Wireless Networking Fundamentals	Chapter 12: Wireless Communication Concepts, Wireless Network Design
5.2: Implement Wireless Security Solutions	Chapter 13: Understanding Wireless Network Security Fundamentals, Examining Wireless Security Solutions
5.3: Configure Wireless Auditing	Chapter 13: Examining Wireless Security Solutions (Wireless Auditing)
5.4: Identify Wireless PKI Solutions	Chapter 13: Understanding Wireless Network Security Fundamentals, Examining Wireless Security Solutions

Table A-1   Objectives-to-chapter mapping (continued)

Domain objective	Chapter and section(s)
Domain 6.0: Designing and Configuring Intrusion Detection Systems	
6.1: Identify the Goals of an IDS	Chapter 10: Examining Intrusion Detection System Components Chapter 11: Developing IDS Filter Rules
6.2: Examine Host-Based Intrusion Detection	Chapter 10: Options for Intrusion Detection Systems
6.3: Examine Network-Based Intrusion Detection	Chapter 10: Options for Intrusion Detection Systems
6.4: Describe IDS Log Analysis	Chapter 10: Examining Intrusion Detection Step by Step (Step 7: Logging and Reviewing Events) Chapter 11: Developing IDS Filter Rules (Log File Analysis)
6.5: Describe Methods of Using an IDS	Chapter 10: Examining Intrusion Detection Step by Step Chapter 11: Installing and Configuring an IDS, Incident Response, Disabling Signatures
Domain 7.0: Designing and Configuring Firewall Systems	
7.1: Identify Firewall Components	Chapter 5: Comparing Hardware and Software Firewalls Chapter 6: Designing Firewall Configurations Chapter 7: Managing Log Files, Improving Firewall Performance, Installing and Configuring Microsoft ISA Server 2006 (ISA Server 2006 Components)
7.2: Create a Firewall Policy	Chapter 6: Establishing Rules and Restrictions
7.3: Define Firewall Rule Sets and Packet Filters	Chapter 5: Approaches to Packet Filtering Chapter 6: Designing Firewall Configurations, Establishing Rules and Restrictions, Authenticating Users Chapter 7: Editing the Rule Base, Managing Log Files
7.4: Examine the Proxy Server	Chapter 5: Working with Proxy Servers, Using Network Address Translation
7.5: Examine the Bastion Host	Chapter 5: Choosing a Bastion Host
7.6: Describe a Honeypot	Chapter 5: Choosing a Bastion Host (Using Honeypots)
7.7: Install and Configure ISA Server 2006	Chapter 6: Designing Firewall Configurations, Establishing Rules and Restrictions Chapter 7: Installing and Configuring Microsoft ISA Server 2006
7.8: Install and Configure IPTables	Chapter 6: Designing Firewall Configurations, Establishing Rules and Restrictions Chapter 7: Managing and Configuring Iptables

B

ADDITIONAL RESOURCES

Information security is a constantly changing field. To keep up with the latest developments, you should visit the Web sites and other resources mentioned in this appendix regularly. Many sites offer white papers, research papers, and other background information on topics such as firewalls, packet filtering, authentication, and encryption. You can find policy hints and resources, disaster-planning guides, and tools to help you do your job. In addition, you should visit these sites to learn about the latest threats. Bugs, security holes, and patches to plug them will be available online long before you read about them in a book.

SECURITY RESOURCES

New threats surface daily, and you need ways to keep up with them. The Web sites in Table B-1 contains resources you can use to enhance your skills and knowledge.

Table B-1   Helpful sites for IT security professionals

Web site	Description
Common Vulnerabilities and Exposures (CVE), *www.cve.mitre.org*	CVE, a dictionary of publicly known security vulnerabilities, helps vendors share information about vulnerabilities so that they can work together.
Symantec Security Response, *www.symantec.com/security_response/index.jsp*	Symantec maintains extensive information, including an outstanding virus encyclopedia and detailed assessments of other security threats.
SANS Internet Storm Center, *http://isc.sans.org*	This site, which is affiliated with SANS, specializes in how to respond to intrusions, incidents, and security alerts. Maps and charts show security breaches reported by geographic region. The site also includes a list of current attack trends, such as frequently attacked ports and recently reported malicious software.
The Center for Internet Security, *www.cisecurity.org*	This nonprofit organization is devoted to developing security standards it calls "benchmarks." Benchmarks are available for Linux, UNIX, and other operating systems.
System Administration, Networking and Security (SANS) Institute, *www.sans.org*	This research and education organization focuses on network security. SANS conducts seminars and workshops on security around the country.
CERT Coordination Center, *www.cert.org*	This group, affiliated with the Carnegie-Mellon Institute, lists security alerts, incident notes, and vulnerabilities on its home page. CERT also offers tips and articles about aspects of network security and training courses.
Forum of Incident Response and Security Teams (FIRST), *www.first.org*	This group is a coalition of security incident response teams working in government, commercial, and academic organizations that seek to promote rapid reaction to security incidents by coordinating communication and sharing information.

Table B-1   Helpful sites for IT security professionals (continued)

Web site	Description
The National Institute of Standards and Technology (NIST), *www.nist.gov* NIST Computer Security Division, Computer Security Resource Center (CSRC), *http://csrc.nist.gov*	NIST is a U.S. federal agency with the mission to develop and promote measurement, standards, and technology to enhance productivity, facilitate trade, and improve the quality of life. The Computer Security Division addresses information security topics. In addition, NIST Special Publications are available for many computer topics and can be useful as standardized guidelines.
Internet Assigned Numbers Authority (IANA), *www.iana.org*	IANA assigns and maintains number assignments for the Internet, including port numbers and protocol numbers. Also coordinates DNS and IP addressing.
Internet Engineering Task Force (IETF), *www.ietf.org/home.html*	The IETF is an international body of network designers, vendors, operators, and researchers cooperatively working toward the Internet's evolution and smooth operation. RFCs are managed primarily by the IETF.
Institute of Electrical and Electronics Engineers, *www.ieee.org/portal/site*	This organization is a major international membership association for computer professionals. Membership isn't free, but the organization offers online courses, information, and professional networking opportunities for members.
Internet Corporation for Assigned Names and Numbers (ICANN), *www.icann.org*	ICANN is responsible for global coordination of the Domain Name System and its unique identifiers.

B

Information Resources

You should also join newsgroups and mailing lists for IT professionals as a way to network with your peers and learn from their experiences. Sometimes you run into a problem that you can't solve, despite poring through manuals and textbooks, searching the Internet, and running numerous tests. Table B-2 lists some resources to check.

Table B-2   Information resources

Web site	Description
SecurityFocus Mailing Lists, *www.securityfocus.com/archive*	SecurityFocus runs security-related mailing lists on topics from intrusion detection to firewalls to honeypots. One of the best features is being able to search archived messages by topic without having to subscribe. However, by joining a list, you can get news daily.
SANS Institute Computer Security Newsletters and Digests, *www.sans.org/newsletters*	The newsletters published by the SANS Institute include a weekly News Bites publication and a weekly Security Alert Consensus listing current security threats and countermeasures. SANS has added a monthly newsletter called OUCH!, which is a consensus security awareness report for end users.
Symantec Security Response Weblog, *www.symantec.com/enterprise/security_response/weblog/*	Symantec maintains a forum about a wide array of security topics open to both the general public and technical experts. Symantec staff post information on the blog occasionally, although they don't usually answer questions.

SECURITY CERTIFICATION SITES

The following sites offer certifications that can be invaluable for finding employment in network security.

Global Information Assurance Certification (GIAC)

The GIAC Web site (*www.giac.org*) provides information about the SANS Institute certification exams. Programs include the GIAC Silver, Gold, and Platinum certifications (in ascending order of difficulty).

The International Information Systems Security Certification Consortium (ISC²)

ISC² (*www.isc2.org*) is an international nonprofit organization dedicated to maintaining a common body of knowledge on security. ISC² prepares and administers two well-known certifications in network security: Certified Information Systems Security Professional (CISSP) and Systems Security Certified Practitioner (SSCP).

CompTIA Certification

The Computing Technology Industry Association (*www.comptia.org/default.aspx*) is best known for the A+ certification track. The CompTIA Security+ Certification exam is also available to establish fundamental security competency in firewalls, encryption, and intrusion detection. In addition, CompTIA offers the Network+ certification, which verifies competence in fundamental networking skills, and Linux+, which tests knowledge of the Linux OS.

The Security Certified Program

The Security Certified Program (*www.securitycertified.net/index.htm*) is the vendor-neutral administrator of the Security Certified Network Specialist (SCNS), Security Certified Network Professional (SCNP), and Security Certified Network Architect (SCNA) exams. For the SCNS certification, candidates must pass the Tactical Perimeter Defense SC0-451 exam, which this book covers. For the SCNP certification, candidates must pass the Strategic Infrastructure Security SC0-471 exam, which is covered in *Guide to Strategic Information Security: Becoming a Security Network Professional* (Course Technology, 2008, 1418836613).

RESOURCES FOR CISCO ROUTER INFORMATION

Most vendors maintain knowledge bases and public forums where users can post problems and get answers and helpful hints from experts and other knowledgeable users. You can join vendors' IT professional forums if you meet certain criteria, such as certification from that vendor. Cisco maintains an extensive knowledge base for its products and provides additional technical and security guidelines. Because Cisco is the de facto standard for routers, many other organizations offer router security information for Cisco products. Table B-3 lists some helpful resources you can investigate.

Table B-3   Security configuration resources

Web site	Resource
National Security Agency, Security Configuration Guides, *www.nsa.gov/snac*	The Router Security Configuration Guide provides guidance on the secure configuration of routers. The NSA also offers configuration guides for OSs, applications, database servers, Voice over IP (VoIP), and other products.
SANS Institute, The SANS Security Policy Project, *www.sans.org/resources/policies*	SANS offers consensus papers on security policy development, including templates and samples.
Cisco, Improving Security on Cisco Routers, *www.cisco.com/warp/public/707/21.html*	This article on improving security on Cisco routers covers logging, secure IP routing, password management, disabling or removing unnecessary services, and more.

Quick Reference for the Cisco Router Command-Line Interface

The Cisco command-line interface (CLI) is the primary tool for managing Cisco routers. It's also used for managing Cisco switches, VPN concentrators, and firewalls. To ensure perimeter security, you must become comfortable working at the CLI. Table B-4 is a brief recap of configuration modes.

NOTE

EXEC is the abbreviation for command executive, which interprets commands entered at the CLI.

Table B-4   Cisco router configuration modes

Mode	Prompt	Common uses
User EXEC (UM)	Router>	View router status and configuration information and provide access to privileged mode
Privileged EXEC (PM)	Router#	Copy, erase, set up, and show router settings
Global configuration (GC)	Router(config)#	Configure clock, hostname, enable and enable secret passwords, and so forth; provide access to line, router, and interface configuration modes
Interface configuration (IF)	Router(config-if)#	Configure interfaces with addressing, access control lists, connection speeds, and other connection details
Router configuration (CR)	Router(config-router)#	Configure RIP, IGRP, and other routing protocols
Line configuration (CL)	Router(config-line)#	Configure lines, such as console, auxiliary, and virtual terminal lines

Table B-5 lists common commands along with the configuration mode you must be in to use the command. Remember that routers offer context-sensitive help, so you can type a command name followed by ? to get a list of possible parameters.

Table B-5 Common Cisco router commands

Mode	Command	Description
UM	enable	Enter privileged mode from user mode
PM	disable	Return to user mode from privileged mode
PM	configure terminal	Enter global configuration mode
PM	line	Enter line configuration mode
GC	line *line*	Configure the line (specifying the line type and number for *line*, such as vty 0 4 or console 0)
GC	interface *interface*	Enter interface configuration mode (specifying the interface type and number for *interface*, such as Ethernet 0)
GC	router *protocol*	Enter router configuration mode and enable routing protocols
GC	hostname *name*	Set the router's hostname
GC	banner motd *message*	Set the router's banner message of the day (motd), with a delimiting character, usually #, at the beginning and end of message text
N/A	Ctrl+Z (key combination)	Return to privileged mode
PM	clock set *hh:mm:ss month day year*	Set the router's time and date
PM	reload	Restart the router
N/A	exit	Log out from the > or # prompt; from other prompts, takes you back one level
UM or PM	quit	Log out of the router
Any	?	Get context-sensitive help for a prompt or command
ROM Monitor mode (rommon> prompt)	config-register *register code*	Tell the router how to boot and change the configuration register settings; specify where the router gets startup information or tell it to boot to ROM Monitor mode
Any	no *command*	Disable the command and parameters (if any) specified by *command*

Chapter 4 explains configuring passwords on Cisco routers in more detail, but Table B-6 summarizes the available commands.

Table B-6   Cisco commands for configuring passwords

Mode	Command	Description
GC	enable password *password*	Set the privileged mode password
GC	enable secret *password*	Set an encrypted privileged mode password
CL	password *password* login	After specifying the line type and number to switch to line configuration mode, set the line password
GC	service password-encryption	Encrypt all passwords on the router

Table B-7 summarizes commands for configuring startup and running settings for Cisco routers. Unless otherwise specified in the table, you must be in privileged mode to use these commands.

Table B-7   Cisco commands for startup and running configurations

Command	Description
hostname *name*	Configure the router's hostname
copy running-config tftp	Copy the running configuration in RAM to a TFTP server
copy startup-config tftp	Copy the startup config in NVRAM to a Trivial File Transfer Protocol (TFTP) server
copy tftp running-config	Copy the configuration from a TFTP server to merge with the running configuration
copy tftp startup-config	Copy the configuration from a TFTP server to replace the startup configuration
copy run start	Copy the working (running) configuration file in RAM to NVRAM; replaces the startup config file
copy start run	Copy the startup config file from NVRAM to RAM; merged with the file in RAM
copy flash tftp	Copy the IOS in flash memory to a TFTP server
copy tftp flash	Copy the IOS from a TFTP server to flash memory
configure memory	Specify pulling configuration information from NVRAM
configure network	Specify loading the running configuration from a TFTP server
configure overwrite-network	Overwrite the existing NVRAM with the configuration stored on a TFTP server
erase startup-config	Erase the current startup configuration
erase flash	Erase flash memory on the router
delete nvram	Erase the switch configuration
exec-timeout *time in seconds*	Set the timeout (in seconds) for the console connection; must be in line configuration mode
logging synchronous	Prevent console messages from being displayed while configuring the console line; must be in line configuration mode

Cisco has a number of commands you can use to see current configurations; common ones are listed in Table B-8. Unless other specified in the table, you can use these commands from user or privileged mode.

Table B-8 Cisco commands for viewing configurations

Command	Description
show clock	Display the clock
show processes	Display CPU utilization information
show interface Ethernet *interface number*	Display Ethernet interface information
show interface serial *interface number*	Display serial interface information
show interfaces	List information for all configured interfaces
show protocol	Show protocols and which interfaces are using them
show history	Display the most recent 10 commands entered
show flash	Display information for flash memory
show cdp neighbor	Display a list of attached Cisco devices; with the *detail* parameter, IP address information is also displayed
show running-config	Display the running configuration; privileged mode only
show startup-config	Display the startup configuration file in NVRAM; privileged mode only
show version	Display version information

Table B-9 summarizes common commands for configuring Cisco router interfaces.

Table B-9 Cisco commands for configuring interfaces

Mode	Command	Description
GC	interface serial *interface number*	Enter interface configuration mode for the specified serial interface
GC	interface Ethernet *interface number*	Enter interface configuration mode for the specified Ethernet interface
IF	encapsulation *encapsulation type*	Specify the encapsulation type for an interface
IF	description *description*	Enter a description for an interface
IF	no shutdown	Enable an interface
IF	loopback	Configure an interface as a loopback for testing
PM	clear interface *interface*	Clear the counters for a specified interface

Table B-10 lists common commands for configuring routing protocols.

Table B-10   Cisco commands for configuring protocols

Mode	Command	Description
IF	ip address *IP address mask*	Set the IP address and mask for an interface
GC	router rip	Enable RIP routing and access router configuration mode
GC	router igrp *AS number*	Enable IGRP routing and access router configuration mode; enter the Autonomous System (AS) number
CR	network *network number*	Use after the router rip and router igrp commands to specify the network number
GC	ip routing	Enable IP routing on the router
PM	debug ip *rip* | *igrp*	Allow real-time monitoring of RIP or IGRP updates
PM	no debug all OR undebug all	Disable all debugging activities
PM	debug all	Enable all debugging activities
UM or PM	show ip route	Display the contents of a router's routing table
UM or PM	ping *ip address* OR *hostname*	Confirm that a host is reachable by IP address or hostname
UM or PM	telnet *ip address*	Start a session with a Telnet server or other remote host
UM or PM	show ip protocol	Display statistics for the IP protocol
UM or PM	show ip interface *interface*	Display statistics for the specified IP interface; if no interface type number is specified for *interface*, statistics for all interfaces configured with IP are displayed
GC	ip route *ip address mask*	Enter a static IP route in the routing table
GC	ip classless	Tell the router to forward packets to a default route when the destination network isn't in the routing table
CR	passive-interface *interface*	Prevent routing updates from being sent out the specified interface

Table B-11 lists commands for configuring access control lists (ACLs).

Table B-11   Cisco commands for configuring ACLs

Mode	Command	Description
GC	access-list *list#* [permit/deny] [source IP address] [source wildcard mask]	Create a standard IP ACL
GC	access-list *list#* [permit/deny] [protocol] [source IP address] [source wildcard mask] [destination IP address] [destination wildcard mask] [operator] [port] [log]	Create an extended IP ACL
GC	no access-list *list#*	Remove the specified ACL
IF	ip access-group *list#* [in/out]	Apply an IP ACL to an interface
IF	ipx access-group *list#* [in/out]	Apply an IPX ACL to an interface
GC	access-list *list#* [permit/deny] [source network/node address] [destination network/node address]	Create a standard IPX ACL
GC	access-list *list#* [permit/deny] [protocol] [source network/node address] [socket] [destination network/node address] [socket]	Create an extended IPX ACL
PM	show ip access-lists	Show all IP ACLs
PM	show access-lists *list#*	Show the specified ACL; if no number is entered, all configured ACLs are shown

Glossary

absorption — A type of loss in which certain materials absorb the RF signal.

access control lists (ACLs) — A series of permit or deny statements applied to inbound or outbound router interfaces for each protocol the router processes. ACLs are used to permit allowed traffic and block denied traffic.

access point (AP) — A wireless device that acts as the base station for a wireless network segment and serves as the bridge between wired and wireless segments.

accountability — The capability to track an attempted attack or intrusion back to its source.

acknowledgement (ACK) — A type of control frame that a receiving station sends when a packet has been received successfully with no errors.

active attacks — Attacks that use active scanning (sending out probe request frames on each available channel) in an attempt to gather information for subsequent attacks.

active scanning — The process of a wireless station sending out a probe request frame on each available channel and waiting for a probe response frame from available APs.

Address Resolution Protocol (ARP) — A protocol included in the TCP/IP protocol stack that maps IP addresses to MAC addresses.

administrative distance — A value calculated by a routing protocol algorithm or assigned by the administrator, used to determine the reliability (cost) of a route. Routing protocols use metrics to calculate an administrative distance.

Advanced Encryption Standard (AES) — An encryption standard that uses the Rijndael symmetric block cipher; it replaced 3DES as the U.S. government standard in 2002.

agent — An IDS component (hardware, software, or combination) that monitors traffic on a specific host.

amplitude — Maximum departure of a wave from its undisturbed state; the height of the carrier wave.

amplitude modulation (AM) — An analog modulation method in which the height of the carrier wave is changed.

amplitude shift keying (ASK) — A binary modulation technique similar to AM that changes the height of the carrier wave. With ASK, instead of both the 1 and 0 bits having carrier signals, the 1 bit has positive voltage, and the 0 bit has zero voltage.

analog RF signal — A continuous RF wave that oscillates between positive and negative voltage.

anomaly detection — A type of detection system based on profiles that sends an alarm when it detects an event deviating from behavior defined as "normal."

antenna — A device used to transmit or receive radio waves. An antenna usually has one end in the air and the other end fixed to the ground directly or via a grounded device. Antennas are generally made of copper wire or other conductive material.

antispoofing — A method of preventing spoofed inbound packets that might contain source addresses matching the internal LAN addressing scheme. Antispoofing uses ACLs on the router that deny or drop packets matching criteria indicating that they might be spoofed.

anycast — An address created automatically when a unicast address is assigned to more than one interface. Anycast addresses are assigned from unicast address ranges and have the same scopes as unicast addresses.

area border routers (ABRs) — In OSPF, routers that have interfaces in multiple areas. *See also* Open Shortest Path First (OSPF).

area ID — A designation to differentiate between different OSPF areas. An area ID can take the form of a randomly chosen integer between 0 and 4,294,967,295 or can be in dotted decimal format like an IP address, such as 0.0.0.0. *See also* Open Shortest Path First (OSPF).

ARP table — A listing maintained by network nodes for routing purposes. Routers also maintain ARP tables, enabling a router to respond to an ARP broadcast with the needed information without having to forward a broadcast. *See also* proxy ARP.

association — A two-step process of being accepted into a wireless network. First, a station listens for beacon frames to locate a network to join, and then it goes through the authentication process. Second, the station sends an association request frame; if it's accepted, it receives an association ID and connection information. A station can be associated with only one network at a time and must be authenticated before being associated.

asymmetric cryptography — A type of encryption in which two different keys are used. A private key is kept by the certificate holder and never shared; a public key is shared among users to encrypt and decrypt communication. *See also* symmetric cryptography.

attack visualization — The process of replaying an attack so that you can see what the attacker viewed.

authentication — The process of determining authorized users' identities through matching a username and password, a fingerprint or retinal scan, a smart card and PIN, and so on.

authentication, authorization, and accounting (AAA) logging — A type of logging that collects information about user dial-up connections, commands, logons, logoffs, HTTP accesses, and similar events. AAA logs are sent to an authentication server.

Authentication Header (AH) — An IPSec protocol that provides authentication of TCP/IP packets to ensure data integrity.

autonomous system boundary routers (ASBRs) — Routers that act as gateways or intermediaries between OSPF and other routing protocols or between other instances of the OSPF routing process. *See also* Open Shortest Path First (OSPF).

Autonomous System Number (ASN) — An integer or IP address representing an autonomous system. ASNs are assigned by IANA and allocated to regional registries. *See also* autonomous systems (ASs).

autonomous systems (ASs) — A network or group of networks controlled and managed by an administrator on behalf of an entity, such as a corporation or university.

availability — Making sure those who are authorized to access resources can do so in a reliable and timely manner.

backdoors — A way of gaining unauthorized access to a computer or other resource, usually through an opening in a program that's supposed to be known only to the program's author.

banners — Messages a router can be programmed to display to anyone logging on to the router.

Basic Service Area (BSA) — The geographical area of coverage for a WLAN.

Basic Service Set (BSS) — An IEEE-defined WLAN configuration in which a group of wireless devices is served by a single AP.

bastion host — A computer on the network perimeter that has been hardened with OS patches, authentication, and encryption.

broadcast — A communication sent to all points on a specific network.

buffered logging — A type of system logging that stores log output files in the router's memory (RAM).

cache — Store data on disk for later retrieval; also a hard disk area where files are stored.

carrier signal — The signal on which a radio transmission is sent.

certification authority (CA) — A trusted organization that issues digital certificates that can be used to generate keys. *See also* digital certificate.

chain of custody — The written record of who handled an object; used as evidence in court.

chains — Sets of packet-filtering rules that Iptables uses. *See also* Iptables.

change management — The process of documenting changes to hardware or software, which helps administrators roll back a configuration correctly if changes have an adverse affect.

chipping code — The bit pattern used in direct sequence spread spectrum *See also* direct sequence spread spectrum (DSSS).

Classless Interdomain Routing (CIDR) — An IP address notation method that uses a slash (/) followed by the number of masked bits for an address—for example, 192.168.6.5/27 instead of 192.168.6.5 255.255.255.224.

cleanup rule — A packet-filtering rule that comes last in a rule base; it covers any other packets that haven't been covered in preceding rules.

clear to send (CTS) — A type of control frame sent in response to a request to send (RTS) frame; it gives the sender clearance to begin transmitting packets. *See also* control frames.

client authentication — The process of granting access to network resources based on a source IP address, computer MAC address, or computer name rather than user information.

client-to-site VPN — A type of VPN connection that makes a network accessible to remote users requiring dial-up access; also called a remote access VPN.

co-channel interference — Interference from two or more wireless access points transmitting with the same frequency.

Code Division Multiple Access (CDMA) — A form of spread spectrum signaling in which sender and receiver share a common code to differentiate their communications from other transmissions.

command console — Software that provides a graphical interface to an IDS.

confidentiality — The goal of preventing intentional or unintentional disclosure of communication between a sender and recipient.

Configuration Storage server — In ISA Server 2006, the server that stores configuration information for all array members in the enterprise.

containment — The process of preventing a malicious file or compromised media from spreading to other network resources.

control frames — A type of MAC frame used to help deliver data frames between stations and control access to the medium.

countermeasures — Strategies that address threats to network security.

cracker — A person who attempts to gain access to unauthorized resources on a network, usually by finding a way to circumvent passwords, firewalls, or other protective measures.

Data Encryption Standard (DES) — An encryption scheme developed by IBM in the mid-1970s that was adopted as an encryption standard in 1977. It's now considered obsolete and is rarely used.

data frames — A type of MAC frame that contains the TCP/IP packet sent over a wireless network or between wireless devices. It carries data from higher-layer applications, such as printer control data or Web pages.

datagrams — Discrete chunks of information; each datagram contains source and destination addresses, control settings, and data. Also called "packets."

default key — A wireless station or AP's key for encrypting messages for transmission. The default key doesn't have to be the same on every station, but the same key must be used for both encryption and decryption.

default routes — A statically configured route that directs all packets not configured in the routing table to a particular route. A packet to a destination that a router has no other table entry for is sent to a default route automatically for processing.

defense in depth (DiD) — A layering approach to security that protects a network at many different levels by using a variety of strategies and methods.

demilitarized zone (DMZ) — A subnetwork of publicly accessible Web, e-mail, and other servers that's outside the LAN but still protected by the firewall.

dependency services — Services a computer system needs to function correctly. Key system processes usually depend on other processes to function.

diffraction — Similar to refraction, except the signal bends around objects in its path, usually objects with a rough surface. *See also* refraction.

diffused IR transmission — An infrared transmission that relies on reflected light rather than a line-of-sight connection between the IR emitter and detector.

digital certificate — An electronic document issued by a certification authority that contains information about the certificate holder and can be used to exchange public and private keys. *See also* certification authority (CA).

digital RF signals — RF signals that oscillate between positive and negative voltage but are broken into discrete segments with many starts and stops in the data stream, instead of a constant stream, as in analog transmissions.

digital signature — An attachment to an e-mail or other message that provides tamper detection and enables the recipient to verify the sender's identity.

direct sequence spread spectrum (DSSS) — A wireless modulation technique that uses an expanded redundant code to transmit each data bit. The spreading code (key) is the chip sequence used to represent message bits, and the key is applied at the data level.

directed IR transmission — A form of IR transmission that requires the emitter and the detector to be pointed directly at one another.

distance–vector routing protocol — A routing protocol that uses mathematical calculations to compare routes based on some measurement of distance, such as hops.

DNS zone transfer — A query used by secondary DNS servers to update their DNS records.

dual–homed host — A computer that has been configured with more than one network interface.

dynamic routes — Entries in a routing table that use routing protocols and routing algorithms to calculate the best path.

electromagnetic (EM) radiation — Electromagnetic energy traveling as a self-propagating wave and spreading out as it moves.

EM spectrum — All forms of EM radiation collectively. EM radiation forms are (from highest energy to lowest) gamma rays, x-rays, ultraviolet light, infrared light, visible light, microwaves, and radio waves.

Encapsulating Security Payload (ESP) — An IPSec protocol that encrypts the header and data parts of TCP/IP packets.

encapsulation — The process of enclosing a packet within another one that has different IP source and destination information to ensure a high degree of protection.

Equivalent Isotropically Radiated Power (EIRP) — The power radiated out by a wireless system's antenna, including not only the intended transmission power, but also unintended gain.

eradication — The process of removing any files or programs that result from an incident, including malicious code or malware, Registry keys, and unnecessary executable files.

escalated — The process of increasing the response to an intrusion to a higher level.

event horizon — The entire length of an attack, from the first packet the IDS receives to the last packet needed to complete the attack.

Extended Service Set (ESS) — An IEEE-defined WLAN configuration in which multiple BSS networks are connected through a common distribution system.

Extensible Authentication Protocol (EAP) — A group of extensible management protocols used in IEEE 802.1x. EAP includes a method of secure key exchange, and wireless stations use it to request port access.

Exterior Gateway Protocols (EGPs) — Protocols used to enable routers to communicate routing information between different autonomous systems.

fading — A form of interference/power loss where the signal is reflected or refracted by the atmosphere, ground, or other obstacles, and the reflected path interferes with the direct path.

failover firewall — A backup firewall that can be configured to switch on if the first one fails, thus ensuring uninterrupted service.

false negatives — Attacks that occur but aren't detected by the IDS.

false positives — Alarms generated by legitimate network traffic rather than actual attacks.

Federal Communications Commission (FCC) — The primary regulatory agency in the United States for wireless communication.

firewall — Hardware or software configured to block unauthorized access to a network.

firewall appliances — Hardware devices with firewall functionality.

firewall policy — An addition to a security policy that describes how firewalls should handle application traffic, such as Web or e-mail applications.

flush timers — Timers that control when a route is flushed from a routing table.

follow-up — The process of documenting what happened when an incident was detected and a response occurred.

footer — A section sometimes added to a TCP/IP packet that tells a computer it's the end of the packet.

free space path loss — The loss of signal strength resulting from the dispersion of the signal over distance.

frequency — The number of times an event occurs in a specified time period; the rate at which an electrical current alternates, creating different radio transmissions.

Frequency Division Multiple Access (FDMA) — An access method in which multiple transmissions are separated by frequencies for each communication.

frequency division multiplexing (FDM) — An RF signaling method that enables multiple users to share a communication channel. Base signals are modulated on different carrier waves and combined to form a composite signal.

frequency hopping spread spectrum (FHSS) — A modulation technique in which the range of frequencies used for transmission changes during the transmission. The time spent on a particular frequency is called the dwell time.

frequency modulation (FM) — An analog modulation technique that changes the number of waves used to represent one cycle, so the number of waves representing a 1 bit is higher than the number of waves representing a 0 bit.

frequency shift keying (FSK) — A binary modulation technique that changes the frequency of the carrier signal.

Fresnel zone — An area in which the RF signal strength can be calculated to determine the signal strength, identify potential obstacles, and determine the potential for multipath distortion between sending and receiving antennas.

fully qualified domain names (FQDNs) — Complete DNS names of computers that include the computer name, domain name, and domain name extension, such as *www.course.com*.

gain — The positive difference in amplitude between signals.

Generic Routing Encapsulation (GRE) — A nonproprietary tunneling protocol that can encapsulate a variety of Network-layer protocols.

hardened — The process of making a computer more secure by eliminating unnecessary software and services, closing potential openings, and protecting information with encryption and authentication.

header — The part of a packet containing source and destination information and general information about the packet.

hide-mode mapping — A NAT mode used to hide multiple private IP addresses behind one public IP address.

holddowns — Timers used to help prevent routers from accepting and entering updates about paths that might be down.

honeypot — A computer placed on the network perimeter to attract attackers and divert them from internal hosts.

hopping code — The sequence of changing frequencies in FHSS that determines the sequence and speed of frequency hops.

host address — The part of an IP address that's unique to a computer in its subnet.

host-based IDS (HIDS) — An IDS deployed on hosts inside the network perimeter.

hybrid configuration — A VPN configuration that combines characteristics of the mesh and star configurations.

hybrid firewall — A product that combines features of hardware and software firewalls in one package.

hybrid IDS — An IDS that combines the capabilities of HIDSs and NIDSs for more flexibility and security.

IDS management server — An IDS component that serves as the central repository for sensor and agent data.

IEEE 802.11 authentication — The process by which an AP accepts or rejects a wireless device's connection attempt.

IEEE 802.11 Wireless Ethernet standards — A series of standards specifying transmission speeds, ranges, and other aspects of wireless networks.

IEEE 802.11i — A wireless security standard intended to replace the IEEE 802.11 WEP-based standard. It uses 802.1x authentication and AES for encryption. *See also* Advanced Encryption Standard (AES).

IEEE 802.1x — A standard developed to provide a means of port-based access control on Ethernet LANs; it has been revised for wireless networks to incorporate authentication and key management.

incident response — The actions taken after a security incident to determine what happened and what countermeasures should be taken to ensure the network's continued security.

Independent Basic Service Set (IBSS) — A wireless network that doesn't use an AP; also known as ad-hoc mode.

infrared (IR) radiation — A type of radiation with a shorter wavelength than radio waves but a longer wavelength than visible light.

infrared transmissions — IR uses infrared light pulses. Infrared transmissions require an emitter and a detector. The emitter is usually a laser diode or LED. The detector is sometimes combined with the emitter and does just what its name implies: It detects IR transmissions and generates the corresponding electrical current for wired communication.

initialization vector (IV) — In WEP's shared key encryption, a 24-bit value added to the beginning of a key to initialize the key stream generated by the RC4 algorithm.

inline sensor — An NIDS sensor positioned so that all traffic on the network segment is examined as it passes through. *See also* network-based IDS (NIDS).

integrity — The goal of ensuring the accuracy and consistency of information during all processing (storage, transmission, and so forth).

intentional radiator — A device that's not the antenna and is designed to generate radio signals.

Interior Gateway Protocols (IGPs) — Protocols used to enable routers in an autonomous system to communicate routing information to each other.

Interior Gateway Routing Protocol (IGRP) — A distance-vector routing protocol that uses a composite metric calculated by factoring weighted mathematical values for internetwork delay, bandwidth, reliability, and load.

internal routers — In OSPF, routers that have all interfaces in a single area and can communicate only with routers in the same area. *See also* Open Shortest Path First (OSPF).

Internet Control Message Protocol (ICMP) — A protocol that reports network communication errors to support IP communications. The Ping command is a common troubleshooting utility based on ICMP.

Internet Key Exchange (IKE) — A form of key exchange used to encrypt and decrypt data as it passes through a VPN tunnel. IKE uses tunnel method encryption to encrypt and then encapsulate packets for extra security. *See also* tunnel method encryption.

Internet Protocol Security (IPSec) — A set of standard procedures that the Internet Engineering Task Force (IETF) developed for enabling secure communication on the Internet.

Internet Protocol version 4 (IPv4) — The IP addressing system currently in widespread use on the Internet, in which addresses are created with 32 bits (4 bytes) of data.

Internet Protocol version 6 (IPv6) — A new version of IP that's gaining support among software and hardware manufacturers and that will eventually replace IPv4; this version calls for 128-bit IP addresses.

Internet Security Association Key Management Protocol (ISAKMP) — An IPSec-related protocol that enables two computers to agree on security settings and establish a Security Association so that they can exchange keys by using Internet Key

Exchange. *See also* Internet Key Exchange (IKE) *and* Security Association (SA).

intrusion — An attempt to gain unauthorized access to network resources and to compromise the integrity and confidentiality of network data or users' privacy.

intrusion detection — The process of monitoring network traffic to detect unauthorized access attempts and sending notifications so that countermeasures can be taken.

intrusion detection system (IDS) — A network security measure that can consist of applications and hardware devices deployed on the network, hosts, or both to prevent, detect, and respond to traffic interpreted as an intrusion.

inverse mask — The inverse of the subnet mask, also called the wildcard mask. In a subnet mask, some octets indicate the network and the rest identify the host. An inverse mask tells the router to pay attention to certain bits and ignore others.

IPSec driver — Software that handles the actual tasks of encrypting, authenticating, decrypting, and checking packets in an IPSec connection.

Iptables — A packet-filtering command-line tool used with the Linux firewall Netfilter.

ISA Server services — A component of ISA Server 2006 installed on array members that performs firewall, VPN, and caching services.

Kerberos — An IETF standard for secure authentication of requests for resource access.

key — An encoded block of data generated by an algorithm and used to encrypt and decrypt data.

Key Distribution Center (KDC) — A Kerberos component that holds secret keys for users, applications, services, or resources; creates and distributes session keys by using symmetric cryptography.

Layer 2 Tunneling Protocol (L2TP) — A tunneling protocol derived from two older protocols, Cisco's L2F and Microsoft's PPTP. L2TP encapsulates PPP packets and is usually combined with IPSec for improved security.

link-state routing protocol — A routing protocol that requires each router to maintain at least a partial network map. Routers monitor link status, and when topology or link state changes, updates are sent to neighboring routers informing them of the change.

load-balancing software — Software that prioritizes and schedules requests and distributes them to a group of servers based on each machine's current load and processing power.

loose source and record routing (lsrr) — An IP option that specifies a set of hops the packet must traverse but not necessarily every hop in the path.

loss — The negative difference in amplitude between signals.

macro viruses — A type of malware that performs the same functions as a macro but tends to be harmful.

malware — Software, such as viruses, worms, and Trojan programs, designed to cause harm, allow theft, or otherwise compromise a computer system.

management frames — A type of MAC frame used to establish and maintain communications between wireless devices or between a wireless device and an access point.

mesh configuration — A VPN configuration in which all participants in the VPN are connected to one another. This configuration is commonly arranged as a full mesh or partial mesh setup.

message digest — A code of fixed length produced by processing input through a mathematical function, usually resulting in a shortened version of the original input. Also called a one-way hash.

Message Integrity Check (MIC) — A mathematical function used in WPA that replaces the Cyclic Redundancy Check (CRC); it's designed to detect tampering in packets. *See also* Wi-Fi Protected Access (WPA).

metrics — Cost values that help routers decide the reliability of a link and include hop count, load, bandwidth, and delay.

misuse detection — A type of detection system that sends an alarm in response to characteristic signatures of known external attacks.

modulation — The process of varying the wave form to transmit a signal, such as modulating between on and off to create 1s and 0s.

multicast — A transmission used for one-to-many communication, in which a single host can send packets to a group of recipients.

Multicast Listener Discovery (MLD) — A core IPv6 protocol that enables IPv6 routers to discover multicast listeners on a directly connected link and to decide which multicast addresses are of interest to those nodes.

multipath — A signal has more than one path from the transmitter to the receiver.

multiple entry point configuration — A type of VPN configuration in which multiple gateways are used, each with a VPN tunnel connecting a different location.

narrowband — An RF transmission on one frequency or a very small frequency range.

Neighbor Discovery (ND) — A core IPv6 protocol used to resolve addresses, locate neighboring routers, and redirect hosts to better routes to reach destination addresses. ND uses ICMPv6 messages to manage node-to-node communications.

network address — The part of an IP address that a computer has in common with other computers in its subnet.

network-based IDS (NIDS) — A set of IDS components specialized for network use. It examines traffic on network segments by using sensors positioned where they can monitor network traffic, management servers, a command console, and databases of signatures.

nonrepudiation — A method for ensuring that the sender can't deny sending a message and the receiver can't deny receiving it.

notification — The process by which SIRT members receive news about security incidents.

Open Shortest Path First (OSPF) — A link-state IGP routing protocol developed to address some problems in RIP. OSPF uses areas to control link-state update boundaries.

open system authentication — This 802.11 authentication method relies on a station having an SSID that matches the network it's attempting to join as the only criteria for acceptance. Its security drawback is that SSIDs are transmitted in cleartext in management frames.

orthogonal frequency division multiplexing (OFDM) — A modulation technique that breaks a high-speed signal into smaller pieces and sends it in parallel across many lower-speed channels.

out-of-band notification — A method of sending news about a security incident on another communication device, such as a pager, rather than via the network.

packet filters — Devices or software that block or allow transmission of packets of information based on port, IP address, protocol, or other criteria.

packet monkey — An attacker who's primarily interested in blocking Web site activities through a distributed denial-of-service attack.

pairwise keys — Any keys used between a pair of devices in TKIP. *See also* Temporal Key Integrity Protocol (TKIP).

pairwise master key (PMK) — The TKIP key used to generate data encryption keys, data integrity keys, and session group keys, among others. This key is used only once at the start of a session.

pairwise transient key (PTK) — The first TKIP key generated by the pairwise master key (PMK) and used for further key generation, according to the cryptographic algorithm in use.

passive attack — An attack that uses passive scanning to gather information for later use in other attacks; also called network reconnaissance.

passive scanning — The process of a wireless station listening on each available channel for an AP's eacon frame, and then moving on to the next channel without sending anything.

passive sensor — An NIDS sensor that examines copies of traffic on the network; no actual traffic passes through the sensor. *See also* network-based IDS (NIDS).

password security — Measures to protect passwords, including selecting good passwords, keeping them secure, and changing them as needed. Using multiple passwords, including screensaver passwords and passwords for protecting critical applications, also helps guard against unauthorized access.

penetration testing — The process of using a variety of tools and techniques to attempt to break into a network. Penetration testing, also called ethical hacking, is used legitimately as part of security audits to identify security vulnerabilities that attackers could exploit.

phase modulation (PM) — An analog modulation technique that changes the cycle's relative starting point when the bit being transmitted changes from 1 to 0.

phase shift keying (PSK) — A binary modulation technique that starts and stops the signal to represent a binary digit.

physical security — Measures taken to physically protect a computer or other network device from theft or environmental disasters.

Point-to-Point Tunneling Protocol (PPTP) — A tunneling protocol used for dial-up access to a remote server.

polarization — The plane on which radio waves propagate; the orientation of the radio waves as they leave the antenna, usually vertical or horizontal.

Power over Ethernet (PoE) — A technology that sends power for the AP unit over unused wire pairs in standard twisted-pair Ethernet cabling.

power-save poll (PS-Poll) — A type of control frame that a station sends on awakening from power save mode; it indicates to the access point that it's ready to receive any frames the AP has buffered for it. *See also* control frames.

profiles — Sets of characteristics that describe network services and resources a user or group normally accesses.

proxy ARP — A service provided by routers when the target of an ARP request is on a different subnet, and the intermediary router returns an ARP reply with its own MAC address designated as the MAC-to-IP mapping for that IP address destination. The router doesn't forward broadcasts, so it acts as a go-between.

proxy server — Software that forwards packets to and from the network and caches Web pages to speed up network performance.

public key cryptography — A form of network authentication that identifies participants through the exchange of public and private keys.

radio frequency (RF) monitor mode — A wireless NIC mode (equivalent to promiscuous mode in wired NICs) that allows a WNIC to capture packets without authenticating or associating with an AP or ad hoc (peer to peer) wireless network.

radio frequency (RF) waves — A type of EM radiation used most commonly for wireless networks.

recovery — The process of putting compromised media, programs, or computers back in service on the network.

reflection — A type of loss in which the RF wave bounces off certain materials.

refraction — Signals traveling through different air masses can be bent rather than traveling in a straight line. The signal changes in response to atmospheric conditions.

Remote Authentication Dial-In User Service (RADIUS) — An authentication method that identifies and verifies users who dial up a central server to gain access to networked resources.

request to send (RTS) — A type of control frame that a station sends when it wants to transmit. The RTS frame sender requests that the medium be reserved long enough for the transmission to be completed and an acknowledgement control frame to be received from the destination. *See also* control frames.

return on investment (ROI) — The total value gained after a solution has been deployed. A positive ROI means the solution has solved more problems than it creates.

Reverse Address Resolution Protocol (RARP) — An address resolution protocol used primarily by diskless workstations that know their MAC addresses when they boot but have no hard disk to store IP addressing information. The workstation boots and sends a RARP request packet to find out its own IP address.

reverse firewall — A device that monitors outgoing traffic instead of trying to block incoming traffic.

roaming — A wireless device moving between access points, or cells, without losing transmit/receive capabilities. Cells are interconnected so that as the wireless device moves between cells, the device/cell negotiates a new connection, depending on signal strength.

rogue devices — Wireless devices installed on a network without authorization or verification of configurations.

routed protocols — Protocols, such as IP, used to provide addressing about a packet being transported. Routed protocols contain Layer 3 addressing information about packets being transmitted. (Don't confuse them with routing protocols, which facilitate communication between routers updating their routing tables.)

routing — The process of transporting chunks of information (usually called packets) across a network from the source to the destination.

Routing Information Protocol (RIP) — A distance-vector IGP routing protocol that uses only hop count as a metric.

routing protocols — Protocols that allow routers to maintain information about network links in the routing tables they use.

routing tables — Lists of routes containing information about neighboring routers, such as the address, metric count, and link state.

rule base — A set of rules for telling a firewall what action to take when a certain kind of traffic attempts to pass through.

scattering — A type of loss in which small objects, such as raindrops, dust, or foliage, scatter the signal.

scopes — Unicast addresses used in IPv6 to identify the application suitable for the address; scopes include global unicast, site-local unicast, and link-local unicast.

screened host — Similar to a dual-homed host, except a router is often added between the host and the Internet to carry out IP packet filtering.

screening router — A router placed between the Internet and the protected network that determines whether to allow or deny packets based on their source and destination IP addresses or other information in their headers.

script kiddies — Attackers (often young people) who spread viruses and other malicious scripts and use techniques to exploit weaknesses in computer systems.

Secure Shell (SSH) — A more secure form of remote access developed to overcome some security limitations of other remote access and management methods.

Secure Sockets Layer (SSL) — A protocol developed by Netscape Communications Corporation as a way of enabling Web servers and browsers to exchange encrypted information.

Security Association (SA) — A designation for users, computers, or gateways that can participate in a VPN and encrypt and decrypt data by using keys.

security workstation — A dedicated computer that deploys a security policy through a centralized firewall to other firewalls that protect branch offices or other networks in the organization.

sensor — An IDS component (hardware, software, or combination) that monitors traffic on a network segment.

server farm — A group of servers connected in their own subnet that work together to receive requests; the load is distributed among all the servers.

service set identifier (SSID) — A unique identifier up to 32 characters that serves as the wireless network name.

session authentication — The process of authorizing a user or computer on a per-connection basis by using authentication software installed on the client computer that exchanges information with the firewall.

shared key authentication — An 802.11 authentication method that uses a standard challenge-response process with shared key encryption. It relies on a wireless station having the correct key to encrypt the AP's challenge text as the criteria for acceptance. Its security drawback is that it uses WEP, which is easily cracked, for encrypting the shared key.

side channel attack — An attack method that exploits vulnerabilities of underlying hardware systems that leak data instead of exploiting vulnerabilities in a cryptographic algorithm.

signatures — Combinations of flags, IP addresses, and other attack indicators that are detected by a firewall or IDS.

Simple Network Management Protocol (SNMP) trap logging — A type of logging that sends notifications of system status changes to SNMP management stations.

single entry point configuration — A VPN configuration in which all traffic to and from the network passes through a single gateway, such as a router or firewall.

site survey — An in-depth examination of a proposed wireless network site designed to determine AP placement and identify stray signals, noise, and obstacles.

site-to-site VPN — A VPN that uses hardware devices, such as routers, to connect two networks; also called a gateway-to-gateway VPN.

socket — A network connection that uses a TCP/IP port number combined with a computer's IP address.

Socks — A communications protocol that provides proxy services for applications that don't normally support proxying and enables applications to set up a secure tunnel by using encryption and authentication.

split tunneling — The term used to describe multiple paths. One path goes to the VPN server and is secured, but an unauthorized and unsecured path permits the user to connect to the Internet or some other network while still connected to the corporate VPN.

spread spectrum — An alternative to narrowband transmissions that spreads a narrow signal over a broader portion of the radio band.

spyware — A type of malware that includes adware, tracking cookies, dialers, and spam.

star configuration — A VPN configuration in which a single gateway is the "hub" and other networks that participate in the VPN are considered "rim" networks.

state information — Data about a network connection, which is typically kept in a state table.

state table — A file maintained by stateful packet filters that contains a record of all current connections.

stateful autoconfiguration — In IPv6, this feature is basically an improved version of DHCP. It's referred to as "stateful" because the DHCP client and server must keep their information updated to prevent addressing conflicts.

stateful packet filters — Similar to stateless packet filters, except they also determine whether to allow or block packets based on information about current connections.

stateless autoconfiguration — A feature of IPv6 that allows the computer attempting to connect to determine its own IP address based on the addressing of neighboring nodes.

stateless packet filters — Simple filters that determine whether to allow or block packets based on information in protocol headers.

static mapping — A NAT mode used to map internal IP addresses to external routable IP addresses on a one-to-one basis.

static routes — Routes that an administrator enters manually in a routing table.

strict source and record routing (ssrr) — An IP option that specifies every hop that the packet must traverse.

stub networks — Networks with only one outbound route.

stub router — A router at the edge of a network with only one way out.

subnet mask — A value that tells another computer which part of a computer's IP address is its network address and which part is the host address.

summarization — A method used to keep routing tables smaller by addressing a block of contiguous networks as a single subnet. Also called supernetting because the network/node boundary in the subnet mask moves to the left rather than to the right, as with subnetting.

symmetric cryptography — A type of encryption in which the sender and recipient exchange the same key. *See also* asymmetric cryptography.

syslog server — A type of server configured to host router log files, particularly when you have large log files. A syslog server can be a UNIX or Windows server or another designated machine.

system logging — A type of logging that sends notifications of system status changes to different locations, including the router's memory buffer, system console port, or syslog server.

target — In Iptables, the command option that determines what action is taken on packets matching specific criteria. *See also* Iptables.

Temporal Key Integrity Protocol (TKIP) — An encryption method devised as a replacement for WEP in WPA. TKIP is based on the same RC4 mechanisms used in WEP but includes a method for generating new keys for each packet. It also incorporates automatic AP-client synchronization of unicast encryption keys, so keys don't have to be changed manually, as in WEP.

Terminal Access Controller Access Control System (TACACS+) — A set of authentication protocols developed by Cisco Systems that uses the MD5 algorithm to produce an encrypted digest version of transmitted data. TACACS+ is usually used to authenticate dial-up remote users.

test cell — A dedicated testing environment, ideally modeled after the production environment, used for testing new software or hardware to detect and correct problems before placing it into production.

three-pronged firewall — A firewall that has three separate interfaces—for example, one to a DMZ, one to the Internet, and one to the internal network.

ticket-granting server (TGS) — The part of the KDC that creates and distributes session keys clients use to access resources. *See also* Key Distribution Center (KDC).

ticket-granting ticket (TGT) — A digital token sent from the Authentication Server to the client. The client presents the TGT to the TGS to obtain a session key to access the resource. *See also* Key Distribution Center (KDC) *and* ticket-granting server (TGS).

Time Division Multiple Access (TDMA) — An access method that uses different time slots to allow devices to share a frequency channel.

token — A small electronic device that generates a random number or password used in authentication.

topology — The way in which participants in a network are connected physically to one another.

Transmission Control Protocol/Internet Protocol (TCP/IP) — A suite of protocols for transmitting information from point to point on a network.

Transport Layer Security (TLS) — A protocol designed to secure Internet traffic. Although it hasn't replaced SSL yet, it offers improvements and is used more widely now for a variety of applications.

trigger — A set of circumstances that causes an IDS to send an alert.

Triple Data Encryption Standard (3DES) — A stronger variation of DES that uses three separate 64-bit keys to process data, making the encryption much harder to break. *See also* Data Encryption Standard (DES).

Trojan programs — A type of program that appears harmless but introduces viruses or causes damage to a computer or system.

true negatives — Legitimate communications that don't cause an IDS to set off an alarm.

true positive — A genuine attack detected successfully by an IDS, in contrast to a true negative or false positive.

tunnel — The connection between two endpoints in a VPN.

tunnel method encryption — A method of key exchange that encrypts both the header and data parts of a packet and encapsulates the packet within a new packet that has a different header.

unicast — A transmission in which one packet is sent from a server to each client that requests a file or application.

Unified Threat Management (UTM) — A term describing products that integrate a variety of security features, such as VPN and remote access services, firewall and intrusion detection functions, and management consoles, into a single application, device, or product.

update timers — Timers that control how often routing updates are sent.

user authentication — The process of identifying a person who has been authorized to access network resources.

User Datagram Protocol (UDP) — A core transport protocol of the TCP/IP suite. UDP is connectionless, meaning it doesn't ensure delivery or provide ordering, as TCP does. UDP is much faster and is useful for transmissions that require speed over reliability. UDP relies on upper-level protocols for error-checking and sequencing services.

variable length subnet masking (VLSM) — A means of allocating IP addressing according to the network's needs that involves applying masks of varying sizes to the same network. This method creates subnets within subnets and multiple divisions of an IP network.

virtual private network (VPN) — A cost-effective way for networks to create a secure private connection using public lines (usually the Internet). VPN endpoints establish connections (tunnels) to transmit and receive data, and then tear the connections down when they're no longer needed. Combinations of encryption, authentication, and encapsulation help ensure the confidentiality, privacy, and integrity of information.

virtual team — A group of people who normally have other jobs and act as a team only during meetings or when an incident becomes serious.

virus — Computer code that copies itself from one place to another surreptitiously and performs actions that range from benign to harmful.

voltage standing wave ratio (VSWR) — A type of loss caused by differences in the equipment itself. For example, if one part of the equipment has a different impedance than others, the signal can be reflected back within the device, and the reflected power can cause the device to burn out.

VPN appliance — A hardware device designed to terminate VPNs and join networks.

VPN client — A router or an OS that initiates a connection to a VPN server.

VPN domain — A group of one or more computers that the VPN hardware and software handle as a single entity. This group uses the VPN to communicate with another domain.

VPN protocols — Standardized communication settings that software and hardware use to encrypt data sent through a VPN.

VPN quarantine — A method created to address the problem of remote clients not meeting an organization's security standards. Quarantine places remote clients in a secured area while they are checked to ensure that software updates and current patches have been applied, antivirus software has been installed and updated, and other policies have been complied with.

VPN server — A computer configured to accept VPN connections from clients.

wardriving — Driving around with a laptop and WNIC in RF monitor mode to detect unsecured wireless signals.

wave — A means of transporting energy from one place to another without physical movement of material.

wave propagation — The pattern of wave dispersal as waves travel from sending to receiving antennas.

wavelength — The distance between two successive amplitude peaks.

Wi-Fi Protected Access (WPA) — A subset of the 802.11i standard that addresses encryption and authentication; it uses IEEE 802.1x or preshared keys for authentication and TKIP for encryption. *See also* IEEE 802.1x *and* Temporal Key Integrity Protocol (TKIP).

Wi-Fi Protected Access version 2 (WPA2) — The encryption and authentication architecture based on the final ratified IEEE 802.11i standard. WPA2 uses preshared keys or IEEE 802.1x for authentication and AES for encryption. *See also* Advanced Encryption Standard (AES) *and* IEEE 802.1x.

wireless networking — Any exchange of data between computers and other devices that uses RF transmission methods instead of traditional wired cables.

worm — A type of malware that creates files that copy themselves repeatedly and consume disk space. Worms don't require user intervention to be launched; they are self-propagating.

Index